CW01210428

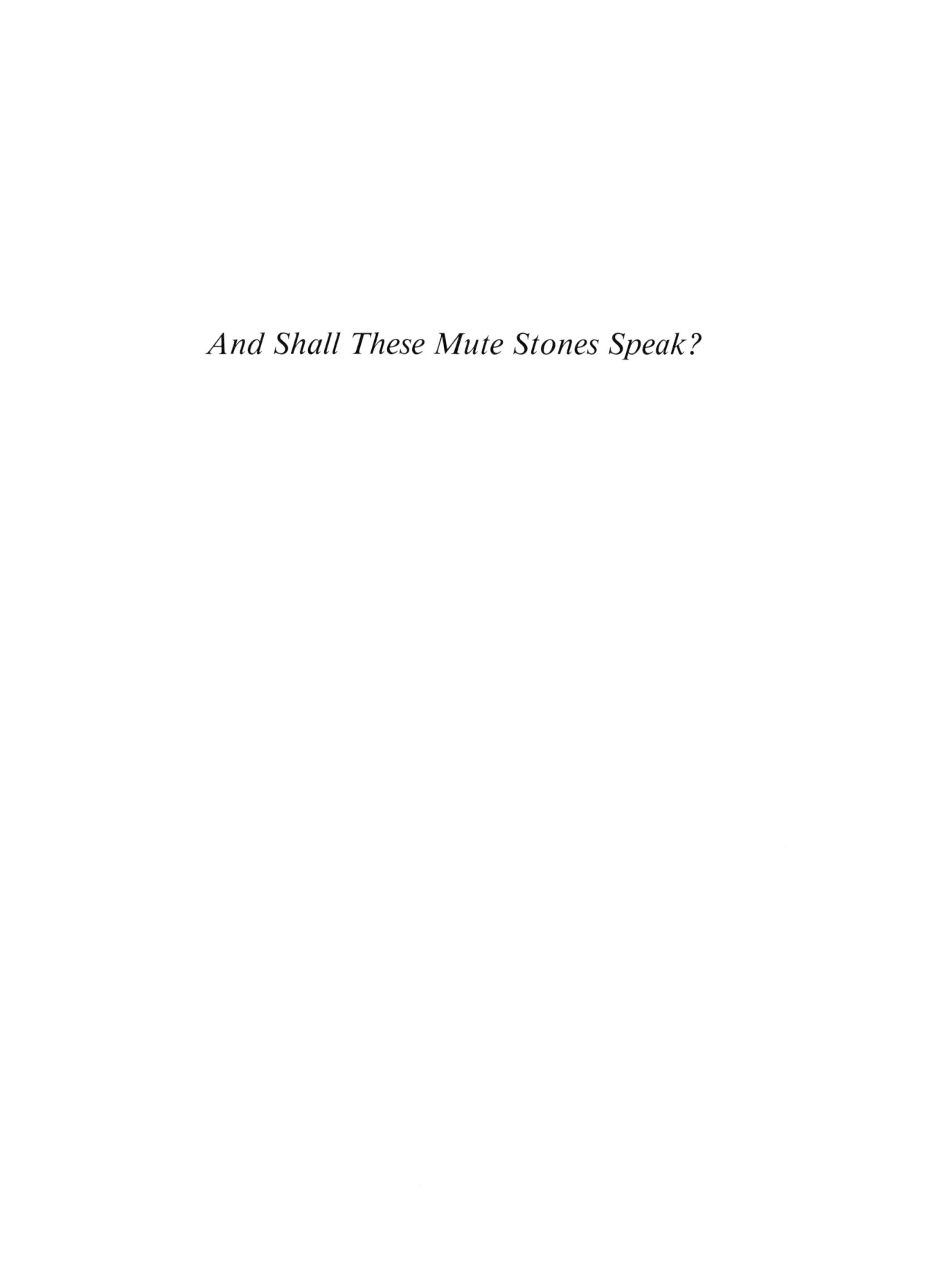

*And Shall These Mute Stones Speak?*

# *And Shall These Mute Stones Speak?*

## POST-ROMAN INSCRIPTIONS IN WESTERN BRITAIN

CHARLES THOMAS

*The second in the series of Dalrymple Archaeological Monographs
published in association with Glasgow Archaeological Society
and the University of Glasgow*

UNIVERSITY OF WALES PRESS
1994

© Antony Charles Thomas 1994

All rights reserved. No part of this book may be reproduced, stored in a retrieval system, or transmitted, in any form or by any means, electronic, mechanical, photocopying, recording or otherwise, without clearance from the University of Wales Press, 6 Gwennyth Street, Cardiff CF2 4YD.

The right of Antony Charles Thomas to be identified as author of this work has been asserted by him in accordance with the Copyright, Designs and Patents Act 1988.

**British Library Cataloguing-in-Publication Data**

A catalogue record for this book is available from the British Library

ISBN 0-7083-1160-1

Typeset by Action Typesetting, Gloucester
Printed at Alden Press Limited,
Oxford and Northampton, Great Britain

I'll sing Aloud, that all the World may hear,
The Triumph of the buried Conqueror,
These Gaping Graves, the *Saviour* shall proclaim
And each Mute Stone th'imprisoned Sinner's Name.

                        Joseph Crabtree, 'Clad All In White'

D.M

F.A.M

SIMVL ACADEMICVS ADVOCATVS H.C
VIXIT ANNOS LXXXIV M.I DIES V
OB TANTAM AMICITIAM
HVNC TITVLVM POSVIT GENER

# Contents

| | |
|---|---|
| List of illustrations | ix |
| FOREWORD | xiii |
| PREFACE AND ACKNOWLEDGEMENTS | xv |
| PRELIMINARY NOTES | xix |
|     1 Sources for the early Insular inscriptions | xix |
|     2 Reproducing inscriptions in print | xx |
| Abbreviations and conventions | xxiv |
| 1  INTRODUCTION: PLACES AND PEOPLE | 1 |
| 2  PERSONAL MEMORIALS IN STONE | 9 |
| 3  HIBERNO-ROMAN TIMES: THE OGAM SCRIPT | 27 |
| 4  IRISH SETTLEMENTS IN ATLANTIC BRITAIN | 41 |
| 5  DEMETIA: SETTLERS AND SOVEREIGNS | 51 |
| 6  DEMETIA: A POST-ROMAN KINGDOM | 67 |
| 7  DEMETIA: 'PASSIM ECCLESIARUM SIGNA AUDIUNTUR...' | 89 |
| 8  VENTURE TO THE INTERIOR | 113 |
| 9  THE BRYCHAN DOCUMENTS | 131 |
| 10  A VISIT TO 'ENYS BRACHAN' | 163 |
| 11  'IN OCCIDENTALE PARTE': WEST CORNWALL | 183 |
| 12  THE GAULISH CONNECTION | 197 |
| 13  THE POST-ROMAN KINGDOM OF DUMNONIA | 209 |
| 14  LANDSCAPE WITH FIGURES: SAMSON AND OTHERS IN CORNWALL | 223 |
| 15  STRANGERS AND BROTHERS | 237 |
| 16  THE DUMNONIAN INSCRIPTIONS: 'KITTENS IN THE OVEN...' | 257 |
| 17  THE DUMNONIAN INSCRIPTIONS: THE NATIVE RESPONSE | 277 |
| 18  THE CHURCH IN THE LANDSCAPE | 305 |

APPENDIX: The Dumnonian Inscriptions: hand-list and concordances        327
BIBLIOGRAPHY        335
INDEXES        341

*Illustrations*

| Figure | | Page |
|---|---|---|
| 2.1 | Menhir with cross, Mabe, Cornwall; 'Maen Waldo', Pembrokeshire | 12 |
| 2.2 | The Davesco stone, Chur Museum, Switzerland | 15 |
| 2.3 | Tombstone of *Eglecta* and *Crescens*, York | 17 |
| 2.4 | Discoidal steles, Languedoc | 18 |
| 2.5 | Roman provincial tombstone, Burgos, Spain | 19 |
| 2.6 | Pictish Class I and Class II stones | 21 |
| 3.1 | The ogam script | 31 |
| 3.2 | Distribution of ogam inscriptions in Ireland | 35 |
| 3.3 | Examples of ogam memorials, Co. Kerry | 37 |
| 4.1 | Irish settlements in Atlantic Britain | 45 |
| 4.2 | Map of Cormac mac Cuilennáin's three named places in Britain | 46 |
| 5.1 | South Wales in late Roman times; *civitates* and rivers | 52 |
| 5.2 | Moel Trigarn from the south | 59 |
| 5.3 | Sketched profile of Moel Trigarn, 1899 | 59 |
| 5.4 | South-west Wales; Demetia, Cedweli and Gower | 60 |
| 5.5 | Southern Ireland; the Uí Liatháin and Déisi homelands | 61 |
| 5.6 | The *Clutorigi* stone (435), Llandysilio West church; The *Maglocuni* stone (446), Nevern church | 63 |
| 6.1 | Demetia; distribution of place-names with element *meidir* | 68 |
| 6.2 | Demetia; a proposed typological sequence of memorials | 69 |
| 6.3 | The initial Irish settlement in Demetia | 72 |
| 6.4 | Ogam-inscribed menhir at Bridell, Pembs. | 73 |
| 6.5 | The *Voteporix* stone (358) | 83 |
| 7.1 | Demetia; distribution of memorials with ogam, (a), (b) and (c) | 92 |
| 7.2 | Demetia; distribution of type (d) memorials, with Christian wording | 93 |
| 7.3 | Demetia; distribution of un-typed memorials | 94 |
| 7.4 | Southern Demetia; Continental imports of pottery and glass | 98 |
| 7.5 | Demetia; distribution of HIC IACIT and angle-bar A | 99 |
| 7.6 | The *Barrivendi* stone (368), Llandawke | 99 |
| 7.7 | Selective indications of Christianity in 6th cent. Demetia | 105 |

ILLUSTRATIONS

| Figure | | Page |
|---|---|---|
| 8.1 | Sketch map suggesting northward expansion of early Demetia | 115 |
| 8.2 | 'Typological profiles' of memorials from Demetia, Dumnonia and Brycheiniog | 116 |
| 8.3 | Usk valley and Llynfi corridor, with inscribed memorials | 118 |
| 8.4 | The *Maccutreni* stone, British Museum | 120 |
| 8.5 | Memorials from Defynnog (328) and Trallwng (342) | 121 |
| 8.6 | Map showing the repetition of Irish personal names, Pebidiog and Brycheiniog, with route | 123 |
| 8.7 | The Crickhowell stone (327) | 125 |
| 8.8 | Map of Brycheiniog with indications of Demetian settlers | 126 |
| 9.1 | Llyn Syfaddan (Llan-gors lake) and the 'garth' of Garth Matrun | 146 |
| 9.2 | Route of Marchell's journey | 148 |
| 9.3 | View of spur with Meidrim churchyard | 148 |
| 9.4 | Location of places, central Brycheiniog | 152 |
| 9.5 | The stone of Anlach, Llansbyddyd | 154 |
| 9.6 | Maplets of Llandyfaelog Fach, Merthyr Cynog, Llan-gors, Llansbyddyd | 155 |
| 10.1 | Map of the Island of Lundy | 164 |
| 10.2 | Beacon Hill, Lundy; 1969 site plan | 165 |
| 10.3 | Lundy memorials (1400 – 01 – 02) | 166 |
| 10.4 | Beacon Hill; view of central *cella* | 168 |
| 10.5 | Beacon Hill; central feature, phase 1 | 169 |
| 10.6 | Beacon Hill; central feature, phase 2 | 170 |
| 10.7 | Beacon Hill; central feature, phase 3 | 171 |
| 10.8 | Beacon Hill; central feature, phase 4 | 172 |
| 10.9 | Beacon Hill; central feature, phase 5 | 173 |
| 10.10 | Map: sea journey from Lundy to Hartland Quay, Devon | 174 |
| 11.1 | Mid and west Cornwall; early Irish settlement | 186 |
| 11.2 | Mid and west Cornwall; Roman coin-hoards pre- & post-AD 284 | 189 |
| 11.3 | Plan of coastal fortlet, Carnsew, west Cornwall | 191 |
| 11.4 | Grave of *Cunaide* - reconstruction | 192 |
| 11.5 | The *Cunaide* stone (479) | 192 |
| 11.6 | View of Trencrom, from below Phillack | 195 |
| 12.1 | Location map, Hayle estuary | 198 |
| 12.2 | *Chi-rho* stone (1502), Phillack church | 200 |
| 12.3 | Typical 'Extended Latinate' (EL) inscriptions | 202 |
| 12.4 | EL inscriptions; vocabulary and distribution | 203 |
| 13.1 | The *civitas Dumnoniorum* | 210 |
| 13.2 | The six ancient hundreds of Cornwall | 217 |
| 13.3 | Generalized distribution of memorials in Dumnonia | 219 |

| Figure | | Page |
|---|---|---|
| 14.1 | Chronology of *Vita Sancti Samsonis* | 225 |
| 14.2 | Route of Samon's visit to Dumnonia | 228 |
| 15.1 | Inscribed memorials of Dumnonia, with ogams distinguished | 238 |
| 15.2 | Intrusive memorials, eastern Dumnonia | 239 |
| 15.3 | The *Iusti* stone (484), St Kew | 241 |
| 15.4 | Map showing repetition of names, Demetia and Dumnonia | 242 |
| 15.5 | Memorials to two sons of *Severus* (373 and 472)? | 243 |
| 15.6 | Demetia and Dumnonia; repetition of personal names and use of angle-bar A. | 244 |
| 15.7 | The *Dunocati* stone (457) and *Vitali* stone (473) | 244 |
| 15.8 | The Camel–Fowey corridor – memorials and place-names | 253 |
| 16.1 | 'Pickwick's Immortal Discovery' (1889) | 258 |
| 16.2 | The Lewannick stones (466 and 467) | 262 |
| 16.3 | The *Latini* stone (470) | 264 |
| 16.4 | *Brocagni* 'Long Cross' stone (478), St Endellion | 264 |
| 16.5 | Memorials of *Enabarr* (488) and *Sabinus* (492) | 266 |
| 16.6 | The Fardel stone (489), British Museum | 267 |
| 16.7 | Mid and west Cornwall – intrusive memorials | 269 |
| 16.8 | The Rialton granite slab (476); a son of *Tribunus?* | 270 |
| 16.9 | The Bleu Bridge stone (462) | 272 |
| 16.10 | Memorial from Tresco, Isles of Scilly (485) | 273 |
| 17.1 | Intrusive and native memorials in Dumnonia | 279 |
| 17.2 | Detail of *Drustanus* inscription (487) | 280 |
| 17.3 | The lost Totnes stone, after Hübner | 282 |
| 17.4 | Memorials from St Columb Major (475 and 1206) | 283 |
| 17.5 | The stone of *Cruarigi* (474) and the Men Scryfys (468) | 283 |
| 17.6 | The *Clotuali* stone (471), Phillack churchyard | 285 |
| 17.7 | William Borlase's sketch of the Redruth stone | 285 |
| 17.8 | The Boskenna (1202) and lost Treveneague (482) stones | 285 |
| 17.9 | Langdon's drawing of the Sancreed pillar (1057) | 287 |
| 17.10 | St Just stones, *Senilus* (483) and *Taetuera* (1055) | 287 |
| 17.11 | Inscribed stones from Exmoor (499 and 1404) | 289 |
| 17.12 | The St Hilary *Noti* stone (481) | 289 |
| 17.13 | Memorial of *Qonfal* at Madron (1048) | 291 |
| 17.14 | Views of mound grave of *Taetuera* | 292 |
| 17.15 | Art on Dumnonian stones: curved lines | 294 |
| 17.16 | Art on Dumnonian stones: 'cartouches' or framing lines | 294 |
| 17.17 | Art on Dumnonian stones: the *chi-rho* cross | 295 |
| 17.18 | Verticality in Dumnonian memorials | 297 |
| 17.19 | Penzance Market Cross | 298 |
| 18.1 | Cornwall: intrusive memorials and Domesday manors | 307 |

ILLUSTRATIONS

| Figure | | Page |
|---|---|---|
| 18.2 | Dumnonia; memorials on Christian sites | 309 |
| 18.3 | Christian sites with place-names *Lan-* | 314 |
| 18.4 | Site plan of the village of Luxulyan | 318 |
| 18.5 | Early cemetery enclosures, Demetia | 318 |
| 18.6 | Pre-Norman *lanns* as parish churchyards, Dumnonia | 319 |
| 18.7 | St Buryan and St Dennis, site plans | 320 |
| 18.8 | Lelant churchyard and *Lan Anta* | 321 |
| 18.9 | Memorial of two princes, *Ioruert* and *Ruallaun*, Llanlleonfel | 323 |

# Foreword

In 1907, the President of the Glasgow Archeological Society, Mr J.G.D. Dalrymple, instituted the Dalrymple Lectureship in Archaeology in the University of Glasgow, to commemorate the fiftieth anniversary of the society. On his death in 1930, the annual payments made over to the university for the remuneration and expenses of the lecturer were replaced by an endowment, the administration of which is vested in the hands of curators, three from the University and three from the Society, under the chairmanship of the Principal of the University. In 1991, the Curators, with the support of the Council of the Society, decided to institute publication of selected lecture-series as monographs. The first Dalrymple Archaeological Monograph was published in 1993: Martin Carver's *Arguments in Stone,* being the Dalrymple Lectures for the session 1990–1. Following the 1991–2 Dalrymple Lectures, delivered by Professor Charles Thomas, there was no hesitation on the part of either the university or the society in eagerly pursuing the prospect of their publication.

The Dalrymple Lectureship is concerned with 'some branch of European archaeology', and this has been interpreted in fairly broad terms over the years. There has been no embargo against the inclusion of the British Isles, although lecturers choosing to focus upon an Insular theme have been enjoined, wherever possible, to make broad connections to Continental Europe. In 1991, Charles Thomas gave as his subtitle to 'And Shall These Mute Stones Speak?'; 'Archaeology, History and the Insular Memorials'. However, form the opening of his first lecture, when he described a plateau in south-eastern France with its menhirs, it was abundantly clear that his theme was to be a far from insular one. During the course of the first three lectures,* Professor Thomas led us with vivid word-pictures (as well as more conventional visual ones) on excursions through Demetia and Dumnonia, pausing at places such as Merthyr Cynog, Lundy, Lewannick and Tintagel, but with flying visits also to Ireland and even Switzerland! At no time, with his guidance, could we have failed to appreciate the significance within the wider European orbit of the rich body of data relating to the Early Christian community of these areas. Nor, despite the lightness of his

---

*The fourth lecture in this series was delivered upon the theeme of 'The Early Christian Inscriptions of Southern Scotland' and is published in *Glasgow Archaeological Journal* 17, 1991–2, 1–10.

touch, could we have failed to appreciate the breadth of scholarly endeavour, taking in linguistics as well as the two primary sources of data referred to in the subtitle.

As chairman for these three lectures, it gave me great pleasure to realize that the academic erudition obviously manifest in Charles Thomas's work could be translated into so immediately approachable (and entertaining) a form for both specialists and non-specialists alike. They certainly fulfilled Mr Dalrymple's wish that the lectures be accessible to the general public. It is the wish of the Dalrymple Lectureship Curators that the fuller version of Professor Thomas's lectures be made accessible to a wider audience of 'ordinary readers' through publication, and they have been happy to support the University of Wales Press in this venture.

The subtitle of Professor Thomas's second lecture in 1991 on 'The Island of Brychan' was 'A Detective Story'. I have had the privilege of reading this book before most other 'ordinary readers'. Like the best detective stories, once begun, it has been most difficult to put down. Would that other aspects of the archaeology and history of this dimly-lit period could be so brilliantly illumined as here!

CHRISTOPHER D. MORRIS

# Preface and Acknowledgements

'YOU ARCHAEOLOGISTS are so *clever*,' sighed a lady recently after I had lectured with colour-slides about Coptic sculpture in Upper Egypt, 'you always manage to work in such nice places.' Agreeing with her, I saw no need to point out that archaeologists are much cleverer than she supposed because they can nearly always find somebody else to pay for the travelling. The fieldwork for this book in Wales, north Cornwall and Devon and elsewhere was indirectly subsidised by the University of Exeter, my employer until 1991, and by St David's University College at Lampeter where I am privileged to be an Honorary Fellow; and I gladly acknowledge this support. Chapters 8 to 10 were first aired in seminar form at the University of York and at SDUC Lampeter; my 1991 Dalrymple Lectures at the University of Glasgow were based on chapters 1 to 7 and 11 to 18. Aside from the stimulus of offering new material to critical colleagues I am indebted to all who made helpful comments. It is now customary for Dalrymple Lectures to be published when possible as books; in this case my existing commitment to the University of Wales Press had precluded this and I am extremely grateful to the Dalrymple Board of Curators – Glasgow Archaeological Society, and the University – for proposing a joint imprint and for a particularly generous subvention that has the effect of lowering the book's retail price to readers. In preparing the material, I thank first my research assistant Carl Thorpe who during 1990–91 visited most of the Dumnonian inscriptions with me, helped with the chalking, reading and photographs and then kindly drew the final versions of most of the line illustrations; and my daughter Susanna Thomas who shared in field-trips to Wales and, both there and here in Cornwall, undertook the professional photography (including fresh coverage of some Cornish stones for the National Monuments Record, RCHME).

The philosopher William James was reputedly asked by a younger colleague at Harvard how he could write a book like *The Varieties of Religious Experience* (1903) and still make sure that the man in the (Massachusetts) street could understand it. 'When you have completed a work' the master told him, 'write a two-page précis of what you wanted to convey. If *you* can understand that, others will. If not, tear it up and start again.' The first version of the present book was finished at the end of 1991. During 1992 further visits to Wales, more fieldwork in Cornwall and (inevitably) second thoughts coinciding with the appearance of such studies as Damian McManus, *A Guide to Ogam*, accompanied a critical reading of my text by two kind friends, Jeremy Knight in Wales and Richard Warner in Belfast, both supplying vital corrections and suggestions for improvement. My gratitude to them especially, as to others who went through chapters or parts – Professor R. Geraint Gruffydd, Dr Morfydd Owen, Dr Richard Sharpe and my (sadly, late) friend Mr Paul Thomas, Treasurer of the Royal Institution of Cornwall – can be measured from the admission that I *did* attempt a two-page summary, found it unsatisfying and muddled and consequently ditched the entire book early in 1993. Thanks to the patience and understanding of Ned Thomas, director of the University of Wales Press, I was allowed February and March 1993 to re-write what is now a new work, not a patched-up revision; and I hope that it better approximates what I wanted to convey. Special thanks, at the Press, go to Liz Powell for her hard work and help as the editor.

Illustrations of inscribed stones, unless otherwise indicated, are drawn by Carl Thorpe or myself from my daughter's (or my own) photographs and field-notes – many would not now be detectable through photographic reproduction. A few, from Professor R. A. S. Macalister's *Corpus*, are shown by courtesy of the Controller, Stationery Office, Dublin. Source material for maps was kindly supplied by the Dyfed Archaeological Trust, the Clwyd–Powys Archaeological Trust, individual friends at Aberystwyth, Cardiff, Carmarthen and Lampeter and such useful things as *Atlas Brycheiniog* (1960), Melville Richards's essential *Welsh Administrative and Territorial Units* (1969), and Professor William Rees's *An Historical Atlas of Wales* (1959 edn.); for Cornwall I am also greatly indebted to my immediate colleagues of the Cornwall Archaeological Unit at Truro who since 1974 have built up our vast and comprehensive Sites and Monuments Register.

Many people have helped with ideas, useful criticisms, answers to tiresome questions, and hospitality, and I should like to record my warm thanks to Professors Leslie Alcock, Wendy Davies, Geraint Gruffydd, Michael Jarrett, Christopher Morris, Nicholas Orme and Malcolm Todd; as well, to David and Gaenor Austin, George Boon, Dr Diane Brook, Angela Broome, David Browne, Dr Stephen Driscoll, Dr Andrew Dugmore, Mrs Bill Glanville, Dr Anthony Harvey, Heather and Terrence James, Cathy O'Mahoney, Dr Morfydd Owen, Dr Oliver Padel, Roger Penhallurick, Peter Powell, Ann Preston-Jones, Dr Mark Redknap, Tomas Roberts, Dr Richard Sharpe, Courtney Smale, David Treffry and Susan Youngs. My colleague in the Tintagel Churchyard work, Jaqueline Nowakowski (who directed the excavations), and my former secretaries Elizabeth Jackson and Heather Oliver, have helped me particularly in a great many ways; and I am grateful as well to the staff at Brecon and Carmarthen Museums and to a lot of kind folk who opened churches, moved pews and helped with photography around Dyfed and Brycheiniog. In venturing occasionally to disagree in very minor ways with any statements by the late Professor Kenneth Jackson, I am still and always will be conscious of how much I owe to his kindness and encouragement to me for a much longer time than my decade of teaching in the same university; he never lost either his interest in and prodigious knowledge of all Insular inscriptions, or his personal excitement on the rare occasions when new examples were discovered, and my early realization that these monuments are also documents telling us about entirely real men and women took firm shape, I think, after a conversation with him in 1957. Like Ralegh Radford, Sir Ifor Williams, Macalister and Nash-Williams, Jackson raised the status of these rough memorials from curiosities to primary records of our *written* past.

The book, like all that I have been allowed to publish, has a target readership; 'the ordinary reader' (p.1) may be an informed enthusiast, final-year undergraduate in a relevant discipline, member of an adult education class or just a person sharing a devotion to our Insular landscape and its astonishingly rich historical depths. This is why the chapter-notes are longer than usual, and also why I resist the temptation to wander off into such exciting topics as the potential evidence for Common Neo-Brittonic orthography contained in a reconstruction of the late sixth-century Brycheiniog narrative (chap. 9), something to be expanded in a separate publication. The intention throughout has been to write a *history* of part of Atlantic Britain from AD 400 to 650, showing how one subject leads on to the next and what parts archaeology, epigraphy, language and landscape analysis can play in the slow construction of a narrative. I am ill-equipped to voice again, let alone to embroider, the noble sentiments as to the unifying purposes of analytical national histories set out by Hector Munro Chadwick in his *The Nationalities of Europe* (1945); this does not stop me sharing a sorrow and annoyance (more than once expressed to me by Mrs Nora Chadwick) at the undue extension of words like 'England, English' or a philosophy of a taught *British* past underlying such book-titles as *Everyday Life in Roman and Anglo-Saxon Times, Roman Britain and the English Settlements,* or *Roman Britain to Saxon England.* There *are* still others of us, west of Offa's Dyke and the river Tamar, and north of Hadrian's Wall; regions where a buzz-word like 'multi-culturalism' has had its own meanings for a very long time indeed. A pictorial *Everyday Life in Demetian and Dumnonian Times* would be beyond me; but here is an attempt to sketch something of its background.

Lambessow, St Clement, Cornwall  CHARLES THOMAS
November 1993

# Preliminary Notes

**1  Sources for the early Insular inscriptions**

The only attempt at a full catalogue of inscribed memorial and commemorative stones in Britain and Ireland has been R. A. S. Macalister's *Corpus Inscriptionum Insularum Celticarum* (Stationery Office, Dublin). Macalister's Volume I (1945) covers 'the Ogam and analogous inscriptions of Ireland, Wales, England, the Isle of Man and Scotland' – though not the Channel Isles or the island of Lundy – and lists 520 monuments, most of which can be dated before AD 700. Volume II (1949) deals with 'half-uncial inscriptions' (i.e., those mainly or wholly in book-hand letters instead of ogam, or Roman capitals), dating roughly from the late-seventh to twelfth centuries. Many of these are not personal memorials, but dedicatory or commemorative, and in the shape of free-standing crosses. In *CIIC*, as Macalister's Corpus is cited, Vol. I includes a few late stones from Cornwall that should properly have been kept for Vol. II; and Vol. II has a few, noted after 1945, that really belong to Vol. I. Numeration is consecutive. In *CIIC*.i (= Vol. I), 1 to 317 are Irish stones; Wales, by counties from Anglesey to Radnor, has 318 to 456; Cornwall (with Scilly), 457 to 487; and Devon, 488 to 494. In *CIIC*.ii the Cornish items, 1043 to 1059, are followed by a single Devon stone, 1060. There is no revision of *CIIC*, but many of the transcriptions and readings of the Irish ogam-inscribed stones have now been corrected by Dr Damian McManus (1991), who has also added (ibid., 65–77) a list of ogam inscriptions discovered since *CIIC*.i appeared. These he numbers (i) to (xx).

Wales has a separate and later catalogue, V. E. Nash-Williams, *The Early Christian Monuments of Wales* (University of Wales Press, Cardiff 1950), cited as *ECMW*. Monuments, grouped by counties, are numbered from one to 415; but each *county* chapter (in which localities, nearly all parishes, are arranged alphabetically) includes early stones as in *CIIC*.i, later inscriptions of all kinds as in *CIIC*.ii, and numerous un-inscribed slabs and stones that bear crosses. Any stone that had been listed in *CIIC* is given its *CIIC* number at the end of the *ECMW* entry. The few Welsh inscriptions discovered since 1950 have nearly all been published, as notes, in *Archaeologia Cambrensis*. It is understood that a revised *ECMW* is in preparation, much-needed because many stones have been moved to new locations since Nash-Williams saw them. The various groups of inscribed stones and crosses from Scotland, which do not figure in this book, pose further problems because *CIIC* by no means listed all of them, and more have now been found.

In the text below, any inscription, or any name or word quoted from an inscription, is prefixed by its (Macalister) *CIIC* number, if it has one – thus, 458 RANOCORI FILI MESGI. Welsh inscriptions may also be cited with *ECMW* numbers (*ECMW* 70 VITALIANI EMERETO) or, if necessary, both references are given; 342 *ILVVETO* (= *ECMW* 70). The reason is that some of the *ECMW* readings, and most of the locality-names, are more accurate than their *CIIC* counterparts.

For south-west Britain the position is now more complicated, through revision as well as new discoveries. A concise *Gazetteer* for all the south-western stones forms an Appendix here (p.327). Because Macalister's system, a closed one, stopped at 1095, arbitrary new high-number blocks are used to label items from Devon and Cornwall. Items from 1200 are inscriptions, probably all older than 700, that are (a) not in *CIIC*, because Macalister did not see them or because they came to notice only after 1949; (b) now lost, or known to have been destroyed, but subject to an acceptable record or reading; and (c) both extant and accessible, with inscriptions that appear to be genuine and early, but now in a condition where they can no longer be read with any confidence. Items from 1400 cover four stones from Lundy and two from Exmoor. Items from 1500 are, like many in *ECMW*, un-inscribed but cross-marked; they range from Exmoor to Scilly. Some, but not all, of these post-*CIIC* stones have been individually published.

## 2  Reproducing inscriptions in print

Inscriptions in Britain and Ireland were written (cut, chiselled, pocked) in two different systems – the *ogam* script (chap. 3), an Irish twenty-symbol system using strokes and notches arranged in four groups of five; and the *Roman* alphabet that was the vehicle for Latin and then for other languages, with the handsome capitals required for public monuments (*capitalis, scriptura monumentalis*) and with other letters modified for writing by hand (here simply called 'book-hands'). An ideal rendering in print should include conventions to denote clearly visible letters; those damaged, but where the reading is more or less certain; others so defective now that we have to guess what they were; and letters assumed to be missing because of flaking-off, or erosion or breaks. It should also show *ligatures* or conjoined letters, a device to aid the cutter or to save space (and cost?), where capitals with obliques (A, V, M) and uprights (D, N, P) can share a stroke. This is indicated by a line or bar above the letters in question, like TV$\overline{\text{MV}}$LO. An illegible letter can be marked by a point, as C...S (three illegibles between C and S). Where parts of a familiar word are missing one can put brackets to exclude outward what can be safely supplied, as FIL)IVS IACI(T. By the sixth century some capitals often appeared in unfamiliar guise; N can be reversed (diagonal or oblique from bottom left to top right) or made to look like H; C or D can be written backwards, and others can be inverted, turned upside-down so that M looks like W. One odd fashion, apparently invented in Demetia before 500 and then copied elsewhere, was to write a final letter I on its side, and this can be shown; i.e. FIL⊢ and not FILI.

Conventions have been kept as simple as possible. Roman capitals are given in the ones we use ourselves and the presence of 'lower case' book-hand, uncial or half-uncial letters specified. All names and words inscribed in ogam are printed in *italic* capitals, thus: 466 *IGENAVI MEMOR*. Inscriptions in Roman capitals often took up more than one line because letters might be as high as 4 in. (10 cm.) for legibility and there was inefficient marking-out. There is a long-standing convention of showing line-divisions by oblique strokes or printer's slashes, thus: 375 TOTOVALI / FILIVS DOTHO/RANTI, which occupies three lines. Names of people whom we meet in inscriptions can be repeated as they were inscribed, 484 IVSTI with ogam *I)USTI*, or cited with genitive endings turned into nominatives and in italics, like *Iustus*.

Neither the ogam script nor the Roman ABC was sufficient to provide separate phonetic symbols, one per distinct sound, for all the sounds in spoken names and words of British, or Irish, or Latin given a British pronounciation. In the inscriptions discussed later, Latin V served for /w/ and also the vowel /u/, long or short; in QVENVENDANI both the V's are /w/, in BARCVNI the V is /u/. Latin letters QV meant /kw/, as in our 'question'; in ogam, *Q* until the sixth century – distinct from ogam *C*, the sound of /k/ – stood for /kʷ/, a slightly different sound with a shorter and less obvious /w/. By the sixth century there was the real problem that many letters no longer reflected the sounds one might associate with the same letters in everyday speech, like familiar Latin. This is a common ailment of language – think of English 'cough, rough, bough, through, though' where -ou- has to stand for five separate vowels or diphthongs and where the -gh is silent thrice and sounded as /f/ twice. We know that final -gh *was* formerly sounded and its equivalents have not been lost in the cognate Dutch or German *kug, rauch, bug, durch, doch*. The British inscriptions show conventions of spelling that were remembered and used but that had become orthographic fossils. On 477, a late sixth-century stone from Cornwall, CONETOCI does *not* rhyme with 'hockey', and never did. The probability is that it stands for an older (inflected, British) male name *\*Cune-dagos* 'Good-Wolf' or 'Good-Hound' (not that the meaning would have concerned its user). The *scriptor* or composer of the message followed an earlier convention linked to the manner in which the British had pronounced some of the Latin consonants, where /d/ and /g/ in these positions still had to be written as T and C because that is how /d/ and /g/ were once represented (when the name 'Tacitus' was actually spoken as 'Tagidus'). Spoken British, the native Celtic language that by the sixth century can be called Late British or Neo-Brittonic, was undergoing many changes on its way to becoming Primitive (or Old) Welsh and Primitive Cornish. There were now consonants whose one-for-one depiction in writing led to other problems. One was 'lenited m', a slurred or softened former /m/ in various positions that had become like a very nasal /v/, or the sounds /m/ and /v/ spoken together as a single consonant. Since it does not exist in English or Classical Latin, phonetically a Greek letter has to be borrowed to represent it, /μ/. For inscriptions, though capital M continued to be used to mean /μ/ until after 500, there came a time when this sound was so clearly seen to be quite different from initial M – as in 470 MACARI where the M is /m/ – that something else had to be found; in the seventh-century 1048 QONFAL the Q must be /k/ and the F can only be for /μ/.

Aspects of this awkward divorce between visible letters and contemporary spoken forms are explained in the text when necessary. The demonstration here is to stress the point that these often rough-looking and deceptively simple inscriptions are far from straightforward. It is not enough to visit them with camera, notebook, chalk and charcoal, rubbing paper or any other aid and then to suppose that an agreed copy of an agreed reading tells it all. There was an almost certain distinction between the actions of the person who cut the letters or strokes, the Latin *marmorarius* (in Rome) or *lapidarius*, and the earlier part played by whoever decided what was to be written, probably charged the bereaved by length, and turned the decision into a pattern to be followed – the *ordinator* or *scriptor*.

Cutters may have been, and probably often were, illiterate; their job was to reproduce, larger-sized, something scratched on slate or wood, or rarely written on a scrap of parchment. They made errors in spacing, missed out letters and miscopied other letters, just as today a keen eye will find small, stupid mistakes in nineteenth-century gravestones. But the purpose of this book is to show how a hundred or more such inscriptions give us approximately-dated names and other information; it is therefore helpful to know their potential defects when used as historical records.

All references to spoken sounds, their values as in Standard English (Received Pronunciation), are between slashes – /kw/ or /p/ or /oo/ as in 'moon'. The only diacritical marks, accents, are marks of length and/or stress on vowels when required. For Irish words and names it is conventional to use the acute accent, as in *dún*, Déisi. In some reconstructed British words the mark of length is a macron or bar above the vowel, *-ōnos*. The asterisk or 'star' before anything – a 'starred' form – means that it is not actually found or attested in a written source, but can be inferred and reconstructed in accordance with what are regarded as established principles of historical linguistics. The symbol < is short for 'is derived from' and

> for 'give rise to'. English 'window' < Old Norse *vind-auga* 'wind-eye, eye of a wall through which the wind blows'. Latin *fenêtre* > *fenêtre* in French and *ffenestr* in Welsh. Those who want to visit Wales and, in looking for inscribed memorials, might need to ask the way, should remember that Welsh employs its own modified Roman alphabetical system. Against English, Welsh is almost wholly a phonetic written tongye, but -ff- is the sound /f/, single -f- is /v/, -g- is always /g/ and never as English 'j', and written -w- within words and names is the vowel sound /oo/ with various lengths. It takes a little care and practice to find out exactly how place-names like LLanllywenfel and Llanwrthwl, not to say Llanynddyfri, are spoken by those who live there.

# *Abbreviations and Conventions*

Apart from abbreviated titles for major reference works (p.335) and periodicals (p. 337) and conventions used in printing inscriptions (p. xix) the following occur in the text:

| | |
|---|---|
| Pr.O,M, | Primitive, Old and Middle stages of the indicated languages. |
| Br. | Breton |
| Co. | Cornish |
| Ir. | Irish |
| W | Welsh |
| s.a. | under the year |
| s.n. | under the name |
| s.v. | under the word |
| V.1,2,3 | Indications of probable date, by thirds of centuries. IV, V, VI, VII are the fourth to seventh centuries AD. 'Thirds' are approximately as V.1, 400–30, V.2, 430–70, V.3, 470–500. |
| nom.,gen. | nominative or genitive forms in languages possessing different (inflected) case-endings for nouns and names. |

# 1
## Introduction: Places and People

THIS BOOK is, I hope, by no means as weighty or mentally indigestible as its chapter-notes and the concluding bibliography might make it seem. It forms a contribution to the early history of two regions of western Britain separated by the Bristol Channel or Severn Sea, and once having in common a language (British) spoken during and after the centuries of our incorporation as *Britannia* in the Roman empire. 'Demetia' and 'Dumnonia', used here, are convenient and historically accurate names respectively for south-west Wales and south-west England in the Roman period and later. Demetia is pronounced with two short E's, as in English 'emetic'. In Welsh it eventually became Dyfed; after the 1973 reorganization of local government throughout Britain, 'Dyfed' was revived as a regional label for the old counties of Cardigan, Carmarthen and Pembroke. I use it mainly to embrace the last two counties of these three, writing either Demetia or Dyfed for variation's sake. Dumnonia, with the first vowel (u) as in Standard English 'bull', may have had a long -o- (to rhyme with English 'ammonia'). This too has partly survived. In medieval Welsh it became *Dyfnein(t)* and some earlier form was borrowed in the seventh century by the Anglo-Saxons when they met the south-western Britons. Hence we find in 851 *Defena-scir*, which has led to today's 'Devonshire'. As a geographical term it covers Devon, Cornwall, and a part of (old) Somerset, and I use it further to include the Isles of Scilly and the small island of Lundy.

The notes and references are for the use of specialists or students who may wish to check what has been written. Some of the archaeological material, particularly from Cornwall, has not been published beforehand, and there are statements and interpretations and estimates of dates that differ from those elsewhere in print. Nevertheless I write first and foremost for the ordinary reader, who needs to look at the notes only for explanations. I readily agree that there can sometimes be no greater bore than an enthusiast, permitted by an indulgent publisher to write at unchecked length about what may amount to a personal hobby. My belief, though, is that dull of mind indeed would be he or she not excited by two such landscapes as Pembroke and Cornwall; and devoid of curiosity, too, not to be interested in those formative early centuries where so much of subsequent history was shaped.

There are, intentionally, three strands in the narrative. They are linked to all those special characteristics that allow us to distinguish Demetia and Dumnonia in post-Roman times (roughly, the fifth to seventh centuries AD) from their earlier state as administrative divisions within *Britannia*, Roman Britain. The first is an attempt to isolate and to describe the principal factors leading to cultural change; the second, examination (in time and space) of the agencies causing any such change; and the third, a demonstration in detail of how one might reach conclusions about the historical truth of the previous two strands. In a shorter form, with names and nouns in place of abstract notions, our three topics will be conversion to Christianity and whatever followed from it; Irish settlements in mainland Britain and the influence of contact with contemporary Europe; and inscribed memorial stones, with what they tell us about languages, names, dated innovations and cultural borrowings. The tools for the job are archaeology, history, language and epigraphy (the last being the interpretation and classification of inscriptions). The outcome could never be, and is not here claimed to be, a set of established facts; established beyond all possible dispute. There are precious few 'facts' in the story of any nation's past until the stage when literacy and historicity have become near-universal. Conclusions are therefore set out only as *models*; propositions that can be claimed as highly probable, because they are based on agreed observations and on credible reconstructions of what, whether or not we accept this, remains an irrecoverable past.

As a block of time past, 'Roman Britain' began in AD 43 and ended according to personal choice; one could use the old date of AD 410 (now fairly meaningless), but with the sub-division from about AD 250 onward being loosely known as 'the Late Roman period'. What should we call the succeeding age? 'Post-Roman' is a useful term, but one perhaps best confined to archaeological finds and sites. I find it preferable in the context of Demetia and Dumnonia and their combined early history to use 'Early Christian' (certainly not the confusing 'Early Medieval'; or 'the Dark Ages', first propounded in 1904 by W. R. Ker when discussing pre-Renaissance literature). It constitutes no objection to admit that in, say, the year 500 not all the inhabitants of Demetia and Dumnonia were necessarily Christians. Many people in Bronze Age Britain never owned, saw or handled any item of bronze, and in Romano-British times a great many Britons never met a genuine Roman official from Italy, used Roman coins or spoke any Latin. Periods of the past may be named by reference to major innovations. The advent of Christianity, its consolidation as the main faith in both Demetia and Dumnonia, and all that followed tangibly and visibly from the adoption of this Mediterranean-based religion together signalled a new, clear, cultural horizon, one that merits a fresh title. Because Christianity as a theological system had a counterpart in the written word, calling for literacy and a knowledge of Latin (at least), internally generated records of the present and recent past − native history − were stimulated. They became possible. Physically, Christianity led to what has now become a full archaeology of places for worship, the disposal and commemoration of the dead, and a symbolic vocabulary expressed as a rather simple art.

But Christianity did not emerge, inexplicably, from the hilly ranges and winding river-valleys of Demetia, any more than from the downs, beaches and little fields of Dumnonia. Nor (in the latter area) was it bequeathed to a post-Roman native kingdom from its Late Roman predecessor, the *respublica civitatis Dumnoniorum*. The Christian faith was introduced; ideas spread from household to household, and new ideas met deeply rooted resistance. 'The advent' (of Christianity, as of any organized religious system) should suggest a band of time, perhaps over two or three generations, at the start of which such ideas are adopted for various reasons by a small though influential segment of a population, and at the end of which a religion has become generally predominant, causing the replacement of structures, graves, art and literature associated with previously held beliefs that can now be stigmatized as pagan or heathen. It does not assist our enquiry to picture missionaries in the Victorian sense of the word, men like the nineteenth-century Dumnonian, Bishop John William Colenso with his powerful influence on the Zulus of Natal; or to imagine at this early stage persons such as – just east of Demetia – William Williams, 'Williams Pantycelin', greatest of Wales's many hymn-writers and a leader of the Methodist revival. Colenso and Williams may have had sixth-century counterparts, but we cannot hope to do more than detect faintly some aftermath of their endeavours.

This may introduce consideration of the second strand, the part played incidentally if not always intentionally by immigrants, colonists and travellers. A major feature of post-Roman (in this instance, rather than 'Early Christian') Wales was the arrival, perhaps originally as casual raiders but subsequently as permanent agricultural settlers, of whole groups of Irish people. How many of them, at what dates, and at which localities are questions to be faced later. There is a certain topicality here. Ireland (the geographical entity) suffered its worst recorded population crash a century and a half ago, when an agrarian people, already struggling with the impossible system of rundale land-tenure, was felled by the incidence of a fungus blight (*Phytophthora infestans*) that wiped out the mainstay potato crops. From a possible nine millions, the populace – devastated by pure famine – shrank further through mass emigration, not always to the United States. Today the 26-county Republic faces a less awful dilemma, but with far more young people than any possible provision of jobs for them there has been another, low-key, mass emigration to neighbouring Britain. The causes are now partly economic and not (as before) mainly those of desperation. The end result is, allowing for greater modern numbers, the same; today, Irish settlements in Liverpool and Kilburn, and around AD 400 in parts of Atlantic Wales and – with Argyll, most successful of all the colonies – of Atlantic Scotland. What were the natures of the causes in the fourth and fifth centuries is unclear. Today the British, in Britain, think that they can distinguish the Irish through gradations of spoken English ('Irish accents', of which there are actually many very different ones), by their forenames and surnames, and rather less easily by their religious followings within Christianity or their politics. In the fifth century, the natives of Wales certainly knew some of these distinctions, spoken Primitive Irish being audibly quite different from spoken Late British, and many (though not all) personal names being peculiar to Ireland. How long these differentials persisted on British soil is open to debate; and there may have been others, for instance detailed aspects of agricultural and pastoral life, that were just as tell-tale at the time but of which we know hardly anything.

In the most general way it has for decades been accepted that within south-east and south central Wales (modern Gwent and Glamorgan) Christianity, as present there in the fourth century, was maintained without any real hiatus into the fifth century and later; that quite a degree of what is called *romanitas*, the whole culture with spoken and written Latin and certain Roman domestic habits current in Late Roman towns, persisted among the better-off and perhaps extended as far to the west as *Moridunum*, now Carmarthen (town); and subsequently that the fourth–fifth century Irish settlers in what became Pembroke and coastal Cardigan adopted both the *romanitas* and the Christian faith of their host country. This does seem to be, broadly, what happened, though it fails to consider relative sizes of native and immigrant populations or to explain just how, in Pembroke firstly, a post-Roman kingdom with a mixed population was established under a ruling kin-group of Irish origin. In a similar way it has long been supposed (one could say here, rightly, but for very inadequate reasons) that Christianity was introduced to Dumnonia – specifically *via* the north-east part of Cornwall and the Atlantic edge of Devon – mainly from south Wales, obviously by people travelling across the intervening seas. This too may be brought into focus under an archaeological microscope, as must be a further and far from negligible topic, the tale of two 'Ventures into the Interior'. One, linked to Demetia proper, led to the rise of a little sixth-century principality in the upper valley of the Welsh river Usk, the heart of the later county of Brecon or Brecknock, *Brycheiniog* in Welsh; it concerns an enigmatic though (it will be argued) historically real person later remembered as 'Brychan'. The other and smaller venture took place within Dumnonia, was likewise involved with people of Irish descent, and affected the 'red lands' or South Hams of present-day Devon.

Is this just a cloud of speculation or does there exist a body of evidence to affirm such claims? We come to the last strand, involving another whole dimension of the past not yet discussed. Archaeology and history, or one might put it as 'archaeological inference and historical evidence', differ in many respects, too many for discussion in an introductory chapter. One of the more obvious is that archaeological work so often, perforce, deals with human anonymity. Skeletons have bones, but they lack names. The remains of excavated houses were once homes in which families passed their lives, but we do not know what they were called. In stating that burial no. 23 is the extended skeleton of a male, aged 40-plus, who had in youth broken his fore-arm and who seems to have died from septicaemia following an abscess on his jaw, we experience the frustration that he must now remain no more than no. 23. Yet in life that man had flesh and hair, spoke a complex language that our united skills can reconstruct only hypothetically and in imperfect form, and led an existence no less emotionally rich than any of ours today.

Between AD 300 and AD 700, perhaps as many as a quarter-million such people lived and died within the confines of Dumnonia. From purely historical sources, how many of them can we name? At the moment, possibly three. Two of those were only visitors; in 384 two heretic bishops, Instantius and Tiberianus, were deposed by an ecclesiastical council at *Burdigala*, modern Bordeaux, and exiled to somewhere than can be identified as the Isles of Scilly (whence, no doubt, they escaped on the first amenable boat). Around 530–40 the British cleric Gildas, censuring five British kings for their personal behaviour, named in his list a Constantinus of Dumnonia, a man by then of mature age. With difficulty, one or two more might be added. If one accepts that the *Life* of St Samson (of Dol) was, at core, composed in the seventh century and contains genuine personal names proper to the early sixth century (p. ...), we have the (Latinized) name *Guedianus* for a Cornish notable of that time, *Juniavus* (or *Uuiniavus*) for a living cleric and *Docco* for another who by then was probably dead. This is not however directly historical. Professor Malcolm Todd points out that *Aemilius* son of Saenius, a sailor on the Rhine, is described on a Cologne inscription as *civis Dumnonius*, a Dumnonian, and there is another tombstone of about 425 at Salona on the Adriatic coast to a lady who was *clarissima femina* 'a most distinguished woman' (i.e., of senatorial family) and also *civis Dumnonia*, though her actual name is lost. Though it is scarcely possible to assert than any surviving place-name in Dumnonia can be securely traced back to this distant time, let alone place-names that contain personal names, that of Domellick – a farmland on the slope of the hill surmounted by St Dennis parish church in mid-Cornwall, itself built within some Iron Age fortlet – is recorded in Domesday Book as *Dimelihoc* and in Geoffrey of Monmouth's *Historia* (early twelfth century) as *Dimilioc*. In this unusual name the first element is Cornish *din-* 'fort'; it is remotely conceivable that this is followed by a reflex of \**Emiliācum* 'estate, or territory, of Aemilius' (a name unlikely to have figured here later than the sixth century), but in no way can this be pressed at all far. Scraping the onomastic barrel with a vengeance, we can only conjure up a paltry few named individuals for all of Dumnonia.

Yet, within this period of the past, there is a way to escape such sterile anonymity; almost we are able to encounter men and women as real as Abbot Aldhelm, Queen Matilda or Horace Walpole. Within Dumnonia (including Scilly, and Lundy) some fifty inscribed memorial stones, and within Demetia rather more out of the larger all-Wales total, may be dated to between 450 and 700 as outside limits. All these inscriptions, a few of which may prove not to be Christian at all, have been closely studied. Inscribed in Roman capitals or devolved forms or book-hand letters or in the Irish stroke-writing called *ogam* and sometimes in both, they make up the oldest written records of the Celtic languages (except for some abbreviated names on native coins of the first centuries BC and AD). They also provide a permanent mirror to contemporary literacy. Ground-rules for dating them to the nearest half-century or third of a century have been painstakingly worked out, though still subject to debate, and the not very common addition of certain specifically Christian symbols alongside the lettering has to be examined as an aspect of our first Christian art.

It is impossible to exaggerate the importance of these monuments, which are at once *archaeological* in respect of being vertically-set, sometimes shaped, stone pillars purposefully sited at the time; *historical*, in that they constitute written records, however simple, and may even name persons independently attested in other historical sources; and *linguistic*, not only because they may reflect contemporary stages of Irish and British but because they reveal the interaction of Insular Celtic with contemporary spoken and written Latin. ('Insular' means 'British and Irish, together'; a useful portmanteau adjective.) Study of the occurrences of individual stones in time and space must now be far more thorough than in the past. As for the inscriptions, almost everything in them consists of personal names, Insular or continuing Roman. Where this leads us is into a realm of explanations. Today, a true-blue Briton called Higginbotham or Armstrong will assume at once that somebody called O'Donovan or Murphy is Irish, or of Irish descent; this may be a generalization from widely known stereotypes but one still likely to be accurate. After Ireland's 1845–9 famines, when many Irish families were induced to settle in west Cornwall as unskilled labourers in the tin and copper mines, some retained their obviously Irish names like Murphy or Burns; some found their names being changed, by mine clerks, to better-known local forms – O'Hagan to 'Higgins', for instance; and some became indistinguishable, because the same name happened to be in use anyhow – Irish 'Teague' (really from the personal name Tadhg, as *ÓTaidhg*, 'Tague, Teigue, Teague', etc.) and Cornish 'Teague' (from *teg* 'good-looking, fair-haired'). Very similar coincidences and confusions can be found centuries earlier. But when within Dumnonia we observe, on stones, that a sixth-century QVENATAVCI bore a specially Irish name and his contemporary CVNOMORI a British one, we must not rest content without trying to explain why both should be found within the restricted compass of modern Cornwall.

Among further aspects one can be singled out now; the location of many inscribed stones on what are recognizable as Early Christian sites. Archaeologists functioning as landscape historians manage to build up maps of what they suspect, or demonstrate through further work, to have been the earliest churches and cemeteries in a region. In certain instances the occurrence of an inscribed memorial, either not moved (or not moved very far, since first set up) may underpin the claim of 'earliest'. But this can reach a stage where the sum of the parts is more enlightening than the study of any single component. Such Christian sites, outward and visible remnants from the adoption stage, the advent, of this religion – still officially the national religion of Britain and Ireland – indicate patterns. In Demetia and Dumnonia, both of which were until recently almost wholly agricultural regions, the patterns may still be ascertained and discussed. What they convey to us is only secondarily linked to the degree of local piety and habits of worship, and much more closely so to recent and more elaborate patterns of market-places, cinemas, fish-and-chip shops and (deserted) rural railway-stations. If we can untangle the messages, they suggest to us where people *lived* – in terms of land-holdings, tiny settlements and defensive homesteads rather than of the familiar medieval village, but as close as we may ever get to the communities of post-Roman times.

The conclusions in this book, which are given at the end of chapters rather than in a final summary, therefore rely heavily upon the interpretation of inscriptions. Here, it seems appropriate to comment on a completely extraneous factor; the urgency imposed by decay. A very large number of these inscriptions on stone can now hardly be made out. Exposure to fourteen centuries of Atlantic rain and wind has not preserved granite and gritstone surfaces, and comparison of some of today's depictions with reliable ones made a century ago reveals that modern erosive elements (acid rain, smoke, exhaust fumes) are causing galloping deterioration. Of the Dumnonian stones, only one (476) has now been moved into the shelter of the Royal Cornwall Museum, another from Devon (489) being in the British Museum's basement. Too many stand by roadside verges and hedges, or outside in churchyards. In south Wales, despite small collections in several museums (Brecon, Carmarthen, National Museum of Wales) and a degree of shelter inside church porches, the picture is not much better. During the years 1989–91 I re-visited, chalked or charcoaled, photographed and drew nearly all such stones in Dumnonia, and was alarmed at so many clear instances of erosion and damage. If this book induces any new priority of care for these unique stone documents, it will have served one purpose.

Demetia, as south-west Wales, and Dumnonia, as south-west England, are not all that far apart; it is only 40 miles as the seagull flies from Tenby over to Ilfracombe. For the worker in the field, going by road and crossing the Severn at the Bridge or at Gloucester, it is more like 400 miles from west Cornwall to Pembroke. Anybody claiming to write with familiarity on the foundation of first-hand study about one region is unlikely to make the same claim about the other, and my knowledge of Demetia in the field is only that of an informed visitor upon many, but long separated, occasions. Given that we already have admirable surveys treating of the post-Roman archaeology and history of much of Wales, as also of Devon and Cornwall, is yet another book necessary? Justification might be offered if we now accept that, mostly in the sixth century, the two regions *were* connected in that people did move from one to the other, that their movements were probably responsible for the spread of Christian ideas, that the inscribed stones in particular form an under-explored source for such historical concepts, and that no study yet published has made sufficient use of the available evidence. The compass of *this* study has been kept within limits — it must introduce the further complication of the early Irish settlements in certain parts of Britain, but the main theme then becomes the interaction of three 'Atlantic' regions within post-Roman Britain and Ireland, in time not straying much later than AD 650. Since it is not intended as a textbook for Demetian and Dumnonian epigraphy as such, an earlier note (p. xx) has explained conventions that permit simplified forms of words and names to appear in the text. Assuming that the reader will probably share the writer's interest in that rare feature of post-Roman study, the survival of actual names of real people, special attention has been given to these; remembering that there will always be a large margin of uncertainty. There are gaps between what *A* was actually called in AD 500, how anyone else chose to reduce that name to writing, what in 1994 we think his name meant, what in 500 he himself (if at all) thought it meant, how it sounded in speech, and where his parents got it from.

There can be no implication that the study of Insular inscriptions has been neglected. It has long been a commonplace to niggle about individual readings, interpretations and inferences in the work of the late Professor R. A. S. Macalister (*CIIC* i and ii); one must affirm that Macalister was a tireless and solitary fieldworker, prolific recorder and would-be preservationist for many decades, in what was only one of his many academic interests. Recent trends in Insular scholarship, where compartmentalization is on the way out and where people can be equally interested in archaeology, history, language and epigraphy, have been towards the complex interplay of the early Insular tongues (Latin among them), fresh and critical analysis of texts, and landscape study aided by aerial photography. Another long look at the inscribed stones, with the historical and social inferences that may be drawn, merely resumes with added ammunition a line of research that attracted many pioneering scholars, among whom the late Professor Kenneth Jackson remains easily foremost.

We can begin with a reminder, sketched in the next chapter, that the inscribed stones of Britain and Ireland are not unique. They are a late Insular manifestation of a custom to be found over most of early Europe (and further afield), and not bound to any one religion. By the time that they had come to be used to display Christian epitaphs, they were a legacy from our communal spiritual past.

# 2
# *Personal Memorials in Stone*

IN LATE SUMMER 1985 I happened to be on a remote limestone plateau in southeast France, three and a half thousand feet up. This huge expanse – desiccated, depopulated, seldom visited – is a land-island cut off by deep river canyons. Upon its rolling surface, under the baking sun, the deep blue skies and the eternal silence, humans are now outnumbered by the griffon vultures, two species of eagles and above all the sheep. The flocks of ewes, kept for their milk from which the queen of all cheeses (Roquefort) is made, wander between the few still-occupied farms. The plateau was not always thus. Remains of four thousand years of land-use lie all across it, a mighty book who runs may read. Low stone walls snake for miles along the ridges, and the markers of this prehistoric countryside are the menhirs; pillars of dolomitic limestones.

I was sitting in the shade of one such menhir, near a spot called Balat de Bioulène, 'valley of the cow-herd', when there was a sound of little bells and a shepherd, with his slow-moving flock, came into view. These men, *li pastrou*, are weather-darkened hermits who roam the hungry acres; he had his stick, his large umbrella with wooden ribs (metal ones attract lightning) and his two snappy dogs. It is almost impossible to meet local informants here and, after tea and civilities, I asked him if he knew the name of the standing-stone, which is an obvious landmark. He told me that its name was *lou tzeiont peiro*. Older people on the plateau speak, besides heavily-accented French, a distinct dialect of Occitan (Languedocien), one that must be explored in order to translate the many significant place-names. *Lou tzeiont peiro* ('géant-pierre') would mean The Giant-Stone, and can be seen as grammatically ambiguous. So with difficulty I asked him, 'Lou tzeiont, ero ece abas, sou aquesto peiro'; 'Was the giant down here, under this stone'? The shepherd, amused by my attempt to speak his archaic tongue, was kindly enough to follow me. He slapped the menhir and replied slowly, as if to an idiot, 'No, no, no. Lou tzeiont e *dedins* la peiro – es *entre* la peiro' (The giant is *inside* the stone – he's in the *middle* of the stone), and with that he had to rejoin his dogs because the sheep, walking at one mile an hour, do not stop until they reach a home field at dusk.

The folklore of these uplands, *les grands causses*, has been fully studied.[1] Mostly it concerns wolves (real wolves, until about 1900) and were-wolves, terrible creatures called *trèves* who are revenants of the newly dead, and the demonology of a real limestone underworld entered through the *avens* or swallet-holes. I can find no legends attached to the menhirs, or to the numerous dolmens; the former may well possess individual names but these are not given ont eh IGN 1:25,000 sheets. I now regret that I did not know enough of his language to question the old shepherd Pratlong (who has since died); but how that simple statement, 'The giant is inside the stone', would have delighted another, intellectual, giant, the Romanian-born, French-speaking, American-based Mircea Eliade, father of religious phenomenology.

On Causse Mejan (*calsa mediana*, the central calcareous upland) in dept. Lozère seventy-four menhirs have been listed and I could add more to these. All, once, had function. Some mark the limits of prehistoric field-systems; or the bounds between the *dévès*, the sparse rough grazing, and the hollows or dolines into which the soil has been washed, and the area laboriously cleared of stones over millennia – *lou balats*. This is not confined to south-east France; there is a near-identical landscape, also with menhirs, in northern Spain above the winding gorges of the river Ebro, and (in miniature) one sees it surrounding Mount Pantocrater on the island of Corfu. It is a limestone phenomenon. But across the French *causses* some of these great pillars, jagged or smooth, as impressive at midday as they are by moonlight, have another function. They mark burials. On Causse Mejan, as on Causse Noir and the gloomy Causse de Sauveterre, they can adjoin ruined burial-cairns or dry-stone cist graves.

In Britain and Ireland, because the earliest (and often the principal) evidence for the adoption of Christianity in a given region assumes the shape of legible inscriptions on large upright stones, it is relevant to consider this background and to move outwards from *les grands causses* to Europe generally. Standing-stones, often called by this eighteenth-century invented Cornish term *menhir* (*men* 'stone', *hyr* 'long'), fall within a complex of all larger re-arrangements and constructions of rocks from the third millennium BC onward. There are the megaliths of the late Neolithic. As well as chambered tombs in mounds or cairns, there are stone circles, stone alignments, and individual menhirs that can be three or more metres tall. In many areas, menhirs may have acted as bound-stones or territorial markers. A nineteenth-century instance of this in the metalliferous mining districts of south-west Britain was the use of small granite pillars, inscribed with suitable code-letters, to define upon the surface the *setts*, the areas underground that had been leased for working. As Eliade pointed out, there seems to be a world-wide incidence (geology permitting) of menhirs that were certainly erected in the remote past, but were not apparently linked to any kind of burial.

That individual upright stones, prominent in any setting, could however mark burials from an early date is apparent not only in parts of France but, in Dumnonia at any, rate, from an excavation at Try, Gulval, in the Land's End peninsula.[2] Here a cist grave at the foot of a three-metres high granite menhir contained pieces of a cremated human skeleton and an Early Bronze Age beaker.

At the same place a strange deposit of horse-bones and a coin of Gallienus (AD 259–68) suggests a very much later interest in the sacred potential of the stone. On the French *causses*, excavations of late Neolithic cist graves have from time to time uncovered similar associations. For later prehistory, among the thousands of standing-stones in Britain and Ireland there are many, somewhat smaller (man-height would be an average) than the vast isolated pillars of primary landscape clearance, where an association with the dead could be alternatively or exclusively suspected. In Ireland, where appropriate surface rock is exposed, small-to-medium vertical stones are legion. They have never been nationally listed (a daunting task) but a good idea of frequency may be gained now from the few and highly-detailed surveys such as those undertaken for County Donegal[3] and the Dingle peninsula (Co. Kerry).[4] Some were ornamented with small incised crosses, perhaps centuries after they were set upright; some bear ogam inscriptions (see next chapter), and we must allow that certain stones were erected specifically to display such additional features. In the absence of large-scale excavation it remains a suspicion, but one well-founded, that the purpose of many an uninscribed upright pillar or slab in Ireland was to mark a human burial.

What is the message contained, generically, in such features, and what connection could there be between the custom of indicating boundaries and land-holdings and (if the old shepherd Pratlong was right) personification of a long-dead notable, human or legendary? Mircea Eliade spelled it out in a classic exposition.[5] To puny men, huge stones are something essentially *other* than themselves. A pillar may be the habitat of an ancestor whose spirit entered into the rock, as in certain cultures it could abide within a megalithic chambered tomb; from this stance, the ancestors were expected to guard the publicly delineated lands that their descendants continued to exploit. The most impressive quality is *permanence*. A stone, as a permanent substitute, can become a body built for eternity. Anywhere, menhirs offer duration without expected end. As long as they stand they portray a modality of *existing*, independent of the brief temporal *becoming* that characterizes man's all too short span on earth. Whether we admit or not, whether we even realize it or not, this is partly why most of us will still spend good money on ordering tombstones. And because all the slabs and pillars and tombstones point upwards, away from that rough soil whence we all sprang and to which, inhumed or cremated, we shall all revert, pillars offer a *modality of ascension* to another sphere of existence. In most faiths (Christianity among these) there is a lossely defined notion that the Otherworld is beyond the sky; in any where it might be regarded as being subterranean, an earth-fast pillar offers an alternative modality of *descent*.

'Christianized' menhirs are known from Britain and Ireland, as well as from Brittany where they are frequently illustrated. The large oval churchyard enclosure at Mabe, near Falmouth in Cornwall, holds a medieval parish church but may mark a pre-Norman cemetery; in 1580 it was *Lavabe* (*lan* 'early churchyard

PERSONAL MEMORIALS IN STONE

**Fig. 2.1** Mabe churchyard, Cornwall; prehistoric menhir(?) with medieval cross **(left)**. Pembroke, near Mynachlog-ddu; a recent memorial menhir, 'Maen Waldo' for Waldo Williams **(right)**. Photos: author.

enclosure' plus *Mabe*). A huge granite pillar, probably *in situ*, stands by the church tower (Fig. 2.1). The reticulated pattern on the granite is natural, but certainly human workmanship is the addition of a linear cross, probably medieval. It brings this prehistoric menhir, too inconvenient to shift, into the ambit of the dominant Faith. For modern times we may look to Dyfed. In Pembroke a picturesque side-road from Mynachlog-ddu to Rosebush crosses, at about SN 135 304, open moorland with a view of the southern flank of the Preseli range. Here there are two large menhirs, north and south of the road, suggestive of territory-markers erected in Bronze Age times. The northern pillar was in fact put up (using a helicopter) in 1989, to commemorate a cystic fibrosis appeal. The southern is rather different (Fig. 2.1). Upon its north-facing side is fixed a polished black tablet with WALDO 1904–1971 (and the menhir, in its small cairn, was indeed only set up after the latter date). It commemorates Waldo Williams, a great man; poet, Quaker, militant pacifist and environmentalist, he was instrumental in defeating an appalling proposal to site a military training-range in the Preseli mountains. On the tablet four lines from his famous poem 'Preseli' recall his beloved hills – *mur fy mebyd* 'the rampart of my boyhood'.[6] The chosen spot was, in life, an actual and symbolic window for him ('Hon oedd fy ffenestr'). It matters not at all exactly where Mr Williams's ashes were scattered. This 1970s menhir is now *him* – Maen Waldo – offering unique permanency to the man, his writings and his life. Only in the intelligibility of the inscription does it differ from pillars with anonymous associations, aeons earlier.

In later chapters, the discussion of inscribed stones in various parts of Wales – Demetia, or Brycheiniog – or in Dumnonia may give an impression that plain pillars and menhirs are all heathen and prehistoric and their inscribed successors all necessarily Christian and the product of more recent times. This is not so, and misses the point. The elements of any inscribed stone when it denotes a human death or burial are public visibility; symbolic permanence; and, as a kind of useful reinforcement, a legible message. The message will convey information, but it is not there *per se* as any act of worship, let alone of Christian worship, and occasionally a Christian significance can only be inferred. The fact that most catalogues or surveys of monuments usually list such things as 'Early Christian stones' is irrelevant, and can beg the question. All this leads to a proposition, one briefly aired in an earlier paper,[7] that may seem to run counter to received views but is none the less indicated by a proper review of the evidence.

There are some fifty Early Christian inscribed pillars or slabs known from south-west Britain, about three times as many in Wales, and two much smaller groups in the Isle of Man and southern Scotland. The mainland British equivalents of the myriad upright stones in Ireland are certainly not lacking, even if a large proportion now serves as gateposts, scratching-posts for cattle, vertical elements in stone walls and coigns or lintels in out-houses. It is quite likely that in both Wales and the south-west there are – generally unrecognized and unlisted – small to medium menhirs of all shapes, erected as late as the pre-Roman Iron Age, that mark pre-Christian burials of notable men and women. On the whole, archaeological attention has tended to focus on the larger menhirs as potential markers that can be accommodated within models of prehistoric partition and allocation of land.[8] On the reasonable premiss that – given the proximity of Britain and Ireland – later instances of a specific and detectable human custom probably imitated, or were inspired by, earlier instances, and should not too readily be explained as cases of independent invention, it will be suggested that Ireland had the precedence in time. In post-Roman Britain the idea of 'personalizing' a given stone memorial with any kind of writing seems to have been, at best, only marginally connected with whatever the Roman occupiers did. It is a fashion that may have been shaped in Ireland before it ever became an aspect of British post-Roman Christian activity. Naturally this raises an implication that there could be inscribed stones, of a sort, within Ireland that were put up during the fourth (if not also third) century AD, and must then be wholly or partly pre-Christian. This, too, is a supportable claim. In later chapters there will be an emphasis on the mental separation of concepts – the knowledge and use of Latin, a penchant for real Roman names, the practice of Christianity and the habit of popular inscriptions – that can be far too readily run together as a single social phenomenon. The really Big Step Forward in the prolonged tale of the human dead and the various stone monuments associated with burial was the addition of *messages*. It is the existence of any such message, elevating the symbolism of the eternal stone to a plane of fresh significance, that may be more important than the message's actual content. It is certainly more relevant, historically, as a development that whatever religious nuances can now be extracted by contemporary analysts.

Something of this is apparent if we turn our attention to early Europe. Here one can find groups of personal stone memorials, linked by having emerged at much the same stage of social development (without going into controversy, this was at an advanced point in the local Iron Age or equivalent). Out of a considerable array we might select instances, none of which can possibly have any connection with Ireland and Britain in Roman times. An intriguing case is that of the south-central Alpine region north from Milan, together with north-east Italy around the head of the Adriatic, and the large south-eastern Swiss canton known (according to linguistic preference) as Grisons, Graubünden, Grigioni or Grischuna. During the final centuries BC this region was home to a north Italic language (Venetic), a Celtic speech that seems to have been an eastern aspect of the better-known Gaulish, and to a non-Indo-European substrate that might be regarded as a northern outpost of Etruscan. Today, continuing this mixed tradition, it is the homeland of a bundle of related sub-languages derived from dialects of Latin – they include Friulan, in that corner of Italy north of a line from Venice to Trieste, and Romontsch, Switzerland's fourth language. The group is known as Raetic (or Rhaetic).

The inscribed stones from here combine many features.[9] A tall slab from Davesco north of Lugano (Fig. 2.2) shows in simplified outline two human figures. One could hardly ask for a better link between people and memorials. The inscription is written in Lepontic, one of several scripts borrowed from the Etruscan civilization to the south. As with other memorial-types having a vertical emphasis – this is in itself a most ancient symbolism, one that brings together the earth and any burials in 'now-space' and the sky above as 'other-space'[10] – we are expected to turn our heads sideways, in this case to the right, and to read upwards. It appears to represent a husband-and-wife memorial. Along the shorter, female, figure can be read the wording SLANIAI : VERKALAI : PALA, and along the male, where there is a hint of a helmet or some martial headgear, TISIUI : PIUOTIALUI : PALA. The common final word, *pala* or *\*bala*, ought to mean

**Fig. 2.2** The Davesco stone, Chur Museum, Switzerland, drawn from photographs; joint memorial of *Slania* (female, right) and *Tisios* (male, left). The inscriptions in Lepontic, read upwards, are written from right to left as shown.

'gravestone, memorial', and it may survive in a Ticino dialect *balon* 'block of stone'. The personal names should be in the genitive case ('of') or dative ('for'). The messages have been interpreted as 'Stone of Slania, daughter' (*-la(i)*) 'of Verkos', and 'Stone of Tisios, son' (*-lu(i)*) 'of Pivotios'. The two people are socially identified through reference to their fathers. Another slab from Stabio, canton Ticino, has a shorter message, ALKOUINOS ASKONETI. The terminations *-os* and *-i* suggest, as in Gaulish, the masculine singular nominative and genitive endings like Latin's cognate *domin-us*, *domin-i*; 'Here lies, or here is commemorated, Alkovinos, son of Askonetos'. The very simple formula appears elsewhere, and Celticists might suppose that the first name ends with an adjective related to Gaulish *-uindos* 'white, fair, etc.'.[11] But there is no reason to see the 'A, son of B' shape of a short memorial as exclusively Celtic at all. Referable to a perception of society, it over-ran linguistic differences. Another slab in Lepontic script from Mesocco reads RANENI UALAUNAL. If this means '(stone) of Ranenos, (son) of Valaun-', the second name invites direct comparison with other personal names of the *Vallaun-* type attested in Gaulish.[12] But the ending *-al* points instead to the entirely non-Celtic genitive or possessive suffix of Etruscan, found with proper names; *Larisal* 'of Lars', *Rasnal* 'of the Etruscan people' (*Rasna*).[13]

In the sub-Alpine region, any borrowing of ideas that produced inscribed memorials must have been from the south. The Davesco stone with its 'pin-men' outlines of Slania and Tisios is later than, and visually cruder than, any Etruscan funerary slab like the well-known sixth-century-BC Volterra stone.[14] This is however a sophisticated example in the same general tradition. It shows a male warrior, and is inscribed up one margin with *mi aviles tites uchsie mulenike*, '(I am) of Aulus Titus. Uchsie dedicated (me)'. The message is 'internalized'; that is, of a sort where the object on view is deemed to be speaking to the viewer. Internalized messages, 'spoken' by stones or pots, were favoured by Etruscans and Romans; if we think them odd in the later setting of European Christianity, we might recall the Alfred Jewel brooch in the Ashmolean Museum, Oxford, with its openwork message AELFRED MEC HEHT GEWYRCAN 'Alfred had me made', and those Romantic funerary wall-tablets that open with such invitations as 'Stranger, look on these Lines...'

The memorials just discussed have inscriptions, and therefore it was intended that they should be read and understood by literate passers-by. Some are additionally pictorial, even minimally so. Writing and art are thus never mutually exclusive, but complementary components of the fundamental *message*; in this manner one can attach an ornamented stone to a dead person more closely and permanently than would be likely through oral tradition, or fallible memory. There is an older Mediterranean idiom, where the personal memorial can partake of the highest expression of contemporary, élite, art. The beautiful sculptured gravestones of Athens in the fourth century BC are relief or semi-relief portraits.[15] If a short inscription happens to supply a name, it is visually a subsidiary feature. When, within the post-Augustan expansion of the Roman empire, derivatives of the Greek, Etruscan and Italic memorial styles eventually reached such outlying provinces as Britain, we can observe further changes; a tendency to expand the inscription into a multi-line message, using abbreviations and formulae to save both space and cost, and the use of pictorial elements (often mere artistic clichés) in whatever area of the surface is not inscribed. In Britannia, a stone from York has a panel flanked by winged figures, and a sad message (Fig. 2.3).[16] Opening with D.M. (*dis manibus*, 'to the shades of the departed', a stock abbreviation), the memorial is to 'Eglecta, aged 30 years, here buried beside Crescens, their son, of 3 years; Antonius Stepanus had this set up to his wife'. Another stone from Housesteads on Hadrian's Wall is topped with a little depiction of a hare, and is to 'Anicius Ingenuus, *medicus ordinarius* of the First Cohort of Tungrians; he lived 25 years'.

Both epitaphs, making allowance for the passage of time, are still socially intelligible. York, *Eboracum*, was a crowded city; disease was common, life-expectancy short, and Eglecta and little Crescens may have been victims of some epidemic. Anicius Ingenuus, the field-surgeon or medico in his military unit, must have been popular with comrades who subscribed for his memorial. The messages, from what was a relatively highly organized world of Roman Britain, place these

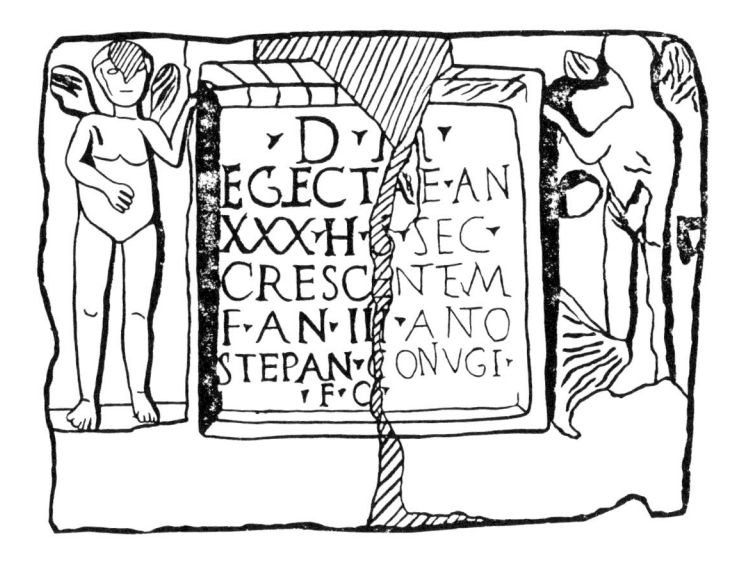

**Fig. 2.3** Tombstone of *Eglecta* and *Crescens* from York (*RIB* no. 695), drawn by R. P. Wright and reproduced by kind permission of Oxford University Press.

people in frames of reference regarded as appropriate. The York stone, from urban life, names the head of the little family; the Housesteads stone, the surrogate military 'family' of the cohort. The warriors in the Lepontic inscriptions are identified through being named as 'the son of' somebody. Messages can thus anchor the dead in *societal time*, a passage of years over several generations where word-of-mouth provides an idea of what had gone before.

But even in their most distant and provincial guises Roman tombstones had this pictorial aspect. It could be symbolic, even space-filling. Stone-cutters, *marmorarii*, could reproduce models lying around their yards, perhaps also show customers the equivalent of patterns. There is a shop sign from Rome that recognizes the customer as the ultimate chooser.[17] It reads D M/TITVLOS SCRIBENDOS VEL SI QVID OPERIS MARMORARI OPVS FVERIT HIC HABES – 'Inscriptions written to order! or anything you might want of stone-cutter's work! The job will be done – you'll get it here!' Such arrangements outlasted Imperial Rome, re-surfacing in later western Christianity. Our own gravestones include stock symbols (the cross, angels, a draped urn). Devices may allude to ancestry or professions, and even a favourite dog or a couple of staves of music can be commissioned. In Scotland, from the seventeenth century, there was a splendid custom of showing tools of the trade; parts of a plough for a farmer, shears and pressing-iron for a tailor, a complete outfit of blacksmith's tools.[18]

Personal memorials on stone without inscriptions of any kind, displays being

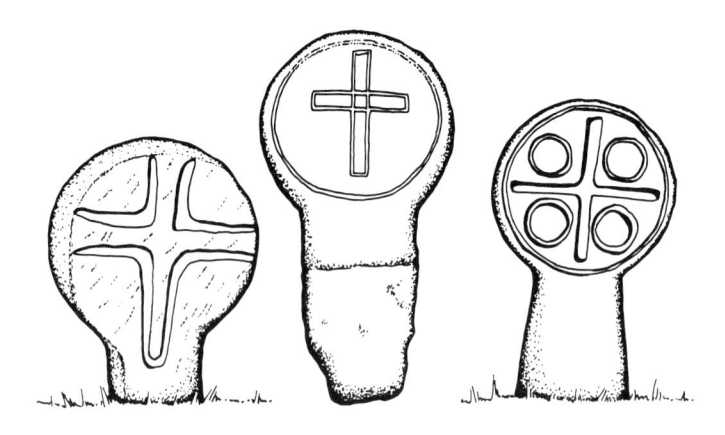

**Fig. 2.4** Uninscribed individual tombstones; discoidal steles from Languedoc, France, eleventh – twelfth centuries (drawn from photographs).

confined to symbolic and representational art, are possible and known; they head a descending scale, at the bottom of which one might notice – in many Middle Eastern lands – rural Islamic cemeteries where the headstones are tiny, often white-washed, but necessarily rather temporary. The tenets of Islam forbid the display of religious art (other than calligraphic passages); such puny stone memorials represent custom, and custom alone, in some locality like an Egyptian village where the inhabitants are also devout and mostly literate. Non-inscribed memorials of the past may reflect a pre-Christian tradition; or (as with Islam) a different view of what a memorial should be; or contemporaneity with orthodox Christianity, but as part of an heretical or idiosyncratic faith (like the Bogomils of medieval Bosnia and Herzegovina, who had their own extraordinary pictorial slabs, pillars and blocks[19]); or, possibly, they indicate no more than poverty, or illiteracy, or both combined. From opposite ends of Britain (Cornwall and Shetland) one can observe, probably of the late seventeenth and the eighteenth century, tiny headstones that have only a little incised cross and one or two home-engraved initials. Again in Europe, the so-called (Fig. 2.4) 'discoidal steles' were used as uninscribed headstones, very probably linked through transmitted memory to quite prominent individuals, over a wide swathe of Languedocian France with an extension into northern Spain and Portugal.[20] These steles (French *stèles*, Latin *stelae*) look for all the world like miniature flattened versions of the large round-headed Cornish and Welsh stone crosses from the twelfth and thirteenth centuries. Local schools or carvers can be detected. The steles revive a shape that goes back to Roman provincial stone memorials, often both inscribed and pictorial (Fig. 2.5). At some documented localities, like the fortified hamlet of La Couvertoirade, dept. Aveyron, it is known that the oldest steles belong to the time when this place was held by the Templars (1158–1312), others being ascribed to its subsequent possession by the Knights Hospitallers.

**Fig. 2.5** Roman provincial tombstone with circular upper motif and rounded top, Burgos, Spain (drawn from photographs).

These distinctions among types of personal memorial raise a great many questions. In a genuine line of descent from the prehistoric or protohistoric menhir erected alongside a grave, and in some Mediterranean lands where marbles and other limestones tend to yield flat-faced slabs instead of rough pillars, can we trace later categories of memorial used, say, by societies that were truly non-literate, having neither the wish nor opportunity to embrace the crafts of reading and writing? Are these to be distinguished from pre-literate societies, occupying a stage where a pictorial-stone tradition was about to be modified under the influence of literate neighbours – perhaps through the adoption of a religion that, like Christianity, was enmeshed in full literacy? Is it possible that one might find a tradition of memorials worked on stone, making reference to individuals solely through pictorial means and bypassing genuine written inscriptions altogether?

The Picts of early Scotland demonstrate the complexity of any such multifarious model. The topic of the Picts, or 'the Pictish problem', can generate (without true cause) a great fog of mystery. The fog is dissipated when we regard the Picts for what they were; an amalgam of tribes, with farmers, herdsmen, warriors, fishers and boatmen, living in the northernmost parts of Britain. They were known collectively to the Romans as *Picti*, and so figure in history from the late third century; if the name means 'the Painted Ones', it arose from Roman observation of tattoo-markings on exposed limbs or faces. Picts were converted to Christianity during the later seventh and eighth centuries. To their west were the *Scotti*, Irish colonists from modern Ulster centred on their kingdom of Dál Riata in modern Argyll. To the south were various kingdoms of the North British between the

Antonine and Hadrianic Walls, by the sixth century mainly Christian as a result of contact with a surviving Church of Romano-British origin in Galloway.[21] Other incoming settlers, the Anglian groups in Northumbria, had during the seventh century spread north to the Firth of Forth (and at one stage, across it). This expansion was roughly contemporary with their own conversion to Christianity, partly from the southern English kingdoms and partly from the (already Christian) Irish settled in western Scotland. The Picts in the early seventh century, possibly half a million strong, may not themselves have been literate (and would not be, until the advent of Christianity had passed) but they had fully literate Christian neighbours.

What can be taken as the Pictish equivalent of personal memorial stones probably arose at this period; there is no precise agreement as to date but, unless the entire phenomenon is seen as some unprecedented side-product of intrusive Christianity, some such bracket as AD 550 to 650 would command majority acceptance. These memorials are initially unshaped boulders or natural slabs and pillars, on which are incised (or pecked) groups of *symbols* – two, three, sometimes as many as five. The symbols are stereotyped; internal embellishment aside, they are outlined designs of fixed character within a range that comprises geometric forms, pictures of real things (mirror, comb, broken sword, etc.), and striking representations of animals, birds, a fish, a snake, and several mythical beasts that have to be connoted by such clumsy names as the Pictish Elephant and the S-Dragon.[22] Stones displaying only these symbols are known as *Class I* (Pictish symbol stones). There is a *Class II*, on which we find most of the symbols but also scenes with humans, more mythical creatures, sometimes a move towards symmetrical disposition. Class II stones are more often shaped and dressed, can be decorated on opposing faces, and combine simple incised lines with low relief. The principal new element is the featuring of ornamental Christian crosses, centralized as the largest element in a display (Fig. 2.6). Aspects of internal decoration on such crosses, and within some of the symbols, can be matched by styles of art current by the mid-seventh century in Christian Northumbria.

It is assumed, though even this is not universally conceded, that we have a typological sequence here. Class II stones, as well as being more elaborate than Class I and in terms of art and sculpture 'better executed' (a subjective judgement), ought to post-date the conversion of the Picts to Christianity. Class I stones, apart from being 'cruder' or 'inferior' and therefore supposedly from a previous, perhaps almost experimental, stage of workmanship, would belong to a time when the Picts were still pagan and when any memorials would have been erected in the spiritual frame of pre-Christian or non-Christian beliefs. If this *is* a sequence, the division in absolute time between Class I and Class II is still being argued. If Class II stones were not erected much before 700, how long before such a horizon did Class I stones appear? What is there to inform us on this point? One line of reasoning suggests that some of the symbols resemble known objects, ascertained

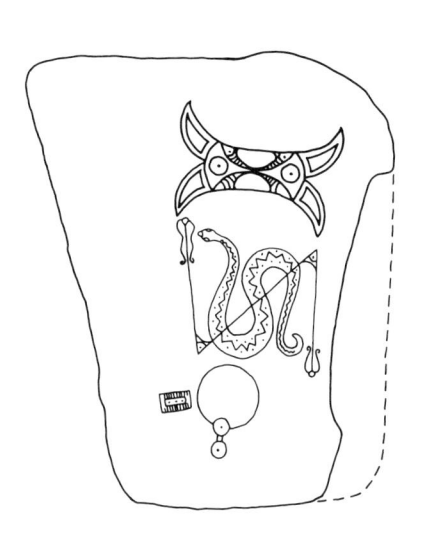

Fig. 2.6 Pictish symbol stones. **Left**, Class I, with Double Crescent, over Snake and Z-Rod, over Comb and Mirror – Dunrobin, Sutherland (drawn by Helen Jackson, and reproduced with Dr Joanna Close-Brooks's kind permission). **Right**, Class II, Ulbster, Caithness (from *Early Christian Monuments of Scotland*, 1903).

from archaeology; these objects are proper to the Pictish material culture during the Roman centuries; some of the symbols, known to us on stone (and, rarely, from metal objects), may have begun as marks tattooed upon human flesh; and in the sixth century, if not in the fifth, pagan and pre-literate Picts may have decided to transfer the currency of their national symbols to personal memorial stones.[23]

The last notion has itself been complicated by many others; that these stones functioned as territorial markers, as indicators of dynastic unions between important families, and even as 'magical' displays with irrecoverable meaning. Champions of these theories, and of others taken from the realms of purest fantasy, continued to defend them with vigour, heat and acrimony. If one stands well back, considering *all* such manifestations of a social art on stone – as it is – later than deep prehistory throughout Europe (and perhaps throughout Eurasia), there are probably enough analogies from within and from just beyond all the zones of Romanization to confirm an interpretation of the Class I stones as some kind of funerary memorial, if only as the least improbable explanation. Aided by a number of recent discoveries from excavations, the idea that Class I stones did accompany actual burials is becoming a favoured reading.[24] It is not aided by the fact that a great many such stones are known to have been moved, some of them several times, since they were originally noticed and recorded.

In the system of literacy used for the Demetian and Dumnonian inscriptions letters or symbols of fixed phonetic value, whether Roman or ogam, are required to perpetuate a dead person's *name*, or his or her immediate parentage. On the other hand, a feature of all known historic societies in Britain and Ireland was the oral transmission of this information, the communal-memory storage and recitation of sequences like 'A son of B, B son of C, C son of D'. Pictorial symbols may have had a complementary function. The instance of modern road-signs, tourist information boards, and packaging symbols can show what a surprising volume of quite specific detail may be conveyed to all and sundry without using writing at all. Given that many Picts, from Late Roman times, had opportunities to see displays of pictorial symbols on Roman monumental stonework heightened by gaudy colours and accompanied by (to the Picts, incomprehensible) lines of writing, a potential collective model existed long before anyone would assume that any Class I stone was carved. By the end of the sixth century the Picts' neighbours among the North Britons, the Irish in Argyll and (not much later) the Northumbrian Angles, were adopting various sorts of inscribed or decorated stone memorials, if only as slabs with primary crosses or the occasional lettered personal name. One would be hard put to sustain the view that the Pictish Class I stones emerged, possibly in the southern part of Pictland, because of a completely independent invention.

Without a digression into statistics, it can be accepted that on the Class I stones the symbols do appear, repetitively, in combinations and conform to what must have been widely known conventions governing their placing and grouping. They are not ideographic, or syllabic. The objection that, having no phonetic values, they could not record names is irrelevant. There is no acceptable alternative to the inference that they were conveying *information*, which – if it had to be particularized, for instance with the allocation of personal names or lines of parentage – may have been supplemented by oral tradition. We can guess, no more, that some of the symbols relate to social status; and that others, probably the zoological ones, to social grouping, the sub-divisions or 'tribes' of the Pictish nation. Bold attempts have been made to translate this symbolic vocabulary.[25] It must be accepted that we lack enough information to pursue this task.

But the proposition that an inscribed personal memorial on stone – 'inscribed' with legible lettering or, as here, with comprehended symbolic motifs – may always have called for a measure of supplementation through orally transmitted data preserved in the locality has a much wider implication; and it explains why even a short discussion of the Pictish stones can be relevant to those of Demetia and Dumnonia. There are many memorials among those of Wales and the south-west that display single names. It is not credible that persons so commemorated lacked parents, or that nobody involved in commissioning a monument knew that A's father was called B. The most likely explanation is that single-name memorials were for priests, clerics, who proposed to discard all earthly parentage ('call no man on earth your father'; Matthew, 23:9). Since in these regions during post-Roman times priests may often have been drawn from the aristocracy the missing details, if sought, could be supplied by any number of people from personal knowledge or from wht they had heard from earlier generations. We cannot suppose the Picts to have been any less conscious of the names and filiations of their local heroes. If we return for a moment (p. 12) to Waldo Williams's memorial, Maen Waldo, casual visitors – and there are many thousands every summer along that road – may well ask, Who was Waldo? The few able to read Welsh might notice, in the second line of verse on the tablet, the words *ym mhob annibyniaeth barn*; 'in every independence of judgment'. This is not the only inscribed stone in Wales to exhibit a poem (p. 104). There will still be folk in nearby Mynachlog-ddu (or their children) who can recall Waldo Williams's father as the village schoolmaster, and tell visitors as much. This is the supplementary oral tradition from the locality. The rest is allusive; one would have to know the poem 'Preseli', and also that *annibyniaeth barn* was a moral quality prized by the poet and fully exemplified in his courageous life. There are very much earlier stones where words and phrases other than personal names may also have required allusive knowledge, for example of Christian Latin.

The present chapter is not designed to trespass upon the detailed content of later ones, but the instance of the Pictish stones raises a further point; their disappearance, as a fashion. This may on a wider canvas be almost as interesting as their appearance. The sole innovatory discussion of recent years has been Dr Stephen Driscoll's, one that addresses this point.[26] Offering new concepts of power and structure within early Pictish society, Driscoll in outline agrees that an individual memorial role is the most likely explanation for the Class I stones, but that their absolute dates – beyond our present grasp – may be less interesting than the question of how, or why, such stone memorials became customary at a particular step in Pictish social development. What conditions, and when, are likely to have led to the erecting of meaningful pictorial memorials to a social élite? These might be linked to a stage in national development 'engendered by the expanding Pictish monarchy'; we possess evidence for the presence of kings among the Picts and of power struggles between Picts and their neighbours. Class I stones, even allowing for huge losses since the seventh century, can never have been widespread and may have been confined to a limited, upper, social element. If the non-literate messages carved on them emphasized such matters as status, affiliation and temporal power within a system of stratified relationships, the very stones 'may have contributed to the maintenance and legitimation of those relations'. So, in a different way, may also have done those few Demetian and Dumnonian memorials that commemorated – as public Christian heroes, meriting public remembrance – the aristocrats of their respective lands.

Driscoll further interprets the display of the Class I stones as a link between 'the social order' of the society that put them up, and 'the cosmic order' – that same society's conceptions of death, any afterlife, power inherent in ancestors, and particular religious myths. But in proposing that such memorials, the seventh-century counterparts of the massive obelisks, Ionic columns and mock temple-facades decorating the graves of nineteenth-century kings and captains of industry, had a *social* function of underpinning a social order as its leaders wished it to be, we side-step the question of *religious* affiliation. The two are separable. For the nineteenth century again, there is many a Christian graveyard in Britain where the costly tombs of professed Christians also exhibit the symbols of Freemasonry (a guild riddled with vaguely Unitarian heresies) and of the Army and Royal Navy (organizations whose members may be paid to kill other Christians). It is not, in Driscoll's view, essential to enquire whether the date-range of Class I symbol stones happened to overlap the introduction of Christianity, because 'the Church was external to the system of power' that the stones may have preached. When, later, the impressive Class II stones, the improved slabs with their centrally prominent crosses, make an appearance, many near-parallels elsewhere in Britain and Ireland help to define them as Pictish cross-slabs, with such likely functions as pointers to open-air worship and assembly, markers of notable Christian episodes and victories, and monuments erected in the initial process of religious foundations. The persistence of (Class I) symbols as accessories to scenes, some possibly of Biblical origin, with human figures is a very secondary appearance. Driscoll suggests that the Class II stones or cross-slabs, established perhaps by the beginning of the eighth century, mark a point in time at which 'the importance of the Church is outstripping that of the ancestors'. In such a scenario continuation of individual, often imposing, stone memorials sited less within religious enclosures than upon secular land-holdings becomes increasingly irrelevant. If we translate this into the setting of other societies within early Britain that had embraced Christianity long before the Picts did so, the (Demetian, or Dumnonian) inscribed memorial with Christian wording and sometimes also Christian art, citing not just the deceased's own name but that of a parent, should also have given way to the general levelling of *all* Christian burials within a consecrated cemetery. This would tend to allot a second generation of cross-incised stones, the larger cross-slabs, to public or dedicatory and commemorative functions alone.

Not only *was* this the case; interestingly, it is more or less what occurred in all other parts of Britain and Ireland (except for the special exception of monasteries, and monastic gravestones). We shall also find that, as in Pictland, the inscribed memorial tradition – certainly in Dumnonia – faded out towards the end of the seventh century. It was not to be revived, in that format, until post-medieval times. The reason for the decline has not been addressed, even if the decline itself has occasionally been noticed. Stephen Driscoll is probably justified in offering, not a theological explanation, but a much more complex social one. The lessons to be derived from this study of the Pictish stones, Classes I and II, can be used to illuminate the quite different inscribed memorials a long way to the south.

This does not solve all the puzzles, by any means. Inside Britannia (in the strict meaning of 'that part of Britain fully subject to Roman occupation, influence, and incorporation as a province in the Empire') native fashions in death as in life generally imitated Roman models, and acordingly can nearly always be dated by reference to the latter. Outside Britannia, where such planks are kicked aside, how do we detect and date the first appearances of any other kind of personal memorial stones? For this, we consider another group of monuments, in their way as challenging as those of the Picts; the ogam-inscribed memorials of early Ireland.

## References

1. For the curious, see A. Bloch-Raymond & J. Frayssenge, *Les Êtres de la Brume et de la Nuit* (Les Presses du Languedoc, Montpellier 1987); an idea of the relevant archaeology is given by Gilbert Fages, *Recherges archéologiques sur le Causse Méjan et ses abords immédiats 1969–74* (Anhilac, dept. Lozère, 1977).
2. Russell & Pool, *CA* 3 (1964), 15–25.
3. Lacy 1983.
4. Cuppage 1986.
5. Accessibly in his *Patterns of Comparative Religion* (1985), chap. vi, and *A History of Religious Ideas, I* (Chicago 1978), chap. 5.
6. Waldo Williams, *Dail Pren* (Gomer Press, Llandysul 1991), 29 – his collected poems, in Welsh. See also Janet Davies 'The Fight for Preseli, 1946', 3–9, and Ned Thomas, 'The Waldo Dialectic', 10–15 (with picture of 'Maen Waldo'), *Planet 58* (Aberystwyth, Aug–Sept. 1986).
7. C. Thomas, 'The Earliest Christian Art in Ireland and Britain', pp. 7–11 in: M. Ryan, ed., *Ireland and Insular Art AD 500–1200* Royal Irish Academy, Dublin 1987).
8. Examples are (Wales), D. J. James, 'The Prehistoric Standing Stones of Breconshire', *Brycheiniog* 18 (1978–9), 9–30; and George Williams, *The Standing Stones of Wales and South-West England* (BAR, Brit. ser. 197, Oxford 1988 – with A. Ward's review of it, *Carmarthenshire Antiquary* 25 (1989), 93–5; for Cornwall, Frances Peters, 'The possible use of West Penwith menhirs as boundary markers', *CA* 29 (1990), 33–42. See now, too, Gareth Morgan in *BBCS* 39 (1992), 155–8.
9. Most are listed in R. S. Conway, J. Whatmough & S. E. Johnson, *The Prae-Italic Dialects of Italy* (Harvard 19033), and M. Lejeune, *Manuel de la Langue Venète* (Heidelberg 1974). Some of the stones are now in the Cantonal Museum, Chur (Switzerland); see Ernst Risch, 'Die Räter als sprachliches Problem', 22–6 (illus.) in: Benedikt Frei *et al.*, *Das Räterproblem in Geschichtlicher, Sprachlicher u. Archäologischer Sicht* (Rätischmuseum, Chur 1984, Schriftenreihe no. 28).
11. *KGP* 121. For the name as a whole, however, *GPN* 387 (n.4) points out that a supposed 'Alcovindo' (inscription at Rodez) should be read as *Aicovindo*.
12. *GPN* 275 (for *-uallaun*). See here generally the excellent short guide, Wolfgang Meid's *Gaulish Inscriptions* (Archaeolingua, Budapest 1992).
13. Giuliano & Larissa Bonfante, *The Etruscan Language* (Manchester 1983). There may be two genitive endings in Etruscan (*-s*; *-l* or *-al*), of which a 'possessive genitive' (as *Ualaun-al*) is partly adjectival – 'Memorial of the Ranenos who-had-Ualaun-as-his-father'.
14. Frequently illustrated; e.g., Bonfantes (1983), fig. 15.
15. Gisela M. A. Richter, *A Handbook of Greek Art* (1959); *Archaic Gravestones of Attica* (Phaidon, 1961).

16. *RIB* no. 695 (Eglecta), no. 1618 (Anicius).
17. Giancarlo Susini, *The Roman Stonecutter* (Blackwell, Oxford 1973), 16 (the stone: *CIL* VI, 9556).
18. Betty Willsher & Doreen Hunter, *Stones – a Guide to some Remarkable Eighteenth Century Gravestones* (Canongate, Edinburgh & Vancouver 1978); Betty Willsher, *Understanding Scottish Graveyards* (Chamber, Edinburgh 1985).
19. M. Wenzel, 'A Medieval Mystery Cult in Bosnia and Herzegovina', *Journ. Warburg & Courtauld Institutes* 24 (1961); Oto Bihalji-Merin & Alozj Benac, *The Bogomils* (1962).
20. See *Archéologie en Languedoc* (annual: Fed. Archéol. de l'Herault, Sete), numéro spécial for 1980 – *Les Stèles Discoidales*: and Robert Aussibal, *Les stèles discoidales Rouergates* (Fed. Interdept. des Sentiers de Pays, St.-Affrique 1982). The only British ones known to the writer are at the twelfth century church of Adel, W. Yorks; illus. Peter Ryder, *Medieval Cross Slab Grave Covers in West yorkshire* (W. Yorks Archaeology Service, Wakefield 1991), 9.
21. Summary, Thomas 1992 (with map).
22. Conveniently in Isabel Henderson, *The Picts* (1967), chap. 5; Anna Ritchie, *Picts* (HMSO, Edinburgh 1991); and (without agreeing any of this author's dates and conclusions) in fig. 1 of A. Jackson, *The Symbol Stones of Scotland* (Orkney Press, Stromness 1984).
23. C. Thomas, 'The Pictish Class I symbol stones', 169–88 in: J. G. P. Friell & W. G. Watson, eds., *Pictish Studies* (BAR Brit. ser. 125, Oxford 1984), with refs. to previous illustrated papers.
24. See, in Friell & Watson (1984), papers by J. Close-Brooks (87–114), J. B. Stevenson (145–50), and L. Wedderburn & D. M. Grime (151–68); also Ian Ralston & Jim Inglis, *Foul Hordes; the Picts in the North-East and their background* (Anthrop. Mus., Univ. of Aberdeen 1984).
25. C. Thomas, 'The interpretation of the Pictish symbols', *Archaeol. Journal* 118, for 1961 (1963), 31–97; Jackson, in n.22 above.
26. 'The Relationship between History and Archaeology', 162–87 in Driscoll & Nieke, eds. (1988).

# 3
# *Hiberno-Roman Times: the Ogam Script*

HER MAJESTY Queen Elizabeth II is said to possess basements in which, catalogued and labelled, are kept all the ritual presents unloaded upon her by visiting heads of state – so that when the Sultan of Melancholia is ushered in, the figure of White Elephants at play carved from a single block of Melancholic alabastrine is already standing on the grand piano, displayed for tactful allusion. In 1977 the analytical catalogue of Roman coins and various gold trinkets found at the huge passage-grave of New Grange, County Meath, drew special attention to the presence among the twenty-five coins (the latest being of Arcadius, *c*.385) of six gold solidi and two uniface solidi pendants, all fourth century.[1] Fantastically valuable in any saleroom today these were pieces of considerable value at the time. The precise context of their deposition at New Grange is not known (most are old finds). Dr Carson's suggestion – votive offerings at a tumulus venerated as a shrine, where 'the most likely depositors of such offerings would have been Irish' – calls for a further explanation as to how such coins had passed into Irish hands, and why selectively abandoned.

    Claire O'Kelly found this unconvincing, pointing out that New Grange, Brug na Bóinne – a neolithic monument – was the mansion (*bruig*) of Ireland's pre-Christian gods *par excellence*; home of the Irish counterpart of I. O. M., Iuppiter Optimus Maximus, in the shape of *An Daghda Mór*, the 'Great Good One'. Her husband Professor M. J. O'Kelly, excavator of the monument, did not exclude the idea that such objects, of such notable worth, were deposited publicly and ceremoniously by enterprising traders (*negotiatores*) from Roman Britain;[2] hoping thereby to secure advantageous positions in fresh markets by showing homage to the indigenous deity. The parallel with ritual exchange of gifts between heads of state is concerned with intrinsic worth, display of 'generosity' as a statement and conformity with ritual; and, too, the facilitation of an *entrée* to another's realm.

    For a very long time indeed it was held as a truism that the Romans were no more present in early Ireland than the reptiles excluded by St Patrick. In the late first century AD Agricola failed to invade and conquer; the odd sailor must have circumnavigated Ireland to explain how Claudius Ptolemaeus in the second century got hold of Irish place- and tribal names to include in his *Geography*; but direct connection with the Late Roman world dated from whenever Palladius was sent by Pope Celestine 'to the Irish believers in Christ, ordained as the first bishop'.[3] The mission of Palladius, accepted as in AD 431, may have been short-lived and confined to an east-coast, Leinster, region (Cos. Dublin, Kildare and Wicklow).[4] It was followed later in the fifth century by the mission of Patrick;[5] the Briton who had been a youthful captive in Ireland, had escaped and probably visited Gaul before returning to Britannia, and had finally returned to Ireland in the capacity of a missionary bishop. Patrick's sphere of activity in his lifetime, obliquely described in his own account (*Confessio*) that is notably short on geographical detail, must be provisionally set in the north-east (Cos. Armagh and Down being the least unlikely). For this once-current assessment of early links of a specifically Christian kind between Ireland and the (Christian) Roman world, Britannia and elsewhere, we must include a separate tradition of the 'pre-Patrician saints of the south'; the belief that locations associated with certain named saints like Ailbe and Ibar, all lying south of the line from the Shannon across to Dublin and including two on the Munster southern coast,[6] represented Christian missionaries from Britain who knew not of Patrick, were independent of Patrick's Ulster activities, and were very possibly earlier — the start of the fifth century if not also or alternatively in the fourth. But the validity of the sources for these people and therefore of any careers at so early a time has recently been seriously challenged.[7]

Hiberno-British, or Hiberno-Roman, contacts from the first to fourth centuries AD — their nature, the evidence for them, the geography and the dating — form a subject in which interest grows rapidly. It was the topic of a major Royal Irish Academy colloquium in 1974[8] and there would be universal agreement that a repeat performance of the meeting, warranted by so much fresh evidence, is overdue. The New Grange gold coins and objects are just some of the many discoveries indicative of material, individuals, even burials and settlement of Romano-British origin in Ireland; the weight of the distribution is, expectedly, in Leinster as the Irish province immediately opposite the Atlantic flank of Britannia but other parts of Ireland have to be included, particularly the north-east with its evidence for Roman-period links across the short sea passage to southern Scotland.[9]

Who were the people involved? Who brought these things to Ireland? Explanations drawn from analogy (as to some extent they still have to be) cluster around two ideas. One is the presence of traders, *negotiatores* or business men; envisaging Romano-Britons, or conceivably also Gallo-Romans, who controlled limited shipping and external markets, wanted Ireland's resources and products and to that end were staffing establishments most probably sited by the mouths of navigable rivers — the 'Great Southern Rivers' of Ireland[10] — and sending their packmen to the interior.[11] The interest attached to this model is that it could further involve localized currency of spoken Latin, Roman writings and enumeration and the employ of native Irish. The other is the supposition, now at last seriously aired, that early Irish society allows for numbers of young men, would-be warrior bands (*fiana*),[12] who may well have served in auxiliary cohorts of the Roman army in Britannia and elsewhere, auxiliaries that commonly included non-Romans of dozens of minor barbaric nationalities. Those who returned, time-expired and with their possessions, weapons or loot, may not have contributed to any stabilizing effect in Ireland's rustic economy and un-Roman ways of living but their *matériel* might certainly be reflected in archaeological finds. This, as the bringing of *romanitas* to Ireland, stands aside from any happenings inferred from the course of Roman Britain's history,[13] or, post-400, from the tract *De Excidio Britonum* by Gildas (p. 89) representing Irish-based raids across the water, in search of plunder or the enslavement of such Britons as the young Patrick.

But the findings of archaeology make only a part of the story. Fifth-century (and later) Christianity in Ireland was a faith whose liturgy and literature had to employ spoken and written Latin. We have no need here to go down an intricate cul-de-sac concerning the manner and the dating of the introduction of a Christian Latin vocabulary to Ireland. Identification of two (or more) stages in the process can rest on whatever chronology is attached to precise sound-changes in Late British and Primitive Irish; and debate on certain points of the sound-changes can sometimes be found to lean on preconceptions about the stages when the Christian vocabulary was introduced – before, during, and soon after Patrick's life in Ireland, itself an episode whose absolute chronology long formed a quite separate battleground.

There are related observations here that have nothing to do with Christianity. The Rock of Cashel, a high limestone crag in Co. Tipperary, is the principal royal seat of Munster and was traditionally captured for the Eóganacht dynasties by Conall Corc at a time that may correspond to Britain's Late Roman centuries.[14] Visited mainly for its Round Tower and lovely little twelfth-century Romanesque cathedral ('Cormac's Chapel'), the Rock is surrounded by a modern graveyard wall. On the east and south-east where the wall is rooted and stepped into the rock, a perceptive eye will note the obvious few points at which excavation would almost certainly find traces of initial fortification.[15]

In the speech of late Roman Britain (Vulgar Latin) it can be guessed that *castellum* was a far commoner term than the textbook *castrum* to denote an authentic Roman fort, and subsequently other kinds of fort. Both in Welsh and Cornish it was borrowed to serve alongside *din* (*dinas, dinan*) as a noun meaning 'fortification'.[16] It was also borrowed into Irish (now as *caiseal*); the further diminutive *caislén* is more widespread in early place-names, but 'cashel' is also an archaeological term, frequently used to denote stone-walled forts and fortlets in contrast to the earthen-banked 'rath'.

The name of the natural citadel of Cashel in Munster, *Caiseal* (*Muman*), is the only one for the royal Irish seats to have this Roman origin; it was 'The Castellum', rather as the legionary fortress in north-west England became, through Old English *ceaster*, 'The Castra', Chester.[17] And this borrowing, which has nothing to do with Patrick, Palladius, pre-Patrician saints and Christianity, accompanies Professor James Carney's exploration of what are seen as among the oldest Irish verse remnants, the Leinster Poems.[18] Latin loanwords occur within them. They include – the Latin and meaning in brackets – *arm* (*arma* 'weapons'), *legión* (*legio* 'legion'), *míl* (*miles* 'soldier;), *trebun* (*tribunus*, 'a (military) tribune'), *múr* (*murus* 'a built wall'), *long* (for (*navis*) *longa*, 'longship, warship') and *ór* (*aurum* 'gold') as well as the surprising *Mercúir* and *Saturn* (*dies Mercurii*, *dies Saturni* 'Wednesday, Saturday'). Professor David Greene added others, assigning them to a loanword stratum that 'could hardly be placed later than the middle of the fourth century'[19] – *corcur* (*purpura* 'cloth dyed purple'), *clúm* (*pluma* 'feather' (as quill?)), *cann* (*panna* 'dish, vessel'), *sorn* (*furnus* 'oven, kiln(?)'), and *siball* (*fibula*, 'brooch, safety-pin'). The trend of this (condensed) collection is perfectly clear. Implied reference to the vernacular of, and life in, Britannia concentrates on military matters, and on Roman technology and trade. Carney pictured 'a non-Christian Ireland, having very close contacts with and knowledge of the Roman empire'. Greene believed that 'trade between Britain and Ireland during the fourth century seems probable.'

The possibility, now approaching likelihood, of correlation between such clear linguistic indicators and the tangible evidence of archaeology must lead on to other questions, arousing just as much attention. Phrased bluntly, they would be these: Were there people in third–fourth century Ireland who spoke and understood Latin as a first or second language? If so, were they many or few, and what *sort* of people? Whereabouts are they most likely to have lived? Did a knowledge of speech also mean ability to read and write Latin?

In this volume the central relevance of such questions (now giving rise to opinions and hypotheses within an expanding spectrum of supposed Latinity in early Ireland) is that – as to about ninety per cent of them – the inscribed memorials, the Mute Stones, of mainland Britain have an Irish origin. Archaeologists are curiously shy about ever postulating 'inventors' to explain any sudden record of innovations, a wariness that probably goes back into the discipline's not-too-distant past when diffusionists and independent-inventionists slugged it out, employing defective evidence for ammunition. Today there must be no hesitation in suggesting, and indeed it now seems inevitable we should suggest, that somewhere in the south of Ireland during the Roman period – the *Hiberno-Roman period* – a clever person or a small circle of clever acquaintances were genuine innovators. He or they invented, or re-invented from the base of others' models and usages, the inscribed legible personal memorial cut on stone.

We distinguish requisites and motives. Required at the start would be a full appreciation of any mode in which a range of signs (squiggles, crows' feet, triangles or letters as we know them) stood, one by one, for a range of perceptibly different sounds; so that C always meant the sound /k/ and nothing else, and C A T meant the conjoined sounds /kat/. If the entire, world, history of writing

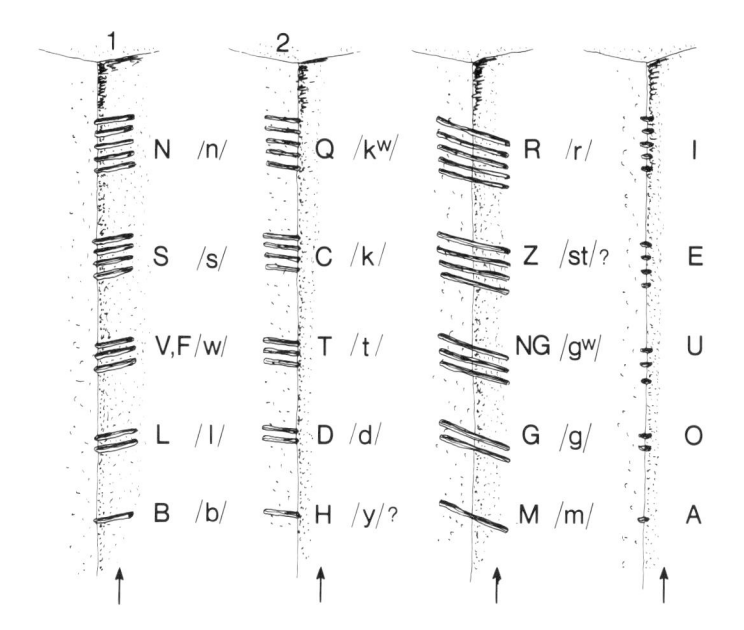

**Fig. 3.1** The ogam script, as it was written on the angles of upright stones (read generally upwards). Capitals: the literary medieval values. Lower-case between slashes: the likely Primitive Irish phonetic values, after McManus, *Guide*. Column 1 is 'the B-surface', column 2 'the H-surface'.

during thousands of years tells us anything it is that though new *symbols* may be dreamt up on the back of an envelope in a single afternoon[20] there is no instance of a phonetic-writing system coming suddenly into being except as a by-product of an earlier, connected, one. As for motives – Why do this? why use such an invention to write people's names on stones, stuck up in the countryside to be noticed, read and probably admired? – the adage *imitation is the sincerest form of flattery* can sum it up. The prime reason for adopting a social custom of this kind is a perceived desirability of imitating what has been done elsewhere; in this case, not only writing but the application of writing to a particular class of monument.

The script known as 'ogam'[21] does not contain organic letters – *organic*, in the sense that the Romans' and our, ABC to Z, letters had evolved from certain early Mediterranean letter-groupings over a long period – but a dot-and-dash system invented in a single operation (Fig. 3.1). A datum line, base-line or 'stem' forms the whole backbone; it may be a real line, like the vertical angle of a slate or limestone pillar (and any straight line drawn on any surface), or it may be imaginary, indicated by placing of symbols. These are four sets each of one to five; for an up-and-down stem, one to five strokes at right angles may run right of the stem, or left of it (2 × 5 = 10), a further one to five longer strokes may be placed at a diagonal across or through the stem (5), and one to five much smaller marks – mere notches – can be placed *on* the stem (5, plus 5, plus 10 = 20). Twenty letters, ABCDEFGHILMNOPQRSTVX, sufficed to perpetuate Cicero's Latin works, an intellectual legacy rarely matched or bettered since 43 BC. Theoretically the whole of his Essays, Orations and Epistles could – with very slight adjustments – be written in ogam. 'If scholars have tended to dismiss the Ogamists as framers of a cumbersome script they have done them a considerable injustice. Subject to all the shortcomings of position-marking as a device, their script is as sophisticated and efficient an example of it as one could create.'[22]

Dr Damian McManus's *A Guide to Ogam* (here, *Guide*) contains not only several semi-concealed and important essays on the nature of writing as such and the ogam script's position within it, but a full history of the many and curious theories adduced as to its origin; readers are referred to the book if they wish to pursue this. There has been no serious doubt for quite a time that ogam arose ('was invented') in the dual context of the Hiberno-Roman centuries and the proximity of southern Ireland to Latin-speaking Roman Britain. For quite a time, too, Jackson's proposals held the field; that the script, used mainly to record proper names, represented contemporary speech in Ireland (Primitive Irish), that its framers knew something of the manner in which Latin grammarians like the fourth-century Donatus were disposed to classify sounds and the letters representing them, and that the inventor may therefore have had a Romano-British connection.[23] In Kenneth Jackson's *Language and History in Early Britain* the inventor was proposed as an Irishman who had been a member of one of the settlements in Britain described in chapters 4 and 5 below, an immigrant to Britain who learned Latin and the theoretically-structured alphabet of the grammarians at a school in Britain. He adapted the Roman alphabet to the ogam notch-system, to be cut on wooden rods imitating (Romano-British) tally sticks. 'The inventor might easily have ... returned to live in Ireland with his kindred, where he then composed this simplified script for the use of the unlettered Irish.'[24]

Since those words (1953) not much of Jackson's theory can be said to have survived criticism (though in 1953 only the most hazy ideas of what could actually have constituted connections between Roman Britain and much of Ireland were in circulation). The typology of ogam does not lend itself to relative dating, though one can dismiss immediately as historically improbable the first century AD, and various older suggestions involving prehistory, 'Druids' and an Elder World of arcane lore. Similarly a contention, still from time to time voiced, that ogam was invented in the fifth century by Christians to commemorate the Christian dead, founders on a whole reef of rocks. Ogam is only a manner of writing, no more tied to any one religion than the Morse Code; fourth-century Romano-British Christians seldom if ever had inscribed memorials; in the fifth century there were almost certainly communities of Christians in British districts like the northern spine (around the Pennines), or the west Midlands, or parts of subsequent Wessex, who neither then nor later had memorials; and finally the incidence of inscribed stones in western Britain is intimately linked in time and space to the Irish settlements. An informed guess is all that can be offered. It would be that the use of ogam was firmly established by the latter part of the fourth century, could well have been current in the earlier part, and could have been invented about AD 300 (or even before).

A sub-topic, that of the physical medium first used to write ogam, is again something of a dead end because though large stones have endured, other impermanent media have not. Nor need the problem be regarded as particularly relevant to ogam's use for memorials; plainly, it could have been written on wood (or skin, or bone, or metal surfaces) with a drawn stem-line, and there is no reason why individuals may not have done this, but a linear stroke alphabet is so plainly adapted for cutting on stone (a) by avoiding the difficult shapes of Roman BCDGQRS – ogam had no sign for Roman P because Primitive Irish did not use spoken /p/; (b) by offering a model that, scratched on a slate or small stone, an illiterate stone-cutter could with diligence reproduce by eye, that there is almost a *prima facie* case for seeing it *invented* for stone.

The five vowels a-e-i-o-u, not distinguished as long or short and not apparently regarded as accessible to diphthongization, made up a range shared between Latin and Irish (and British). The values of the fifteen consonants are usually set out according to a classification that is a medieval, not a fourth-century, system. In writing on an upright stone the convention was to start at the bottom and write *upwards* (p. 11) – with a preference for the left-hand angle, facing the stone – and if necessary to continue over the top, or else to use the right-hand angle. In this mode, the first one-to-five group of notches, working upwards, B L V (or F) S N, lie to the *right* of the (angle or) stem, the 'B-surface'; the second group, H D T C Q, to the left or 'H-surface'; the longer diagonal strokes, which have to be folded to appear on front and side, are M G NG Z R.

It has long been accepted that Primitive Irish before and after 400 had no /v/, and that the supposed V or F symbol stands for /w/. McManus has now shown that other, original, values can be identified; Fig. 3.1 shows these against the later conventions. Q is distinct from C (the sound of /k/) because it stood for /k$^w$/, not quite the same as QU in Latin *quis, quaero*. The outcome is that the postulated original values not only serve to represent the phonemic quality of Primitive Irish (as opposed to later Old Irish, or Middle Irish) but reflect the consonant-system of the language at the date when ogam was invented.

What has to be addressed therefore is a time-and-place setting for the invention, other than that proposed by Kenneth Jackson. We have several clues; one is that some ingenuity, coupled to a clear analytical interest in language and almost certainly a capacity to 'doodle on paper' (i.e., from a knowledge of Roman writing-practice), underlies construction of a group such as B-L-W-S-N instead of B-C-D-F-G.[25] Another is the strong likelihood that suggestive visual models did comprise the incremental Roman numerals (I II III IIII V VI VII VIII) and the tally-stick system that continued in use up to our own medieval Exchequer, and rune-inscribed wooden merchants' labels from the quays at Bergen;[26] the fact that Roman tallies and labels have not survived does not mean that, in a waterlogged context, some may not one day be found. A third observation is that ogam was not the only case where an 'artificial' script was invented within the penumbra of the Roman empire and Latin literacy; the Germanic runes, a different system of incremental or varying-direction strokes and probably several centuries older than ogam, are related in principle.[27] The last clue, as to place of origin, is contained in the distribution of ogam inscriptions in Ireland (Fig. 3.2), one that can only imply a home in south-west Leinster, or the south of Munster from Co. Waterford west to Co. Kerry.

There is not much to be gained from speculating at length with so little firm information, but such combination might point to an Irish person of intellectual bent and native learning, sited at a place providing all the models of spoken and written Latin,[28] with mercantile apparatus of enumeration and tally-labels, during a relatively settled period; say, from *circa* 250 up to the turmoils of the 'barbarian conspiracy' in the 360s. Jackson's returning immigrant recedes, and will recede completely after later chapters here, as an improbable product of fifth-century Demetia. As for place, do we have in mind nothing less than a Roman-controlled trading establishment, temporarily integrated into its neighbourhood, near the outflow of one or other of the large rivers: the area of Cork, and Cork harbour, or around modern Youghal, or Waterford? This is not a problem to which any neat archaeological solution could ever be expected.

So much for invention; purpose and application are separate headings. If we concede that one aim, possibly the over-riding one, was to provide a simple way in which the personal and family-or-tribal names of selected *prominenti* (deceased) could be blazoned from stones sited at appropriate points in the landscape,[29] we face the question: what could have prompted such an idea in fourth-century Ireland? The likelihood that religion was involved is slender. The time is too early for Christianity, and the inchoate network of beliefs inherited from prehistory (in so far as they can be made out from Old Irish sources) were not of a kind to yield theological and eschatological imperatives. It may seem that the only possible answer lies, again, in some imitation of Roman ways. Here the individual lettered tombstone is indicated; but, with this, we are back to the larger collections of such things inside the Empire – military establishments along the *limites* or frontiers where legionaries and auxiliaries alike could be commemorated by comrades and regimental burial-clubs, on Hadrian's Wall or against the Rhine. (An extreme position – not adopted here, but mentioned in case anyone else should raise the idea – would be that some putatively early (fourth-century) inscriptions did not commemorate the dead at all. It is constantly pointed out that ogam stones have not been found in direct association with graves or pagan burials, though as constantly supposed that this results from later interference and the known removal of stones; in fact their function as epitaphs has been assumed, epigraphically from analogy,

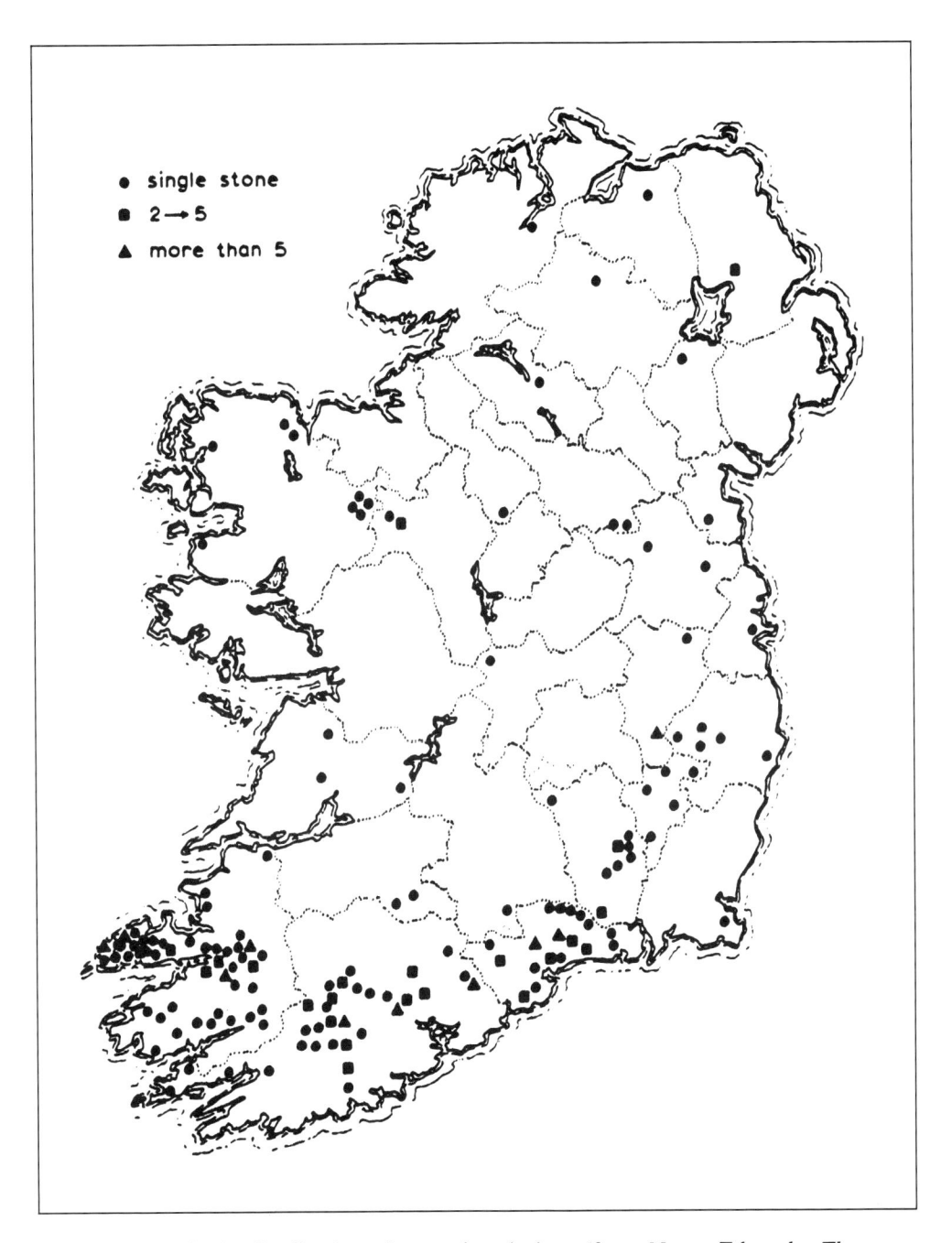

**Fig. 3.2** Ireland: the distribution of ogam inscriptions (from Nancy Edwards, *The Archaeology of Early Medieval Ireland*, 1990, fig. 47, drawn by Jean Williamson and reproduced with Dr Edwards's kind permission).

and contextually from links between later fifth and sixth century inscriptions and Christian sites. If one reverts to Roman models, choosing to argue that the 'Of A, son of B' named in ogam on a pillar was *alive* when the stone was set up on his land or the boundary-point thereof, then an exemplar could be not a Roman individual tombstone but another and common category of Roman inscriptions, 'building-record' slabs naming those who completed a particular task — and, conceivably, the *arae* or altar pedestals.[30])

Assuming that the Irish stones were originally funerary, we are encountering a feature on which Jackson and others have often commented — the *shape* of the message found in what may be the oldest ogam inscriptions, where the dead man's name is given in the (Primitive Irish) genitive and where a word is missing: (Tomb, Stone, Pillar, Memorial) of X, son of Y. It is impossible to see this other than as a repetition of Roman formulae (see further, p. 95); there is otherwise no intrinsic reason to have commenced an inscriptional fashion in such a way. If one accepts the proposal of Warner and others that direct Irish contact with the Roman *limites* (or just possibly legionary fortresses and out-stations) took the shape of auxiliary service, the level at which lettered tombstones offered a model would have been that of the centurion or (for auxiliaries) the *praefectus cohortis* rather than of the *tribunus* or *legatus legionis*. The confusing multiplicity of Roman personal names — *nomina*, *cognomina* and the rest — was one that might readily be assimilated to a non-Roman society where A was formally also A son of B, or A son of a segment of the tribe of God X.

Fig. 3.3 illustrates samples of such ogam inscriptions, showing both the method of imposing ogam upon a stone and typical cases of the resulting messages. How many passers-by could ever read such an inscription — 'read' in the sense of translating the markings into the component sounds of a man's name and filiation in speech — we cannot begin to tell, except to suspect that the number would increase rather than decrease through time. More to the point is that establishment of, and acceptance of, this strange custom in fourth-century Ireland — southern Leinster and Munster — must be posited to explain its transfer overseas. This, too, need occasion no surprise at all. Transmutation in the nineteenth century of the Church of England, with relatively little alteration, to Australia and New Zealand led gradually to the construction of parish churches and even cathedrals differing from their English prototypes only in scale and geological components — not in plan or appearance — and the home-country tombstone could be reproduced without change in style or wording. Earlier, the eighteenth-century ornate tombstones of south-west Britain re-appeared across the Atlantic in New England.[31]

The study of ogam in all its branches, 'ogamology', has had a bad press at times because like all quasi-cryptic scripts it fell prey to undisciplined theorists and, worse, to the lunatic fringe. Damian McManus effectively rehabilitated it in his *Guide*. In this book the transmission of an ogam inscriptional tradition from

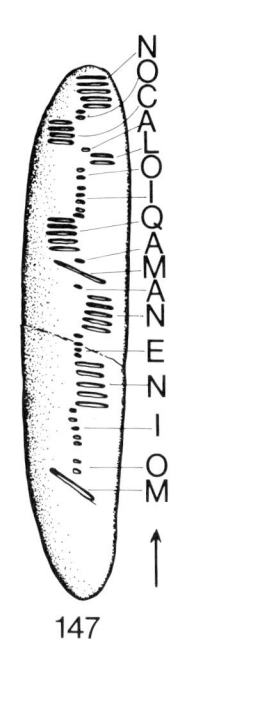

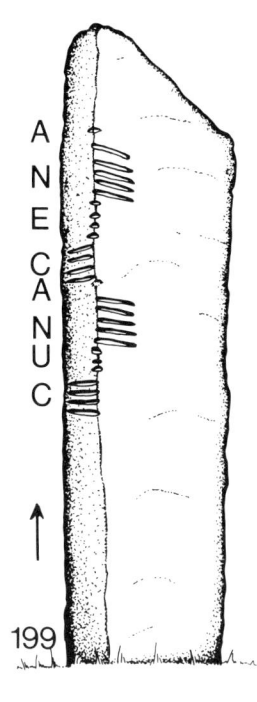

**Fig. 3.3** How monumental ogam was used (drawings based on *CIIC*). **Left**, 147 Ballineesteenig, Co. Kerry, on worn sandstone block with imagined stem-line, *MOINENA MAQI OLACON*. **Right**, 199 Coolmagort, Co. Kerry, on grit slab with sharp angle as stem-line, *CUNACENA*.

fourth-century Ireland to fifth-century Wales and then to sixth-century Dumnonia could, on its own, offer material for a prolonged publication. It cannot of course be separated from other things – Death, Latin, the Roman scripts, the choice of personal names, the persistence of tombstone formulae and the impenetrable long-gone factors of family pride, mourning, intrigues and superstition (the last before its replacement by Christian doctrine). It is virtually certain now that the first exportation of the ogam-inscribed memorial was from southern Ireland to south-west Wales, and not long after AD 400. Our following chapters can provide the background, and then the evidence.

# References

1. R. A. G. Carson & Clare O'Kelly, 'A catalogue of the Roman coins from Newgrange, Co. Meath', *PRIA* 77 C (1977), 35–55 illus.
2. From conversations with the late Professor O'Kelly; he had come to see this as the most persuasive interpretation of his finds.

3. Prosper of Aquitaine's *Chronicle*, s.a. 431. Palladius may have come from Auxerre (*CRB*, 300–1); if so, sailing from the Loire?
4. Map (very tentative), *CRB* 305, fig. 57.
5. Patrician dates are not agreed but the weight of informed views at present favours the 'late' Patrick (as described with dates in *CRB* chaps. 13 and 14). On this scheme, he returned to Ireland around 450-plus.
6. *CRB*, fig. 57, map.
7. Richard Sharpe, 'Quatuor Sanctissimi Episcopi: Irish Saints Before St Patrick', pp. 376–99 in: D. Ó Corráin et al., eds., *Sages, Saints and Storytellers* (= James Carney Festschrift) (Maynooth 1989).
8. 'Colloquium on Hiberno-Roman Relations and Material Remains', *PRIA* 76 C (1976), 171–292, ten authors.
9. The leading proponent and synthesist is Richard B. Warner (Belfast), the most important papers being: 'Some observations on the context and importation of exotic material in Ireland (etc.)', *PRIA* 76 C (1976), 267–92; 'Ireland, Ulster and Scotland in the earlier Iron Age', pp. 160–87 in: A. O'Connor & D. Clarke, eds., *From the Stone Age to the Forty-five* (= R. B. K. Stevenson Festschrift) (Edinburgh 1983); 'Ireland and the origins of escutcheon art', pp. 19–22 in: Michael Ryan, ed., *Ireland and Insular Art* (Dublin 1987); and 'Cultural Intrusions in the Early Iron Age: Some Notes', *Emania* 9 (1991), 44–52. Warner's Early Iron Age, with named divisions, runs from third cent. BC to fourth cent. AD.
10. Warner, map, 277, fig. 3, in *PRIA* 87 C (1976); this paper also gives (283) his terminology of period-divisions.
11. An inscribed fine-stone stamp, as would be used by a travelling herbalist or oculist, from Golden Bridge, Co. Tipperary, is one such clue. See J. D. Bateson, 'Roman Material from Ireland: A Re-consideration', *PRIA* 73 C (1973), 21–97 (p. 74, no. 25).
12. Cf. Professor P. MacCana's definition (*Celtic Mythology* (1970), 108) as 'a roving band of professional warriors'; Warner, op cit. n. 10 above, 282 and n. 32, looks at this possibility of 'Irish mercenaries serving with the Roman army'.
13. S. S. Frere, *Britannia* (rev. edn., 1978), index (476) under 'Irish raiders'. Few, if any, British Romanists now seem to be *au fait* with current discoveries and ideas in Hiberno-Roman studies.
14. Byrne 1973, chap. 9 ('Cashel').
15. The writer's *in situ* observations (five visits since 1950); a simple, well-placed section may one day be feasible.
16. W. *castell*, Co. *castell* (Padel 1985, 42–3, suggesting some late extensions of meaning).
17. Strictly *castrum* (sing., neuter) – plur. *castra* ('fortifications') must have been a common colloquialism, later dominant.
18. 'Three Old Irish Accentual Poems', *Ériu* 22 (1971), 23–80; the Leinster poems at 65 ff., Latin borrowing at 69–70.
19. 'Some Linguistic Evidence Relating to the British Church', pp. 75–86 in: M. W. Barley & R. P. C. Hanson, eds., *Christianity in Britain, 300–700* (Leicester 1968) – Greene's list at p. 81.
20. A classic modern example is the script not unlike Pitman's shorthand invented to write the language of the Canadian Inuit (Eskimos), one that appears in official publications – this agglutinative syllabic language with its three vowels (a, i, u) is readily expressed in a ti-ta-tu, li-la-lu, it-at-ut system of syllabic hooks and triangles. For some interesting earlier inventions among minority languages see S. Robert Ramsey, *The Languages of China* (Princeton Univ. Press, 1987), part II.

21. Ogam is used here throughout; other spellings are ogom, ogham (OIr. *ogum*, RIA Dict.).
22. *Guide*, 14 (2.7, end).
23. *ECNE* 200–3; *LHEB* 151–7.
24. *LHEB* 157, a view not subsequently altered.
25. For a reasonable explanation of how this may have come about, see *Guide*, 3.9 (after Carney). See now also, for earliest phonetic values, P. Sims-Williams, 'Some Problems in Deciphering the Earliest Irish Ogam Alphabet', *Trans Philological Society,* 91.2 (1993), 133–80.
26. R. I. Page, *Runes* ('Reading The Past' ser.), British Museum (1987), pl. opp. p.6.
27. *Guide*, Chap. 2, especially 2.4.
28. This may introduce (though Chap. 3 is not intended to explore it) another important sub-debate within 'ogamology' – the extent to which Latin was known in pre-400 Ireland in such settings as those postulated here (and elsewhere). Increasingly, congruence of archaeological and linguistic inferences favours the position adopted by Dr Anthony Harvey – see his 'Early Literacy in Ireland: The Evidence from Ogam', *CMCS* 14 (1987), 1–15; 'Latin, Literacy, and the Celtic Languages Around the Year AD 500', pp. 11–26 in: C. J. Byrne, M. Harry & P. Ó Siadhail, eds., *Celtic Languages and Celtic Peoples* (St Mary's Univ., Halifax, Nova Scotia 1992); and (summary) 'The Ogham Inscriptions and the Roman Alphabet: Two Traditions or One?' *Archaeology Ireland*, 4.1 (1990), 13–14. See also Jane Stevenson's 'The Beginnings of Literacy in Ireland', *PRIA* 89 C (1989), 127–65.
29. Most recent summary of possibilities; *Kinship*, 261–2 (and elsewhere, *passim*, in the context of land tenure).
30. A handy guide – R. G. Collingwood & Ian Richmond, *The Archaeology of Roman Britain* (rev. edn., Methuen, London 1969), chap. xi. On altars (quadrangular in section and therefore physically like natural limestone pillars and slabs in parts of Ireland) the dedicator's name is in the nom. – *Aurelius Quirinus, praefectus, f(ecit)* 'made this'. Building-stones on the other hand often show personal names in the gen., notably when legionary sub-units are named – cf. *RIB* 1632, near Housesteads, *c(enturio) Iuli Candid(i) fecit*, citing the century *of* Julius Candidus. For auxiliary units the generic name is genitive plural – e.g., *RIB* 1823, *coh(ors) I Batavorum*, some Batavi working on the *vallum*.
31. Edmund Vincent Gillon, Jr., *Early New England Gravestone Rubbings* (2nd edn., Dover, New York 1981), citing also Harriette M. Forbes, *Gravestones of Early New England* (Boston 1927). It is abundantly clear that these eighteenth-century immigrant stone-cutters, specialist families with apprentices, brought pattern books with them from the Old Country.

# 4
# Irish Settlements in Atlantic Britain

MUCH HAS BEEN WRITTEN about society in Ireland during Britain's Roman centuries.[1] Comparatively little is known in a way that would satisfy economic historians. The absence of anything like the small towns or larger cities of Britannia is taken for granted. Within an Irish economy whose nature is inferred from excavations and casual finds an emphasis on cattle-ranching, pastoralism with short-distance transhumance and (arguing back from literary sources) possession and acquisition of cattle as wealth allows one possible scenario – the problem of an increasing imbalance. This would have arisen between the needs of a steadily growing population organized into far too many *tuatha* (the petty kingdoms or 'tribal areas'[2]) and the finite capacities of good land where so much was bog, mountain, karst or still forest. Archaeology's aim is to define open and defended living-places in such a system together with their likely extents of life-supporting land, from which models for this segment of the past can be proposed and tested. Despite the present quite healthy state of Irish field-archaeology[3] this aim addresses an unending task, unlikely to be tackled as a matter of priority.

One aspect of early Ireland surprisingly poorly documented is that of the Irish as sailors – not on rivers and lakes but in a deep-water capacity. Yet it was in this capacity that contact between Ireland and Roman Britain took place, unless it was all one-way. Leaving aside the special case of trade (p. 27) there was of course less stimulus for Britons to consider settling *en masse* in Ireland than there might have been for Irish to contemplate a neighbouring island known to hold the material rewards that followed Romanization. It is conceivable that the lure of such rewards, their existence known or imagined as the outcome of a British trading presence, featured at a period when land-hunger or pasture-shortage pressed upon the Irish – in an Ireland hemmed on all sides by the sea. Did this help to prompt emigration in groups?

If so, this is to be divorced historically from the raiding activities of coastal barons and entrepreneurs; just as from the chance (if not probability) of individual Irishmen, somehow swept up into the Roman auxiliary forces, occasionally coming back with tall tales of Empire. The raiders' easy capture and enslavement of youth from Britannia's open countryside bore no closer relation to contemporary Irish pastoralism than the work of twentieth-century gang-masters does to traditional English mixed farming. Patrick's *Confessio*, in this respect unique as a fifth-century source, tells how he and the *servos et ancillas* 'labourers and maid-servants' on his father's country estate were captured in one such raid.[4] Possibly it also hints that the raiders' aim was to get back to Irish shores as rapidly as possible.

In his stupendous though exasperating book[5] Dr John Morris's chief contribution was to look at early historic Britain and Ireland from the vantage-point of the whole Late Roman world. He observed what he believed to have been a distinction common to many areas – 'all along the frontiers, the third-century enemies of Rome were raiders who went home again, however deeply their raids penetrated; but in the later fourth century and the fifth Rome everywhere faced bolder enemies, migrating peoples on the move, eager to settle within Roman territories.' This may hold good for Europe in general but is too wide a conclusion to accept unmodified here. On Patrick's evidence only, supported by the dates of bullion hoards in Ireland's north,[6] Irish raids into (north-west) England went on until well after 400. Morris's sequence happens to suggest the right dates for one of the settlements; that which took place in south-west Wales.

Still a useful presentation of historical sources is Cecile O'Rahilly's slim book of 1924.[7] It avoids, as do all later treatments of the theme, exploration of the *motives* for colonization. Why should any Irish have wished to settle permanently in Britain, individuals or groups? What could be unattractive about their own green island, of which Bede was to write that it was superior to Britannia in its healthiness and milder climate, flowing with milk and honey, stocked with vines, fish, birds and hunted for its deer?[8] In the memoir of his father-in-law, Tacitus had written (and some Irishmen may have read) how the great Agricola claimed that Ireland – 'tolerably well known from [British] merchants who trade there' – might be conquered with one legion and supporting troops.[9] *Might* be; but the logistics of the invasion may have appeared too daunting, and there was no reason therefore to flee Ireland in order to escape a Roman subjugation. Tacitus's further note that Agricola had welcomed an Irish prince, driven by a rebellion from his homeland, gives about the only case of a credible reason for (swift) emigration. Nor can the gap in our knowledge be said to have been filled by Myles Dillon's 1971 O'Donnell Lecture at Oxford.[10] The explanation of the Welsh settlement, given by a courteous scholar and scion of a distinguished Irish family to his (in part, Welsh) hosts, was that 'the Irish came to Dyfed and Gwynedd as friends and allies of the British in the struggle against Rome. The mass of the British people must have feared and hated the Romans who had robbed them of liberty and self-esteem. I find myself hating them, too, as I read the story...' To the Briton Gildas in the sixth century, the mass of the British (lately, Roman) people feared and hated the Irish who raided them. To Roman historians of this century, who would probably regard Liberty as a small price to pay for the privilege of Roman citizenship, Irish groups in Britain were *foederati*, federates, tribesmen allowed to settle under treaty in order to protect Britannia's flank from their unredeemed fellow-tribesmen.[11] *Quot homines, tot sententiae*. All we can guess is that, eventually, more persuasive explanations for Irish settlements in late Roman Britain – if ascertainable at all – will emerge from socio-economic studies about populations and land-use.

The various post-Roman (or end-of-the-Roman-period) colonies of Irish along western Britain, from Scotland almost to Scilly, have been addressed now a great many times,[12] and those not concerned with Demetia and Dumnonia are mentioned only briefly. Settlement in western Scotland north of the Clyde and on some of the Isles was centred on modern Argyll and gave rise to the kingdom of Dál Riata.[13] Persistence of spoken Irish, so introduced, gave rise to Scottish Gaelic and, as eventually the dominant power over the Picts and some of the North Britons, the *Scotti*, or Irish incomers, gave their new land its commonest extra-territorial name.[14] In south-west Scotland, Galloway, a smaller-scale drift across the narrows from Antrim and a dispersed settlement is detectable from place-names and archaeology, but not really before the sixth century and then in a mainly Christian context.[15] The Isle of Man, left to itself in Roman times, was recognized as a sky-line feature from several shores; *Manavia* was known but not Romanized.[16] Culturally, it was an extension of Britain's Cumbrian shore and Lancashire coastal plain and since the Manx language emerges as an isolated descendant of Irish it follows that Man was settled, overwhelmingly, probably from Ulster. The later imposition of an important little Norse kingdom makes it hard to say much about Man's post-Roman story.[17]

Along that traditional shipping-route of Dublin to Holyhead, Irish groups went to north-west Wales; Anglesey, and the 'pig's ear' peninsula of Lleyn or Llŷn in Caernarfonshire. With other place-names like Mallaen and Dinllaen it reflects forms of the Irish word for Leinster and the Leinstermen.[18] Further evidence, as in Demetia, comes from the presence of Irish names on inscriptions and to a limited extent from early history and hagiography.[19]

In south-west Wales, Demetia or Dyfed, all that we know of the Irish settlements there tells us that they fall into a category all their own; and this is not being claimed simply because of the writer's special interest. The quality of the evidence for them could be described as in some respects unique. Lastly it is possible – no more than that – to suggest a small and isolated settlement in the west of Cornwall, something which will be taken up in chapter 11. Fig. 4.1 (p. 45) is a rudimentary map, in no sense a detailed distribution, to show the consistent Atlantic-shore pattern of all these colonies. It covers, probably, a period from the late fourth to the early seventh century AD. There is a remote chance that a few other very small settlements took place – on the Cumbrian coast? on the Cheshire–Lancashire shoreline? in Cardigan Bay? – for which no evidence has come down to us.[20]

For the presence of Irish in Demetia, it is helpful to consider this in terms of two phases, the earlier exemplifying Morris's raiders active within the Roman period and the later covering a longer period of actual settlement and the conversion to Christianity. The only general Irish perception of the first, and it is both retrospective and oblique, is to be found in the work called *Sanas Chormaic* or 'Cormac's Glossary'.[21] This was compiled by Cormac mac Cuilennáin, who was killed in 908 when king of Munster at Cashel, in Tipperary, and reputedly had also been a bishop. In it, etymologies of hundreds of words, many archaic and obscure, are explained through anecdotes. One, attached to the phrase *mug-eime* 'slave of the hilt', tells how the first lap-dog in Ireland — probably a whippet — was obtained by an ingenious ruse, and the explanation involved Irishmen visiting Britain. For this a quasi-historical background is supplied, set centuries earlier in the seductive and peculiarly Irish variety of 'dream-time', an age of ancient kings — in this instance Crimthann Már mac Fidaig, king of Munster and an all-Ireland potentate. If Crimthann son of Fidach ever existed the traditional genealogies would suggest that it was far back in the Roman centuries. Cormac's entry depicts the Irish as powerful in Britain, dividing Britain (*Alba*) up among them, settling there and constructing houses and fortresses.

The next part of the entry is frequently cited, but not always explained. Three place-names are given; the unusual thing is that two of them, both of forts, are given in two versions, the first being British — probably taken from Old Welsh — and the second Irish. 'Dinn Tradui, that is, Dún Tredúi; that is, *tredhúe* "of three d.'s" of Crimthann mor son of Fidach king of Ireland and Britain up to the Sea of Icht'. (*Icht* is the Isle of Wight, Latin *Vectis* — this means 'as far as the English Channel'.) The next place is not a fort but a *cell* 'church, monastery', *Glasimpere*; Glastonbury, a place that in Cormac's time had a fascination for the Irish and even an association with St Patrick.[22] The third is a fortress again, 'Dind map Lethain in the lands of the British of Cornwall' (*i tírib Bretan Cornn*) and this (in Irish) was Dún maic Liatháin because, it is explained, the word *mac* 'sons' in British is *map*.

These three places, linked to the name of Crimthann and to a time when the Irish were lording it in parts of Britain, including Cornwall specifically, may have been all that Cormac knew or else all that it was thought necessary to include by way of illustration. That the two fort-names are given first in British and then, as it were, in translation is curious enough; does it suggest that, being in Britain, their real names were naturally British, that Cormac had access to some British source, and even that the names were still current? Was there even a British tradition that these forts had been used, if not necessarily first constructed, by militant Irish a very long time before the ninth century AD?

Glastonbury is a real place. So, presumably, are the forts; it will be shown later that they can be identified, the first with reasonable confidence, the second only tentatively. The likelihood is that they were never the nuclei of settlements — colonists who were basically farmers and herders were after land, not enclosed

**Fig. 4.1** Irish settlements or colonies in Atlantic Britain, from late fourth century AD onwards; areas affected shown in generalized form.

hill-tops – but more in the nature of symbols; prominent features, held for very short periods, in districts that were initially raided, and features whose names (in either language) could then be worked into heroic recitations subsequently set in the heroic age. The first fort is in Wales and the second, as Cormac knew, in Cornwall. It has not been noticed that, as seen from Cashel, the three names may be in a sequence; north to south in an arc, perhaps in what were thought to be increasing distances from the Irish shore (Fig. 4.2). And this is an appropriate place to say that there is no warrant at all for the oft-repeated idea that Dinn *Tradui* (in British) is the same name as a Cair *Draitou*, or *Draithou*, contained in a list of twenty-eight cities of Britain[23] that appears in the ninth-century British compilation ascribed to 'Nennius' nor, if this is a later version of it, the Din*draithou* of the medieval Welsh Life of St Carannog (p. 80). Dindraithou at any rate seems to have been in Cornwall, not Wales, and the two names do not mean the same despite a superficial likeness.

Nothing from British tradition, Welsh or Dumnonian, mirrors what Cormac wrote. As we shall see, certain Lives of saints, mostly compiled a few centuries after Cormac's day, reiterate a theme of travel between Wales, Ireland and Cornwall, but only in the context of individual pilgrims and Christian activities.

# IRISH SETTLEMENTS IN ATLANTIC BRITAIN

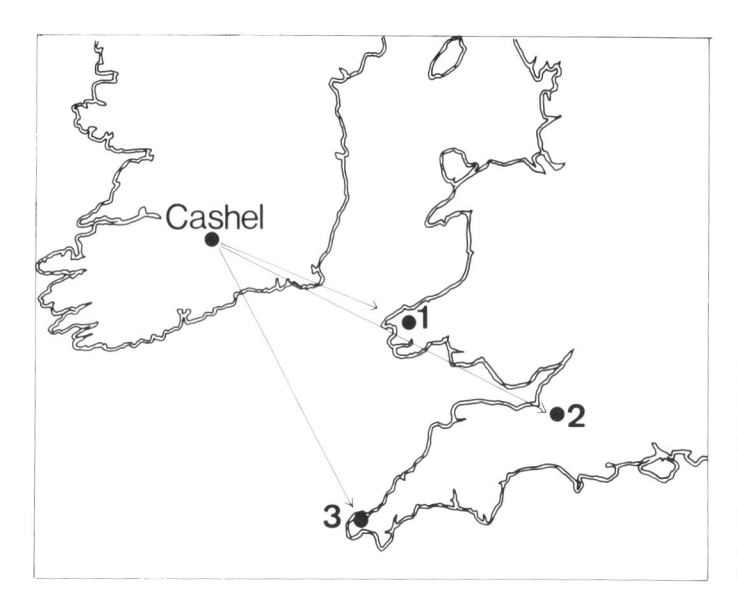

**Fig. 4.2** Sketch map; Cormac mac Cuilennáin's three named places in Britain, as seen from late-ninth-century Cashel. 1, *Dún Tredúi* (?Moel Trigarn, Pembs.). 2, Glastonbury, Somerset. 3, *Dún maic Liatháin* (?Trencrom, west Cornwall).

Gildas's précis of what, around 500, was remembered of the history of Britain a century and more earlier mentions the Irish; but without specific geography, and as one component in a mélange of hostile barbarians. Modern scholarship is not that much better placed. The details, temporal and geographical, of the permanent and eventually dominant colonization in Dál Riata have to be pieced together from annals and chronicles that dwell on selected names, on certain kinds of happenings like battles and sieges and the happy accident that one early Life (of St Columba) is set in the right place. The early Irish in Galloway – Wigtonshire and Kirkcudbrightshire – have been inferentially reconstituted, devoid of any group-names or dates, from studies of place-names and from archaeology. In the Isle of Man all this is even more shadowy; the existence of the Manx language and the large corpus of pre-Scandinavian place-names suggest an island entirely Hibernicized. Only the high probability that its inhabitants in the pre-Roman Iron Age and the Roman period were British speakers and looked back to Lancashire rather than to Ulster, and two or three fifth–sixth century inscriptions with British names, allow us to postulate an Irish settlement of a British island.

The existence of substantial numbers of families, under their chieftains, coming from Ireland into post-Roman north-west Wales and south-west Wales is not in doubt; the radical difference between these regions, and the Isle of Man and western Scotland, is that they are still Welsh-speaking. This may not be simply a question of comparative weights of sheer numbers, as the greater example of England shows — the advent between the late fourth and the sixth centuries of, perhaps, a hundred thousand immigrants from north-west Europe led to the replacement of a language spoken by, perhaps, three or four million Britons.[24] For an even more marked example of how unimportant a factor the disparity of numbers can be, we might think of the history of spoken and written English in the Indian sub-continent. Socio-linguistic theory will not however help us to explore precisely what happened in Pembrokeshire in AD 400–500. Nor, oddly enough, can conventional archaeology offer much aid. By the eighth century, studying Britain (by then partly English) and Ireland together, it is quite true that at the summit of the archaeological pile-up we have superb personal ornaments of gold, silver and gilded bronze with various inlays and intricate ornament, that distinct art-historical styles exist and regional ateliers and master-craftsmen can be postulated, and that a brooch can be described as Irish, Pictish, Northumbrian or Kentish in respect of its more-than-probable origin. At the level of farming tools, most low-grade personal weapons, rural craft equipment and what some auctioneers now call 'kitchenalia', no such clear distinctions exist; a small iron knife is a knife is a knife regardless of what language its holder happened to speak. Some archaeologists have gone so far as to talk about 'an Irish Sea Culture', meaning that a common pre-Roman Iron Age background led to more or less the same range of everyday things in Ireland and Atlantic Britain. This can be extended from rustic activity to rustic existence. The appearance, from perhaps as far back as the late Bronze Age, of a single phenomenon, that of the *enclosed defended homestead,* had led by the end of the Roman period to a myriad such sites mainly distinguished by what we choose to call them — the little duns and circular earthworks of Scotland, the thousands of Irish *dúns* and raths, the enclosed hut-groups and concentrics of north Wales and other 'raths' and *caerau* in the south-west, and the rounds of Cornwall. Irish farmers and pastoralists of sufficient standing and with enough resources and human capital to inhabit one of these at home would probably have looked for, or reproduced *de novo*, a similar establishment in a new land. Especially when diagnostic small finds are few or non-existent, how can we always tell? Laymen sometimes assume that all this points to early societies in a state of perpetual conflict. In fact, it is infinitely more likely that the substantial farmer and land-possessor with his immediate family and dependants protected his home against the unfree, the bandits and in many areas the wolf — the influence of the menace of the wolf upon domestic construction is a European topic in itself.[25]

It *is* possible not only to define but to describe an Irish settlement in Demetia. In the place of archaeology, we have to turn to a most cautious dissection of fragmentary historical sources, and to a class of evidence literally writ in stone — the contemporary memorial inscriptions.

## References

1. Cf. relevant chapters in N. Edwards, *The Archaeology of Early Medieval Ireland* (Batsford, 1990); J. P. Mallory & T. E. McNeill, *The Archaeology of Ulster* (Institute of Irish Studies, Belfast 1991 – chap. 6 applicable beyond Ulster); and H. Mytum, *The Origins of Early Christian Ireland* (Routledge, 1992, chaps, 4 & 5 – though note here Richard Sharpe's critical review, *Early Medieval Europe* 2.1 (1993) 88–9). Nerys Thomas Patterson, *Cattle-Lords and Clansmen. Kinship and Rank in Early Ireland* (Garland, N.Y. and London 1991) contains much of interest for those working in early agrarian history and archaeology.
2. 'Tribe, tribal', etc., are used for convenience only; see Francis John Byrne's essential guide, 'Tribes and Tribalism in Early Ireland', *Ériu* 22 (1971), 128–66.
3. Best followed in selected journals – *Archaeology Ireland* (1, 1987– ), *Emania, Bulletin of the Navan Research Group* (1, 1986– ), *Journal of Irish Archaeology* (1, 1983– ) and *Ulster Journal of Archaeology* (*UJA*) (3rd ser., 51 (1988– ).
4. *Confessio*, i; for this writer's view of the geography (Carlisle and hinterland), see *CRB* chap. 13.
5. *The Age of Arthur* (1973); here, 155–63.
6. Michael Dolley in *PRIA* 76 C (1976), 181–90; Patrick's captivity from around 430, *CRB* 320 (and, with this 'late' dating, other writers).
7. *Ireland and Wales. Their Historical and Literary Relations* (Longmans, 1924).
8. Bede, *HE* i.1 – the whole passage is derivative but reflects Bede's obvious sympathy for the (by then, Christian) Irish and their land.
9. Tacitus, *Agricola*, cap. 24.
10. 'The Irish Settlements in Wales', *Celtica* 12 (1977), 1–11.
11. This is suggested in R. B. Collingwood and J. N. L. Myres, *Roman Britain and the English Settlements* (1936 edn., 282–3), even found a place in *LHEB* (at 154) and was adopted by Leslie Alcock in his *Arthur's Britain* (1971), 124–5. Most Celticists dismiss this as pure speculation. W. Davies (1982, 88–9) favours the possibility of 'internal Irish political problems' as stimulating emigration; if allied to socio-economic ones, many would agree with her.
12. C. Thomas, 'The Irish settlements in post-Roman western Britain: a survey of the evidence', *JRIC* n.s. 6 (1972), 251–74, is now hopelessly out of date.
13. John Bannerman, *Studies in the History of Dalriada* (Edinburgh 1974); Alfred P. Smyth, *Warlords and Holy Men – Scotland* AD *80–1000* ( = New History of Scotland 1; Edward Arnold, London 1984), chaps. 2–4.
14. Extra-territorial names are what a given country is called by others, or in other languages (Écosse, Schottland); intra-territorial, those used only within it, like Deutschland as opposed to Germany or Alemania.
15. John MacQueen, 'Kirk- and Kil- in Galloway place-names', *Archivum Linguisticum* 8 (Glasgow 1956), 135–49; W. H. F. Nicolaisen, 'Scottish place-names: 24, Slew- and sliabh', *Scottish Studies* 9 (Edinburgh 1965), 91–106; C. Thomas, discussion covering archaeology, pp. 177–83 in *Medieval Archaeol.* 11 (1967) (Ardwall Isle report).
16. *PNRB*, 40–41, with the view that *Manavia* has the sense of 'mountainy island'. Others however might prefer a connection with the divine name *\*Manau* and some oceanic deity.
17. *LHEB* 72–4; McManus, in *Ériu* 37 (1986), 5. Dr Molly Miller's paper 'Hiberni reversuri', *PSAS* 110 (1979–80), 305–27, while as always stimulating, does seem to use a sledgehammer to crack a nut.
18. The place-names: *BBCS* 22 (1966), 37–41 (note, in Welsh). Leinster possessed a marked

early identity; R. Ó hUiginn, 'The Literature of the Laigin', *Emania* 7 (1990), 5–9.

19. *LHEB*, 172, gives its author's view (not followed here) about Irish retentions of a role as 'separate entity' and of their language.
20. See J. D. Bu'lock, *Pre-Conquest Cheshire 383–1066* (= History of Cheshire, vol. 3; Cheshire Community Council, 1972).
21. Whitley Stoke's edition, *Three Irish Glossaries* (Williams & Norgate, London & Edinburgh 1862) has been used here. For a recent description of its nature and context, see Paul Russell in *CMCS* 15 (1988), 1–30.
22. See relevant essays in Lesley Abrams & James P. Carley, eds., *The Archaeology and History of Glastonbury Abbey: Essays in Honour of the Ninetieth Birthday of C. A. Ralegh Radford* (Boydell, Woodbridge 1991).
23. Conveniently, text and translation in John Morris, *Nennius. British History and the Welsh Annals* (Phillimore, London & Chichester 1980). For the medieval Dindraithou, see p. 45 above; it, and Cair Draitou, contain OW (or OCo.) *\*traitou* 'strands, beaches'. The List (ignoring Morris's 'translation' of it) contains some seventeen Roman places, the rest being apparently notable native centres or fortresses. 'Cair Draitou' *ought* to be the Dumnonian royal citadel, used in the fifth to sixth cents., on Tintagel Island; but this is flanked by only one small insignificant beach, the Haven.
24. Contemporary realistic view of fourth-cent. population of Britannia and un-Romanized Britain; the onus is on Anglo-Saxonists to show that the English settlements were substantially greater, if indeed as great, as a figure of this order.
25. 'Last wolves'; Scotland, Sutherland 1743; Wales, uncertain, but an attempted extermination in tenth cent.; Cornwall, Rospeath in Ludgvan, reign of Henry VIII; Ireland, supposedly Wicklow 1770 – Macalister, *The Archaeology of Ireland* (2nd ed., Methuen, 1949, at p.14), suggests that Mallow, 1790s, is possible. Two generations ago, elderly folk on the SE France *causses* (p. 9) remembered the severe winters when starving wolves in pairs actually entered the farm-places; semi-subterranean *bergeries* in which ewes were penned all winter, like the massive upper-floor dwellings (with internal wells), were not entirely against the weather. Wolves attacked all livestock *and* isolated humans and in Europe carried rabies. Archaeologists sometimes overlook this menace as a factor in monument-layout.

# 5
# *Demetia: Settlers and Sovereigns*

STUDENTS OF EARLY historic Wales, whether historians, historical linguists, archaeologists or landscape-analysts, enjoy today an unrestricted access to accurate maps at many scales and to expert place-name gazetteers. They can teach themselves to think spatially – to correlate mentally the images of maps with memories and notes of corresponding fieldwork. Air photography can elaborate the correlation (though the aircraft is usually a poor substitute for a pair of boots). It is not easy to grasp the fact, though it is vital we do so, that virtually the whole of this referential frame was denied to the occupants of post-Roman Britain. With rare exceptions, and then only in a few cases like practical mariners in respect of coastlines, men could know little about their home geography. Compass points were linked to the sun and the seasons, specification of distances to estimates of how long would be needed to cover them on foot or horseback. Despite their practical knowledge of surveying and of what might be called simplified urban and rural planning, the Romans too have not left us anything save the most vague indication of how Roman Britain, Britannia, was divided; either into the four *provinciae* (of the civil *dioecesis Britanniae*) or into the twenty or more *civitates*, the fiscal and administrative 'cantons' of unequal size.[1]

Southern Wales in Roman times contained the *civitas* of the Silures, which included the later Glamorgan and Monmouth; and to its west an inferred *civitas* of the Demetae.[2] *Moridunum*, now below modern Carmarthen town, was its centre. A recognized boundary or frontier was required if only for taxation purposes, and natural features would form the obvious choice. It has to be a guess that Demetia, as we can call it, extended north of the Teifi across modern Cardiganshire. The frontier with the Silures is a matter of debate. Their *civitas* must have gone as far west as the valley and outflow of the river Neath (Fig. 5.1), just as Demetia must have gone as far south-east as the valley and outflow of the river Towy, *Afon Tywi*. One could suggest that the natural division between them was the intermediate river Loughor, immediately separating small territories – the Gower peninsula south, the Kidwelly district, Cydweli, on the west – that in post-Roman Wales had separate area-names and probably identities. Names of rivers that have survived from great antiquity, if not just chance survivals, are likely to have been those that had special importance; the names mattered because, before and during Roman times, the rivers served as bounds to tribal areas and then to

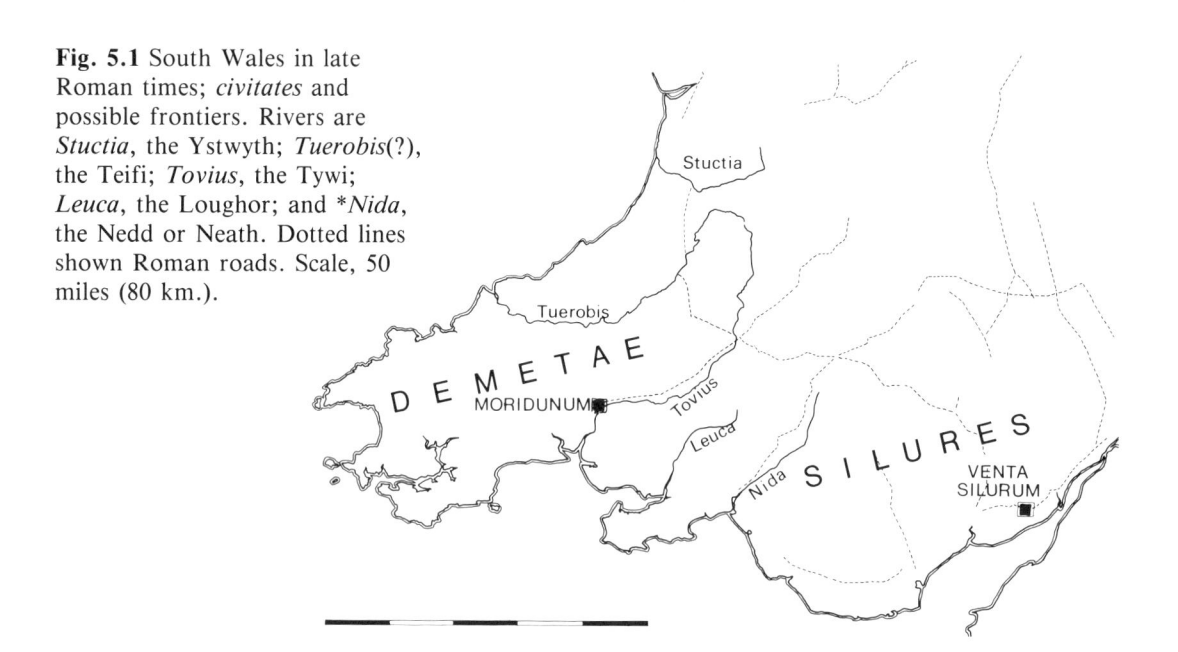

**Fig. 5.1** South Wales in late Roman times; *civitates* and possible frontiers. Rivers are *Stuctia*, the Ystwyth; *Tuerobis*(?), the Teifi; *Tovius*, the Tywi; *Leuca*, the Loughor; and *\*Nida*, the Nedd or Neath. Dotted lines shown Roman roads. Scale, 50 miles (80 km.).

*civitates* or *pagi* within them. In that light (Fig. 5.1) the *Stuctia* or Ystwyth[3] is a credible northern limit to Demetia. South and east the name of the Tywi is recorded (Tovius);[4] that of the Neath (*\*Nida*?) has to be inferred from the settlement-name *Nidum*,[5] the town of Neath, *Nedd* in Welsh; but the intervening river Loughor, *Afon Llwchwr*, has a known Roman name as *Leuca*.[6]

It would be difficult to produce a thick volume on Roman times in the *civitas Demetarum*. The topic is one where work is in progress, the gradual progress reflecting the limited resources and the few archaeologists on the ground. An official visiting Moridunum in the fourth century would have regarded lands to the north and west as native territory, Roman only because it all lay within the Empire. Yet it is historical, not hypothetical, that – apparently during the fifth century – this became a British kingdom and that a Romano-Celtic name Demetia, giving Old Irish *Demed* and a Welsh Dyfed (<*\*Deµed*), was carried over. The heartland may have been between the rivers Teifi and Tywi, but post-Roman Demetia was certainly larger than that. It differed in two very important respects from what happened to the former *civitas* of the Silures. First, there was never a single 'Siluria'; we may not know all the contemporary names of the several small kingdoms that arose within this rather larger *civitas*, but the indications are that that there *were* several of them.[7] Second, while in south-east Wales generally (i.e., the old Glamorgan and Monmouth) there was a notable degree of continuity from a Romanized and semi-Romanized, even Roman Christian, past into new principalities, the background remained that of indigenous Britons – proto-Welsh – who could build on pre-400 institutions, language and letters. Demetia lacked this Roman past, and was also to be subjected to a lasting intrusive element: the Irish.

Our fundamental text is Old Irish and runs translated, with a few additions, as follows:

> Eochaid, son of Artchorp [or Art Corb] went over the sea with his *clann* into the territory of Demed; and it is there that his sons and grandsons died. And from them is the race of Crimthann over there – of which, Tualador (*Teudos*), son of Rigin (*Regin*), son of Catacon (*Catgocaun*), son of Caittienn (*Cathen*), son of Clotenn (*Cloten*), son of Nae (or Noe) (*Nougoy*), son of Artur (*Arthur*), son of Retheor (or Petor) (*Petr*), son of Congar (*Cincar*), son of Gartbor (*Guortepir*), son of Alchol (*Aircol*), son of Trestin (*Triphun*), son of Aed Brosc, son of Corath, son of Eochaid 'Allmuir' the son of Artchorp.[8]

The author is not known. It comes from a story that may have been worked up from earlier oral recitations and that was apparently composed about 750, called 'The Expulsion of the Déisi' (expulsion of an Irish tribe from one part of Ireland to another). There are a number of versions of this story (= ED) in manuscripts of different dates.[9] ED was intended to explain the reasons behind the fate of the Déisi and includes this passage, describing how part of the tribe migrated to *Demed*, Welsh Demetia. The leader of the momentous happening was called Eochaid, a common Old Irish personal name, distinguished as Eochaid *Allmuir*, 'Over-Sea' – *transmarinus*, 'd'oûtre-mer'. The names are set out as a genealogical string (A, son of B, son of C, son of D, etc.) going back to Eochaid the founding-figure. The word *clann* has shades of meaning, but the mention of *a maic ocus a hui* 'his sons and grandsons' directs us to translate 'immediate descendants, whole family'.

Seamus Pender has pointed out that ED calls these Déisi who went to Demetia 'the race of Crimthann over there',[10] meaning that they were so known in Ireland during the eighth century, even if there is no trace of such a description in any Welsh source. He wondered if there had been a separate group of Cenel Crimthainn elsewhere in Wales among Irish emigrants, or whether such a group accompanied Eochaid and the Déisi, or even if a Crimthann other than the king Crimthann Már mac Fidaig was intended. It may seem more likely that the statement is figurative – rather as if J. R. Green had written of the British in India 'And so the race of Alfred took the tongue of Shakespeare and Milton to the dusky continent'. Since, around 900, Cormac mac Cuilennáin apparently still thought that Ireland's first forays into Britain had led to Crimthann Már becoming king of both Ireland and Britain as far as the Channel, and possessor of at least one fortress there, any earlier narrator could have known of the same tradition.

The extract from ED describes an emigration from Ireland without saying exactly where it set out, and then purports to give a descent through thirteen names from Eochaid to a 'Tualodor'. The names in italics and in brackets come from a Welsh source, one that provides only the supposed genealogy; it is among other such genealogies, long and short, compiled in the tenth century and found in an early twelfth-century manuscript.[11] It differs from ED in that its oldest two names matching the Irish ones are *Aircol map Triphun* (alongside *Alchol* and *Trestin*) – other Welsh names given after these, i.e., going back in time, are not found in the Irish version. The Welsh list also continues beyond, i.e. later in time than, *Teudos/Tualodor*. It brings us into history; Margetiut the son of Teudos, a known king, died in 796, Ouein the son of Margetiut in 811, and Ouein's great-great-granddaughter Elen was the wife of king Hywel Dda who acceded to Dyfed in 904 and died in 949–50. The Welsh version was therefore completed or updated at a fully historic stage.

The coincidence of the Irish and Welsh lists over so long a course is remarkable. Nor does it concern us if the relationship between them in their written guises is described as 'almost certainly a literary one'.[12] In some fashion, the same twelve-name sequence had been preserved over nearly 300 years in south-west Wales and in a province of Ireland (probably in Munster). One can read into this an inference that the Déisi in Dyfed 'kept in touch with their homeland until at least the eighth century'[13] but what it really shows is a two-way traffic; Irish *literati* and Welsh *literati* were exchanging information.

What exactly *is* the list? Principally, the kings of Demetia; some have Irish names, most do not. It is not a genealogy at all, even if there is one possible father-and-son pair in it, Guortepir son of Aircol. It is a regnal list – a catalogue of successive rulers. Its preservation in redactions that must be partly independent, in separate countries with differing languages, lends a certain confidence to any belief in its accuracy. Like all such regnal lists it has to be used with caution. In giving what some people thought to have been the correct order in which kings of Demetia, from Eochaid Allmuir, held that position (and we assume these *are* the kings; neither version says so) there is no guarantee that reigns with dual or parallel rulers are not included. In early Celtic society, kings were normally chosen on the basis of their membership of kinship or descent-groups.[14] This does not of itself preclude a son following his father, but for various reasons it renders that arrangement less likely than a nephew succeeding an uncle or a transfer of rule between cousins considerably separated by age.

The Welsh list has other names representing stages before Triphun (who belonged to the later fifth century). It gives them as (Triphun) '...map Clotri map Gloitguin map Nimet map Dimet map Max(im) guletic (map) Protec (map) Protector (map) Ebiud map Eliud (map) Stater (map) Pincr misser map Constans map Constantini magni map Constantii et Helen...'. Now nearly all of this is unredeemable fantasy, and to treat it seriously as a quarry for calculating timespans and absolute dates is a pointless exercise.[15] The last part, lifted from Classical history, is an add-on about Constantine the Great and his supposedly British mother Helen,[16] and Maxim or Macsen Guletic (*gwledig*) is the usurper Magnus Maximus of 383–8. Of the paired names, *Nimet* and *Dimet* can only represent *Demet* (Demetia); *Protec* and *Protector*, which are hardly names, recall the epithet on the memorial of the real sixth-century Guortepir, 358 MEMORIA VOTEPORIGIS PROTICTORIS (p. 82); *Ebiud* and *Eliud* are both poor ghosts of a written Eochaid (as 'Eciud'?); and 'Stater' with 'Pincr misser' is too far gone to merit investigation. But the first two names, *Clotri* and *Gloitguin*, are runners out of a very different stable. Both are old 'heroic' British names, *Cluto-rigi* and *Cluto-uindos*, and it is likely that they came at the end of a first version of the Welsh list.[17] If so, they ran parallel to the Irish names earlier than Triphun (as Trestin) – Aed Brosc, Corath and Eochaid himself.

ED falls into a class of Irish 'wandering' stories and its whole narrative need not concern us too much. It is a rambling explanation about why the Déisi were driven out of east-central Ireland and ended up somewhere in the south-east coastal plain, where they became listed as *Déisi Muman*.[18] Seamus Pender considered it 'a fiction based upon the facts that there was a small region of Brega (a plain in county Meath, north of Tara) whose population were called Déssi and a large region of Munster inhabited by a number of communities collectively called Déssi, the word "Déssi" meaning "subject communities".' He added that, as a very broad guide to antiquity, 'nothing Christian or relating to Christianity comes into the Migration story' – though what chronological significance could now be attached to this is open to debate.

Is Eochaid Allmuir's migration an event that can be dated at all? Is the double regnal-list open to dating? Dr Molly Miller's lengthy investigation of 'the patrilineage of Dyfed, with its reported marriages' concluded that a 25-year generation interval, abstracted from the nineteen stages between Triphun and a king Owain who died in 988, would put Eochaid's arrival 'approximately within the years 400 × 425'.[19] The whole base of her calculation is flawed from the start if one does not accept her view of what the list actually represents. Nevertheless it ought to contain an inherent chronology. Dr James's tables (with 33.3-year and 30-year alternatives for generations? or reigns?) do not help us because he, more so than Dr Miller, treats the Welsh names earlier than Triphun as if they were of real people, not as the late fictions they almost certainly are.[20]

There could be several approaches to the problem but, abandoning here and now any idea that the dual list is either a patrilineage or any kind of genealogy, a useful first step is to assign the names to types: capitals are used for the Irish forms.

| | | |
|---|---|---|
| 1 | EOCHAID ALLMUIR | Irish |
| 2 | CORATH[21] / Gloitguin | Irish / British |
| 3 | AED BROSC / Clotri | Irish / British |
| 4 | Triphun (<*Tribunus*) TRESTIN | Roman (borrowing) |
| 5 | Aircol (<*Agricola*) ALCHOL | Roman (borrowing) |
| 6 | Guortepir GARTBOR (358 *WOTECORIGAS*) | British (+ Irish (ogam)) |

| | | | |
|---|---|---|---|
| 7 | Cincar | CONGAR | British |
| 8 | Petr | PETOR | British (biblical, 'Peter') |
| 9 | Arthur | ARTUR | British |
| 10 | Nougoy | NAE, NOE | British (biblical, 'Noah') |
| 11 | Cloten | CLOTENN | British |
| 12 | Cathen | CAITTIENN | British |
| 13 | Catgocaun | CATACON | British |
| 14 | Regin | RIGIN | British |
| 15 | Teudos | TUALADOR | British |
| 16 | Margetiut ('Meredith') d.796 | | British |
| 17 | Ouein ('Owen') d.811 | | British |

This exposes several minor horizons. One introduces Roman-originating names (4, 5). The next is the end of any Irish aspect (6) which is also the start of British (Demetian, Welsh) names; and the third gives us two presumably Christian names, because biblical – 8 and 10. Some of these ideas will occupy us later.

There is no known way in which over so long a procession one can estimate either an 'average' reign in the absence of a known starting-date; or obtain such a date by hypothesizing such an average, multiplying it by the right factor and subtracting the result from AD 811. Voteporix or Guortepir or Vortipor was a mature man (*canescente iam capite* '(your) head already whitening') when Gildas wrote about him, a man old enough to occupy a throne stained with his murders and adulteries. If this was in the 540s, such a man could have died in 550×560 and a date in the middle third of the century, VI.2 for short (p. 262), is appropriate for the details of his inscribed memorial stone. He was also *boni regis nequam fili* 'O bad son of a good king', giving the implication that he was the son of the previous ruler Aircol (see p. 81). Aircol then reigned in VI.1 and would have been born in V.3 or just within V.2. A five- (or four-) reign stretch from Aircol back to Eochaid, both inclusive, must put us in a patch of time – say, a decade or two – centred on 400. This would contain Eochaid's arrival and the start of his rule. If we want to look for a moment of political opportunity, the years after 383 when Magnus Maximus, *Max(im) Guletic* above, famously led a military adventure abroad taking troops with him would suit.[22] Since it would be unwieldy to hedge every further allusion to Eochaid with a thicket of conditionals, the provisional model will be that of a man born in Ireland in the second half of the fourth century who headed a one-way passage to Demetia in 390×400, and then reigned and died there within V.1.

So much for the inception of an intrusive kingship, of which so far we have nothing save a list of names; what of the post-Roman kingdom? Where did these Irish Déisi land along so extensive a coastline, a good hundred miles and more from the mouth of the Teifi right around to the mouth of the Tywi; how many of them are there likely to have been, for how long after Eochaid's arrival do we suppose they continued to land, and was this anyhow the first time that groups of Irish had wandered around the Demetian countryside? Questions like these are always omitted, probably because it is assumed they cannot be answered and therefore there is no point in posing them. Excessive timidity at one end, the limits of inference at the other, support a tightrope along which we tread with care.

The last question above brings us back to any fourth-century raids preceding Eochaid and his *clann*, and therefore to what Cormac wrote, and to Dinn Tradui or Dún Tredúi. Was this possibly a vacant pre-Roman stronghold, not too far from beaches where boats might be left and guarded – a stronghold suited to a temporary camp and bridgehead? Pembrokeshire is the greater part of a block-shaped peninsula (Fig. 6.3, p. 72), its south-east segment being the western portion of Carmarthenshire. Across the north of Pembroke runs the high ridge of Prescelly, Mynydd Preseli, the end of a great arc of upthrust that widens eastward to become the Cambrian Mountains. Here and there Preseli rises to over 1,500 feet; under exceptionally clear conditions it has been reported as just visible from Ireland. No archaeologist would want to claim that Mynydd Preseli is fully explored. It is a dramatic region whose safeguarding was eminently worth the struggles of Waldo Williams (p. 12) and so many others, and a mysterious one. Carn Ingli, on a detached bloc north of the Gwaun Valley (centre at SN 063 374), is crowned with the Neolithic equivalent of a small hill-top defended enclosure – low ramparts of piled stones between crags. It figures in the medieval Life of the Irish saint Brynach,[23] of Nevern, as the *mons angelorum* 'hill of angels' where this ascetic met and conversed with entities other than humans. Visitors to so evocative and other-worldly a spot, where one can be for hours and see nobody, may not be surprised to learn that it is also a point of magnetic anomaly, inducing reversed polarity in compasses.[24]

Greatest of the Preseli fortifications is Moel (or Y Foel) Trigarn (Fig. 5.2), 'bald hill of the three cairns'. Twelve hundred feet up, commanding a view northward that embraces miles of coastline, this is a three-acre enclosure with a wide-spaced outer rampart and a subsidiary (later?) enclosed area; in plan, just about trilobate, but not trivallate.[25] The etymologist, whether really Cormac or not, who wrote '... *Tredúi*, iss ered tre *dúe*...' wanted to explain the name as 'three' and the plural of OIr. *dóe*. This word[26] usually, but not invariably, signified a *vallum*, rampart, large bank or circumvallation. In a law tract it appears as a synonym for *fert*, normally 'mound, burial-mound', and other usages suggest a semantic origin in the area of 'construction'. Inside the fortified surround, three vast cairns (each the size of a collapsed apartment-block) crown the summit, and mark the skyline from north and from south (Fig. 5.3); hence the place-name. Inconclusive last-century diggings,[27] among numerous hut-platforms, showed an Early Iron Age occupation, but there was the odd visitor after this; finds of later date include the rim of a Roman mortarium.[28] If we could expect to start looking for Dún Tredúi in any part of Atlantic Britain, opposite Munster, where the Irish settled and where settlement may have been preceded by short-term raiding, we look to Pembrokeshire; within it, Moel Trigarn is far and away the most persuasive candidate and indeed there is no other. A final comment must be that, while *Dún Tredúi* can represent some fourth to fifth century Primitive Irish place-name, and while British *din-* <*duno-* corresponds to Irish *dún* <*dūno-*, 'Tradui' cannot be a real Primitive Welsh compound; we would expect *tri-* (as in *Tri*garn, which no doubt *is* from Primitive Welsh), nor does any antiquity-name in Wales seem to hold a cognate to Irish *dóe*. A possible inference is that the original Irish name was current in speech for centuries and (with *din* for *dún*) was simply adopted as if it were a native name, alongside and then ousted by (Moel) Trigarn.[29]

In the ninth-century British compilation attributed to 'Nennius' there is a section, largely fabulous, about the origins of the Irish people.[30] After brief mentions of various Irish land-takings in *Dalrieta* (Dál Riata, Argyllshire) and *Eubonia insula* (? Isle of Man) comes the assertion *filii ... Liethan obtinuerunt in regione Demetorum et in aliis regionibus id est Guir Cetgueli*, 'The Sons of Liethan were in control in the region of the Demeti, and in other regions, that is Gower and Cydweli.' The geography of this is clear enough (Fig. 5.4). The passage continues with ... *donec expulsi sunt a Cuneda et a filius eius ab omnibus Brittannicis regionibus*, 'up to the time when they were driven out, by Cuneda and by his son (sons?), from all the British regions'.

It would require an extra chapter — one that will not be inserted here — to discuss the context and possible sources of these statements; but, where the fifth century is concerned, neither is historical and the second is an exaggeration. The 'Sons of Liethan' were another Irish tribe, Uí Liatháin (already noticed in Cormac's Dún maic Liatháin, placed by him in the lands of the Britons of Cornwall, p. 44). In the south of Ireland their home is regarded as adjoining that of the Déisi Muman. The testimony of 'Nennius' cannot, for Demetia, replace the older Irish source ascribing settlement there to the Déisi under Eochaid. That source neither mentions, nor specifically excludes, the Uí Liatháin as participants in a settlement around 390×400; but it does specify *crich Demed* 'territory of Demetia' and nowhere else in Wales. We go back to the early Irish as sea-travellers. For the Uí Liatháin who like the Déisi had access to coast and harbours (Fig. 5.5), the remote possibility that this group initiated a minor settlement directly over the sea in west Cornwall will be examined in chapter 11 later. There is nothing that informs us whether or not Uí Liatháin families accompanied Déisi families to Demetia but, for the moment, their early presence in Gower and Cydweli can probably be accepted.

So far, the departure-point of Eochaid's migration with his followers has not been refined and, beyond stating that it must have been in the extreme south of Ireland, it may not be possible to say more. In following chapters, there is an assumption that groups from the Déisi Muman certainly, and (in so far as they could ever be identified) from the Uí Liatháin as well, hailed from that region where the use of

**Fig. 5.2** View of Moel Trigarn from the southern approach, showing how the three vast cairns dominate the skyline (photo: author).

**Fig. 5.3** Sketched profile of Moel Trigarn, with **(below)** close-up drawing of the three huge cairns; both by Miss Edwards, a member of Revd Sabine Baring-Gould's 1899 excavation party (reproduced from *Archaeologia Cambrensis*).

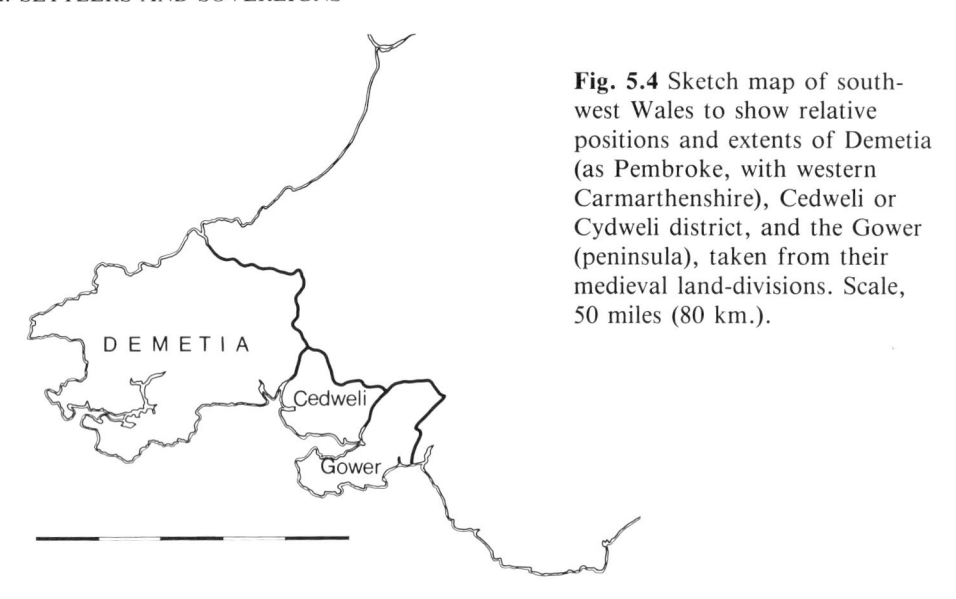

**Fig. 5.4** Sketch map of south-west Wales to show relative positions and extents of Demetia (as Pembroke, with western Carmarthenshire), Cedweli or Cydweli district, and the Gower (peninsula), taken from their medieval land-divisions. Scale, 50 miles (80 km.).

ogam script on stone memorials was established. If this seems to beg the question of whether the custom was extant already by *circa* 400, chapter 3 explained why a belief in this could now be entertained. A difficulty in recent decades has been to reconcile the idea of an initial settlement in Demetia in the fourth (let alone late third) century, the presence of so many ogam inscriptions and undoubtedly Irish names in the area so settled by the Irish, and the dating of all such inscriptions – with Professor Kenneth Jackson's support – no earlier than the second half of the fifth century. One unusual response to this dilemma was Professor R. de Valera's thesis that ogam-inscribed memorials were invented, in Demetia, by Irish colonists (following what models? we are not enlightened on this) and were then imitated over much of southern Ireland as part of a reflux-movement associated with the spread of Christianity.[31]

Two other papers have, independently, proposed an early settlement of Irish around 400 – from Waterford, across to Pembroke and then a second wave, about a century later, coming from Wexford (Ó Cathasaigh) and mainly affecting modern Cardiganshire (Coplestone-Crow).[32] Both papers are important but, however well developed, their arguments start from certain premisses – the date of the first inscriptions in Demetia, the dates and historicity of the travels of the Déisi after expulsion from Brega, and the value to be accorded evidentially to medieval Lives of saints and patterns of dedications – that this present book is inclined to reject.

The positions in Ireland of tribal homelands (Fig. 5.5) are approximate, and argued back from place-names and area-names like those of the old baronies. The Sons (*mac*) or Direct Descendants (*uí*) of Liathan, either a distant but once-living hero or a minor pagan divinity, are placed in an area containing an ogam inscription, 273 *CALUNOVIC(A) MAQI MUCOI LIT(ENI)*; one of ten found in what

Fig. 5.5 Map of the southern part of Ireland, provinces of Leinster and Munster, with selected modern cities and towns, and the approximate fourth–fifth centuries homelands of the Uí Liatháin and the Déisi Muman peoples. Scale, 50 miles (80 km.).

sounds like a pre-Christian burial enceinte at Drumlohan, Co. Waterford.[33] *Litenos* may stand for the tribal eponym, and *MUCOI LITENI* (only example) may have marked a particularly favoured kin-group.[34] Without prejudice to absolute date – the ten ogam stones from Drumlohan are fairly similar, with no repeated names, and need not necessarily range over any long period – it seems hard to support the idea that an inscription like 273, whether set up after or before AD 400, reflects Christianity. It gives the impression of being one of ten or so pagan slabs or pillars, housed in some special pagan funerary shrine, with only the appearance of *writing* on it linking it to a wider world; but we must postpone expansion of these ideas for the moment.

Here, the outline model proposed is that fourth-century raiding parties, who may have set out from the modern Irish counties of Wexford or Waterford or (east) Cork, landed on the north coast of Pembroke where there are suitable beaches – and a major harbour from Ireland still at Fishguard – and that Moel Trigarn, as Dún Tredúi, served once or more times as an occasional fortified base. Was this then also the stretch of coast where Eochaid Allmuir landed, and did the first gradual colonization fan out from here – along the northern front of Preseli, around and beyond the western end of the whole ridge, and through valleys to the southern slopes? 'Dual' colonizations aside, can we not agree the likelihood that small-scale arrivals continued during much of the fifth century? What an outline model would also entertain is the idea that, certainly from 400 to 450, Irish newcomers under their own leaders like Eochaid (who within the colonized part could be represented as 'kings') co-existed with a much larger number of Britons in central and southern Pembrokeshire, children and grandchildren of the former *cives*; Roman citizens of the *civitas Demetarum*. If after 400 rule over these British fell into the hands of native grandees, the names of Clotri, *Clutorigi*, and Gloitguin, *Clutuinn*, would indeed suggest indigenous, parallel, fifth-century kinglets.

But here, most unusually, a subsidiary model could be proposed and even tested. The Welsh version of the regnal list from B. L. Harleian MS 3859, shorn of its imaginative appendages ('Nimet, Dimet' *et al.*), suggests a tradition in which – from a British viewpoint – the Déisi-descended *Triphun* was preceded by the two British names, *Clotri* before Triphun and *Gloitguin* before Clotri; names absent from the Irish version. Supposing that, under Triphun as a sole ruler, a large part of Pembrokeshire became through agreement or inter-marriage (conquest need not inevitably be adduced), the sole fief of the kings chosen from the Irish-originating kin-groups, this would have occurred within 450×500; and Clotri's life would have centred on V.2, the middle third of the century. Any children of his could have allied themselves with settlers of similar status. There may actually be epigraphic witness to this. Built now into the outer south wall of Llandysilio (West) church, at a village south of Preseli and more or less in the centre of Pembrokeshire, is a memorial slab inscribed CLVTORIGI / FILI PA̅VLINI / MARINI LATIO – 435, *ECMW* 315 (Fig. 5.6). It is in Roman capitals, may have been designed as three horizontal lines on a medium-size slab, and could epigraphically be dated to 450×475. It reads '(Monument) of Clutorigi, of the son of Paulinus Marinus from Latium'.[35] For the moment, we are less concerned about whether the style and wording indicate a Christian monument (they are, as it happens, neutral in this particular respect) and more with the fact that the person named is quite possibly the *Clotri* of the regnal list. His father's name is not 'Gloitguin', nor need we expect it to have been that of his predecessor; those who erected the memorial, a correct fifth-century Latin statement cut in Roman capitals, were concerned to stress that he was the son of a Roman citizen from the last days of Britannia, a 'Paulinus Marinus' who hailed from Latium.[36] By 'citizen' we could

**Fig. 5.6 Left**: 435, CLUTORIGI/FILI PAVLINI/MARINILATIO, built in the south wall of Llandysilio West church. **Below**: 446, MAGLOCVNI FILI CLUTORI (with ogam *MAGLICUNAS MAQI CLUTARI*), now built into a window-sill inside Nevern church. (Photos: Susanna Thomas.)

perhaps picture a *magistratus*, a *decurio*, from the *ordo* or council of the civitas.[37] If any son or daughter of Clotri was adopted by marriage into a Déisi-descended family and was eventually accorded an inscribed memorial of appropriate type, then such a stone ought to reflect appropriate differences. And indeed one does – twelve miles northward, over Preseli, and now built into a window-sill at Nevern church (446; *ECMW* 353 – Fig. 5.6). It commemorates

MAGLOCVNI FILI CLUTOR ↦ 'Maglocun' (later Welsh *Maelgwn*) 'of the son of Clutori', and this is duplicated along the edge, in ogam, and in a careful Irish translation (*MAGLICUNAS MAQI CLUTARI*) showing that his relatives treated him as they would any notable of their own kin meriting such a memorial.[38] This is a classic 'type (b)' inscription and, with 435, will be mentioned again in a suitable context. Here, the two stones are displayed in advance because — a rare instance — they seem to verify a reasoned historical inference from a documentary source.

This slight digression into the technicalities of inscribed memorials shows just a glimpse of what can often be inferred from them. Demetia is rich in such monuments. If we are to attempt any closer definition of this post-Roman kingdom, the inscriptions (with a few other categories of evidence) offer the best approach and may shed light on historical aspects not so far discussed; Latinity, Christianity, any independent references to kings named in the dual lists, and the likely extent of Demetia — in relation to neighbouring kingdoms — in the sixth century.

## References

1. Barri Jones & David Mattingly, *An Atlas of Roman Britain* (Blackwell, Oxford 1990), chap. 5, various maps — note 'approximate boundaries' of *civitates* in Wales, map 5.11.
2. Inferred, because no inscription actually naming it survives; Demetae (*PNRB*, 333), for some odd reason, was a *feminine* plural.
3. *PNRB* 462; *stuctia* — 'bent, curved, winding' gave rise to Ystwyth.
4. *PNRB* 474.
5. *PNRB* 425.
6. *PNRB* 388–9; *Leucarum* is identified as a Roman fort at Loughor. In Fig. 5.1 here, the name of the river Teifi, *Tuerobis* — probably a corrupt form — follows *PNRB* 480. See however *PNP* 21, s.n. 'Teifi'.
7. W. Davies 1982, *passim*; the power of geographical determinism here, where N–S valley systems produce such 'natural' smaller territories, has been particularly apparent in all local-government groupings.
8. The starting-point, *EWGT* 4 (and notes, 124), with refs. to the published editions; here, the text is as Bartrum's (from Rawlinson B.502), with a few variants from the later Laud 610. To allow comparison with the bracketed italicized forms, OIr. gens. have as far as possible been converted back to noms. — Gartbuir to Gartbor, Catacuind to Catacon, etc.
9. Pender 1947, Ó Cathasaigh 1984 & Richards 1960 between them provide the necessary passages. See Ó Cathasaigh 1976, 156, for a useful short bibliography.
10. 1947, 211; developed in 1984, 25–6.
11. London, British Library Harleian MS 3859; see *EWGT*, 9–11.
12. Nora Chadwick, *Studies in the Early British Church* (Cambridge 1958), 122 n.2. Though she did not specify this, names 4 to 15 (pp. 55–6) were passed from Wales to Ireland in the eighth cent. as a written roll. This is shown by such errors as 'Trestin' for 'Triphun', where Insular script -p- was misread as -(long)s-, and the two verticals of -h- as -ti.
13. So Jackson, *LHEB* 154–5.
14. See further discussion in chap. 9, pp. 146–7 below.

15. J. W. James, 'The Harleian MS 3859 Genealogy II', *BBCS* 23 (1969), 143–52. On this sort of treatment, cf. David Kirby's astringent remarks in *BBCS* 27 (1976), 81–114 ('British Dynastic History...'), *passim*.
16. See *CRB* 41–2 for the literary setting of 'Helen'. The names earlier than 'Clotri map Gloitguin' seem to come from a quite separate source, but one whose original sense was hopelessly lost when the tenth cent.(?) genealogists got to work. 'Prwtech m.Ewein m.Miser m.Custennin' is tacked on, in a JC 20 brief (*EWGT*, 45–6), after 'Ayrcol lawhir m.Tryphun m.Ewein Vreisc' (the last-named being somehow based on Aed *Brosc*: Miller 1977–8, 39 ff.). The sequence Protector–Piner–Miser–Constantinus–Helena also figures in the fully medieval *Vita S. Petroci* from the Gotha MS (*EWGT*, 28–9).
17. This is suggested because there is an obvious break following *Gloitguin*, with the four pairs of 'names' next, and then the usual validating Late Roman 'ancestors'. The actual graphs, *Clotri* (cf. p. ...) and *Gloitguin* (scribal error for *Cluitguin*?), are perhaps no older than the 9th–10th cents.; this does not rule out the likelihood that some earlier (7th?) record existed in which *Clutuuin*, as a fifth-century Demetian British notable, was provided with some named Late Roman forbears.
18. 'Of Munster'; *Mumu*, gen. *Muman*.
19. Miller 1977–8 ('Date-Guessing and Dyfed').
20. Her paper seems open to an unwonted number of criticisms; she repeats the misidentification of Dinn Tradui as Dindraithou, re-sites 'Dún mac Letháin' (*sic*) *contra* the explicit statement that it was in Cornwall, and in proposing a marriage of Triphun to a daughter of 'Clydwyn' (Gloitguin) conflates the latter with a homonymous Brycheiniog *Clytguin* named in *DSB* (see p. 141 below) – another man, from another kingdom, and almost certainly from the following century. (For an extreme case of what can be done with this perplexing list, one that builds on earlier and wholly unreal calculations, see K. D. Pringle, 'The Kings of Demetia', two parts, *Trans. Cymmrodor.*, (1970), 70–6, & (1971), 140–4.) Dr Miller's claim (op. cit., 35, n.2) that the Demetian list is a straight pedigree and that 'A king-list is quite a different sort of document, and the genre appears to have been unknown in Wales' is by no means substantiated. It would be safer to describe this, as also that of Brycheiniog (chap. 9), as a king-list or regnal-succession list, within which there may be father-to-son, or father-in-law to son-in-law (Teuderic, Anlach), couplets if such happen to be attested independently at early dates.
21. Note that 'Corath' may be non-existent (see further, p. 79); *Corath* is the Rawlinson B.502 reading, while Laud 610 has *Corach* (? = OIr. *corach*, adj.; *CGH*, index, lists only a single *Corach*, better reading *Conrach* (Lec.)). This does not affect the names in parallel from Triphun/Trestin onwards, but would tend to reduce the fifth-century rulers, Eochaid to Aircol, to four only.
22. This was argued, historically, by Leslie Alcock; *Arthur's Britain* (1971), 123–4. Older views – the third century AD used to be favoured – need no longer bother us.
23. *VSBG*, 2–15; for Carn Ingli as a name, see *PNP* 163.
24. *Expertus dico* – a visit in autumn 1991 when I happened to have a boxed surveying compass with me; needle pointed variously due S and due E. Archaic rocks, strongly magnetic, have been tectonically displaced – the phenomenon is known elsewhere.
25. Air views – pl.7 in D. Moore, ed., *The Land of Dyfed in Early Times* (Cardiff 1964); *Antiquity* 35 (1961), pl.xxxvi.b. View of cairns; pp.43–5, Mick Sharp's, in Peter Fowler & Mick Sharp, *Images of Prehistory* (Cambridge 1990). The name; *PNP*, 193–4.
26. RIA Dict. D, 244, 3 *doe*; tract, *Ancient Laws of Ireland*, iv (Dublin 1879), 144.
27. By Sabine Baring-Gould and friends, *AC* (1900), 189–221.
28. *BBCS* 4 (1928), 268; also coin of Faustina II (before AD 175), D. W. Crossley's invaluable gazetteer in *BBCS* 20 (1963), at 189.

29. Of course this is speculative, as it can only be; but if Cormac's dual fort-name pairs, British/Irish, had not existed it is even more difficult to know why he included them than to speculate how he obtained them in the first place.
30. Here, from John Morris, *Nennius*...(Phillimore, 1980), 20–1, 62.
31. S. P. Ó Ríordáin, *Antiquities of the Irish Countryside*, 5th edn., revised by Ruadhri de Valera (1979), 26, 146.
32. Ó Cathasaigh 1984; Coplestone-Crow 1981–2.
33. CIIC.i, p. 267 – the stones are nos. 272 to 281. The particular barony ('Decies Without Drum') in fact contains Decies < *Déisi*.
34. Another 'ancestor' seems to have been Echu Letháin, descendant of the prehistoric 'Eógan, Mug Nuada', slave of the god Nuada and eponym of the Eóganacht dynasties of Munster; Byrne 1973, 168, 183–4, 291. See also L. Ó Buachalla, 'The Uí Liatháin and their Septlands', *JCorkHAS* 44 (1939), 28–36.
35. *Marinus* (uncommon) occurs as *Julius Marinus*, centurion, tombstone at Maryport, *RIB* no. 858. OW Clotri, Clodri is from the oblique (gen.) stem *Clutorig-; *Clutorix should have > Clodyr, Clydyr (not, as far as the writer knows, attested). On the slab, cemented into the church wall but apparently entire, there is no trace of any final -S (CLVTORIGIS). The name was written CLVTORIGI – gen., and probably nom. as well.
36. The geographical qualifier, unusual here, must have been deemed important; either the Latium around Rome, or some British district?
37. Another fifth-century Briton, Patrick, 'Patricius', also had a native name (Sochet < *Sucetos*: Muirchu's *Life*), a father and grandfather with Roman names (Calpornius, Potitus) and a father who was curial, a *decurio*, probably with the Carvetii at Carlisle (*CRB*, 310–11).
38. The likely significance of 446 ('mid to later fifth-century', *LHEB* 174: a date 475–500 would suit, historically) has not been noticed. *Maglocun* is British, not Irish – *LHEB* 174; *Guide*, 113, 6.21 – and *Clutori* must also be – *Guide*, ibid., calling it 'indefinite', because OIr. *Clothri* exists as well as OW *Clodri*. As a type (b) full bilingual inscription, 446 is one in which an accurate ogam PrIr. translation was seen to be required (others show Irish names with Latinized British versions). A mid-fifth cent. *Clutorigi* at one place, and a British-named son of *Clutori*, late fifth, only twelve miles away, are bound to look as if connected; and linked also to an OW *Clotri*, recorded in Harl. 3859 as a notable in Demetia, and just before the later fifth cent. *Triphun, Aircol*.

# 6
# *Demetia: a Post-Roman Kingdom*

WHEN THE REVEREND W. Meredith Morris compiled his model glossary of the spoken Welsh in the Gwaun Valley, skirting the north-west frontage of Mynydd Preseli and debouching at Fishguard, he recorded everything that he had heard and gave full notes and examples.[1] There are standard Welsh words for 'road, street, track, lane', etc., but Morris encountered *feidir*; '(1) A narrow lane overmantled with thick growth. (2) A private road leading from the farm buildings to the fields.' The initial F- is /v/ and could therefore come from lenited /b/ or lenited /m/; there is a reference to a 1688 translation of *Pilgrim's Progress* where 'lane' is rendered *moidir*. Sir John Rhŷs suggested that *meidr*, *meidyr* could represent older \*moudr, or \*boudr, 'which would be the Welsh representative of the Irish *bóthar*, "a road".' Bóthar, to be seen on any Dublin street-sign, was explained by T. F. O'Rahilly as coming from \*bou-itro, 'cow passage';[2] a feature intended for, and used for, the passing to and fro of livestock. Welsh \*boudr, \*beudr, cannot have quite the same source and it is possible that, as with Cornish *bounder* (p. 185), the second part goes back to *tir* 'land'. The first is certainly 'cattle' (\*beu), as also in *beudy* 'cow-house'. That, as British terms, these may be early ones is suggested by their near-exact correspondence to Cornish \*bou, dialect 'bowjy' (cow-house; *bou*, *ty*) and the place-name feature *bounder*.[3]

Melville Richards's map of place-names with *feidr*, *foidir*, *moidir*, showed them 'almost wholly confined to North Pembrokeshire' with five examples in the west of Cardiganshire, just across the river Teifi (see Fig. 6.1, from his article).[4] Other place-name distributions plotted by Professor Richards were the rather more extensive patterns involving *cnwc* 'hillock', a borrowing from Irish *cnoc* as distinct from the native Welsh cognate word, *cnwch*.[5]

The recorded extent of names containing *cnwc/cnwch* is important, and can be used below (p. 115), but slightly more important here is the difference between the currency of a term for a very common natural feature – which is likely, anyhow, to be widespread – and that of other words directly related to a human activity that, if at all specialized, may be confined to a smaller area.[6] It is suggested that the early range of meanings of a Welsh \*boudr, as for *bounder* in Cornwall (map, Fig. 11.1), may have been complex and specific. This was a new term within a new land-use emphasis; pastoralism, focused on domestic cattle that constituted wealth.[7] What the incidence of subsequent *feidir* in Dyfed may show is

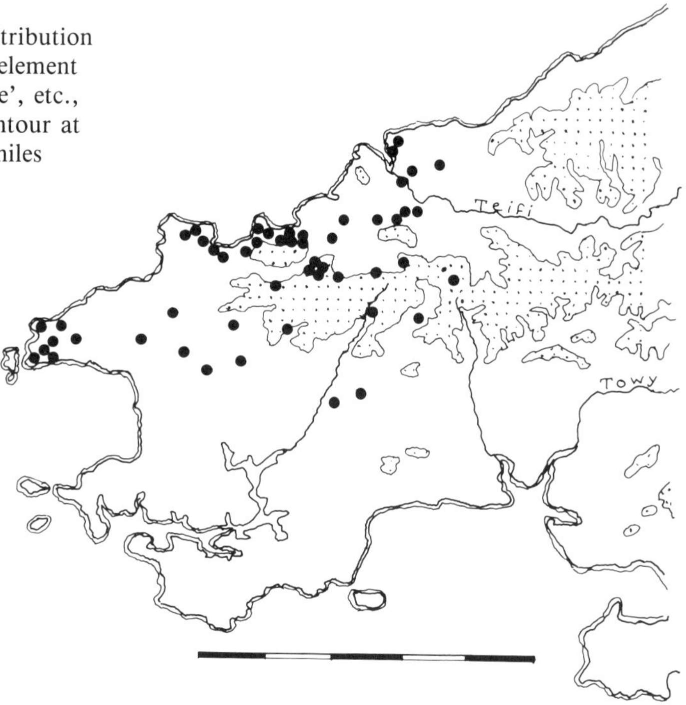

**Fig. 6.1** Demetia; the distribution of place-names with the element *meidir (feidir, feidr)* 'lane', etc., by Melville Richards; contour at 600 ft added. Scale, 25 miles (40 km.).

approximately where such practices could have arisen because of Irish settlement.[8]

For the three recent counties of Dyfed – Pembroke, Cardigan and Carmarthen – the whole body of the pre-700 inscribed memorial stones has a westerly emphasis and, in that crude respect, looks towards Ireland and E. G. Bowen's 'Western Seaways' rather than to sub-Roman south-east Wales. But even if it was possible to collate for individual stones Nash-Williams's (*ECMW*) largely epigraphic dating, and Jackson's (*LHEB*) largely linguistic one, and then to impose firm third-of-a-century labels like V.3 or VI.2, a time-layered distribution would not necessarily reveal *origin* as opposed to *duration*. In any case, such a collation involves accepting many estimates of age that can now fairly be challenged.[9] There is another way; to treat monuments that are admittedly also historical, written, records *as* archaeological monuments and to look for a typology, or identifiable stages in formal and stylistic development through time.

Excluding a very few memorials that would stand outside this, and can be referred to an intrusive Continental fashion manifested as the 'extended Latinate' (EL) stones with their special vocabulary (p. 203, Fig. 12.4), the following typology – which will later be extended to the stones of Dumnonia – is now put forward. Fig. 6.2 offers a simplified key. Type (a) memorials are those exhibiting

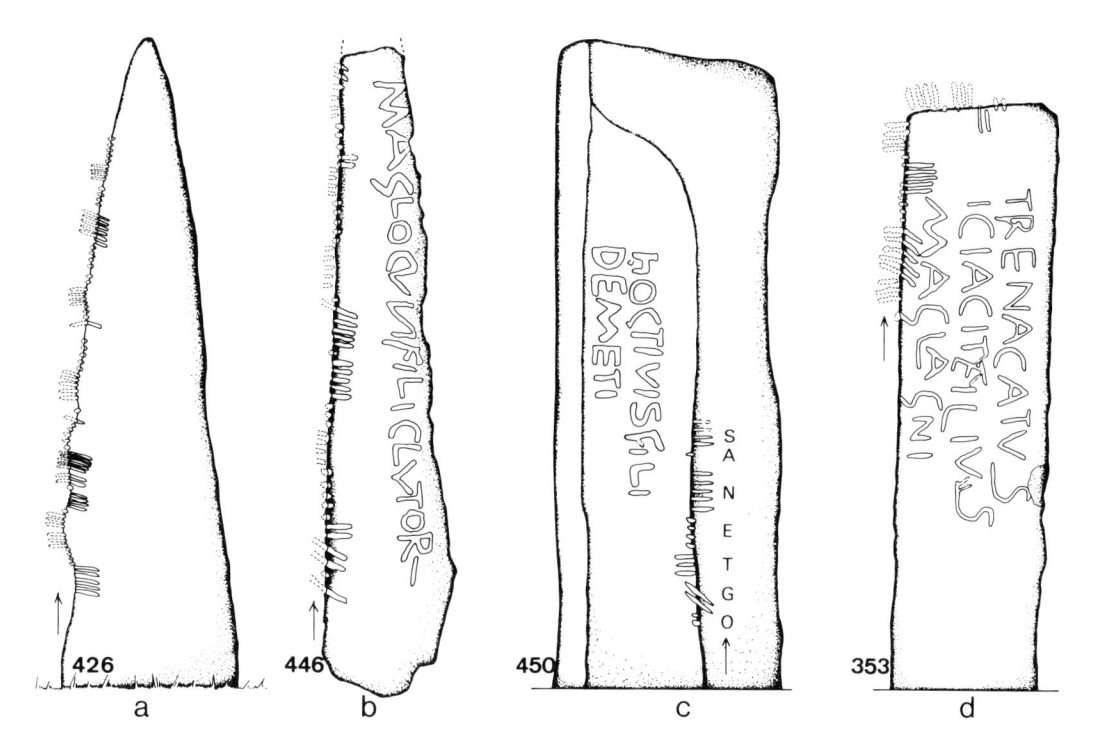

**Fig. 6.2** Demetia; a proposed typological sequence of memorials. Type (a), ogam only; 426, the Bridell 'menhir' (see Fig. 6.4). Type (b), full bilingual; 446, Nevern church, MAGLOCVNI FILI CLVTORI, ogam *MAGLICUNAS MAQI CLUTARI*. Type (c), ogam confined to name of deceased; 450, St Dogmael's, HOGTINIS FILI DEMETI, ogam *OGTENAS*. Type (d), where the Latin contains HIC IACIT or Christian wording; 353, Rhuddlan, with ogam confined to *TRENACCATLO*. Drawn partly from *CIIC*, corrected from photographs.

nothing but the ogam script; anything else on these stones, like incised crosses, represents later additions unconnected with the epitaphs. Type (b) comprises memorials usually known as 'bilinguals', those where a message in ogam and in Irish is accompanied by one of the same content (and, usually, length) in Roman lettering, capitals and occasional book-hand letters, and in Latin. Without prejudice to which half 'translates' the other, ogam Irish MAQI 'of the son', a formulaic genitive of PrIr. *maqqas* /mak$^w$k$^w$as/ 'son', corresponds to Latin FILI, the normal post-400 Insular written form of *filii* 'of the son'. There is a recognizable sub-set of type (b) when the bilingual is very short, confined to a single name, and when often the name in one of the versions has an added qualifier. Type (c) memorials have the Roman-lettered, Latin, inscription in full – in the shape Of-A, FILI of-B, for instance – but only the first name, the deceased, as 'A' or 'Of-A' is repeated in ogam. In the type (d) memorials the new element is the presence of any Latin wording – and HIC IACIT 'here he (or she) lies' with variations is the commonest of these – that indicates a Christian memorial. This is not to say that types (b) and (c) stones may not also commemorate baptized Christians, but we have no *direct* indication that they do so. On a few type (d) memorials, the name of the dead person in ogam may still be given. Finally there are a good few stones with Roman lettering only, the inscriptions generally short and in the style Of-A, of-the-son of-B, which are described here as 'untyped'.

This is a hypothetical typology of the visible shapes of the messages, regardless of anything else to be inferred from individual names and words, on stones put up and displayed to carry such messages. Other series, and other potential characteristics that might permit inferences, run alongside it. Most of these inscriptions are written up and down a face, vertically disposed, as anything in ogam has to be because of the demands of that script; it follows that anything set out in *horizontal* lines may have departed from such a norm for particular reasons, and it probably follows that one peculiar feature, putting the last -I horizontally in respect of a word or name (indicated here as ↦), was a trick invented in Demetia in the later fifth century as someone's unusual response to the general emphasis upon verticality. There is a further divergence among all the names in that some are patently 'continuing-Roman', carried over from the fourth century and earlier, some distinctively Irish, some distinctively British and a few not easily assigned to either language.

The premiss followed here is that the inscribed memorial is a monument-type introduced to Demetia by Irish settlers and that it was not previously current in Demetia; and that types (a) to (d) *are* a typological sequence, but one with overlapping steps. It may be interesting, since neither Nash-Williams nor Jackson chose to perceive any kind of sequence along these lines, to see approximately what dates they would have assigned to the stages; this has been painstakingly worked out from *ECMW* and *LHEB* and is summarized in abbreviated form (V = 5th century, VI = 6th, etc.).

| Type | ECMW | LHEB |
|---|---|---|
| (a) | V to early VI | (not mentioned in this respect) |
| (b) | V, slight preference for late V, to early VI | Mid-V or late or end V to early VI |
| (c) | V to early VI, and occasionally later | Late V to early or mid-VI |
| (d) | As for (c) | End V to early or mid-VI (428 seen as 'early VII') |

If this tells us anything, it would be that Nash-Williams was less ready to be specific about the date of any individual stone within his 'Group I, 5th to 7th centuries' on grounds of epigraphy, physical shape, formulaic character or anything else than Professor Jackson who, on grounds of linguistic developments foremost and epigraphic ones secondly, did arrive at a stepped typology matching the proposed (b) to (d) without realizing it, or presenting conclusions in that way. What neither was prepared to do before 1949 (Nash-Williams) or before 1950 (Jackson) was to discuss dates for stones corresponding here to type (a), or to step outside the constraints of views then held about the chronology of the ogam script. The proposition now is that, in Demetia, some of the type (a) stones are V.1; from any time after the arrival of Eochaid Allmuir. This is no more susceptible to proof than are current ideas about when the ogam script arose and when ogam first appeared on stones in Ireland (p. 33), but it might be thought to be typologically indicated; and it might be thought to accord with views as to what certain type (a) memorials really represent.

The map in Fig. 6.3 brings together what, at the moment, seems to be the only evidence tending to locate (substantially, within the northern part of modern Pembroke, dominated by the Preseli ridge) the first settlements, and then the land-taking expansion or the 'colonization' of Irish families and any extended groupings of them. The place-name element *feid(i)r* is carried over from Fig. 6.1, and the memorials are those of types (a), (b) and (c) only. Four type (d) memorials which do exhibit ogam as well as Roman lettering – 353, 358, 428 and 433; all are probably sixth century – are omitted because they possess a further characteristic (the words HIC IACIT, or versions of them) implying overtly Christian sentiments, and will be included along with eight or nine others that, though also type (d), lack ogam, in a subsequent discussion within chapter 7. Questions of relative dating of the three types (a), (b) and (c) examined now, and how an overall chronology might accord with any other linked to the successively-named rulers from Eochaid Allmuir onwards, may however be postponed until we look at concise descriptions of the relevant inscriptions.

For the type (a) stones, four on the north side and two (Caldey Island 427 and Llandawke (Llan-dawg) 368) on the south, three of the northern ones did contain ogam but the inscriptions today, through wear and damage, are illegible or fragmentary;[10] 348 simply cannot be read as *TRENALUGOS* (Macalister), 439 appears to have two names but neither *EF(E)SS(A)GN(I) ASEGNI* (*ECMW*) or *I?( )SS( )ASO...* (*Guide*) allows much comment, and the gate-post from a 'rath' near Brawdy, 423, may say no more than *M(A)Q(I) QAGTE* (*ECMW*) or *..AQ..QA..GTE* (*Guide*) with a good chance that it contains *MAQI*. Far and away the most important, however, is 426 in the churchyard at Bridell. The stone (Fig. 6.4), more than three metres high, looks like (and probably was) a menhir, of which there are plenty in this region along the south side of Preseli, employed for a memorial. An incised encircled outline cross was imposed on one face, probably in the tenth–eleventh century. The long ogam inscription up one side and over the top is *NETTASAGRI MAQI MUCOI BRIECI*.[11]

The pillar, so inscribed, can be matched by dozens in Counties Waterford and

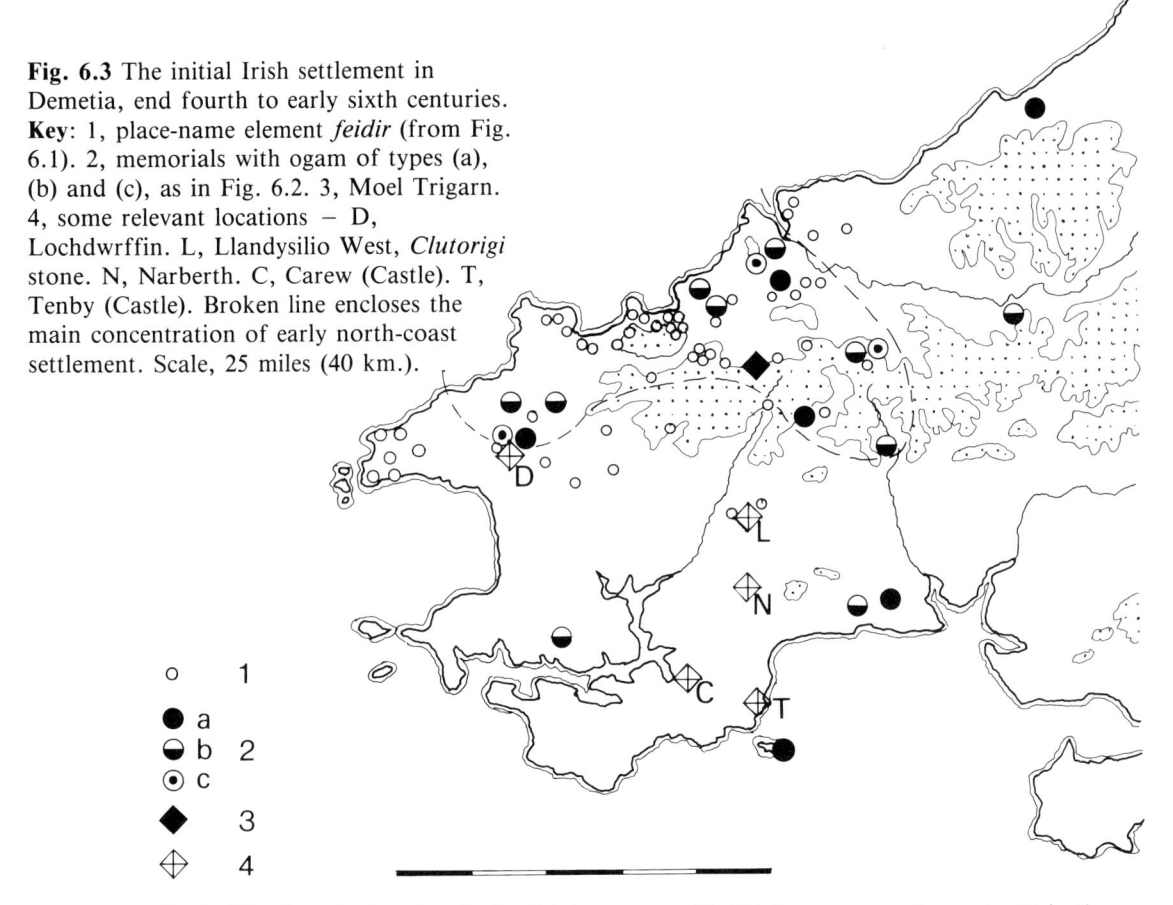

**Fig. 6.3** The initial Irish settlement in Demetia, end fourth to early sixth centuries. **Key**: 1, place-name element *feidir* (from Fig. 6.1). 2, memorials with ogam of types (a), (b) and (c), as in Fig. 6.2. 3, Moel Trigarn. 4, some relevant locations – D, Lochdwrffin. L, Llandysilio West, *Clutorigi* stone. N, Narberth. C, Carew (Castle). T, Tenby (Castle). Broken line encloses the main concentration of early north-coast settlement. Scale, 25 miles (40 km.).

Cork. The inscription is wholly Irish, ogam with Irish names and words. It is the memorial 'of Netta-sagras; of a son of the sept, or kindred, of Briec(?)'. Considerations in giving it a likely date include the earliest time at which such a prominent stone, perhaps for a notable who accompanied (or soon followed) Eochaid himself, could be imagined – here, $390 \times 400$ plus a reasonable interval between arriving and dying; accepting the idea that models for it existed in (pre-400) south-east Ireland; and accepting that it may pre-date other types of memorial, (b) and (c), which on the whole began near the middle of the fifth century. There is good reason to suggest that 426, the Bridell pillar, must be one of the earliest of the kind put up on mainland British soil, falls within V.1 and could be as old as $c. 420 \times 430$. It should, on balance, be regarded as non-Christian. In *Netta-sagras* 'Champion' (<*neitos*) '-of-Sagras' and, instead of a father's name, a tribal or sub-tribal ascription *mucoi Brieci*(?), older pagan deities may well be exhibited.[12] Without anticipating chapter 7 below, one has to face a need to offer more positive views than some held forty years back – 'In Wales the Irish colonists must have become christianized, if they were not Christian already on arrival',[13] or 'The Irish could hardly have been already converted when they first came to settle in Britain, but in the intervening period they must gradually have become so...'[14]

It would be insupportable to pose an absolute link between paganism and the use of ogam *per se*; type (d) stones alone controvert that idea and, as Jackson pointed

DEMETIA: A POST-ROMAN KINGDOM

**Fig. 6.4** The ogam-inscribed, type (a) menhir (with cross added much later) in Bridell churchyard, Pembs. Photos: Susanna Thomas.

out, 'There is no reason to suppose that there was anything about the Ogam script essentially repugnant to Christianity, and that an ogam inscription means that the man commemorated must have been a pagan.'[15] Stone 426 at Bridell, if inscribed in V.1, is claimed as 'pagan' (non-Christian, locally pre-Christian) because we have no evidence that native Demetians were generally Christian at this early phase and because there is as yet no cogent reason to think that the Déisi under Eochaid were, either. Ogam as a script was a way of writing, not a way of worshipping. In this connection we can look at a type (b) stone in the 'single-name' sub-set, 456 from Steynton in south-west Pembroke. Re-used for a tenth–eleventh century cross slab, its original short bilingual was ogam GENDILI and, with this, GENDILI in eroded but more or less capital letters (*not* 'half-uncials'; Macalister). This seems to be less of a name, and more of a title or epithet, like calling some florid extrovert 'Squire'. Late Roman Latin *gentilis* had come to mean 'heathen', when applied by Christians to non-Christians.[16] As a spoken fifth-sixth century nickname of appellation, /gendil/, spreading from Vulgar Latin to Late British and here simply given the usual genitive case-marker -*i*, GENDILI is what one would expect in, say, V.3. *Was* he a pagan? *Was* he of Irish ancestry? Was he, if pagan, prominent enough to merit the inscribing of the word by which most people knew him, in both scripts, supplied by someone who could write both and thought this appropriate?

Two other type (a) stones are 368, at Llandawke, and 427 'found in the ruins of the priory' on Caldey Island — which, as Ynys Bŷr, seems to have housed a small monastery by about 500 (p. 228). The Llandawke ogam is on a stone with a secondary use for an unconnected inscription. 368 BARRIVEND⊢/FILIVS VENDVBARI/HIC IACIT is type (d), Christian, uses angle-bar A (p. 96), and belongs to the sixth century; the type (a) message is hardly likely to be *later* than this. Ogam goes up both angles of the pillar, making it uncertain whether it should be read 'D, *maqi mucoi*' or '*maqi mucoi* D', but the agreed reading is MAQI MUCOI DUMELEDONAS; splitting of the stone has removed what would have been a second name. Incomplete, this is as Irish as 426 Bridell, *Dumeledonās* (with -*aidonas*) being an Irish genitive form.[17] The Caldey stone, 427, again one re-used for a ninth-century cross-slab, is not entirely legible — MAGL(IA?) DUBR(ACUNAS? MAQI ...)INB, *ECMW*, or more cautiously MAGL(I) DUBAR..., *Guide*.

Among the type (b) bilinguals, the two other single-name ones, 432 and 445, probably *are* late (late fifth, earlier sixth) examples and may really represent inscriptions that could also be seen as type (c) — first name only in ogam. Stone 445, at Nevern churchyard, has two lines across a tall slab, horizontally, VITALIANI / EMERETO, and up one edge ogam VITALIANI. The name is continuing-Roman, probably of an early sixth-century cleric, *emeritus* implying 'having deserved (his eternal reward)'.[18] The ogam translates part of the Latin here. Stone 432 from Jordanston in north-west Pembroke has ogam *DOVAGNI* and, in two lines, TIGERNACI/DOBAGNI; an Irish personal name,[19] in one version preceded by *tigernac-, adjectival(?), 'land-owning, lord-like' (?).

There are seven full type (b) bilingual inscriptions. Looking at them as a group, we might firstly note that in so far as the character of the names is determinable (and all the inscriptions show two names, the deceased and his or her immediate ancestor) the seven pretty well reflect a mixed population. One shows two continuing-Roman names (430); another, two British names (446, at Nevern; this is the son of *Clotri* mentioned earlier, p. 62); three, both names Irish (372, 378, 442); and then an Irish(?)-named daughter of a British name (362) and an Irish-named son of another British name (449). With these we ought to be, and epigraphically and linguistically could be, in the later fifth and earlier sixth century. A further point to make is that six of the seven stones now stand in churchyards (the seventh is said to come from a chapel site, Capel Mair – 372, Llangeler). Before jumping to any conclusion that this supplies an otherwise un-evidenced Christian status for all of type (b), one must bear two things in mind. Firstly, in most of Wales there is an old and in its way praiseworthy habit of moving visibly-inscribed memorials from farms, roadsides and waste places into churchyards, even into church porches and interiors. Secondly, while accepting that a menhir like 426 Bridell stands *in situ* within an ancient-looking curvilinear churchyard having a mighty bank along one side, a typical *lann* (p. 101), the sequence may really have been; Iron Age and Roman-period Demetian cemetery (short cists, N–S dug graves, cremations or whatever) – use of the same, from *c*.400, by Déisi settlers – subsequent, post-conversion, use for Christian graves – ovoid enclosure around consecrated nucleus of cemetery, sixth century – first stone church within this, eighth–tenth centuries (including adding of cross to the 426 pillar) – medieval church – present church.

The type (b) memorials (Irish names only) begin with 378, Llanwinio, BIV̄AD⌐/AVI BODIBE/VE; AVI 'of a grandson of', not FILI as read by Macalister, with an eroded ogam[20] *BIVVA ... AVVI BODDIB...* The AVI(/awi/) is a 'Latin' imitation of *AVVI* (/awi/). Llangeler (372) is also incomplete because the stone has a central part broken out; the two vertical lines are DE(CAB)ARBALOM / FILIVS BROCAGN⌐ and the ogam, which may once have repeated both, *DECCA(IBAR VALB...?; Brocagn(as)*, 'Little-Badger', is an Irish name that we shall meet again more than once (pp. 113, 135). The slab, 442, at Mathry, lost for several centuries and found again in 1937, now shows what is left of a recorded five-row horizontal inscription in capitals, with ligatures; (MAC)/CV DICCL(I?)/FILIVS/ CATIC/VVS. There *was* a long ogam inscription, mostly trimmed, which probably (though not of course certainly) repeated this early sixth-century memorial.[21]

At Clydai, 430, ogam *ETTERN(?I MAQI VIC?)TOR*, with ETTERN– F̄ILI VICTOR(IS?), the Roman names Aeternus and Victor(ius?), confirms that the type (b) usage extended to non-Celtic names. Stone 449, St Dogmaels, a very large pillar, has SAGRANI FILI / CVNOTAMI and its ogam equivalent *SAGRAGNIS MAQI CUNATAMI*; while *Sagragn(as)* contains the name-element as in 426 NETTASAGRI plus the Irish diminutive *-agn(as)*, **Cunotamos* would seem to be British.[22] Lastly the stone from Eglwys Gymyn in the south-east of Pembroke, 362, reads AVITORIA / FILIA CVNIGNI; 'A, daughter of *Cunignos*', a British name corresponding to Irish *Cunagnas* – the ogam *INIGENA CUNIGNI AWITTORIGES* shows PrIr. *inigena* 'daughter' and the woman's name, though not elsewhere attested, might (with one extra vowel-notch) have appeared as a correct genitive singular, *Awittorigeas*.[23]

There are only three type (c) inscriptions. 422, Brawdy, is not entirely legible; the eroded lettering is VEND(O or A)FILI V(?) / ?GNI, and the ogam *VENDOGNI*. If O (so the *Guide*) has replaced A under Latin influence – the stone is possibly sixth-century – the Irish name **Wend-agnas* (**uind-* 'fair, white', etc., with diminutive) is shown. Another from St Dogmaels, 450, is also not an exact correspondence; it reads HOGTIVIS F̄ILI / DEMETI – the -IV- is obviously meant to be ligatured ĪN, for HOGTINIS – and ogam *OGTENAS*. This peculiar name may be written with Irish genitive *-ās*; with DEMETI, are we to read *Demetius*, or a name based on *\*Demetia*, or something British resembling the former? Lastly at Clydai, 431, we have on a slab defaced with a much later cross-design DOBITVCI/FILIVS EVOLENG(I, or ⊢), and ogam *D(O)V(A)TUCEAS*, the latter the subsequent Irish name *Dubthach*.[24]

In the rest of this book readers will not be asked to struggle through quite so many transcriptions bunched together, but these have been given in detail in order to show what is involved in reading the epitaphs – each one, after all, is a near-permanent record of some man or woman whose complete life-story would enable us to reconstruct much that is lost forever – and to demonstrate, in Demetia, how unusually fully the stones portray the inception of a native state. On the map, Fig. 6.3, apart from the four markedly southern memorials and the outlying 348 in Cardiganshire and 378 eastward beside the Teifi, the faint dotted line that can enclose the other thirteen also encloses the main concentration of *feid(i)r* place-names and Moel Trigarn. If this is a focusing-down in *space*, then in *time* we are looking at memorials, all or nearly all of which would be appropriate to c.450–550, with a few of type (a) before 450. Do we see, effectively, a picture of the Déisi settlement as it was through most of the fifth century and during the time of Eochaid and the next two or three named rulers? The indication is that the initial landing, or at any rate many of the landings (if, as is likely, there were many, when one or two boat-loads came across), took place on the north coast between Fishguard and Cardigan. There are some very obvious and easy points for entry, like Newport Sands; and, if Moel Trigarn is also Dún Tredúi, Irish people knew the way and knew the country to be expected.

Of all the land between the Teifi and the Tywi in the fifth century, one-third in the hands of the Irish would leave two-thirds in those of the native Demetian British; and, during that century, the names preserved as Clotri and Gloitguin (p. 55), it was argued, represent native rulers. The map therefore includes the position at Llandysilio of the memorial 435 of the *Clutorigi*, son of Paulinus Marinus from Latium, who may well be 'Clotri'; and, going southward, positions of possible royal estates or centres for a combined kingdom in the sixth century near Narberth, and in the seventh under the medieval Carew Castle.

Continuing that model earlier proposed (p. 69) of the memorial fashion itself as an Irish introduction, first manifested through type (a) ogam-inscribed uprights, what ought we really to read into the types (b) and (c) bilinguals? The demonstration that, in combining ogam script and Roman letters, it seems to have been immaterial if people's names were other than obviously Irish ones shows that these can properly be called, or also called, *biliterals*. It is virtually certain that many other stones have perished; it has long been agreed generally, and the character of many individual names support it, that we observe commemoration of nobles, land-holders and priests and not of peasants. We have no option but to regard the inscriptions we possess as representative of an unascertainable total. The biliteralism goes with memorial-pillars themselves, with the employment of ogam, with verticality and with the custom of identifying people by their fathers or kin-groups as an aspect of *style*; of funerary fashion.[25] It was done; certain learned persons knew how to set out an inscription for cutting or chiselling, and also still knew (but through ogam, and through an Irish interest in the structure of Primitive Irish) old declensional endings like genitives in -*ās* and -*ō* (<*os*). Loss, during successive generations after Eochaid Allmuir and his contemporaries, of spoken Irish may have been swifter than loss of any knowledge of, or any taste for, ogam – manifest in the sequence (a), total; (b), corresponding versions; (c), (d), partial; un-typed, none. Until (probably) VI.1, ogam if not *de rigeur* was at a certain level of society desirable, if only to re-state Irish roots. If 'Maelgwn', son of a native king Clotri, was commemorated in both scripts and his name Hibernicized at Nevern, 446, we could guess that his father had had the sense to ally his family with another from the Déisi nobility. On his particular stone, as on all of them except the few of type (a), the unanswered question concerns the source, with date(s) of its adoption, of that one component not attributable to the Irish immigrants; the Roman alphabet as the vehicle for written (and spoken) Latin. It is not enough to say that the *civitas Demetarum* formed part of Roman Britain, that Latin was Britannia's dominant language if not also a *koine* or second vernacular along with British, and that anyone who wrote anything at all did so in the Roman alphabet, *capitalis* or book-hands. Nor are we to suppose that Irish learned men (who may have known a lot *about* Latin) suddenly pressed an isolated biliteralism on their mourning compatriots. Fifth-century Pembroke beyond *Moridunum*, like fifth-century west Devon and Cornwall beyond *Isca Dumnoniorum*, may in respect of *romanitas* have been what old-style Cornish local preachers, without irreverence, called the Land's End peninsula and its people: 'we down here in the ass-end of the world'. Among the Demetian memorials, we have to define this innovation as 'the horizon of Latinity' and, with other cultural horizons (of Christianity, and then historicity), fit this into the unfolding story.

Since, meanwhile, Fig. 6.3 goes a little way towards showing the location and size of Irish-settled Demetia as the first step in a fifth-century kingdom, what of its rulers? The sequence of kings from Eochaid Allmuir to (Welsh) Guortepir, \**Voteporix*, and beyond was given in the bare format of that dual list, and again through a diagram (p. 55) indicating apparent steps and changes in a long catalogue. Are there, additionally, independent early references to any of them? How independent of each other are the Irish and Welsh versions?

An overdue analysis can show that, as a source of information, the dual list is more complicated than it might seem. The first few names (end of fourth to mid-fifth century) were preserved in Demetia by *filid*, learned men among the Déisi, and at the same time in the Irish homeland. To-and-fro contact could have been kept up, just as long as casual transmarine settlement was taking place.[26] It is probable that further names of kings in Demetia, up to *Votecorix in the sixth century, were known in Munster. In Demetia itself the succession was preserved in memory, or written down (or both), to a later stage when Irish personal names were no longer used. At the point marked by (Irish list) Tualodor mac Rigin and (Welsh list) Teudos map Regin — since Margetiut son of Teudos reputedly died in 796, this point fell in the later eighth century — a roll of twelve names (Triphun to Teudos) was supplied from a Welsh source to an Irish recipient. That such a transmission occurred no later is clear, because the Irish list stops here. That it went from Wales to Ireland is also clear because any subsequent textual corruption hardly disguises the fact that *Trestin, Alchoil, Retheoir,* etc., are not real Irish names at all but miscopying of written Old Welsh names. In Wales, genealogists then continued a king-list or regnal succession up to the time of Hywel Dda. The recensions we have to use now (the twelfth-century MS Rawlinson B 502 and MS Harleian 3859) are even later, but still comprehensible.

We can infer, first, that the Déisi settlers preserved their own king-list for the fifth and sixth centuries in the knowledge that its earlier affinities were of Irish origin, and second — this is just as significant — that (as with the Irish in Ireland) there would have been circulating, orally and then in written form, *other* lists or genealogies relating to *other* descendants of Eochaid Allmuir, providing good contexts in societal time for nobler families and those who claimed to be (or were recognized as being) of royal kin-groups, This second inference can be made because at least one such other list can be reconstructed. It must have passed, around 500–550, from Demetia to the smaller inland state of Brycheiniog. It was preserved in that kingdom's records and when, in the eleventh century, interested parties from *Nantcarban* or Llancarfan in Glamorgan wanted to add certain relevant details to the Life of their patron, St Cadog, we can suppose that they were able to obtain a copy from Brecon — presumably from a pre-Norman community there whose establishment was to be replaced in the twelfth century by the Priory. Parts of this (or of a similar) genealogy had in fact been used, centuries beforehand, in the 'Brychan Documents' discussed here in chapter 9.

The purpose of the Llancarfan recitation[27] was not to delve into the remote Demetian past but to validate the noble, indeed royal, ancestry of Cadog in the Life (*Vita Sancti Cadoci*, or *VC*). Cadog's father was the prince Gwynllyw, son of and successor to Glywys the ruler of Glywysing (roughly, Mid Glamorgan); his mother was Gladusa the daughter of Brychan, the eponymous king of sixth-century Brycheiniog, which lay immediately north of Glywysing. Brychan's mother had been the indigenous princess Marchell and his father, the preceding king, an incoming Demetian nobleman of apparent Irish (Déisi) descent called Anlach. For the cult of Cadog it was important to specify the claim that the saint's mother's father did really come *de optimis prosapiis regum Hibernensium* 'from the best stocks of the Irish kings'. For us, the value of what was set out – this separate short piece, which in all probability *is* a genealogy, since its concern is to denote blood-ties and not to recite an imagined succession of kings – is that it may supplement and correct the earlier part of the dual Welsh-Irish list.

The Brychan Documents are *De Situ Brecheniauc* (*DSB*), containing a narrative that (it will be argued later) was composed late in the sixth century, and *Cognacio Brychan* (*CB*), a kind of paraphrased copy of *DSB* also written within Brycheiniog but probably several centuries later. Both make limited use of Demetian-originating material. Neither mentions Eochaid Allmuir, because both tap in, as it were, to the Demetian king-list at a point later than Eochaid's generation. In *DSB*, *Anlach* is a 'king of Ireland' and son of 'Coronac' (read *Cormac*). In *CB*, where there is a particular concern to stress the noble background of St Cynog, Brychan's firstborn son and Anlach's grandson, another source may have been used because *Anlach, filius Gornuc* (= Cormac), continues with 'Gornuc' as *filii Eurbre de Hibernia*. The version expanded slightly in *VC* comes as a descending, not ascending, genealogy and for some reason omits Anlach's father of *DSB* and *CB*. Cadog is the son of *Gladusa*, daughter of *Brachanus* (Brychan), son of *Anlach*; Anlach, son of *Urbf*, son of *Brusc*, son of *Briscethach*. Here the close correspondence of (*CB*) *Eurbre* and (*VC*) *Urbf* suggest that the -f- of *Urbf* has escaped from a line of writing with *Urb f(ilius)*. Of the earlier names in *VC*, 'Brusc' points to Aed *Brosc*; and 'Briscethach' to compression of some such original written guise as ...\**Bruisc (maic) Echach* 'of (Aed) Brosc son of Eochaid'.[28]

If the proposed interpretations in chapter 9 are correct, Anlach was never as *optimus* as being a king in Ireland, but was the principal figure in a group of aristocratic Demetians, mostly if not entirely of Déisi stock, who migrated from Demetia to Brycheiniog at the end of the fifth century. His pedigree was recorded as Anlach, son of Cormac, son of Urb or Eurbre, son of (Aed) Brosc, son of Eochaid (Allmuir). We are not immediately concerned now with Anlach and his forebears except perhaps to note that in the obvious correction of the scribal errors *DSB* 'Coronac' and *CB* 'Gornuc' his father's name Cormac (<\**Corbmac*) may show the not infrequent habit of repeating a name-element borne by a famous ancestor (Eochaid's father Art *Corb*). It is this coincidence, of the likely inclusion of the names of Aed Brosc and Eochaid with their appearance in the dual list, that is of special interest. There is a distinct chance that a separate genealogy, transmitted from Demetia to Brycheiniog at some point between the sixth and eighth centuries, preserves an older aspect of the first few Déisi immigrant rulers than do the versions in the MSS (Rawl. B 502, Laud 610) giving the Irish side of the dual list. It calls into question the name 'Corath' (Laud 610, *Corach*) that appears between Aed Brosc and Eochaid in the ascending-pedigree format of the Irish version of the dual list.

This writer regards 'Corath' or 'Corach' as a disposable ghost-name, a ruler created out of a mere epithet.[29] Names older than Triphun/Trestin are recorded only from the Irish side; this is confirmed by the epithet in Eochaid *Allmuir*, since his description as 'Over-Sea' would be meaningful only from an Irish standpoint. If *brosc* represents an intimately descriptive term[30] adhering to Aed's name and treated as part of it, *corach* may be a second such title, perhaps acquired late in life or in retrospect. If, too, it carries any such sense as 'striker' with an implication of fame as a warrior, we can observe that in the twelfth-century Cardiganshire Life of St Carantoc or Carannog the names of the four *Scotti . . . duces* 'Irish war-leaders' who overcame Britannia are given as *Briscus* (with Thuibaius, Machleius and Anpacus).[31]

With this closer look, the rulers of early Demetia are pared down to: Eochaid, who if he landed in the late fourth century should have died in the earlier fifth; Aed *Brosc* (also *Corach*?), stated in two (but not necessarily independent) sources to be his son; Triphun; Aircol, who seems to be a figure of the end of the fifth century; and then a *Guotepir, perhaps by inference Aircol's son, who died probably in VI.2. From the Welsh side only, in Harleian 3859, a Clotri (<CLVTORIGI, 435?) and a preceding 'Gloitguin' may in some fashion run parallel to Aed Brosc and Triphun. Now very unusually, for Insular kings at so early a period, three of these people in a row are mentioned elsewhere – Triphun, Aircol, Guotepir or *Voteporix*. The one remaining point to be strongly emphasized is that, while the two names Triphun < *Tribunus* and Aircol < *Agricola* can be explained as regular derivatives, in Irish and British respectively, of known Roman originals there is no evidence whatsoever that in contemporary speech these men were called 'Tribunus' and 'Agricola'. This does not of course mean that learned persons, who might have written 'Brosc' as BRVSCVS and did write the genitive of what underlies 'Guotepir' as VOTEPORIGIS, could not have been able to reconstruct TRIBVNVS and AGRICOLA as sixth-century epigraphic forms. It will be suggested subsequently that, for the former man, precisely that happened with 327 TRILVNI (cutter's error) and 476 TRIBVNI.

A secondary recension of the c.1095 Life of St David by Rhigyfarch[32] refers to happenings *in tempore regis Triphuni et filiorum eius* 'in the days of king T. and his sons'; the milieu is Demetia, but this has been lifted from a near-contemporary Life of St Gildas by Caradoc of Llancarfan.[33] Gildas preaches every Sunday in his sea-side church, in the district called *Pepidiauc* (the north-west tip of Pembrokeshire), *in tempore Trifini regis*. Among the Llandaff charters, one commences with a time-annotation, *regnante Aircol lauhir filio tryfun rege demetice regionis* 'in the reign of Aircol *lauhir* son of Tryfun, king of the Demetic territory' (citation of Aircol's parentage here need have no independent inferential value).[34] This introduces his epithet *Lauhir* 'Long-hand', the sense of which is usually taken to mean 'generous' (as in our own 'open-handed').[35] Other Llandaff documents mention him as *rex Aircol, Aircol lauhir* and – from the Life of St Oudoceius[36] – *in demeticam regionem tempore Aircol lauhir regis eiusdem regni*. Unconnected with these is a reference to him in the thirteenth-century Black Book of Carmarthen.[37] Here, the *Englynion y Beddau*, 'Stanzas of the Graves', are short mnemonic verses that are 'witness to a wealth of stories and traditions current in pre-Norman Wales, but now for the greater part lost for ever'.[38] One line, unhappily devoid of any more specific geographical detail, reads *bed Airgwl yn Dyuet* 'the grave of Aircol in Dyfed', implying perhaps a well-known spot or memorial.

Because of the mention of his supposed generosity, rather than the dual list's assertion, Aircol has been taken as the *boni regis* 'of a good king' whose *nequam fili* 'bad son' is the *Demetarum tyranne Vortipori* (= Guotepir) addressed by Gildas in *De Excidio Britonum*.[39] The date of composition of *DEB* can be, though it should not be, the fixed point to which the chronology of the dual list can be anchored. For the purposes of the present work *DEB* is seen as a sixth-century writing, with a probability that 540, plus rather than minus a decade, is the date of the textual references involved (though also with an awareness – not further explored now – that *DEB* may have been completed nearer to 500). If we turn back to the combined evidence so far rehearsed, from all sources, for the succession of persons named as rulers or notables in early Demetia a simple table can be set out:

(*a*)(*b*) Eochaid *Allmuir* son of Artchorp

| (*a*) Aed *Brosc* (?*Corach*) son of Eochaid | | | |
|---|---|---|---|
| Urb(f) son of Brusc | (reign of Aed) | | (*d*) Gloitguin |
| *Cormac son of Eurb(re) | (*c*) Triphun | | Clotri (435 CLVTORIGI son of PAVLIN(VS)) |
| Anlach son of *Cormac | Aircol | | 446 MAGLOCVNI son of CLVTORI |
| Brychan son of Anlach | Guotepir son of Aircol (as 358 VOTEPORIGIS) | | |

– where (*a*) is the *pedigree*, Eochaid to Brychan, built up from *DSB*, *CB* and *VC*; (*b*), Eochaid to Guotepir, the Irish version of the *regnal list*; (*c*), Triphun to Guotepir, the Welsh version; and (*d*) the sequence from the Welsh version (Harleian 3859) continued from inscriptions.

This cannot be given as a fixed synchronology because dating rests on three assumptions; the time of Eochaid's arrival, the likely date of the *DEB* reference to *Vortipor(i)* as alive and elderly, and the estimates of dates for the memorials 358, 435 and 446. None the less the sequences of names are arguably correct here. If we work on the provisional belief that Eochaid Allmuir arrived from Ireland in late IV and died in Demetia in V.1 (or possibly early V.2), and agree that over a short period reign-lengths and generations will not necessarily coincide, the contentions that Brychan (chap. 9) and Guotepir (below) were broadly contemporary, born in late V.3 and died in mid-VI, cannot be excessively misplaced. As for the proposed identifications of the separate British rulers in Demetia – if that is what the names in (*d*) represent – the memorial 435 CLVTORIGI is arguably a sub-Roman inscription (Fig. 5.6) set up in V.3, and that of his supposed son 446 MAGLOCVNI is a type (b) memorial some thirty or forty years afterwards.

The memorial attributed to Guotepir, found at Castell Dwyran near Narberth, reveals a number of interesting facets. It is a partial bilingual, like type (c), but because it contains a specifically Christian term must be classed as type (d). It reads 358 MEMORIA / VOTEPORIGIS / PROTICTORIS, three horizontal lines of capitals below an equal-armed cross in a ring. The ogam reads upwards, *VOTECORIGAS* (/wotecorigas/, gen.). We have here: (i) restriction of the ogam to the deceased's name, even on a royal memorial perhaps favouring a date no earlier than VI.2; (ii) the use of *memoria*, a word from the intrusive 'extended Latinate' vocabulary; (iii) the presence of a primary Christian motif, the ringed cross (Fig. 6.5) that, whatever others may have said in print about this, shows every sign of being integral with the inscription and not a later addition;[40] (iv) a learned treatment of the Roman-lettered name, giving it a mock-Latin genitive termination; and (v) similarly learned treatment in ogam of an otherwise unattested Irish name.[41]

To the possible question by this stage – Are all these men supposed to have been real people of an actual historical past? – the obvious response is, Why not? By usual standards there is a surprising amount of information here and little reason to doubt that, though we have it from MSS of the twelfth and later centuries, such details were fixed in writing in both Wales and Ireland long before the Norman period. In this respect the Demetian rulers show up well when compared with a figure such as the *dux* Arthur, the very location of whose campaigns and battles in sixth-century Britain cannot be agreed. The geography is consistent. Eochaid's primary settlement is likely to have been within the northern third of Pembrokeshire. If Triphun is to be linked with *Pepidiauc regio*, the old cantref of Pebidiog[42] in north-west Pembroke, is it a coincidence that one of the three place-names with the prefix *loch-*, taken by Melville Richards to show Irish influence, occurs here in the shape of Loch*dwrffin*, which may even contain Triphun's name?[43] The grave of Aircol lay in Dyfed; he was king of the Demetic *regio*. A curious prologue to a Llandaff charter places Aircol's court at 'Liscastell', the chief place of the kingdom (*caput totius demetice regionis*).[44] The stone of *\*Voteporix* or Guotepir was found at a site, sounding from its description like the vestiges of somewhere both royal and Christian,[45] near modern Narberth in mid-Pembroke; Narberth is the Mabinogi *Arberth*, traditionally such a capital within early Dyfed. In chapter 9, Anlach the descendant of Aed Brosc journeyed, it will

# DEMETIA: A POST-ROMAN KINGDOM

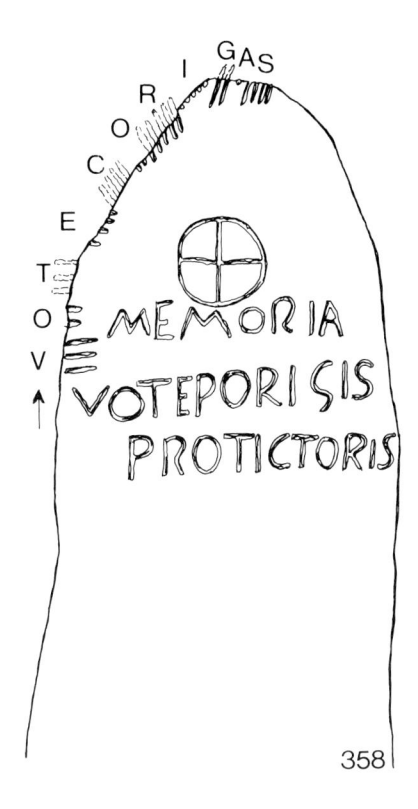

**Fig. 6.5** The *Voteporix* stone, 358, drawn from photographs in Carmarthen Museum. The ogam employs an imagined stem-line on the irregular rounded surface. Note suggestion, top line, of -MO- lowered to accommodate the previously-carved encircled cross.

be shown, from Demetia to Brycheiniog and perhaps from Pebidiog within Demetia. The limited associations of the earlier names (Eochaid, perhaps Aed Brosc, Triphun) lie in northern Demetia; with Guotepir, and perhaps Aircol if 'Liscastell' lies anywhere near Tenby, we move southwards into the field indicated by Fig. 7.4.

The fifth-century kingdom of Demetia *can* therefore be accorded a shape, and a skeletal dynastic history. Evidence for acculturation into post-Roman Britain, more closely into post-Roman southern Wales, is another question. Tracing the attainment of *horizons* from the evidence of history, epigraphy and archaeology offers a useful model, but this chapter confines itself to mention of the first horizon only; Latinity. In this light the names Triphun and Aircol, as reflections of the inferred *Tribunus* and *Agricola*, are not horizon-indicators because we cannot exclude the likelihood that they were names introduced from Ireland by the Déisi in that form. For Britannia, as for other western portions of the Empire, though Latin was the language of the Church its currency preceded conversion to Christianity. The attainments of the horizons of Latinity and Christianity could and did coincide in certain regions, but not automatically so, and not here.

If a fourth-century *civitas* centre at *Moridunum*, Carmarthen, can be postulated so can an *ordo*, a curial class of Romanized Demetians as provincial citizens, and very probably provisions for some schooling in Latin. The memorial of *Clutorigi* (435) marks one whose father was Paulinus Marinus 'from Latium' (*Latio*), and one for whom an inscription was cut in horizontal lines of capitals; uneven in size, but firm letters deeply cut and as legible as a pre-400 Romano-British monument. This may well have been in 450 × 475 (Fig. 5.6). How long an interval, if any, should we envisage until the appearance of Demetian type (b) memorials on which Irish epitaphs were 'translated' into Latin formulae, or Roman-lettered names given parallel Irish versions – with Irish and British and even continuing-Roman names, like 430 at Clydai with *Etternus* and *Victor* (and the same in ogam)? There are in all thirteen memorials of types (b) and (c). It is possible to argue from the epigraphic styles that some of them were set up before AD 500. Four exhibit horizontal I (⊢), a convention probably invented at the time such bilinguals came into fashion. Not one shows angle-bar A, another trick that had a Continental origin, is found on a number of Demetian stones and was secondarily diffused to Dumnonia; but may not have reached Demetia until about 500 (Fig. 7.5).

As for Aircol and Triphun, models for the former name (in Ireland) could at a stretch include romantic revival of the name of the first-century Emperor who (so Tacitus informs us)[46] gave shelter to an Irish prince obliged to flee his homeland. Given its royal usage, was this name then adopted in Britain as 'Aircol' (/airgol/)? An *Agricola* was *praefectus* in Gaul in 418, consul with Eustathius in 421; would this have been known in Demetia and if so would it have mattered a jot to the Demetians? Prosper of Aquitaine's *Chronicle* noted that in 429 the pope Celestine sent St Germanus (of Auxerre) to Britain to combat the teachings of *Agricola Pelagianus* – a follower of the heresiarch Pelagius[47] – because this man, son of a Pelagian bishop Severianus, had been corrupting the *ecclesias Britanniae*, the Christian communities, with the dire influence of his dogmatics.[48] The name 'Severinus' does figure on a memorial from Whitchurch, Carmarthenshire (373), with SEVERINI / FILI SEVERI – see Fig. 15.5 – but this is at least a century on from AD 429. The little that could be said about the visit of St Germanus would not include his presence anywhere in south-west Wales.

Triphun is patently a name here; or, when so used by a fifth-century ruler, a name rather than the military and civil title *tribunus*. If 'Aircol' cannot be explained easily, the chance that 'Triphun' was brought from Ireland follows from its appearance in the archaic Leinster poems as a descriptive term. The king Mes-Delmonn is a *trebunn trén tuathmar* 'mighty tribune of many peoples'.[49] Progression from a borrowed use of this kind to adoption as a proper name may be quite speedy.[50] Demetians who knew enough to recognize its origin in Latin *tribunus* would have rendered it, epigraphically, as TRIBVNVS (p. 270); that would leave a *spoken* /trifu:n/ or /trivu:n/ unaffected.

If we define 'attainment of the horizon of Latinity' by the settlers of Déisi origin as meaning, not the universal adoption of spoken Vulgar Latin and written Latin as means of communication, but simply a new emphasis — led by composers of inscriptions — in fashions for names and titles on significant memorials, we may be able to site this horizon within V.2. Assimilation between population-groups would have widened access to the remnant Latinity of those Demetians who looked back to the days before 400; Demetians whose fathers bore Roman *nomina* and *cognomina*. A few of the type (b) memorials, relevant as they may be to those who died two generations after Eochaid's arrival, bear witness to this. While the spread of a fashion for Latinity, for a display of Roman names, may have involved some small first element of the Christian faith — were the composers of these inscriptions all laymen, or not? — this need not imply any deliberate and aggressive dissemination of Christianity. Epigraphy, history and archaeology may better inform us when such dissemination took place. Meanwhile, there rests a suspicion that in Demetia the horizon of Latinity preceded, perhaps by several decades, a general attainment of the horizon of Christianity. In this particular landscape, the Church must be the subject of a separate analysis.

## References

1. W. M. Morris, *A Glossary of the Demetian Dialect* (1910; facsimile repr., Llanerch, Felinfach 1991).
2. *Celtica* 1 (1946), at 160.
3. Padel 1985, 27–9.
4. In his 'Welsh MEID(I)R, MOYDIR, Irish BÓTHAR "lane, road"', *Lochlann* 2 (Oslo 1962), 128–34.
5. Richards 1960 — the basis (*GPC*) is *knukko*- 'lump, protuberance, knob', cf. OBr. *cnoch*.
6. A good modern case — Cornish place-names with 'Wheal' (Wheal Alfred, Wheal Busy, etc.), a word for 'a working' (*wheyl*), are confined to medieval-to-modern shaft mines in the metalliferous-ore districts.
7. For cattle and pastoralism in early Ireland see, as an introductory guide, Byrne 1973, chap. 4, and A. T. Lucas, *Cattle in Ancient Ireland* (Boethius Press, Kilkenny 1989).
8. This takes into account the caution (Richards 1960, 152) that 'the blank area in S. Pembrokeshire is a good indication of the way in which earlier Welsh names have been almost completely submerged by successive waves of ... Norse, English and Flemish.'
9. As in Dark 1992; some of his reservations are certainly held by others, and have been (quietly) for some years now.
10. Macalister seems not at his best (or conversely at his most imaginative) in certain parts of Wales; readings here lean more on *ECMW*, further corrected by Dr McManus, *Guide* and (for some) also by the author's visits, 1989–91. Sadly we must accept that some ogams are by now, effectively, illegible.
11. *BR)IECI(I?* is probably 'the least insupportable' version (see *Guide*).
12. For *mucoi* (etymology very uncertain), see *Guide*, 111, 119–20.
13. *ECMW*, 4.
14. *LHEB*, 175–6; earlier, Jackson, *ECNE*, 200 ff.

15. *LHEB*, ibid.
16. So used in fourth-century Britannia; lead curse-tablet, Roman Bath, starts 'seu *gentilis* seu Christianus' ('whether heathen or Christian') who had stolen Annianus's six silver coins; R. S. O. Tomlin, p. 232, no. 98, in: B. W. Cunliffe, ed., *The Temple of Sulis Minerva at Bath*, vol. 2 (Oxford 1988). The graph -ND- in GENDILIS, presumably /nd/, looks like preservation, in a name, of 4th-cent. British Latin /gendilis/ for the adjective *gentilis*; this may have preserved it from *nd* > *nn* (*LHEB*, 511–13), and the -D- need not imply lenited *d* /ð/.
17. *Guide*, chap. 6 n.14, n.50; *Dumelas* is Irish.
18. Latin *emeritus*, used secularly of a time-expired military man; this single-name epitaph, suggestive of a priest and from a very early Christian location – Nevern (in Welsh, Nyfer) – uses it here deliberately (for Insular inscriptions, uniquely) in this sense.
19. *Dub* 'black, swarthy?' and diminutive -*agn(as)*.
20. Macalister (*CIIC*) read more ogam than this, but it is extremely hard to see now how he did so; the repeated name-element here is *\*biwa-*, Irish *béo* 'living, alive'. AVI (not FILI) is certain.
21. Nash-Williams, ECMW no. 346, wondered if the ogam was a separate independent inscription (why?). McManus, *Guide*, shows this is probably sixth-cent. because MACCV shows delabialization – i.e., the /kw/ of MAQI has here eroded to mere /k/.
22. *Guide*, 113, 6.21; because CVNOTAMI is continued as Welsh *Cyndaf*, but there is no corresponding Irish derivative.
23. *Guide*, pointing out the arrangement that puts the two versions of her name together – 'Daughter of C, of A' / 'A, daughter of C'.
24. *Guide*, 67; this is a gen. (-*eas*) and certainly the best reading.
25. There are no real, modern parallels. Partial examples would be use of dates like MDCCCLXXVIII on memorial-tablets; in west Wales (if this happens), commissioning of all-Welsh tombstones for non-native speakers; in Cornwall (where this does now happen), insertion of Revived Cornish phrases among English tombstone wordings.
26. On this theme, note now John Carey's suggestions (*BBCS* 39 (1992), 24–46, at 45); 'an impressive array of evidence in both Ireland and Wales suggests that Twrch Trwyd and the Ychen Bannog derive from *dindshenchas* brought to southern Wales by Irish settlers; these colonists came from east Munster, in the vicinity of Cashel'. If transmission of literary themes took place in the fourth to fifth cents., genealogical information could just as easily have been passed.
27. See *VSBG*, 118–9.
28. The connection between Aed *Brosc* and such manifestations as 'Briscus' and 'Brusc son of Briscethach' has of course often been noticed; the most illuminating discussion is Patrick Sims-Williams', *BBCS* 29 (1982), 618–9 with numerous further references.
29. Vendryes, *Lexique*, C.204–6, *1 cor* ('coup, tour, mouvement tournant' etc., as a noun); derivative adj. *corach* 'qui frappe', as in *cath-chorach* 'qui aime engager la bataille' (from a Leinster poem in Rawl. B 502, 116.39 – see *CGH*, 9).
30. *Brosc* presents difficulties; it seems to have been taken as an otherwise unattested OIr. cognate of OW *breisc* 'stout, fat' (see GPC, s.v. *braisg*). See *BBCS* 29 (1982), 619 nn.1 & 2. The exact meaning is probably not recoverable.
31. *VSBG* 142–3.
32. James 1967 (= *VD*), text at 4, and earlier at xxxi.
33. Hugh Williams, *Two Lives of Gildas, by a Monk of Ruys and Caradoc of Llancarfan* (Cymmrodorion Record Ser., 1899), at 88–9.
34. W. Davies, *Llandaff* 148, s.n. AIRCOL LAUHIR.

35. *EWGT*, 226 (as Llawhir); 'generous' remains an assumption of its meaning, but surely a reasonable one.
36. *Llan Dâv*, 130.
37. A. O. H. Jarman, *Llyfr Du Caerfyrddin* (Cardiff 1982), 44 (line 220).
38. Thomas Jones, 'The Black Book of Carmarthen "Stanzas of the Graves"', *Proc. British Academy* 53 (1968), 97–137; text, 132–3, and his comment here, 116.
39. This is the only contemporary statement that one Demetian king was the son of an earlier, presumably preceding, ruler. Aircol is not named, but it is hard to see what other *rex* could be meant.
40. Close inspection (the stone is displayed in Carmarthen Museum) shows that the top line may have been cut immediately after the cross-motif was carved, because – see here, Fig. 6.5 – the letters – MO – in MEMORIA are lower-topped than flanking E and R as if to accommodate the lower circumference of the ring.
41. Jackson (1982, 31–2: longer discussion in *LHEB*) saw this as parallel contemporary name-forms, *Voteporix* (British), *Votecorix* (Irish). The former (nom.) would lead to /wodebir/, which is what 'Guotepir' miswritten as 'Guortepir' represents. Those who knew this was once a nom. in *\*rig-s* composed -RIGIS on the analogy of Latin *rex, regis*. But if the man's name was primarily British, ogam /wotecorigas/ is simply a pedantic translation into a likely Primitive Irish form. This may suggest, not bilingualism, but a learned person in the royal entourage. See also *LHEB* 749.
42. Richards, *WATU*, maps 85 and 86.
43. Richards 1960, with relevant map; the site, at SM 855 303, is probably a former bog with pool at a stream junction. Did it ever contain an Irish-style crannog, as at Llyn Llan-gors? See *PNP*, 273.
44. *Llan Dâv*, 125; precisely what place is meant seems to be unknown. *PNP* sheds no light on this puzzle.
45. The story of this stone's discovery, an important account, is given in *AC (1895), 303–13*.
46. Tacitus, *Agricola*, 24 ('unum ex regulis gentis exceperat'; the man is not named).
47. *CRB*, 53–60, for the background.
48. Prosper wrote this as *dogmatis sui insinuatione corrupit*.
49. Carney 1971, 69–70 (see *CGH* 20, 118.a.35); Byrne 1973, 134.
50. Apart from the obvious 'Rex' and 'Roy', cf. the twentieth-century cases in North America, and secondarily in Britain, of 'Duke', 'Earl', 'Count' and 'King' as titles of well-known musicians; and now the widespread use of Earl, at any rate, as a normal baptismal name.

# 7
# *Demetia: 'Passim Ecclesiarum Signa Audiuntur ...'*

'ON ALL SIDES are to be heard the evidences of churches', proclaimed the author of the life of St David, *Dewi Sant*.[1] Rhigyfarch was writing *Vita Beati Davidis* (*VD*) about 1095, using 'the oldest manuscripts of our land'; worn texts, *ex antiquo seniorum stilo conscripta* 'written in the archaic fashion of the elders'. Rhigyfarch's Dyfed had been Christian for centuries and the chief see, where his father Sulien served as bishop, was *Menevia* (St David's) – near the place where the national saint built his monastery at *Rosina Vallis*. The intrusions from Munster or Leinster were almost if not entirely forgotten. *VD*, as a sacred biography, stands virtually within the medieval period.

We are given no particular reason to suppose that during the early years of the fifth-century Irish settlers, Déisi or Uí Liatháin, were Christians. If at the time there had been any Christians within Ireland opposite south-west Wales they would have been few and far between; Romano-British traders and their immediate converts, rather than Irish auxiliaries returning from military service and throwing their weight around. Yet, from the sixth century, Demetia can be pictured as just another Christian kingdom. The words addressed by Gildas to king Guotepir, as to his four coeval rulers in what had been *Britannia Prima*, are crystal clear. Part-agents of the nation's miseries, these monarchs who set themselves up as *reges* but were little better than barbarian *tyranni* 'usurpers' were steeped in past sins, the more appalling because they *were* all of them notionally Christians. Adulterer and murderer, widower accused of violating his daughter, Guotepir was nevertheless to be accorded an inscribed memorial bearing not only the Cross encircled and a label (*memoria*) normally confined to the epitaphs of priests or holy persons, but the grandiose title of *Protector* – whatever his surviving relatives and followers meant it to signify.[2] His good and generous father Aircol may lurk, un-named, in the Life of the Demetian saint and bishop Samson (chap. 14). Samson's father Amon, a noble, and son of a man of the same social importance, underwent a Christian marriage, attended church, gave alms and was included by name in a list of benefactors[3] to be read aloud at Mass. He ended his career in Cornwall as head of a monastery founded by his son Samson; a son who, where his father was involved, reads very like the tail that wagged the dog. Amon was reportedly once an intimate of his king. The chronology of Samson's life suggests that Aircol was the king in question and that, if so, Aircol had been fostered in a noble Christian household.[4] Whatever weight is attached to mentions of Aircol in various Llandaff charters, allusions to Aircol *Lauhir* are in his capacity as grantor of estates to the Church.

How far back we may push this Christian horizon is uncertain. Adoption of the Faith in royal and noble circles is likely to have preceded any more general conversion of the people. If the regnal sequence is followed the likelihood is that Aircol was born at a date after 450. There is no independent reason to think that he was a son of Triphun. If Irish custom pertained he could have been a younger relative, a cousin, and separately a grandson or great-nephew of Eochaid, just as Brychan's father Anlach may have been a great-grandson of Aed Brosc. The slight geographical clues (p.80) that Triphun himself was to be linked to north-west Pembroke, the *Pepidiauc regio* inland from Porth Mawr and St David's, direct attention to this corner of Demetia as one where conversion may have been resisted until the sixth century.

Late compilation though it is, the Life of St David revives for us from those *antiquo stilo conscripta* a credible portrait of a society in spiritual flux. David's father, Sant king of Ceredigion, assaults a much younger Demetian virgin Nonita. Even while she is pregnant the unborn child is menaced, Herod-fashion, by a certain nearby ruler, *quidam ex confinio tyrannus*, who is warned by his heathen magicians and prophets (*magi*) about the spiritual power of the boy who is to come. The ruler is not named. Is Triphun implied? Some years afterwards when David and his companions, now ordained priests, return to the pleasant spot of *Rosina Vallis* where they are to build their monastery, paganism is still rampant. In the tale of Baia or Boia who lives within mutual viewing-distance in his *arx* or defended residence – probably the fortified hillock called Clegyr Boia[5] – we get a sharply defined vignette of an unredeemed Déisi chieftain, a district Godfather, horrified at the notion of Christian rivals on his private territory. Slaves armed with swords are despatched as a show of force, but are enfeebled *en route* and must confine their assault to shouting obscene taunts. Boia's wife then sends all the maidservants to cavort in the nude around Rosina Vallis, hoping to inflame the distracted brethren. Divine intervention arranges for some personal enemy to ambush Boia and slay him; heavenly fire consumes his *arx*. With this the ungodly are routed. Pagan tyrant and magicians, surly chieftain with his Lady Macbeth, foul-mouthed followers and shameless wenches are alike written out, and the monastery – most interestingly described in considerable detail as the centre of a large mixed farm[6] – is set on an eventual path to its famed quasi-archiepiscopal status, and today its real cathedral.

The point is that, whatever written scraps or half-remembered stories Rhigyfarch used (and, as *Vitae* go, his composition is skilled), in this western end of Dyfed a conversion to Christianity is shown as having been neither instantaneous nor automatic. In so late a work there can be no inherent chronology. Conflicting entries in *Annales Cambriae* provide 601 for the death of

David, *Menevensis archiepiscopus*,[7] and 458 'thirty years after Patrick's leaving Menevia' for David's birth. Oddly enough the earlier date, if certainly nothing like a contemporary entry, better suits a putative Triphun as a still-pagan king of V.2, and better suits as well a late fifth-century foundation of a monastery in this part of Demetia — despite unvarying statements that St David was a figure of the sixth century.

There is no doubt that, in the main, Christian stimuli came to Demetia from an easterly direction. Anna, the pious wife of Samson's father Amon, hailed as his social equal from the next province; not named, it must have been east of the river Tywi, though for the fifth century it would be hard to assign area-names within this very long stretch of south Wales, later housing several small kingdoms (like Glywysing, p. 104). If there is any basis to the idea, given to us by 'Nennius', that Cydweli and Gower underwent minor settlement by the Uí Liatháin while the Déisi were colonizing Pembroke, one must stress that these two districts contain almost nothing matching the inscribed memorials of Demetia. There is an isolated type (a) stone from Loughor, with a battered ogam that may read 405 *GRAVICA* — so Macalister, though more cautiously *(. L .)LICA* in *ECMW* no.228 — carved on a disused quadrangular Roman altar from the station or auxiliary fort at *Leucarum*.[8] Where are other witnesses to Irish immigrants? The odd memorial in the valley-approaches leading over Fforest Fawr to Brycheiniog, northward and inland, may be relevant (chap. 8). For fifth-century, sub-Roman, Christianity we look further eastward still. Among the first indications of any monastery in southern Demetia must be an establishment on Caldey Island, *Ynys Bŷr*, as a small offshoot — perhaps shortly before 500 — from Llanilltud Fawr (p. 227).

The sixty-plus early (*ECMW* Group I) inscribed stones of Demetia, mostly in Pembrokeshire with some in Carmarthenshire, offer the main way — in some respects the only way — of delineating at least part of the course of events here in the fifth and sixth centuries. As field monuments, their archaeology resides in patterns of siting and in their connections with ecclesiastical or secular locations. As inscribed records the epigraphy, controlled by the typological model set up earlier (p. 69), and the linguistic nature of individual names allow restrained inferences about Demetian society through time, during two centuries or more. This last aspect is concerned with distinctions, between identifiably Irish or British names, and the use of continuing-Roman ones. Bilingualism, in the sense in which this word might pertain to parts of contemporary Wales, must be played down. The absence of textual evidence (apart from a few place-name elements), or of specific early references to currency of a 'foreign' vernacular, and the retention of non-British names, do not together suggest a bilingual scenario. Personal names in particular are susceptible to explanations indicated by modern analogies.[9]

Figure 7.1 is simplified from an earlier map. It shows the pattern of inscriptions — types (a), (b) and (c) — that exhibit ogam, and in this respect form a sequence;

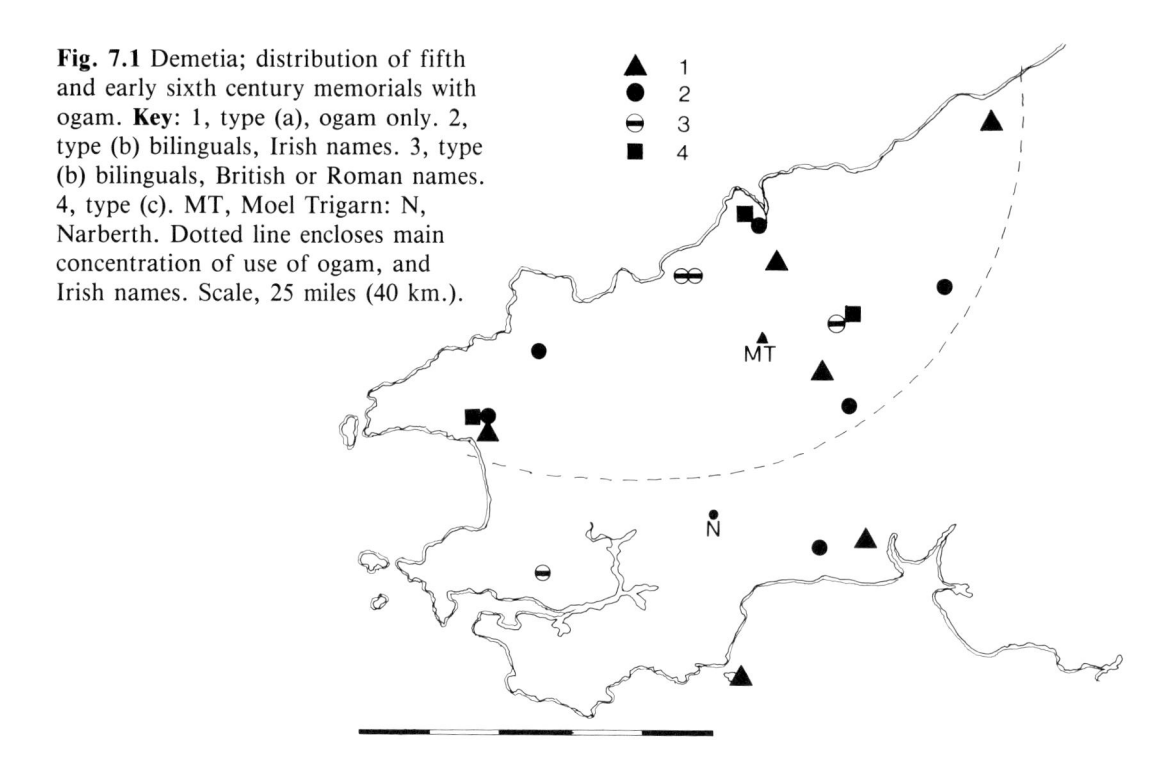

**Fig. 7.1** Demetia; distribution of fifth and early sixth century memorials with ogam. **Key**: 1, type (a), ogam only. 2, type (b) bilinguals, Irish names. 3, type (b) bilinguals, British or Roman names. 4, type (c). MT, Moel Trigarn: N, Narberth. Dotted line encloses main concentration of use of ogam, and Irish names. Scale, 25 miles (40 km.).

ogam-only, to full bilinguals, to deceased's name alone in ogam. A few of these are fifth-century memorials. The northerly emphasis supports a belief that Irish settlers landed, at first with Eochaid Allmuir and gradually thereafter, 'between Strumble Head and Aberystwyth'[10] (Strumble Head is the promontory sheltering on its east the fine natural harbour of Fishguard). This could be refined to a concentration on the thirty miles between Fishguard and New Quay, allowing the likelihood of use of Porth Mawr or Whitesand Bay south of St David's, and apparently also around to the much larger indentation on the south Pembroke coast between Tenby and the sandy estuarine outflow of the river Tywi; the island of Caldey was certainly settled by 500.[11] In Figure 7.1 virtually all the personal names are demonstrably Irish, the few exceptions being the type (b) memorials, both at Nevern (Nyfer), of 445 VITALIANI, a Roman name and probably an early cleric, and the (446) MAGLOCVN, son of CLVTORI who (it was earlier suggested) was a son of a native potentate *Clotri* absorbed by marriage into a Déisi family; and the peculiar 456 GENDILI memorial at Steynton, p. 74.

The maps in Figs. 6.3 and 7.2 refer to inscriptions that must be dated mainly to the sixth century though there may be a few slightly older than 500 and there certainly are a few later than 600. Fig. 7.2 shows the type (d) inscriptions, four of which exhibit ogam[12] and nine of which do not.[13] Type (d) memorials contain the phrase (HIC) IACIT 'here lies (he, she, or the body of)', or other words specifically suggesting a Christian epitaph, as in 358 MEMORIA (of *Voteporix*) and 448 RINACI/NOMENA (possibly for *nomine*). While those with ogam expectedly exhibit Irish names – 433 ANDAGELLI, 428 TRENAGUS (I?), 353 TRENACCAT (L)O – others

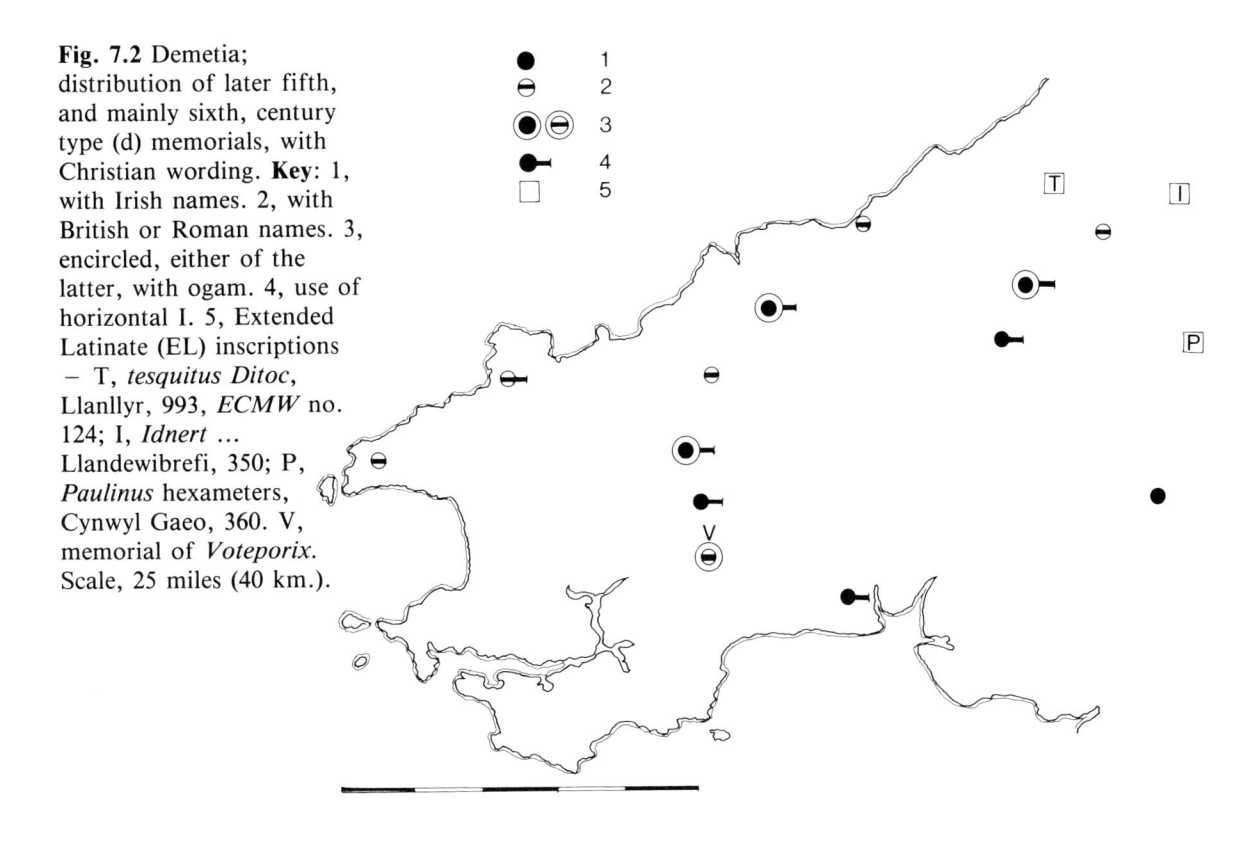

**Fig. 7.2** Demetia; distribution of later fifth, and mainly sixth, century type (d) memorials, with Christian wording. **Key**: 1, with Irish names. 2, with British or Roman names. 3, encircled, either of the latter, with ogam. 4, use of horizontal I. 5, Extended Latinate (EL) inscriptions – T, *tesquitus Ditoc*, Llanllyr, 993, *ECMW* no. 124; I, *Idnert* ... Llandewibrefi, 350; P, *Paulinus* hexameters, Cynwyl Gaeo, 360. V, memorial of *Voteporix*. Scale, 25 miles (40 km.).

may not do so. A lost stone from Meline, 443, apparently read HIC IACIT CAMVLORI(X) BRANNVS and, like the short (clerical?) epitaph 355 SILBANDVS IACIT from Silian church, it shows British names. The three-line memorial in St Nicholas church just west from Fishguard, 451 TVNCCETACE VX/SOR DAARI HIC IA/CIT, suggests a lady with a British name, *Toncetaca ( = Latin *Fortunata*: 'Lucky') who was *uxsor* 'the wife of' an Irish-named Christian(?).[14]

A line enclosing all the symbols for type (d) stones with ogam and Irish names in Figure 7.2 – a line the reader can supply mentally, or pencil in – would show a shift of emphasis (away from Fig. 7.1), both southward and south-easterly; on the one part, now affecting central Dyfed and not just the northern part of it, and on the other, constituting a grouping that lies closer (than the pattern of type (a) memorials) to likely Christian influences. By 'influences' we must understand the following: foundation, around 500, of small monasteries, or small churches for communal attendance with near-resident priests; contact overland, and along the southern coast, with sub-Roman Christianity in what is now (old) Glamorgan; and contact with that south-eastern portion of Demetia most likely to have contained families who, a few generations earlier, were Romanized, lived within a day's easy travelling to and from *Moridunum* (Carmarthen), and may have themselves been exposed, if only through Latin schooling, to fourth-century Christianity.

Figure 7.2 also shows, north-east side, three inscriptions (one, not a personal memorial at all) that have extended Latin wording, permit some interesting

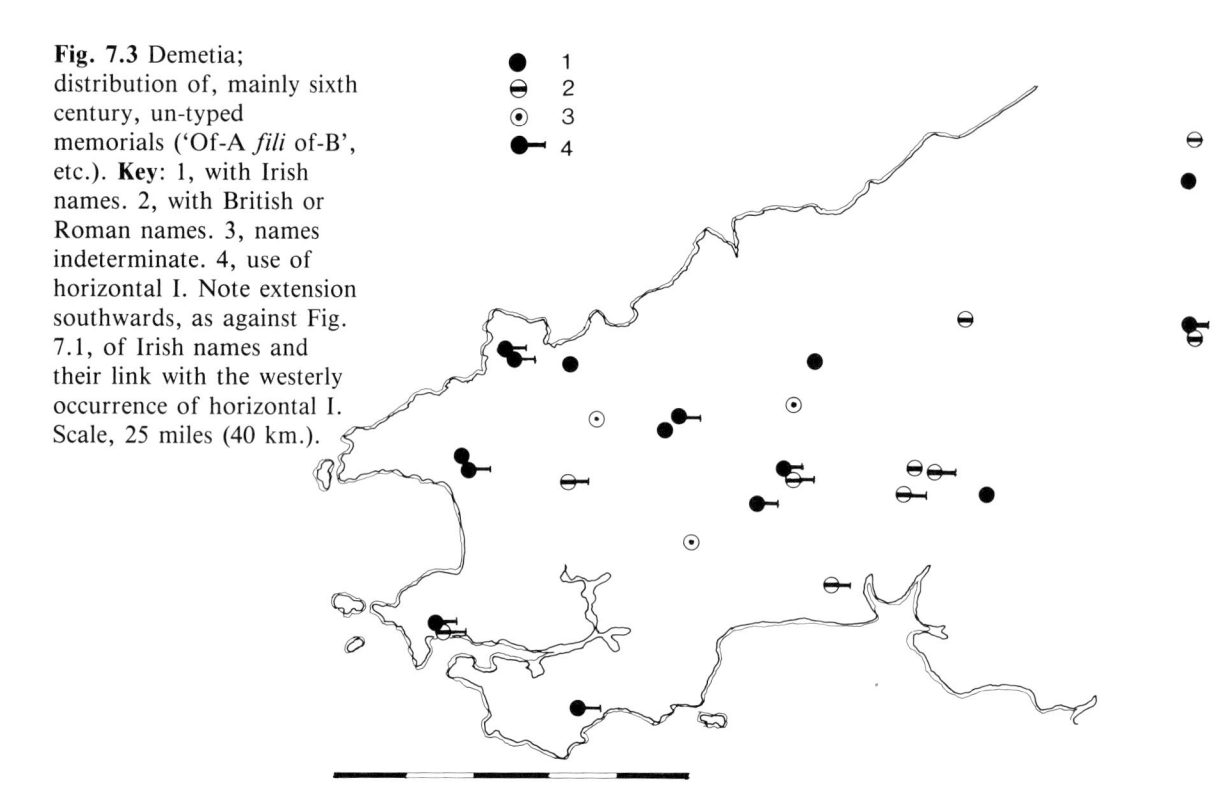

**Fig. 7.3** Demetia; distribution of, mainly sixth century, un-typed memorials ('Of-A *fili* of-B', etc.). **Key**: 1, with Irish names. 2, with British or Roman names. 3, names indeterminate. 4, use of horizontal I. Note extension southwards, as against Fig. 7.1, of Irish names and their link with the westerly occurrence of horizontal I. Scale, 25 miles (40 km.).

inferences and are markedly Christian; they are sixth and seventh century, and will be noticed separately later.[15]

Our third map (Fig. 7.3) amplifies the picture. It shows the distribution of a further twenty-seven memorials categorized as un-typed. In these the norm is a vertical inscription of two or three lines, in the form 'Of-A (*relationship*) of-B' but with almost all the possible permutations in the range 'A, *or* of-A / FILI *or* FILIVS / B, *or* of-B'. Five show individual names alone.[16] In the remaining twenty-two, the personal names exhibit (where identifiable in this light, as most of them are) a mixture of differences; there are a few continuing-Roman names, some that are Irish (*Quenuendani, Corbagni, Maquerigi, Ercagni, Curcagni, Macutreni, Macudeceti*) and some just as obviously native Demetian or British (*Mavoheni, Totavali, Lovernaci, Regini, Cuniovende*). These are distinguished in Fig. 7.3, which suggests that in the sixth century there were more people using Déisi-derived Irish names in north-west and west Pembroke than there were eastward into Carmarthenshire. Such a pattern could be expected, if it reflects a gradual, southerly, spread of descendants of the Déisi settlers.

Simply as they stand, the inscriptions on the un-typed memorials reveal how, after the fifth century, the use of (and awareness of) conventional or correct grammar breaks down. The same could be said of those in Dumnonia, and the same brief analysis will serve for both areas. Jackson pointed out that a message like (352a) DOMNICI IACIT FILIVS BRAVECCI – literally, 'Of-Domnicus, he lies, son of-Braveccus' (and therefore, literally, nonsense) represents something where the words 'body of' and 'he was' have to be understood.[17] *(Corpus) Domnici iacit; filius Bravecci (fuit)* 'The body of Domnicus lies here; he was a son of Braveccus' would be grammatical and correct. But the sheer variety of departures from such an ideal suggests that far less attention was paid to this than to the public display of names, arranged in formulaic guises regarded as customary, as appropriate to heads-of-families of a certain standing, and as making little if any concession to what – in the fourth century – might have been taught in Britannia's urban schools by Latin grammarians. A long way behind the sixth-century un-typed memorials lay the formula introduced from late fourth-century Ireland, 'Of-A, of-the-son, of-B' where (in Irish settings) it is true that a missing word 'stone' or 'monument' might have been implied. It was suggested (p. 36) that if the genesis of the ogam-inscribed memorial lay in imitation of Roman practice there are explanations for this formula. On a Roman tombstone, following D(IS) M(ANIBVS), itself an invocation 'to the shades of the departed', the name may be in the genitive meaning 'and to the spirit OF Aelius Martius' or dative as a further invocation 'and TO Aelius Martius', allowing, within Christianity, a fourth–fifth century word like *memoria* (of Aelius Martius) to be supplied mentally by readers and onlookers.[18] South Welsh examples from Caerleon of tombstones citing names in the genitive could be (*RIB* no.359) *D M Gai Iuli Decumini veterani Legionis II Augustae*, and (*RIB* no.374) *D M Iulie Senice uicsit annos LX*, respectively for an old soldier and a lady. The Demetian memorials are not directly derived from these but, ultimately, their inscriptional format may go back to the same origin.

What inferences can be extracted from Figures 7.2 and 7.3 together? In the first place they depict aspects of Demetia in the sixth century, and are witness to a society of (?) five to ten thousand folk who, four to six generations after Eochaid, were 'integrated' and spoke Late British or Neo-Brittonic, with a few people knowing a little Irish and rather more some Latin. Retention of old personal names in families was nothing exceptional, but need bear no relation to ethnic or linguistic origin.[19] An anthropologist might note that, among forty-two memorials, only four mention females – 349 *Velvoria* (filia) and 356 *Potentina* (mulier), both nom., and 451 *Tuncetace* (uxsor) with 454 *Cuniovende* (mater), both gen. – and that three names are British, with Potentina a Roman one. Several memorials show linguistic mixture; Tuncetaca as wife of Daar (British/Irish?), TALOR⤑ ADVENT⤑ (361 as son of MAQVERIG⤑ (part-Roman/Irish), 376 Vennisetli as son of Ercagn(as) (probably British/Irish[18]), 429 Solinus son of Vendon(us)<*Wendagnas* (Roman/Irish), and 455 Camulorigi son of Fannuc (British/Irish).[20]

Secondly, while type (d) stones are demonstrably Christian in sentiment, most or all of the un-typed ones may also be. Absence of HIC IACIT would not, after *c*.500, of itself make them non-Christian. A quick trot around any churchyard or municipal cemetery today will show gravestones omitting any words that are specifically Christian, as opposed to being mere commemorative formulae. Conservative fashion may be one explanation – Of-A, of-the-son of-B was considered enough, Christian character being implicit in the site of burial. It may be trite to point out what every serious student of inscriptions, Roman, Insular and medieval, has always agreed; that, however these memorials were costed, the combined efforts of *scriptor* and *lapidarius* using either ogam or Roman lettering are virtually certain to have been charged for totals of strokes, notches and letters.[21] Allied to this is a third observation concerning the epigraphy of un-typed memorials in particular. If (as it were) we stop the tape running, if we freeze-frame the sequence at the year 500, the Demetian memorials afford a unique opportunity to see a funerary fashion dominated by precedent, and resistance to any real change. This is relevant to later chapters because it demonstrates the package that was taken by families and individuals and reproduced in Dumnonia *as it was at this stage* – a single type (a), a few types (b) and (c) still, type (d) as an indicator of recently adopted Christianity, and then the un-typed forms. Epigraphically the vertical disposition was the norm; there are very few, and doubtful, attempts at horizontal lines (361?, 440, 436??). Use of the sideways final (rather than medial) I, as ⊢, is seen on four type (d) memorials, all with Irish names; as it is also on eighteen of the un-typed ones, regardless of name-forms, and with a generally southern emphasis (as if the fashion was something long-established, spreading as the use of memorials themselves spread southwards). Conservatism, as Jackson constantly emphasized throughout *LHEB*, was linguistically endemic, as the persistence of generalized Vulgar Latin case-endings (-*i*, -*us*, -*e*, -*a*) and others that supposedly represented British (-*i*, -*a*) and Irish (-*o*, -*as*, gens.) proves. Nobody used these in sixth-century converse any longer. Nobody read aloud, from stones, medial -T- and -C- as if they were /t/ and /k/ either. In fourth-century Britannia, for both spoken Latin and British, they had represented /d/ and /g/, so that 'Tacitus' was /tagidus/ but had to be written TACITUS; and by now these letters occasionally had to stand for the lenited sounds /ð/ and /ʒ/. About the only epigraphic innovation of note, brought in from Christian Gaul, the Atlantic side of France, in (?) VI.1 was a little sub-fashion for angular or angle-bar A, no doubt thought very smart; this, too, spread around in a minor way. There are no occurrences of it on any types (b) or (c) stones, which would generally have been too early; two on type (d) and five on un-typed memorials, suggest that use of angle-bar A was again diffused originally in south-west Demetia. This also was taken south across the Severn Sea to Dumnonia (see Fig. 15.6).

Statements that innovations like angle-bar A, the words MEMORIA and NOMENA used or misused on Christian messages, and even the type (d) HIC IACIT formula, were 'brought from Christian Gaul' – the nearest part of the Continent where all these were current by V.3 in epitaphs – are not mere deductions. The Gaulish connection is considered more fully in chapter 12, but for southern Demetia we may rely upon hard archaeological evidence. Four sites have now yielded material dated to the late fifth, sixth and seventh centuries, in the shape of pottery and glass, that was exotic, imported, provenanced, and formed part of a larger traffic in these items; between post-Roman Atlantic Britain (with much of Ireland), and not only Atlantic Gaul but the eastern Mediterranean and North Africa.

The locations are Caldey Island and, intervisible form it on a high outcrop spur in the coastal flats west of Laugharne, Coygan Camp (excavated in 1963–5 by Dr Geoffrey Wainwright);[22] Longbury Bank, cave-fissures in a limestone ridge in the Ritec estuary just NNW of Penally and a mile west from Tenby, a place where material from a vanished surface site has collapsed into fissures and holes below;[23] and now, from current excavations, an extensive defended site on a low spur in the river Carew's creek, below the medieval Carew Castle.[24] Two separate groups of imports, only a few finds in each, are involved – separate as to source, and as to date. Mediterranean items include Phocaean Red Slip bowls, form 3 (source: modern Turkey), from Caldey, Coygan Camp and Longbury Bank, represented by odd sherds; amphorae of B.i (probably Aegean) from Coygan and Longbury; and of B.iv (Sardis, Turkey) from Longbury. The likelihood is that these do not represent continuous importation but refer to one or two landings in the early sixth century. From northern or Atlantic France, there is a fragment of Class D ware from Longbury; pieces of Class E pottery from Carew (two vessels at least), Caldey (one), Longbury (two) and an isolated rim sherd from Brownslade Burrows, west of Castlemartin and about two miles south of Rhoscrowther.[25] Tiny pieces of Merovingian(?) glass were found at Longbury. This Gaulish material is more likely to be seventh century than in the sixth.[26] Class D ware may however be pre-600.

If this is set out on a simplified map, showing also the incidence on type (d) and un-typed inscriptions of angle-bar A and the use of 358 MEMORIA and 448 NOMENA, one can include those inscriptions in which HIC IACIT – closer to a Gaulish model than either IACIT or IC IACIT – also features. To this might be added the little that can be guessed as to the whereabouts of Demetian centres of power in the sixth and seventh centuries; the place at Castell Dwyran where the memorial of Guotepir was discovered, the putative defended spur below Carew Castle, and in all probability the coastal fortress described in the ninth-century poem *Etmic Dinbych* 'The praise of Tenby', so brilliantly dissected by Sir Ifor Williams.[27] That this *caer... yn yr eglan* 'fortress on the promontory' is represented by the headland site of the Norman castle at Tenby seems unquestionable. A fourth place meriting inclusion, despite the lateness of the record, must be somewhere mentioned in a Llandaff charter as *liscastell* (p. 82), described as a seat where Aircol Lauhir was gathered with his court, *curiam suam,* and as *caput totius demeteci regionis* 'the chief place of all Demetia'; on no very clear authority it is placed at Lydstep, some five miles WSW from Tenby by the coastline.[28]

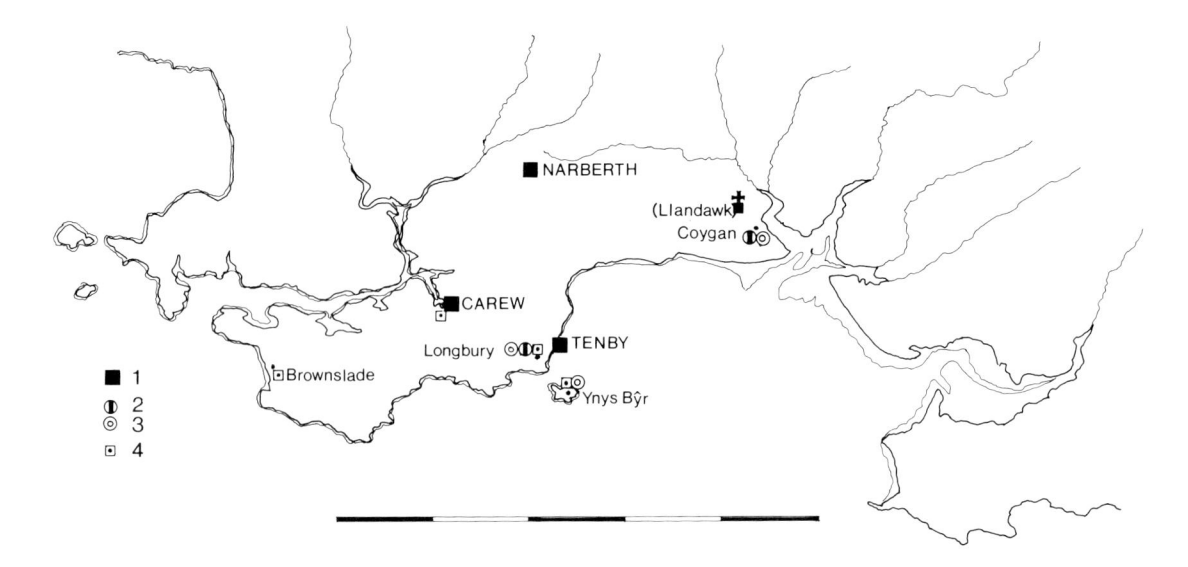

**Fig. 7.4** Southern Demetia; Continental imports (pottery and glass) of the sixth – seventh centuries. **Key**: 1, relevant secular locations. 2, Mediterranean amphorae ('Class B'). 3, Mediterranean red-slip wares ('Class A'). 4, Gaulish pottery (Classes D and E) and Merovingian(?) glass. Scale, 25 miles (40 km.).

The outcome (Fig. 7.4), perhaps to be pictured as relating to the period 500 × 650, suggests that the balance of power in Demetia had moved southward, that the wide bay from Tenby to the Tywi estuary was accessible to trading vessels with interesting passengers – indeed, we know it was, from the Life of St Samson[29] – and that imports of *matériel* were matched by invisible ones, rendered manifest when cut epigraphically. If a single memorial can be found to illustrate much of this, it would be the type (d) pillar, 368, from the churchyard at Llandawke now housed in the church. It began as the recipient of the type (a) ogam *MAQI (M(ucoi?) DUMELEDONAS*, well back in the fifth century. A family that need not have been related then appropriated the memorial, a tall thin rectangular-section slab. The *scriptor* probably set out a three-line model:

    BARRIVEND ⊢
    FILIVS VENDVBARI
       HIC IACIT

employing horizontal ⊢ for the first name, angle-bar A twice, and HIC IACIT – a full epigraphic display. The *lapidarius* started on a broad face, between the ogam notches down each angle; managed to copy Roman capitals, but not all at the same height and, making an error common among illiterates by cutting S backwards or inverted, he ran out of space, and had to put a smaller HIC IACIT on one narrow side. It is also possible that the model had VENDVBARRI (two R's). Father and son

**(Left) Fig. 7.5** Demetia; model for diffusion of two end fifth or early sixth century epigraphic fashions, HIC IACIT and angle-bar A (involving perhaps Christian centres at Penally and Ynys Bŷr, 'P' and 'Y'). **Key:** 1, type (d) memorials with HIC IACIT. 2, type (d) and untyped, with angle-bar A. 3, HIC IACIT and angle-bar A together, 368 Llandawke. 4, all other type (d) and un-typed – N, 448 *Rinaci nomena*, M, 358 *Memoria Voteporigis*. 5, Continental imports (see Fig. 7.4). Scale, 25 miles (40 km.).

**(Right:) Fig. 7.6** Memorial now in Llandawke church, 368; type (d), BARRIVENDI/FILIVS VENDVBARI/HIC IACIT (*CIIC* drawing, corrected from photographs), re-using an unconnected and older type (a) ogam-only memorial. Note the clear angle-bar A's.

share name-elements. Both names mean 'fair-haired' and, on balance, can be seen as Irish rather than British.[30] Llandawke churchyard is a mile and a bit north of Coygan Camp. BARRIVENDI was laid to rest in late VI.1 – say, 510 x 530, after angle-bar A and HIC IACIT were established conventions, but not much after that – and he may have been the part-time reoccupant of the Coygan fortlet (useful perch to command so much coastal-flat grazing) and recipient of the odd imported gift from a greater lord not long before his death. His memorial (Fig. 7.6) was erected either by his inland home; or in the first (or the chief) Christian burial-ground in the vicinity.

In this sixth-century Demetian landscape, so rich in its Early Christian memorials, where are all the *ecclesiarum signa*, the signs of churches on all sides, with which the chapter opened? There is no church building, no small stone-walled rectangular affair with an eastern-end altar and little slit windows, surviving from so early a period; nor in Dumnonia, either, would we find any such structures conceivably older than the eighth century. The pattern is one of *sites* – enclosed cemeteries, foci for worship involving buildings that may have been impermanent and of wood; or larger agglomerations of huts and cells, to be called 'monasteries' mainly because of who lived there and what went on in such places. Nevertheless we can turn to the three extended, narrative, Latin inscriptions indicated in Fig. 7.2 as a foretaste. Two refer to sites rather than to people. In the church at Llanddewibrefi, the broken slab or pillar (350) reads (or once read; the inscription is recorded, *ECMW* no.116) HIC IACET IDNERT FILIVS IA(... / QVI OCCISVS (F)VIT PROPTER PR(AEDIVM/ ... / SANCTI 'here lies Idnert, son of Ia ..., who was slain *propter praedium* of the holy ...'. The Latin words are *praedium* 'estate, private land', and *propter*; either 'near, hard by' or else 'for the sake of, on account of'. The inscription is sixth century (VI.2 or VI.3) and it is irresolute whether a Christian, violently killed, would be more likely to have been noticed through the *place* of his demise, or given such a memorial because he died 'for the sake of'; defending church property. In either event the *praedium* stands; a *sanctus* owned real property in God's name and a Christian was buried, either nearby, or (if the property consisted of a bounded, consecrated cemetery with structures attached) within it.

The second stone is later (seventh century, probably after 650) and inscribed in book-hand, rounded half-uncial letters, but it records the stage before the full ownership of a *praedium*; its initial gift. It stands at Llanllyr, near what must have been the north-eastern limit of Demetia, and reads (*ECMW*, no.124) *tesquitus Ditoc / Madomnuac O/ccon filius Asa/itgen dedit* 'The little piece of waste-land of Ditoc, that Occon son of Asaitgen gave to Madomnuac'. There is an encircled cross above the four vertical lines of lettering and a second such cross, with stem, on the side of this five-foot pillar. The gift was a Christian one, to a holy \*'Mo-domnōc, use for a burial-ground being the obvious explanation, and three of the names are Irish.[31] Unusual is the fact that Occon felt the need to commemorate his benefaction so publicly on stone, like an Alderman Bloggs giving the Old Tanyard to his Fellow-Citizens as a Playground in Perpetuity.

An inference that other such gifts of plots were being made can be found, not in cut lettering, but in place-names. In the Life of St David (*VD*), the youthful David is sent to Paulinus, saintly head of a monastic school somewhere in south (south-west?) Wales, *in insula Wincdilantquendi*.[32] The grotesque-seeming name, another one exhumed by Rhigyfarch from scraps of manuscript (*in vetustissimis patrie scriptis*, 'the oldest bits of writing in the country'), can be split into 'Wincdi', a descriptive noun-phrase rather than a true place-name, and 'Lantquendi'. *Pace* Dr J. W. James as editor, *insula* can imply 'an isolated place' rather than an actual island (in water). Lantquendi, if read aright from what may have been written down before 600, is *lant-* ( = \**land* > *lann*) 'enclosure with monastic establishment, monastery' as well as 'enclosed cemetery', followed by a personal name (gen.). Compounds of this shape are discussed further in the setting of Dumnonia (chap. 18); they cover two categories at least. In one, a holy man or monastic founder is indicated, possibly before his death, usually afterwards; the *lann* of Paulinus would become known as 'Llanbeulin'. In another, the name marks either a forgotten predecessor-cleric or, probably, a lay donor and former Christian proprietor (like Occon giving Ditoc's *tesquitus* to Saint Madomunac). In \**Land-quendi*, where the personal name is an Irish one,[33] this may be what is implied; a late fifth or early sixth century benefactor. In fact, this may be the older name of Llanddeusant, south-east from Llandovery, Paulinus's rather lonely little hillside monastery and church.[34] An archaic Demetian place-name, preserved in a Demetian Life, supports the testimony of a Demetian narrative inscription (*ECMW* 124). Christian descendants of the Déisi settlers, still using Irish names and now part of a land-owning caste, were giving parcels — if sometimes only a *tesquitus* or a mountain-side — for burial-grounds and churches.

It was previously suggested that, in Demetia, a horizon of Latinity may have been reached both earlier than, and separately from, a horizon of Christianity. The latter concept was however mentioned without further explanation. Such expressions as 'conversion to the Faith' and 'the advent of Christianity' sound well, but are necessarily vague; what are they likely to have meant in this particular context? Where and how should this second horizon be placed within the reconstructed outline of Demetia's history, AD 400 to 600? There is the risk of a circular argument if one leans too hard upon the typological sequence of the Demetian inscriptions. A cautious model (finding support in (e.g.) what Bede's *Historia* tells us, often in great detail, about the conversion of various English kingdoms) might interpret *conversion* or *advent* as a band of time, at the start of which Christianity is introduced by 'missionaries' successfully influencing kings; and at the end of which, Christian ideas having percolated outwards and socially downwards from an initial royal acceptance, a given kingdom or *regio* exhibits Christianity as its dominant faith, something reflected in archaeology, art and epigraphy as well as through direct historical testimony. In Demetia the starting-point may have fallen during the lives of king Aircol and Samson's parents Amon and Anna — say, in late V.2 or early V.3. This does not imply, immediately, a detectable and specific Christian archaeology (Aircol's own grave, *bed airgwl in dyuet*, p. 81, may have been out in the countryside, not in a consecrated cemetery). Nor — and clearly not until the deaths of the first converts — will there have been an immediate reflection in epigraphy. While some of the types (b) and (c) memorials could theoretically pertain to Christians, it is only with the type (d) and un-typed memorials, few of which can safely be regarded as older than the end of V, that we observe plainly Christian epitaphs; memorials for *nobiliores*, the holders of land, and presumably including people who gave plots to the Church and supported peripatetic priests. If these stones denote the end of an 'advent' phase, an end centred perhaps on 480 to 500, it is a phase that happens to coincide with the first hints of detectably Christian establishments. We may envisage the appearance of small communities, whose religious influence may have taken a number of forms; early manifestations of 'outreach', as such influence can be so unhappily described nowadays. Nothing of this was peculiar to Demetia. The probability is that it mirrored what had been taking place during the fifth century in south-east Wales. Education, by religious communities or the first monasteries, of royal and of well-born children – *Dewi Sant* and Samson were typical pupils – produced the next few generations of *sancti*, saints, and since the Latin language was the vehicle for Christianity this education naturally exploited any earlier horizons of Latinity. (Naturally, too, it facilitated the subsequent attainment of a *third* horizon, historicity; systematic records of a regional or national past, in narrative or annalistic format, and in written Latin.) Next, Christianity led to tangible outcomes; the dotting of the (Demetian) landscape with *primary Christian sites*. The most readily detected now are curvilinear cemetery-enclosures, for which the word *lann* (<\**landa*) was adopted as a label; places that could serve as preaching stations and eventually the surrounds for small churches. This is why nomenclature, extension of *lann-* with proper names, involves names of saintly heads of communities, notable priests linked to specific spots, or lay donors (and, rather less often, geographical or locative terms, like Lanivet in Cornwall: p. 252). Thirdly, Christian influence can be seen in epigraphy. The abandonment of ogam, the use of *hic iacit, memoria* etc., and even the prestige of new letter-forms, mark decisions by *scriptores* or *ordinatores* – not the decisions of the native mason with his mallet and simple iron tools. By the end of the fifth century such *scriptores* must have been, in the main, priests.

'Historicity', just mentioned, the third significant horizon, can been seen here, as it can be in Wales generally and in Dumnonia, as an outcome of a combination of Latinity, Christianity and an uncertain weight of external stimuli. Regional or national rather than individual in emphasis – the Lives of saints, as proto-biographical ventures, seem to mark a secondary development – historicity belongs to a stage at which persons thought it *desirable* (it may, slightly earlier, have been *possible*, another matter altogether) to construct narrative statements about the past, distant or recent; and to do so of course mostly from corporate memories, orally-transmitted ideas. In any nation's story this must be a tremendously important step.[35] We are not concerned with historical truth, or with complex motives (claims about descent, claims to territory, restatement of origin-myths), or with the linked endeavour of *annals* and *chronicles* (registers of happenings, in correct order, liable to be re-worked backwards from the most recent of successive entries) that takes us into a further area of *computistics* (how absolute dates, consular, Incarnation or from any other cycle, were calculated and affixed to annalistic items).

Not much more on this can be said in respect of Demetia, save to voice the suspicion that since the horizon of historicity was apparently reached in the smaller kingdom of Brycheiniog by VI.3 (see chap.9) there seems no sound reason to deny it to sixth-century Demetia, even if nothing relevant has survived; if so, David's monastery at or near modern St David's, Mynyw or *Menevia*, is a likely centre. Precisely in what form early narrative records were made and preserved has to remain a matter of speculation. Unfortunately, too, romantics among us must abandon the notion that they were written at this early stage in anything but Latin (on papyrus or vellum or parchment, using various book-hands). The native tongue, Late British or Primitive Welsh, would have been confined to the reproduction of proper names and names of places. But this is why, from the Life of St David, a postulated sixth-century Menevian **uinndilantquendi* could be so fascinating. As well as providing what must be the oldest-known occurrence of *lant*[36] — a form preceding the *lann* of the Brychan Documents (p. 137) — Rhigyfarch may have dredged up, with his *vetustissima scripta*, a fragment of the very attainment-moment of a lost Demetian historicity.

No comparable analysis of these three horizons is possible, as this book's closing chapters will show, for Dumnonia. In that other and larger Atlantic peninsula, stretching from *Isca Dumnoniorum* to the Land's End nearly thrice the distance from *Moridunum* to St David's, neither Latinity nor Christianity took real root in what is now Cornwall, at least, before the early sixth century; and they did so then principally because both were introduced by settlers from Wales. Dumnonian historicity is nowhere apparent. Until the later ninth, or the tenth, century (by which time the independent British kingdom of Dumnonia was effectively finished), none of the few early monasteries can be regarded as a suitable or probable centre. The monastery of St Petroc at Bodmin is the only candidate, but not before its tenth-century prominence. The Dumnonian failure to attain indigenous historicity can probably be attributed to the absence of appropriate Christian seats of literacy; one reason for their absence might be described as historico-geographical. East of Demetia, and in touch overland and by sea, were major centres of learning like Llanilltud Fawr, rooted in the sub-Roman fifth century as potential foci for the dissemination of culture. East of Dumnonia, on the other hand, lay only a scattering of, at a guess, small fifth-century 'kingdoms' that arose and fell leaving few traces; that, west of the Cotswolds and Dorset, retained almost nothing of fourth-century Romano-British Christianity; and that, constituting as they did about a quarter of England south of the Trent, may have been cut off from south-east Wales when the Anglo-Saxon drive westwards culminated in 577 with the victory at *Deorham*, Dyrham.[37] In the Severn-basin region, over into (old) Monmouth ('Gwent') as on the eastern side, there had been a sub-Roman, Latinate and Christian world;[38] within which the eponymous 'Glywys' of Glywysing (p. 78) may really have hailed from Roman Gloucester, a *glevensis* from *Glevum* proper. After Dyrham, we can only guess in how great a degree south Wales and the whole long stretch of south-west Britain went their divergent cultural ways.

The third extended inscription located in Fig. 7.2, found near Cynwyl Gaeo (361: *ECMW* no.360), again illustrates many of these points. Now broken, defective and preserved at Carmarthen Museum it was once a thin (*c.* 7 in.) natural slab measuring about 3 ft. by 3 ft. as an off-square or rhomboid. The fact that the five horizontal lines of lettering occupy the *lower* half shows that, improbable as an upright, it may have roofed one-half of a large cist grave; and have been thus legible from above, at ground level, Continental (and Roman) fashion. It is entirely in capitals. Omitting ligatures and supplying present gaps from older records, it reads: SERVATVR FIDAEI / PATRIEQ(ue) SEMPER / AMATOR HIC PAVLIN/VS IACIT CVLTOR PIENTI/SIMVS AEQVI − 'A guardian of the Faith, of his homeland always a lover, here Paulinus lies; most conscientious observer of all that is right'. Application of scansion allows this to be verse; two hexameter lines (break after *Amator*). The wording and short phrases stand close to those in the Continental corpus of inscriptions, some taken over from Classical poetry.[39] A date in late VI.1/early VI.2 − say 520 × 540 − is likely.

The temptation to assign this epitaph to the 'Paulinus' who figures as an older contemporary of David in *VD* has to be resisted. *Paulinus*, or alternatively *Paulus*, was not uncommon as a Christian name, Welsh inscriptions to the fore.[40] The saintly Paulinus of *VD*, if also of Llanddeusant (= *Lantquendi*?) died and was buried at St Pol de Leon according to Wrmonoc, unless (as is quite possible) Wrmonoc's Life conflated a Welsh Paulinus with another who genuinely travelled. *This* 'Paulinus' of the inscription may however have been a prominent and noble layman, buried not at a church but on his own estate. The slab came from a field at Maes Llanwrthwl, several miles south-south-east of Cynwyl Gaeo, or Caio. Allowing slightly for hyperbole from family and retainers, this lengthy and impressive memorial must point to a good man, a local champion who was also a Christian − it is not impossible that his contemporary estate can still be traced.[41]

Here in eastern Demetia we see Latinity, Christianity, external models and internal literacy mingled; unless the slab, found centuries ago, belonged to a private *lann* relating to the farm-name Maes *Llan*wrthwl we could expect most such subsequent memorials to be found in churchyards. The *scriptor* is likely to have come from an established house not too far off; Llandeilo, ten miles south down the Dulais valley, or Llanddewibrefi twelve miles north across the hills, or even Llanddeusant ten miles south-east. But this serves to introduce a final topic;

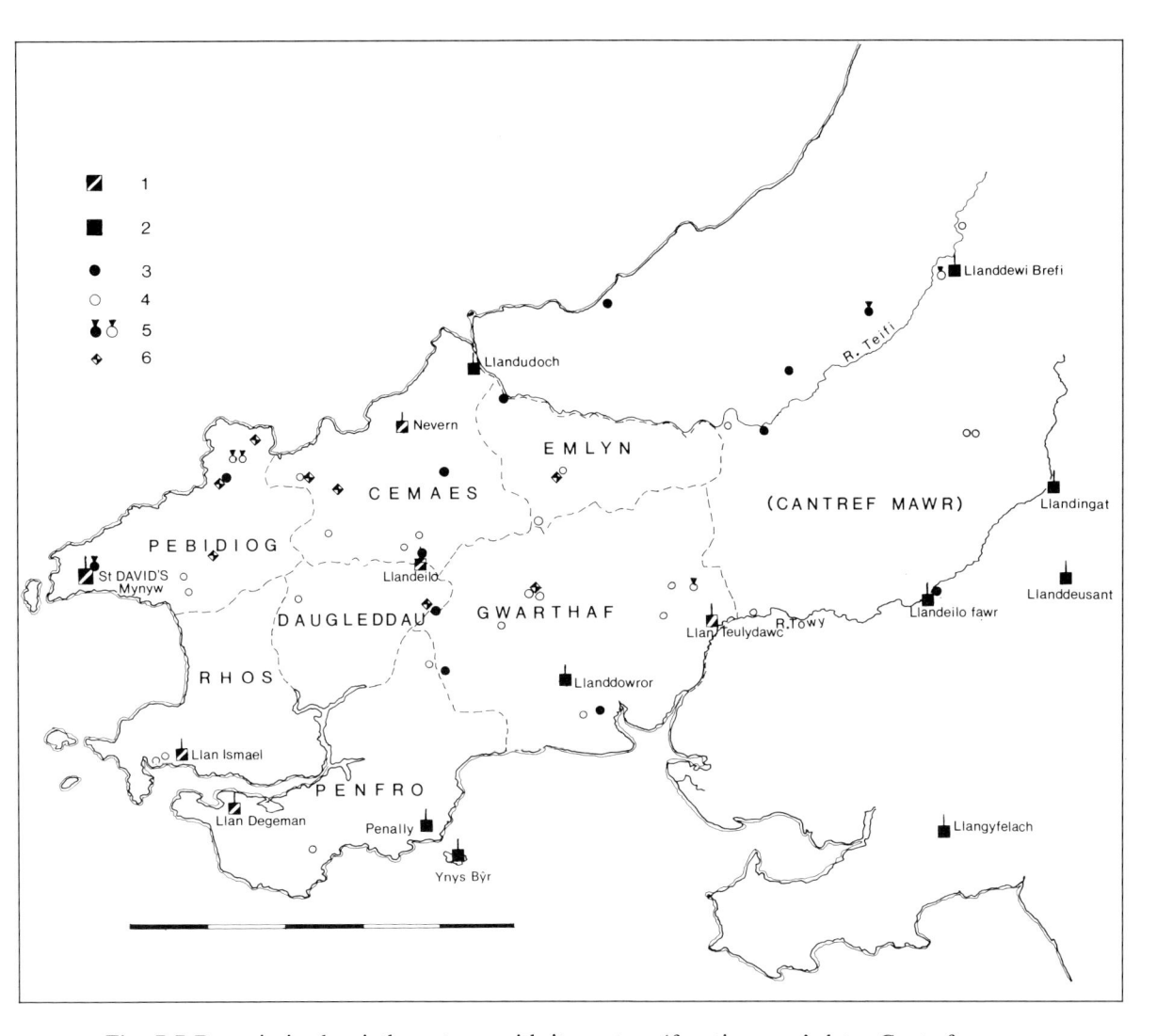

**Fig. 7.7** Demetia in the sixth century, with its eastern 'frontier zone', later Cantref Mawr; selective indications of Christianity. **Key**: 1, the ancient 'bishop-house' churches (Charles-Edwards 1971) with the seven early Demetian cantrefs. 2, other putatively early churches. 3, Type (d), certainly Christian, with un-typed, possibly Christian, memorials (4). 5, single-name memorials (for clerics?). 6, early church sites suggested by Lewis (chap. 7, note 51) from *ECMW* Group I or Group II stones.

where *were* all these churches? And it must at once be confessed that the time is not ripe for a proper answer; years of arduous investigation await us. A medium has to be found, between one map showing all the churches and chapels – hundreds of them – with any claim to antiquity, and another with about five or six dots on it. The final map here, Fig. 7.7, is selective and can be regarded as no more than a general indication, its oldest sites being perhaps from *c.*500, of the more important places named in Demetian contexts.

Materials towards an investigation present themselves in a number of ways, each complementing the others. From literary sources – hagiographical, and thus mostly post-700 and retrospective – it can be assumed that by VI.1 and VI.2 monastic churches existed at St David's (*Rosina vallis, Hodnant*; not originally either *Mynyw* or *Menevia*, though these can be used[42]), Penally (*Penn-allun*, modern Welsh *Penalun*), Caldey Island (*Ynys Bŷr*[43]) and, in eastern Demetia, Llandeilo Fawr, Llanddewibrefi[44] and Llanddeusant. Just as significant are the 'Seven Bishop-Houses of Dyfed',[45] ancient and superior churches whose placing seems to relate to territorial divisions. (The full history of the older, sub-county units in Wales – the cantref and its sub-unit the commote – is complex enough as a subject on its own.[46] For the original Demetia between Teifi and Tywi, modern Pembroke contains, along the north, west–east, 1 Pebidiog, 2 Cemais and 3 (part of) Emlyn; south-west of these, a once-double cantref of 4 Rhos and 5 Daugleddau, with 6 Penfro south of them. Modern Carmarthen is larger, with the east part of Emlyn; 7 Cantref *Gwarthaf* ('upper') below that; and its eastern half having, north to south, Cantref *Mawr* ('great'), Cantref *Bychan* ('small') and Cydweli, 'Kidwelly'.) The numbered cantrefs are those once holding bishop-houses or episcopal churches, headed by 1 *Mynyw*. In so far as they can be located, others are, 2 (or 3) *Llan Geneu*;[47] 4 *Llan Ismael*, St Ishmaels'; 5 *Llan Teilaw*, the almost-forgotten little church of Llandilo or Llandeilo Llwydarth, near Maenclochog on the southern slopes of Preseli; 6 *Llan Degeman*, now Rhoscrowther; and 7 *Llan Teulydawc, Llandeulyddog*, Old Carmarthen.

Archaeologically, very early sites might be fixed where names in *Llan-* correspond to churchyards of suitably curvilinear and archaic nature in which significant memorials appear to have been located; others, detectable at ground level, often reveal much more when seen from the air.[48] Certain church sites are patently of interest even when little or no documentation survives. Meidrim, some few miles west from Carmarthen on the original (?) road westward, occupies an inland spur- or promontory-fortlet[49] and is named as a staging-post in the oldest narrative element of *DSB* and *CB* (p. 149). One can also draw attention, in the area of inscribed memorials, to a few places exhibiting monuments (types (b), (d) and untyped) with single names, some of them almost certainly of sixth-century priests. At Nevern, 445 VITALIANI EMERETO / VITALIANI, the man who had 'earned his reward', is the best-known. Two at St Nicholas in north-west Pembroke, said to come from a nearby Llandridian, are 452 PAAN⊢ and 453 MEL⊢.[50] For two others, 374 CVNEGN⊢ and 355 SILBANDVS IACIT, we may have eponyms of churches; Llangynin (*lann, \*Cunin*) and Silian respectively. And, though this is another topic not explored at length, we must recognize the incidence within Nash-Williams's *ECMW* Group II of a great many stones, slabs or pillars, uninscribed but displaying primary incised crosses: linear, encircled as on 358 VOTEPORIGIS, and with expanded or ornate arm-ends ( = terminals). This feature, commencing not before VI.2, has to be seen as yet another importation from Ireland. It is in contrast to the 'art' of the sixth and seventh century memorials of Dumnonia, where the far fewer instances (p. 295; Fig. 17.17) derive separately from the Gaulish *chi-rho* motif, in Wales found only on the small group of memorials in the north-west. Obstacles in linking crosses with, say, un-typed inscriptions of the mid-sixth to mid-seventh century is that it is hardly ever possible to be certain that crosses are not secondary; pious additions by descendants, for instance. In an important paper John Lewis has shown the strong probability that many now-small church sites can be regarded as foundations of the early period simply because of the incidence of un-unscribed cross slabs.[51]

The absence of any specific pattern in Fig. 7.7, which (as pointed out) is a location map rather than a true distributional presentation, may hint that – during VI and VII – Christianity as revealed by churches, cemeteries and monasteries was uniformly present; as one might suppose on other grounds. For the time being we see such places as just some of the *ecclesiarum signa* making up the outward and visible signs of a Christian kingdom.

In Western Scotland (Dál Riata) and the Isle of Man, the Irish settlers introduced their language permanently and at the expense of indigenous ones; whence Scottish Gaelic and Manx. What was different in Demetia? Were relative numbers of incomers and natives so disparate? Allowing for current debates on the precise datings of sound-changes, in V.3 and VI.1 the spoken forerunners of Irish and Welsh differed in degree – in sound, more than in vocabulary – and not radically, as English and French. To hit the 'head of the son' of a chieftain, a hapless mistake, would be *penn maip* if one was British, *cenn maic* for an Irish miscreant. Yet, the retention of non-British personal names aside, British triumphed and went on to become Old, Middle and Modern Welsh. The answer may be a matter of which side of an extremely delicate balance finally tips down and stays down. Dr James Mallory, facing the problem of how a proto-Celtic language established itself in prehistoric Ireland, adduces Fredrik Barth's study of sociolinguistic contact in the old North-West Frontier Province of India, where Pathans and Baluchs are intermingled.[52] One can quote Mallory's summary: 'The successful language was that spoken by those (the Baluchs) who were poorer, less well-equipped, and with less of a military reputation than their richer neighbours (the Pathans). The success of what might appear to an archaeologist as the weaker party ... was attributed to their social structure which more easily incorporated and assimilated displaced people in an unstable border situation.' *Mutatis mutandis*, something of this is applicable to the Déisi, who carved out estates, spread across Demetia and provided early kings (but lost out, linguistically); and to the Demetians who within two centuries assimilated them entirely. Finally, if anyone wonders what has happened to the Demetians, children of two Islands, the answer is: Nothing. They are still there – far more so than the western

Dumnonians, where the Cornish as miners, inventors and entrepreneurs, spread out across the British Empire during the last 150 years, leaving gaps to be filled by the English. Writing recently,[53] Francis Jones produced the remarkable figures that from 1530 to 1603 the High Sheriffs for Pembroke and Carmarthen (annual offices), in all 122 people, included only thirty-four of non-Welsh origin; among the Welsh, twenty-five claimed descent from the ancient princes of Dyfed, and a further fifty-eight from early chieftains, survivors of the class of *nobiliores*. In 1964, the Lords Lieutenant of the two counties were both descendants in the male line from the eleventh-century Cadifor Fawr. Outside the handful of pocket duchies in western Europe there can be few such demonstrations of continuity; here, from a *regio* that took shape when the Emperor Justinian I was ruling at Byzantium.

## References

1. James 1967; notes, text and variants, translation (but, alas, no index).
2. So much rubbish has been written about PROTICTORIS that this author will refrain from adding to the heap; for an antidote, see Jackson, *ECNE*, 208. We cannot have any idea why his commemorators chose this, surely unmerited, 'obscure, but nonetheless well-established, Roman rank or commission'. Jackson's curt belief that they simply wanted him to look very Roman and very important can well serve as a dismissive explanation.
3. See p. 150; this is a remarkably early direct reference to an Insular case of *nomina in sacris diptycis scripta*.
4. The implication (*Vita Samsonis*, chap.1) is that both parents were from families that could act as *altrices* 'foster-families' to youths from elective royal kin-groups; in the chronology proposed here, Amon may have been an older 'brother' to the young Aircol, not of Aircol's natural father's generation.
5. The fullest treatment of the setting, with maps, is Professor E. G. Bowen's *Dewi Sant – Saint David* (bilingual text; Univ. of Wales Press, Cardiff 1983). For the name, see *PNP* 289, with references.
6. Even if this is based on the economy of an eleventh-century bishop-house estate at St David's, it is eminently worth study.
7. *Menevia* (Mynyw) is the district immediately around St David's.
8. RCAHMW *Inv. Glamorgan,* vol. I pt.3 (1976), 37 (no.845) and pl.2.
9. The writer, lecturing at Edinburgh from the mid-50s to 1967, taught the first-generation children of Scottish mothers and Polish fathers who had settled in thousands from the Polish Resettlement Corps, Forestry Corps, 2nd Corps, etc. A few boys had Polish names; girls, rarely; unless devout Catholics attending special Sunday classes they knew virtually no Polish. Surnames were already being assimilated (e.g., Sienkiwicz to 'Sinclair'). The Poles integrated rapidly in specialized occupations – coalmining, manufacture of linoleum, bespoke tailoring, furniture repair and antiques. Half a century on from 1943–4, assimilation is complete, and it is the maternal indigenous personal names that have virtually ousted the paternal intrusive ones (admittedly the latter presented orthographic and phonetic problems, greater probably than any between Primitive Irish and Neo-Brittonic or Latin).

10. Lewis 1976, 178–9.
11. Should anyone wonder why Caldey was selected, its archaeology and geography reveal a self-contained unit with hundreds of acres for pasture, cereal-growing and of course fishing and sea-birds; Roscoe Howells, *Caldey* (Gomer Press, Llandysul 1984, full bibliography).
12. 353, 358 (VOTEPORIGIS), 428, 433.
13. 352a at Llangwyryfon 6 miles south of Aberystwyth is isolated and not shown on the maps here; 448 contains (RINACI) NOMENA; 354, 355 (and 352a) have IACIT; 368, 370, 436, 443 and 451 have HIC IACIT, and 369 has (HIC?) IACET. The further decline to IC IACIT, and even just IC, found in Dumnonia (chaps. 16 and 17) has not yet taken place.
14. *LHEB*, 273; the Irish cognate in a later form occurs in ogam, 172 TOGITTACC, *Guide* 5.11.
15. 360 Cynwyl Gaeo, SERVATVR FIDAEI ..., early sixth; 350 Llanddewibrefi, IDNERT ... OCCISVS, later sixth; 993 (*CIIC*.ii), Llanllyr, *Tesquitus Ditoc* ..., seventh.
16. 374 CVNEGNI (British), 356 POTENTINA (Roman, fem.), 351 DALLVS DVMELVS (Irish), 452 PAANI (Irish), 453 MELI (probably Roman).
17. *LHEB*, 622 ff.
18. Excellent background account; Lawrence Keppie, *Understanding Roman Inscriptions* (Batsford, London 1991), at 105–6.
19. A further modern analogy – the writer's numerous great-uncles, born between 1859 and 1881, were called: (Germanic kings) Albert, Ernest, Frederick, George, William; (Norman or Plantagenet) Telfer (<*Taille-fer*), Richard; (Anglo-Saxon) Edgar; (Methodist or biblical) Charles, Joseph, Josiah. Paternal and maternal families have been almost exclusively Cornish, rising through mine-management and the professions. The only British name was Arthur, the only Cornish ones Bostraze and Vivian. Some of them spoke Afrikaans, Malay and Portuguese and, marginally, Arabic and Welsh. None knew German (or Norman-French!). Correlation here between name-origin, speech range and ethnicity is non-existent.
20. For more light on *Fannuci, Fanoni* (<*\*Swann*-), see p. 267 below.
21. Cornwall, 1993; going rate for inch-high machine-cut letters on slate, £1 a letter (rather more on granite). Prices elsewhere are doubtless higher. For a widow to add IN TREASURED AND LOVING REMEMBRANCE OF, a stonemason's stock phase, would cost £33, about five per cent of the price of a modest funeral all-in.
22. G. J. Wainwright, *Coygan Camp* (Cambrian Archaeol. Assoc., 1967).
23. Detailed references to sites, Edwards & Lane 1988; the finds, Euan Campbell, ibid., 124–36 illus., updated by him in *AC* 138 (1989–90), 59–64 illus. ('New Finds ...'); see also (Longbury Bank) notes in *Archaeology in Wales* 29 (1989), 64–5 – more Phocaean Red Slip Ware, B ware and Merovingian glass.
24. Under excavation; information kindly provided by David Austin.
25. This is a stray find from 1921–31; the writer is very grateful to Cathy O'Mahoney, SDUC Lampeter, for drawing attention to it.
26. General discussion of the present context of the Mediterranean imports, Thomas 1989, and of the Gaulish ones – Class E ware, etc. – C. Thomas, 'Gallici nautae ...' *Medieval Archaeol.* 34 (1990), 1–26. It should be emphasized that these Mediterranean scraps, even the Longbury Bank assemblage being negligible alongside the many thousands of sherds from Tintagel, cannot be more than leavings from a rich man's table – somewhere in coastal Demetia there ought to be a major royal citadel of VI with a far larger quantity of imports. Superficially, Castle Hill at Tenby, under the Norman castle, as the location of the poem *Etmic Dinbych*, suggests itself; physically this is very like Tintagel Island on a smaller scale (see next note).
27. See his 'Two Poems from the *Book of Taliesin:* (i) The Praise of Tenby', pp. 155–71 in:

Rachel Bromwich, ed., *The Beginnings of Welsh Poetry. Studies by Sir Ifor Williams* (Univ. of Wales Press, Cardiff 1980).

28. Baring-Gould & Fisher, *LBS* iv. 236 (behind which must lie someone's reason for supposing so); a substantial and visible defended site ought to be involved. See *PNP*, 698.

29. See p. 204 — learned Irishmen, returning from Rome, stop off at Caldey, 'Piro's Island', at some date within VI.1.

30. With some reserve, *contra* Richards 1960 (who omits it from his 'Irish' list); *LHEB, passim*; and Sir Ifor himself (note 27 above, at p.24), but with the support of *Guide*, 6.10, etc. A reason is that *\*barros* 'top, summit, etc.', represented by PrIr. *\*barras*, here *sensu* 'top of head, hair, topknot, crest, scalp', was continued in WCo. in a geographical use (cf. mountain name Berwyn, or W. Bargod, Co. Bargus 'top of the wood' (*coet*)); personal names with *barr-* 'hair, scalp' are Irish, not British — 'Finbarr' is in fact VENDUBARI (<*uindo-barras*), and (p. 251) even the *Berwin* of *DSB* could be explained as from the Irish form *\*barro-uindas*.

31. Rhys, in *AC (1896), 119–21*; see also Hogan, *Onomasticon*, 202 for 'Cell mo-Domhnoc', perhaps in Cloyne diocese, east Cork. The same name appears in *VD*, cap. 41, as a disciple of David called Midunnauc (var. Midumnauc, Modomnoc, Modomnoch); if the same man, subject of some Cardiganshire legend, then retrojected into the Life anachronistically by Rhigyfarch (critical treatment of whose work, by Mrs Chadwick, figured in *SEBC*, 136 ff. *Tesquum* is 'an augural term of uncertain sense ... by non-technical writers interpreted as a tract of wild or desolate land' (*Oxford Latin Dict.*). It would be interesting to know where, at this date, a Demetian *scriptor* found the highly obscure diminutive *tesquitus*. Appreciation of early generosity must be tempered by a recurrent observation that a great many enclosed cemeteries *were* sited on marginal, unworkable or useless land. For the other names (not elsewhere attested?), Asaitgen appears to comprise OIr. *assait* (Vendryes, *Lexique*, A-96, 'accouchement, parturition') with suffixed *-gen* ('begotten', etc.); for Occon, cf. in *CGH* such names as Ocan, Occoman (= Ogoman), *Ochon (= Onchon) — or simply an epigraphic, nominal version of *ócán* (*óc* plus dimin.) 'Young-Man'?

32. 'Wincdi' (the *-c-* is impossible) must be *\*uinn* plus *ti*, proto-form of (GPC) *gwyndy* 'blessed abode, holy house, church', citing Lland. *ygundy teliau* (*Llan Dâv* 120, 'Braint Teilo') and, better, *ar wyndei* from Cynddelw's 'Marwnad y Owein Gwynet' (*Llawysgrif Hendregadredd*, p. 95). Rhigyfarch probably misread *uuinndi* as *uuincdi*.

33. The (pre-delabialization) *Qu-* /kw/ may imply a written source of (?) early VI. Was this a *\*Quenadeccas*, alongside 263 LUGUDECCAS, OIr. *Luigde*, gen. *Luigdech* (*Guide*, 6 n.17)? See perhaps *CGH*, 248: Rawl. 154 a 28, *m. Ceinnetich* (var. *Ceindech*, Lec. BB). In what Rhigyfarch found, *-quendi* may have been a Latinized gen. (*quendici*?).

34. See G. H. Doble, *St Paulinus of Wales* (1942). The 'two saints', *deu sant*, in Wrmonoc's ninth-century Life were Notolius and Potolius, with whom the youthful Paulinus founded a family hermitage, later a monastery with church. The name of their home *regio*, given as 'Brehant Dincat', contains a word translated by Wrmonoc as *guttur* 'windpipe', explained in the belief that Wrmonoc equated 'brehant' with an OBr. cognate of OW *\*brouann*, later *breuant* 'neck, larynx, etc.' (see *GPC*). Despite entry of *brehant* in Fleuriot *GVB*, 89, and *LHEB* 443 n. 3, 460, it would be at best dubious and at worst a ghost-word. The writer proposes that Wrmonoc's *written* source, obtained as he tells us from *transmarini*, originally read *\*bronant dincat* — the *bro* or district (p. 216) appended to or controlled by Nant Dincat (*Llan Dâv* 154–5; explained here, p. 124). As a record of an area-name this may, like *Wincdi Lantquendi*, be sixth-century. Geographically the Tywi, Bran and Gwydderig valleys north and east of Llandovery are indicated. Other Irish names from VI.1/VI.2 in this eastern frontier-belt of Demetia to set alongside 'Quendi' and 'Dincat'

(p. 124) are 369 *Curcagnus* (Llandeilo), 361 *Maquerigi* at Cynwyl Gaeo.

35. In so choosing to define a 'horizon of historicity' I gladly acknowledge the stimulus gained from many articles by the late Dr Molly Miller, who saw its huge importance. It is a matter of lasting regret that she never found time to analyse the Brychan documents (*DSB, CB*), because she would undoubtedly have anticipated the conclusions presented in this book (see Chap. 9).

36. Because it traps the word, like a butterfly, in its flight from British (Gaulish, Romano-Celtic) *landa* ('Vindolanda'), through fifth-cent.(?) apocope as *land*, into sixth-cent. *-lant-* (written), /land/ (spoken), and then *lann* through assimilation of *-nd* to *-nn* – 'probably finished by the end of 6th', *LHEB* 511–13.

37. *Anglo-Saxon Chronicle,* s.a.; defeat of three British-named kings associated in the entry with Gloucester, Cirencester and Bath.

38. Readers (beyond Wales itself) familiar with Professor Wendy Davies's main works (1978; 1979; 1982) might wish to add the following – G. C. Boon, 'The Early Church in Gwent, I: The Romano-British Church', *Monmouthshire Antiquary* 8 (1992), 11.24; Jeremy K. Knight's sequel, '... II: The Early Medieval Church', ibid., 9 (1993); J. K. Knight, 'Excavations at St Barruc's Chapel, Barry Is., Glamorgan', *Trans. Cardiff Naturalists' Soc.*, 99 (1976–8 = 1981), 28–65; same author, 'Glamorgan, AD 400–1100: Archaeology and History' in: H. N. Savory ed., *Glamorgan County History*, 2 (Cardiff, 1984); and G. C. Boon, 'Traces of Romano-British Christianity in the West Country', *Trans. Bristol Gloucestershire Archaeol. Soc.*, 110 (1992), 37–52.

39. Brief discussion, *ECMW* 108–9 and footnotes.

40. North Wales, 325 *vasso Paulini* (but possibly P. of Nola, d.431?); south-east Wales, 410 *Paulus*, 407 pater, *Paulinus*: Dyfed, 435, *Paulinus Marinus* as father of *Clutorigi* (? Clotri). Another in Dumnonia; parish of Paul, near Penzance (but 1288 *sancti Paulini*); any number in Brittany. The cantref of *Peuliniog*, some way west of this inscription, may imply another important lay 'Paulinus'.

41. See ingenious and convincing reconstruction, Professor Glanville Jones, pp. 313–18 in: H. P. R. Finberg, ed., *The Agrarian History of England and Wales, I.ii* (AD 43–1042) (Cambridge 1972). Doble (op. cit., n. 34 above) also thought this inscription 'sounds more like the epitaph of a virtuous and pious layman' (p. 14).

42. As stressed by Mrs Chadwick in *SEBC* (see note 31 earlier).

43. The writer accepts without the usual reservations that the *insula* of *Piro* (*Vita Samsonis*, cap.20) was Caldey; the only possible alternative (Gateholm) lacks any of the supporting evidence.

44. This is apart from the historicity of any mid-VI 'Synod of Brevi', on which see Ludwig Bieler, ed., *The Irish Penitentials* (Scriptores Latini Hiberniae, v: Dublin 1963), 3, and text, for reservations.

45. Charles-Edwards 1971; partly mapped, W. Davies 1982, fig.53.

46. It can be followed in the admirable maps, Richards, *WATU*, and Rees, *Atlas*.

47. Llan Geneu cannot be St Dogmaels (Llandudoch); a distinct possibility would be, for 2 Cemais, Nevern, since this name (Welsh *Nyfer*) is only a locative taken from the small river beside the place (*PNP*, 131–2).

48. See plate in W. Davies 1982, fig.11, Eglwys Gymyn; Terrence James, in Edwards and Lane 1992, at 62–76, with air photographs and plans; Mark Redknap, *The Christian Celts* (NMW, Cardiff 1991), 38 (Llan-gan), 39 (Llangynog).

49. The author is grateful to Heather James (Dyfed Archaeol. Trust) for pointing this out and providing detailed maps; churchyard entrance crosses the slight outer slope from ditch to bank-face.

50. *Paan(i),* despite its initial p-, should be an Irish name; Hogan, *Onomasticon,* 209, *Cell-Phaain,* 'Kilfane', and *Paan* in Book of Ballymote. See RIA Dict., which notes *págán* <Latin *paganus* (and, for a separate British connection, *Paan* in the perplexing list of, mainly Irish, saints claimed as sons of *Brachan* (Brychan; here, chap. 9), *EWGT* 32–3). *Mel(i)* is presumably a Roman name, Melus.
51. 'A survey of the Early Christian monuments of Dyfed, west of the Taf', pp. 177–92 illus. in: G. C. Boon & J. M. Lewis, eds., *Welsh Antiquity. Essays presented to H. N. Savory* (NMW, Cardiff 1976). Llantrisant (Cards.) should be added, on the strength of three recently-found cross slabs; *AC* 126 (1977), 64–8, illus.
52. In *Emania* 9 (1991), at 58; see also J. P. Mallory, *In Search of The Indo-Europeans* (Thames & Hudson, 1989), 260–1. References are to Barth's *Features of Person and Society in Swat* (London & Boston 1981) and his 'Ethnic processes on the Pathan-Baluch boundary' *Indo-Iranica* (Wiesbaden, 1964), 13–20.
53. 'Welsh and Norman in the Early Ruling Families', pp. 40–2 in: D. Moore, ed., *The Land of Dyfed in Early Times* (Cardiff 1964).

## 8

## Venture to the Interior

'BRYCHEINIOG – the Welsh name of the old county of Brecon or Brecknock – lies east of Carmarthenshire and differs from Demetia in many respects. It is entirely land-locked. Most of it is at a much higher altitude, up to 2,000 feet and more. Its heartland, the broad valley of the river Usk flowing through Cantref Selyf, is like a Welsh Andorra, ringed about on most sides by mountains. Whereas after the early sixth century the kingdom of Demetia contracted, Brycheiniog may have briefly absorbed a small state of Buellt ('Builth') on its north; and lastly 'Brycheiniog' was not its original name at all but a new one accruing from that of its best-known king. Though often described as 'the semi-legendary' Brychan he was a real person who seems to have lived from V.3 to VI.2, bore an Irish-originating name (<*Brocagnas*, 'little-badger'), died and was buried elsewhere on an island, and was eventually remembered by another name. His mother was an indigenous princess, his father a Demetian for whom a descent from Aed Brosc was claimed, and rather more can be said of him than of most Welsh rulers before the great Hywel Dda. This chapter and the following two are concerned, for a change, with Brycheiniog and king Brychan. If they read like a Dark Age romance or a post-Roman detective tale, it would be as well to remind ourselves that it may be no more than an everyday story of protohistoric people, and nothing out of the ordinary. What *is* extraordinary is that inferences arising from the epigraphy of the Brycheiniog stones, and the evidence that can be prised from medieval documents, together form a concord; one allowing an outline history of Brycheiniog, 450 to 600, to be set out here and now for the first time – and, very fittingly, in a Welsh publication.

There are some seventeen early inscribed memorials, *ECMW* Group I, in Brycheiniog. It has long been common knowledge that seven or eight of them bear ogam; typologically, two of type (a), three of (b) or (c), and three of (d). Four stones have been found since *ECMW* was published. Recognition of this incidence of ogam, of a few obviously Irish personal names and of the general drift of the Brychan documents (chap. 9) has led to statements like 'the establishment of Irish dynasties in (Dyfed and) Brycheiniog . . .', 'at the same period' (*sc.* of the Déisi settlement) 'a further Irish colony was established in Brycheiniog as the ogham-inscribed stones there bear witness', and 'the kingdom of Brycheiniog could well have been established by an Irish dynasty'. If we substitute, throughout, *influenced* for *established*, and *Demetian* for *Irish*, a greater probability is nudged forward.

From *Moridunum* to the little city of Brecon in a straight line is about forty miles; from St David's, over eighty. Ystrad Tywi, a long slice of broken country east of the river Tywi or Towy (and west of the rising ground to the hills containing Brycheiniog proper), was not part of Dyfed. It was incorporated, perhaps late in VI, within a southward-expanding Ceredigion (Cardigan) and later still was part of a broader area named Seisyllwg.[1] The presence of persons from Demetia, as (it will be suggested) they must have been, in Brycheiniog cannot be regarded as part of a casual drift eastward; sending a son to take in the next parcel of land. It was an event, one that must have required conscious decision, and movement over a distance (several days' travel on horse, as we shall be told, p. 147). A Venture to the Interior is a correct description. Our sources comprise this small but highly informative set of inscribed stones, and so-called Brychan Documents (chap. 9). The inscriptions inform us approximately *when* this occurred (in a relative time, that must be converted to an absolute estimate), and also *whence* came some of those caught up in the venture. It is not impossible that the documents supply partial answers about *who* they were, and *why* they migrated.

We can clear some potentially confusing ideas out of the way at the start. It can be said – anticipating what follows – that, accepting the reality of a limited folk-movement from Demetia to Brycheiniog late in V.3, this formed no part of a domino effect; nor would the most tentative chronologies for post-Roman western Britain allow that. A map (Fig. 8.1) based on Professor Melville Richards's distribution-map of Irish place-name elements, the few early inscriptions east and north-east of the river Teifi, and possibly whatever was remembered in the preamble to the late *Life* of St Carannog,[2] makes it clear that fifth-century Irish settlement affected the southern half of the county of Cardigan. When, as *Ceredigion*, founded by an eponymous Ceredig from the north Welsh royal kin-group of *Cunedag* or Cunedda,[3] this British kingdom comes into late sixth or seventh-century focus, it does so at the expense of any Demetian claim to territory beyond the natural bound of Afon Teifi. The regnal succession of the dual list (chapter 6) indicates no catastrophic break after Guotepir. If people went east to Brycheiniog it was not as refugees from the ravening hordes of the Ceredigion British; nor, by the same token, can one assume that the further migration of Demetians to what is now north Cornwall, described in later chapters, constituted a similar flight. Nor, beyond this, does it seem remotely likely that the arrival of a few hundred Demetians (who within a century seem to have been as fully absorbed into Dumnonian society as the Déisi descendants were into Demetian) triggered a migration, from the southern shores of Cornwall, to Armorica in numbers sufficient to implant Late British as the seed for Primitive and Old Breton.[4] It is safer to view all such inferred movements as manifestations of what the Germans compactly sum up as a *Volkswanderungszeit*, a time after the collapse

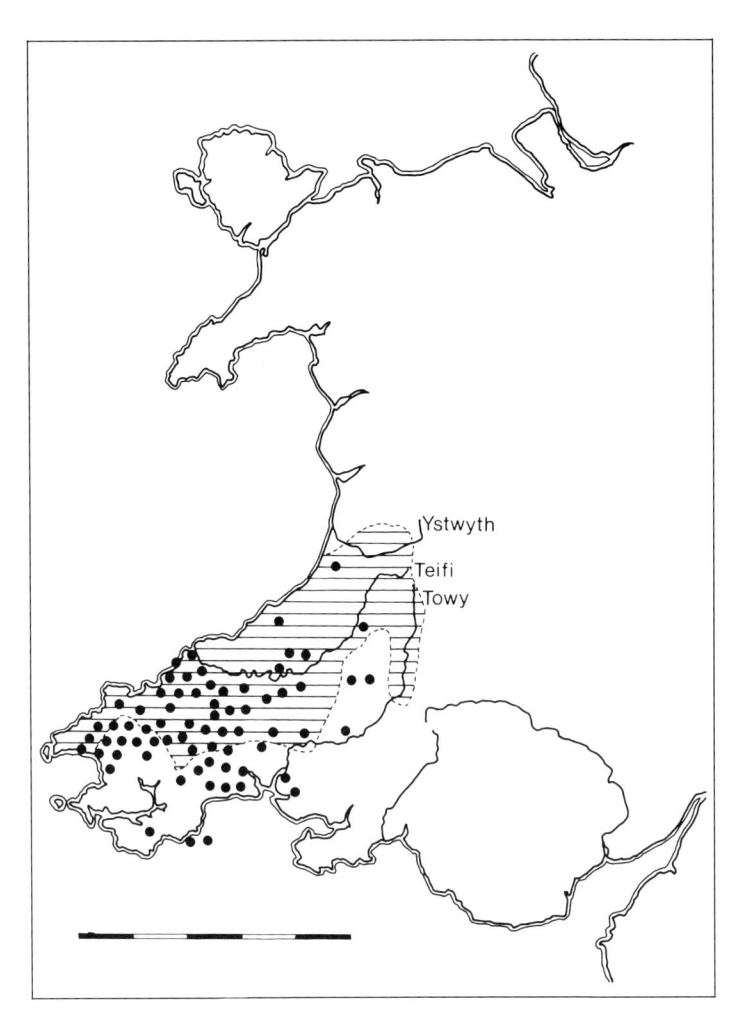

**Fig. 8.1** Sketch map (relevant rivers indicated) suggesting fifth – sixth century expansion of Irish-settled Demetia north of the Teifi. Lined area, all place-name elements (*meidir, cnwc,* etc.), after Melville Richards. Dots, all memorials with ogam and/or Irish names. Scale, 50 miles (80 km.).

of the Empire when groups, not individuals, were on the move. In British and Irish protohistory we do not use the term 'Migration Period'; there are times when it might seem not wholly inappropriate.

The Brycheiniog memorials can be considered in detail, since there are so few of them. There is a preliminary perspective that may be useful. In previous chapters we considered sixty-one inscriptions from Demetia; later, a further fifty-one from south-west Britain (fifty-five in all, but four are fragmentary or illegible) will be consulted; and there are seventeen in Brycheiniog. The typological sequence-model, type (a) through to un-typed messages, appeared to be valid for Demetia; predictive application to Dumnonia will suggest that the types are in the

# VENTURE TO THE INTERIOR

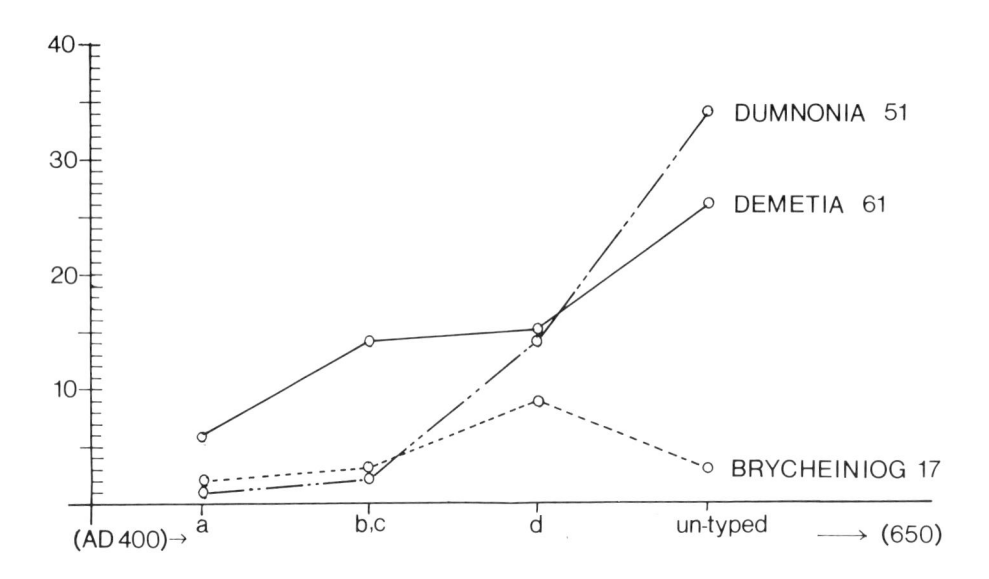

**Fig. 8.2** Diagram; 'typological profiles' of memorials from Demetia (total of 61), Dumnonia (51) and Brycheiniog (17). Vertical axis, numbers of each type, types (b) and (c) being amalgamated. Horizontal axis, likely sequence of types through time.

correct order. The diagram (Fig. 8.2) amalgamates (b) and (c) – ogam bilinguals – as variants of each other, but distinguishes them from (d) with HIC IACIT and Christian wording and, for convenience, from the un-typed ones. Bearing in mind that individual monuments vary within likely date-bands according to numerous criteria, simple curves for the three regions can be set together.

Where Demetia and Dumnonia are concerned the inference would be that the Dumnonian memorials start later – probably not much before 500 – because the fashion was only then introduced; the introduction coincided with a rapidly-increasing adoption of the Christian faith, and this fashion was maintained into the seventh century, most inscriptions being dated to 550 × 650. This is the conclusion that a separate study of the Dumnonian stones would produce. The larger number of ogam-inscribed stones in Demetia, from type (a) to some of type (d), reflects a proximity to the Irish source of ogam as a vehicle of expression. The Brycheiniog inscriptions produce an earlier line, close to that of Dumnonia, for the same reason; introduction not before the end of V, and distance from the main ogam-using region. The rise, again, marks the use of memorials in an early sixth-century Christian context; the falling-off, abandonment of a fashion whose main strength lay in Demetia, one that was never more than a marginal aspect of social funerary-commemoration in Brycheiniog.

Fig. 8.3 is a map of early Brycheiniog, the nucleus being a 25-mile stretch along the upper valley of the river Usk which, eastwards, turns slowly south and reaches the coast at Newport, having passed the legionary fortress at *Isca*[5] or *\*Castra Legionis*, Caerleon. The centre is modern Brecon, at the south end of the broad corridor between mountains running north-north-east up to the river Wye at Glasbury. This corridor, traversed by the river Llynfi, was home in the fifth century to a predecessor of Brycheiniog – a small sub-Roman British kingdom whose name comes to us as *Garth Matrun*. The upper Usk was accessible from south-east Wales; and the sub-Roman Christianity (and *romanitas*) of the whole Severn basin was linked by a Roman road coming north-east past *Gobannium*, Abergavenny, to the fort of Brecon Gaer or Y Gaer (probably *Cicucium*)[6] and, moving to higher ground south of the narrowing valleys, continuing to *Alabum*(?), the Roman fort on the north side of Llandovery. The route then went west to the Dolaucothi gold-mining complex near Pumpsaint (*Luentinum*), thence north to *Bremia* (Llanio, near Llandewi*brefi*, from the same river-name); from Llandovery a rather more important Roman road went down the north side of the Tywi to *Moridunum*, Carmarthen. A little too much weight has been placed, particularly by historical geographers and students of hagiography, on the role of Roman roads after the fourth century as the *only* routes along which people and ideas could move overland; but it can be accepted that Caerleon and Brecon Gaer, at least, must have been so linked after 400, and the Usk valley system may reveal one way in which sub-Roman Christianity may have reached Demetia.

The Brycheiniog inscriptions are in two groups. One group is related to the Usk valley and, if reflecting introduction from Demetia, points to the old Roman road *via* Llandovery (the present A40 runs slightly north of this up the winding valley of the Gwydderig, a tributary of the Tywi). The other consists of inscriptions from the higher reaches of the southward-draining river valleys like the Taf Fawr, the Mellte and the commencement of the river Neath. This enormous block of high land, Brecon Beacons or Fforest Fawr, constituted Cantref Mawr, by pre-Norman times the southern uplands of Brycheiniog. South of the mapped area lies, not Gower with its faint tradition of a minor Uí Liatháin colony, but the coastal plain or 'Vale' of Glamorgan. Here very few early inscriptions are recorded. Though it is unwise to pose anything like a rigid sub-grouping, the nine Brycheiniog stones in this southern cluster between them seem to represent isolated land-taking in the lonely sheepfarming valleys, draining south from Fforest Fawr.

The earliest inscription is that near Brycheiniog's western end, marked as 003 on the map.[7] Found in 1954 by Canon Jones-Davies of Llywel, at nearby Aberhydfer, it is a tall sandstone slab with a prominent line of ogam up one face. Before the ogam was cut, this face was chamfered, and tooled all over with pock-marking; it damaged but did not entirely obliterate an *earlier* and unrelated

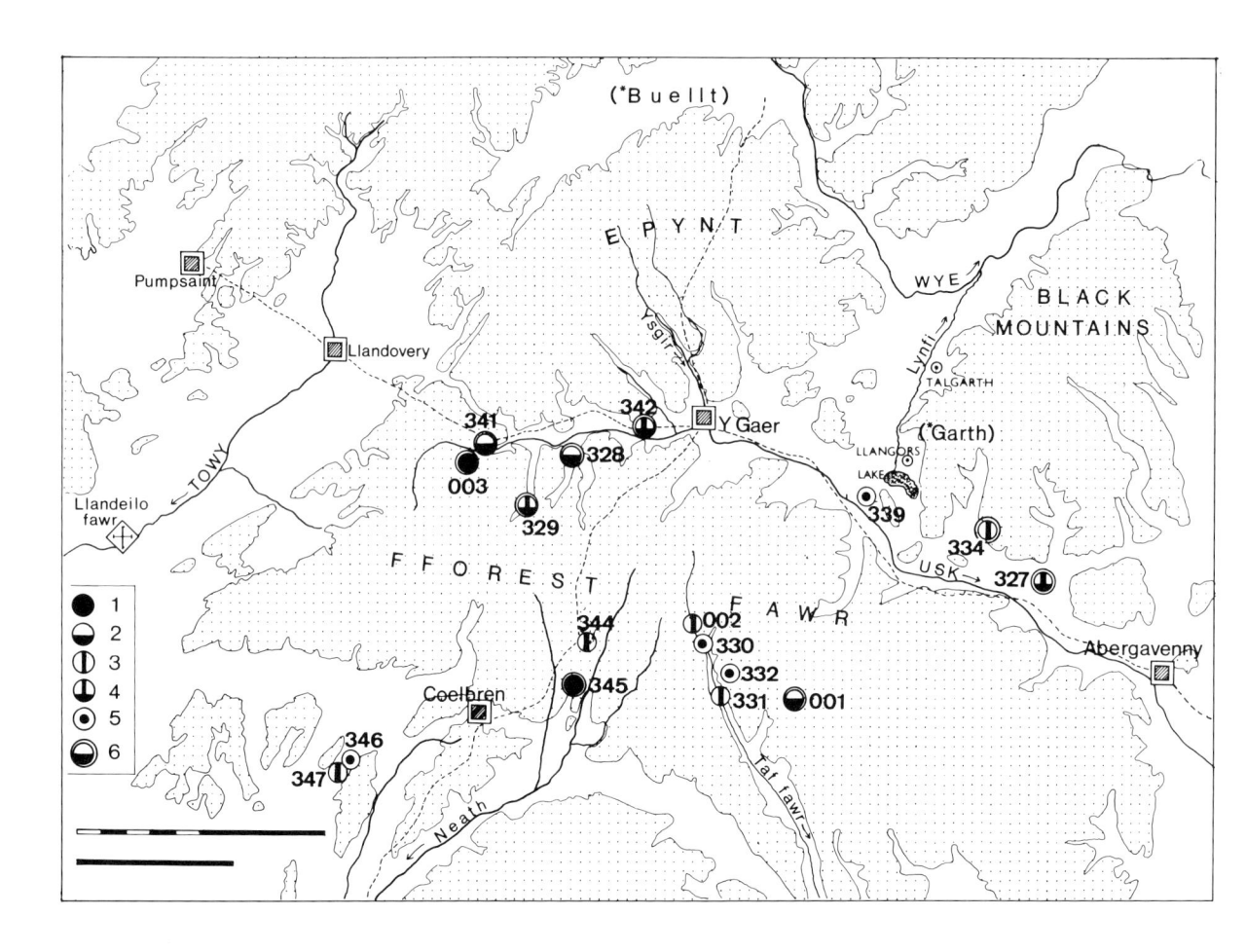

**Fig. 8.3** The heartland of Brycheiniog, the upper Usk valley and the Llynfi corridor, with inscribed memorials. Hatched squares, Roman sites; dotted lines, Roman roads. **Key**: 1, type (a) memorials. 2, types (b) and (c). 3, type (d), and 4, type (d) with ogam. 5, un-typed memorials. All memorials with Irish (Demetian-originating?) names are encircled (6). Contour at 800 feet. Scales, 10 miles over 10 km.

inscription, four (or five?) lines of horizontal Roman capitals. With great skill Dr Roger Tomlin has partly restored this[8] as ..CIVS/....VS/.AVR/.ANVS/..? and suggests that some such wording as *(Lu)cius (fili)us (T)aur(i)anus (hic iacit)* would have produced what can be made out. Though this is, formally, a type (d) message and a Christian one, it may be as early as V.2 – not long after the middle of the fifth century – and it goes with a very few other Insular inscriptions[9] that we must call truly sub-Roman. If *hic iacit* and related words are shown, they reflect early and isolated contact with Christian Gaul. Proximity to the Roman highway at a point about ten miles west of Brecon Gaer[10] allows the idea that this inscription – for a person who might well have been born around 400 – alludes, not to the first of the Demetians or Brycheiniog-natives[11] using commemorative inscriptions, but to the last of the Romans.

The ogam, 003 TARICORO, is type (a), and shows a genitive in -o; the actual name is not attested.[12] It introduces us to five further inscriptions, all bilingual (341, 329, 328, 342, 327), that can be examined from west to east. From Trecastle, 341 (*ECMW* no.71) has the rare distinction of being in the British Museum, and on prominent display there. The vertical single-line inscription of this type (b) memorial is M̄ACCVTRENI SALICIDVNI, with ogam *MAQUITRENI SALICIDUNI* (Fig. 8.4). The lost stone from Crai, known only from Edward Lhuyd's 1698 drawing (329: *ECMW* no.42), was in four lines and of type (d); CANN̄TIANI ET / PATER̄ ILLIVS M̄ACCV/TRENI HIC IA/CIT, with ligatures as shown, and with an indeterminate accompanying ogam (possibly confined to the first name). Inscription 328, *ECMW* no.44, is in the church porch at Defynnog. A slab of reddish and rather crystalline stone, it is eroding badly along the angles and one end (original base) bears a ninth-tenth century double cross. Macalister read the two-line vertical capitals as RVGNIATIO / FI)LI VENDONI. This (as also in *ECMW*) is incorrect; spacing allows a better reading to be D?)RVGNIATO / FI)LI VENDONI (Fig. 8.5)[13]. There may have been an ogam above this, mostly trimmed away and eroded, and a few strokes can be seen; whether it was full (type (b)) or only the first name (type (c)) one cannot say.

The handsome pillar (Fig. 8.5) in the church of Trallwng, on the north bank of the Usk, has a long-stemmed incised ringed cross whose stem comes down between the two vertical lines of lettering; it is not impossible that this was intentional and contemporary (in VI.2). The inscription (342, *ECMW* no.70) is CVNOCENNI FILIVS / CVNOGENI HIC IACIT, and the long ogam, *CVNACENNIVI ILVVETO*. The consensus is now[14] that it contains a minor error, for *CVNACENNI (A)VI* . . ., and the wording will need further discussion (below). The last of these bilinguals comes from much further east near the limit of early Brycheiniog, from farmland just north-east of Crickhowell. Like the Trallwng inscription it is type (d) and reads – 327, *ECMW* no.43 – TVRPILLI IC IAC (with IT placed above IAC)/ PVVERI TRILVNI DVNOCA (with TI below). The ogam is defective; with McManus (*Guide*, 67), *TURP(I)L(LI)* ....... *L(?)..N..* is all that this writer could make out (but see p. 124 later).

Finally, in the Usk valley, there are two other, Roman-lettered only, eastern memorials. Inscription 339, *ECMW* no.68, stands by a roadside and is badly worn and in markedly rustic captials; a single vertical line reads N(EMNI)I FĪLĪVS VICTORINI. The tall pillar, 334, *ECMW* no.54, set into the outer south wall of the church at Llanfihangel Cwm Du, is carefully inscribed with slightly ornate letters – capitals with quasi-serifs and three instances of angle-bar A with forked top – and is the latest of the eight; perhaps VII.1. It reads CATACVS HIC IACIT / FILIVS TEGERNACVS.

Among the nine southerly inscribed stones in Fig. 8.3, the only type (a) is 345, now in Cyfarthfa Castle museum at Merthyr Tydfil, found in the open near Ystradfellte – *ECMW* no. 74. A long-stemmed cross was added much later. *GLUVOCA* can be read, the illegible continuation probably taking the form of *maqi B*. The new type (b) single-name stone found, or rediscovered after search, in

**Fig. 8.4** The Llywel or Trecastle memorial, a type (b) with MACCVTRENI SALICIDVNI; on the (inverted) reverse, unexplained pictorial scenes (sixth – seventh cents.? later? Biblical?). British Museum; reproduced by kind permission of the Trustees.

**Fig. 8.5** Memorials from Defynnog (328, church porch; **left**) and from Trallwng (342, inside church; **right**). Photos: Susanna Thomas.

the Cwm Criban valley has a defective ogam (001, M..Q..D..C..D..), for which Sir Ifor Williams suggested the likely vowels as *Maqi-deceda(s), and this may have been accompanied by an obliterated Roman-letter equivalent.[15]

If nothing at all were known of the Demetian inscriptions described in earlier chapters, or of the reasons for supposing an end-of-IV Irish settlement in Pembroke, it would be apparent from the Usk valley inscriptions that — ogam apart — the personal names call for explanation. As they stand, without conversion to Latin or PrIr. nominatives, they give us (from west to east) *Taricoro; Maccu-Treni (Saliciduni); (D)rugniato,* son of *Vendoni; Cunacenni (Ilwweto),* son of *Cunogeni; Dunocati; Catacus* son of *Tegernacus;* and probably *Maqi-Decedas.* Roman names accompanying these are *Cantian(n)i, Turpilli* and *Victorini.* The only more or less certain British name is (339) *Nemni(us)* or *Nimniuus.* All the other non-Roman names in this small inland *British* kingdom are either patently of Irish origin or, if at all indeterminate — like *Cunacennas* and *Cunogeni* — probably Irish because they are accompanied by ogam. Two names are given locatives; 341 *Saliciduni* appears to mean 'Of the Fortress of Willows' (though no Welsh fort-name **Dinhelyg* is recorded), and in 342 the proposed reading AVI ILVVETO 'a descendant of **Ilwetos*'? suggests either personification of the area-name of the commote of *Elfed*, part of eastern Demetia lying north-west from Carmarthen, or preferably a British personal name **Ilwetos* 'the Eloquent'.[16]

The range of dates is from (probably) V.3 for the ogam TARICORO, through VI.1 and VI.2 for the remainder, up to the (VII.1?) Llanfihangel Cwm Du stone, 334 *Tegernacus* — for which compare, though Irish rather than British, the Pembroke 432 TIGERNACI DOBAGNI, ogam DOVAGNI. If the stones commemorate intruders from a distance, a reasonable interval must be subtracted; such persons are not likely to have hobbled into hilly Brycheiniog as crutch-assisted geriatrics. An 'intrusion', whatever that means, can be tentatively supposed as around 480 x 500. As for its source, Fig. 8.6 supplies the most likely one. It does so, not with the idea that any one man could be commemorated in two places, but with the probability that specific names circulated in limited segments of society; kin-groups, even only large families. On this basis we note four stones from the north-west of Dyfed — Pebidiog — with the names 425 *Macutreni*, 422 *Vendagni*, 432 *Tigernaci* and 440 *Macudeceti*. None need be later than VI.1.[17] Two such names, 428 MACVTRENI, ogam MAQITRENI, and SOLINI FILIVS VENDONI (429), also figure just south of the Teifi; but 428 at Cilgerran is 'early seventh century' (so *LHEB*) and 429 at Clidey is, from its lettering, VI.2 and not V.3/VI.1.

It is just possible that the *(D)rugniato*, son of a *Vendon(us)* at Defynnog church (328) was a son of the *Vendagni* (**Wendagnas*) who appears commemorated on the rather crude stone from Caswilia at Brawdy (422); otherwise, only wider family links can be postulated. But this epigraphic evidence, which is consistent as to the character of names, the relative dates and their estimated absolute ones, and the appearance of ogam and the expected types of memorial, points to one main

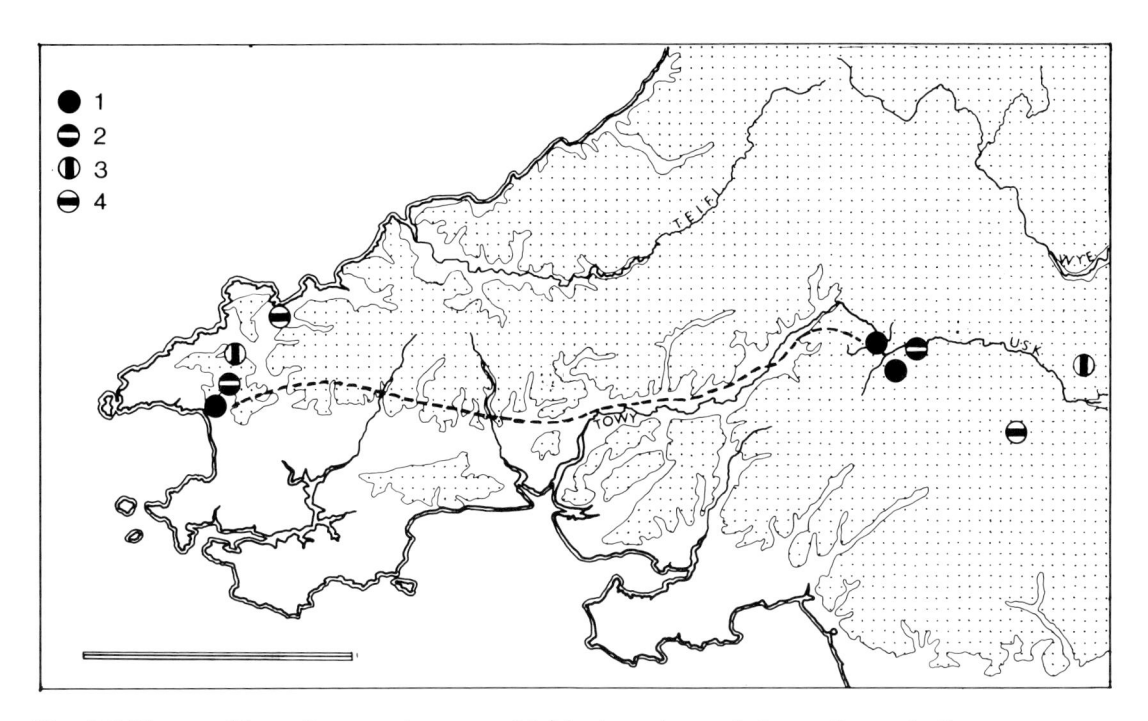

**Fig. 8.6** The repetition of personal names of Irish character, as between the west of Demetia (Pebidiog) and Brycheiniog. **Key**: 1, *Maqi-treni* (425, 329, 341). 2, *Vendo(g)ni* (422, 328). 3, *Tigernacus, Tegernacus* (432, 334). 4, *Maqi-decedas* (440, 001). Dotted line shows probable route of transmission in V.3 and VI.1. Scale, 25 miles (40 km.).

episode; when a group of Demetians — in a position to do so, of a social grade meriting such monuments, and probably together and at the one time — migrated from the supposed fief of Triphun (p. 80), late fifth-century Pebidiog, across some eighty miles to the desirable valley land of Brycheiniog. The likely date, and the presence of four type (d) inscriptions among the eight, would propose this group of people as being Christian. Rhetorical questions as to why the Demetians came, so far and probably together — and, since we deal with *surviving* monuments, the chance that these mark only some of the party — can be left to chapter 9. It would seem that the incursion was remembered and, if not fully explained, described.

The Crickhowell stone (327) now in Brecon Museum is more complex and more interesting than the *CIIC* and *LHEB* entries suggest. The lettered part reads TVRPILLI IC IACIT PVVERI TRILVNI DVNOCATI. At face-value, this could be rendered '(Stone) of Turpillius; here he lies: (stone) of a son of Trilunus Dunocatus'. Objections to this interpretation are three-fold. Contextually; this is an imposing stone with a long dual inscription (costing perhaps a couple of sheep, let alone the labour to move and erect the pillar). It was found on farm-land. Is it really more likely to mark a *puer* 'young son, non-adult boy' than a landed proprietor on whose estate it was to be displayed? Linguistically; 'Trilunus' is an improbable name – not a known Roman one, or a Latin *nomen*, nor in Irish or Welsh does any likely reflex of it occur. The word *puer* is not used in Insular inscriptions in this sense, and the entrenched currency of *filius* as a formulaic copula alternating only with ogam MAQI makes the straightforward meaning 'son' almost impossible. Epigraphically; the inscription was incompetently cut, perhaps by an illiterate. Though clearly marked about 18 in. up with a stop-line to allow for the footing of the slab in the ground, the surface defeated the cutter who, unable to space his straggling uneven capitals (with reversed N's and inverted D), had to squeeze in -CIT superscript and -TI subscript. The ogam, if cut at the same time, is probably unreliable, and had to be continued over a jagged summit (Fig. 8.7).

This writer suggests that the *scriptor's* model read, not TRILVNI, but TRIBVNI; and that a faint-looped B was thought to be an L, an error transferred from lettering to ogam. The sense would then be '(Stone) of Turpillius; here he lies; (stone) of a *puer* of Tribunus; (also of a son) of Dunocatus'. *Puer* in the secondary sense of 'young attendant, page, *puer regius*'[18] is what Turpillius when young had been to Tribunus, and 'Tribunus' was the Demetian king *Triphun* (as probably also on 476 ... FILL⌐ TRIBVNI (of V.1?) in Cornwall, p. 268 below). There are two reasons to regard the name *Dunocatus* separately. Unlike Aircol *Lauhir*, Triphun is nowhere recorded as 'Triphun *Dincat*' (and in any case *Dunocatus* is a proper name, not an epithet or title).[19] Second, there is good reason to see another *Dunocatus* (who may well have been father of *Turpillius*) elsewhere in early Brycheiniog; as the eponym of the church-site at Llan*dingad*, Llandovery (as its lay donor?), as the proprietor of a mountain-valley estate called *Nant Dincat*, north of Trecastle,[20] and as a man named in the earliest stratum of the Brychan Documents (p. 141).

The ogam on 327 is now largely missing. The first word can be agreed as TURPILLI (vowels hardly detectable). The final word or name shows only ..L..N.., and may be TRILUNI, copied straight from the letters. The link-word is *not* MAQI; how *pueri* was rendered in Irish, and ogam, is open to question but one likelihood is that it was as CELI.[21] As to the date, a man buried here as an estate owner in VI.1 or in early VI.2 – and a type (d) bilingual inscription is unlikely to be later – could very well have served at a north Pembrokeshire *curia regis Tribuni* in V.3, ceasing when Aircol began to reign, and then coming to Brycheiniog with his father Dunocatus. Those who read this interpretation as a too-ingenious one are invited to find another explanation for *puueri* instead of *fili*; to say in what *language* the name 'Triluni' is supposed to exist, and where else it can be found; and to examine the actual stone and form an opinion of the stone-cutter's competence.

The inscriptions from the valleys draining south out of Fforest Fawr (Fig. 8.3), apart from 345 and 001 with their ogams, show a limited spread of the commemorative fashion among, probably, farmers and pastoralists occupying the

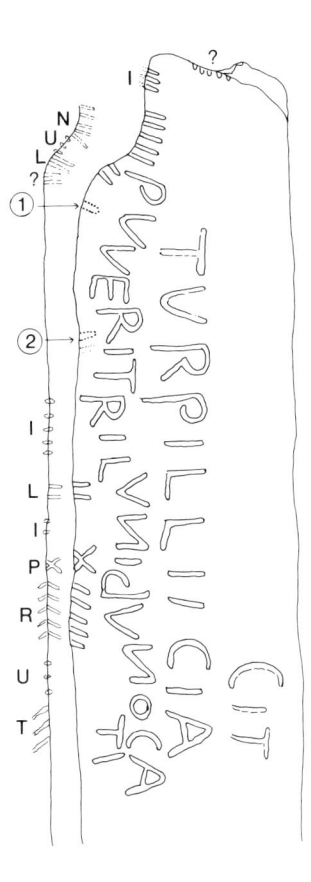

**Fig. 8.7** The Crickhowell stone (327), Brecon Museum; J. O. Westwood's 1877 *Lapidarium Walliae* drawing, simplified. Queries: ogam not now detectable. Encircled 1; possibly part of *I* rather than *R*. Encircled 2; possibly part of *L*, or *S*.

smaller lateral valleys off the main ones. Three are un-typed, four type (d), some now fragmentary. The picture is one of isolated memorials dating no earlier than VI.2. Personal names, Roman or British, point to small-scale adoption of a style of commemoration introduced in VI.1 from outside (and to the Usk valley) though the possibility of stimulus from what is now (old) Glamorgan cannot be dismissed. The longest inscription – *ECMW* numbers in brackets – is 331 (41) from Abercar, A)NNICI FILIVS / IC IACIT TECURI IN HOC TVMVLO, the last three words 'in the grave' being an aspect of a widened Christian vocabulary of Continental origin associated with horizontally set EL (extended Latinate) inscriptions – Fig. 12.4. Inept late handling of a type (d) message is shown on the very tall Maen Madog menhir at Ystradfellte.[22] The inscription, of *circa* 600 or later, is DERVAC⊢ FILIVS / IVST⊢ IC IACIT with the clumsy capitals inverted and reversed all over the place (344; 73). The recently found Nant Crew stone[23] is of interest because of (002) CAMAGLI HIC IACIT NIMNI(?). The first name is British *\*Catu-maglos*, caught here (with syncope of *\*CA(TA)MAGLI*) on its way to the Welsh *Cadfael*. The inscription is perhaps VI.3, and the *father* on this stone (*\*Nimni(us)*?) may also be the *son* of Victorinus, whose name appears as 339 (68) N(EMNI)I, *Nemni(us)*, on the roadside at Scethrog which is only ten miles northward. If so, the type (d) memorial of *Camagli* is more ostensibly Christian than that of his father. All the Brycheiniog stones, epigraphically, can add little to what has been written earlier;

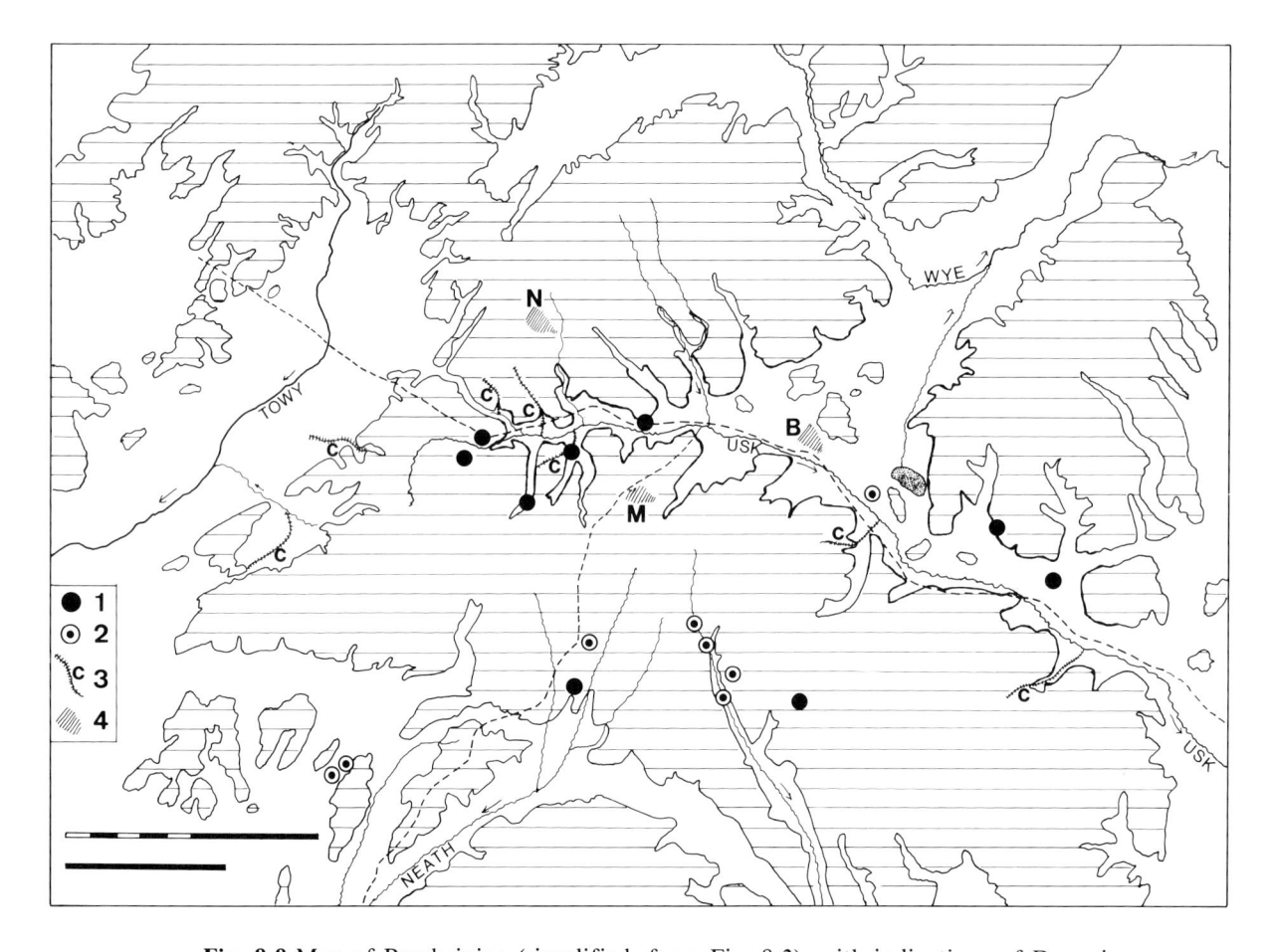

**Fig. 8.8** Map of Brycheiniog (simplified, from Fig. 8.3), with indications of Demetian settlers. **Key**: 1, memorials with ogam, and Irish names. 2, memorials with British and/or Roman names. 3, stream names Clydach, Cleidach, possibly of Irish type – R. J. Thomas, *Enwau Afonydd a Nentydd Cymru* (1938), chap. 1. 4, approximate location of 'Demetian' estates – N, Nant Dincat; M, Mynydd Frynych; B, Mainaur Aber Brynich. Contour at 800 ft.; scale, 10 miles over 10 km.

if horizontal ⊢ continued to be reproduced, and if there are occasional appearances of sixth-century angle-bar A (as on the incomplete 332 (40) ..P)ETA FIL(IA..)) the source is again Demetia.

Siting of individual stones conveys relatively little information about the contemporary Christian landscape. There are at least half a dozen churchyard sites in central Brycheiniog for which an origin in the sixth century might be argued. Several have produced *ECMW* Group II uninscribed cross-marked stones, but none an indisputable association with a contemporary memorial. For the ogam-inscribed, Irish-named, stones in the Usk valley the spacing of those so far discovered might suggest erection of prominent and legible memorials, in each case on the estate or holding of the family whose adult male leader is being signified.

Over-riding for the moment questions as to *function* — as territorial signposts, agreed boundary markers, or publicly legible claims to tenure, all quite consistent with a Christian personal epitaph whose design was commissioned from a local priest — the impression is that the Brycheiniog pattern is like another, demonstrable in more detail, involving prominent memorials of VI.1 and VI.2 around the Camel estuary in north Cornwall. These will be identified in chapter 16 as also of prominent Demetians, commemorated on a group of estates that comprised the best available land, later becoming large Domesday manors.

Any implication that we see in central Brycheiniog and parts of Dumnonia the sixth-century influence of dominant immigrants, early counterparts of all those agrarian-reformer landlords in England and Wales who during the eighteenth and nineteenth centuries so busily corresponded with Coke of Holkham, Young, Davy, Fraser and all the old Board of Agriculture luminaries, invites here a further question. Given that several score Demetian *nobiliores* arrived in the Usk valley around 500, was the land they took up un-used, under-exploited, ill-exploited, or in the occupancy of others who were obliged to move over? What social machinery might explain how newcomers could acquire hillside sheep-runs, upland and south-facing agricultural parcels and access to water and trackways (unless possibly in a grossly depopulated district)? Translated into twentieth-century terms the answers would be by straight purchase, direct transfer of capital, or borrowed money. That will hardly serve for post-Roman Brycheiniog. Unlike Demetia, where the Melville Richards's plottings of name-elements such as *feid(i)r* or *cnwc* probably do reveal an intimate link between the countryside and the linguistic aspects of its exploiters, about the only toponymic clue in Brycheiniog is the incidence of many stream-names terminating in velar suffixes like -*ach*, considered to represent Irish-type naming.[24] Some few years ago however, C. B. Crampton in the course of highly detailed fieldwork identified substantial tracts of a specialized upland settlement type, with unusual (and what, for convenience, he would call 'Irish') clusters of nucleated fields.[25] Crampton believed that these 'could have originated during the fifth and sixth centuries' and he looked to models in Irish patterns of first-millennium land exploitation. Though his hypothesis has undergone some critical erosion since 1967, there can be little doubt that Crampton's approach deserves to be resumed; the inscriptions do portray a new element within the population at a known date, those people were almost certainly agriculturalists, and the possibility follows that detectable innovations took place.

In this chapter 'the native population' of what was to become another kingdom with a mixture of peoples, Brycheiniog, has scarcely figured. Yet we can be certain that it existed, and in its thousands, before a Demetian set foot off the Roman road from *Alabum*; that Christianity was present if attenuated, and that continuing-Roman names were being used. By VI.1, two horizons (of Latinity and Christianity) had been attained. There must have been a social reaction, a general awareness, to the advent of men from the furthest corner of Demetia — if, as analysis of the memorials may indicate, that was their provenance. Nor is there any reason to see these immigrants as slaves, tinkers, the sixth-century version of potato-pickers, when their very presence comes to us epigraphically in the shape of parochial chieftains. On the face of it, the chance that Brycheiniog might also by now have attained the horizon of historicity, or would attain it by VI.3, seems too remote to contemplate seriously. But we have access to written material, largely unrecognized for what it is, that may well represent later sixth-century historicity. The so-called 'Brychan Documents' are there to inform us, and in so doing also to perplex us, as to some of the questions that neither epigraphy nor archaeology can address unaided.

## References

1. See appropriate map, Rees *Atlas* pl.22, and W. Davies 1982, 110.
2. *VSBG*, 142–3; see also *Vita* II, cap.3 (ibid., 148–9), advance to the Gwaun valley.
3. Purposefully avoiding discussion of 'Cunedda's Move' and related problems, the author points now to the *only* authoritative recent treatment; Professor R. Geraint Gruffydd's paper 'From Gododdin to Gwynedd; reflections on the story of Cunedda', *SC* 24–5 (1989–90), 1–14.
4. Cf. *LHEB*, early chapters, for the Breton migration(s).
5. *PNRB*, 376–8, for longer treatment of this minor linguistic topic.
6. *PNRB*, 307 (and ibid., under names, for the other places mentioned). See now also P. Sims-Williams, *CMCS* 26 (1993), 36, for a further name 'Caer Fong'.
7. The three new finds are cited here as 001, 002 and 003 only for immediate reference. For 003, R. S. O. Tomlin, 'A Sub-Roman Gravestone from Aberhydfer near Trecastle', *AC* 124 (1975), 68–72 illus.
8. Op. cit, pl. x and figure; the stone is now inside Llywel church.
9. Whithorn, 520 *Latinus*; Carnsew, Cornwall, 479 *Cunaide* (see here at p.193); in Demetia, 435 *Clutorigi*, if dated to V.2/early V.3, p. 136 above; and probably 498 at Chesterholm, *Brigomaglos*. This list omits a whole group of likely sub-Roman memorials, confined to north-west Wales.
10. But, for absence of post-Roman indications at Brecon Gaer, see Edwards & Lane 1988, 24. The place is fully described and illus. in RCAHMW *Inv. Brecknock*, pt. ii (1986), 135–46.
11. *GPC* has a word *Brycheiniwr*, 1870, 'a Breconshire man' – a venerable native speaker (Merthyr Cynog, 1989) assured this author that he had never heard it used, or knew that it existed. Is it literary?
12. As OIr. *\*Tairchor*, gen.*Tairchuir*? but both elements occur; cf. 458 (Cornwall) RANOCORI, *CGH* 740–1 (*Tairmesc*, etc.), and Hogan, *Onomasticon* 212, Cell *Tairri* (< *\*Tari-rig-*?).
13. The second -I- (..ATIO) is not there, and never was; this is a gen. in *-(t)o*, *Guide* 6.24, cf. 215 *ALATTO*. One (missing) initial is needed. D might be indicated by 167 *DROGNO*, 31 ?*DRUGNO* (with *CGH* 597, *Drón*?) – see RIA Dict., D, 405–6 s.vv *drong*, *Drong*, and (cognate) Fleuriot, *GVB* 152, *drogn*. The translating word, Engl. 'throng', must itself be another distant cognate.

14. *Guide*, 67, following *LHEB*; the difficult *ILVVETO* is discussed below.
15. D. P. Webley, 'The Ystrad (Brecon) Ogam Stone. A Rediscovery', *AC* 106 (1957), 118–9 illus.
16. 'Elfed, Elvet' *appears* to be <*elmet-* ('area with elm-woods') like the name of the British kingdom in the Pennines – J. F. G. Hind in *BBCS* 28 (1980), 541–2, comments by Eric Hamp, *BBCS* 30 (1982), 42–3. Since in the Demetian name *Elmet by this date the -m- would be lenited /elµed/ the question here and elsewhere is how this sound could be conveyed in writing. *LHEB* 480-6 did not entirely resolve this. If ogam *ILVVETO* is not for /ilµeto, elµeto/ (gen.), what does *VV* convey? *LHEB* 185 n.1 prefers Sir Ifor Williams's different interpretation, *THSC* (1943–4), 155. For a seventh-century Dumnonian inscription where lenited -m- (as a nasal bilabial?) seems to have been rendered by -F-, see p. 291 (no. 1048). Admittedly the *sense* of 329 *(A)VI ILVVETO* is not very likely to represent the notion of 'descendant of a *place*' as opposed to 'of a personal name'.
17. On 422 (at Brawdy) Macalister's drawing shows strange rounded half-uncial letters; the lettering is almost all gone and these are misleading and imagined. VENDOGNI implies a stage earlier than VENDONI (-gn> -nn). *ECMW* reads the second name not as 'HOCIDEGNI' but as V......NI and the first name as VENDAGNI.
18. *Oxford Latin Dict.*, *puer*. 5. See also David Dumville, *CMCS* 10 (1985), 41 and 42 n.13, on *puerculus*, *c.*750 = 'disciple'(?).
19. *Duno-catu-* 'Battle-fortress. Stronghold-of-Battle'; giving rise to both W *Dincat* and Ir. *Dunchad*. It is assumed that the Irish form, *ex* Demetia, is represented here.
20. *Llan Dâv* p. 370, location (upper Cilieni valley; a side-coombe).
21. *Guide*, 6.27, and examples in *CIIC*.i; on the stone, where the angle with ogam is badly worn, a single remaining B-surface stroke might be part of CE(L)I, but not of *MAQI*, since M is a diagonal through-stroke and Q five strokes on the H-surface. Less likely would be a word corresponding to 325, *ECMW* no. 33, VASSO 'servant, disciple' – W *gwas*, Ir. *foss*, usually referring to followers of saints – which would contain medial -S-, four strokes on the B-surface. J. O. Westwood, *Lapidarum Walliae*, pt. II (Oxford, 1877), pl.XLI; pt. III (1878), 73–4, text, saw the stone in 1846 and seems to have detected ogam TURP( )LI ...... (L?)LUN... which he gives in his drawing. For this early use of the additional X-like ogam character to denote the /p/, see Patrick Sims-Williams in *CMCS* 23 (1992), at 41–42.
22. A small area around Maen Madog (or Madoc) was excavated some years ago – (Sir) Cyril Fox, 'The Re-erection of Maen Madoc, Ystradfellte, Breconshire', *AC* 95 (1940), 210–6; no burial was found and the adjacent Roman road, Sarn Helen, was apparently overgrown when the pillar was put up.
23. D. P. Webley, 'The Nant Crew Stone: A New Discovery', *AC* 107 (1958), 123–4, illus.
24. There are many cases of a word *clydach* 'stream'; if really from Irish, perhaps PrIr. *clout- and adj. -ac-* (cf. OIr. *Cluad*, for the river Clyde: *PNRB*, 309–10), with a loose sense of 'the washing, the cleansing'. See now *PNP*, 7–8, and R. J. Thomas's *Enwau Afonydd a Nentydd Cymru* (Cardiff 1938) – in Welsh; 'Names of Rivers and Streams of Wales' – which devotes its first chapter to this, though unfortunately without maps.
25. 'Ancient settlement-patterns in mid-Wales', *AC* 116 (1967), 57–70; see also for related palaeo-environmental matters, Crampton & D. P. Webley in *BBCS* 20 (1963), 326–7; (1964), 440–9; earlier, 18 (1960), 387–96; and as background T. M. Thomas's essential study 'The Geomorphology of Brecknock', *Brycheiniog* 5 (1959), 55–156.

# 9

## The Brychan Documents

*D*E SITU BRECHENIAUC 'About the Circumstances of Brycheiniog' (*DSB*) and *Cognacio Brychan* 'The Kin of Brychan' (*CB*) are, superficially, medieval Latin tracts whose subject-matter suggests composition at or near Brecon. *DSB* is known from a larger manuscript collection that may have been put together around 1200, perhaps at Monmouth Priory some thirty miles away.[1] *CB*, which is at least as old as this, is known only from a transcript made at Brecon by Sir John Price (or Prise: 1502–55), a Visitor to the Monasteries at the time of their suppression, and a scholar and collector of manuscripts who lived in what had been Brecon Priory.[2]

*DSB* and *CB* are relatively short compendia – miscellanies, or collections of supposed facts about Brycheiniog's distant past. They differ, but more in style and arrangement than in subject-matter.[3] It is likely that the last version of *DSB*, which is all that we have, was written out after the foundation of St John's Priory at Brecon (between 1110 and 1125) by an Anglo-Norman brother who had trouble with many Welsh names. The document he was copying, and the separate text of *CB* that Price saw, owned, and wrote out in the sixteenth century, were pre-Norman, pre-1100; both probably belonged to a religious community at Brecon of which we know very little except that after the Norman conquest of south Wales it was replaced by the larger Priory, whose magnificent church is the core of what since 1923 has become Brecon Cathedral.[4] This pre-Norman monastery – a house of secular canons? – may not have been sited at Brecon much before the tenth century, after the English of Mercia had attacked Brycheiniog.[5] If its document-store included what we can call the national records, the prototypes of *DSB* and *CB* were among these; and it has long been agreed that aspects of the *DSB* text must pre-date the (?)Monmouth Priory, Vespasian A xiv, exemplar. But neither *DSB* nor *CB*, as originals, need have been composed or housed at what is now Brecon, the centre of the Norman lordship (and the later county). It can be suggested that before the tenth century their home was an older monastic church at Llan-gors, now a large village six miles east of Brecon, and just north of 'the Lake of Llan-gors' or Llyn Syfaddan (a large shallow expanse of water, a central feature of pre-Norman Brycheiniog).

Llan-gors is only a locative name – *llan*, plus *cors* 'marsh, swamp, reed-bed' – and the curvilinear churchyard enclosure with its Norman church of St Paulinus may once have been *Lann-beulin*. This is the best candidate for a royal ecclesiastical centre; royal, because so close to the *crannog* or artificial island by the north shore of the lake. From the evidence of current excavations[6] this crannog was used by rulers of Brycheiniog in the ninth century, and it is where in 916 x 919 Aethelflaed's troops from Mercia destroyed 'Brecenanmere' – some feature in the 'mere' of *Brecen-*, Brycheiniog, capturing the king's wife and thirty-three other people.[7] However, ancient though Llan-gors may be as a church-site and as the centre of a large royal estate, it need not have acquired that status until the early eighth century.[8] There are aspects of *DSB*, at least, that may point to a still earlier date of composition; and indications that, as the home of any written record of the foundation of Brycheiniog, Llan-gors was preceded by a still older church. If so, it was not far away; on the far side of the lake, where the southern shore bends to form a kind of southward arm and there is a rounded spur or *tal*, a kind of 'brow'. Here, today, stands the church of Llangasty (Tal-y-Llyn), the *llan* of 'Casty' on the brow of the Lake. Church and yard are modern – the scholarly John Loughborough Pearson worked here in the 1850s as architect – but somewhere in the immediate vicinity a very early Christian site indeed may await discovery,[9] and 'early' in the sense of *circa* 500. Like Llan-gors church as *Lann-beulin* it may have had its own name; if so, possibly the *lann* of the Twelve Holy Men.[10] And it would have been here, associated with a priest whose continuing-Roman name was apparently *Castanius*, that we can tentatively place local attainment of the horizon of historicity in the later sixth century.

Brycheiniog, on the evidence of the first inscription upon the Aberhydfer stone (003: p. 118 earlier), had some contact with sub-Roman, Christian, south-eastern Wales. The nature of the various early sixth-century type (d) memorials discussed in chapter 8, with the record of such names as *Annicius, Iustus, Victorinus* (and also *Castanius* and *Marcella*), allows us to suppose that Christian and Latinate horizons existed in what was to become the kingdom of Brycheiniog by around 500. What is now to be proposed is that, somewhat later but still before 600, and geographically perhaps in the neighbourhood of Llangasty, a resident priest composed in Latin from oral tradition one of the first instances of conscious and deliberate narrative local history known in post-Roman Britannia; certainly the first such in Wales. It may have occupied only the equivalent of two or three pages; but together with a few shorter written pieces it went to make up a little miscellany that, *via* Llan-gors, reached medieval Brecon, attracted interest and was thought important, was copied into a Norman-period collection mainly of Lives of saints and – with re-spellings, re-copyings, minor additions and minor errors – can be read today as the Vespasian A xiv text of *DSB*.

The sister-text, similarly embedded in another miscellany that contains more or less the same items in slightly different order, we know as *CB*; and we are dependent on Sir John Price's transcription of it (to which he added a few short notes of his own) for the sole copy. The distinction between *DSB* and *CB*, in a nutshell, is that *DSB*'s narrative might (like Gildas's slightly earlier *De Excidio* of the mid-sixth century) be called sub-Roman; whereas *CB* is a later paraphrase, still in Latin but written within the Old Welsh period (in the modified sense of from the eighth to the mid-twelfth century). As to absolute dates, the *DSB* narrative – which is, correctly, more of a foundation *history* than a foundation *legend* – concerns happenings of *circa* 480 to 500; the latest items in its original stratum appear to be notes of the burials of Brychan's sons, Cynog and his younger half-brother Rein, both of whom must have been dead by 560 × 570; there is no mention of any later king of Brycheiniog; and while the notes include a notice of Brychan's burial, the narrative has no reference at all to the subsequent (mid- or late seventh century, p. 174) enshrinement of his remains. A working hypothesis is that the *DSB* narrative was composed about 580. One's impression is that the *CB* narrative, paraphrasing this, is at least two centuries later – late eighth or early ninth – or could be later still; without having a secure, unrevised and unimproved, first text of it, we are deprived of clues that might allow closer dating.[11]

Here, for ease of allusion, the prototype of *DSB* (the narrative, with – see below – the genealogy of Cynog, the List of 'Sons' and the note of royal burials), assumed to possess a late sixth-century provenance in the vicinity of Llangasty, is described as 'B.1'. The next stage, suggested as at Llan-gors from the eighth to the tenth century, is 'B.2'; and it remains uncertain whether or not *CB* is a late B.1 product, or a B.2 product (in point of time) and also whether or not a text of it was also held at Llan-gors. The third stage, 'B.3', represents both miscellanies when held at Brecon; from the tenth century, probably, and certainly both before and after William de Braose's conquest and the foundation of the Priory in the first half of the twelfth century. It is inherently likely that, during B.3 – certainly as regards *DSB* in its ultimate, Vespasian A xiv, format – and possibly during B.2 as well, both documents were successively copied, if only to preserve 'master copies', with up-dating of the spellings of certain names, inevitable minor mistakes arising from misreading of letters, and also with brief additions or insertions of an explanatory nature. These are *glosses*, attachment to personal names of epithets, short comments, the names of places and the names of spouses and offspring. By the end of B.3, the miscellany common to both *DSB* and *CB* comprised: *1.* a history of the formation of the kingdom of Brycheiniog, with particular emphasis on Brychan and Cynog, perhaps closing with a memorandum about four royal graves; *2.* a genealogy of Cynog;[12] *3.* a list of twelve male names (other than those of Brychan and Cynog); and *4.* an eventually rather confused list of twenty-four (or so) female names, analysis of which shows that it began as *two* lists, possibly intended to contain a dozen names each.

These scanty records, the 'title-deeds' of the kingdom of Brycheiniog, had been compiled from popular knowledge and were in no sense secret; nor do they reflect all that would have been circulating. At least one separate written genealogy (a real one, not a regnal list) of Brychan's paternal descent existed (see p. 79). The *DSB* author probably chose to omit folk-tales that could then have survived for centuries, up to the post-medieval period. Items *2, 3* and *4* above, because they were replete with personal names, had a particular attraction to genealogists; and much later they were copied, but before Norman times, into a Glamorganshire collection (preserved in a fourteenth-century MS)[13] where Welsh was largely substituted for the older Latin words and phrases. Item *2*, at some stage labelled *Ach Kynawc Sant* 'The Descent of Saint Cynog',[14] was of wide interest because of this saint's fame; and some longer form of it was apparently obtained from Brecon(?) in the late eleventh century for inclusion at Llancarfan in the Life of St Cadog, who was Brychan's grandson, because it referred to the ancestry of Cadog's mother Gladusa.[15] Indeed, the *Vita Cadoci* and one or two other Lives written in south-east Wales at this period have other stories figuring Brychan and Brycheiniog, because these Lives were concerned with adjoining kingdoms.[16] Still others were current, to be gathered up by Giraldus Cambrensis and Walter Map, in the twelfth century;[17] and as folklore some survived late enough to be written down by the antiquarian herald Hugh Thomas, who died in 1714.[18] Only the narrative element of *DSB*, however, can be regarded as something akin to history composed in the late sixth century. As for the Brycheiniog royalty, clumps of 'genealogies' (in fact, regnal-succession lists) naming men who lived long after Brychan were, obviously, only completed after the deaths of the latest-named figures within them.[19]

If we now go back to the anonymous author of the *DSB* narrative — and let us assume an isolated priest, a successor to Castanius, living and ministering near modern-day Llangasty in the later sixth century and having some status in the Brycheiniog royal household — we may picture him as deciding (or as being asked to decide) to write down the really significant national events of the previous three or four generations. No special problem would be presented regarding composition in Latin. Spelling (within limits), the rules of grammar and syntax and certain graphic conventions were constant over the western half of the former Empire. There was, for any cleric, the lodestone of the Bible; represented mainly if not invariably by the *editio vulgata*, the Vulgate Latin text prepared by St Jerome (d. 420) and his assistants to replace the many divergent *vetusta Latina* or 'Old Latin' part-Bibles that had circulated in fourth–fifth century Britannia. There were secular classics that a would-be stylist might want to imitate; and the *DSB* author, whom we might now call 'the priest of Llangasty', *was* something of a stylist who favoured obscure words and, to us, tortuous phrasing — putting *Quamobrem opereprecium est quatinus pelliciam vestem nate mee conquiramus* where a simpler soul might have written *Ergo necesse est ut pelliciam vestem filie mee obtinemus*. Were literary models available in sixth-century south Wales? Why not? When Samson from Demetia, admittedly a man who in V.3 had been given a formal Latin education at Llanilltud Fawr (p. 227), travelled across Dumnonia on his way to Brittany in the 530s, his whole wagon-load of baggage included, beside his *spiritualia utensilia* (his eucharistic vessels), '... *atque volumina*' – his books and writings.

The writing out, the agreed spellings, of names of persons and places was another matter altogether. Spelling, as used for Old Welsh after *c.*750, was only gradually fixed by appropriate models[20] and before this in Wales must have been as much subject to variation – within the range of Roman letters ABCDEFGHILMNOPQRSTVX – as the contemporary display of names on inscribed stones; and the Priest of Llangasty and his fellows, and their predecessors, were almost certainly the *ordinatores* or *scriptores* of these late fifth to seventh century memorials. An example would be the name of the kingdom's eponym, 'Brychan' himself. The *DSB* narrative suggests that he was given an Irish name – Primitive Irish *\*broc(c)-*, a word meaning 'badger', with the diminutive ending *-agnas*.[21] It occurs as BROCAGNI (316, Co. Derry, probably late V); in Wales, 372 BROCAGNI (from Llangeler, type (c), end of V or VI.1); and in Cornwall as 478 BROCAGNI – see p. 263 (type (d), slightly archaic, end of VI). By the sixth century the internal *-gn-* was becoming spoken /nn/ and this is shown, with apocope (loss, as in speech, of all the final inflected terminations), in the ogam 187 BROCANN (Co. Kerry, VI.3 or later). In a Welsh Latin writing of VI.3 the name might have been written as *broccanus* or *broccannus* (nom.), using the convention of *-cc-* to show that the sound /k/ was meant. However, we may guess that between vowels, in speech, this /k/ was becoming spirantized; that is, getting closer to the spirant, like '-ch' in Scottish 'loch' (written /X/ here), and during his adult life the king Brychan, who may have been born about 490 and who died about 550 × 560, was no doubt locally called something akin to 'Brochán' – that is, /broXa:n/, with slight spirantization of the *-ch-* between vowels, and slight compensatory lengthening of the final vowel. Old Irish genealogies spell this name as *Broccan* or *Brocan*. In Wales, where the graphs or written conventions – actually digraphs, two-letter conventions – *ch* (for /X/) and *th* (for /Θ/, as in 'think'), which conceivably had been first developed in Irish learned circles, entered the repertoire during the sixth century,[22] we must guess that a written *brochan* replaced an older *broccan*. Hence, with a new realization of the first vowel, we find 'Brachan' and even a Latinized *Brachanus* in both *DSB* and *CB*, as B.2 replacements. Later still, during B.3, the first vowel was represented by written *y*, normal in Middle Welsh for the obscure sound (like -e- in 'the, report') and so we find ourselves with 'Brychan' – a name that does *not* rhyme with English 'stricken'. By a remarkable chance, what seem to be very early written Latinate forms of *DSB* were somehow conveyed in writing from Brycheiniog to a monastery in what is now north Devon by the seventh (or eighth) century, and were preserved long enough to appear in a twelfth-century Life written by an English monk. They gave us *Brocannus* (twice) and *Broccannus* (once), just as postulated. The accompanying *Broccannioch* – the name that eventually but regularly became Brycheiniog — supplies that of the kingdom.

Though, like this postulated sequence *broccannus*, through \**broccan*, \**brochan*, *brachan*, to 'Brychan', many of the *DSB* names must have been up-dated, just a few seem to conserve the original sixth-century graphs. If so, they shed an interesting light on how a literate, but possibly isolated, sixth-century cleric set about reconciling (in written *Latin*) contemporary spoken forms and the extant conventions employed to show such names on memorials. If we had the inscribed memorial of Brychan's British grandfather, from around 500, his name would have been cut as TOTORIGI or TOTARIGI (gen.). By *c*.580 it may have been spoken, in Brycheiniog, as /tu:dərig/ or, more probably, with slurring or lenition of the intervocalic -d-, /tu:ðərig/, and even with lenition, on the way to dropping it altogether, of the final -g, /tu:ðəriʒ/.[23] This is resolved into long first vowel; then /d/, or its lenition as /ð/; then a short middle obscure vowel /ə/; and at the end the weakening sound /ʒ/, inadequately signified now by -gh in 'Ugh!' or 'Faugh!'. But how in the *sixth* century, not in the ninth or tenth, was a man to reflect this through the Roman ABC, which possessed no dedicated symbols for lenited consonants? Our author almost certainly did write the name *teuderic*. He used -eu- for the long vowel /u:/; we have to guess that the -d- between vowels meant, to him, the lenited /ð/ since, if he had written *teut-*, the second, intervocalic -t- would have signified the sound /d/, as it did on sixth-century memorials. If he was aware that this particular name had been an oblique-stem form, \**Touto-rigi*, of the British \**Touto-rix* 'king of the tribe, or people', then he wrote a final -c to represent the original /g/, however this letter was by then being spoken (or not sounded). So *Teuderic* was in fact a logical compromise between a hypothetical, monumental *capitalis* rendering, TOTARIGI, and what Brycheiniog folk actually said in 580. Two or so centuries later the author of *CB* chose to write *teudric* because syncope had taken place (the obscure middle vowel had disappeared). But now we find a hint that the authority of these early written forms outlived developments in speech. For the MS Jesus College 20 the *CB teudric* was copied, in late pre-Norman days, as 'Tewdric' and in later manuscripts as 'Tewdrig'. As a man's name, this was still in use, but certainly not spoken thus; one of the Old Welsh Lichfield Gospels, or Book of Chad, memoranda gives it as it would have become by *c*.800, written 'Tutri' (that is, /tu:dri/).[24] All this runs parallel with a Demetian name discussed earlier in these pages (p. 62); CLVTORIGI, fifth century, then probably the same name (and man?) on the sixth century 446 at Nevern, CLVTORI, ogam CLUTARI — the O and A both for the obscure sound, /ə/ — and finally in manuscript format as 'Clotri' (for /klodri/, if not /kludri/). In Brycheiniog, the original written *teuderic* with a variant or miscopying as *teudiric* was preserved, because in the eleventh century this was used (as *Teudiric(us)*) in the Llancarfan *Vita Cadoci* to set out Cadog's genealogy — son of Gladusa, the daughter of Brychan, the son of Marchel, the daughter of Teudericus.[25]

These are selected cases. Not all of the original written forms have survived.

*Kynauc*, with its *K* and *y*, has replaced \*Cunac or \*Cunauc. In the list of twelve male names, *Kynon* (in *DSB* and *CB*) may have earlier been \*Cunon or \*Cunen, which on a contemporary memorial would have been CVNEGNI (as a man of this name was so commemorated; 374, a Carmarthenshire stone). But if careful analysis can show that the primary *DSB* narrative holds written name-forms (Latin, British, Irish) in the Latinate spellings we could expect for the postulated date, that will increase confidence in the claim that it *is* a sixth-century product. If so, the *dramatis personae* were real, had lived, had been known to informants older than *DSB*'s author; and the events therein described, however darkly, belong to history rather than to legend.

The main component, the narrative story, of *DSB* is given here to be read as a straightforward passage in translation, not as a text set out for linguistic or diplomatic analysis; the reader need not be concerned with the Latin original. This *DSB* story has been mentioned in fairly dismissive terms, as if incomprehensible.[26] It does not strike one as legendary. If its writer was obliged to construct what he could out of talking to grandchildren and great-grandchildren of personalities once concerned with what became Brycheiniog, this *is* one avenue towards the creation of legend; but we must allow him to have been attempting to compose history. The primary text is *DSB*. Brackets show, in italics, sentences that seem certainly ( ) or probably ( ?) to have been added in B.3; late 'improvements'. To help the reader, the present writer has inserted in square brackets [ ] an occasional explanatory word or phrase implied by the sense. Modern, or restored, forms of place-names are added, in brackets and italicized, as (*Llanfaes*). A. W. Wade-Evans's printed editions of the *DSB* and *CB* texts contain readings not supported by the actual manuscripts, nor are his translations entirely happy; the fresh versions given here have been made from the manuscripts, Vespasian A xiv and Domitian 1, though a few nouns for which no clear single-word English equivalents exist are left untranslated in italics and explained in footnotes. The division into sections is for convenience only; it is uncertain if, or how, the originals were sub-divided. In order to show to what extent it is a paraphrase of *DSB*, the *CB* text in translation follows.

## (DSB) About the Circumstances of Brycheiniog

1. 'Brycheiniog' first took its name from Brychan.

2. [*Marchel and Anlach*]
In the earliest times [of which we know], Teuderic was the king of that district. He was formerly living in Garth Matrun; and from there he set out with his commanders, and his elders, and all his household, and he went to Bran coyn (*Bryn gwyn*) near Lann Maies (*Llanfaes*). Then Teuderic said to Marchel, his daughter: 'The force of this great coldness is attacking us like some wild boar!

Because of this, it is most desirable that we look for a garment of fur for my daughter, lest she be burdened with the harshness of the frost. And so I shall send her to Ireland, with three hundred men [and twelve maidens], to Anlac son of Cormac, king of that land, that she may be wed to him.'

And therefore Marchel set out with the three hundred men, to Lan Semin (*Glansefin*), and there on the first night a hundred men died through the severity of the frost. On the second night, moreover, she came to Methrum (*Meidrim* or *Mydrim*), and at that place the same number as previously perished. On the third night, she came down to Portmaur (*Porth Mawr*), to a place known to be more sunny. And thence, with the hundred men left to her, she journeyed across to Ireland.

And, with her surviving retinue, she came at last to Anlac, king of that land. He, receiving her with great ceremony and joy, joined her to himself in lawful wedlock, proffering her a solemn oath that — if she should bear him a son — he would go back to Britannia with her, namely so that the boy would not be deprived of an hereditary realm. And by the same token Anlach gave to twelve of his *cubicularii*[27] [the twelve girls] or hand-maidens, each one of them to the men in accordance with their rank by birth.

After this, Marchel bore a son, and called him 'Brachan'.

3. [*The Return*]
And so Anlach came back [to Britannia] with the queen Marchel and the boy Brachan; and with the following *duces*[28] – Kerniol; and secondly Fernach, from whom is named Enifernach (\**Menid Fernach* > *Mynydd Frynach*); thirdly, Lithmilich, from whom is named Mainaur Oper Birnich (\**Maenor Aber-Brynich*); fourthly, Lounoic. Brachan tarried at Benni (*Y Fenni-fach*).

4. [*Brychan's schooling*]
And he was sent to Drichan, from whom 'Din Drichan' is named. For Drichan himself taught Brachan (*whence is said 'Brachan Brecheniauc'*) from the time when he was four years old. (*In the seventh year Drichan said to Brachan 'Bring me my spear.' For Drichan, near the end of his life, had become blind. And while he [Brachan] had been lying there, watching, a certain wild boar came from the woodland, and stood next to the bank of the river Ischir (Y*sgir*), and there was a stag behind it in the river, and also under the belly of the stag a fish; which three [creatures] portended for Brachan a future, happy with abundant wealth. As well as this, a beech-tree was standing by the shore of this river, and in it bees were making honey. Drichan said to his ward, Brachan, 'Behold, I give you this tree, with the bees and honey, full as it is with gold and silver too' and may the grace of God, and His love, remain with you always, here and evermore?*).

5. [*Brychan and Cynog*]
And afterwards, Anlach gave his son Brachan as a hostage to a king (of Powis = Powys). Eventually, in the fullness of time, Brachan violated Banadliuet,

daughter of Benadel. She moreover, becoming pregnant, bore a son by the name of Kynauc, who was taken away to *castra* (= *Castan*) and was baptized. When this had been done, Brachan, having taken an *armilla* from his arm, gave it to his son Kynauc. (*This selfsame saint Kynauc is very famous in his homeland Brecheniauc, and the armilla itself up to the present time is kept among the most precious relics of this aforesaid kingdom.*)

6. [*The descent of Kynauc*]
This is the genealogy of saint Kynauc, son of Brachan. Brachan the son of Marchel, Marchel the daughter of Teuderic, Teudiric the son of Teudfall, Teudfall[29] the son of Teuder (= *Teuderic*, repeated), Teuder the son of Teudfal (= *Teudfall*, repeated), Teudfal the son of Annhun, king of the Greeks.

7. [*The royal burials*]
The grave of Brachan is in the island, which is called Enys Brachan, which is next to Mannia (*Damnonia*). The grave of Rein, son of Brachan, in Landeuailac (*Llandyfaelog Fach*). The grave of Kanauc, Merthir in Brecheniauc (*Merthyr Cynog*). The grave of Anlauch, before the door of the church of Lanespetit (*Llansbyddyd*).

8. [*Brychan's wives*]
Three wives had Brachan — namely, Praust, and Ribraust, and Proistri.[30]

## (CB) The Kin of Brychan

1. (*The Kin of Brychan, whence is said 'Brecheyniawc'* — *part of Demetia, that is of Suth Wallia* (= South Wales).)

2. [*Marchel and Anlach*]
Teudric, king in Garthmathrim, came to Bryncoyn (*Bryn Gwyn*) next to Lanmaes (*Llanfaes*) with his commanders, and his elders, and all his household, having an only daughter, called Marchel, and to her he said, 'I fear for your health, on account of this impending plague that is threatening us' — to ward off which, the said Marchel had a kind of girdle of animal-skin, because there was a belief that whoever wore around their middle parts an animal-skin might thereby ward off infection from the plague — 'because of this, you are to set out for Ireland.' (*So perhaps God will grant my wish, that you may be able to survive.*)

And her father allotted to her three hundred men, and twelve girls, daughters of an *architriclinus*,[31] instead of maid-servants, who might all conduct her thither. Setting out, then, Marchell on the first night found lodging at Llansemyn (*Glansefyn*), and there a hundred men died in that night. She rose in the morn, cursing the place of that stay, and set out, troubled as much by the danger as by remorse; and by the second night reached Madrum (*Meidrim* or *Mydrim*), and, as before, here a hundred men died. Rising as quickly as possible in the morning, [she was] by the third night at Porthmaur (*Porth Mawr*) and, avoiding the death of [any more of] the men, with a hundred men and her handmaidens she came to Ireland.

Having learnt of her arrival Anlach son of Gornuc (= Cormac), king of that place, hurried to her with a large retinue befitting a king. And, having learnt the reason for her coming, king Anlach was delighted, and he took her in marriage as much for her beauty as for her connection by birth (for she was the daughter of a king). And king Anlach swore that he would go back with her to Britannia, if she was able to bear a son. And king Anlach married off the aforesaid twelve girls, giving away each one of them in wedlock. And so as the days rolled by it happened that Marchell conceived and bore a son, for whom his father ordained the name 'Brachan'.

3. [*The Return*]
Thus when Brachan was two years old, his parents took him back to Britannia, and they tarried at Benny (*Y Fenni-fach*).

4. [*Brachan's schooling*]
And Drichan took the boy to be fostered, and he was with him seven years.

5. [*Brachan and Kynauc*]
And afterwards, (*war having broken out between kings*) his father gave him as a hostage to the king (*of Powys*), by name Banadyl; where, time dragging heavily upon him, he violated the daughter of the aforesaid king, called Banadylued, who conceived and bore a son whom he had carried away to saint Gastayn (= *Castain*) (*whose church now stands by the Mara* (= the Lake of Llan-gors)), who baptized him, calling his name 'Kynauc'.

And everyone recognized, from the *armilla* that had been taken off, with which Kynauc was endowed, that he was the son of Brichan.

6. [*The descent of Kynauc*]
This is his genealogy – Kynaucus the son of Brachan, the son of Anlach, the son of Gornuc (= Cormac), the son of Eurbre of Ireland; and that on the part of his father. On his [father's] mother's part, Brichan the son of Marchel, the daughter of Teudric, the son of Teithphal (= Teudfall), the son of Teithrin (= Teudric), the son of Tathal (= Teudfall), the son of Annun the Black King of the Greeks.

7. [*Brachan's succession*]
Afterwards, with Brachan growing up in the way of good qualities, (*the war came to an end, and peace between the kings was restored*). And some time later still, his father Anlach died; while he was hoping to inherit his parents' realm, he [Brachan] called a meeting with the *nobiliores*[32] of the realm, about the matter of his inheriting it. And they, seeing what a great measure of ability, handsomeness and nobleness he displayed, raised him up to the kingship.

8. [*Brachan's wives*]
During the time that he had been ruling, and controlling the realm entrusted to him with the utmost good government, he joined to himself three wives in

succession, whose names are these – Eurbraust, Rybraust, and Proestri (*by whom he had a great issue, namely thirteen sons, whose names are these ...*).

9. [*The royal burials*]
Brichan lies in Mynau (*Menevia*, St David's) in the valley which is called Vallis Brichan. Anllach lies before the door of the church of Llanyspydyt (*Llansbyddyd*). Reyn, son of Brichan, lies at Llanvayloc (*Llandyfaelog Fach*). The grave of Kynauc, in Merthyr Kynauc in Brecheiniawc (*Merthyr Cynog*).

\* \* \* \* \*

As a prelude to discussion, it is useful to turn here briefly to the list of twelve male names (the 'List of Sons' or 'The Sons of Brychan' in previous commentaries about the two documents). It is not strictly part of the narrative, and only in *CB* (para. 8 above) is it 'spliced on' by adding a gloss to the note of Brychan's three wives.

An inserted sub-head in *DSB* (in Vespasian A xiv) reads *hec sunt nomina filiorum Brachan de Brecheniauc* 'These are the names of the sons of B of B'; it represents no more than a B.3 inference and an appropriate guide-line. The *contextual* links with *DSB*, nevertheless, are threefold. The original, simply a list of twelve men, may be as old as (and perhaps a decade or so older than) a *DSB* narrative of *c*.580. The list, it will be suggested, shares a Llangasty (or vicinity) provenance with *DSB*. Thirdly the first name certainly, and the second probably, do represent sons of Brychan, mentioned (like their father) in a Christian rather than historical setting.

In neither *DSB* nor *CB* is this list given correctly; the odd name has been omitted, contiguous names are re-cast as father and son, and extra confusion is given by the addition of short explanatory glosses on names, some perhaps added as early as (late) B.1 or (early) B.2. Set out in parallel, without glosses, the *DSB* and *CB* versions provide the following:

|    | (*DSB*)    | (*CB*)           |
|----|------------|------------------|
| 1  | Rein       | Rein *Drem Rud*  |
| 2  | Clytguin   | Clytwyn          |
| 3  | Arthen     | Arthen           |
| 4  | Papay      | Kynon            |
| 5  | Kynon      | Papay            |
| 6  |            | Run              |
| 7  |            | Marthaerun       |
| 8  | Dynigat    | Dingat           |
| 9  | Paschen    | Pascent          |
| 10 | Chybliuer  | Kyfliuer         |
| 11 | Berwin     | Berwyn           |
| 12 | Rydoch     | Ridoc *gwindouut* |

– the B.3 allusion, in *CB* para. 8 above, to *tredecem filios* 'thirteen sons' being justified in that instance because the list of twelve is preceded by the name of Kynauc.

The content and to some extent the original order of names are confirmed by the MS Jesus College 20 version, headed *Enweu y meibyon ereill y Vrachan* ('Names of the other sons of Brachan' – i.e. other than *Kynauc*, Cynog). This appears to be a B.3 derivative of the *CB* version. It supplies the twelves names as:

| | | | |
|---|---|---|---|
| 1 | Rein *dremrud* | 7 | Marchara..un |
| 2 | Clytwin | 8 | Dingat |
| 3 | Arthen | 9 | Pascen |
| 4 | Papai | 10 | Cyblider |
| 5 | Kynon | 11 | Berwin |
| 6 | Runan(n) | 12 | Reidoc |

There is regular 'stratigraphy' of glosses within the final B.3 texts. The fiction that all these men were Brychan's sons having gained ground, and suitable headings to that effect having been added, all the names in *DSB* have *filius Brachan* added to them, the JC 20 list imitating this with *m(ap) Brachan*. In *CB* (and JC 20) a few 'sons' are made grandsons – Arthen father of Kynon, Dingat father of Pascent and (JC 20) of Cyblider. Common to all three is a similar gloss, noting that Clytguin or Clytwin had as sons the two saints Clydauc and Dedyu (Dettu, Ditu).[33] If these are the B.3. additions, probably within the B.2 phase were added the geographical glosses ('*qui est*', '*inde dicitur*', '*in*', '*apud*') to be examined in a moment; these relate certain of the men to the outside world, and to known localities. The only additions to single names in B.1 are likely to have been the title, or nickname, *drem rud* for Rein; and similarly *windouith,* (*CB*) *gwindouut*, for Ridoc(h).[34]

It is quite feasible to offer reconstructions of the lists, as they would have appeared (separately, in *DSB* and *CB*) in the B.2 phase. A caveat here is that even the un-glossed *DSB* list cannot be the original; at most it was a late sixth century transcript of a missing original, a transcript then appended to *DSB*. In these reconstructions place-names that have been up-dated in B.3, or are B.3 replacements for older and different names, or should simply be left blank, are in square brackets.

| | | |
|---|---|---|
| 1 | Rein *dremrud* | (*CB*) *qui post patrem suum regnavit* 'who reigned after his father' |
| 2 | Clytguin | (*DSB*) *qui invasit* [ ] 'who invaded?' |
| | | (*CB*) *(a) oresgynnaud* [ ] 'who conquered, overcame?' |
| 3 | Arthen | |
| 4 | Papay | |
| 5 | Kynon | (*CB*) *qui est in* [*manan*] 'who is in [*Manan*]' |

| | | |
|---|---|---|
| 6 | Run | (*DSB*) *qui sanctus est in occidentali parte predicte* [*mannie*] 'who is a saint in the western part of the aforesaid [*mannia*]' |
| | | (*CB*) *ipse sanctus ycallet in* [*manan*] 'himself a saint *ycallet* in [*manan*]' |
| 7 | Marthaerun | (*CB*) *apud Keueilauc* 'at Cyfeiliog' |
| 8 | Dynigat | (*CB*) *apud Llandeuery* 'at Llandovery' |
| 9 | Pascent | |
| 10 | Kyfliuer | (*DSB*) *inde dicitur merthyr Chebliuer* 'whence is named Merthyr Cibliver' (= *Llan Dâv* 32, 44, 346) |
| | | (*CB*) *ab eo dicitur Merthyr Kyfliuer* |
| 11 | Berwin | (*DSB*) *in Cornwallia* |
| | | (*CB*) *apud Cornubiam* 'in Cornwall' |
| 12 | Ridoc *uindouith* | |
| | | (*DSB*) *in* [*francia*] *inde dicitur Ton Ridoch Windouith* 'whence is named Hill of Ridoch Windouith' |
| | | (*CB*) *in* [*francia*] *inde dicitur collis Ridoc gwindouut* |

The inference to be drawn is that, if one starts with a sixth-century list or roll of names of twelve men, deemed for any reason to be persons worth commemorating, these glosses were added some two centuries or so later (in B.2) as a record of what happened to some of them. Rein, Brychan's second son, succeeded him as king; Clytwyn, probably Rein's brother, invaded or conquered some region on behalf of Brycheiniog. Nothing could be added to the names of Arthen, Papay and Pascent. Of the others, some were to be associated with places in Wales – Cyfeiliog, a commote in Montgomeryshire; Llandovery, where the southern church is called Llandingat; Merthyr Cibliver, a lost site somewhere in Glamorgan; and a hill named for Ridoc 'Uindouith', possibly in Erging in Hereford.[35]

We are left with three names, associated with localities seemingly not in Wales at all. Kynon had gone to (*CB*) 'Manan'; Run had become remembered as a saint in the same region, the aforesaid 'Mannia' (which is what a *DSB*, B.2, gloss may have had against Kynon's name) and, further (so *CB*), Run – in the western part of 'Mannia' – was specifically located *ycallet* 'in the wood' (better, 'in "The Wood"'). *Mannia, Manan*, at this B.2 stage, represent *Dumnonia* (variant, *Damnonia*), or south-west Britain; the 'western part' of which, Cornwall, is more directly given as Berwin's location with the (*CB*) *apud Cornubiam*.[36]

The Dumnonian traces of Kynon, Run and Berwin as sixth-century migrants from Wales to Cornwall are discussed in chapter 15, later; for such traces can indeed be found. Their inclusion here is just one of many clues. This enigmatic list – which could have been completed in the latter part of the sixth century – records some of the secular and Christian heroes, the Great and the Good, of early Brycheiniog. It opens with (probably) two sons of Brychan himself, the others being contemporaries either of Brychan or of the generation of Rein and Clytwyn.

143

The subsequent B.2 locational glosses mark a continuing interest in their known fates. The fantastic B.3 embroideries, added at a period when the original purpose of the list had been forgotten, do at least stress the intimate link with the kingdom's eponymous founder, or re-founder. We have sufficient here to indicate that purpose (p. 150 below), but may now return to the broader sweep of the *DSB* narrative.

The putative author, the Priest of Llangasty, wrote within a Christian *milieu*. Lurking within his short account of the parentage, birth, upbringing, succession and reign of Brychan is a more subtle theme. The composition reflects at several points (as of course does that of the later *CB* paraphrase) imitation of the Vulgate text of the Gospels.[37] But we might detect a possibility that, while he adhered to a sequence of events preserved through personal memories or transmitted orally, some slight licence was taken – for the most pious of motives – in hinting at parallels between the life of Brychan, and that of Our Lord. We may be asked to envisage Marchel, *Marcella*, the virgin only-daughter of the king, alongside Mary the Holy Mother; the generously inclined Anlach, and then Brychan the only son, as the complement in the royal Holy Family. Marchel's voyage westward is hardly the Flight into Egypt, though the author of *CB* may have had Herod's edict in mind since he chose to specify the infant Brychan returning to Britannia when two years old; but in *DSB*, shifting the focus a generation forward, we read of Kynauc (later, the kingdom's premier saint) being taken as a baby to Castanius for baptism besides, or even in, the lake of Llyn Syfaddan, as the child Jesus went to be baptized by John in the Jordan. In *DSB*, too, the deliberate textual juxtaposition of the baptism at Llangasty and straightway Brychan's public recognition of Kynauc as *filius suus* – the future *sanctus*, but a figure to be implicitly rejected of men in favour of his half-brother Rein – echoes the sequence in Matthew's Gospel account; immediately after Christ's baptism by John, there is the descent of the Spirit as a dove and the Heavenly voice proclaiming *Hic est filius meus* (*dilectus in quo mihi complacui*).

The narrator's intent was to link the essence of an agreed recent past with a Brycheiniog at the time of writing; in arguing for a late sixth century date, it seems sensible to suggest that *DSB* was composed within the kingship of Rigeneu, successor to (possibly, son of) Rein Dremrud the son of Brychan.[38] In giving a précis of supposed facts about national origins, with a Christian emphasis and in a slightly mannered Latin reflecting the author's knowledge of the Bible and (probably) a limited range of secular classics,[39] the composer of *DSB* had to aim at a concise narrative open to external scrutiny and in accord with internal group-memories and beliefs. One has to say that he realized such an intent rather well. What is being described is a transition, from a very small sub-Roman kingdom (of Teuderic) to an enlarged realm under his grandson, with a new name being acquired from that grandson's own as a ruler whose legitimacy and Christian standing form matters for emphasis. The transition fell with, and may have been partly spurred on by, a natural catastrophe; marked by a spell of exceptionally cold weather, it must have occurred within the memories of aged men (or children of such men) to whom the *DSB* author could speak, in which case we have to regard it as a genuine event. Coincidentally the indigenous ruler had an only daughter, a solitary heiress. A marriage to a man of similar rank, but from another and distant place, was arranged. Suitably attended, the daughter was sent westwards to meet her future husband and she remained with him until a male heir was born. The family returned; so did a party of aristocratic girls who had accompanied her, who had also been provided with appropriate husbands, and who brought those husbands back with them, as immigrants who now acquired specified estates. In due time the immigrant husband of the princess succeeded his father-in-law as king. Meanwhile his son, fostered with a local sage from the ages of four to eleven, as was the custom, was placed as a princely hostage with a neighbouring potentate, with whom there may have been border skirmishes. While there as an adolescent he fathered a son of his own who, brought home for baptism and accorded a premature public recognition as a future king, was then denied this role and fulfilled another as a famous *sanctus*. The youthful father, following his own father's death, was recognized by the *nobiliores* as a suitable king. He took a legitimate wife; their offspring included Rein, who was to succeed him, probably Clytwyn, and certainly at least one daughter, Gladusa. The narrative closes by reciting the burial-places of Brychan's father, saintly son Kynauc (Cynog) and royal son Rein. The concluding lines, claiming that Brychan himself was buried elsewhere – outside his kingdom – must constitute an admission of fact, one that could hardly be changed to contravene general knowledge. Here the inference is, not that the hero-king was deposed, but that he *died* elsewhere, and at this period the likely explanation would be that he had sought to end his life as a Christian ascetic. And this is what took place. 'Enys Brachan' is known, as is Brychan's original grave, his name-in-religion and the final resting-place of his enshrined remains.

There have long been, and doubtless will continue to be, many who describe the *DSB* narrative as a foundation-legend, and Brychan as a legendary (or 'semi-legendary') king. If nothing of *DSB* had been made up, arranged, and written down before the eleventh century such a claim would have substance. The indications are, though, that its narrative precedes the Norman conquest of Brecon by a good half-millennium; it forms a coherent and credible historical account. Nearly all of it is comprehensible and explicable. By now, readers will have guessed that in *DSB* and *CB*, *Hibernia* 'Ireland' means, not the Emerald Isle, but the Déisi-settled area of Demetia – specifically, its north-west corner, later Pebidiog (Fig. 7.7). Teuderic's small kingdom lay in the Llynfi corridor, NNE from Brecon city (Fig. 9.4), and its fifth-century name *Garth Matrun* harks back to its pre-Christian, late-fourth-century roots. The *garth* 'mountain-spur' is the frowning height of Mynydd Troed, a western spur of the Black Mountains (Fig. 9.1), with

Fig. 9.1 Llyn Syfaddan (Llan-gors lake), near Llangasty, looking north; background, right, the mountain spur that may be the 'garth' of Garth Matrun and Talgarth. Photo: author.

modern Talgarth – place at the 'brow of the garth' – below it. This district was spread out below the Garth of the *Matrona*, 'The Great Mother', a goddess probably personified by the lake of Llan-gors, a fish-rich and life-supporting water whose other title (Llyn Syfaddan) appears to conceal an alternative 'divine' name.[40] In the fifth century, the kinglets Teudfall (<*Touto-maglos*) and Teuderic (<*Touto-rigi*) claimed descent, as did virtually all Welsh dynasties large and small, from a Roman notable. The distinction in their case was that their Validating Ancestor was not plucked from the House of Constantine, but was an Antonius Gregorius – in some fashion, remembered as having been a swarthy man – who really existed.[41] It is conceivable that his last post was as provincial governor, *praeses*, of Britannia Prima at *Corinium*, Cirencester.[42] A gold armilla (armlet or torc), seen and described in some detail in the twelfth century at Brecon by Giraldus Cambrensis, may have formed a legacy to his descendants who, after *c*.400, succeeded in setting up their own principality amid the Brecon uplands. The narrative suggests that the armilla was passed down, not exactly from king to king, but through each nominated successor (the Welsh *gwrthrychiad*). It appears that the armilla's transmission stopped with Cynog and that for the next seven centuries it was linked to his name.

In V.3, the horizons of Christianity and Latinity are marked by a location alongside the sacred lake, and by such names as *Castanius* and Marchell; *Marcella*, not just Latin but overtly Christian.[43] We are told nothing leading us to picture Teuderic himself as Christian. For his daughter, depicted as an only child, the absence at home of any appropriately ranking bridegroom may have made it desirable to arrange a marriage with a Demetian *nobilis*, Anlach son of Cormac. It is unlikely that Anlach was himself ever a king, but we may suppose he was within the *derbfine*, the four-generation group of agnatic descendants, of Aed Brosc (probably his great-grandfather), and thus *rígdamnae* – one, under Irish custom and law, in theory eligible to be chosen for the Demetian kingship, in Anlach's lifetime a throne held probably by Triphun (p. 81).[44]

The journey to Demetia is presented to us in several lights. The details of the actual travelling, on horseback, could be realistic and factual, and relate to a known route. The trip involved three stages of twenty-four, twenty-six and thirty-seven miles (Fig. 9.2), (*DSB*) *Lan Semin* marking the fording of the river Tywi near Llangadog, and *Methrum* probably the use of the fortified spur, now Meidrim churchyard (Fig. 9.3), as an overnight bivouac. The arrival at 'Porth Mawr' signifies the north-west extremity of Demetia, introduction of this beach being required because the fictitious journey across to *Hibernia* follows.[45]

After the union of Marchell and Anlach, within a year or so the birth of Brychan is followed by the Return to Britannia. Since so important a happening in the history of Brycheiniog is unlikely to have been wholly forgotten the author attempts to validate it, from surviving tradition, by adducing details and names. Anlach's family was accompanied by twelve (or so) noble companions, represented as the husbands – then, or later – of twelve (or so) Brycheiniog girls of equal social rank. Only four of these men's names could be remembered (or have survived successive transcribings of *DSB*). The Priest of Llangasty if he wrote about 580 is describing a Return that had taken place nearly a century beforehand. The names are given an 'Irish' sound, with typical velar suffixes (endings in -*c*, or -*ch*). *Lounoic* (scribal error for *Lonnoic*, gen.?) recalls 194a, Co. Kerry, ogam LLONNOCC, and *Lithmilich* possibly something like the attested OIr. *Leit(h)mech*. Of the estates named, *Enifernach* (as an interlinear note by Sir John Prise shows that he realised) begins with OW *(m)eni(d)*, now *mynydd* 'mountain' – this may be the hilly Mynydd Frynych south of the Usk, opposite Trallwng.[46] The *mainaur* (*maenor*: 'estate, demesne') called *Oper Birnich* lay by the *aber* ('outflow, confluence') on the Usk's north bank of the small Brynich stream, just south-east of Brecon. Had we all the names of these incoming *duces* and their estates, undoubtedly more of the latter would be co-terminous with the larger farms, manorial and tenanted, on both banks of the upper Usk basin.

What, then, *are* these names? Where are the others? The minor answer is that

THE BRYCHAN DOCUMENTS

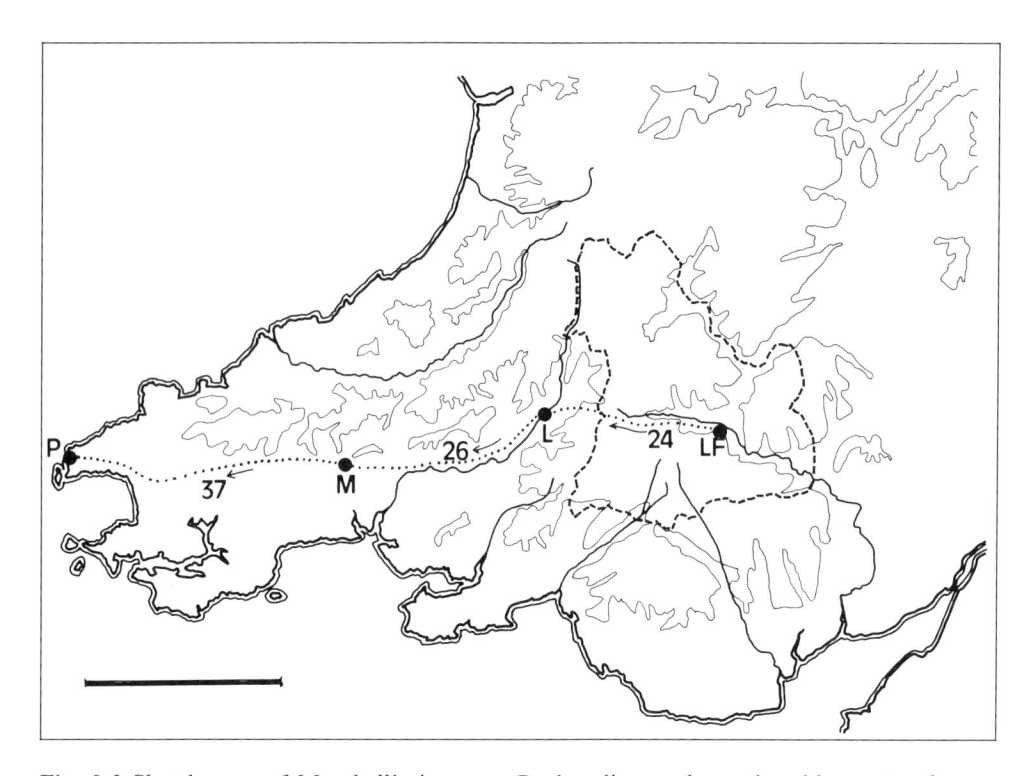

**Fig. 9.2** Sketch map of Marchell's journey. Broken line encloses the old county of Brecknock; dotted line, her route westward with intervals in miles from Llanfaes (LF) to Llansefyn (L), Meidrim (M) and Porth Mawr (P). Contour at 600 feet; scale, 25 miles (40 kms.)

the two actually recorded are relatively near Llangasty (about five miles to the west) and that other names may lie hidden in local place-names, obsolete or surviving.[47] The major answer is that the route of Marchell's outward journey (Fig. 9.2), in reverse, is that postulated for the end of the fifth century in connection with the presence, in the Usk valley, of persons migrating from Demetia; possibly (so Fig. 8.6.) from Pebidiog in particular. We can only guess, without much point, whether or not exactly twelve *nobiles* made the move, plus an uncertain total of women, children and dependants. The names listed on p. 122 supply, graven in stone, at least some that a late sixth-century author could not recover and – allowing a time-lag between arrival, and death, and also for memorials to members of the second (and third) generation – the estimated dates for such memorials accord with a suggestion that Marchell's journey, Brychan's birth and the Return occurred around AD 490 plus or minus a decade.

The meaning of the brief stay at *Benni, Benny* – taken to mean the farm-hamlet of Y Fenni (Fach) just west of Brecon city – eludes us. These may just possibly

**Fig. 9.3** Meidrim (or Anglicized, Mydrim), Carmarthenshire, approached by the old road from the east; the wooded spur above present village, site of small promontory fort with present church and churchyard. Photo: Susanna Thomas.

be B.3, Brecon-interest, insertions; the Priory had lands here, and a chapel of *Benni* licensed in the thirteenth century might have originated in pre-Norman times.[48] Brychan's seven-year stay with Drichan, on one or other side of the small river Ysgir, is an instance of fosterage.[49] The colourful recitation of the boar, stag, fish, beech-trees, honey and bees may have circulated separately as a bardic poem,[50] but it is drawn from a wider symbolic repertoire whose other manifestations were discussed by A. W. Wade-Evans long ago.[51] A further glimpse of aristocratic custom comes with the placing of the boy Brychan (aged nine? aged eleven? older still?) as *obses*, resident hostage, in the family of a neighbouring chieftain or petty king.[52] When a B.3 redactor of *CB* tried to aggrandize this by talking of *orta guerra* 'war having broken out', he was using Anglo-Norman, not sixth century, phraseology. In *DSB*, 'Benadel' (the *CB* 'Banadyl') – MW *banadil* 'broom-plant, *genesta*' – and his daughter Banadylued ('broom-blossom', i.e. golden-haired) may represent only local aristocrats; they became royalty later in *CB*, with Banadyl elevated as *regi de Powys*(!) – the political geography of B.2, the ninth or tenth century. The site of Brychan's stay as an *obses* is more likely to have been in a small fifth–sixth century state, perhaps once the equal of *Garth Matrun* but later the inferior of Brycheiniog. This was *Buellt*,[53] later Builth, 'the cow-pasture land' reached from the Usk valley by crossing the Mynydd Epynt plateau, going north along the line of today's B 4520 road past Upper Chapel and the extinct Drovers' Arms — a most ancient track, one that gave Epynt its name. The reported refusal of the Brycheiniog *seniores* to recognize Cynog as an acceptable heir-apparent and successor to his father may have been linked to a view of Cynog's mother Banadylwedd as a rustic nobody. Paucity of early historical sources hardly assists us here, but the *DSB* and *CB* glosses against the name of Clytwyn, *qui invasit* . . . and *(a) oresgynnaud* . . ., cannot possibly in the sixth-century original have been followed by (*DSB*) *totam terram Sudgwalliae* or (*CB*) *Deheubarth*. These are vain boasts, added in B.3. The original area-name may well have been that of *Buellt*.

We turn back to the list of twelve male names (p. 141). One at least is continuing-Roman, to set beside *Castanius* and *Marcella* — Pasc(h)en(t), *Pascentius*. Most are British; Rein, Clytwyn, Arthen, Kyfliuer.[54] A few may be of Irish origin — Berwin (cf.368, Llandawke, BARRIVENDI, p. 99 earlier). In the name Dynigat, *CB* Dingat, we may perhaps observe not only one of the Demetians returning with Anlach, but the aristocratic (327) DVNOCATI on his son's memorial from Crickhowell, the proprietor of a *maenor* at *Nant Dincat*, and the eponym (as lay founder?) of the ecclesiastical site at Llandingad, within modern (and medieval) Llandovery.

This may afford the final clue. The list recites names of those who, in one way or another, were destined to be recalled not just as notables or heroes but as *Christian* notables or heroes. They could have become *sancti* 'saints' like Run, and probably Kyfliuer; a father of saints, like Clytwyn (who also conquered); and benefactors to the Church, the givers of land, founders of sites that later held churches (like Dynigat?), supporters in kind. What we read is a surviving *diptych*, a roll to be recited during the sacrament of the Mass entreating prayers for their souls (and such a recital may well have been preluded with the names of both Brychan and Cynog).[55] St Jerome's fourth-century words, *publice diaconus in ecclesia recitat offerentium nomina* 'a deacon shall read out aloud in the church the names of those to be recalled in the Mass', supply enough authority for a liturgical practice that by the sixth century may have been introduced to Brycheiniog through *Castanius* (or whoever else the name of *Castanius* signifies) from fifth-century sub-Roman observances further down the river Usk in south-east Wales. Early written items, early hagiographical traditions, involving the number twelve (or multiples thereof) must always raise the suspicion of Biblical influence — Our Lord's disciples, as a start — but in this case, for any reason, a genuine sixth-century written roll of *nomina in sacris diptycis scripta* may have totalled a dozen. And if here, during VI, there really was an extremely early small church, a building for public worship associated with 'Castanius' and sited near the lake, it may until the mid-sixth century have been the kingdom's *only* church. We could even point to one of its names. Somewhere upon the hillside, east of Llangasty, was a spring — *finnaun doudec seint* 'Fount of the Twelve Holy Men' — presumably within, or on the edge of, church land. In the Book of Llandaff, the *lann i doudec seith*[56] is the church-site itself; and it would have acquired this unusual title through the local fame of the *duodecim sancta nomina*, the Twelve Holy Names of Brycheiniog therein commemorated.

This book omits discussion of the longer list of twenty-four (or so) female names, appended to both *DSB* and *CB*.[57] They are not central to a demonstration that inferences from the inscribed memorial stones and a reading of the reconstructed *DSB* narrative fall together as a reflection of sixth-century happenings. The female list ('of Daughters of Brychan', inevitably) is certainly bipartite and one can simply point to the appearance of *Guladis*, or *Gladusa*, daughter of Brychan and mother of St Cadog; a reference to a *Bethan* who, like Kynon, Run and Berwin in the list of men, was said to be *in Mannia* (*DSB*), *apud Manau* (*CB*) — that is, in *Damnonia*; and a strong probability that, contained within a tangle of names and glosses that is extremely hard to unravel, we do have a group of twelve (British) female names originally regarded as a counterpart to the defective roll of the *duces* who returned with Anlach. In this respect, they may once have been thought to represent the twelve *puellae, vice pedissequae*, who travelled to Demetia with Marchell; and, in terms of social anthropology, could perhaps be construed as prominent women within late fifth-century Garth Matrun, marriage to whom somehow legitimized the acquisition of real property in the Usk valley.

If the environmental, or climatic, episode with which the *DSB* narrative opens is to be seen as an actual happening of the very late fifth century, partly remembered nearly a century afterwards, can any explanation be suggested? What we are told is the coincidence of a need to find a husband for Marchell with a period of exceptionally cold or frosty weather, *algor (DSB)*, attacking humans with boar-like ferocity (*aprine*), calling for garments of sheepskin or wolfskin (*pelliciam vestem*), severe enough as a *frigus*, a 'coldness of death', to carry off two batches of a hundred men each, and relieved only at the sunnier (*apricior*) and thus warmer sea-level locale of Porth Mawr. When, rather later, *CB* was composed, a collective memory of long-past disasters led to the substitution of *pestilentia*, plague — almost certainly from knowledge of the *magna mortalitas*, the pandemic of the 540s that had reached Wales[58] — but nevertheless with retention in *CB* of the now-meaningless *perizoma de corio animalis* 'girdle of animal-skin' worn by Marchell; in accordance with reported popular belief as a specific against, not frost, but infection.

One possible interpretation is that, around 490, the limited area of Garth Matrun (the Llynfi corridor, Fig. 9.4) and the upper Usk basin, hemmed in by so much higher ground whose slopes formed the grazing and the pastures, was subject for a year or more to a phase of dust-veil, 'dim summers', effects; the localized

**Fig. 9.4** Central Brycheiniog; locations of places named in text. Broken line, extent of twelfth-century Norman Lordship of Brecon (= approx. tenth-century Brycheiniog?) – from I. W. Rowlands, in *BBCS* 30 (1982), 123 ff. **Key**: 1, ecclesiastical sites. 2, mainly secular sites. Outline contour at 800 feet; scale, 10 miles (16 km.).

result of a volcanic eruption elsewhere that precluded proper summers and at this height above sea-level led to frost-marked, long, winters of unusual severity. Two recent linked papers by Baillie and Warner, focusing upon early Ireland, have considerable relevance here.[59] 'Bad' episodes of the past, even of the remote and prehistoric past, may leave traces. Airborne volcanic dust can be detected in deep pollen or peat sampling, and in cores through lake and estuarine muds; from the 'signatures' or precise mineral content of such particles it is sometimes possible to say which known and dated eruption of which particular volcano (here, probably in Iceland or North America) was involved. There is another indicator. Dust-veil years will restrict the growth of trees, producing in (say) oaks an absence or faint trace only of the annual growth-rings; and from the Irish dendrochronological record Professor Baillie finds a PORG (period of restricted growth) covering a decade in the 540s AD. Richard Warner's stimulating discussion offers an archaeological model, suggesting that such 'bad' episodes in Ireland's past have been followed by phases of archaeologically detectable cultural change 'including a high level of innovation and intrusion', with much building, evidence for warfare, rituals associated with water and wet places and general activity manifest in archaeological finds.

Something of this, curiously, might be applied to Garth Matrun as it became Brycheiniog — intrusion certainly (from Demetia), some fighting possibly (with Buellt?) and, if we seek water-associated ritual episodes, the siting of a centre for an innovative and intrusive religion (Christianity) actually *at* the Lake, a feature at the heart of the kingdom personified if not deified as *Matrona, Samotona*. A 'bad' episode, climatically, could also have embraced during, before, or after a dust-veiled phase one of the periodic blightings of Llyn Syfaddan, in the shape of partial or total eutrophication.[60]

For Christianity, and for such developments after the initial attainment of a Christian horizon not long before 500, the narrative points obliquely to the presence of further church-sites and/or consecrated burial-grounds (the latter, notably, likely to have been marked by the place-name element *Lann*-). The map, Fig. 9.4, may be a pointer to the expansion of Brycheiniog (and the progressive eclipse of some secular focus of Garth Matrun where Talgarth now stands[61]). In *DSB, Lann Maies* (Llanfaes) is named, though not as a religious site; the note of the royal burials points to later sixth-century cemeteries at Llandyfaelog Fach and Llansbyddyd, and also at Merthyr Cynog — where the *merthyr* in this name may not be a sixth-century feature,[62] but whose format as a large curvilinear enclosure suggests a monastic settlement, one where Cynog's corporeal remains would be enshrined (Fig. 9.6). Along both sides of the Usk, west of Brecon, one could add both Trallwng and Defynnog on the strength of early memorial stones. For the period after 600, there are occasional uninscribed cross-slabs (*ECMW*'s Group, or Class II). These include one that still stands in the parish churchyard at Llansbyddyd (Fig. 9.5), and is still pointed out as marking the burial of king Anlach[63] — it may well be late seventh or eighth century, a Christian afterthought for a man whose burial-record in the narrative is oddly specific (*ante ostium* 'before the doorway'; i.e., outside the church).

The sole point at which the *DSB* text looks outside Brycheiniog, apart from reference to Demetia as *Hibernia* in the context of Marchell and her travels, is in the list of the twelve men's names. Here, if the locational glosses are B.2 and not B.1, some of them may still have been added in *writing* by 700, recording

**Fig. 9.5** Llansbyddyd churchyard; *ECMW* Group II cross-ornamented slab (no. 63), perhaps late seventh or eighth century, said to mark the burial of king Anlach. Photo: Susanna Thomas.

information that was known a good century before this. The most intriguing annotations are those for Kynon, Run and Berwin, implying that during the sixth century rather than the seventh these three – if not also others un-named – had left inland Brycheiniog, reached the south Welsh coast (at Newport? Swansea Bay?) and crossed the Severn Sea to Dumnonia, but to Cornwall rather than Devon. Tidings of their arrival and, in Run's case, a closer destination (in the western part of 'Mannia'; in some famous 'Wood' in 'Manan'), trickled back to Wales. What was lost during the seventh century was any clear Brycheiniog knowledge, not of the existence of the greater south-western peninsula (Cornwall

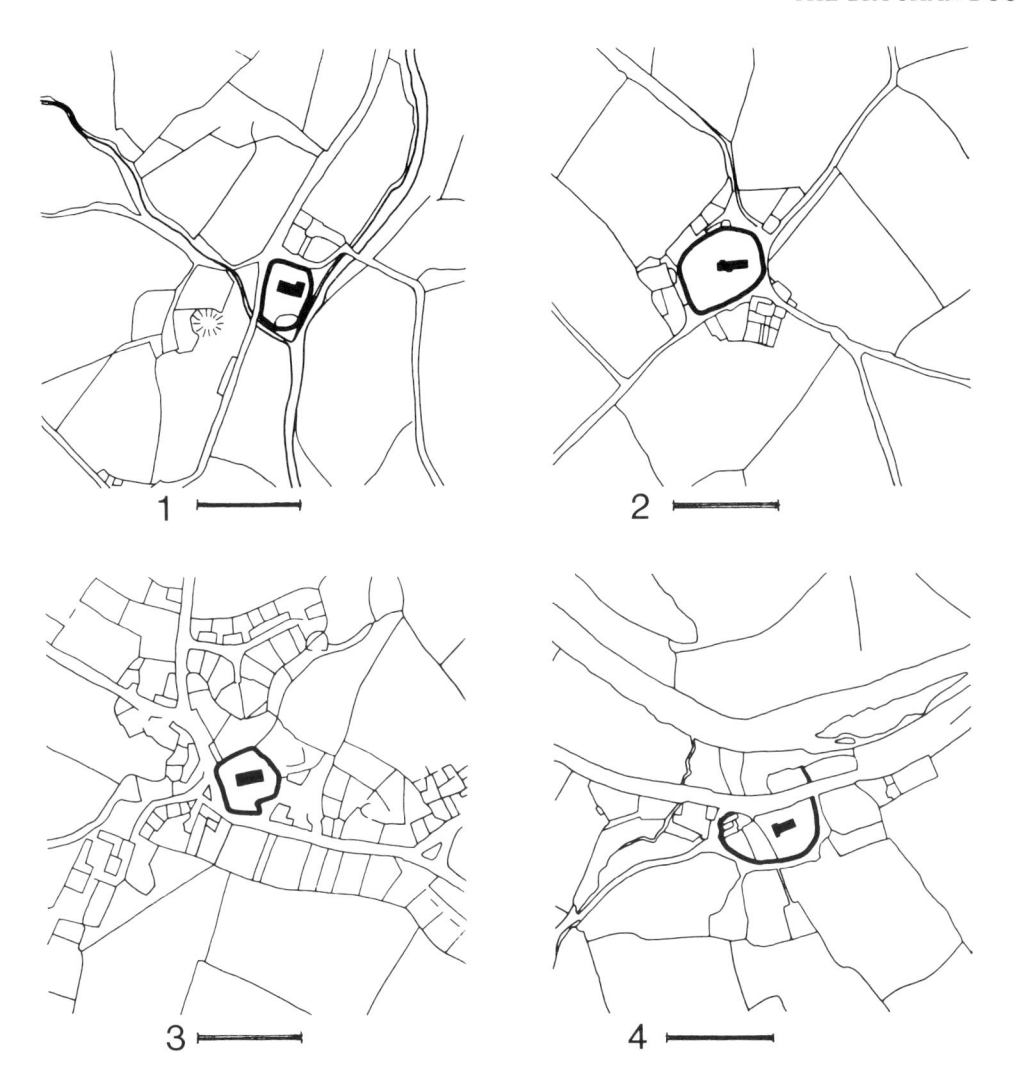

**Fig. 9.6** Brycheiniog; enclosed developed cemeteries, now village churchyards (llannau), from maplets kindly supplied by the Clwyd-Powys Archaeological Trust.
1, Llandyfaelog Fach. 2, Merthyr Cynog. 3, Llan-gors. 4, Llansbyddyd. Scale bar for each, 100 metres.

with Scilly, Devon, and most of Somerset, home to other British), but of its post-Roman Latinized name in the scribal variant *Damnonia*. This did not preclude transmission, possibly through Demetia and Demetian transmarine contacts, of the area-name *Cornubia* (for Berwin), a label that may have become current only by VII.3;[64] but B.2, and then B.3, copyings of the glosses to the Twelve Saintly Names somehow yielded in place of the original *Damnonia* all the 'Mannia, Manau, Manan' variations that have for too long consistently defied

155

explanation.[65] It would of course be tempting to link any sharp break in communication between the Britons of south-central and south Wales, and those of south-west Britain, to the Anglo-Saxons' westward advance to the Atlantic shores of Britain and the English victory at *Deorham* (Dyrham) in 577 with the capture of sub-Roman Gloucester, Cirencester and Bath. This may be too simple. It is equally possible that sea-contact, direct from Demetia (Tenby Bay) to the north Cornish coast (the Camel estuary) died away during VI.3 and was hardly ever renewed; a movement from Demetia to Dumnonia, described here in later chapters, took place but then came to a full stop.

Probably before 600, news of the death and burial of the absent Brychan had reached Brycheiniog. In his *patria*, the grave was duly recorded as being on an island; its true name was uncertain, and *Enys Brachan*, 'Island of Brychan' (so *DSB*) was the obvious substitute. It is virtually certain that nobody else from Brycheiniog had ever been there. All that anyone knew was that the isle was *iuxta Damnoniam*, 'next to Dumnonia', and this was therefore noted. It was, in fact, the Isle of Lundy. Brychan, by then a man probably in his sixties and a simple brother, under another name, in a small island community had died there. In 1969, more by chance than by any design, his grave was discovered — opened, and empty — in the course of an archaeological excavation. The circumstance of its finding, and the rest of Brychan's story, must form a separate chapter.

## References

1. British Library, MS Cotton Vespasian A xiv. On its Monmouth Priory provenance see Silas Harris, *J. Hist. Soc. Church in Wales*, 3 (1953), and Kathleen Hughes, pp.67–85 in: K. Hughes (ed. posthum. D. N. Dumville) *Celtic Britain in the Early Middle Ages* (Woodbridge 1980).
2. British Library, MS Cotton Domitian 1; and see N. R. Ker, 'Sir John Prise', *The Library*, 5th ser.,x (1955), 1–24. Prise also copied most of *DSB*, since at the time he apparently owned a version of it.
3. See further, n.11. Texts of both *DSB* and *CB* appear in *VSBG*, 313–19. Wade-Evans's translations were given in *Trans. Brecknock Soc.*, 1 (1930), 7–24, and earlier diplomatic editions with translations and notes appeared in *Y Cymmrodor.*, 19 (1906), 18–50. These were not entirely reliable; Wade-Evans missed out some significant interlinear notes by Prise. Older editions and commentaries (Phillimore, Sabine Baring-Gould, *et al.*) need not concern us. The present writer has used enlarged (British Library) photocopies from both MSS.
4. Obliteration through rebuilding may have been near-complete; for the historical background see D. M. Gwynne-Jones in *Brycheiniog* 24 (1990–2), 23 and n.7, and the Brecon city essays in *Brycheiniog* 25 (1992–3). The Priory's dating here follows Dr F. G. Cowley (*The Monastic Order in South Wales 1066–1349*, Cardiff 1977, *passim*).
5. *Anglo-Saxon Chronicle,* Mercian register, s.a.916 (*recte* 919).
6. Interim notes in *Antiquity* 63 (1989), 675–81; *Medieval Archaeology* 34 (1990), 250–1, 35

(1991), 235–6, and 36 (1992), 305–7; illus. account, pp.16–25 of Mark Redknap's *The Christian Celts* (NMW, Cardiff 1991). The startling quality of the small finds, seen at Cardiff through Dr Redknap's kindness, makes it abundantly clear that the crannog was a high-status site with ecclesiastical connections.

7. See n.5 above; this is the only possible interpretation of the entry.
8. So, implicitly, Wendy Davies 1979, at 98; a Llandaff charter, grant of Lann Cors with *territorium*, tentatively assigned to *c*.720.
9. Any serious search might begin at the farm-holding called Llan, at SO 133 259, a short way inland (south) from the present church.
10. *Llan Dâv* 255, *Lann i Doudec Seith* (*sic*), with (146) an associated spring, *Finnaun i Doudec Seint* – see further, p.151.
11. This chapter (with chaps. 8 & 10) presents conclusions only; for fuller explanations, readers are referred to my *The Brychan Documents: A Critical Analysis* (SDUC, Lampeter, forthcoming 1994). Relationship of *CB* to the older *DSB*, even when obvious B.3 and Anglo-Norman inserts have been pruned, is complex and puzzling. Main distinctions may be summarized. (a) *Stylistic*; *DSB* is closer in flavour to certain fifth or sixth-century Insular Latin writings (Patrick, Gildas, Muirchu) with sentences mostly linked by enclitic *-que*, and patterned use of meaningless conjunctions (*vero, autem quidem*, etc.) in second or third place. *DSB* seems to echo parts of the Vulgate Latin, e.g. Genesis, iv (very closely), Matthew, iii (less so). *CB* introduces main and subsidiary phrases with *Et...*, makes greater use of full relative clauses, and tends to repeat stems (*vitandam, vitaret, vitata*). (b) *Lexical; DSB* probably uses rather more obscure words best matched in secular sources (e.g., Catullus?), *CB*'s choice being on the whole biblical (though Ovid, *Metamorphoses*, may have been known). (c) *Orthographic*; an uncertain area because of up-dated spellings in successive copyings but (with names) *DSB*'s Latin forms seem the older – Brittanniam (*CB* Britanniam), Annhun (*CB* Annun, *Antonius*), and epenthetic vowels in *DSB* are lost in *CB* – Dynigat (*CB* Dingat), Teuderic (*CB* Teudric). Note *DSB* Lann maies (disyllabic still, from *mages(ta)*), but *CB* Lanmaes – diphthong? Generally too *DSB* medial or final *-i-* is rendered in *CB* by *-y-* and certain dentals are treated differently. (d) *Content; CB* omits (as of no special interest?) names of returning *duces* but *inserts* extended genealogy of *Kynauc*, Cynog; offers fresh explanations for certain items; elevates 'Banadyl' to kingship; and re-locates Brychan's grave at St David's – all these apsects imply a remove in time, greater than could be noted in *DSB*, from the original happenings.

Both authors were plainly familiar with the Vulgate and both presumably wrote at churches or monasteries. However if *DSB* is to be assigned to Llangasty, or thereabouts, in late VI, *CB* as a subsequent paraphrase (repeating some 80% of content, but only some 40% of the actual *DSB* wording) seems indicative of somewhere else in Brycheiniog. Merthyr Cynog is a possibility, Llan-gors rather more probable. The central text of *CB* may well have reached pre-Norman (B.3) Brecon quite separately from *DSB*.

12. The modern St Cynog, still principal patronal figure of Brycheiniog, appears in *DSB* and *CB* as *Kynauc(us)*, etc; final *-c* represents /g/. The first *DSB* graph would have been *Cunac* or *Cunauc*; the name is British, adjectival and hypocoristic, 'Hound-like, Little-Hound, or Little-Wolf'. Cf.397 Penmorfa, Caerns., type (d) of VI – FILI CVNALIPI CVNACI IACIT BECCVRI.
13. MS Jesus College 20 (= JC 20), Bodleian: see *EWGT*, 42–4.
14. JC 20 heading; 'Llyma'r mod y treythir o *Ach Kynawc Sant*'.
15. See *VSBG*, at 118–19. The late Hywel D. Emanuel's crucial study ('An analysis of the composition of Vita Cadoci', *Nat. Libr. Wales Journal*, vii (1951–2), 217–22) argued

16. E.g., *Vita S. Gundleii* ('Gwynllyw'), cap. 2 – *VSBG*, 172 ff.
17. Walter Map, *De Nugis Curialium* (transl. M. R. James: new edn., C. N. L. Brooke & R. A. B. Mynors, Oxford Medieval Texts, 1983), 153–5, story about Llyn Syfaddan – earlier edn. (*Cymmrodorion Record Ser.* ix, 1923) has (Sir) J. E. Lloyd's splendid notes on folklore, 77–82. Giraldus: *Itinerarium Cambriae*, I.2 (and elsewhere) – see also Raikes, in *Brycheiniog* 22 (1986–7), at 39–41.
18. Cited in *LBS* ii. 266–8, an extraordinary tale about St Cynog.
19. *EWGT*, 11, 81–3; in later centuries the Brycheiniog lines (plural) were involved with those of neighbouring kingdoms, notably Demetia. The post-700 part of one list, *EWGT* 45 (from JC 20), is persuasively restored by D. N. Dumville, *CMCS* 10 (1985), 48–52.
20. A helpful summary, stressing continuity of much of OW orthography from what must have been conventions of V–VII, appears in *CMCS* 7 (1984), 117 ff.
21. Though the story implies that 'Brychan' was given an Irish name, by his Irish father, in an Irish-settled *regio*, the British may by this time have already borrowed PrIr. *\*broccas* (later WCo. *broch*, English 'brock' as loanword) as a taboo-substitute for the old *\*tazgos* – see A. Mac an Bhaird, Ériu 31 (1980), 150.
22. See *LHEB*, 565–70 (linguistic development of Pr.WCBr. *pp, tt, cc,* to *f, th, ch* – 'middle or second half of VI') and, for the introduction of digraphs, notably British memorial TH, CH, to denote such, Anthony Harvey, pp.56–66 in: D. Ó Corráin *et al.*, eds., *Sages, Saints and Storytellers* (= Carney Festschrift), Maynooth 1989 – esp.63, para,(b), tending to favour 'an Irish origin for the convention' (of writing *ch, th,* etc.). Some support for Harvey's mild criticism of Jackson's dating (ibid., n.39) might be found in certain memorials, if rightly dated. From Dumnonia, 460 VAILATHI / FILI VROCHANI (un-typed, Irish names – so *LHEB* 566, VI.2 or VI.3) and now 1206, with DOVITHI (type (d), British names, probably VI.2?), show introduction of CH and TH for monumental use by VI.2, and perhaps during VI.1, presumably from Demetia; cf. there 375 DOTHORANTI and 365 LVNARCHI, both Carms., both of VI (*LHEB*, 365 as VI.3, 375 as VI.2/3). What this may allow is that, in *DSB*, such digraphs as seen in Marchel, Drichan, Methrum and ('List of Sons') Arthen are primary and genuine, and reflect usage well-established by c.580. In the 'List of Sons', if the names are really of VI (p. 150), note that Ridoch *Windouith* (*\*uuin, douith*) precisely matches the Cornish 1206 DOVITHI (= W *dofydd* 'lord, The Lord'). The final *-ch* employed in *DSB* for Anlach, Fernach, Lithmilich, Birnich (though not for 'Coronac' (= Cormac)) may be a slightly different convention (so Sims-Williams, elsewhere) designed to give such names a distinctly 'Irish' appearance in writing.
23. These comments are a necessarily tentative incursion into a vexed area (cf. *LHEB*, 433–60), but if *DSB* contained – as seems likely – *Teuderic*, not *Teuteric* (with the second *t* = /d/), lenition of the voiced dental ought to be implied; treatment of the final stop, if /g/, again apparently written as *-c*, may well be partly explained by the *DSB* author's likely knowledge of the older British form of the name. After all, someone in Demetia in V.2 (or V.3) knew enough to ordain CLVTORIGI for the memorial no.435; as did a later *ordinator* for 358 VOTEPORIGIS.
24. *LHEB* 448, 456; see also *CMCS* 7 (1984), 95.
25. See n.15 above: *VSBG*, 118–9 (*VC*, cap.48) – two Brecon-originating genealogies became slightly muddled here (*1*, Cadocus – Gladusa – Brachanus – Anlach – Urbf, etc.; *2*, Cadocus – Gladusa – Marchell – Teudiric(us) – Teitfall, etc.) but the specific names *Teudiricus* and *Teitfall* (read probably 'Teutfall') suggest a *DSB*-type source.

26. John Morris, *The Age of Arthur* (1973), 126–32, '... the crazily-perverted documents of Brecon ... nonsense even wilder than is usual in medieval story'. Morris had turned Teuderic into a Gothic mercenary general, re-conquering west Wales for Arthur before retiring to a sunset home in Cornwall, where he re-emerged as 'King Teudar' (p. 187).
27. *Cubicularii*, 'servants of the bed-chamber' (so Cicero, possibly the source), but 'office-holding intimates, chamberlains' more closely attending a king than *seniores* or *duces* may be intended.
28. *Duces* was earlier translated as 'commanders' (the *duces* and *seniores* accompanying Teuderic to *Lann Maies*) because there it might suggest aristocratic followers still young enough to lead in battle, as opposed to *seniores* as the king's counsellors (by whatever right). In this case, the implication seems to be 'men of substance prepared to emigrate, with their king, and assert themselves in a new land'.
29. Teudfall must represent *\*Touto-maglos* 'prince of the tribe, people'; one would have expected rather *\*Teudfael*, which may in fact have been originally written. For the graph -f- as lenited *m*, /μ/, a pretty early instance if used c.580, cf. the Madron stone 1048 QONFAL (dated within VII) from Cornwall, p. 291 subsequently. Here, and in *CB*, and of course in all later derivative texts, the simple *Teuderic son of Teudfall* sequence appears to have been repeated, as if somebody felt that two additional generations were required.
30. *Praust, Prawst* is otherwise attested (*EWGT*, 209, refs.; *TYP* 277), and Sir Ifor Williams (*CT*, 68) regarded its general sense as 'worthy'. A second 'wife' for Brychan, after Cynog's birth, to explain the different status of Rein (and Gladusa, and possibly Clytwyn) is obviously meant; the other, apparently inexplicable, two names look like inventions. For compounds, however, an *Onbraust* appears as a king's wife in a Morgannwg charter, *Llan Dâv*, 132, 140.
31. *Architriclinus*, 'master of a feast', from the Vulgate (John, ii. 8–9).
32. Here, *nobiliores* suggests members of whatever gathering, one that surely included the royal kin-group, had to be concerned with approving a king's successor. Since it cannot be certain what native terms are rendered by sixth-century Latin *nobiliores, seniores, duces*, throughout this book *nobiliores* is loosely used to imply persons of free, aristocratic status.
33. St Clydog is the patron of Clodock, Herefords. (probably the *Merthir Clitauc* of *Llan Dâv*); St Dettu, possibly of Llanddetti, by the Usk south-east from Brecon.
34. For *windouith*, see n.22 above; OW *drem rud* 'red-face, red-eyed' is also found in Brittany – *CB* 126, Daniel *Drem-rudd* 'au visage rouge' (so Loth). Cf. Sir Ifor William's note, CAn. 386 (line 1466), and see also G. P. Jones in *BBCS* 3 (1926), 34.
35. This supposes that *francia* ('France') is a B.3 scribal error for, possibly, *ercicg* 'Erging', a sub-Roman kingdom in Herefordshire.
36. *DSB*'s 'Cornwallia' here is at the earliest an eleventh century form; for *Cornubia*, see n.64 later.
37. A demonstrative sample only – *DSB*: Marchell's fur garment, *pelliciam vestem,* Mark i.6 (John the Baptist), *Joannes ... zona pellicia circa lumbos eos* (known also to the *CB* author, who has *perizoma de corio animalis ... circumdaret lumbos eos*). The birth of Brychan, (*DSB*) *peperit filium vocavitque eum Brachan,* goes with Matthew i.23, *et pariet filium ... peperit filium suum primogenium ... et vocavit nomen eius Iesum*. *CB*, on the other hand, using *conciperit et peperit filuum* (Brychan), *concepit et peperit filium* (Kynauc), is closer to Genesis iv.2 (*concepit et peperit Cain*) and iv.17 (*concepit et peperit Henoch*).
38. There is no mention in either text of Rigeneu (a British name; *\*ri, ceneu* 'whelp of a king') who appears in the Brycheiniog succession in JC 20 as *Rigeneu m(ap) Rein dremrud*.
39. *Tripudium*: Tacitus, *Histories,* v.17 (*tripudiisque,* wild dancing by primitive Germans);

*pedisequa*, lit. 'foot-follower; girl who walks behind mistress; hand-maiden', Cicero, *De Oratore*, with *ancillulam pedisequamque*, a 'little maid' and 'waiting-woman' contrasted. The Vulgate NT uses *ancilla,* not *pedisequa.*

40. 'Syfaddan' has not really been explained (cf. Peter Powell, in *Brycheiniog* 22 (1986–7), 40, citing twelfth-cent. form *Syvadon*). This author would now suggest that, with shift to penult stress, it goes back to British \**Samo-ton(a)*, divine female personification of the summer months (\**samo-*) as the best fishing period.

41. *Antonius Gregorius* ('*Niger*') is indicated as the original for (*DSB*) *Annhun rex Grecorum,* (*CB*) *Annun nigri regis Grecorum* (and see *EWGT* 170, index, for later derivative refs. to 'Annun Ddu, king of Greece', etc.). By VI, *Gregor(ius)* was being confused with a British reflex of Latin *Grecorum* – cf. modern W *Groegwr*, plur. *Groegwyr*, 'Greek(s)' – and *niger, ddu,* need only imply a darker-than-British complexion. In AD 313–4 an Antonius Gregorius, *vir perfectissimus*, was *praeses Thebaidos* (Thebes, Middle Egypt: see *PLRE* i.403). If by some extraordinary chance the same man was in Britannia by IV.2, the genealogical 'padding' in *DSB* may suggest a realization that two or more extra generations between Antonius and Teudfall had to be denoted.

42. The writer is most grateful to Professor Michael Jarrett for this ingenious and attractive idea.

43. Marcella was a fourth-cent. Roman lady praised by Jerome (*Epistolae*, 127); her name, like *Marcellus*, gave rise to later Welsh names (*EWGT*, 202).

44. Anlach was discussed earlier (Chap. 6, p.) in the context of the Demetian regnal-list. Here, for *DSB*, one need only re-state that – if, as likely, an actual great-grandson of Aed Brosc – Anlach was probably born *c*.465–70, would have married Marchell *c*.485–90, and as a youth in Demetia would have lived at the time of Triphun, and possibly the start of Aircol's kingship. To place Anlach, Brychan's birth, the Return, etc., (say) a half-century later than this would be to go against too many other independent date-estimates.

45. For the Pebidiog end of the journey, there is a 'Caer Farchell' (RCAHMW *Inv. Pembrokeshire*, 336, nos.976–8, with a field called 'Parc-y-castell' – see *PNP* 287, 313, citing *Caervarchell*, 1341) at SN 795 270, eight miles ENE from St David's. 'Tradition' (but how old?) 'associated the place with ... Marchell the mother of Brychan', *PNP* 287.

46. Fan Frynych (*ban*, isolated peak) at SN 95 22 was, in 1572, called *Kraige Verenigh*; the writer is much indebted to Mr Peter Powell, of Brecon, for expert guidance on Brycheiniog place-names.

47. Llanhamlach, a parish three miles east of Brecon, has no known patron. Theophilus Jones (*Hist. Brecknock*, iv.15) notes a *c*.1800 spoken form 'Llanhamwlch' (*sic*) and provided his own folk-etymology of Llan-aml-llech. It allows a slight suspicion that \*-*milich*, or whatever real Irish name of VI is embedded in *DSB*'s *duces*, was used here in a pre-Norman *lann* compound for an early estate with its church or cemetery.

48. Miss Morgan's note, *AC* (1903), 210–11; exact position unknown. See also Theophilus Jones, *Hist. Brecknock*, ii.111–12. Y Fenni *Fach* ('little') is simply to distinguish the place from 'Y Fenni', a modern Welsh name for Abergavenny. An older notion that *Benni* was a native name for the Roman fort of Y Gaer, or Brecon Gaer, a mile further west (so *AC* (1903), 352, Baring-Gould) arose from the mistaken belief that this had been the Roman *Bannium* or *Bannio* (*recte*, the Roman fort at Abergavenny, *Gobannio*, *PNRB* 307).

49. For the name *Drichan* (British), cf. Loth, *CB* 127, *Drihic(an)*; Fleuriot, *GVB* 135, 152, *derch, dre(h)* 'aspect, regard, apparence'. There is no other subsequent record of any fort, Din Drichan.

50. So Canon Thornley Jones, in *Brycheiniog* 17 (1977), 17.

51. *Life of St David* (SPCK, London 1923), 60–61; cf. also *VD* cap.2. For the blind, elderly

and (?)moribund Drichan's spear (*lancea*), see J-M. Picard, 'The strange death of Guaire Mac Áedáin', at pp.370–1 in: D. Ó Corráin *et al.*, eds., *Sages, Saints and Storytellers* ( = Carney Festschrift) (Maynooth, 1989), which offers a plausible key to this particular piece of symbolism. The whole episode may however be a B.3 insertion.

52. A full study of early Insular hostage-placing as between rival rulers, a custom perhaps derived from Mediterranean civilizations (W. Dinan, *Monumenta Historica Celtica I* (1911), *passim*), would be of great interest. Predicament of well-born children so exchanged, governed by set conventions (O'Curry, *Manners and Customs of the Ancient Irish* (1873), vol.i, cccl–ccclv) would have been analogous to inter-tribal fosterage – Jackson, The *Oldest Irish Tradition* (1964). See now, too, Charles-Edwards, *Kinship*, 78–82. *DSB*, in mentioning this without comment, may imply that such social mechanisms within Insular society were, in VI, normal and expected.

53. Henry Lewis, *BBCS* 8 (1936), 229; *\*bou* 'cow, cattle' and *\*gelt* 'grass, pasture'. Epynt is from *\*epo-sent-* 'horse-path'.

54. Clytwyn<*\*Cluto-uuin-* = 'Of-Fair-Renown'; Arthen<*\*Artu-gen-* = 'Bear-begotten'(?); Kyfliuer, intensive *cyf-*, *liuer* 'painter, dyer, colorist'.

55. *Diptyca* or *tabella*, brief catalogues of the dead, held names of church-founders, benefactors, holy elders and (elsewhere) bishops and martyrs. Jerome's words (In Ezech., 4.18) describe one way of introducing the public reading into worship; Cyprian (Epist., 12.2) explains how such commemorative rolls were drawn up.

56. The spring may be the one, overgrown on the hillside, at SO 157 271 (finally located, 1991). See *Llan Dâv* 146, 255, for these; reading there *in cantref Talgard* (Talgarth), for the erroneous *Talacharn*, another commote altogether west of Afon Tywi in south-west Carmarthenshire.

57. These are examined at length in my *The Brychan Documents: A Critical Analysis* (see n.11 earlier).

58. *Annales Cambriae*, s.a. 547, with death of Maelgwn of Gwynedd, the *Maglocune* of Gildas, *De Excidio*, 33. Generally taken to have been bubonic plague, this pandemic spread from Africa or Asia, *via* Byzantium, probably arriving in Britain – with seaborne trade? – in 542/3.

59. M. G. L. Baillie, 'Dark Ages and Dendrochronology', *Emania* 11 (1993), 5–12; R. B. Warner, 'Tree-Rings, Catastrophes and Culture in Early Ireland: Some Comments', ibid., 13–19. So far, no episode dateable to 480–90 has been identified; but the kind of event envisaged might be like one of 536–7 described by Cassiodorus and others, when a 'dim sun' effect in the Mediterranean lasted for some eighteen months (D. J. S. Schove & Allan Fletcher, *Chronology of Eclipses and Comets AD 1–1000* (Boydell Press, 1984), 95–7; 'a volcanic eruption in 536 is almost certainly the explanation of all the reports'). Non-archaeologists, perhaps unaware of recent developments in this important potential for absolute dating (applicable to historic as well as prehistoric times), may like to consult the following: C. Burgess, 'Volcanoes, Catastrophe and the Global Crisis of the Late Second Millennium BC', *Current Archaeol.* 117 (Nov. 1989), 325–9; J. J. Blackford *et al.*, 'Iceland volcanic ash and the mid-Holocene Scots pine (*Pinus sylvestris*) pollen decline in northern Scotland', *The Holocene* 2.3 (1992), 260–5 (acid pollution from Hekla (H-4) eruption, *c*.4000 BP); A. J. Dugmore & A. J. Newton, 'Thin Tephra Layers in Peat Revealed by X-Radiography', *Journ. Archaeol. Science* 19 (1992), 163–70 (Icelandic tephra identified in N. Scottish peats); Mike Baillie, 'Using Tephra to date the past', *Current Archaeol.* 134 (May–July 1993), 134–5. (I am grateful to Dr Andrew Dugmore, Edinburgh, for his help here.)

60. See R. L. Raike's study of the lake, *Brycheiniog* 22 (1986–7), 22–35; what may be a

twelfth-century occurrence is mentioned by Giraldus Cambrensis.
61. In the Prologue to *Vita Cadoci* (*VSBG*, 26–7) Brychan's court (*curia*) is placed here (*que vocatur Talgard*); there must still in the eleventh century have been some local tradition to this effect.
62. Names in *merthyr* (like Co. *merther*; Padel 1985, 164) probably commence later than those in *lann*; from Latin *martyrium*, in its fourth-century sense, the meaning is 'place claiming corporeal relics of (a named saint, confessor, martyr or bishop)'. See also Tomos Roberts, pp.41–4 in Edwards & Lane 1992. Llandyfaelog (*CB* – *Llanvayloc*) has as a site been re-modelled but the setting of thirteenth–fourteenth cent. yews marks the older ovoid enclosure, in which the cross-slab *ECMW* no. 49 (tenth cent.) may have stood in a pre-Norman church. The name is *Lann*, hypocristic *-te* (> *de, dy* 'O-Thou') and *Maeloc* <\**Maglacos* 'princely one'. Rather than denoting a dubious 'St Maelog', can the \**maglacos* have simply referred to Rein, as donor to the Church of a site from a royal estate? Llansbyddyd, (*DSB*) *Lanespetit*, may be a locative name with an early form of W *ysbyddad* 'thorn-bush, hawthorn?' rather than the suggested connection with *hospitium* (W *ysbyty*).
63. *ECMW* no.63; pointed out as such (1990) by village children; the near-certainty that they had been taught this at school is itself a continuity of a tradition known, *c*.1800, to Theophilus Jones at Brecon. J. O. Westwood seems to have been told it marked Brychan's grave (!).
64. Late British \**Cornouia*, Latinized as *Cornubia*. A poem of *c*.700 attributed to Aldhelm (*Monumenta Germaniae Historica, Auctores Antiquissimi*, xv, 523–8, lines 9–10) has 'usque diram Domnoniam / per carentem Cornubiam' – the first-known record of the word.
65. Older suggestions included the Isle of Man, Anglesey, and *Manau* (of the Gododdin) in south-east Scotland.

(*Note added in proof*) In *CMCS* – from this vol., now *Cambrian* Medieval Celtic Studies (Aberystwyth) – 26 (November 1993), 27–64, Patrick Sims-Williams ('The Provenance of the Llywarch Hen poems: A Case for Llan-gors, Brycheiniog'), writing entirely independently of this book's chaps. 8 and 9 and concentrating his attention upon the eighth to eleventh cents., rather than (as here) the pre-700 period, offers cogent reasons for selecting Llan-gors as the (B.2) litarary centre of Brycheiniog. This important paper, to which readers with any Brycheiniog interest are referred, hardly explores the 'Brychan tracts' (*DSB, CB*) but otherwise reaches many of the topographical conclusions given above. Note especially 52, map 2, and summary, 62–3.

# 10

# A Visit to 'Enys Brachan'

THE ISLAND of Lundy lies out in the Bristol Channel or Severn Sea, sixteen miles from Ilfracombe. Long, thin and high, three miles N–S but only half a mile wide, Lundy's main characteristics are its isolation and visibility. This elongated granite plateau, rising to 463 feet OD at Beacon Hill (with the Old Lighthouse), can be seen on most days from Dyfed's shores and from much of the Devon and Cornwall coast down as far west as Tintagel. Exceptionally from the top of the Old Light – 500 feet up – the shadowy line of Preseli can just be made out (Fig. 10.1).

The name is Norse – 'Puffin Isle', *lundi, ey* – like many of the island names in the south-west; Caldey, Skomer, Gateholm, etc. What Lundy was called by the British of Wales and of Dumnonia is something of a puzzle. There is no full history because there are almost no documentary records.[1] An outline of its ecclesiastical past is just possible.[2] A tiny church of St Helen, or Helena, stood here in the thirteenth century; by the sixteenth this was under the aegis of Cleeve Abbey in Somerset, though earlier almost certainly under that of Hartland in Devon. Much-battered foundations of a granite cell, internally 14 by 25 feet, are still visible at Beacon Hill. In 1896 a large and incongruous modern church was plonked down on Lundy; 'it would be elegant enough for a London suburb', commented A. E. Blackwell.[3]

In the walled graveyard atop Beacon Hill, next to the disused (1819) Old Light and the Trinity House keepers' quarters, burials took place both within and outside the remains of St Helen's little church until very recently. The enclosing granite dry-stone wall was built by Trinity House. What its line fails to hide, at least to the trained eye, is the fact that the walling was partly imposed on a much older and in part still curvilinear enclosure defined by a low bank and outer ditch; a characteristic *lann*. On the south-west sector a stretch of it survives, just inside the stone wall (Fig. 10.2). Implications that this site is what it appears to be, a pre-Norman cemetery enclosure, are confirmed by the presence of four inscribed memorials, all granite, two of them quite small. 1400 OPTIMI and 1401 RESTEUTAE must have been lying around unobserved for centuries; 1403 TIGERNI was unearthed in 1905 when a grave was being dug, and 1402 POTITI was found in the 1960s. None is *in situ*, though none can have been moved very far, and the first recorded positions are shown in Fig. 10.2.

A VISIT TO 'ENYS BRACHAN'

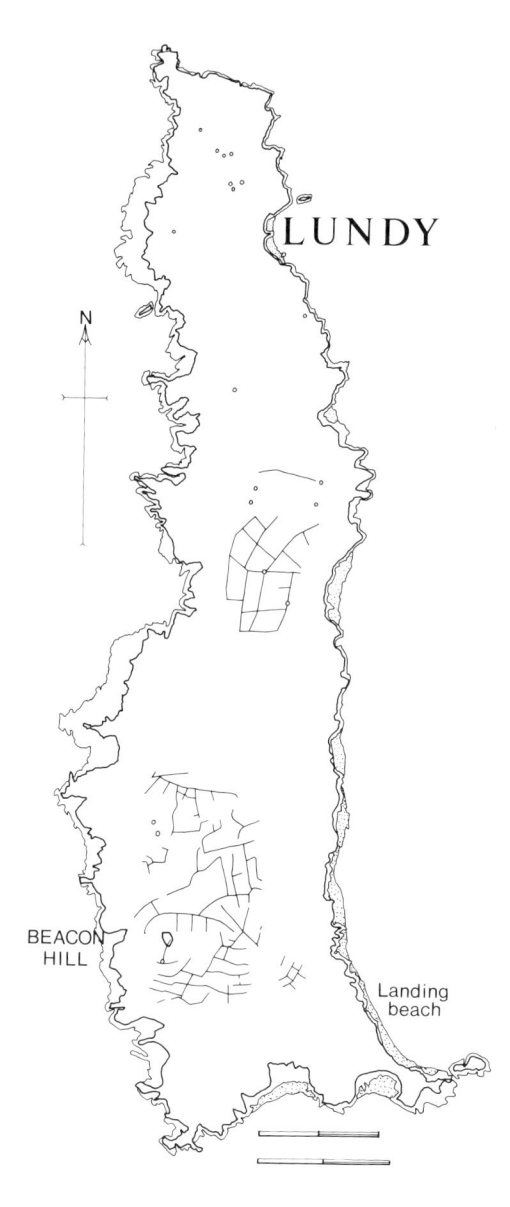

**Fig. 10.1** Outline map of the island of Lundy, showing two 'Celtic' field-systems (1960s fieldwork only: small circles, probable huts) and position of Beacon Hill enclosed cemetery. Scales, 600 yards above 600 metres.

Lundy, once in private ownership, was bought for the National Trust in 1986.[4] Since 1947 the Lundy Field Society, a small but active body, has been giving space in its annual *Report* (journal) to occasional archaeological papers alongside those reflecting a main concern with biology and geology. The society, supposing (rightly) in 1986 that a new management regime would lead to extra building, physical change and increased tourist numbers, thought it desirable to find out if any context for the four inscribed stones at Beacon Hill could at this late stage be discovered; and accordingly a small-scale excavation took place in summer, 1969.[5]

On the ground – close-grazed pasture and pieces of rather stunted granitic heathland – there are signs of two separate 'Celtic' field-systems with their little

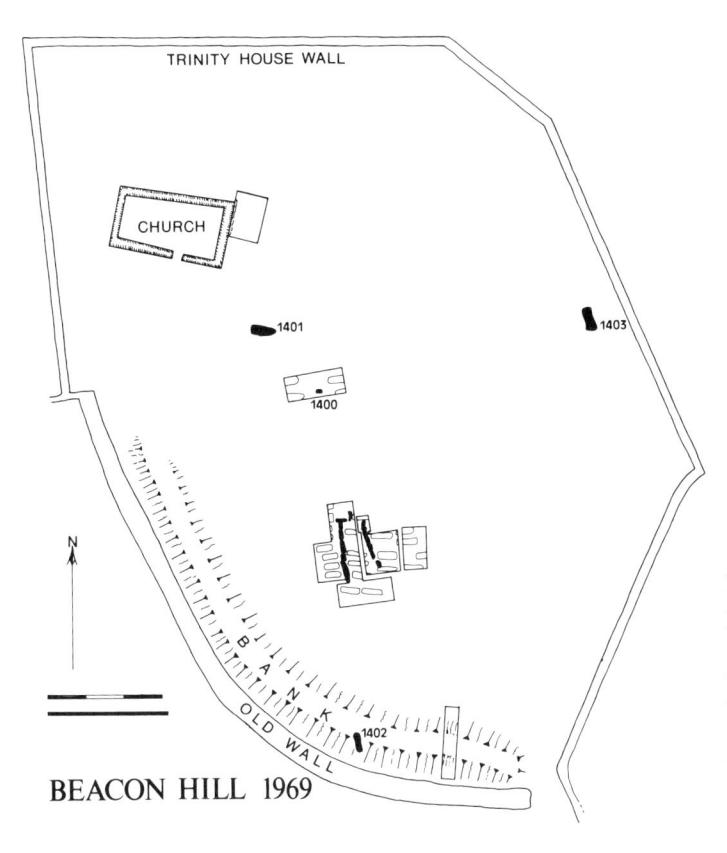

**Fig. 10.2** Beacon Hill; 1969 site plan (simplified) showing foundations of St Helen's small church and positions of four 1969 cuttings. First-known, though probably all recent, positions of the four inscribed stones are given. Scales, 30 feet over 10 metres.

banked and lynchetted plots and the odd circular hut-foundation revealed by low banks. One such system, superficially a peasant farm-holding of the late Iron Age or Roman period, partly underlies Beacon Hill and indeed the faint remains of a lynchet (a division between fields, on a slope, arising when displaced cultivated soil is banked up) run across the enclosed graveyard.

The inscribed stones comprise three that, typologically, are single-name memorials all in capitals; two lettered horizontally, the third vertically – and a much larger, though sadly broken, granite pillar with a two-line vertical inscription, an un-typed memorial of the 'Of-A FILI Of-B' kind. Though strictly speaking these could all be called Dumnonian they are more akin as a group to the memorials of Demetia. 1400 O/P/TIMI is in three lines with a horizontal groove below, the 'O' being notably larger than the other letters, 1401 REST/EVTAE, in two lines, is enclosed between top and bottom horizontal grooves and has a separate circle above the lettering, somewhat oblate because the top of this small pillar slopes backward. 1402 POTIT(I is a single vertical line, headed again by a circle, but one that contains a cross; very like that seen on 358 VOTEPORIGIS (of VI.2). The fourth stone now reads ...)IGERN⊣/(FIL)I TIGERN⊣ and may be no

165

**Fig. 10.3** Inscribed memorials, Beacon Hill, Lundy (on 1401 it is uncertain, from erosion, whether second line ends -A or -AE ligatured). The 'painted *chi-rho*' insertions on 1400 and 1401 are hypothetical only. Drawn from 1969 rubbings and photographs.

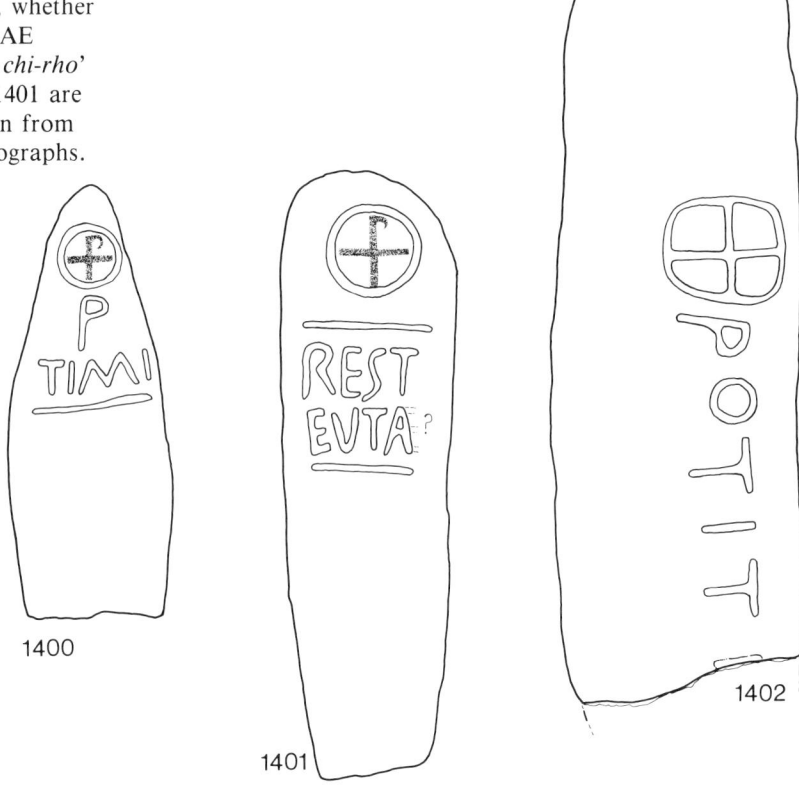

1400

1401

1402

earlier than the late sixth century; the incomplete first name would have been of the type *Contigerni, Vortigerni*, etc.

The memorials 1400–1–2 are single-name ones, two of the names being Roman and male.[6] 1401 *Resteuta* appears to be British and feminine.[7] As a single-name horizontal inscription, it and *Optimi* go along with (e.g.) 445 VITALIANI/EMERETO (horizontal) at Nevern and it is assumed here that *Optimus* and *Potitus* were clerics – priests or monks. Memorials 1400 and 1401 are best described as sub-Roman; within a small and dispersed class also containing the fifth-century, horizontal, memorials of CLVTORIGI, 435, at Llandysilio West and the part-named person on the Aberhyder stone (p. 119) defaced by TARICORO – both V.2. This writer suspects (Fig. 10.3) that the O of OPTIMI contained a linear cross with small *rho*-loop (p. 199), not chiselled or cut but *painted*, rather in a reminiscent Roman fashion; that the circle above REST/EVTAE repeated this, imitatively; and that the ringed cross above POTITI is a still later simplified version of it.

The influence or inspiration behind 1400 and 1401 certainly, and partly behind 1402 POTITI, is Continental or Gaulish rather than Demetian (see chap. 12), but mediated through south-east Wales. If OPTIMI is regarded as probably not later than *c.*500, RESTEVTAE a little after this and POTITI of the same general date as the memorial of *Guotepir*, 358 (i.e., c.550), and if the two masculine names at any rate are regarded as those of ecclesiastics, Beacon Hill and any other adjoining location can be tentatively interpreted as the home of a small community — an island monastery — that came into being around 480 x 500. Now this is much the same constricted phase, the end of the fifth century, that one would allot to the foundations of a larger island monastery on Caldey, *Ynys Bŷr* (p. 228); and in Dumnonia, near the north Cornish coast, of a place later known as *Lann Docco (p. 229), modern St Kew. Ynys Bŷr was an offshoot of St Illtud's larger sub-Roman monastery at Llanilltud Fawr. The monastery associated with *Docco* in all probability was a similar offshoot of another of the south-eastern Welsh houses. We can suppose that Lundy — in a straight line, only fifty miles or a fair day's sailing from the Glamorgan coast at Porthcawl — possessed a similar origin.

Lundy's complete absence as any kind of Christian site from the early Insular record may be linked to the strong chance that it ceased to function as a religious house in the seventh century and was too remote and small to be remembered as one such.[8] There were other little island monasteries scattered around the Severn Sea — like *Ynys Echni* (either Flat Holm or Steep Holm) and, if it could be shown to be so by excavation, Gateholm as well — and in each case we may envisage a mainland mother-house. One Welsh name for Lundy seems to have been Ynys Weir (or Wair), an otherworld island on the horizon where Gwair, a figure in an early Welsh tale, was imprisoned;[9] it is quite possible that such a name arose in, and was originally confined to, Demetia.

The excavations of 1969, which failed to locate likely original stances for any of the four inscribed memorials — they have all been moved, probably several times — were mainly directed at opening a central area in the southern part of the enclosure where the tops of an alignment (N–S) of upright granite slabs protruded through the grass. By the close of a month's work it was apparent that the cemetery holds at least a hundred (undated) long cist graves of Early Christian character; probably more. Thirty were exposed in the central area alone. Some were made, or used for burial, in modern times. The axis of each grave was east–west and some were so small as to indicate their use for children; monastery or not, Beacon Hill had all the features of a lay cemetery. Because the dark moist granite soil is strongly acid, no human bones or teeth had survived (or would ever survived, unprotected, for more than a century or so).

The observed sequence in the central area, relatively well stratified, could be detected and described though much of it was puzzling and in 1969 this writer failed to understand what it implied. The upright granite slabs, several very large (Fig. 10.4), were the taller components of a rectangular setting that enclosed several cist graves. The lowest levels revealed that, as well as having been laid out in the middle of an older field-system, the Beacon Hill cemetery incorporated at least one native Romano-British circular hut, finds from whose occupation were recovered within the central area. The pottery, coarse and handmade and including

# A VISIT TO 'ENYS BRACHAN'

**Fig. 10.4** Lundy, Beacon Hill, 1969; view of central *cella*, partly excavated, showing (arrowed, left) burnt patch of wall-rubble by grave 3; W side of *cella* with (nearest) S slab swung around; and (arrowed, right) the roofless primary burial, grave 23. Photo: M. Cooke.

bits of *briquetage*, the débris of large salt-evaporation dishes, matched similar finds of the first century BC to second century AD from sites in west Somerset. It represented the domestic utensils of a peasant farmstead.

In 1990 the entire excavation archive, fortunately including some hundreds of colour slides, was re-examined at length. A new and much more interesting interpretation, taking into account aspects of Early Christian field-archaeology that were hardly appreciated twenty years beforehand, suggested itself and was then confirmed from the original recording. The reader will not want a mass of tedious detail and the outcome is therefore summarized in a five-stage sequence, each stage being given a separate drawing.

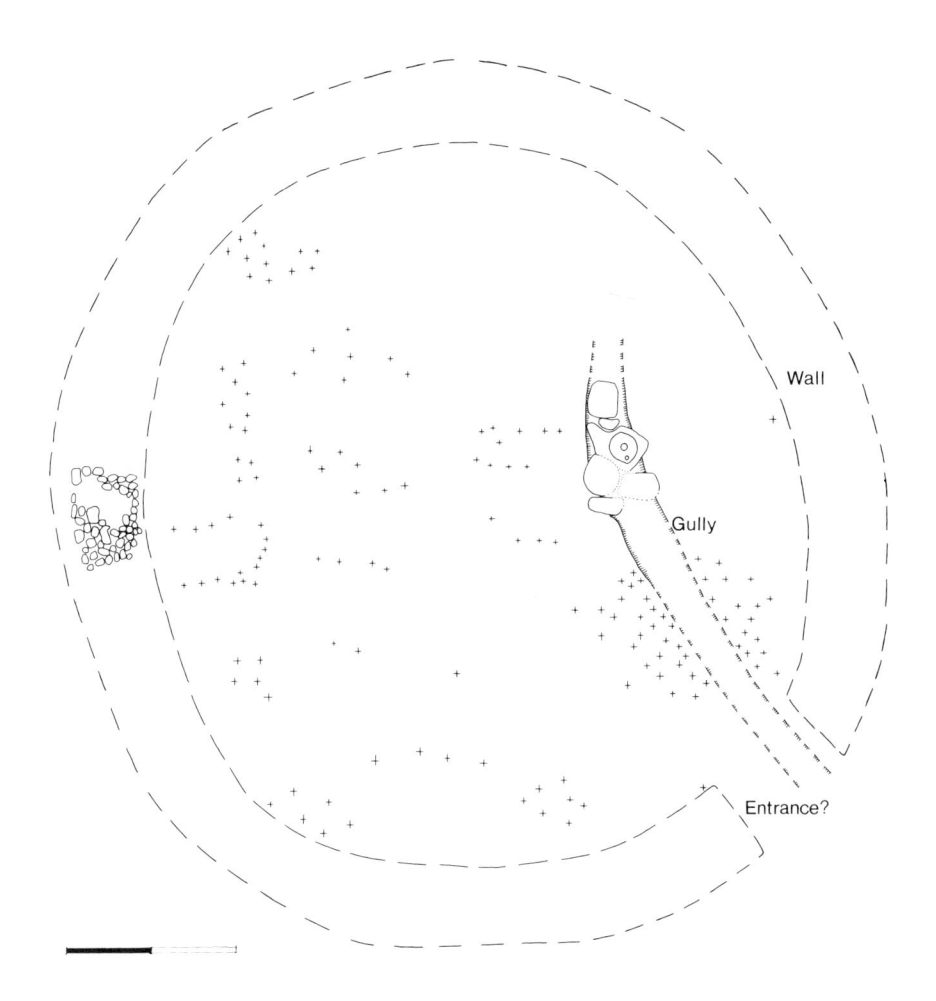

**Fig. 10.5** Beacon Hill; central feature, phase 1. Small crosses mark all finds, mostly pottery; double broken line, likely outline of hut with entrance, drainage-gully (granite quern left lying on cover slabs) and remnant patch of rubble core (*left*) below small burnt area. Scale, 2 metres.

(Fig. 10.5) The living hut found within the cemetery was doubtless deserted and roofless by the fifth century but still visible in outline. The pattern of finds allowed its circular shape to be plotted, with an internal diameter of some 20 feet; low walls would have been (from countless analogies) double-faced of granite slabs retaining a wall-core of smaller stones. An entrance was probably on the south-east with a drainage-gully from the interior going out through this doorway and down a slight slope.

(Fig. 10.6) When the area was chosen for a burial-ground, most of the double walling was dismantled, the largest slabs being used to make a rectangular

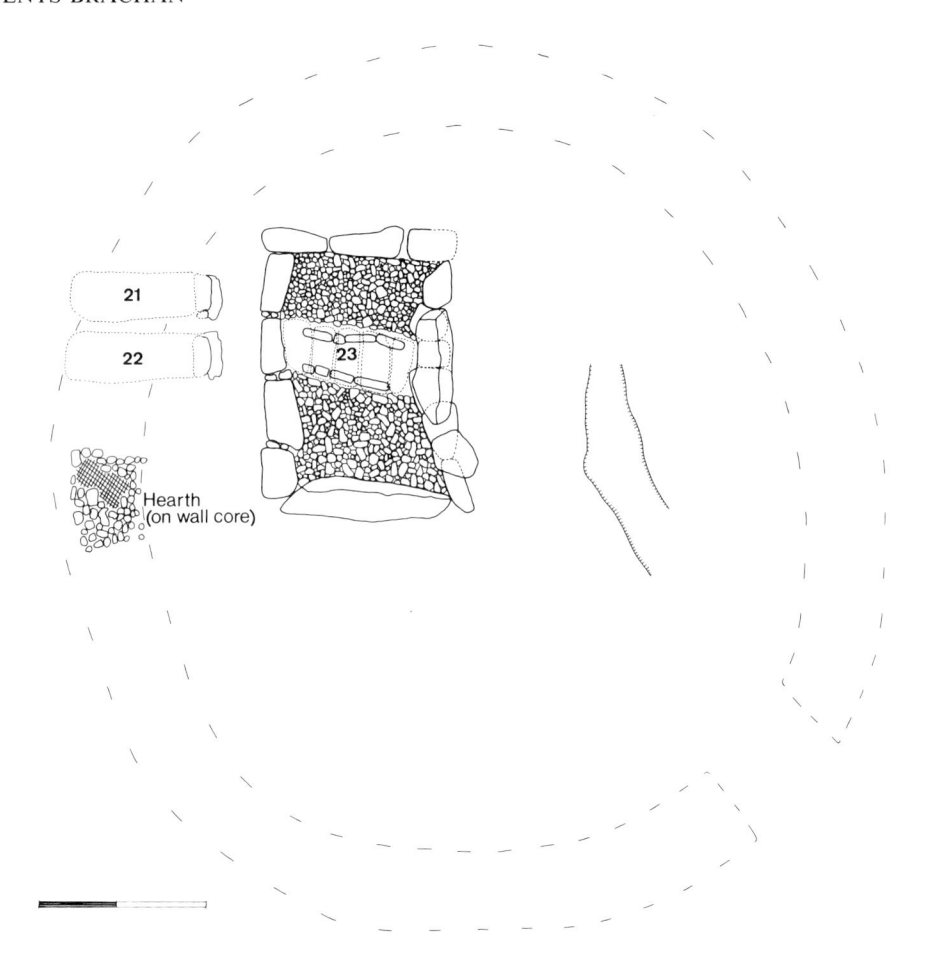

**Fig. 10.6** Beacon Hill; central feature, phase 2. Dismantling of hut walls to construct *cella* housing main burial (23); small fire on patch of rubble core; possible addition of burials 21 and 22.

surround measuring externally about 11 feet N–S and 7 to 8 feet E–W; smaller slabs would have been in demand to construct the sides and lids of cist graves. For the surround, the slabs on the west long-side were the taller; on the east long-side, an upper row may have been placed along the uprights to level the heights opposite each other. Within this rectangular space a cist grave was built. It was given side-slabs and (when finished) covering-slabs, but no end-slabs, the inner faces of the surround acting as such. The grave, little more than 5 feet long internally, had to be squeezed into a traverse space that was perhaps not quite as long E–W as had been intended. The whole of the interior, above the completed and roofed grave, was completely filled with a mass of small granite pieces, rising to the level of the top of the enclosing slabs. For this cairn, about 3 feet high and comprising several tons of loose stone, the wall-fill of the dismantled hut would have been used.

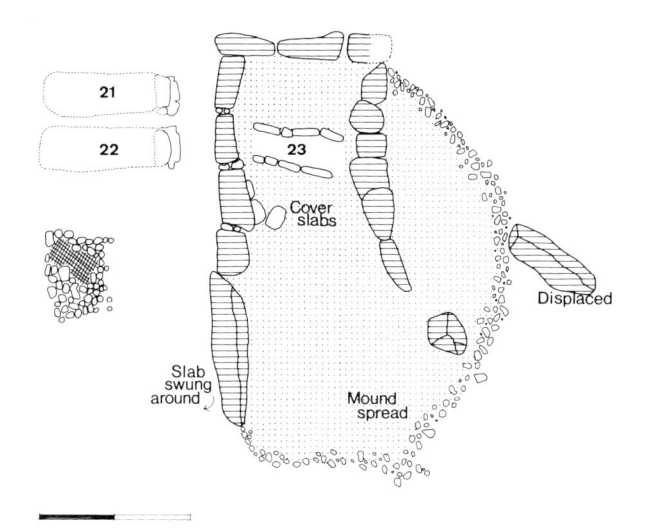

**Fig. 10.7** Beacon Hill; central feature, phase 3. Opening of the *cella*; large slab at S end swung around, cairn filling shovelled or thrown out to S, SE and E, cover-slabs of grave 23 removed.

Outside the rectangular surround and just to its west a patch of small stones, marking and filling a dampish hollow, represented wall-filling that had not been robbed. On this a fire had been lit, leaving a blackish area and some of the granite reddened and heat-cracked.

This focal grave or central burial in its laboriously built setting is what is called a 'special grave' in the immediate sense of differing from all the others and being constructionally more elaborate.[10] It combines three elements; visual above-ground prominence, the layout of a rectilinear space or *cell* (in other provinces of the Late Roman Empire, a feature known as a *cella memoriae* 'the cell of the grave-monument'), and the superimposition of a great heap of stones constituting a *mound grave*. The last two features, cell and mound, can occur separately. Expressed here in native style using local stone, neither need have arisen within the funerary practices of late Roman British Christianity.

A special grave in its *cella*, a visible Christian monument, had functions beyond that of housing a dead person. It is normal to find during survey or excavation some indication that the inherent sanctity of such a grave led to further graves being placed as closely as possible next to it; thus juxtaposed, the dead within them stood a better chance of sharing in prayers offered by pilgrims or visitors and, given that the Second Coming and Resurrection could be seen as an imminent cosmic happening, would be favourably placed next to the tomb of a *sanctus* to ensure participation when 'this corruption shall have put on incorruption' and 'the dead shall be raised incorruptible'.

(Fig. 10.7) After an interval, impossible to determine archaeologically but perhaps from fifty to 100 years later, the *cella* was broken open. From the east-side wall, the upper stones were dragged off. The largest slab of all forming the south

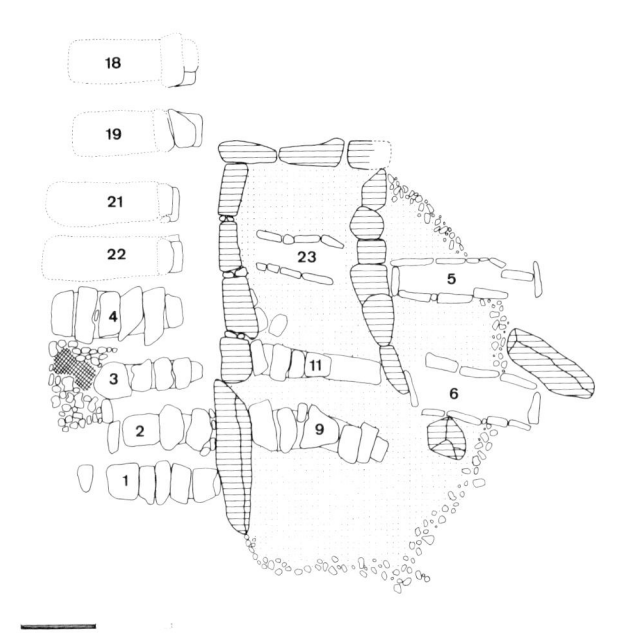

**Fig. 10.8** Beacon Hill; central feature, phase 4. Further burials after opening; graves 5, 6, 9 and 11 set into spread of rubble, graves 1, 2 and 3 (for children?) set against removed S slab and (3) intruded into burnt area; graves 4, 19 and 18 probably added.

short-side was uprooted and swung around through ninety degrees. This allowed the exposed cairn of smaller stones to be picked or grubbed or handled outwards, spread to the east and south, until the central cist grave was exposed. Its covering slabs were lifted off and left in the rubble just south of it. Whatever was then found in the tomb, probably no more than some extremely decayed bones, was removed. The grave was not rebuilt because it had served its purpose. The episode must not be regarded as senseless vandalism or impiety. It is explicable; given the likely setting, it could have been expected; and there is a Christian Latin term for it, *translatio*.[11]

(Fig. 10.8) In no way did this lessen the attraction of the *cella* as a focus for burial. More graves were placed close to it. Nos. 1 and 2, hard against the shifted slab, with 3 and 4 cut into the stony patch where a fire had been lit, all had small plain headstones. (Nos. 2 and 3 are small enough to have been the graves of children.) Nos. 21 and 22, side by side, may have been constructed there against the west (head) end of where the central burial lay in the *cella*, even before the opening of it. Four adult graves – 11 and 9 south of the *cella*, 5 and 6 to its east – were at a slightly higher level because they were actually dug down into the spread of the rubble, and therefore post-dated the opening and the removal of the fill.

(Fig. 10.9) In the last phase, all the other graves are included. The making of no. 20 involved the removal of slabs at the north-east corner of the *cella* to get as close as possible to the now-empty central grave. On the south side 10 and 17, with

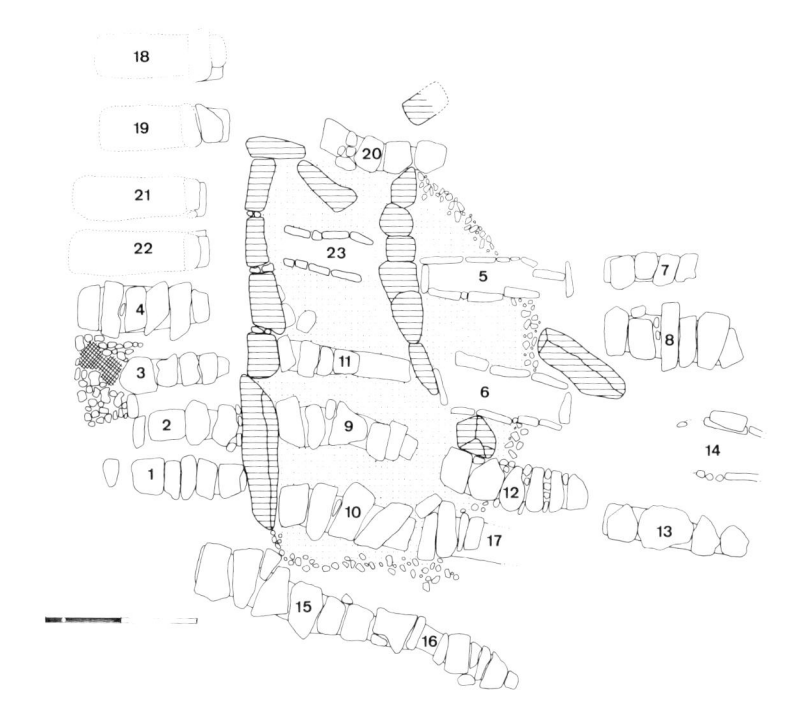

**Fig. 10.9** Beacon Hill; central feature, phase 5. Continued addition of burials focused upon 'empty' grave 23 and its *cella*; note pair of 'tandem' graves (10–17, 15–16) sharing end slabs, and insertion of 20 into N end of the *cella*, with slab removed.

15 and 16, are paired, having shared end-slabs. The precise time-order of the numbered graves is irrecoverable but cannot have differed essentially from what has just been described.[12]

The only supportable interpretation of the sequence is that the *cella* was made to house the burial of a Christian of particular importance, sanctity and 'specialness'; it was built by Christians, on the spot, who were sufficiently versed to combine the outward traditions of focal graves, rectilinear *cella* and superimposed mound (protective or ritual). The epigraphic evidence on Lundy suggests that such Christians belonged to an island community originating in the late fifth century, their memorials indicating likely contact with south Wales. Special graves were not generally sited in the open, unconsecrated countryside. This in its turn implies that the *cella*, even if primary to the other burials that subsequently clustered about it, was secondary to the burial-ground as a whole (regardless of at what stage its curvilinear enclosing-bank was laid out or added) and therefore likely to have fallen in the sixth century.

The reason for the breaching of the *cella* and the grave was that the corporeal remains, what was left of body and skeleton, were destined to be enshrined. Reverently picked out, washed and wrapped, the remains would next be housed in another kind of container. It might be a grave-like structure, even a *sarcophagus* (one-piece stone trough) with a stone lid. Its stance would be above ground, or

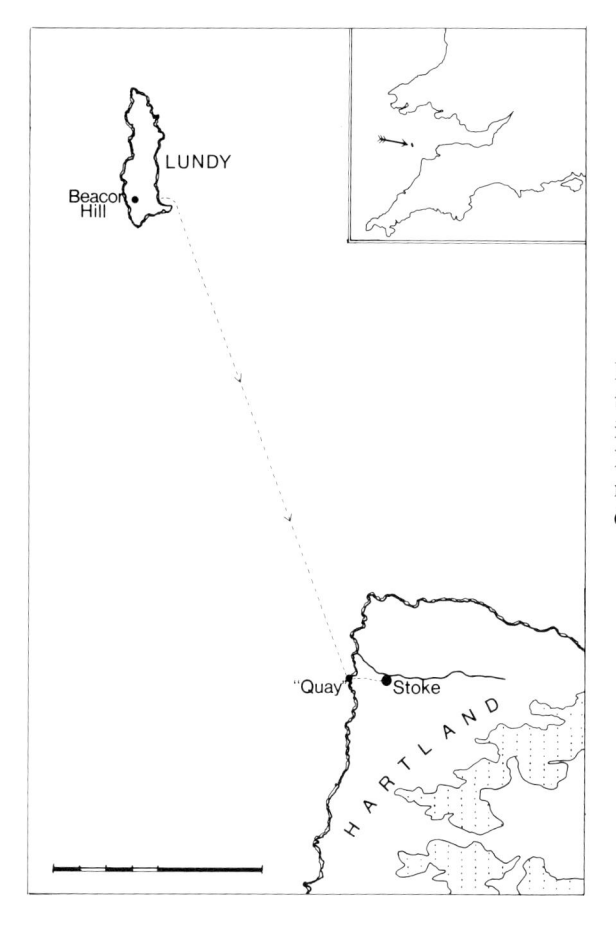

**Fig. 10.10** The sea journey from the island of Lundy (position, inset map) to Hartland Quay landing, N. Devon, about 12 miles directly. Land contour at 600 feet; scale, 8 kms (5 miles).

buried only so deep that the lid would be visible, accessible and under certain circumstances removable. The process of *translatio* is widely documented for Atlantic Britain and Ireland, as secondarily also for Christian Northumbria, and it reached a peak of fashion in the seventh century.[13] Given the inference that Christian activity on Lundy probably began in V.3, and that the *cella* is a secondary feature of the sixth century, we may perhaps see this enshrinement, half a century to a century afterwards, as falling within the seventh. The new 'coffin' or stone shrine would by the seventh century have been housed within a church. It is not impossible of course that this was on Lundy, but it is also most unlikely and there is nothing whatsoever to suggest it. Another and more powerful church would have claimed the relics; and if the evidence can be read correctly another did so.

As for the components of this special grave – the setting of upright slabs, the superimposed cairn of stones – these, individually, may betray fifth-century Christian customs known in south-east Wales (if not also in other Welsh regions) and around the Severn Sea. It is a very approximate but useful guideline in the field-archaeology of post-Roman Atlantic Britain and Ireland that monuments of square or rectilinear plan are far more likely to be derived from Roman and ultimately Mediterranean models than are monuments of curvilinear (round or oval) plan, like the *lann*, generally rooted in the native Late Iron Age. The *cella* is probably a derivative of the open-air mausoleum, roofed or unroofed, found in Late Roman cemeteries to house graves of those distinguished by social status, membership of a substantial burial-club, or family esteem.[14] In the Life of St Illtud, a twelfth-century work drawing partly on a much older composition,[15] St Samson's burial (at Llanilltud Fawr) is described; the *clerus* (monastic brothers) interred the body *in cimiterio*, but *in medio quadrangularium lapidum erecte insistentium* 'in the centre of quadrangular stones – i.e., stones set in a square or rectangle – standing upright'.[16] That sounds familiar enough, as a simple description. The cairn, the mound-grave, and with it the traces of a fire or open-air hearth alongside the burial, are recurrent features and are discussed further (p. 205).

From Lundy we move now across the sea, twelve miles SSE, to the narrow, difficult, but still-used landing place at Hartland Quay, one of very few along a coast described as 'perhaps the most vicious cliffs in the whole of the south-west, broken only occasionally by small, rocky coves'[17] (see map, Fig. 10.10). A road takes us a mile inland to the church of St Nectan, centre of Stoke St Nectan village in the huge parish of Hartland, still a rural and under-explored district of Dumnonia. The church, a magnificent edifice of the fourteenth century with the second highest tower in Devon, is the latest of a succession of churches here. The churchyard, by whose down-hill northern exterior one can trace (in woodland) slight remains of an earlier enclosure, is on the southern flank of an east–west valley, that for the 'Abbey River', opening to the sea. The evidence from Hartland's history suggested (rightly) to Professor Susan Pearce that '... Stoke was in origin a British monastery, like St Kew [here, p. 229] and others further west in Cornwall, founded between, say, 500 and 560, and endowed with what remained, essentially, the monastic estate until the 1540s. Its founder was Nectan, and his relics lay in the monastic complex, apparently until the Dissolution.'[18]

A mile north-east, the Augustinian house of Hartland Abbey came into existence by 1189. Here, soon after this, a Life of St Nectan was composed, and joined to an older story about the discovery or *Inventio* of his shrine and an account of various miracles brought about through his relics.[19] The Augustinians had inherited the ancient foundation at Stoke and of course the name of 'Nectan'. The author of the Life had limited access to local traditions of this person and also to some written (Latin) material that must have been preserved, since long before the Norman conquest, by a small clerical community at Stoke. This can be dimly discerned in Domesday as a house of secular canons – descending ultimately from the postulated British monastery – refounded (probably with the building of a new church) in the 1050s by Gytha, wife of earl Godwin and mother of king

Harold, supposedly in thanksgiving for Godwin's safe delivery from shipwreck.[20] (The endowment, *Harton* or *Heortigtun* first named in Alfred's will of *c*.881,[21] is represented by the 17,000-acre Hartland parish.)

The Augustinian monk knew almost nothing about the saint. His brief composition opens with a *regulus*, king, called *Broc(c)annus* who lived long ago in the furthermost parts of Wales and from whom a province took the name of *Brocannioch*. As we have already seen, the only possible source for these as written forms would have been the Brycheiniog narrative in its sixth-century state (p. 135), and their reproduction in twelfth-century Hartland is virtual confirmation of a postulated British house here in the seventh century, one that obtained a copy of all or part of the Brycheiniog story from Wales.[22] Whether the Augustinian author found at Stoke Church an actual seventh-century document or (more likely) a later one into which certain names and details had been accurately transcribed we cannot say, nor is this vital. The Life of Nectan tells us that 'Brychan', to give him his usual name, was married to *Gladwisa* (= his daughter *Gladus*, in *DSB*), but left to live in Ireland for twenty-four years occupied with good deeds arising from his Christian faith. On returning, finding 'Gladwisa' still living, he fathered upon her twenty-four sons and daughters. A list is given; it bears little or no relation to the Brycheiniog rolls, male (12) and female (2 × 12, 24), though buried within it is *Canauc*, suggestive of a B.1 version of Cynog's name (as *\*cunauc*). All were later to be holy martyrs or confessors in Devonia or Wallia or Cornubia. Heading the list is the first-born son *Nectanus*, 'Nectan'. Nectan when still in Wales was inspired by God to imitate *Antonius*, most famous of the early desert fathers of Egyptian monasticism.[23] Bidding farewell to his family, abandoning a kingdom that *sibi iure hereditario debebatur* 'was owed to him by hereditary right', and travelling down to the nearest coast (*ad littora pergens vicina*) he sailed off alone over a calm sea and arrived at a certain wooded solitude in north Devon called *Hertilonde*. Building a hut he dwelled there, in vegetarian asceticism, praying and doing good works. As news of his worthiness trickled back to his homeland, all his brothers and sisters left home and came to join him as hermits, both in Devon and Cornwall but especially in Cornwall (*Cornubia*). Eventually two robbers beheaded him, and Nectan was buried in his hut, near his fountain (*iuxta fontem*; this detail was introduced to authenticate a spring, still visible close to Stoke church). 'His tomb (*sepulcrum*) is raised up in the middle of the chancel (*medio choro*)' of the church at *Stoke*; this describes some Norman shrine of Romanesque type placed within a twelfth-century church, almost wholly expunged by the fourteenth-century rebuilding but represented by a magnificent late Norman font.

The associated writing, *Inventio Sancti Nectani Martyris*, is an older composition inherited from the pre-Norman Stoke community and, as copied, originating in the tenth century. It purports to explain just why a medieval shrine of Nectan's corporeal remains could have been exhibited in the church, both before and after the foundation of Hartland Abbey (which possessed an integral church of its own but supported the adjoining parochial foundation at Stoke). Supposedly during Aethelstan's reign (924 × 939) an English-named priest *Brictricus* (Brihtric) was commanded in a dream to enter Nectan's *basilica* and to dig up the floor towards the north side, where he would find the body of the holy martyr buried, and then to place the remains in a more conspicuous position to be paid due honour. Brictric's story, even after two more such dreams, met with disbelief. In the end his fellow clerics consented to take up their *ligones* 'mattocks' and to excavate the earthen floor inside the church as indicated. Finding nothing, they gave up and left; but Brictric dug away on his own, and found *lapidem barbaris figuris insculptum*, a 'stone carved with uncouth designs'. It was the decorated stone lid of a sarcophagus, apparently with an access-aperture plugged with a small round stone,[24] and – chastened by Brictric's faith and its reward – the community lifted the remains (including, allegedly, the martyr's staff or *baculum*) which together with the shrine-lid were incorporated in a new high altar. A description of refurbishing the whole church during the Crediton bishopric of Lyfing (1027–46) then follows – or, more probably, was added to the text at the time of an actual late eleventh-century re-foundation by queen Gytha.

The *Inventio* is a more important source than the *Vita*, not just because it was written rather earlier but because it describes in credible and intelligible ways the following sequence. There was a church at Stoke, as part of a monastery within a *lann* whose British name is lost to us, in the seventh century. Within it, probably left of (north of) the east-end altar against the inner wall, a stone 'sarcophagus', more likely to have been a cist grave, held the remains of the martyr named as *Nectanus* and was covered at floor-level with a long slab bearing incised ornament; rather more than just a cross.[25] A plugged hole permitted access to the relics which had been thus re-interred or enshrined, as a *translatio* of the seventh century. Rebuilding or enlargement of the church subsequently obscured the lid, though some knowledge of its existence was retained. In an early tenth-century further rebuild, the lid and burial were discovered and a further translation took place, probably into a composite altar with the lid as *mensa* or frontal. At the same time an account of the finding (the *Inventio*) was written; and when, *tempore* the foundation of Hartland Abbey, Stoke church finally became a large Norman cruciform, the pre-Norman arrangement – holding by now nothing but dust – was transformed into yet another shrine-coffin set in the Norman chancel.

There is no 'Nectan' mentioned anywhere within the Brycheiniog documents, nor is an early male saint of this name attested separately for Brycheiniog or south Wales. The medieval cultus of Nectan and his twenty-three brothers and sisters, in whose several names any number of churches, chapelries and wells over a large swathe of north Cornwall and north-west Devon are dedicated, does not concern us. Admittedly, it is difficult to explain,[26] but patently it seems to be linked to the pre- and post-Norman claims of Hartland as centre of a massive Dumnonian *paruchia*. What is suggested, nay claimed, is that the poor fragments interred around 600 × 650 below the floor of a little stone-walled British church – hardly *basilica* – at Stoke were those exhumed from the central burial in the Beacon Hill *cella*; that on Lundy this burial took place about 550, give or take the odd decade, the relics being later seized by Stoke as a superior house at a time when any establishment on Lundy may have been coming to a close; and that the burial was represented at seventh-century Stoke (and at Hartland, in the twelfth century and up to the present) as that of the martyr 'Nectan'. But Lundy was *Enys Brachan*. 'Nectan' has no independent existence, because 'Nectan' was king Brychan.[27] This was known; which is why his body was accorded a special grave and, both before and after *translatio*, attracted so many satellite burials. The tidings of his death and burial were conveyed, doubtless through some such monastery as Llancarfan, to Brycheiniog in the period *c*.550 to *c*.580 (between the death, and the Priest of Llangasty's writing). The news of this seventh-century enshrinement as Nectan at Stoke, on the other hand, never reached Brycheiniog because, by then, such contact had been severed. When in much later times it was thought desirable to produce a Life of St Nectan – any kind of Life, to support the visible shrine and the antiquity claimed for Stoke – there were scraps of Latin, obtained from south Wales perhaps even as long ago as the beginning of the seventh century. Names like Brocannus, Brocannioch, Hybernia, Gladwisa (? \**gladuuisa*), possibly also Canauc and Anton(ius), could be made out. Most of it was by now completely incomprehensible, and, with the long lists of barbaric Old Welsh names, all that was clear was that, embarrassingly, *Nectanus* figured nowhere. The cobbled version – by the tenth-century canons, not the twelfth-century Augustinian who simply used it – therefore began afresh with its own list, headed by *Nectanus* (as *beatus Nectanus primogenius fuit*). For the rest, where in some fashion it was realized that a total of twenty-four men and women[28] was required, one solution might be that just about every patronal saint in that whole region of Dumnonia who was traditionally thought to have been of Welsh origin was included in a fairly desperate catalogue, pruned to produce the authentic twenty-four.[29]

Why the name 'Nectan', *Nectanus*? Commentators who may or may not have pointed out that this is a 'Goidelic' form of a name failed to understand what this implies. In Dumnonia we should have expected a British (PrCo., OCo.) reflex like \**Neithan*; it is first attested (in Primitive Cumbric, so Jackson) on a southern Scottish memorial of *c*.700 as NEITANO[30] and, away from Hartland, we can notice a fourteenth-century *Nythan(us)* = /nee-than/ and a seventeenth-century *Nython* both from mid-Cornwall.[31] What we have from Hartland or Stoke (or Lundy) is PrIr. \**Nekt-anas*, OIr. *Nechtan*[32] and its preservation throughout would alone tell us that it was first introduced in that form. From the radical \**nikto*-, probably 'washed; washed clean' was developed OIr. *necht* 'clean, pure, white'[33] and in a Christian setting possibly meaning 'washed' (as in 'washed in the blood of the

Lamb'). Old Welsh *Neithon* is found, but rarely[34] and not in any Brycheiniog connection. When Brychan decided to adopt this, and it was his name-in-religion, a new name signifying a second life, his knowledge of it would have come from Demetian Christianity.

Imperfect as it must be, the outline of the Nectan story reveals the outline of what took place. We can picture Brychan, *Broccann*, whose birth (in Pebidiog) must be placed to 480 × 490, as a Christian king whose queen ('Praust' in *DSB*) may have died; whose first-born son Cynog, a royal priest, may then have been forming his own small monastic settlement up in the hills; [35] whose second son Rein was of an age to succeed him; and whose daughter Gwladys[36] had been given in a dynastic marriage to the prince, now himself king, of the kingdom next down the course of the Usk.[37] This description is not mere guessing. For the greater part one can rely on a historical source of the late sixth century, the Priest of Llangasty's account. We have to suppose that Brychan in his fifties or sixties handed his throne, with the consent of his *nobiliores*, to Rein and decided to adopt the existence of a *miles Dei*, a soldier of God in the nearest substitute for the deserts of Upper Egypt – the ocean. It is quite likely that he travelled down the Usk and departed Wales for ever from Newport, the outflow, beside which his royal son-in-law possessed a seat.[38] Because it is unreasonable to see such a man sailing off into the unknown blue there is the implication that the existence of a community on Lundy was known (hence the earlier suggestion that it was an outpost of a south Wales foundation); and by the same token we may suspect that a mainland Christian foundation at Stoke, perhaps not before late VI, originated in Wales as well – the monastery at Llancarfan associated with (if not necessarily founded by) Brychan's grandson Cadog comes to mind.[39] Brychan was not the only person from his kingdom to travel south over the sea, since the Priest of Llangasty recorded the presence in Dumnonia of others (Run, Kynon, Berwin, Bethan) – not Brychan's relatives necessarily, still less his 'children' in any sense, but compatriots and contemporaries and (except for Kynon) also Christian pilgrims.

On Lundy, this man passed as Nectan. It is possible that his stay there was briefly preceded by a landing on the Devon coast, as the *Vita Nectani* claimed, except that the Life had a particular interest in placing its martyr-saint next to the eponymous church and makes no mention of any island. It is not really possible that those on Lundy failed to include people who knew who *Nectan* was, or had been. His death called for a tomb appropriate to his status, and the next visitor from or to Wales carried the news of it to shores from which the tidings (before the 580s) reached Brycheiniog. The island was not known by any particular name and 'Enys Brachan' had to be supplied. In the *patria*, that was the end. A Brycheiniog priest, writing forty or fifty years after Brychan's departure – 'abdication' sounds incongruous, but that is what it was – knew only of the king as father of the national saint, and a supporter of the Faith. We can even doubt whether at the time of a seventh-century *translatio*, not much if at all before a stage when the Hartland community would be diluted with English converts from Wessex, there were memories at Stoke other than those linked to the name of Nectan. And perhaps it is fitting that, thirteen centuries afterwards, the final link between this Demetian-born king of Garth Matrun and the pseudonymous saint who rested in Dumnonia should be set out, with the help of certain *vetustissima scripta*, by the very same Dumnonian who — unwittingly — laid open the grave of Brychan for the second time.

**References**

1. Histories: J. R. Chanter, *Lundy Island, A Monograph* (Exeter, 1887); R. Perry, *Lundy, Isle of Puffins* (Lindsay Drummond, London 1940); Anthony & Myrtle Langham, *Lundy* (David & Charles, Newton Abbot 1970).
2. A. E. Blackwell, 'Lundy's Ecclesiastical History', *Trans. Devonshire Assoc.*, 92 (1960), 88–100; thorough and reliable digest.
3. Ibid., 93. It acts as 'parish' church, though Lundy is not a full parish.
4. This safeguard — it was up for auction — was made possible through Mr Jack Hayward's timely munificence; Lundy is managed, for the NT, by the Landmark Trust and is open to visitors.
5. Directed by the writer, for the LFS, with students from the Universities of Leicester and Edinburgh. See C. Thomas, P. Fowler & K. Gardner, 'Lundy, 1969', *Current Archaeology* no.16 (1969), 138–42; same authors, 'Beacon Hill – Early Christian Cemetery', *20th Ann. Rep., Lundy Field Soc.* (Exeter 1970), 14–17; and now also C. Thomas, 'Beacon Hill Re-Visited – A Re-Assessment of the 1969 Excavation', *42nd Ann. Rep., Lundy Field Soc.* (1992) 43–54 illus.
6. Optimus: *PLRE* i.650 (Flavius Optimus, *praeses*, Phrygia, in IV); Potitus: *PLRE* i.721 (*vicarius urbis Romae* in 379–80), also of course St Patrick's grandfather, *Conf.* 1.
7. This presents difficulties. As a starting-point, REST/EUTA is visible and certain. Ligatured final AE is just admissible (if barely detectable) and would go with Welsh 413 CAELEXTI, 414 AETERNI as an epigraphic form — it is also likely that a fem. gen. would end in -AE (for -E) and not nom.A. As a name it is probably British, if influenced by Roman *Restituta*. For *rest- 'run, roll along(?)', cf. Gaulish *Restu-marus, KGP* 258, and the OBr. (eleventh cent.) *Restue*, Loth, *CB* 159.
8. There is however a remote possibility that the medieval ascription to *sancte Helene de Lundey* (1335) drew on a Hartland tradition, the 'Helen' here, as at St Helen's, Isles of Scilly, being a much older *Ilid* (male: 'Elidius'), said by William Worcestre to have been a Welsh bishop. If so, this would be a pointer to a Welsh mother-house; but which one?
9. *TYP*, 228–9, and notes, 231–2; cf. R. S. Loomis, 'The *Spoils of Annwn,* An Early Welsh Poem', chap.ix in his *Wales and the Arthurian Legend* (Cardiff 1956).
10. The Insular 'special grave' concept was first isolated and defined in *ECANB*, chaps. 3 and 4, with reference to Irish and North British instances.
11. C. Thomas, *Bede, Archaeology and the Cult of Relics, Jarrow Lecture 1973* (Jarrow 1974).
12. To the obvious question, Why no C-14 date here? the answers are (1) no uncontaminated samples, (2) no money — this was a 1960s university summer dig, nine people, 5 weeks,

£340(!), and (3) a C-14 determination would not necessarily have yielded so high a probability as the historically determined estimate of AD 550 plus or minus twenty years.
13. *Bede, Archaeology and the Cult of Relics* (note 11) cites the many such dated happenings recorded by Bede and others.
14. For south-west Britain, in the Late Roman municipal cemetery outside Dorchester, Poundbury: C. S. J. Green, *Poundbury — A summary of recent excavations at Poundbury, Dorchester* (Dorchester, 1979), and (post-Roman) at Wells Cathedral: Warwick J. Rodwell, 'From Mausoleum to Minster; the Early Development of Wells Cathedral', pp.49–60 in Pearce 1982, a volume with (pp.61–76) a further account by Christopher Sparey Green of the Poundbury mausolea.
15. *VSBG* 216–7; the blatant anachronism of the aged *Iltutus* burying his much younger ex-pupil Samson (who died in Brittany) disguises an account of Illtud's own funeral, presumably in the earlier *Vita* postulated by Canon Doble.
16. The addition of the *cruce lapidea superposita*, the (shaped?) stone cross incised with some mark of a bishop placed on this grave, alludes to the writer's (twelfth) century, not to Illtud's (early VI).
17. Pearce 1985, 263 (and map, fig.4).
18. Ibidem, 266.
19. Text (from the Gotha MS) with far-ranging notes, Paul Grosjean, 'Vie de S. Rumon, Vie, Invention et Miracles de S. Nectan', *Analecta Bollandiana,* 71 (1953) 359–44. English translations, G. H. Doble, *The Life of Saint Nectan* (2nd impr., Bideford 1949).
20. There is no full modern history of Hartland; see R. Pearse Chope, *Farthest from Railways* (Hartland, 13th edn., 1973, etc.); Pearce 1978, 197–9; Orme 1992, index, 228 s.n.
21. Sawyer, 422, no.1507.
22. It is not possible to say what was transmitted, but the names in *Vita S. Nectani* of Gladwisa and Canauc show that at least the *incipits* of the Brycheiniog lists of men and women were known.
23. Inspiration from Egypt is a commonplace in other Lives (cf. *Vita S. Davidis*, cap.13) but *Antonius* might suggest expansion of a B.1 *Antun* (*niger rex Grecorum*) noticed in a copy of the Brycheiniog document.
24. Text reads *remoto lapide qui cirografum obstruxerat* ('having removed a stone that had been blocking the *cirografum*'), whereupon a sweet and fragrant odour issued from the tomb, etc. An original phrase like *velut cirografi sigillum* has been misunderstood and compressed ('stone ... as it were like a round seal on a deed'). Circular access-apertures occur on covers and sides of shrines; cf. *ECANB* chap.5 and *Bede* ... (Jarrow Lecture), note 13 above.
25. The best-known surviving seventh-century ornate shrine cover is the one at Wirksworth, Derbyshire (*ECANB*, 158 with references); later Dumnonian lids were plain, like the tenth-century cover of St Materiana's shrine — unrecognized, on the floor of Minster church by Boscastle. A hint of what *barbaris figuris* might have meant if Welsh artistry lay behind this is given by the inverted reverse of the Brycheiniog slab, 341 MACCVTRENI SALICIDVNI (p. 120), now displayed in the British Museum; extraordinary pictures (*CIIC*.1, p.327), perhaps seventh century, that may indicate Biblical stories.
26. Orme 1992, 45–51 with map, is a full and reasoned discussion of the problem. Whatever the rationale, it sheds no light at all on Lundy, Wales, or historical matters earlier than Norman times.
27. (A personal note.) As trifling evidence that intuition can be a better guide than deduction, I record here that an absolutely certain conviction that 'Nectan' was Brychan hit me suddenly in the north aisle of Stoke church, May 1990, when sheltering from a rainstorm and vainly examining the interior stonework for pre-Norman fragments. The supporting

arguments printed here were worked out later. I find not the slightest reason to abandon that conviction, and a great many reasons to retain it.

28. If so it might suggest that the (B.1) copy of the Brycheiniog document held (and this could be suspected, p. 151) the list of twelve male names and *only* the 'A' list of twelve females.
29. Olson & Padel, 1986, 66; Orme 1992, 46 ('manifestly compiled in part on gender lines') – men and women are approximately equal, though gender of several names is not entirely clear. Possible Welsh influence or assistance in compilation may be suggested in that eight of the twenty-three names after Nectan contain initially or terminally the element *-wen(n)* – embracing OW, OCo.*-uinn* (masc.), OW (& OCo.?) *-uenn* (fem.,<**uind-ā*), 'fair, holy, *sanctus* (*-a*)'; Wencu, Wensent, Wenna, Wynup(?), Wenheden, Adwen, Morewenna, Merewenna (doublet?). These look quasi-hypocoristic, rather than actually nominal.
30. Not in *CIIC*.i – K. A. Steer (with note by Jackson), *PSAS* 101 (1968–9) 127–9, pl.9a, found at Peebles; late seventh or early eighth century.
31. Sub-parochial chapel, St Winnow, 1384, as *parochia sancti Nythani*; chapel in Cubert parish, 1630, of 'St Nython'. Modern spellings like 'St Nighton' (waterfall, near Tintagel) are literary and late. On an eleventh-century bone(?) seal, known from an impression and assigned by Francis Wormald to the pre-Conquest community at Stoke – this may be the seal alleged in the *Inventio* to have been found in the shrine-coffin, probably because it was kept in a later shrine as a relic by association – is a couped head and the legend 'Sigillum Nehtanus'. Interestingly this shows in the *-ht-* of Old English orthography a realization of what would have been the spirant /χ/, *Nechtanus*; complete retention of the seventh-century spoken original. See F. Wormald, 'The Seal of St Nectan', *Journ. Warburg Institute* 2.1 (1938–9), 70–71.
32. *CGH*, 711–12, many instances of *Nechtan*, gen. *Nechtain*.
33. Vendryes, *Lexique, M N O P* (1960), N–6, *necht*.
34. *EWGT*, index, 206.
35. At Merthyr Cynog, a substantial *lann* with Norman church, now in a shrunken hamlet. For its curious inclusion among hill-forts, see RCAHMW *Inv. Brecknock* ii (1986), 44; a site-plan would have been of rather more use and value than the small location-map.
36. It could be pointed out that this, the girl's name Gwladys (Welsh) and Gladys (English loan), had a quasi-symbolic origin, 'She of the *patria*, homeland' (*gwlad*), and in VI may have resumed the theme of Marchell as a 'White Hope' of the kingdom.
37. Gwynllyw husband of Gwladys, father of Cadog, was (*Vita S. Gundleii, VSGB* 172 ff.) the son of king Glywys, eponym of *Glywysing*, and himself later eponym of a sub-kingdom *Gwynllwg, anglice* 'Wentloog'. *Collis Gundleii,* 'Gwynllyw's Hill', commands the mouth of the Usk at Newport and is now crowned by his major church (St Woolo's). The writer is grateful to Jeremy Knight for pointing out the significance of this site in such a sub-Roman context.
38. Direct sailing, Newport to Lundy, would be (skirting Penarth and Barry) about sixty-three miles, with Lundy in sight for the last forty.
39. *Vita Cadoci*, by far the most important of the Welsh Lives in the Vespasian A xiv collection, still awaits (a) disentanglement, and textual 'deconstruction' as here applied to the Brycheiniog tracts; with (b) interpretation, accepting that its core is historical and not invariably legendary. Cadog's life, as a grandson of Brychan, falls within VI. 2 and VI. 3. *VC* contains suggestions that the monastery at Llancarfan pre-dates this; and the writer regards Llancarfan, Llanilltud Fawr, probably Llandough and possibly one or two more as a south-eastern group of V.3 foundations.

# 11
## 'In Occidentale Parte': West Cornwall

ANY LATE ROMAN or post-Roman contact between the Irish – setting out from Ireland's own shores – or between Irish settlers already in Britain and the far south-west remains obscure and perhaps unidentifiable. It was not a topic featured in contemporary literature. 'So the impudent Irish pirates [*grassatores*] returned home, though they were shortly to return', commented Gildas in the 540s.[1] *Grassatores* were footpads, street robbers, the criminal scum of any large city; this term of abuse taken from Old Rome itself may have been acquired from Cicero. This is one British view of events; like most of Gildas, devoid of precise geographical information. It goes with other mentions[2] of the Irish (*Scotti*) and Picts as *tetri greges* 'loathsome gangs' emerging from dank crevices like maggots attracted by sunlight. In time, we view this as following the departure of the Romans, after a last vain British appeal to Rome and after a famine. There had been a final rally of Britons and for the moment the barbarians, repulsed, crawled back home; following not just day-raiding, but long or short periods in Britain as unwelcome intruders. The date, as David Dumville demonstrates, may be about 450–55. Can this be accepted? Could any of it be germane to south-west Britain? It would seem to be a good half-century too late for the Déisi in Demetia and somewhat too early for the *Scotti* in Dál Riata. However we need not expect accuracy of date from sixth-century Britain. E. A. Thompson's chilling dismissal[3] of so much of intellectual life in an abandoned Britannia comes to mind. 'The most frightening feature in the picture drawn by Gildas is ... the destruction of knowledge itself. Knowledge of the outside world and knowledge of the past had been wiped out of men's minds.' Wherever in Britain he lived and wrote, Gildas had heard of Dumnonia as a kingdom and region. The past in question was only a few generations before his own; but it is impossible to say if his remarks about the Irish, as raiders or settlers who came and went at will, were meant to embrace south-west Britain.

Nearly five centuries after Gildas, we are permitted another glimpse (from Ireland) in that brief passage from Cormac mac Cuilennáin (see earlier, p. 44). It is implied that the *grassatores* of Gildas, before any temporary departure, had been in a position to exercise *cumachta mór* 'great dominion' in parts of Britain. Symbolizing their success were two named strongholds – Dún Tredúi, which has been tentatively equated with Moel Trigarn in Demetia, and Dún maic Liatháin, placed by Cormac in *Cornn* 'Cornwall'. A (late) Irish source thus purports to specify a region within Britain, whereas Gildas does no more than to indicate Britannia as a whole.

Those seeking to explore this further face a familiar dilemma. *Were* there early Irish settlers in Cornwall in the fourth or fifth century? There is just sufficient reason to hypothesize such a happening. On the ground, it is uncertain how one would begin to confirm its reality. Similar circumstances arise elsewhere at the same period. Few would doubt the reality of an inferred, and mass, emigration from Dumnonia (if not also from Wessex) to *Armorica*, Brittany during the fifth to seventh centuries. It is dimly apparent from history and from place-names, and more clearly so from the oldest stage of the Breton language as an Insular implant.[4] To date, there has been no compelling archaeological demonstration that it ever took place, nor is it very easy to understand how it could be so demonstrated. Failure has encouraged an extreme French view, fuelled a little by *amour propre*, that no such immigrations occurred and Breton is a survivor of Gaulish. Again, there is a lesser-known episode in which a further-flung migration – from Britain? from the British who settled in Brittany? – produced a sixth-century Christian enclave in north-west Spain, in the countryside where Asturias gives way to Galicia. At a synod at Braga in 572 a bishop representing a see of *Britonensis ecclesia* signed as 'Mailoc'. This Celtic name was earlier British \**Maglācos* ('Princely One') and it is gratifying to discover that this aristocratic incomer is not yet forgotten.[5] The modern village of Santa Maria de *Bretoña*, 10 km south from Mondoñedo, commemorates the post-Roman diocese. In E. A. Thompson's opinion[6] 'no mere handful of Britons' was involved. North of Bretoña the broad valleys, like sunnier versions of Bodmin Moor or north Devon, are replete with unexplored 'Celtic' field-systems below today's stone-hedged farms and cosy little hamlets. It is a prime archaeological resource, an expected agrarian landscape, but where does the fieldworker begin? There is as yet no tangible evidence that the see of the Britons is more than a romantic dream.

Cormac mac Cuilennáin's place-name, Dún maic Liatháin, implies a particular link between the Uí Liatháin and the lands of the Britons of Cornwall; if so, to be distinguished from any record of Uí Liatháin bands in Cydweli and the Gower (p. 58). Though the evidence to be reviewed in later chapters below is ambiguous, the indication is that any intrusive post-Roman settlement in *mid-* and *north-east* Cornwall was, first, never directly from Ireland but from Demetia with its own Irish-descended colonization and second, therefore connected with the Déisi. We are left, then, with *west* Cornwall. The only north-facing port of entry of any size here is Hayle, now a small town around the estuarine mouth of a river of the same name.[7]

From Hayle to Cork harbour, landfall to landfall, is 165 miles. In the nineteenth century the many Cornish mine-captains – three from my own family among them – who went to open up the copper ventures in Cork used to sail from Hayle to Bristol, and thence on a Cork-owned line across to Ireland. But then (and earlier and later) in the small-cargo trade, unstructured sailings between Hayle or St Ives and Cork were thought nothing out of the ordinary. In the seventeenth century the St Ives fishing-boats that 'did usually saile to the Coast of Ireland and take ffish and Herrings there'[8] were no larger and, undecked, no more seaworthy than the kind of craft (a large curach?) with which we can credit the early Irish. Distance raises no objections.

By late Roman times the economy of west Cornwall was almost wholly agricultural; streaming for alluvial tin and possibly some inshore fishing would be the exceptions. Land use was dominated by a scattering of small defended enclosures, marked in place-names by the element *ker-* (*car-*, *caer-*), in English 'round'. These rounds resemble the many 'raths' of Demetia, with which they shared a not very complex rural system of agrarian and pastoral living. Surrounded by lay-outs of small and often rectilinear fields, lynchetted (terraced) on slopes and with walls whose size reflected the extent of necessary stone-clearance, the rounds were the enclosed farmsteads containing circular double-walled homes. We can just perceive the social gradations; an 'unfree' class in dispersed and undefended huts, singly or in groups, the round-dwellers as extended families owning or occupying units of landscape (to be represented later by the place-name element *tref-*), and chieftains and rulers who may have used more prominent hill-forts. Cereal cultivation, accounting for only a fraction of the exploitable land, went alongside extensive pastoralism of domesticated animals.

Some time ago the writer recognized[9] that the Cornish word *bounder* (translated as English 'lane') matched in its fuller range of meanings the Demetian dialect *meid(i)r, moydir* (*\*boudr*) examined by Melville Richards (p. 67). In Cornwall a definition might be 'farmland not enclosed into fields, but used as access (i) from a farmstead to a highway, (ii) from one farm, or part thereof, to another, (iii) from a farmyard to open grazing, and (iv) from one parcel of grazing to another'. There are minor problems in agreeing the etymology of *bounder*,[10] but no serious doubt that it contains *\*bou-* 'cattle' or that the semantic parallel with Pembrokeshire Welsh *\*boudr* holds good.

The map, Fig. 11.1, includes the known distribution of *bounder*, some examples of which have since the eighteenth-century become encapsulated in growing towns.[11] The markedly western emphasis is not necessarily to be correlated with the demise of spoken Cornish, last retained in the far west (most markedly perhaps in the Lizard peninsula). Many of the examples will be medieval (pre-sixteenth century) and it seems to be genuinely a west Cornish feature. The pattern cannot be claimed to mirror the extent of some hypothetical land-seizure by the Irish, and we are observing diffusion of a particular word through time and space. But one might guess that, as in Demetia, the original term (a long way behind the attested *bounder*) was linked to an emphasis on pastoralism, like the native Irish notion of 'road' (*bóthar*) deriving from 'a path for cattle' (*\*bou-itro*), and was an innovation

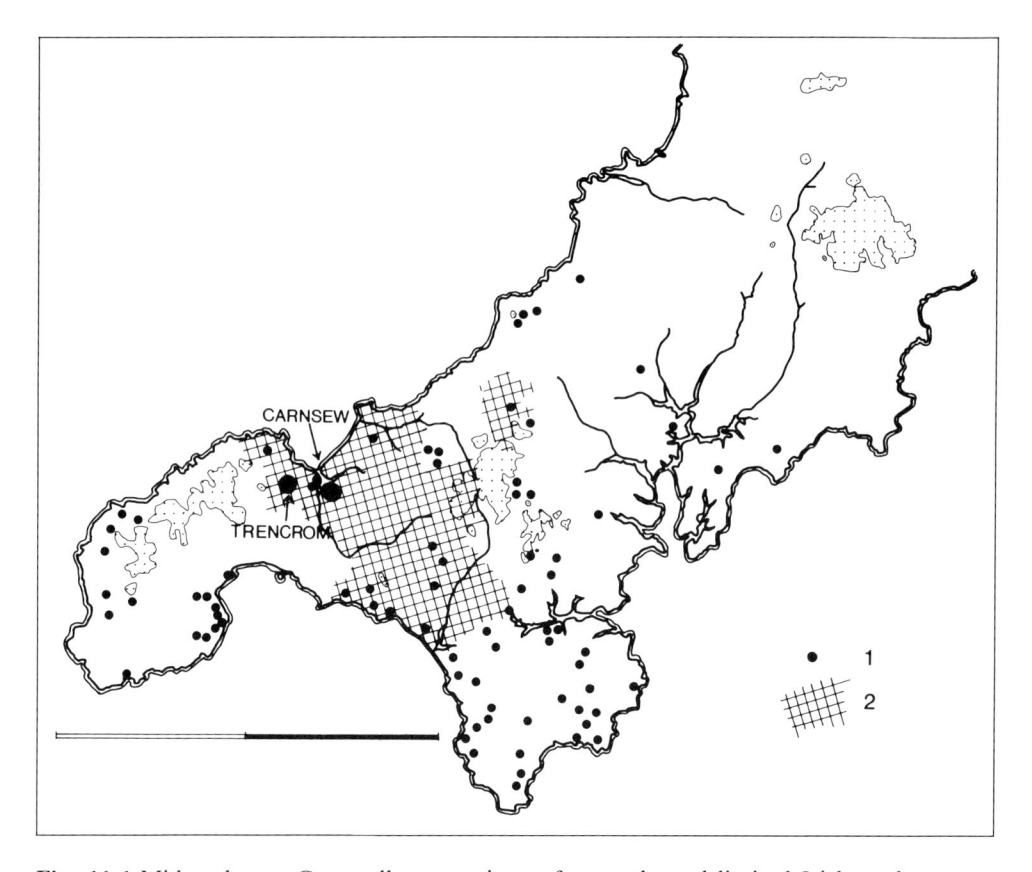

**Fig. 11.1** Mid and west Cornwall; suggestions of an early and limited Irish settlement. **Key**: 1, place-names with element *bounder* 'lane'. 2, parishes with interlinked 'Irish' patronal saints. Black circles mark forts at Trencrom ('Din map Letan'?) and Carnsew. Scale, 20 miles (32 kms).

arising through contact with Irish settlers having their own priorities in land-use.

The other main symbol on the map, the cross-hatched area, is included with every reserve. It marks a block of ecclesiastical parishes (as they have been since the late eleventh or early twelfth century) whose patronal saints, or whose patrons of two or more ancient chapels in such a parish, are all connected. They have been represented either as 'brothers and sisters' or as companions in the same party. They were Irish, of royal or noble birth; on arriving from Ireland their reception was hostile, and opposition from a native tyrant (usually the folkloristic 'King Teudar') could lead to swift martyrdom. This is the stock-in-trade of Cornish hagiography as a written source, and ecclesiastical and parochial folklore as an oral one, but it is intensified by the many links between the names. Sources include the (fourteenth century?) life of Guigner, Fingar or *Gwinear*, patron of Gwinear, by one Anselm;[12] some notes by William Worcestre[13] who in the 1470s saw versions of (now lost) Lives featuring *Uny, Herygh* and *Hya*, patrons of Redruth and (Uny)Lelant; St Erth; and St Ives and Wendron – and then John Leland's notes of the late 1530s.[14] He mentions a Life of *Breaca* (patron of Breage), possibly a different Life of Gwinear, a life of Hya or *Ia* ('S.Ive's legende') and other lost *legenda* that brought together *Sinninus* (of Sithney), *Germochus* 'the king' (Germoe), *Elwen* or *Elwin* (Porthleven in Sithney) and *Crewenna* (Crowan). When any details of arrival from Ireland occur, the landing-place is given variously as the port which is called *Heul* (Hayle), or near to it at a shore beneath *Reyver* (Riviere, p. 198) where the Cornish tyrant Teudar had a *castellum* 'almost at the est part of the mouth of Hayle ryver on the North Se' (Leland). It is implied that Uny and Hya came to the same spot, because of William Worcestre's record that their shrine-tombs, in Lelant and St Ives churches, were on the northern sea-shore.

These colourful little *legenda*, preserved and read aloud at a dozen or more local churches until the Reformation, were padded out with rustic marvels (cows, killed and quartered, re-assembled themselves) common to the whole run of Insular (and Breton) hagiography. The lost Life of St Hya had some passage, which Leland read, about '*Iva* and Elwine, with many other' landing at *Pendinas* (the so-called Island, and harbour, of St Ives) and a church there built by 'one Dinan, a great Lord in Cornewaul'. This typifies the twelfth-century accretions. A Norman family, descendants of the Conqueror's military leader Turold or Thoroldus, played a major role in Cornwall's affairs; they acquired the fief of Car*dinan* (Cardinham, near Bodmin), took a new name from it, and down by St Ives held a substantial manor bordering the town.[15]

The drawing of inferences from what is at best partly preserved folklore – however holy – holds little appeal for the archaeologist, who tends to assume an inherent credibility only for things that can be seen and touched; or for the linguist, who tends to forget that the conventions used for linguistic reconstructions *are* conventions, not scientific principles. We must tread warily. The common theme of landings from Ireland by Irish men and women of social standing, at or near Hayle mouth in St Ives Bay; the similarity of subsequent adventures; and, in map form, contiguity in life, in death and then enshrinement, and in parochial dedications – together hint at a former belief, old and blurred by the time of the Reformation, in some central happening. This concerned the long-ago arrival by sea of 'foreigners', all of them perceived as Irish, not all of whom found a ready welcome, and some of whom were opposed by a local ruler. The saints (as they became) belong to parishes, and to chapels (some, demonstrably pre-Norman), that are found in a restricted area of west Cornwall, an area suggestive of an inland south-easterly spread from the shores of St Ives Bay. And that is all that should be said, except (Fig. 11.1) to superimpose the area in question upon the distribution of the *bounder* names.

The postulated tradition has no indication of date. It is a cardboard past with kings, soldiers, peasants, cows, rivers, and heads being cut off. Some of the remembered names (including a few, patrons of sub-parochial chapels, not given above) are vaguely Irish-looking – Erygh or Erth (*Erc*?), Breaca (*Brecc*?), Hya (*Iar*?), with shifts of gender; others, just as vaguely British-looking (Gwinear, equated with Irish *Fingar*; Gothian or Gwithian (*Guedian*?); Derwa). Was a historical kernel of past reality too far back in time for the transmission of incidental details? Cormac's fortress in Cornwall, Dún maic Liatháin, belonged to the age of Crimthann Már, a heroic past at least as old as the Roman centuries of Britain (p. 44). There is one piece of archaeological evidence that might be considered. It is the pattern of the deposition of hoards of Late Roman coins (Fig. 11.2).

These, often very extensive, gatherings of low-denomination coinage start to appear in the third century AD. It has long been noticed that they seem to be concentrated in the districts where easily worked alluvial tin was obtained from the streams that had always drained the higher mineralized zones.[16] It is extremely doubtful that here, in the far end of Dumnonia, Roman coins had any circulation and currency as *money*. The hoards suggest payments by middle-men, or *negotiatores*, within an officially controlled monopoly. They were frequently crammed into pots or metal vessels, and concealed under boulders or in holes in the ground; one potential value was simply a supply of convenient good-quality bronze for the making of brooches or other items. In Fig. 11.2 the upper map shows hoards deposited, on coin evidence, between AD 253 and 284. The lower map shows those of later times, with a few where the latest coins go up to AD 423. In the second map, there is a hint of concealment in places that are not all by tin-streams (like those around the Helford – arrowed on the map), but are peripheral to the shaded area, putatively the zone of (fourth? century) Irish settlers.

If one considers any hypothesis of an early Irish settlement in the west of Cornwall, and in view of the distance a settlement rather than raid might be imagined, three questions arise. One, now covered, is what part of west Cornwall could be involved; landings in St Ives Bay constitute a provisional answer. The second concerns the place named by Cormac, long after its existence, as an Irish stronghold in Cornwall; in its British version, *Din(d) map Lethain*. There is slightly more incentive to seek it in west Cornwall than in any other part. The third is the explanation of a small coastal fortlet at Carnsew, on the western shore of the Hayle river-mouth, where there was a fifth-century inscribed Christian memorial accompanying a burial, and bearing a name that may be Irish.

Jackson suggested[17] that Cormac was aware of Old Welsh and that he 'unconsciously partly Hibernicized' his translation of the Irish Dún maic Liatháin; that 'in Primitive Cornish the name was doubtless Din Map Letan'. These may represent *literary* equivalents. For Irish place-names Hogan's *Onomasticon*[18] gives a great many examples of compound place-names having the shape *X of the*

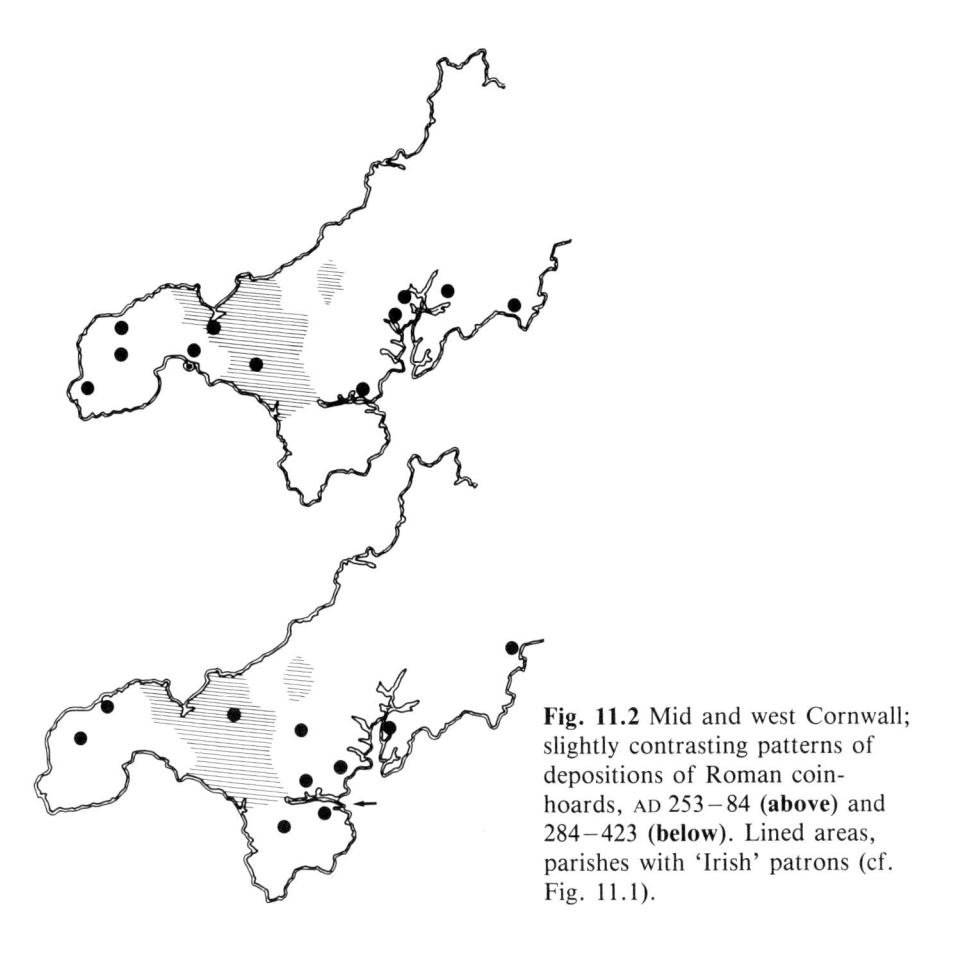

**Fig. 11.2** Mid and west Cornwall; slightly contrasting patterns of depositions of Roman coin-hoards, AD 253–84 **(above)** and 284–423 **(below)**. Lined areas, parishes with 'Irish' patrons (cf. Fig. 11.1).

*sons of A, Y of the sons of B;* Clonmacnoise (*Cluain mac Nóis*) springs to mind at once, and there are others with Dún (*Dún mic Chonchobair*, etc.). No instance is known of any Cornish fort-name (nor any place-name) compounded with Primitive Cornish *map* 'son', or its unextended plural *\*maip* (nom.), *\*map* (gen.).[19] There is no objection, as such, to the belief that a place-name of Cormac's era (*c.*900) or indeed putatively of much earlier times[20] could survive long enough to be recorded, recognized and interpreted. Here of course the 'sons' in question were not a Cornish tribe. One could guess that any corresponding *spoken* form in Cornwall is more likely to have resembled *\*Din Lētan*.

In Cornish names there is a degree of interchangeability between *caer*, which implies a man-made fort, and *din* (var. *dinas*, dimin.(?) *dinan*), which seems to have carried a further sense of 'fort-like; fortifiable; potential stronghold' and even 'hill'.[21] (The writer's own view is that *din* tends to refer to fortresses that are larger, were perceived as ancient and important, or were coastal promontory-forts;

and *caer*, often to forts on hill-slopes rather than summits, and multivallate forts perceived as enlarged instances of rounds.) The relevance is that a Cornish tenth-century charter[22] does happen to name a *Caer Lydan*. It is however in mid-Cornwall; and *lydan* might be construed here as 'wide; wide-in-outlook; having wide views from it' (British and Gaulish *litan-*, Old Cornish *lidan*, Old Breton *letan, litan*). In fact it may now be impossible, without a battery of dated forms, to say whether a name comes from *lidan* 'wide' or a supposed reflex of an Irish *Liathan, Liatháin*.

None the less, there is the twelfth-century verse romance *Tristran* (as for 'Tristan and Yseult') by Beroul; the shadowy author may have been a native of northern France familiar with Cornwall, and writing in Norman French.[23] Among the earlier treatments of the Tristan romance his is alone in having so many detailed references to Cornwall, with recognizable forms of place-names. Miss Ditmas's suggestion[24] that Beroul may have written in part under the patronage of Robert de Cardinham or Cardinan, of the Anglo-Norman family mentioned earlier (p. 187), has much in its favour. In a passage (lines 2221–35) where Tristan and Yseult meet to discuss their tragic love and predicament, Tristan exclaims that he would like to talk to his uncle King Mark and to assure him that nothing dishonourable had occurred. He says that Mark 'has not a knight in his realm, *not from Lidan right up to Durham*, who if he wished to say that I had a love of you out of dishonour would not find me, armed, in the field'. The words *ne de Lidan tresque en Dureaume*, a figure of speech like 'from Land's End to John O'Groats', are meant to imply the whole span, south to north, of Mark's kingdom; and they are spoken at the Cornish, not the Durham, end of that span. In the text *Lidan* is repeated (line 3562) simply as a place for an overnight stay, but it may be a textual slip for *Dinan*; 'Dinas lord of Dinan' (a compliment to Robert of Cardinham?) is Mark's seneschal and a subsidiary hero. We must not press this too far; but, if Lidan as opposed to Durham was an acceptable trope for geographical extremes, west Cornwall – or west of that district, mid-Cornwall down to the Truro river at Malpas, that Beroul seems to have known at first hand – is indicated. Was a *(Din) Lidan* still prominent, still pointed out, in the twelfth century? Which fort might it have been?

Before looking at possibilities, we can discuss the third question, mentioned earlier (p. 188); the nature of the small coastal fort at Carnsew, commanding the mouth of the river Hayle. It occupies the front or bluff of a low cliff between the estuarine inlet on the west and, on the east, a former marshy stretch that curved around into Hayle's East Pool or *Est Lo*, below Phillack church (Fig. 12.1). 'Carnsew' is *carn du* 'black rock' from an exposure of the dark slate bedrock here. The fort, as an archaeological site, was twice butchered in the nineteenth century. The eventual Penzance–Paddington main line (double) was taken through a deep cutting that gashes right across the fort. Later, the remains were philanthropically landscaped to form a kind of park, with seats, flagstaff and *Aussichtspunkt*, for

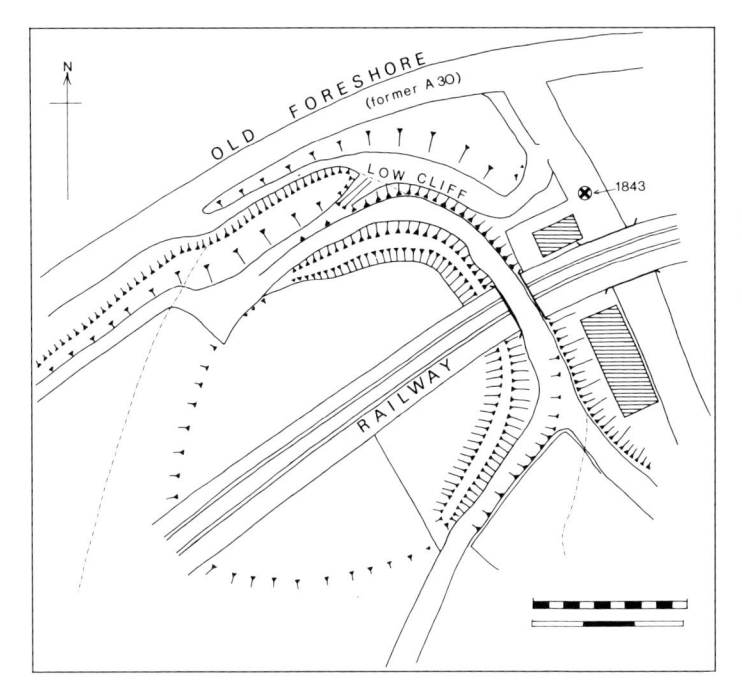

**Fig. 11.3** Carnsew, Hayle, west Cornwall; sketch plan (1990) of remains of small coastal fortlet. Encircled cross marks most likely spot of 1843 discovery of grave and memorial (479). Scales, 100 feet over 30 metres.

the good people of Hayle (who still call it, rather oddly, 'The Plantation'). Despite these twin assaults and the absence of any excavations or analytical survey, it is possible to give (Fig. 11.3) a reliable sketch-plan made in 1990. If one could remove the trees, bushes, terraces, paths and gates and reverse the Victorian damage, Carnsew – though not large – would appear as quite impressively sited, and rather more than a fortified look-out.

In 1843 a side-road was planned at sea level on the eastern side of the bluff; it was part of a system of carriage drives and walled ravines connecting Henry Harvey's residence to Harvey's Foundry, enabling him to travel in a carriage from home to work and back again shielded from the gaze of the vulgar. In the course of the work, an interesting discovery was made at the point marked 'X' on the plan. It is best described in the words of Harvey's friend Richard Edmonds, civil engineer of Penzance and recipient of a first-hand account when he paid a visit.[25] 'At a depth of about four feet from the surface, and immediately beneath a thin stratum of sand' Harvey's men had found an inscribed granite pillar 6 feet long, a foot wide and 8 ins. thick. It had perhaps been traversely fractured twice when it fell originally, and was found lying prone; it seems very likely that the inscribed face was uppermost and therefore spotted. This face was 'much weather worn'. Just north of the stone was a grave, six or eight feet long (by report) and aligned east–west, excavated into the hard ground under the 'thin stratum of sand'. It was formed of 'unshapen and uncemented stones', some placed on edge to define the grave and some laid over these to form a covering; a cist grave. It was filled with

191

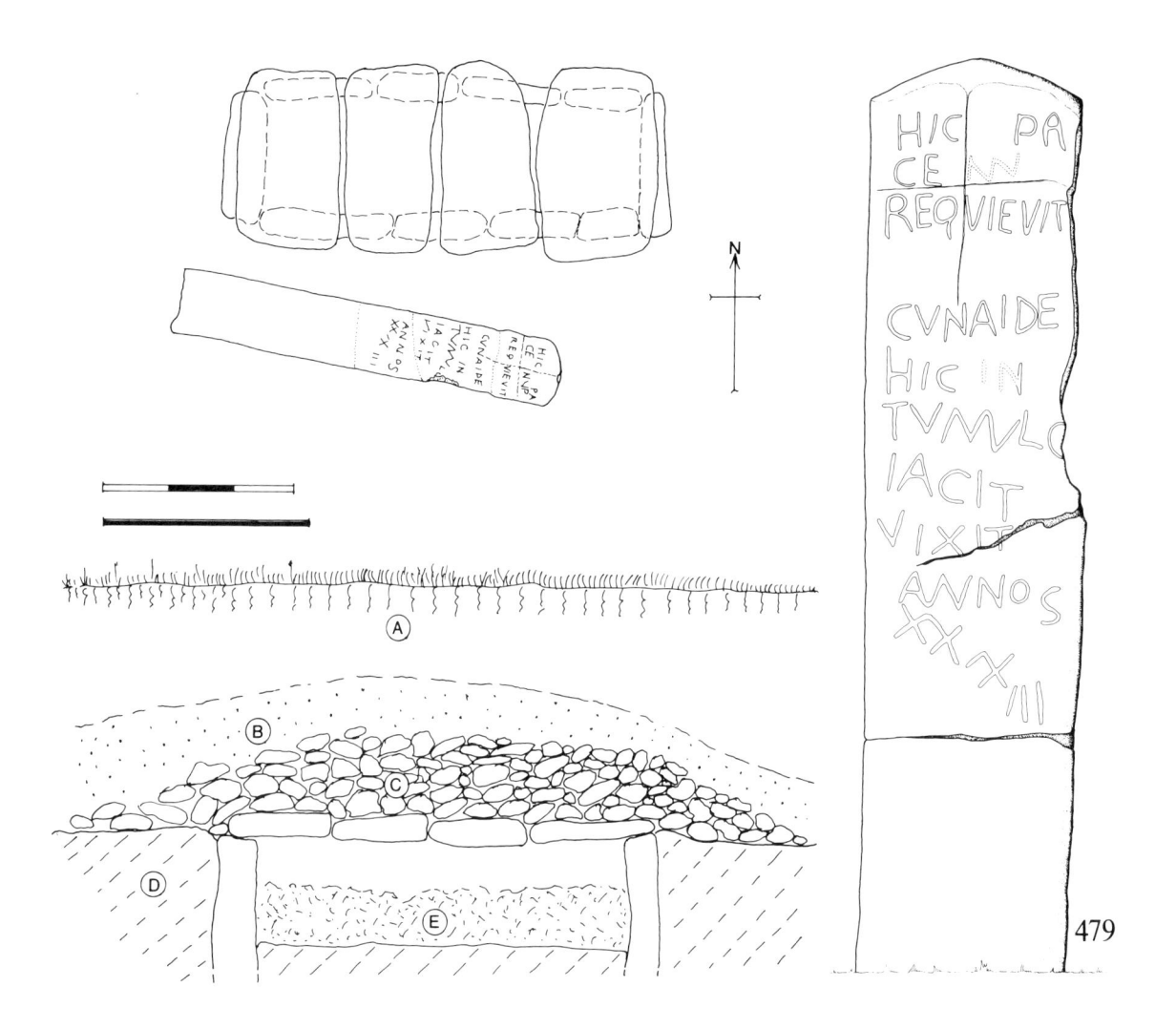

(left): **Fig. 11.4** Reconstruction from Richard Edmonds' 1843–4 description of the Carnsew grave. **Above**, plan, assuming that memorial originally stood at W (head) end and had fallen with inscribed face upwards. **Below**, section. Contexts are A, upper ground (grass, subsoil); B, layer of blown sand overlying C, mound or cairn of smaller stones; D, old land surface, granitic 'rab' or gravel; E, sand, ashes and charcoal found when grave was opened. Scales, 3 feet over 1 metre.

(right): **Fig. 11.5** The Carnsew memorial, 479 CVNAIDE, drawn *in situ* 1990–91. Note the transverse cracks or breaks (jagged lines) and the natural 'cross' of mineral veins on upper part of this narrow granite pillar.

a mixture of 'sand, charcoal and ashes', and the whole was entirely covered with 'a loose heap of stones, the top of which was considerably beneath the surface of the soil'. Edmonds, a keen antiquary in his spare time, gave a full and intelligible account and Fig. 11.4 is a reconstruction based on his words. The inscribed stone, which must already have been fractured, 'fell into three parts' when the workmen moved it and Mr Harvey caused it to be fixed into a wall alongside his new road. Later, it was moved again with further minor damage, and cemented (where it is now) into a wall by a path in the upper part of Carnsew fort, an inaccurate reading being given on a slate plaque alongside it.

Though in 1844 the inscription must have been more legible than it is now, it was badly misread. It was examined again in 1891 by Revd William Iago, generally competent in this field (p. 257), who nevertheless managed to insert two non-existent lines of text.[26] R. A. S. Macalister also had difficulties.[27] Finally an accurate transcript was attained, after many visits, by the late J. J. Beckerlegge.[28] This was in 1948, since when the stone has been not very carefully re-cemented. Exposure has rendered the surface extremely difficult to examine or rub; after prolonged checking in 1990 and 1991, the reading in Fig. 11.5 (which agrees with Beckerlegge's) was produced and drawn from many photographs. It is as definitive as one may now hope to be. The whole inscription, in ten lines, is (479) HIC PA/CE NUP(er) /REQVIEVIT / CVNAIDE / HIC (IN) / TV$\overline{\text{MV}}$LO / IACIT / VIXIT / ANNOS / XXXIII – 'Here in peace lately went to rest Cunaide. Here in the grave she lies. She lived 33 years'. NVP is now almost undetectable (the concluding letters (er) must be supplied); IN has virtually perished since 1843 and the -O of TVMVLO is almost obliterated by an old gash.

Superficially, *Cunaide* looks like a Latinized feminine genitive, with *-e* for *-ae*, though the sense requires it to be nominative and, since the rest of the inscription is correct Latin, a simple mistake seems unlikely. Whether this name, which the *ordinator* of the stone probably obtained orally, was really *Cunaida* instead of *Cunaide* is unknown. Jackson commented[29] that it seems to be 'a Latin genitive singular feminine of the Primitive Irish name *\*Cunaido*, and not a British name at all'. For the moment it stands alone. The epigraphy and other implications attached to the inscription will be examined in the next chapter. Here, all we need note is that it is a Christian memorial, certainly within the fifth century and probably not later than 450–75; that it accompanied an oriented cist, under a mound, just outside and below a coastal fort; and that whoever Cunaide was, her social position entitled her to a long inscription and a form of 'special grave'. In view of what has been argued earlier, it must be thought improbable in the extreme that any Uí Liatháin settlers or their immediate descendants, in west Cornwall during the late fourth and earlier fifth centuries, were already Christian; nor, for that matter, any Dumnonians. Who then had converted whom, and whence came the inspiration? That too must shortly be addressed.

The small fort at Carnsew is not a suitable candidate for Dún maic Liatháin, or subsequently a native name *\*Din Letan* (*Ledan, Lidan*). It is probably too small ever to have attracted a *din-* name and, in the setting of all of west Cornwall, quite insufficiently prominent. Inspection suggests a specific role – from it, one gets a fine view of the river-mouth dead ahead, and all of the estuarine widening, and in the fifth century the tidal water must have lapped a narrow beach at the very foot of the bluff (constructional work here in 1990 showed ten-plus feet of sand below a foot of modern topsoil). This is a practical, fortified, bridgehead possibly adapted from a pre-Roman defensive work; if we are to picture sporadic settlement by bands arriving on west Cornwall's north coast, Carnsew is somewhere that early leaders among settlers might well have wished to acquire and hold.

Dún maic Liatháin, whose name could be remembered in ninth-century Munster (and may, as 'Lidan', have still been known in twelfth-century Cornwall) must have been a far more prominent hill, a landmark in west Cornwall, and – like Moel Trigarn, if that were Dún Tredúi – in part a symbol, as a notable stronghold briefly occupied in a phase of late Roman raiding. It may have figured in some heroic tale set in the distant age of Crimthann Már mac Fidaig, the sole details being the belief that it was in Cornwall and that it could be ascribed to the exploits of the Uí Liatháin. These do not automatically render it unreal, but the obstacle is that any original (post-Roman) names, current in Primitive Cornish, of most major Cornish hillforts have simply not survived. Probably during the late first millennium AD and increasingly so by the eleventh to thirteenth centuries, they were re-named for land-holdings on their slopes or at their feet, later with the English suffix 'hill' being understood.

One could guess that Beroul's *Lidan* lay west of the Hayle estuary in the high ground of West Penwith, the final Land's End peninsula, and that (like Moel Trigarn) any Dún maic Liatháin is likely to have been closer to the northern than to the southern coast. This would direct us to two possibilities (one shown on Fig. 11.1); Chun Castle, and Trencrom or Trecrobben Hill. Both now bear the names of the farms below them (*chy (an) oon* 'house of the downs, high moors'; *tre(v) an crom* 'farm-holding of the humped or curved (hill)'). Both may well have had older names in *din*. Chun Castle has massive stone ramparts and, it is known from minor excavations a long time ago, originated in pre-Roman times; it was in some fashion re-occupied, with a post-Roman (sixth century?) episode marked by pottery and some tin-smelting.[30] Trencrom, which has never been excavated, was conceivably a neolithic *enceinte* rebuilt as an Iron Age multivallate hillfort, inside which numerous circular hut foundations are visible. Archaeological details are not very relevant, since a short occupation in the fourth or early fifth century within either fort would not necessarily have left detectable traces.

Trencrom is not only intervisible with Carnsew; from anywhere within a good distance eastward, as one approaches the Land's End, it dominates the western skyline (Fig. 11.6). (Chun, on the other hand, is on a rounded ridge and becomes impressive only at a short distance.) It can be no more than a guess but, if any such place existed, Dún maic Liatháin might be identified as Trencrom.

With this, we reach the limits of inference. At some future date, Carnsew fort may be excavated, in which case any more-than-temporary occupation during the fifth (and sixth?) century ought to be readily detectable. Distributionally, one

**Fig. 11.6** The hillfort of Trencrom, dominating the view westward from the end of Hayle's East Pool below Phillack (see Fig. 12.1); a winter's morning view. (Photo: Susanna Thomas.)

could guess now that as a minor 'centre of power' Carnsew should have been involved in the receipt, by sea, of Mediterranean imports in the early sixth century.[31] As for the Uí Liatháin, or people from any other named tribe or population-group of south-coastal Ireland, the hypothesis that there may have been limited settlement in west Cornwall cannot be proved, but is not in conflict with what clues can be extracted. Entirely separate is the topic of the *character* of Cunaide's memorial inscription. It stands alone in Early Christian Cornwall. The personal name and the find-spot of 1843 may have Irish connections; the inscription does not, and it directs us elsewhere.

## References

1. *De Excidio Britonum*, 21 (Michael Winterbottom's translation).
2. *DEB*, 19.
3. Thompson 1984, 115.
4. Summary in *LHEB*, chap.1.
5. A gift-shop with Celtic-looking goods, Artesania Maeloc, may be seen (1991) in Santiago; the author's enquiry whether 'Maeloc' was the *obispo muy distinguido y muy antiguo de Bretoña* was met with delight, and astonishment that anyone outside Galicia had ever heard of him. For the name, see *LHEB* 646; and Sims-Williams, *BBCS* 38 (1991), 20–21.
6. E. A. Thompson, 'Britonia', in Barley & Hanson 1968, 201–6.
7. Padel 1985, 127; the name means 'estuary'.
8. J. Hobson Matthews, *A History of St Ives, Lelant, Towednack and Zennor* (Elliot Stock, London 1892), 339.
9. 'The Irish settlements in post-Roman western Britain; a survey of the evidence', *JRIC* n.s. 6 (1972), 251–74.
10. Padel 1985, 27–8.
11. Examples – Vounderveor (Lane), Penzance, once serving sea-shore common grazing, and Boundervean, Camborne, the old N–S access lane across the medieval glebe-lands.
12. G. H. Doble, *St Gwinear, Martyr* ( = Cornish Saints 9; Long Compton 1926).
13. Harvey 1969, 115.
14. Toulmin Smith 1907, i. 187–90.
15. The manor of Ludgvan; the family controlled it until about 1250.
16. See the relevant chapters in Penhallurick 1986.
17. *LHEB*, 155.
18. Hogan, *Onomasticon*, 266.
19. The later analogic plural *mebyon* is similarly absent.
20. Cf. O. J. Padel, 'Predannack or Pradnick, in Mullion', *Cornish Studies* 15 (1987), 11–14, suggesting British *Britannākon*, 1196 Bridanoc 'the British one', early name for the Lizard.
21. Padel 1985, 84 (s.v. *dyn*).
22. Sawyer, no.770, originally AD 969, referring to Lamorran south-east of Truro.
23. Alfred Ewert, *The Romance of Tristran by Beroul, 2 vols.* (Blackwell, Oxford 1939–70).
24. E. R. M. Ditmas, *Tristan and Iseult in Cornwall* (Forrester Roberts, Brockworth (Glos.) 1969). The classic study is now O. J. Padel, 'The Cornish Background of the Tristan Stories', with numerous refs., *CMCS* 1 (1981), 53–80.
25. 'Sepulchral monument, discovered on Carnsew cliff, in Hayle, Cornwall, in December, 1843', *12th Annual Report, Royal Cornwall Polytechnic Society* (Falmouth 1844), 69–71.
26. Unpublished; Iago MS, Royal Institution of Cornwall, Truro.
27. *CIIC* i, pp.457–8; he made HIC IN / TVMVLO out of the top two lines, though in other respects was correct.
28. 'The Ancient Memorial Inscription on the Stone at Hayle', *Old Cornwall* 5 (St Ives 1953), 173–7 illus.
29. *LHEB*, 329 n.1; I have failed to discover the source of Jackson's 'Pr.Ir. *Cunaido*', or on what basis he postulated it.
30. The 1920s work was by E. T. Leeds (see *Archaeologia*, LXVI, 205 ff., and LXXXI, 26 ff.); discussion, much later, of some of the finds – sherds of B i amphora (early sixth?) and grass-marked pottery (late sixth or seventh) – in C. Thomas, 'Evidence for post-Roman occupation of Chun Castle, Cornwall', *Antiquaries Journal* 36 (1956), 75–9 illus.
31. This is shown in Thomas 1989, especially the maps, Figs. 3 & 4.

# 12

# *The Gaulish Connection*

A MILE NORTH-EAST from Carnsew, standing in the lee of the high dunes that separate Hayle's East Pool from the sea, is Phillack parish church (Fig. 12.1). When major rebuilding took place in 1856–7, the pious enthusiasts in charge (William White the architect, Frederick Hockin[1] the rector-cum-squire) were rewarded with many exciting discoveries. They found the neat granite altar *mensa* of the original Norman church; a priest's tomb-slab of the same date; an eroded granite Crucifixion panel[2] that may have been the altar frontal from some pre-Norman church on the spot; and a glass phial, said to have contained the dried blood of the patroness 'Piala' (duly walled up again). Lying around in the churchyard, revealed when tons of blown sand were carted away, were several post-Norman granite crosses, a coped grave-cover (eleventh century?) late in the 'hogback' series, and a large coarse pillar of granite with the inscription (471) CLOTVALI / MOBRATTI (p. 284). The impressive array of antiquities confirmed the great interest of the place. Phillack churchyard has since the fifth or sixth century been a Christian focus, apparently developed with a succession of churches, and as a cemetery it may have been sited on (or overlapping) a pre-Christian burial area with short stone cists of Iron Age character.[3] But neither the supposed Irish female martyr 'Piala', nor still less the subsequently-adopted 'St Felicitas', has any bearing on the original dedication. As Lynette Olson and Oliver Padel have now shown,[4] in the tenth century the (male) patronal name was *Felec*. British rather than Irish, it should be cognate with the rather obscure Welsh noun *ffelaig, ffelyg* 'lord, chieftain, leader, governor, etc.'[5] It may be a case where the patron's name – if not simply adjectival – represents, not a saint, but the original donor of the consecrated site. Should this imply in the neighbourhood a post-Roman notable, we are back to the legendary Cornish 'King Teudar' of various medieval Lives, persecutor of all the Irish saints, with his sand-engulfed palace at Riviere (tenement adjoining Phillack churchtown).[6] Even if this is just folklore, there is elsewhere enough reason to see Phillack as a significant locality. Claims for the antiquity of the churchyard derive neither from the 1856 finds, nor from the King Teudar stories (which are still remembered at Hayle and Phillack). In 1973, when some road-widening led to a necessary clipping-back of the line of the churchyard wall on its southern curve,[7] small-scale excavations took place. From the lowest levels, below a deep sequence of recent graves, then medieval and pre-Norman

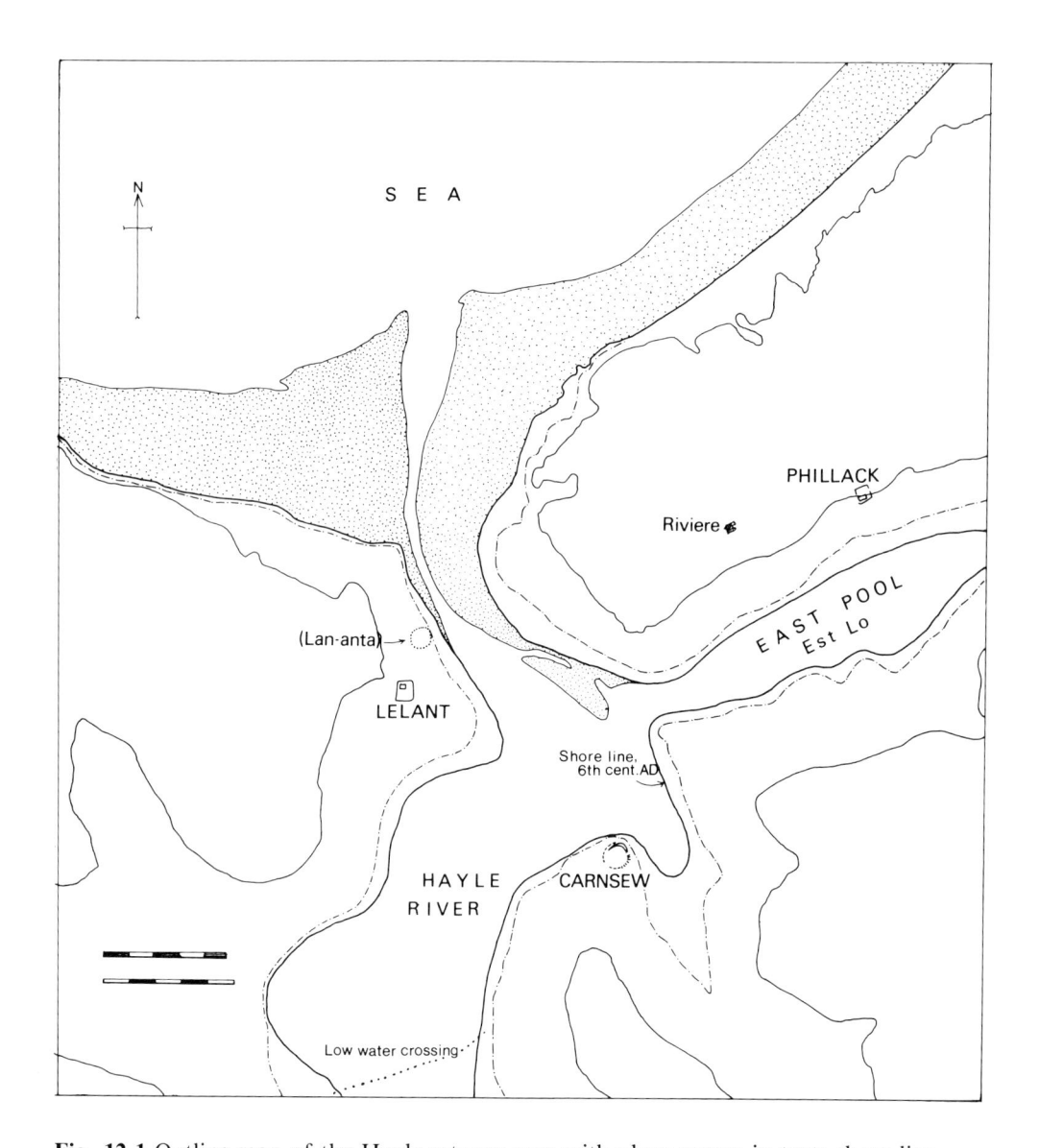

**Fig. 12.1** Outline map of the Hayle estuary area with place-names in text; shore line (mean sea-level) as it was in the sixth century AD, contours at 25 and 50 feet above present OD. Scales, 500 yards above 500 metres.

long-cist burials, came a single rim-sherd of an imported East Mediterranean red slipware dish (Phocaean Red Slip, Form 3). Its date is late fifth or early sixth century, and it is referable to the wider importation of such items into post-Roman Dumnonia;[8] here, perhaps connected with the status of Carnsew.

In 1856, inner church walling that was probably of Norman date had to be dismantled; fortunately spotted in time was a small piece of shaped, worked, granite. This was inserted above the doorway of White's new south porch in a place of honour. Rectangular, it has a low-relief circular boss on which, incised with a V-section cut (which, from long immurement, is still fully visible), there is the motif of the *chi-rho* in its first, fourth and early fifth century, form. The *chi-rho* is a monogram of our own capitals X and P, which are also the Greek capitals for *chi*, an aspirated sound /kh/, and *rho*, the sound of /r/. These are the starting-letters of *Christos* 'the Anointed one; Christ'. As an easily reproduced symbol we find this used in fourth-century Roman Britain, antedating the appearance of the linear Cross on inscribed memorials and other objects in Britain and Ireland.[9] A modified second form, drawn like a cross or plus-sign (+), the top of the vertical arm being hooked or looped to the right to represent the *rho*, generally replaced the XP form in the late fifth and sixth centuries.

This minimal inscription (1502) shows the *chi-rho* on a flat boss, raised slightly above the coarse granite backing (Fig. 12.2). It is important to note that the *rho*-loop is actually a hook ('open') and not closed, as in the letter P. Careful examination (from the top of a ladder) suggests that the boss is original, and that there was no tinkering with the piece in 1856. Its thickness, into the wall, cannot be ascertained. One problem is in deciding just how this little stone was used. The only, generally similar, other west Cornish *chi-rho* of this kind (1501) seems to have been larger, on a flat piece of granite roughly shaped as a gable-cross, found at the (pre-Norman?) chapel of St Helen, Cape Cornwall;[10] unhappily it was lost some time ago and we know it only from drawings. Such *chi-rho* motifs, sometimes flanked by the Greek letters *alpha* and *omega*,[11] appear within wreaths and circles as flat-relief decoration upon stone sarcophagi (one-piece coffins) in fourth–fifth century Gaul, and they can head multi-line inscriptions on tombstones from Gaul, other provinces of the late Empire and North Africa. At Phillack we can hardly imagine that the *chi-rho* piece was somehow cemented to the summit of a narrow pillar, like that of the Carnsew inscription in Fig. 11.5. Was it possibly incorporated at the top, or head-end, of some formally constructed grave?

If genuine – and, on balance, we can assume that it is – the Phillack stone should be fifth century, perhaps not much later than mid-fifth. Its open, hooked *rho* (instead of the looped variety) is a significant starting-point. Generally if not invariably in the limited art of Roman and sub-Roman British Christianity the closed *rho*, the more 'correct' depiction, is used.[12] The distinction was made by Alison Frantz in a classic paper of 1929.[13] The open *rho* originated in Eastern Christianity during the fourth century; in the Western provinces, for historical reasons, it was adopted in the southern part of Spain, and also in that part of Gaul – the huge, southern *diocesis Viennensis* with *Lugdunensis Prima*, the territory centred on the modern city of Lyon – particularly influenced from an early time by the Church in the East. Here, the open *rho* was the commoner type. It could be modified further, becoming more like the tailed capital R, or being assimilated to depictions of the pastoral staff as a crook. Examples abound, many of them

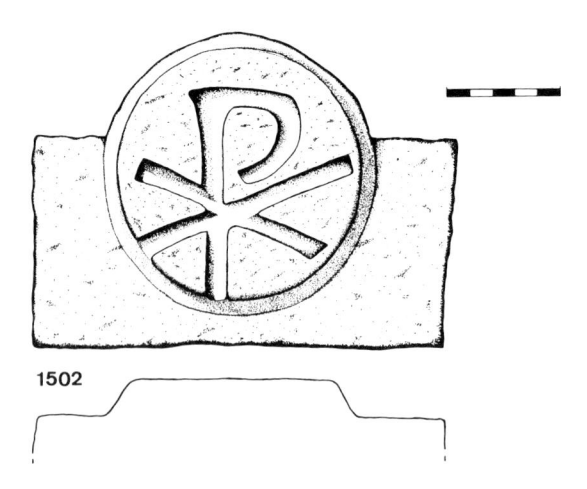

**Fig. 12.2** The small, fine granite, stone with slightly raised boss and 'open-looped' *chi-rho* (1502) built into upper gable of south porch, Phillack church; drawn *in situ*. Scale, 5 centimetres.

wreathed or encircled, and we might suppose that on the Phillack stone the outline of the low boss is itself a form of encirclement. A conclusion is that, if one looks to a Continental source, it would (for the closest) be Atlantic France south of the Loire estuary.

Phillack church is near enough to Carnsew for us to accept that the *chi-rho* fragment and the Cunaide stone – otherwise-isolated manifestations of fifth-century Christianity around a remote shore – are almost certain to have been connected. The Carnsew inscription, which is unlike those series from Demetia and Brycheiniog earlier discussed, belongs to a restricted class to which one might be tempted to give the label 'long-winded'. 'EL', meaning 'extended Latinate', is a more dignified term. Common to them are the following. They are inscribed in Roman capitals, and there is no ogam. The inscriptions, in horizontal lines, are multi-line; a minimum five lines might be the qualifier (Carnsew, *Cunaide*, has ten). The phrase HIC IACIT, with minor variation, is always included: HIC IN TVMVULO (also with variants) and a statement of age at death may be present. There may be two or more personal names, not necessarily given in the 'A son of B' formula. Where any motif heads one of these inscriptions it is of the fourth–fifth–sixth centuries *chi-rho* series, and there may occasionally be horizontal lines along with lettering.

These EL memorials, only a dozen or so, differ from almost all other Insular inscriptions in clearly being derived from external models. They can be differentiated at once from the products, within south Wales generally, of that other continuing Latinate (even a continuing *Christian* Latinate) tradition whose adherents were able only to transmute Irish ogam *A MAQI B* into Latin A FILI B; were manifestly under the sway of the Irish-originating, ogam-related preference for verticality; and, to stress a Christian context, could add only the occasional HIC IACIT or even a token HIC, IC. The *wording* of the EL inscriptions introduces an expanded and very different vocabulary, with (in both south Wales and Dumnonia) the extension of words to memorials not strictly of EL type.

The model for this range is readily found in the Christian epitaphs (later fifth and sixth centuries) of Gaul, and the phraseology is matched by the development of funerary inscriptions in other provinces (Iberia (Roman Spain and Portugal), North Africa, the Rhineland, Switzerland). British occurrences are mapped in Fig. 12.4. Continental stones display these words and phrases in combinations.[14] At Vienne we can find HIC REQVIESCIT IN PA/CI LUPICINVS / QVI VIXIT ANNOS NV/MERO XXXV... HIC QVIESCIT / IN PACE IOVENALES / QVI VIXIT ANVS ...; at Lyon, the stone of Ursus (AD 493) with IN HOC TVMVULO REQVIESCIT / BONE MEMORIAE VRSVS / QVI VIXIT IN PACE ANNVS (etc.); from Camiac (Gironde) a fragmentary HIC IACET PECV/LIA IN PACAE (fifth cent.); and for a certain Leo, at Köln (Cologne), later in the sixth century, IN OH TVMOLO / REQIESCET / IN PACE BONE / MEMORIE / LEO VIXET AN/NVS (etc.). Nash-Williams, in *ECMW*, long ago noticed[15] the likely Gaulish background of the Welsh EL inscriptions, though he avoided the question of how a fashion centred around Lyon and Vienne – both some way from Gaul's Atlantic coast – should appear in the Bristol Channel and Irish Sea regions.

In the Carnsew inscription (Fig. 11.5) the lettering is in clear capitals, there are no blunders and the ligaturing is minimal. The past-tense form REQVIEVIT 'she has gone to rest' (from *requiescere*) is correct but in this guise very unusual.[16] It could be argued, possibly, that a physical model (for many lines of capitals on a tall narrow slab) might have been provided by any late Roman route-marker or milestone, and one is preserved in the parish church at St Hilary, not far from Carnsew.[17] But on such milestones the inscriptions are grossly contracted, formulaic, and (at the period) probably unintelligible to local people. The innovations are the *length* of the memorial statement and the extended Christian phrasing. For the EL class as a whole, a sample of which (taken uncorrected from *CIIC*) appears in Fig. 12.3, one can observe a predominance of Roman names, among memorials of what were nearly all Christian Britons. 360 *Paulinus* from Cynwyl Gaeo was noticed earlier (p. 104). On Anglesey we find 323 *Saturninus*, patron and eponym of Llansadwrn church, and 320 *Secundus*; from mid-Wales, 421 *Rostece* (feminine, genitive, for *Rusticae*); from south-west Scotland, 516 *Viventius* and *Mavorius*. There is another aspect. 360 *Paulinus* may have been a pious layman rather than priest, but from north-west Wales 393 *Carausius* and certainly 391 *Senacus*, a presbyter (PRSB) buried CVM MVLTITVDINEM FRATRVM, were clerics; 325 *Bivatigi(rnus)* on the long Llantrisaint inscription was a SACERDOS, as were (516) the SACERDOTES Viventius and Mavorius. As for the Gaulish element, some of these EL stones are topped with upright *chi-rho* symbols; the encircled one on 516, from Kirkmadrine in Galloway (Fig. 12.3, no.7) is the open *rho* of Gaulish type.[18] Bivatigirnus (325) was described as VASSO PAVLINI, using a (?) Gaulish rather than British *uasso* 'servant, disciple'.

THE GAULISH CONNECTION

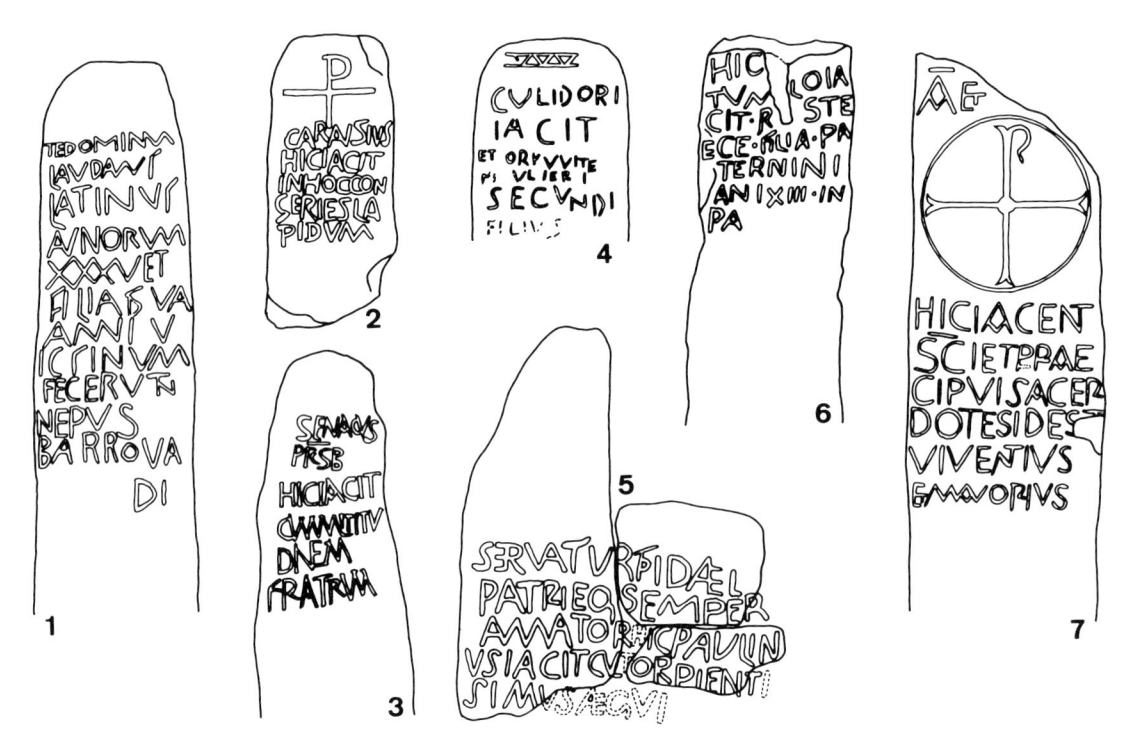

**Fig. 12.3** Representative 'Extended Latinate' inscriptions (EL), mostly drawn from *CIIC*. 1, 520 Whithorn. 2, 393 Penmachno. 3, 391 Penllech. 4, 320 Llangefni. 5, 360 Cynwyl Gaeo. 6, 421 Llanerfyl. 7, 516 Kirkmadrine. Nos. 1 and (possibly) 4 might be called 'sub-Roman British'; the rest, influenced by Continental models.

We detect a modest beginning to subsequent combinations of memorial inscriptions and Christian art. One odd feature of the *Cunaide* stone (Fig. 11.5) is that its upper face shows a natural cross, the horizontal being a thin vein of tourmaline in the granite, and the vertical a crack along a quartz inclusion. Whether this was perceived or not, we cannot tell, but lettering of the first three lines was disposed to fit around this 'cross'. On the Lundy stones (Fig. 10.3), which are far too curt to be regarded as EL, but which should be related to this class rather than to the Demetian vertical style, both 1400 (*Optimi*) and 1401 (*Resteuta*) have horizontal border-lines. This is rare in Wales, but appears as a double line with inner zigzag and a lower single line on an Anglesey stone (320). Firmly cut lines – originating perhaps in guide-line rulings – above, between or below rows of lettering, and also rectilinear framing of 'justified' texts, feature on pagan Roman tombstones. There is a late (early fourth century?) isolated example from Carlisle, memorial of the Greek *Flavius Antigonus Papias*.[19] Continuance of such ornament in Continental inscriptions was commonplace.

Alongside a loose acceptance that the special characteristics of these EL memorials (whose revealing distribution can now be added, Fig. 12.4) ought to be

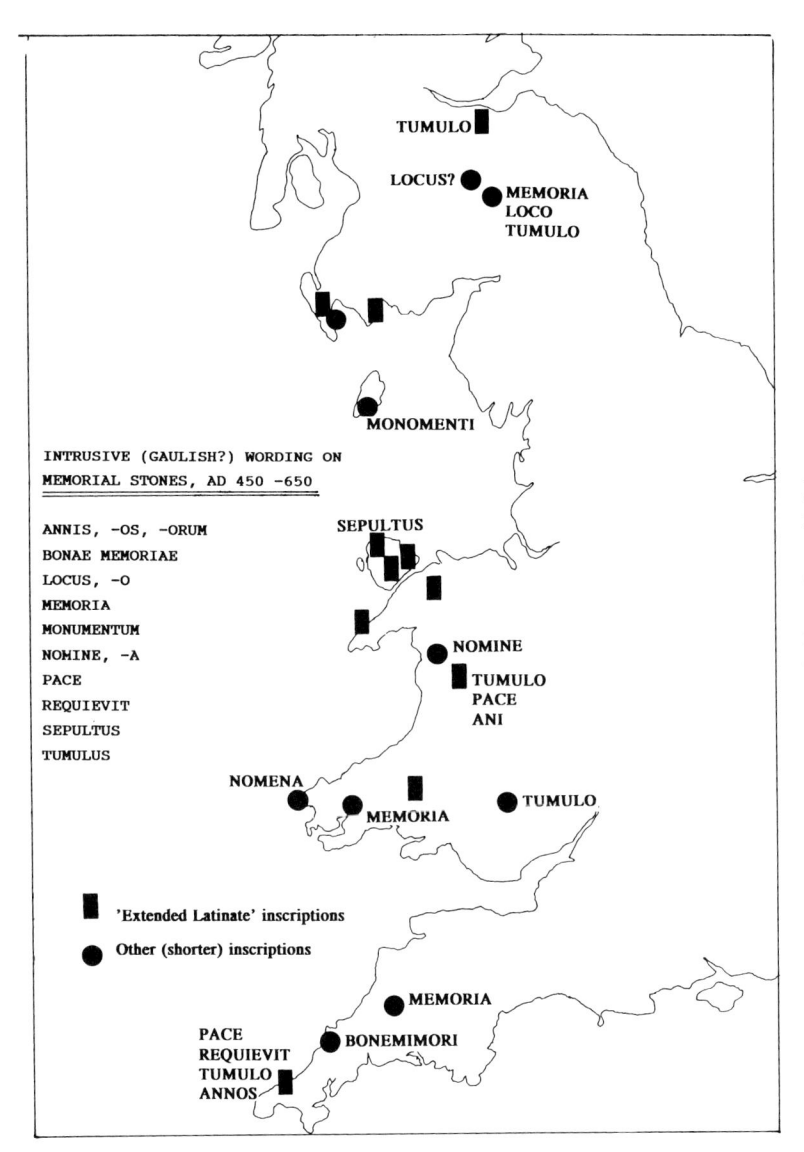

**Fig. 12.4** Extended Latinate inscriptions in Atlantic Britain, later fifth and sixth centuries; distribution, showing elements of intrusive Christian Latin vocabulary.

INTRUSIVE (GAULISH?) WORDING ON MEMORIAL STONES, AD 450 –650

ANNIS, -OS, -ORUM
BONAE MEMORIAE
LOCUS, -O
MEMORIA
MONUMENTUM
NOMINE, -A
PACE
REQUIEVIT
SEPULTUS
TUMULUS

■ 'Extended Latinate' inscriptions
● Other (shorter) inscriptions

attributed to Gaulish influence, there has been an even looser explanation of them as the work of 'Gaulish missionaries'. This is little better than a substitute answer. Historical and literary inferences offer the rudiments of a framework in which contact between Britain and Gaul during the fifth century can be supposed.[20] The supposition implies travels by sea and, given the Atlantic emphasis of Fig. 12.4, fairly lengthy trips. Much the same pattern of coastal contact, but including Ireland, can be argued from finds of domestic wheelmade pottery (Class E ware) of Gaulish – though, within Gaul, still unlocated – manufacture; but this particular commerce, possibly a sideline in the shipping of wine in barrels or casks, though now resting on firm archaeological foundations really belongs to the period after AD 600.[21] Here, we are concerned with events that began before 500. On the evidence of the inscriptions it has been argued[22] that two, at least, of the Kirkmadrine stones in south-west Scotland (516, 517: 518, though with Gaulish features, is not a memorial and is slightly later) commemorate members of a party of clerics who were themselves either Gaulish immigrants or churchmen who had stayed in some part of that country. The same should probably be claimed for some districts of north-west Wales, and earlier (p. 99) it has been proposed, in an epigraphic context, that there may have been a similar introduction of ideas into Demetia, the inscriptional evidence for which has not survived. As for Hayle, with its Carnsew and Phillack monuments, the river-mouth is one of the few natural inlets on Cornwall's north coast; it is difficult *not* to imagine the mid-fifth century arrival here of a ship from Gaul, very possibly busy with un-spiritual commerce, but carrying a passenger (or passengers) with the fire of the Gospel in the belly and the knowledge of Gaulish epigraphic fashions in the head.

W. H. Davies found certain insights in the writing of Gildas.[23] There is a passage that describes, at scathing length, shortcomings of British *presbyteres* about or soon after AD 500. Certain men had been buying orders of priesthood, and paying to be consecrated as local territorial bishops – the sin of Simon Magus.[24] Close friends, in unhappy Britain, drew the line at so scandalous a practice. Such 'beasts of the belly' in their pride and greed 'send urgent messages ahead, and take a positive pleasure in sailing across seas and traversing wild lands in order to attain at least such a glory ... Then, with great pomp and show (or rather, madness), they return home; making their gait, which had been erect before, still more erect.' Gildas may have known cases where the rank of bishop had been purchased abroad, in some lax district of Gaul or perhaps Spain. Davies comments that these words show a reflux of sixth-century churchmen 'returning as proud prelates and obviously a fertile source of Gallic influences'. Given all the other clues, we may well accept this.

In the small list of specific words shown in Fig. 12.4, HIC IACIT (Christian in import, and also a mid-to-late fifth century borrowing from the Continent, but too widely spread to be diagnostic) is omitted. The few (sixth century) occurrences of *nomine/nomena* and *memoria* are of interest. Apart from the northernmost, the rather irregular EL Yarrow Stone near Peebles (515), these are not on EL stones; from Wales, 416 EQVESTRI NOMINE and 448 RINACI NOMENA are short and vertical, while the Demetian (358) MEMORIA / VOTEPORIGIS / PROTICTORIS and the Dumnonian (466) INGEN/VI /MEM/ORIA both additionally have ogam names and, though horizontal, are only three and four lines. This is an innovation, but somehow differently so. *Nomine* (for which *nomena* is probably an error), 'by the name (of)', 'in the name (of)', may treat *nomen* 'personal name' as equivalent to 'soul, spirit, spiritual individuality, good name, repute', with the chance of a (written) affection from the unrelated word *numen* 'divine nature' – used normally of divinities and emperors. Though in Britain *nomine* and *memoria* ('visible memorial, grave', with perhaps 'marked grave, special grave') may have been mediated through Gaulish contact there is the possibility that they reflect another minor introduction from the Mediterranean – North Africa, Italy, the East – where these terms would be more at home. On a group of Irish ogam inscriptions, confined to the south-west (Cos. Cork and Kerry), linguistically and epigraphically late – i.e., later fifth and sixth century, and probably all Christian – the opening word is the nominative ANM (representing Primitive Irish *anmen* 'name', a cognate of *nomen*). This may carry the sense of '(Inscription) of-A, of-the-son of-B', but again the limited occurrence hints at an introduced idea, where Latin *nomen, nomine,* was re-cast in Irish.[25]

Should one have in mind the agency of British (and Irish) pilgrims to the Holy Places, causing on their return an imitation of holy memorial models noted afar,[26] there is a separate archaeology of such postulated travels in the shape of the presence at many British and Irish coastal sites, in the late fifth and sixth centuries, of East Mediterranean and North African imports (pottery containers and fine-ware dishes) in considerable quantity.[27] Perhaps a related clue may be something for which we can return to the grave of Cunaide discovered at Carnsew in 1843 (p. 192; Fig. 11.4). Features here included a superimposed heap of stones over the cist (a *mound grave*) and the unexplained presence *within* the grave of ashes and charcoal. Mound graves, or reported cases of such, are scattered up and down early western Britain at this period; apart from those known archaeologically, there is epigraphic evidence – 393 (Penmachno, Caerns.) has CARAVSIVS / HIC IACIT / IN HOC CON/GERIES LA/PIDVM, 'C. lies here in this *congeries lapidum* (heap of stones)'. There are references to burials under mounds and cairns in early Welsh sources. While in the northern half of Britain in post-Roman times this could have been part-perpetuation of a native habit of some antiquity – the Picts of north-east Scotland, for example, appear to have used low burial cairns at quite a late date[28] – in the southern half we must allow the possibility of external models. What *can* be said at this stage is that a poorly defined connection exists between EL (and related) memorial stones, mound graves and perhaps other kinds of 'special graves'; the burials of prominent people; and Christianity. The postulated first tomb of Brychan (p. 171) was a 'special grave' with a mound grave in it, in a cemetery from *circa* 500 with particular memorials; the stone (393) of Carausius with its *congeries* is an EL stone, as is Cunaide's with *her* mound grave, and as also seems to have been the EL 'Catstane' near Edinburgh (510, commencing with IN OC TVMVLO).

The last component in this interesting nexus is evidence for the presence, by the graveside and perhaps at the time of the actual burial, of a funerary meal; a *cena*, where the relatives solemnly partook of food and drink, probably cooking the foodstuff, possibly using the exposed surface of a grave as a *mensa* or table and thus reproducing, *al fresco*, the essence of the Last Supper to speed a Christian soul towards its Maker. Where it differs from the present-day custom of providing 'baked meats' for mourners after a funeral is that it apparently took place *at* the grave, in the burial-area. There may be slightly later literary allusions. Dr Richard Sharpe draws attention[29] to a chapter in Adomnán's Life of St Columba (of Iona); this refers to western Scotland in the late sixth century, and the death of a native layman with whom the Iona monks had been in a dispute over rights to hunt seals. Columba had, forgivingly, despatched the man a present of a fat beast and six pecks of corn. The recipient Erc was however found dead and 'the gifts sent were used up *in exequiis ejus*, at his funeral rites'. As Dr Sharpe says, this can only refer to a funeral feast but we are not further informed as to its shape.

The Early Christian *cena*, something that could be repeated on subsequent anniversaries of special occasions, was certainly a Mediterranean aspect of death; it is depicted in tomb frescoes, there are archaeological reflections such as deliberate holes allowing drink to be poured down into a grave, and small D-shaped altars for tomb-chapels that imitate the larger tables in *triclinia*, Roman dining-areas.[30] Some of the early Fathers drew adverse attention to occasional gluttony and excessive drinking at such events.[31] Whether the custom reached Christian western Britain *via* Gaulish contacts, or *via* Mediterranean traders and returning pilgrims, we do not know; evidence that it did reach Britain is increasing. The 'ashes and charcoal' in Cunaide's grave imply, not her cremation, but gradual filling of the grave through chinks and gaps by remains of a fire alongside it. At Tintagel churchyard, north Cornwall, the 1990–91 excavations that exposed (2 metres down) the level of the first Christian cist-graves – *circa* 500 and later – revealed alongside one of them a burnt patch, an open-air fire. Mature-oak charcoal (therefore, unfortunately, already old when burned) yielded a radio-carbon estimate centred on AD 403, consistent with a sixth-century date for the event;[32] this was confirmed by the discovery, impacted into the burnt area, of sherds of an early sixth-century imported Mediterranean amphora, which would have been brought over (with beer? milk? even some precious imported wine?) from the adjoining secular citadel on Tintagel Island.[33] We saw earlier, on Lundy, how traces of a similar little open-air fire were found hard by the central 'special grave', assigned to Brychan's mid-sixth century burial (p. 171; also shown in Fig. 10.6).

The features from the Hayle area in the fifth century, Cunaide's EL inscribed memorial and burial and the Phillack *chi-rho* stone, not only accord best with the idea that an isolated introduction of Christianity – by sea, and from (most probably) Gaul – took place, but can introduce the larger topic of other such introductions, and the persuasive body of evidence that this was epigraphically reflected. In west Cornwall there is nothing much to add; any earlier settlement of a limited number of Irish, discussed in the preceding chapter, is something resting upon a set of inferences. Christianity and the Irish incomers are (so far in this narrative) in touch only through the Carnsew inscription, and then solely if we accept (with Jackson) that the name *Cunaide* (or *\*Cunaida*) was Irish rather than British.

None of this concerns the mainstream of the Dumnonian conversion to Christianity. That is to be sought elsewhere in the south-western peninsula. A further study obliges us to look again towards Demetia (if not also towards Brycheiniog). Once more, the evidence starts with personal memorials and is then to be amplified by conventional archaeology. The rest of this book is concerned with such a search.


**References**

1. Hockin, who paid, appears in Francis Kilvert's Diary; see Richard Maby & Angela Tregoning, eds., *Kilvert's Cornish Diary* (Alison Hodge, Penzance 1989).
2. C. Thomas, 'A new pre-Conquest Crucifixion stone from west Cornwall', *Antiq.J.* 41 (1961), 89–92 illus.
3. These were poorly reported in the last century; C. Thomas, *Phillack Church. An Illustrated History . . .* (British Publishing Company, Gloucester 1961).
4. Olson & Padel 1986, 48–9.
5. So *GPC*, 1281, s.v.; the word is originally adjectival.
6. Cf. W. H. Pascoe's study, with many valuable local details, *Teudar. A King of Cornwall* (Dyllansow Truran, Redruth 1985).
7. Brief note, *CA*12 (1973), 59.
8. Thomas 1989, 16, and maps, figs.3 & 4.
9. *CRB*, 86 ff., with illus.
10. Main record, J. T. Blight, *A Week at the Land's End* (Longman, London 1861), 179 illus.
11. *CRB*, 89; the allusion ('first and last') is to Revelations, i. 8, xxi.6. (Vulgate: *Ego sum Alpha et Omega initium et finis*).
12. *CRB*, figs.4–7.
13. 'The Provenance of the Open Rho in the Christian Monograms,' *American Journal of Archaeology*, 2nd ser., 33 (1929), 10–26.
14. Examples chosen here from: Monique Jannet-Vallat (et al.), *Vienne aux premiers temps chrétiens* (1986), J.-F Reynaud, *Lyon aux premiers temps chrétiens* (1986), both *Guides archéologiques de La France*; J. F. Knight, 'The Early Christian Latin Inscriptions of Britain and Gaul: chronology and context', pp.45–50 in: Edwards & Lane 1992; Günter Ristow, *Römischer Götterhimmel u. frühes Christentum* (Wienand Verlag, Köln 1980).
15. *ECMW*, 8, 10, 55 and 93.
16. Krämer 1974, 41 n.605 – the present tense (*requiescit*) is usual in the Rhineland series. Spain includes however (cf. Vives 1969) no.67, REQVIEVERVNT (Toledo, fifth cent.), no.500, REQVI(VIT (Lisbon, AD 522) and no.487, REQIEVIT (Mertola, AD 510). At Carnsew, does the unusual *nup(er) requievit* perhaps imply a memorial erected some little while after the burial?
17. *RIB* no.2233 (Constantine I, 306–7).
18. See now Thomas 1992, illus., for a fuller discussion.

19. *RIB*, no.955 – described as 'probably Christian' on the strength of the words PLVS MINVS (indifference to earthly age).
20. Summarized in C. Thomas, 'Gallici nautae de Galliarum provinciis (etc.)', *Medieval Archaeol.* 34 (1990), 1–26.
21. Ibid., with further references.
22. Thomas 1992. These and the other Scottish inscriptions are now examined at length in my paper 'The Early Christian Inscriptions of Southern Scotland', *Glasgow Archaeological Journal* 17 (1991–92), publ. 1994, 1–10.
23. W. H. Davies 1968, 149, n.107; from *De Excidio,* 66–8, here given in Michael Winterbottom's translation.
24. 'Simony' – purchase or sale of things spiritual.
25. McManus, *Guide* (see Index, 200, s.v. ANM); suggestion first arose with J. Vendryes, 'Sur un emploi du mot AINM "nom"', *Études Celtiques* 7 (1955), 139–46.
26. John Wilkinson, *Jerusalem Pilgrims Before the Crusades* (Aris & Phillips, Warminster 1977); E. D. Hunt, *Holy Land Pilgrimage in the Later Roman Empire AD 312–460* (Oxford 1982).
27. Summary with maps, Thomas 1989.
28. P. J. Ashmore, 'Low cairns, long cists and symbols', *PSAS* 110 (1979–80), 346–55; see also various papers (87–151) in J. G. Friell & W. G. Watson, eds., *Pictish Studies* (*BAR* Brit. ser. 125, Oxford 1984).
29. Adamnan, *Vita Columbae*, i.41; see Sharpe 1994.
30. Conveniently exemplified at Salonae; Ejnar Dyggve, *History of Salonitan Christianity* (Instituttet for Sammenlignende Kulturforskning, ser.A.XXI: Oslo 1951).
31. Tertullian, *Apologeticus*, 39 (on the correct approach to the 'Christian feast'); cf. J. Stevenson, *The Catacombs* (1978), 96–8.
32. Nowakowski & Thomas 1990, 13–14, figs. 6 & 7; the date, GU-2798, 1650 ± bp, calibrated (2-sigma) as AD 250 (403) 530.
33. Sherds of a British B ii (Carthage LRI, Keay LIII, etc.) amphora; more of this, as of several others (B i, B ii, B iv), were found in the 1991 season in similar contexts (Nowakowski & Thomas 1992).

# 13

## The Post-Roman Kingdom of Dumnonia

ONE DISTINCTION between the two peninsulas, Demetia and Dumnonia, has lain in the survival of their respective early names. It was quite acceptable in the present century to publish a glossary of the *Demetian* dialect.[1] The later 'Dyfed' could be rehabilitated for a 1973 region or super-county and for use in such titles as The Dyfed Bakery or Dyfed Archaeological Trust. Dumnonia had been fragmented by the ninth century – in aspect and feeling, Devon and Somerset soon became wholly English – and in any case only a hopeless pedant would use the name 'Dumnonia' for anything today. Cornwall, demarcated by the long river Tamar and its extended coastline, isolated economically and socially, preserved its language (a derivative of Late British) until Hanoverian times; that part of Cornwall's population, perhaps only a third, which could truly be described as Cornish[2] thinks of itself as Cornish first and foremost, English reluctantly, British occasionally, but 'Dumnonian' never.

Dumnonia is much larger than Demetia; two hundred miles from Scilly to the edge of Mendip. In Roman times the *respublica civitatis Dumnoniorum*[3] embraced Cornwall, Devon and part of Somerset. The eastern bound, against the cantons of the Dobunni and Durotriges, is not defined; modern maps of Roman Britain omit hard frontiers[4] and we have to guess that natural lines, like a river in the Somerset Levels or the river Axe to the south, were the markers. The centre of administration, *Isca Dumnoniorum* or Exeter, was linked by a major road to the rest of *Britannia*, Roman-governed England and Wales, but Isca was in no way central to the whole *civitas* (Fig. 13.1).

The name of the native peoples, Dumnonii, has been explained as derived from a divine name *Dumnōnos*.[5] Though Rome took the area-name *Dumnonia* as an ethnic term for the whole peninsula the probability is that, west of the Tamar, *Cornovii* denoted those who centuries later were to become the Cornish. A place-name, reconstructed tentatively as *Durocornovium* (if so, British *Duro-cornouion* 'the *duro* (defended place?) of the Cornovii'?) cannot be located[6] but should have been in north-east Cornwall.

Dumnonia, about which there is a fair amount of archaeological information, may be considered as having lain firmly within Britannia. In Late Roman times it was part of the province of *Britannia Prima* (Wales and the west) with a capital at *Corinium*, Cirencester. It was marginal to the more civilized, more Romanized,

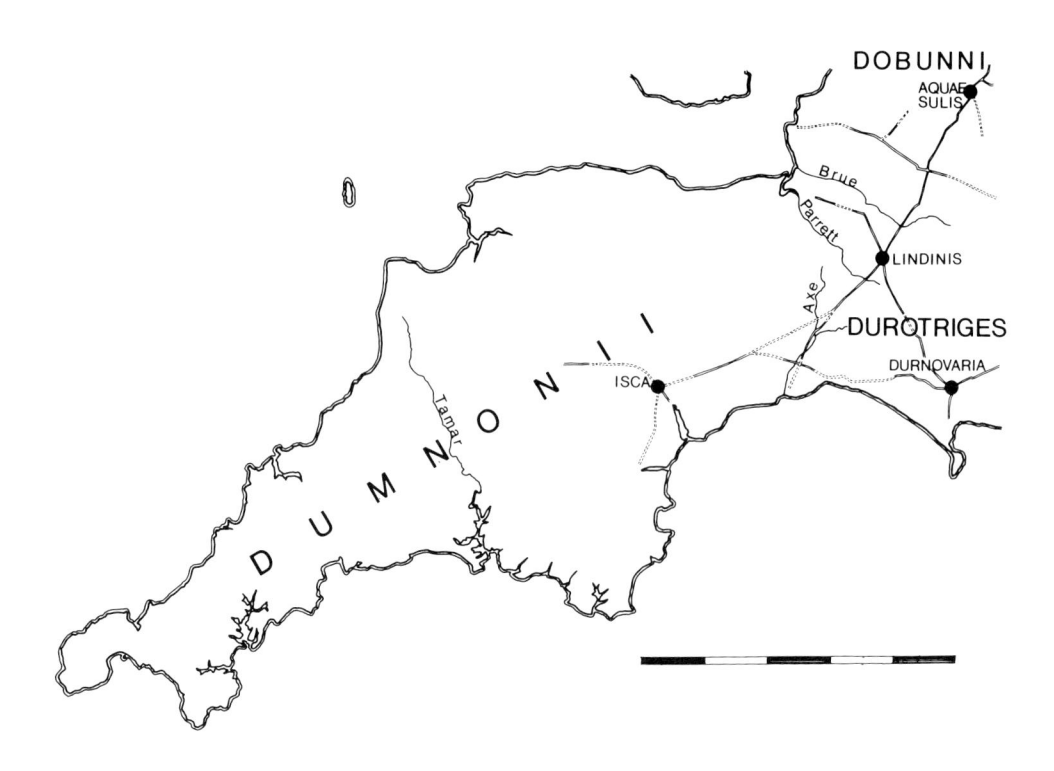

**Fig. 13.1** The *civitas* of the Dumnonii in late Roman Britain; its eastern boundaries may have been the rivers Parrett and Axe. Towns are *Isca* (*Dumnoniorum*), Exeter; *Durnovaria*, Dorchester; *Lindinis* (*Durotrigum*?), Ilchester; and *Aquae Sulis*, Bath. Scale, 50 miles (80 kms). Roman roads, certain or probable, are included.

zone to the east. The external interest, as we saw (p. 188), lay in the peninsula's mineral wealth. There are various summary accounts of Roman Dumnonia[7] and there are surveys of what is known or inferred about the peninsula in post-Roman times.[8] As for religion, there is no point in speculating about continuity from Romano-British Christianity in Dumnonia, since there is no evidence that such existed.[9]

As in much of northern and western Britain (including Wales) the political complexion after the early 400s was the fifth-century emergence, in circumstances of which we know little, of fiefdoms, baronies, areas dominated by war-lords or whatever, that by the sixth century may be styled native 'kingdoms'; in that their rulers would, in Latin, have laid claim to the title *rex*. In the ghost-towns of lost Britannia, on lowland estates, perhaps in a few ecclesiastical centres, there were those like the sixth-century British cleric Gildas who could call such potentates *tyranni* – 'usurpers' rather than tyrants, because they had usurped a civil power once vested in city-based magistrates or the councils (*ordines*) of the former *civitates*. Dumnonia was such a kingdom. How it became one is not clear. Malcolm Todd suggests [10] that 'the geography of the peninsula will have tended to encourage bids for local power' – in other words, that over so long a tract of land it would not be easy to win swift and universal recognition as any kind of monarch; and also that 'a more or less unified kingdom may have developed relatively late, perhaps not before 500'.

Our knowledge of any post-Roman Dumnonian kings is at no point dependent upon a Dumnonian record. Oral recitation or bardic poetry, apart, there is no reason to think that one existed. The information comes to us piecemeal from Welsh material and it can be extracted from analysis of that material alone.[11] There is nothing to match the Irish and Welsh regnal lists for early Demetia. D. P. Kirby notes that the topic of post-Roman Dumnonia 'has a legendary fascination against which secure historical information relating to the kings of the Cornish Britons appears tantalizingly meagre'.[12] We can start by singling out three levels, or categories, of any such kings, treating all the references for the moment as of equal validity.

The earliest concerns the *semi-legendary ancestors*. This level typifies what was a well-nigh obligatory and retrospective genealogical bond, artificial or not, between a post-Roman line and its Roman roots in the fourth (or third) century, back to a time when names had become fixed in the concrete of Roman historiography. It is common to virtually all the lists. For Dumnonia, the principal name is that of Cynan or Conan (Meiriadoc) who accompanied Magnus Maximus, emperor in 383–8, with the Roman legions from Britain to the Continent. Whether or not any of the native kings of post-Roman days were truly descended, directly or obliquely, from fourth-century usurpers and generals is immaterial. The observation is that from an early stage it became desirable to claim as much; hence, to give a mantle of *romanitas* (and, in the case of any claimed descent from Constantine I, Christian *romanitas*) to a British dynastic group. In his preface to Dr B. L. Olson's recent study of early monasteries in Cornwall,[13] Dr David Dumville voiced the hope that a parallel work on the secular organization of early Cornwall might follow it, adding that 'such a work is greatly needed by Celtic historians'. One can warmly echo his hope and his opinion; the reality is that we have insufficient information, and only just enough to allow some controlled inferences and cautious suggestions.

The second level is of kings who can be designated *historic*; persons named in more than one source (documentary or epigraphic) in relation to a given realm, preferably by sources that can be regarded as independent and that may also indicate something approaching an absolute date. With the third level we move to tradition. These are *folkloristic* figures whose names are found only in subsidiary and late contexts. They cannot usually be slotted into any sequence, for the very good reason that they are un-dated, and may be fictional.[14] One could allow them another adjective; supernumerary. An ideal regnal list, by thirds of centuries, would have to include people who may have existed but who were no more than extra and subordinate rulers. Dumnonia was large. There is some evidence for sub-divisions within it, and sub-divisions point to subordinate rulers. Because the terminology comes to us in Latin (*regulus, comes, dux*, etc.)[15] and would be unspecific if we tried to translate this back into British it is seldom safe to go further than noting occurrences.

A list of Dumnonian kings is found in the manuscript, Jesus College 20, and also in the *Bonedd Y Saint* tract.[16] It gives three names, Gwrwawr, Tudwawl and Kynwawr, that are British and in a typical 'heroic Celtic' mould (\**Uiro-māros* 'Great-Man'). If these were successive rulers in the later fifth century, the next name is Custennin, or Custennyn Gorneu (*Corneu* = (probably) 'of-Cornwall').[17] His name is Roman − Constantine, *Constantinus* − and here, a stage or generation later than in Demetia, is the horizon of Latinity (p. 84−5). A loose equation in time is possible with the Demetian Guortepir (358 VOTEPORIGIS). The equation is present because Constantine counts as historic. He was harangued by Gildas in the same passage as Guortepir of Demetia; *immundae leaenae Damnoniae tyrannicus catulus* 'usurper-whelp of Dumnonia, filthy lioness'.[18] If we look more closely, there is a clear implication that a king who could dress or act as an abbot (and in that guise dispose of his nephews) and had earlier put away a lawful wife was at least middle-aged when Gildas wrote. The *Constantinus Cornubiensium rex* 'C., king of the of Cornish' in Rhigyfarch's Life of St David[19] was a ruler who came in obedience to the sixth-century saint. This (fictional) episode may be drawn from a source independent of Gildas's writings; it is not however necessarily independent of an *Annales Cambriae* entry, under its year 589, noting *conversio Constantini ad Dominum* 'the conversion of C. to the Lord', ostensibly a record of some last-moment entry into a monastery or spectacular public repentance of an aged sinner. Though in the south of Wales that may later have been read as a reference to Constantine of Dumnonia, there were other kings of the same name.[20]

After Constantine the list continues with Erbin (not necessarily Latinate; it need not be from *Urbanus*) and then a Gereint who can be temporarily distinguished as 'Gereint I'. The name may be taken from *Gerontius*, said by the historian Zosimus to be of British origin,[21] a Roman general who accompanied troops to Gaul in 407 and who may have been perceived as a military hero. The 'sons' and/or 'grandsons' of Gereint (I), who may have been at best no more than members of the same kin, include men with Biblical and Roman names − *Selyf* (Solomon), Iestin (*Justinus*) − and with others that are British; Kyngar, and Cattw (Cato, Gadw, Gadwy, Latinized as 'Catovius'). Repetition of the name Gereint, as that of a historic king and one, if related at all, two or three generations on from the first Gereint is glimpsed at the end of the seventh century. Gereint (II) was the *Geruntius rex ... per Domnoniam* who about 705 was sent a long letter by Aldhelm, then abbot of Malmesbury.[22] One or other of the two Gereints (possibly the later) figures in a later Welsh heroic poem that seems to remember him, heading *guir deur o odir diwneint* 'brave men from the land of Dyfneint (Dumnonia)' falling in battle at *Llongborth* – identified mainly because of name-similarity with Langport on the river Parrett, a place that may have been on the frontier of Roman Dumnonia.[23]

The folkloristic kings or sub-kings include the 'Teudar' who persecuted the Irish saints in and around St Ives Bay (p. 186), and others known from similar late or un-historic settings. The Cotton Vespasian A xiv Life of St Carannog has the saint crossing the Severn Sea to Dumnonia, in times when *Cato et Arthur regnabant in ista patria* 'Cato and Arthur were reigning in that country'.[24] The final appearance of 'Cato' is as *Cador, dux* of Cornwall, in Geoffrey of Monmouth's twelfth-century History of the Kings of Britain. A figure of very wide currency is a king Mark, appropriately defined by O. J. Padel[25] as 'a true pan-Brittonic character of folklore', and central to the Tristan and Yseult stories. Mark is part of a three-way tangle between history, hagiography and epigraphy, in the attempt to identify him with the 487 CVNOMORI on a Dumnonian inscription (a person who may not have anything to do with the Kynwawr <(?*Cunomāros* 'Great-Hound' of the Dumnonian list); this can be disentangled later (p. 280).

There is not much to be gained from exploring this further; and nothing at all from trying to reconstruct a genealogy with relatively dated generations, because even the historic kings of Dumnonia could never be fitted into anything better than a regnal succession with gaps. Their medieval representation as fathers and sons in material of Dumnonian origin re-cast in Wales does not affect the likelihood that (with rare exceptions) these were successive rulers chosen from particular kin-groups (cf. p. 56 earlier).

Their geography is also most uncertain. The description of the early sixth-century Constantine as *Corneu* might be thought to imply a particular association with Cornwall. It could reflect no more than a tradition about his birth, and when Gildas alleges that he was involved with black deeds 'in the bosom of the church ... at the holy altar ... in the guise of an abbot' (*sub sancti abbatis amphibalo*) the pointer at this early date would be to a sub-Roman ecclesiastical centre on the eastern fringe of Dumnonia.

In the discussion of Demetian kingship (chap. 6) *Arberth*, near modern Narberth, and then possibly Carew, were suggested as likely royal centres. Dumnonian tradition offers us nothing until the twelfth century, when Beroul could set a seat of King Mark at Tintagel, and Geoffrey of Monmouth two citadels of *dux* Gorlois, at Tintagel and at 'Dimilioc' (St Dennis, some way inland; p. 320). Even then, the reference to Tintagel in relation to Mark as the king of Cornwall may have been a re-location. The writer harbours a suspicion that the

Mark–Tristan–Iseult theme, an opening depiction in which is of a Dumnonia obliged to make tributes to a hostile Ireland, may have first taken shape in a simpler oral recitation in pre-Norman *west* Cornwall.[26] This would leave untouched any separate traditions, with other names, concerning Tintagel; Geoffrey of Monmouth's *Historia* shows how an existing hero (Arthur) could, for art's sake, be given a spectacular new setting.

Search for a fixed post-Roman centre or capital of Dumnonia may be pointless. Medieval and later models of 'central rule' do not apply. The physical geography of the whole elongated region provides a basis for inherent divisions; for example, Cornwall west of the Tamar, and large parts of modern Devon north and south of Dartmoor. Place-name evidence might allow a Roman-period *Cornouii as a sub-people; how can we be sure there were not others, the original Dumnonii being confined to a region west of the Exe in, say, Devon's South Hams? Richard Warner makes the interesting suggestion[27] that, perhaps from the late fifth century, several autonomous tribes within Dumnonia had their own royal kin-groups, from any one of which an 'over-king' (say, for Cornwall) could be supplied; and that, later, a 'high king' may have been identifed among remembered names. The simultaneity of many kingly names, among people who had not reached any sort of horizon of historicity, would make it impossible to construct a proper regnal list out of a handful of such names, some historic, some of the kind described above as folkloristic.

The model of peripatetic kingship, a mechanism whereby a large kingdom like Dumnonia was ruled simply from whatever point a major or superior ruler with his court happened to be at a particular time, has been gaining ground; and Dr Thomas Charles-Edwards in a recent discussion has sharpened our perception of it.[28] The core of this is given in one sentence; 'In the whole of the British Isles all but very minor kings kept on the move in order to survive; itineration was an essential economic basis of kingship.' We need not examine the thesis in relation to Anglo-Saxon or Welsh royal history (or even its partial exemplifications as late as Tudor times). Some such explanation, as of a naturally imposing 'high-status defensive settlement' (i.e., a royal citadel) occupied only occasionally by a king and his entourage, several hundred people who were supplied with food from a surrounding district, can now be put forward[29] for the coastal promontory or 'Island' at Tintagel. This is postulated on (plentiful) archaeological evidence; until Beroul and Geoffrey of Monmouth, no names can be attached to it. If this was a place where during the sixth century kings of Dumnonia might repair for a few months in a summer there should be others. The enigmatic 30-acres walled site at Oldaport, up the estuary of the south Devon river Erme, is certainly a possibility.[30] Malcolm Todd's interpretation of the initial rectangular enceinte as 'a civilian, private, fortification' within the Roman period might allow the notion that its enlargement was also private, but post-Roman and kingly.

The evidence that Dumnonia *was* divided well before the Normans into lesser areas comes from Cornwall, the least Anglicized part and the final long peninsula where such evidence is most likely still to be detected. It is not as clear-cut as in the case of the smaller Demetia, where Thomas Charles-Edwards again has examined[31] a spatial coincidence between seven pre-Norman bishoprics, and the seven cantrefs;[32] concluding that 'the *cantref* appears to have been the successor of the ancient *tud*, the old small kingdom ruled over by a *tudyr* (<\**toutorix*) or a *breyr* (<\**brogorix*).' Cornwall also has a system of internal divisions, the so-called 'hundreds'. Since 1973, the local-government districts look back in approximate shape, and partly by name, to a pre-Norman system.[33] By the eleventh century the hundreds totalled nine, but they can be presented as an original six because the two eastern ones had become tripartite and bipartite.

This is an immensely difficult topic.[34] From the twelfth to nineteenth centuries nomenclature of the hundreds wavered between the old area-names, as they seem to have been originally, and others borrowed from those of the paramount manors within them. Thus Penwith, the westernmost, could also be 'Conerton' from a powerful manor with extensive rights on the eastern side of St Ives Bay. Sites of two of these hundredal manors (Conerton, near Gwithian; Winnianton, by Gunwalloe church) are known,[35] and both have yielded pottery of the tenth to twelfth centuries. To a limited extent this goes with Charles Henderson's belief that 'the original six divisions were created at once and did not grow up casually from Celtic tribal divisions. Evidence of this is found in the fact that the four western hundreds all meet together at one point...' Though one would not now accept this, it may well have been that definite *borders* between the hundreds, in an attempt to rationalize the totals of the homesteads or main agrarian tenements in each (the *trefs*) along the lines of the Welsh cantref (= *cant* 'hundred' plus *tref*) and the southern English hundred, were created over a short period. This may have been in or soon after the reign of Alfred's grandson Aethelstan (925–39). The emphasis upon paramount manors at the time of the Domesday survey could reflect a fixing, for many purposes, of hundredal centres.

Nothing of this negates the likelihood (in this author's opinion) that the ultimate origin of the hundreds lay in post-Roman times, but as *areas*; the dividing-lines between which were customary and loose, and in fact could never be fixed until a later relationship was possible with networks of tithings, 'proto-parishes' and manors. How any such areas were named is another matter. There must have been a cognate to Welsh *tud* (<\**touto*; 'all-the-people' (who elect, or matter, or have a certain status); hence, 'tribe') because of later Cornish *tus* 'folk', used as a suppletive plural for *den* 'man, person'. One of the old hundreds, Powder, was *Poureder* in 1130. This may be from \**ereder*, plural of *aradar* 'plough', and a prefixed *pou-* 'district, province' which as Old Breton *pou* could be glossed by Latin *pagus*.[36] A curious early name for the west Cornish parish of Breage (with its 'St Breaca', p. 187) was still in use when John Leland went there in the 1540s. He noted[37] 'Pembro wher the paroch church is', 'the South Se is about a mile from Pembro', 'an hille in Pembro paroch, vulgo S. Breaka' and 'Trenewith a litle from the paroch (chirch) of Pembro, wher the paroch chirch (was) or ever it was set at Pembro.' The compound here, *pen* and *bro*, is found in Demetia because it became the larger area-name of Pembroke (Sîr Benfro in Welsh), implying 'the end, or extremity, of the land (*bro*)'. This will not serve at Breage, which is not at the end or extremity of anywhere, and the other meaning of *pen* 'head, chief' (in the abstract) is indicated – 'head-place of the *bro*'. What the latter was – part of the hundred of Kerrier? – is anyone's guess, and long before Leland there may have been a local perception that the hill-fort above Breage, Tregonning Hill or otherwise Castle Pencair (as 'the head or principal fort', *pen, caer*, and not 'end-of-the-fort', *pen* (*an*) *gaer*), had served as a district headquarters. None of this is at all conclusive but there is enough to suggest that, unless they were no more than colloquialisms, terms like Primitive Cornish \**bro* (<\**broga*; 'boundary, division between clear opposites', hence 'defined territory') referred to socio-geographical tracts smaller than Cornwall as a whole.

An outline map of Cornwall (Fig. 13.2) can show some of this early geography. For the nine (medieval) hundreds, the lost single name behind 'East' and 'West' became redundant when the English divided it into East and West 'Wivelshire' (the 'two-fold shire' or *Twy-feald-scir*). The Cornish word for 'hundred' was *keverang*, which has been tentatively explained[38] as meaning 'military assembly' and thus 'district operating as a unit for military service', rather like the English *wapentake* as a label for a hundred in some of the old Danelaw counties. Possibly it implies not the sixth century, certainly not the fifth, but a subsequent time when independent Dumnonia had to face an expansionist Wessex. Nevertheless, the very much older Common Celtic element of obligation to serve in a warband, as a concomitant to tribal membership, free status and the holding of land, *is* still there. The hundred-name of Trigg, with its tripartition into (reduced) Trigg, west; Lesnewth, central; and Stratton, east (Fig. 13.2), appears in the seventh-century Latin Life of St Samson (chap. 14) as *pagus Tricurius*. *Pagus* may or may not equate with *pou*, but the actual name must be from \**tri* 'three' and \**corio* 'warband, army'; hence probably 'rallying point for army' and eventually 'tribal centre'.[39] The points were probably old hill-forts, like Helsbury for Trigg and Warbstow Bury for Lesnewth. 'Helsbury' is named for the hamlet below it, Helstone in Trigg (*hen, lys*, English *-ton*); Lesnewth means 'the new *lys*' (*lys* + *nowyth*) replacing some *lys* that had become *hen* 'old, obsolescent'. The word *lys*, Welsh *llys*, is perhaps not readily translated but can be rendered as 'court, early administrative focus'.[40] If ten or so *lys*- names, accepted as containing this element (and nine of these were the names of manors at the time of Domesday), are added to Fig. 13.2, we may begin to have some slight idea of customary sub-divisions even smaller than the hundreds. But, because of the complete uncertainty

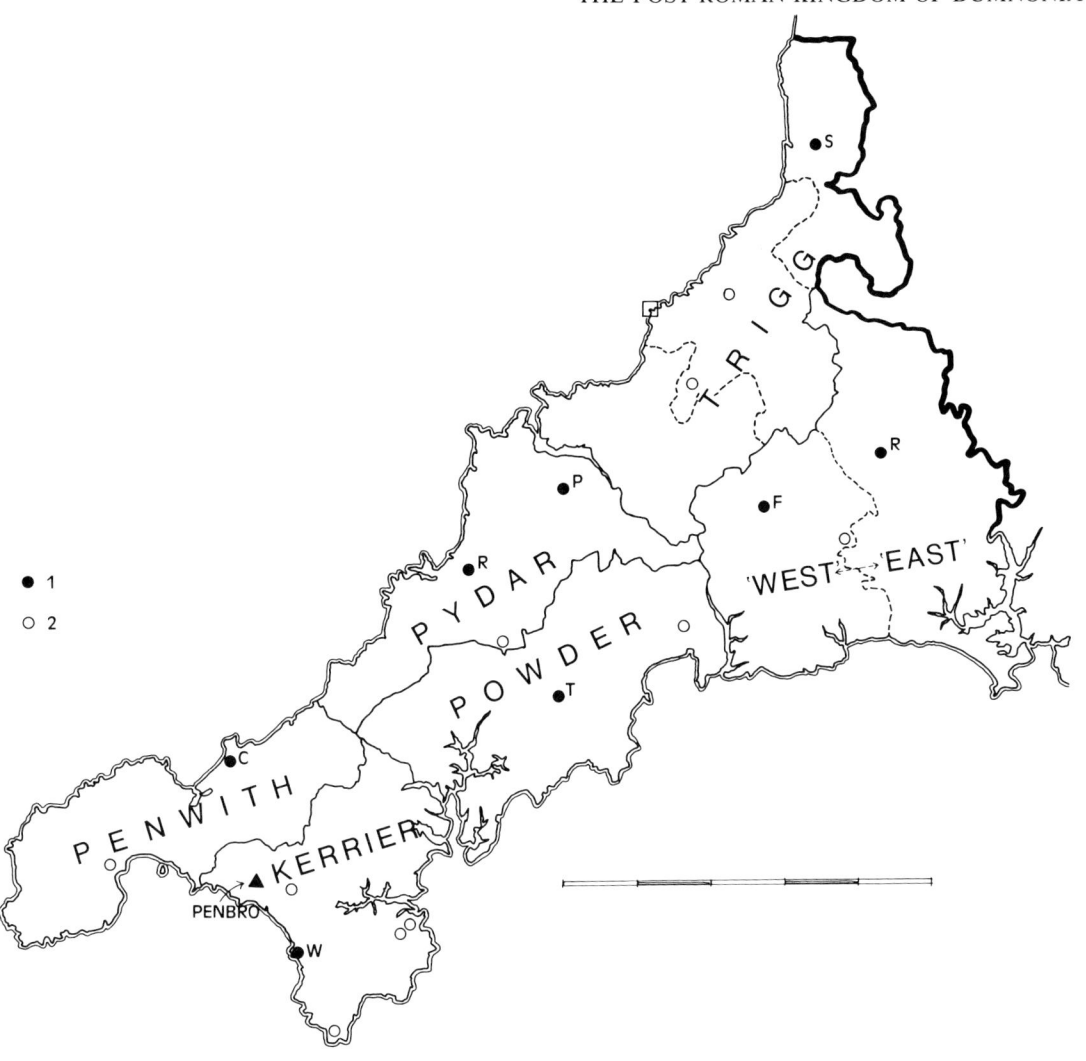

**Fig. 13.2** Cornwall, late first millennium AD, with the six ancient hundreds – Trigg, subsequently Trigg, Lesnewth and Stratton, and the possibly once unitary 'West' and 'East' (Wivelshire). **Key**: 1, paramount manors, Domesday. *Penwith*, C, Conerton; *Kerrier*, W, Winnianton; *Pydar*, R, Rialton (P, Pawton, secondary); *Powder*, T, Tybesta; *Trigg*, S, Stratton; *West*, F, Fawton; *East*, R, Rillaton. 2, place-names in *Lys-*, *Lis-* (selected), possibly early administrative centres? Scale, 25 miles (40 kms).

that attaches to the relative dates of more than one system of territorial division, the whole subject takes on a slightly kaleidoscopic air. It would for example be exciting, though impracticable, to explore a hint that on the map (Fig. 13.2) about two-thirds of what became Cornwall, the four old western hundreds, together constituted either a very large *pagus* or a block of *pagi* in fourth-century Dumnonia. That idea might arise if the name of the north-eastern one, Pydar, was thought to perpetuate British *\*petuariia* 'one-fourth; a fourth part'.

Apart from what Gildas may have implied about Constantine of Dumnonia, a supposedly Christian ruler who had transgressed the tenets of his faith, where in the early Dumnonian story does Christianity figure? The position is much as it was for Demetia. The hard evidence comes first and foremost from the detailed study of the inscribed memorials. We find little or nothing Christian in Dumnonia during the Roman period, and no trace at all west of *Isca Dumnoniorum*;[41] the sole exception to this, the Carnsew and Phillack stones, has already been explained as an isolated intrusion. We cannot suppose that early Dumnonian Christianity owed anything to sub-Roman Christianity much further eastward, in southern England. At the moment (1993) the earliest, native, Christian site may be the excavated part of the parish churchyard at Tintagel, if indeed this represents (p. 296) the consecrated burial-place of those who occasionally took up residence on Tintagel Island. That claim does not explain how or when Dumnonian rulers (at some time after AD 500) had become Christians, still less how their subjects had been converted.

Two comments may preface the long analysis of all the inscriptions. The obscurity of post-Roman Dumnonia *is* momentarily illuminated, not by what Gildas wrote (or omitted), but by another document; one whose light sweeps across the centre of Cornwall, as the beam from a powerful lighthouse travels over the waves of a bay at night. This is the *Vita (Prima) Sancti Samsonis*, the Life of the Demetian saint Samson whose final centre is at Dol de Bretagne. The Life is so important that it must be examined as a preliminary to any study of the memorials. The second comment opens with a pictorial message (Fig. 13.3). The inscriptions of Dumnonia cover a large area. The four from Lundy (1400–1403) have, like 478 Carnsew and 1502 Phillack, already been mentioned, but there is not room to show them; nor two from Exmoor (499, 1404) that will be briefly mentioned (p. 288). Excluded because they are outside the scope of the book are the (seventh to ninth century) inscriptions from Wareham, Dorset; they are of great interest, may well be connected with a surviving British enclave and have been fully recorded,[42] but this was not a Dumnonian enclave. Also omitted is a pre-Norman (eighth century?) inscription from Holcombe, Somerset, the linguistic nature of which is uncertain.[43]

While the map, Fig. 13.3, is probably the most complete and the only accurate one of its kind yet published, it contains a cautionary message. The bald, two-dimensional portrayal is meaningless. Were one to insert an imaginary line right up the centre or spine of Dumnonia, there would be slightly more dots to the north than to the south. Far more information is required. Application of the methodology used to examine the inscriptions of south-west Wales should however yield meanings – episodic and temporal groupings, and perhaps answers to the questions; when, whence and how did Christianity reach Dumnonia?

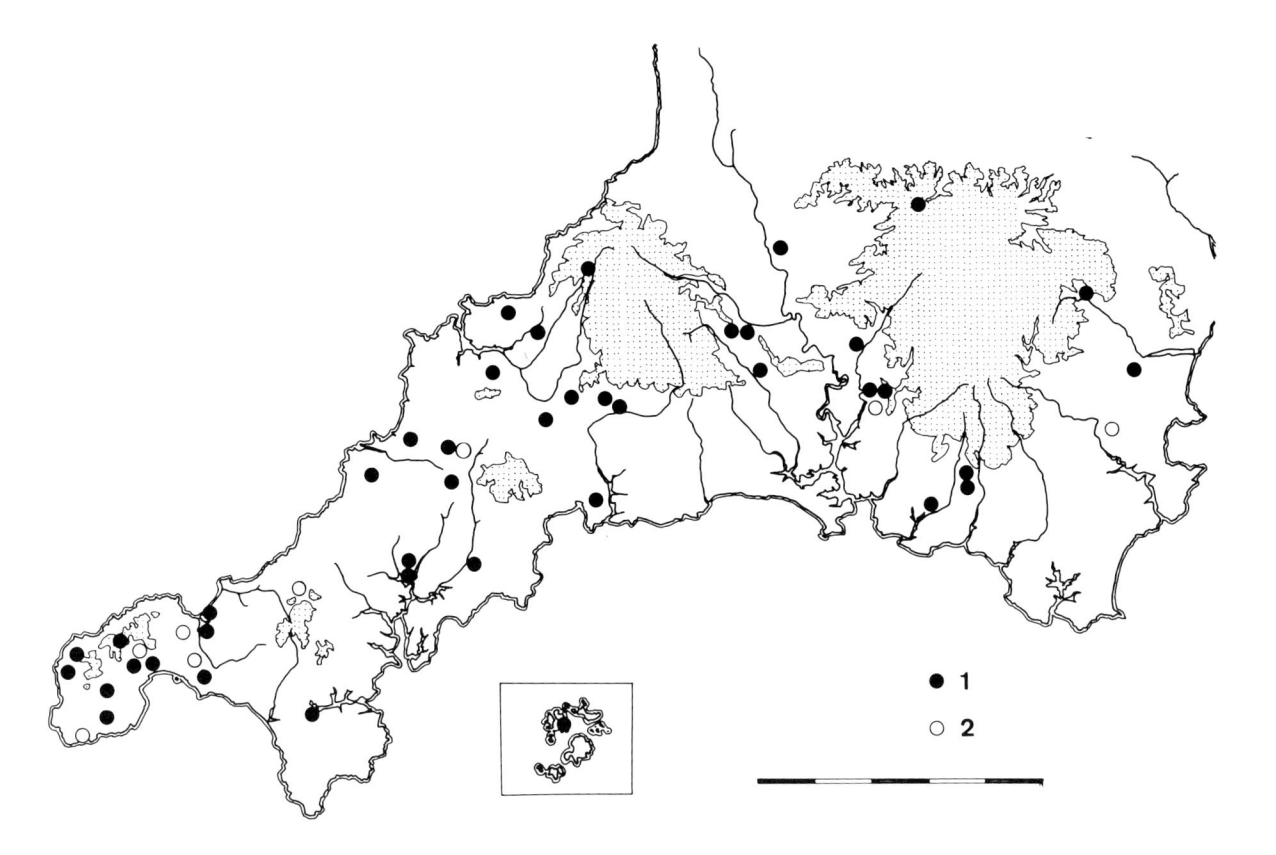

**Fig. 13.3** Post-Roman Dumnonia – Cornwall, Scilly (inset), Devon, part of Somerset. Undifferentiated distribution of fifth–seventh century inscribed memorials, excluding four on Lundy and two from Exmoor. **Key**: 1, extant and legible. 2, lost or destroyed but acceptably recorded *or* extant, apparently genuine, but now illegible. Scale, 25 miles (40 kms).

## References

1. W. Meredith Morris's *A Glossary of the Demetian Dialect* (Tonypandy 1910), from the Gwaun valley in north Pembroke.
2. Using the definition 'born in Cornwall, with one or both parents and at least two grandparents also born in Cornwall', the real figure may now be even lower.
3. So inscriptions on Hadrian's Wall (*RIB* nos. 1843, 1844, fourth century).
4. Todd 1987, figs. 7.1, 9.1; Jones & Mattingly 1990, map 5.11.
5. See *PNRB* 342–3; the root is *\*dumno-* 'deep, (?) mysterious', with the common suffix- (ō)nos, *-(ō)na* (fem.) apparently implying divinity or aggrandisement. There is no connection whatsoever with (post-medieval) shaft mining in Devon and Cornwall.
6. *PNRB* 350; this was just possibly a Roman *statio* at Tintagel, as suggested in Thomas 1993.
7. Thomas 1966, for the native economy; Fox 1973, chap. viii; Pearce 1978; Todd 1987, chap. 7 (the most authoritative).

8. The fullest is Pearce 1978, going up to the tenth–eleventh centuries.
9. *CRB*, chaps. 12–15, notably the maps showing Dumnonia as a blank.
10. Todd 1987, 237.
11. Kirby 1976, 88–9, offers a realistic appraisal of the position (as against, perhaps, S. M. Pearce, 'The Traditions of the Royal King-List of Dumnonia', *Trans. Cymmrodor.* (1970), 70–6).
12. Kirby, op. cit.
13. In Olson 1989, at ix–x.
14. But with the proviso that 'folkloristic' references are not all necessarily un-historic; merely very much harder to interpret.
15. Charles-Edwards 1989; also James Campbell, *Bede's Reges and Principes* (Jarrow Lecture 1979: St Paul's Church, Jarrow 1980).
16. *EWGT*, 42 ff., 54 ff. (nos. 26, 27 and 76).
17. *TYP* 314–5, 355–60.
18. Jackson 1982, 30–31.
19. *VSBG* 159; James 1967, 14, 38.
20. See *TYP*, 314–6.
21. *TYP* 355 ff.; for the name, see also *PLRE* ii.508.
22. Text in Haddan & Stubbs, iii.286–73.
23. Text (21, *Gereint fil' Erbin*) in A. O. H. Jarman, *Llyfr Du Caerfyrddin* (Univ. of Wales Press, Cardiff 1982); notes (in Welsh), ibid., 104–5; its possible tenth-century date, Thomas Jones, *BBCS* 17 (1956), 246.
24. *VSBG* 144–5.
25. Padel 1981, 73.
26. The clues – location of *hryt eselt* 'Ford of Eselt (= Isolt, Yseult)' in the Lizard area, tenth century (Padel 1981, 65–7); Carn *Marth*, south of Redruth (if not *margh* 'horse'); the idea that the 'Irish element' relates to west Cornwall, as in chap.11 earlier.
27. Unpublished; *in litt.*, 1992.
28. His 'Early medieval kingships in the British Isles', pp. 28–39 in: S. Bassett, ed., *The Origins of Anglo-Saxon Kingdoms* (Leicester 1989).
29. Summary, with further refs., in Thomas 1993, chap.6.
30. Todd 1987, 260–2; site report, M. E. Farley & R. I. Little, 'Oldaport, Modbury; a Re-assessment of the Fort and Harbour', *PDAS* 26 (1968), 31–6 illus.
31. In his 'The Seven Bishop-Houses of Dyfed', *BBCS* 24(1971), 247–62.
32. These are shown in Rees, *Atlas*, pl.28.
33. Districts (with hundredal names in brackets) are: Penwith (Penwith), Kerrier (Kerrier), Carrick (Powder), Restormel (Pydar), North Cornwall (Trigg, Lesnewth and Stratton), Caradon (East and West).
34. W. M. M. Picken, 'The Names of the Hundreds of Cornwall', *Devon & Cornwall Notes & Queries* 30.ii (April 1965), 36–40; important still is Charles Henderson's 'A Note on the Hundreds of Powder and Pydar', pp.108–24 in: *Essays in Cornish History, Charles Henderson* (ed. A. L. Rowse & M. I. Henderson, Oxford 1935).
35. But remain unexcavated; they seem to have been pre-Norman hamlets, possibly with some 'large-house' component not yet recognized.
36. *GVB* 289; Padel 1985, 193.
37. Toulmin Smith, i.187, 191; earlier forms are *Eglospenbro* 1284, *Penbro* 1338, *Sancte Breace de Penbro* 1356.
38. Padel 1985, 56.
39. *PNRB*, 318–9; Padel 1985, 64–5.

40. Padel 1985, 150–1.
41. For the odd relevant find from Exeter, see CRB 108, 168.
42. The entry – four stones only – in CIIC.ii, 1061–1064, is now superseded by RCHM England, Dorset Inventory, II (South–East), pt.ii (1970), 308, 310–12 illus., discussion by C. A. Ralegh Radford and K. H. Jackson.
43. S. Foster, 'Early Medieval Inscription at Holcombe, Somerset', Medieval Archaeol. 32 (1988), 208–11 illus.

# 14

# *Landscape with Figures: Samson and Others in Cornwall*

SAMSON, A DEMETIAN, had been given a Biblical name – that of the giant Danite who, betrayed by scheming women, was in his last hour granted strength by God. Samson's mother was called Anna. This may have been for the New Testament prophetess;[1] it seems as likely to have been for the supposed mother of the Blessed Virgin.[2] These are potent reminders that a Vulgate or pre-Vulgate text of the Bible,[3] and perhaps other Christian literature, was known in south-east Wales in the fifth century AD. The name of Samson's father, Amon, may have been British, rather than Roman (Ammonius), or that of the obscure Hebrew king included in the genealogy of Jesus.[4] Amon's setting was the ruling circle of Demetia. It was common knowledge (*pro certo scimus* 'we know for sure', claims the Life) that Amon was by birth a Demetian, was like Anna a Christian, and was also the son of one who had been an *altrix* – in Classical Latin, this would imply 'foster-parent', so 'an intimate courtier' at the very least – to the king (p. 89). We are within the successive reigns of Triphun (Tribunus) and Aircol Lauhir (Agricola). Anna was from the same exalted background but in the next kingdom eastward, *provincia proxima*; the forerunner of Glywysing? Joseph Loth's idea that Anna's sister (who was to marry Amon's younger brother), named in the Life as 'Afrella', was really called *Aurelia* is a persuasive one.[5] In Late Roman *Britannia Prima* the Aureliani made up a noble family, one with whom both the sub-Roman Ambrosius Aurelianus and Gildas's (unlocated) sixth-century king Aurelius Caninus were presumably connected. All this common knowledge about the saint's origins suggests, on his mother's side, a credible glimpse of fifth-century Christian *romanitas* in south-east Wales. The Demetian royal entourage was, through such contact, just acquiring the same. It may not be accidental that several times the narrative of the Life portrays Anna as consistently more devout than her husband.

The Life of St Samson of Dol in Brittany, the *Vita (Prima) Sancti Samsonis*, is a tale compiled at a Breton monastery in the seventh century about a Christian from Demetia who, in the early sixth century, crossed Dumnonia on his way to the Continent. In the fashion of his day the un-named author included an element of imagination (what he thought might have happened or should have taken place) alongside his representation of fact (what he had been told really happened). He had no reason always to indicate a distinction, nor today can we always detect one.

There are problems arising from textual transmission from the lost original, through a ninth-century copy with interpolations, to some twenty versions dating from the tenth and later centuries.[6] The author who may have been connected with a monastery at Dol (now a small city on Brittany's northern coast, dominated by St Samson's huge granite cathedral) seems to have been elderly.

It is neither a case of a blind conviction nor of wishful thinking, but of a reasoned balancing of probabilities, to accept that the narrative core of the Life is a genuine seventh-century writing, one that described genuine happenings of the previous century. What tips the balance is that the author, instead of starting with a string of miracles, provided a prologue in which he explained his sources. This Prologue is long and complicated – complicated enough to make a diagram helpful (Fig. 14.1) – but not muddled. We are meant to read it with care, as indeed it was composed.

The author had learnt much about Samson through meeting a religious and venerable man (the 'Old Man'), who had lived nearly eighty years, hence very close to Samson's own times, in a *domus ultra mare* 'a monastery beyond the sea' (from Brittany; i.e., in Cornwall) that Samson himself had founded. The author would seem to have visited this monastery, and other parts of Cornwall, and possibly also Wales. The Old Man assured the author that Samson's own mother had related various things to a very holy deacon, who was not only the Old Man's uncle (the 'Uncle') but also a cousin of Samson. The Uncle was called *Henoc*. Henoc himself, as a contemporary of his cousin Samson, had composed written works that described Samson's activities in both Brittany and *Romania* (other parts of France, if not further afield, may be implied); these, Henoc *ultra mare adportavit*, 'carried to beyond the sea'. This seems to mean that Henoc, the Uncle, wrote down such memoirs during a stay in Brittany and then took them back to Cornwall – *ultra mare*, from Dol, signifies as much. The Old Man read them (*legere faciebat*) piously and with great care. He did so when dwelling in this monastery in Cornwall, *ante me* ('before my time' has been suggested, rather than 'in front of me, in my presence', though either interpretation is possible). It seems very probable that the author saw and even copied the Uncle's writings, when visiting the Old Man.[7]

In short, the author lived too late ever to have met Samson, and he never met Samson's cousin Henoc, the Uncle; but he did go from Brittany to Cornwall, met Henoc's nephew the Old Man, and was treated both to *oral* information (which had come, through Henoc, from Samson's mother and would have covered the family background and childhood) and *written* information (which Henoc could have supplied directly about Samson's subsequent career and Continental activities). This provides a post-Roman biography in a certain mode where author and subject are in fact unusually close and the *relative* time-sequence inspires some confidence. Let us imagine today in 1994 a man of fifty who wants to write a biography of Douglas Hyde, poet, Gaelic activist and first President of Ireland.

Hyde was born in 1860 and died in 1949. Our would-be biographer meets a man of eighty (born in 1914) who in his youth did once or twice meet Hyde, and whose own uncle (born about 1870) was not only Hyde's relative but an intimate colleague; a colleague whose available diaries from 1893 to 1940 record a great many details about Hyde's words, thoughts and deeds. The biographer is now lucky enough to obtain from the man of eighty his uncle's diaries. We would all regard the ensuing biography as likely to be accurate and illuminating. The work is demanding, and the book might eventually be published 140 years after Douglas Hyde's birth. The chances are that the *Vita Samsonis* was also 'published' about 140 years after Samson's birth; if so, by an author himself born less than a century after Samson.[8]

What is the *absolute* time-sequence? From the background details the milieu would seem to cover the later fifth century for Samson's parents and birth, the sixth for the rest of his life, and the earlier seventh for the appearance of the *Vita*.[9] If one accepts Kathleen Hughes's belief that the saint is to be identified with the Samson, bishop and signatory at a council held at Paris in some year between 556 and 573,[10] he may have died in the decade $560 \times 570$. Canon Taylor's computistics[11] yielded, from various details, 521 as the year of Samson's consecration as a bishop. Assuming that he was then at least thirty, his birth may have fallen in $480 \times 490$; and given the sequence of events portrayed by the Life the very brief visit to Dumnonia took place in $525 \times 535$. Fig. 14.1 shows how these estimates might accord with belief in a seventh-century date for composition of the original *Vita*, and – from earlier chapters – an appropriate Demetian temporal setting for Samson's parents.

The Dumnonian visit, a month or so's progression across Cornwall from north to south, supplies four important facts about that region in the sixth century. First of all it locates the commonest landing-place from south Wales at this period, and probably at most others. Second, it mentions a monastery that had already been founded, perhaps one or two decades earlier. Thirdly, it offers a glimpse of a slow movement from native paganism to a general adoption of Christianity, suggesting that in this respect Dumnonia was a half-century behind Demetia. Lastly it describes, though it fails to locate it precisely, a *second* monastery, founded in Cornwall by Samson before leaving for Brittany; the monastery where the author's informant the Old Man was to spend a lifetime.

The *Vita* introduces the phenomenon of monasteries in Cornwall and it makes references to others in Wales. They form a separate and parallel tradition to be set beside the Christian sites so far mentioned, mostly in relation to Demetia and Brycheiniog; those were nearly all consecrated cemeteries, 'developed' by the insertion or addition of churches, buildings intended as foci for communal worship. Practical considerations have precluded us from saying much about actual *churches* of the late fifth, sixth and later centuries. Save under most exceptional circumstances we cannot hope to recover evidence about the size,

| TIME-SCALE (DECADES) | SAMSON son of Amon and Anna | AMON marries Anna | HENOC ('UNCLE') son of sibling of Anna(?) | 'OLD MAN' nephew of Henoc | 'AUTHOR' monk at Dol |
|---|---|---|---|---|---|
| 460 | | Born, Demetia | | | |
| 470 | | | | | |
| 480 | Born, Demetia | Marries Anna | | | |
| 490 | Schooling, Llanilltud | | Born? | (Sibling of Henoc born) | |
| 500 | | | | (parent) | |
| 510 | | (Anna, details) > | (memory) | | |
| 520 | Consecrated as bishop | | | Born? | |
| 530 | Cornwall: founds Mon. | Cornwall: made head of Mon. | Cornwall: deacon | Cornwall; boy in Mon. | |
| 540 | Brittany | Dies? | Brittany | | |
| 550 | | | Re-visits Mon., leaves writings | | Born? |
| 560 | Council at Paris? Dies? | | Dies? | (conversation, > copies) | |
| 570 | | | | | |
| 580 | | | | | |
| 590 | | | | 'nearly 80' (conversation & writings) | Visits to Wales & Cornwall |
| 600 | | | | | > (copies) |
| 610 | | | | | Composes Vita, Dol |
| 620 | | | | | |

Fig. 14.1 The chronology of Samson, his family, certain relatives, and his biographer. All dates are tentative, but assume the decade 525×535 for the visit to Cornwall and the foundation of Samson's monastery ('Mon.'). The symbol > indicates likely stages in the transmission of information, according to the 'Author' of the *Vita*.

shape and appearance of these constructions. Cemeteries, many of which seem to have been formally enclosed by curvilinear banks, ditches and walls – perhaps in the later sixth and seventh centuries, as secondary aspects of these monuments – are much more easily recognized in the landscape. We may wish to continue to describe them as 'primary' Christian sites, and many undoubtedly contain potential sequences from sixth-century burial areas to twentieth-century parish churches. But it must be accepted that the monastery, large or small, in its various physical forms, similarly belongs to a primary Christian landscape in Britain and Ireland.

*Vita Samsonis* contains quite a few named places. It does not say so, but by the sixth century it is likely that the ground-plan of a monastery might resemble that of a large enclosed cemetery. The barrier against the outside, sinful, world for a community of ascetic and celibate Christians seeking to attain true spirituality through prayer and contemplative works could be an actual one. A monastery might be founded within an existing enclosure, like some deserted fortification. Before leaving Wales for Dumnonia and Brittany, Samson with his father Amon and two others discovered a *castellum admodum delicatum* 'rather a pleasant little fort' near the Welsh shore of the Severn, and then lived within it as a small private monastic community. The episode may be symbolic but it is a fairly typical one.

A monastery, socially, was manifested as a voluntary grouping of men (or women) under a chosen head; for men an abbot (*abbas*), who was not necessarily also of the grade of bishop. The occupation of a deserted plot or remote property, or the receipt of one as a gift from a magnate or pious well-wisher, seems to have accompanied a general attitude that the abbot himself could function as lay 'owner' of the establishment, treating it as a piece of real property whose conduct was his to ordain, and which could be passed on to his own kin. In the *Life*, Samson's monastery somewhere near the south coast of Cornwall appears to have been at a site granted to him by influential locals; the saint ordered his own followers to undertake whatever construction was necessary and then, before sailing for Brittany, he placed his father Amon in charge of the new foundation and left instructions for its spiritual conduct.

Shorn of many diversions and miraculous anecdotes, as it would be further pruned if all the post-auctorial additions and insertions could be identified and expunged, the Life's narrative is straightforward. Samson was sent, as a small boy from Amon and Anna's Demetian home, to the combined *magnificum monasterium* and *schola* 'school' of *Eltutus*, St Illtud. This is Llantwit Major, Llanilltud Fawr in Welsh, close to the Glamorgan coast and perhaps a foundation linked to his mother's family. The educational side harked back to sub-Roman culture. Samson learnt his twenty (Roman) letters – ABCDEFGHILMNOPQ RSTVX – in a day. As a monastery, Llanilltud may have existed for several decades before Samson's enrolment; not much longer. The educational aspect however may have been continuously available, with small private schools and grammarian tutors, since well back in the fourth century.

A quarter-century after the primary schooling, Samson had been ordained as a deacon and then as a priest. He went, or was sent, to a certain island on which there was a smaller monastery *nuper fundata* 'lately established'. It seems to have

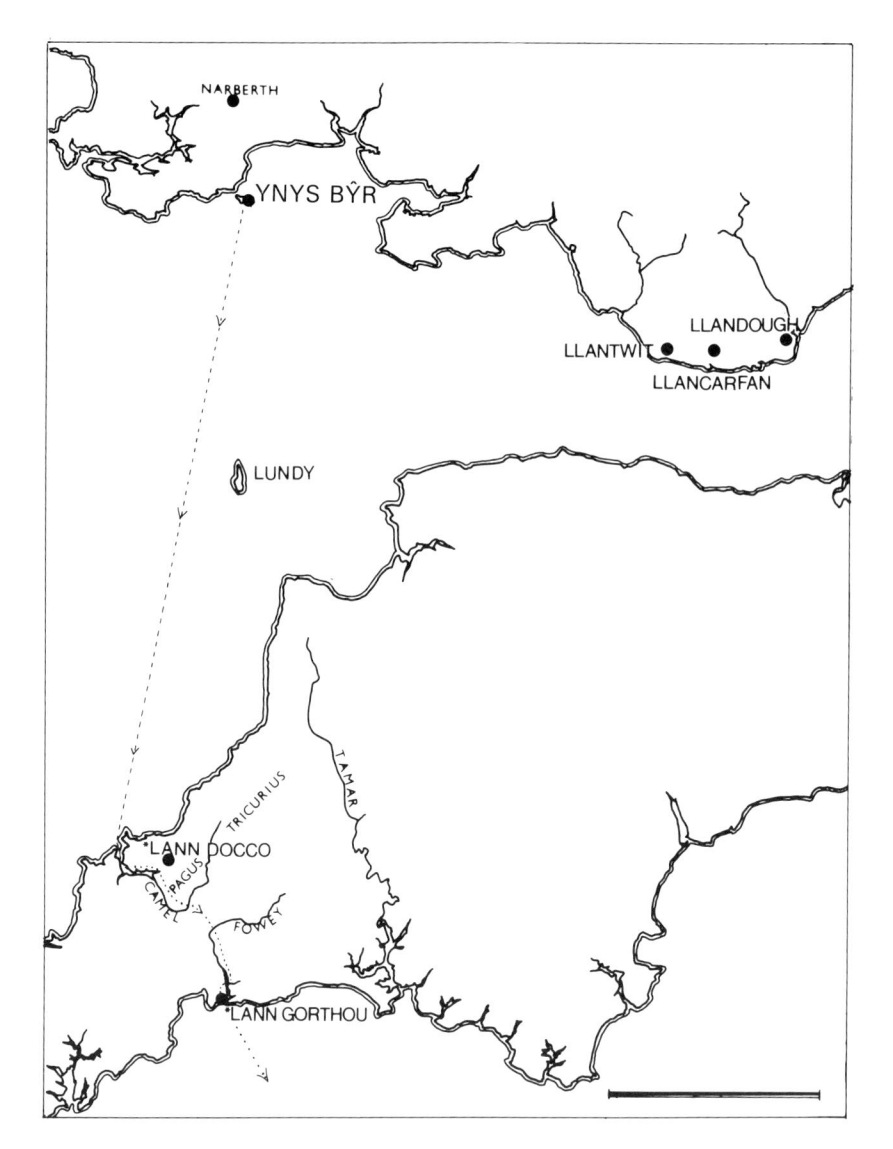

**Fig. 14.2** Map: the geography of Samson's visit to Dumnonia. Scale, 25 miles (40 kms).

been a subsidiary of Llanilltud, and it was under the *sanctus presbiter* Piro, or Pyro. The statement that it was *non longe* 'not all that far' may refer to ease of travel, not to measured distance. This island with Pyro, *Ynys Bŷr* or Caldey as it is generally thought to have been, lies 50 miles westward along the coast from Llanilltud's nearby natural harbour of St Donat's (Fig. 14.2). This is about the same distance as from St Donat's to Lundy (p. 167). The actual site, if it was indeed on Caldey, would be difficult to identify[12] but recently recognized finds tend to confirm this place as having been a site of significance at the appropriate period.[13]

Samson, following Piro's death, remained for a time on the island as the community's abbot. The *Vita* has an episode in which Samson visits Ireland; this must certainly be regarded as a later interpolation.[14] We then find the saint once more at Llanilltud and, after his old master St Illtud has died, predictably being invited to assume the abbacy there together with his consecration as a bishop. Since Samson is by now implicitly in his thirties, the date may be around 520–30. But the episcopal elevation is a preliminary to a Divine call in the shape of an angelic apparition. Samson is to go overseas, as a pilgrim. He sets sail accompanied by his father Amon, who had earlier repented of sin, embraced celibacy and been tonsured; and also by a band of clerics and retainers. The goal may have been Europe but the route thither lay across Dumnonia (as, most probably, it had done for pilgrims from Wales in the previous century).

A rigorous analysis of the Dumnonian episode has now been offered by Dr B. Lynette Olson.[15] The map, Fig. 14.2, can provide the setting. Samson and his party arrived without incident ('a favourable wind ... a happy passage') *ad monasterium quod Docco vocatur*. They landed on the east shore of the Camel estuary and were actually in the neighbourhood of this monastery. It lay at St Kew, either where the church now stands or not far away. This is the *Landochou* of a tenth-century charter, by then the *monasterium* of two saints, Dochou and Cywa;[16] the latter was the later and dominant 'Kew'. Samson did not visit the monastery. Its brethren, hearing of the arrival, sent the wisest of their number, Uiniavus,[17] who gently refused Samson's request on the grounds that the community, having declined from a former standard, had become unworthy and preferred not to be denounced by so holy a visitor. Samson then sent his ship away, arranged for a cart (*plaustrum*; an agricultural wagon may be implied) to transport his holy vessels and books across the peninsula, and acquired a couple of horses to draw a *currus*, a smaller vehicle that he 'had brought with him from Ireland'; an interesting note, if this means that the Déisi-descended nobility of Demetia were still using light carts of an Irish pattern.[18]

The journey south, up one or other side of the long valley past Wadebridge and towards Bodmin, took the visitors through *pagus Tricurius*, part of Trigg (p. 217). On a hill eastward, they came across locals engaged in a patently non-Christian ceremony; they were dancing (?) like Bacchantes and worshipping an idol, performing some mummery in its honour. Samson descended from his *currus* and more closely observed both the idol, which may have been of wood, and on the summit of the hill an abominable image. This may have been a bedecked standing-stone. 'On which hill I have been myself,' the author adds, 'and I have marvelled at, and felt with my own hand, the sign of the Cross that Saint Samson (with his own hand, and with a bit of iron) carved on that standing-stone' (*in lapide stante*).

Samson with two companions confronted the revellers who were headed by their chieftain (*comes*), Guedianus. The locals sought to excuse themselves by explaining that they were celebrating the mysteries of their ancestors, and that this was nothing wrong. At that moment a boy, driving horses at a gallop, fell headlong from his mount and lay there as if lifeless.[19] The natives cried out and wept. Samson promised that, were they to agree to destroy the idol, he with God's help would bring the youth back to life. They consented, and after two hours of prayer Samson was able to restore the injured rider, alive and sound, to his fellows. At this, the abashed revellers destroyed their idol and prostrated themselves at the saint's feet.

The *comes* Guedianus now obliged everyone to come forward and *omnes ad confirmanda eorum baptismata* 'all were to affirm (or to re-assert) their baptism'. With the statement that they regarded Samson as a Heaven-sent angel, who *venit eripere nos de nostro errore* 'comes to snatch us back from our erring ways', the passage is meant to depict these Dumnonians as apostates, or Christians lapsed into paganism. This may or may not be a genuine tradition; at most, it could mean that they were aware of the precepts taught at Docco's nearby monastery, or that the leaders among them had been recently or nominally converted. A stock miracle is to follow. The whole party, Demetians and natives, travel on, the revived *puer* having now promised to become one of Samson's clerical followers. Samson is invited to rid the land of a fearful serpent dwelling in a cave in a certain fair neighbourhood, which turns out to be two days' journeying away; near the south coast. This is easily and dramatically effected. For those who want to visit it, the cave is on the *west* bank of the river Fowey, Samson and party having travelled down the *eastern* side; it still exists, fortunately devoid of the awful reptile.[20]

There is no mention in the episode, apart from Uiniavus and the monastery that was Docco's, of any churchmen; this land, unlike Demetia and Gwent, has no bishops, abbots, monks, churches and large monasteries. The highest secular individual is Guedianus, some kind of chieftain, but a chieftain apparently with an armed following or war-band (*exercitus*). When Samson, aided by the lad whom he had revived, ousted the serpent from its lair, it was this lad who rushed to tell the *comes* and his *exercitus* what had happened. The outcome was that the Dumnonians approached Samson and invited him *apostolicum excipere obsequium* 'to accept an apostolic honour'; that is, to become their bishop. We could be in Darkest Africa in the days of Livingstone; the miraculous and powerful Christian wizard must be induced to remain at all costs. It is at this point that Samson, declining, accepts instead (implicitly) a site for the construction of a monastery, somewhere *prope antrum* 'near the cave' which, now that it is vacant, the saint appropriates as a temporary hermitage. The monastery is completed. Amon is charged with its governance. Samson's cousin Henoc, who transpires to be among the party, is admitted as a deacon; and then Samson, Henoc, and 'very many monks', the balance of the original travel-group, take sail for a *portum in Europa*, and out of the story for the time being.

What, supposing the above to be credible in outline if not in all the details, does the *Vita* allow us to infer? The arrival at the Camel estuary pinpoints the most convenient landfall. Thomas Phaer's 1559 report[21] observed that 'This Haven of Milforde' (Milford Haven in Pembroke) 'lieth agenst Patstow in Cornewall'; it was still known as the regular crossing in Tudor times. The suggestion that Docco was dead, his community now headed by another, and that it had departed from some former standard of moral excellence must give an impression that this monastery had been in existence for some ten or twenty years before Samson landed. We may have a record of a foundation here of about 500, at much the same time as was suggested (p. 167) for another small monastery on Lundy. Docco, as a name, is a hypocoristic or 'pet' form, from its shape with a geminated -*cc*- and final -*o*. (Fortuitous modern parallels are 'Jacko' from John, or 'Robbo' from Robert.) The Life of St Cadog actually mentions someone as both *Dochou* and *Docguinnus*,[22] contemporary of Teilo and Illtud and thus pictured as living in the later fifth century; he may be the same person as the Cornish eponym.

We cannot hope to identify the hill where *comes* Guedianus and his Bacchantic rustics were engaged,[23] but might note that a menhir with a visible 'cross' can occur naturally, because of the way that granite surfaces fracture, or display veining. Nor is Docco's monastery to be found. One cannot say if it is represented by the St Kew churchyard, whose present shape is not particularly revealing, or – as W. M. M. Picken has justifiably suggested[24] – by somewhere in and around the present farm of Lanow or Lannowe (whose name comes from *Landochou*). It reminds us that a medieval churchyard is not invariably a direct development from an Early Christian monument.

The monastery founded by Samson before his departure, the *domum quam ipse solus Samson fundaverat* 'house that Samson himself alone founded' of the Prologue, was the establishment headed by Amon; the home for many years of the author's 'Old Man' (nephew of Henoc and perhaps also great-nephew of Amon); and at some stage a base for the author of the Life when visiting Cornwall. It was on the south coast, two or three days' travel from the Camel estuary, and it was near a cave plausibly located in the Fowey river's west bank. These facts alone oblige us to dismiss at once any suggestion[25] that it was at St Samson's, South Hill, which is miles away and inland, near Launceston; the churchyard at South Hill contains a sixth-century inscribed memorial (p. 278) but the dedication there must be a coincidence. The favoured candidate has always been the churchyard of St Samson's, Golant, which stands on a hill-front just up from, and west of, the river Fowey about three miles upstream from the river's land-sheltered outflow alongside Fowey (town). The cave, whence the serpent was expelled, is admittedly in this bank, near Golant village and about half a mile from the church. In fact, within Cornish ecclesiology it is by now almost a dogma that Golant churchyard *is* Samson's monastery.[26]

Dogma or not, this may be a wrong identification. The very attractive church at Golant – St Samson or St Sampson, both forms being used – was until 1507 only a chapelry to the much more important Tywardreath (St Andrew's, a former Priory) and had no burial rights. The present church is entirely a structure of 1509. There is not the slightest trace of any earlier building, nor does the churchyard's shape suggest any enclosure of pre-Norman origin. It is hardly conceivable that any Christian site in Cornwall, ostensibly dating from the sixth century, would resemble Golant. The writer proposes, instead, the present parish church of Fowey itself.

Fowey – the parish and the (in part, visibly medieval) harbour town – takes its name from that of the river.[27] In 1311 the church here was *Langorthou*. The possibility that this represents *\*lann* ('churchyard enclosure'; perhaps 'monastery') and a plural *\*corddou* is of some interest, because *\*cordd*, like *\*cor* (< *\*corio-*; the element present in the area-name *Tricurius*, 'Trigg', p. 217 earlier), should exhibit the meanings of 'war-band, army' as well as 'tribe, clan'. If Langorthou represents a pre-Norman *\*Lann-gorddou*, we are not too many centuries in time from a potential origin, indicated in the Life; that Samson's monastery stood on a spot made over to him through popular acclaim, and by the *exercitus* 'army, war-band' of the *comes* Guedianus. The patron saint is Fimbarrus, today equated with the better-known St Finnbarr of Cork; but it was shown earlier that this name is a secondary inversion of that of *Berwen* or *Berwin* (p. 143), who in Wales was represented as a sixth-century 'son' of Brychan and who was said, in Brycheiniog, to have gone to *Cornwallia* (*DSB*). We could reconcile these traditions by supposing that Berwin, following Amon and Samson from Wales, was a subsequent head of Samson's monastery and that his burial (and name) was commemorated in a later church; while the whole site, the eventual churchyard, retained its older locative name commemorating a traditional gift to its founder.

Fowey church with its very tall tower is mostly of the fourteenth and fifteenth centuries; a handsome circular Norman font shows that this church has replaced some twelfth-century structure, doubtless cruciform. Today it is hemmed in by houses, while inland and immediately north-west is a steep cliff-like rise to the battlemented front terrace of Place House. If we regressed to the sixth century, south-east and east of the church there would have been a hundred yards or so of gentle slope, with bushes and scrub giving way to shingle and then a sheltered strip of beach – a natural slipway. Inland, the constructions at Place – a medieval fortified house with successive re-modellings – may have obliterated the first burial-ground. From notes made by J. T. Treffry of Place in 1840[28] it would appear that he himself discovered 'a great number of bodies' in east–west cist graves, 'which, in my excavations round Place, I have from time to time dug up.' Attached to Samson's actual monastery (which need not have been larger than the present churchyard, with an extended cemetery below and around Place House lying inland and uphill from it) may have been a grant of land. What suggests this is a record (so Treffry) that *tempore* Richard III a *vill de Langurthou* or *Langurthowe*, separate from and adjacent to the *vill* or town of Fowey, occupied ground (including Place) west and north-west of the church.

As for St Samson's, the parish-name Golant has the sense of 'valley of the (religious?) feast or festival'[29] and there might be an implication that a connection with Samson and his ridding the river-bank cave of its serpentine monster formed the traditional basis of some periodic celebration. The church at Golant probably *was* within the general geography of the saint's cult, and one cannot overlook the point that Beroul's twelfth-century *Tristran* singles out both the church of Saint Samson and the manorial farm of *Lancien* (Lantyan, 2 miles north on the same side of the river) as locales of special importance.[30] On the ground, none of this affects the observation that somewhere beneath the church of St Fimbar, *olim* Berwin, with its churchyard, the grounds and buildings of Place House and some of the land beyond it, Samson's *monasterium* should be located.

Analysis of the *Vita Prima Sancti Samsonis* may have left an impression of an early sixth-century Cornwall in which nothing much of Christian significance was happening. But its clerical Breton author, like his primary and secondary informants the Old Man and his uncle the deacon Henoc, was concerned only with a narrow swathe running across from the Camel estuary to the Fowey estuary. There are many revealing undertones. When Samson, from some beach near Docco's monastery, dismissed the vessel that had brought him, there is an implication that transmarine trips from Wales were commonplace. Nor are we talking about curachs or punts. This *navis* had carried, as well as crew, tackle and provisions, Samson with Amon and Henoc and perhaps twenty or more others; the dismantled *currus*; Samson's own equipage; and presumably, for the rest, what was necessary for all those prepared to emigrate for good. The *Vita* lays emphasis on the status of Amon's whole family as Demetian *nobiliores* who, Christian or not, would be travelling with personal servants.

Elsewhere in Cornwall at the date of Samson's visit — let us represent it as being in AD 530 for convenience — we may be able to detect, at very localized levels, other families arriving from Wales (but going no further) who also happened to be Christian, literate, and already in the habit of commemorating heads of such families with inscribed memorials. This subject can be taken up in following chapters. The lack of easy communications (save for a few old and major trackways like the Camel–Fowey route), the virtual isolation of any one agrarian valley-settlement from any others and, in the *Vita*, the marked absence of any reference to any Dumnonian more important than the *comes* Guedianus must all be considered. We can draw dots on maps until our eyes swim, but their overall pattern and the connections between them exist only in our twentieth-century perceptions.

When Samson was in Cornwall, a knowledge of Christianity had reached Carnsew and Phillack, from outside, but may not have spread further. The work at Tintagel (Island and churchyard) allows the probability that Christian burials were beginning to appear there, but in connection with a peripatetic kingship (or 'over-kingship') of a notional Dumnonia whose existence and occasional impact may have left a great many of Cornwall's 40,000 or so inhabitants in happy ignorance. What mattered most was the local sub-king or baron, 'King Teudar' or

Guedianus. Visitors by sea were much more interesting and potentially more lucrative. For the entire north Cornwall coastline, and the Severn Sea to which it belongs, Samson's *Vita* underlines the dominance of the southern coastal belt of Wales. Here we must look for the inspiration – the initial missionary thrust, if one can use those words – behind the establishment of small island monasteries at *Ynys Bŷr,* Caldey, and at Lundy; probably the departed Docco, whose proto-monastery cannot have been far from where he first landed; Samson himself; and, at home, the rise in south-east Wales of such major establishments as Llanilltud and Llancarfan. Behind *these*, as a figure without parallel in Dumnonia, looms the primary *Dubricius*, St Dyfrig; territorial and diocesan bishop, somewhat in the Roman mould, of a sub-Roman diocese and a kingdom with real estates, churches, reading and writing.[31] It was Dubricius *papa* who, canonically with two other bishops, placed Samson in the episcopal chair not long before the Cornish visit;[32] Dubricius, the bishop of Llandaff, who with Cadog administered the last rites to Cadog's saintly royal father Gwynllyw;[33] and Dubricius who, in the Life of Samson's old abbot and mentor Illtud, we find named as *pontifex* 'pontiff' of the region.[34] When Samson stepped ashore somewhere near John Betjeman's St Enodoc, little of this sub-Roman Christianity as exemplified in south Wales had yet reached Devon and Cornwall. It was however in process of arriving, detectably so; and the inscribed memorials of Dumnonia go far to show us when and where this happened.

**References**

1. St Luke ii.36.
2. This is not Biblical; it comes from the second-century Apocryphal *Protevangelium*, or 'Book' of St James. Her cult (as *Sainte-Anne*) subsequently flourished in Brittany; continuing interest in Wales is suggested by the *Vita Cadoci* (cap. 46; *VSBG* 118–9) where the genealogy of Gladusa starts with 'Anna' *quam dicunt periti consobrinam esse Marie virginis* 'whom the learned say to be the cousin of the Virgin Mary'.
3. Gildas (sixth-century) still knew the Vetus Latina version.
4. St Matthew i.10. See also Patrick Sims-Williams, *BBCS* 38 (1991), 24–5 (name of a famous Egyptian ascetic?).
5. Loth 1914 (see n.6 below), 15.
6. Robert Fawtier, *La Vie de Saint Samson, Essai de critique hagiographique* (Champion, Paris 1912); Joseph Loth, 'La vie la plus ancienne de Saint Samson de Dol d'après des travaux recents; remarques et additions', *Revue Celtique* (= *RC*) 35 (1914), 269–300; reply to Loth by Fawtier, *Annales de Bretagne* 35 (1921–23), 137–70, and further comments from Loth, *RC* 39 (1922), 301–33, and *RC* 40 (1923), 1–50 – the prolonged interchange is for the specialist. Long essay and English translation, Thomas Taylor, *The Life of St Samson of Dol* (SPCK, London 1925); best recent assessment, Olson 1989, chap.ii (supporting her remark that 'a critical edition of this work is very badly needed').
7. Olson 1989, 10; the prologue's Latin is tortuous, but (*contra* Dr Olson's most careful translation) I am sure that *ante me* must mean 'in my presence'. The author's aim was to stress the authenticity of Henoc's writings, and to indicate that he had actually seen (and read?) them.

8. Compare a larger and slightly later quasi-biography, Adomnán's *Vita S. Columbae* (now Sharpe 1994). Columba lived from *c*.521 to 597. Adomnán, abbot of Columba's foundation at Iona, lived from *c*.628 to 704 and finished the Vita in 688 × 692. He went to Iona only in the 670s, three-quarters of a century after Columba's death. He claims both written and oral sources; it is, at least, doubtful that any direct oral tradition about Columba reached him through fewer than two links of informants.
9. This may seem contentious, but it would take into account that the dating in Fig. 14.1 is supportable on more than one ground.
10. In *CMCS* 1 (1981), at 4–5. Dr Hughes argued, though not perhaps as convincingly as was usual for her, a later seventh-century dating.
11. Taylor 1925 (n.6 above), xi.
12. Roscoe Howells, *Caldey* (Gomer Press, Llandysul 1984) is the best general account, and one that addresses this problem well. See also *PNP*, 567.
13. E. Campbell, 'New Finds of Post-Roman Imported Pottery and Glass from South Wales', *AC* 138 (1989–90), 59–63; in Tenby Museum, sherd of East Mediterranean Phocaean Red Slip (early sixth cent.?) and base of Gaulish Class E jar (seventh cent.).
14. Padraig Ó Riain, 'Samson alias San(c)tan', *Peritia* 3 (1984), 320–3, thinks with good reason that this Irish episode 'seems more at home in the ninth than in the early seventh century'.
15. Olson 1989, 9 ff.
16. Olson 1989, 91–2; W. M. M. Picken, 'The *Landochou* charter', pp. 36–44 in: W. G. Hoskins, *The Westward Expansion of Wessex* (Dept. of English Local Hist., Univ. of Leicester, Occas. paper 13, Leicester 1960).
17. 'Who was also named among them in the British language 'light' (*lux*)', cap.47. The author chose to see the name (MS var. *Iuniauus*) as if from Pr. Cornish & Breton *\*uinn*- 'fair, white, light'; see also Loth 1914 (note 6 above), 295–6.
18. For the *currus*, see David Greene, 'The Chariot as described in Irish Literature', pp. 59–74, with Liam de Paor's drawing (like an Irish or Cornish donkey-shay), in: C. Thomas, ed., *The Iron Age in the Irish Sea Province* (CBA, London 1972). Richard Warner points out (*in litt.*, 1992) that the reconstruction is probably closer to an early medieval vehicle (as depicted on Irish cross-bases) than to an Early Iron Age chariot.
19. R. B. Warner, in his 'The Drumconwell Ogham and its Implications', *Emania* 8 (Belfast 1991), 43–50 (at 49–50) posits an early Irish connection between horse-racing as an aspect of popular assemblies, stones as markers, and (subsequent) cross-markings of such stones; he suggests (*in litt.*) that the *Vita* may conceal a Cornish parallel.
20. Olson 1989, 14 n.27, full and helpful account of her visit.
21. In *BBCS* 24 (1972), at 498.
22. *VSBG* (cap. 22, at 68–9, 72–3). G. H. Doble (see D. Simon Evans, ed., *Lives of the Welsh Saints* (1971), 212 n.6) saw *\*Lann-Docco* as a daughter-house or offshoot of a Welsh foundation (Llandough?).
23. Baring-Gould & Fisher, *LBS* iv.156–7, made some colourful guesses (and took considerable liberties with the text, too).
24. Op.cit., n.16 above, at 41.
25. Olson 1989, 13–14, airs this idea without much enthusiasm.
26. Olson 1989, 13–14, citing earlier such references; local guides have long claimed this as an established fact, beyond question.
27. Pronounced in both cases 'Foy'; the name seems to be from *faw* 'beech' (Latin *fagus*).
28. 'An account of a British Sepulchral Urn, discovered in the neighbourhood of Place'. *Report of the Royal Institution of Cornwall* (Truro 1840), 63–7. This may be yet another

spot where prehistoric and pre-Christian burials preceded a Christian cemetery.
29. Padel 1985, 106 (s.v. *gol* 'feast, fair').
30. Padel 1981, 60 ff., with his further discussion as 'Some South-Western Sites with Arthurian Associations', pp. 229–48 in: R. Bromwich, A. O. H. Jarman & Brynley F. Roberts, eds., *The Arthur of the Welsh* (Cardiff 1991).
31. Wendy Davies 1982, figs. 34, 53 and elsewhere in her writings.
32. *Vita Prima S. Samsonis*, caps. 33–5, 44.
33. *Vita Gundleii* (in *VSBG* 180–1).
34. *Vita Iltuti*, cap. 15 (*VSBG* 215).

# 15

## Strangers and Brothers

In the discussion of the inscribed memorials of Demetia (chap. 6) it was suggested that a typological sequence could be perceived. This was indicated in Fig. 6.2. A few ogam-only stones were ascribed to the early fifth century; complete bilinguals followed them in the later fifth and perhaps the beginning of the sixth century; and insertion of only the deceased's name in ogam, within a longer Roman inscription, was a sixth-century fashion. The shorter corpus of Brycheiniog stones conformed to the last two stages (chap. 8). The use of ogam, it appeared, fell away sharply after the first half of the sixth century.

The distribution-map of all recorded inscriptions in Cornwall and Devon (Fig. 13.3) was presented earlier to show how without further analysis it actually tells us very little. If it is now repeated (Fig. 15.1) with the new distinction of those stones containing any ogam, a further meaning begins to emerge. Six stones are involved. One alone, 488 Buckland Monachorum ENABARR (with secondary usc), is an ogam-only inscription. Three – 484 at St Kew, 466 at Lewannick and 489 at Fardel – are (rather short) full bilinguals; and the last two, 467 also at Lewannick and 470 at Worthyvale, repeat the deceased's name in ogam alongside a longer inscription.

488 ENABARR is not likely to be early fifth century (around 400, this name might have appeared in the nominative as ENABARRAS or even ETNABARRAS (Pr. Ir. *etnas* 'bird', *barras* 'top of head, scalp'; 'Crest-like-a-Bird')). It shows loss of final syllable.[1] With 484, 466 and 489 it may be later fifth or earlier sixth century, and the others – 467 and 470 – are either of this date, too, or (470) slightly after $c.550$.[2] A provisional bracket from the end of the fifth to the second half of the sixth will serve. On these six stones, in relation to the ogams, there are eight names. Four are Irish – definitely Irish – which removes them at once from the native Dumnonians. Four (*Ingenuus*, *Iustus*, *Latinus* and *Macarius*) are Roman. So far, the only instance of a continuing Roman name used in Dumnonia before the mid-sixth century has been that of the ruler Constantine, and the picture derived from the last three chapters has not suggested a Dumnonian world, sufficiently Romanized before 400 or subject to any remnant *romanitas* after that date, in which personal names other than British ones would be expected at a social level below local kingship.

What the map (Fig. 15.1) notably fails to show is inscriptions (apart from the

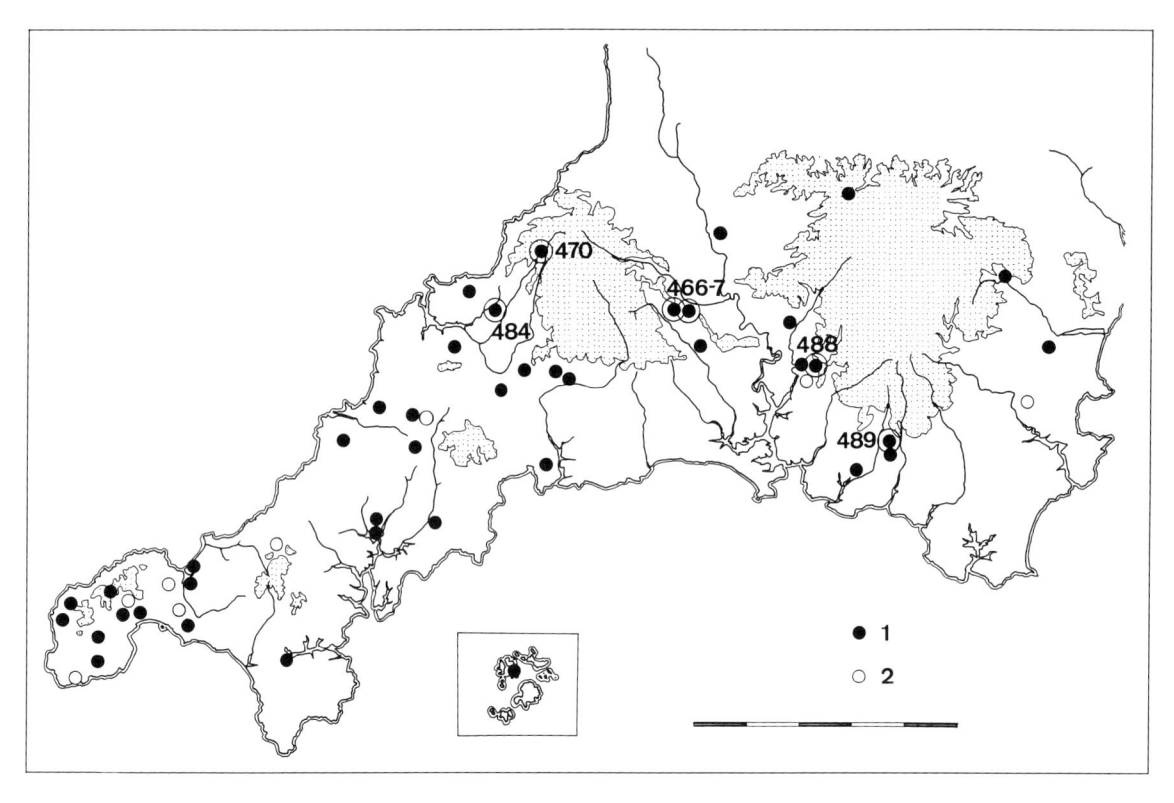

**Fig. 15.1** Post-Roman Dumnonia; the inscribed memorials, as for earlier map (Fig. 13.3) but those with ogam now encircled (*CIIC* numbers shown).

isolated and early 479 *Cunaide* at Carnsew) in the *west* of Cornwall that could be associated with settlement, however minor, of an Irish people like the Uí Liatháin whose homeland lay firmly within the Irish ogam belt. This does not mean that Irish names never appear on stones in west Cornwall; they do, but in Roman letters and Latin guise, and not before the middle of the sixth century. As for the occurrences of ogams linked to Irish and Roman names in north and east Cornwall and south-west Devon, if we look for the same combination elsewhere in the period 475 to 550 it would be pointless to consider any part of Ireland. Patently the source is Wales; more specifically, it may lie in Demetia.

A further elaboration of the base-map, Fig. 15.2, begins to clarify this. Omitting as for the moment irrelevant inscriptions in west Cornwall (west of the Fal estuary), it picks out all those stones that can now be described as seemingly *intrusive*; having non-Dumnonian characteristics. These include, of course, any use of ogam; Irish names; and Roman names (the last two separately or together). We can also indicate inscriptions, seen to be in the majority, where the memorial can be construed as overtly Christian. The signs of this would be use of terms like HIC IACIT or (466 only) MEMORIA; and for the moment also the appearance of a single name, any reference to parentage of secular background being omitted.

If the refined distribution is now treated as a conventional archaeological

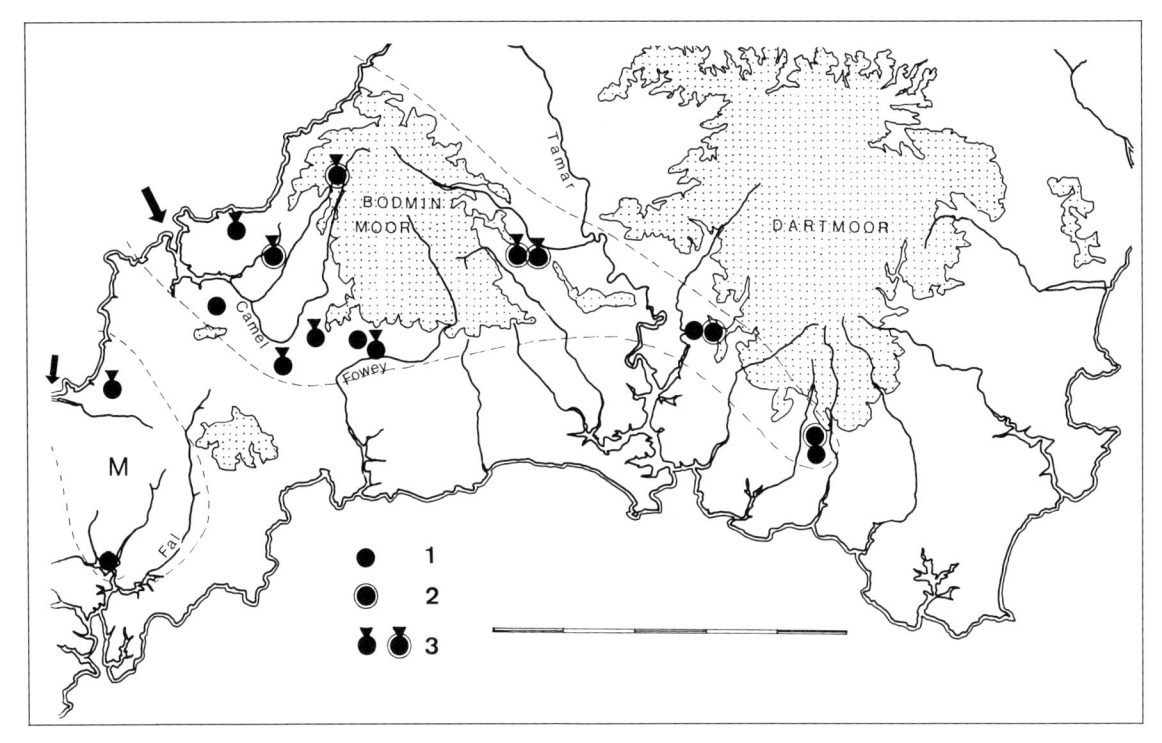

**Fig. 15.2** Map, east Cornwall with the 'Camel–Fowey corridor' and south Devon with the South Hams (M = mid-Cornwall). Intrusive memorials only, *c*.500 onwards, are included. **Key**: 1, Irish and/or Roman names. 2, use of ogam. 3, indications of Christian status — as type (d), or single-name memorials. Scale, 25 miles (40 kms).

distribution-map, of a cluster of intrusive and innovative features falling within a given period in a given area, some further conventions can be usefully exploited. Dotted lines can emphasize groupings. Since the area is nearly all maritime and 'intrusion' may imply coastal entry, a proper knowledge of the physical geography allows likely points of entry to be arrowed.

The outcome is, cartographically, an extension of the conclusions drawn from analysis of the Dumnonian episode in Samson's *Vita*. The Camel estuary is indicated as the prime entry-point, with an initial spread along the river-valleys leading east and south-east from it. (There may be a smaller access – smaller arrow – in mid-Cornwall, the Gannel just west of Newquay.) We might detect a further diffusion around the south of the high block of Bodmin Moor, into the broad valley of the Tamar and across into the dairylands south-west of Dartmoor. Dates for individual inscriptions are not shown, because the band of time depicted here is possibly no more than a century.

Several aspects that could affect further suppositions to be drawn from this map need to be described, preceding an analysis of the memorial stones. In the first place there is the *quantitative* aspect. Mid-Cornwall apart, this map shows only thirteen stones; these are the ones that happen to have survived from the fifth and sixth to the present century and one can only guess what fraction they represent — a fifth? a tenth? a fiftieth? — of all such memorials erected at the period. Accepting that a memorial referring to an extended family working a holding of land may have been commissioned and set up only when its 'head' or eldest male died, and also that not every family necessarily partook of the fashion, it is impossible to estimate (from the total of intrusive stones) just what kind of total of intrusive people they might represent. There are checks imposed by other factors. Given that we envisage immigrants, permanent settlers expecting to acquire not barren moorland but sufficient better-quality land to support families, a figure like five thousand would be excessive; and there was also the effort and hazards involved in a seaborne move. Given the known total of memorials, multiplied by the various factors already mentioned, five hundred to a thousand folk all told, over a century or so, might be a supportable guess.

The *temporal* aspect arises with attempts to date inscriptions closely, as indices of settlement. There must have been a time-lag. Families emigrating do so preferably when led by young, or young middle-aged, fathers and uncles, not by geriatrics; memorials to leaders date from their passing to the Otherworld, not from their arrivals in new lands within this one. Finally there is the *religious* aspect. Most of the memorials shown in Fig. 15.2 can be called Christian, and about a third may commemorate priests; spiritual, not family-group, leaders. Taken with the nature of the personal names, we can interpret them as evidence for an intrusive society that was predominantly or wholly Christian as well as Latinate. This is the stage of cultural development postulated for Demetia, with its appropriately mixed population, by the end of the fifth century. We might then expect not only the presence of those memorials actually recorded, but of primary Christian sites as well. We should look to *these*, rather than to the marginal influence of visitors from Gaul and certainly instead of towards ideas derived from any part of sub-Roman southern England, as the main witness to Dumnonian Christianity during the sixth century.

The monastery of Docco and, in its own way, Samson's monastery on the southern coast fit well within this model. One inscription, 484, reads IVSTI in Roman letters (within a 'cartouche', Fig. 15.3) and has *I)USTI* in ogam alongside it. Granite, but not a pillar, it is more like a large 'pillow-stone' to sit above the head end of a grave. It was found just outside the churchyard at St Kew. If this is for a cleric, it was surely for one of the brethren in Docco's monastery, who may not have died before the mid-sixth century (and may well have been living there when Samson passed by).

When we try to find support for this model of a mainly Demetian settlement, the cumulative benefit of studying the inscriptions in large groups instead of one by one becomes noticeable. The memorials of south Wales and those of south-west

**Fig. 15.3** The memorial of *Iustus*, 484, from St Kew (Landocco?), now in parish church; IUSTI, in cartouche, with ogam *(I)USTI* above. (Photo: author.)

Britain are not separate bodies of evidence for happenings in the fifth and sixth centuries, divided geographically as they may be, but parts of a single continuum. The personal names, Irish or Roman, found in Dumnonia can as a start be matched with those found in south Wales. Names from nine Dumnonian inscriptions are met within Demetia (and, three times, in Brycheiniog). The map, Fig. 15.4, might be interpreted as showing Demetia as the area of origin, and both Brycheiniog and Dumnonia as the recipient regions. While it remains uncertain how much weight can be laid on it, the currency of the names involved can never have been enormous.[3] The pattern should be more than coincidental.

Naturally there is no suggestion that any two inscriptions, one from each side of the sea, refer to the same person; no one can be buried and commemorated in two places at once. There *is* the argument that Fig. 15.4 could denote repetition of names favoured in particular kin-groups and that members of such groups in Wales moved to Dumnonia. One instance allows us to go further. The stone at St Breoke just west of the Camel (472) is the memorial of VLCAGNI FILI / SEVER⊢, the large letters using two faces of the pillar (Fig. 15.5). It may not be much, if at all,

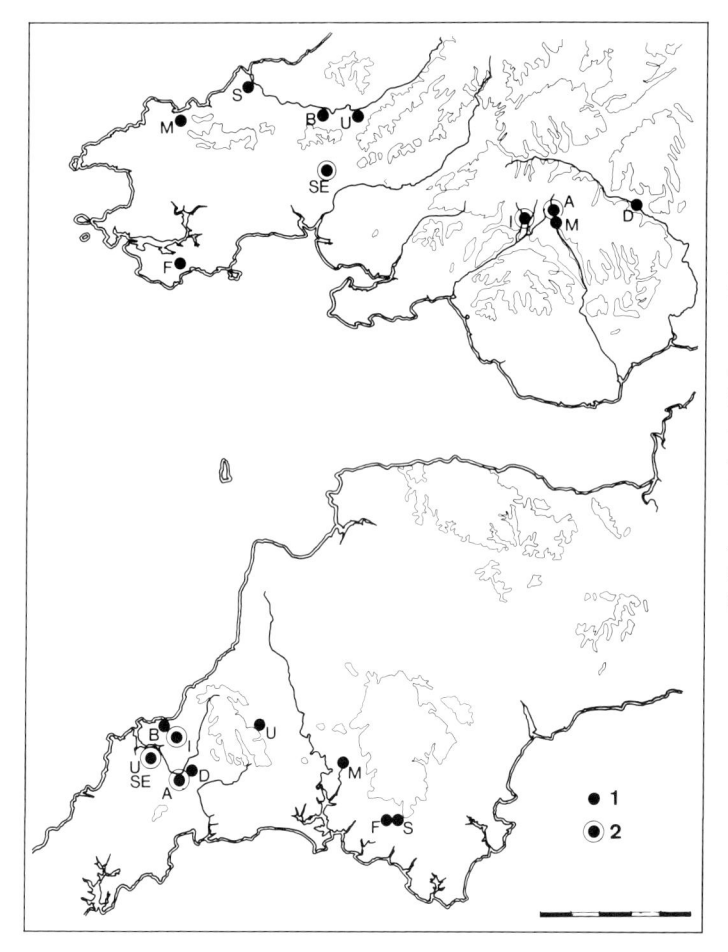

**Fig. 15.4** Repetition of names, as between Demetia (and Brycheiniog) and Dumnonia (cf. also Fig. 8.6). **Key**: 1, Irish names – B, *Brocagnus*; D, *Dunocatus*; F, *Fan(n)onus*, *Fannucus*; M, *Maqi-Decedas* (and variants); S, *Sagra(g)nus*; U, *Ulcagnus*. 2, Roman names – A, *Annic(i)us*; I, *Iustus*; SE, (sons of?) *Severus*. Scale, 25 miles (40 kms).

later than about 500. The name Severus is quite common from Late Roman times[4] but there is a second stone at Newchurch, Carmarthenshire (373, *ECMW* 171), of very similar epigraphic style and about the same date, with SEVERINI / FILI SEVERI. Even the formula 'Of A, of-the-son of-B' is constant. It is hard to resist the idea that Ulcagnus and Severinus were brothers. There is a likely parallel in the memorials to SOLINI FILIVS VENDONI (429) and to )RVGNIATO FILI VENDONI (328) shown in Fig. 8.5. Both 'families' are represented in the area of the Déisi settlement. If these are pairs of brothers, in each case one has a Roman name and the other an Irish one. Both families had attained the horizon of Latinity and probably also of Christianity. In each case it was the (elder?) son with the Roman name who lived and died in Demetia, and the (younger?) with the Irish name who emigrated – like a Victorian remittance-man sent to try his luck in the Colonies.

A rather more intricate clue, drawn from palaeography rather than epigraphy,[5] reinforces this demonstration. Most Insular inscriptions used the same Roman capital A as we do now. An older form, 'open A' with no cross-bar (like inverted V) is seen on some Roman milestones and very rarely on inscriptions like the west

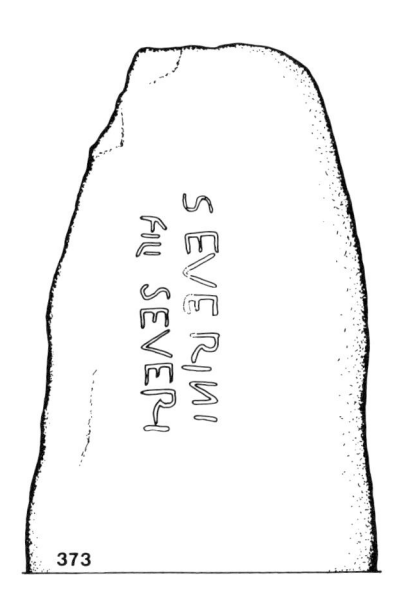

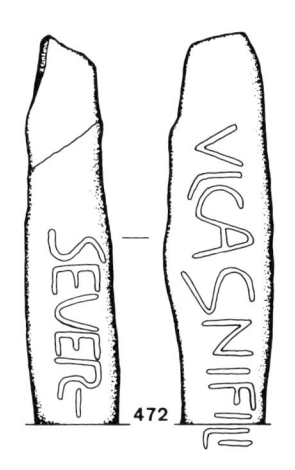

**Fig. 15.5** Two sons of *Severus*? **Left**, 373, Severinus son of Severus, Carmarthenshire; **right**, 472, Ulcagnus, son of Severus, Cornwall.

Cornwall Men Scryfys (468) with the first A in the dead man's name, RIALOBRAN↵. In the later fifth century yet another kind, 'angular' or 'angle-bar' A in which the cross-bar is a shallow open V, appears on Gaulish stones (like VRSVS at Lyon, dated to 493, and PELEGER at Vienne, AD 502). If the Carnsew CVNAIDE stone, with ordinary A, had a Gaulish model its likely date (450–75?) may suggest that angle-bar A was not by then commonly in use.

The angle-bar A is simply an embellishment, a 'fancy' way of writing Λ, that seems to have originated in the Western provinces[6] and spread from manuscripts to the much larger *capitalis quadrata* or monumental script. Its appearance in Atlantic Britain is undoubtedly linked to the chain of Extended Latinate (EL) memorials, also showing Continental features, discussed in chapter 12. The Kirkmadrine (south-west Scotland) memorial of the two priests Viventius and Mavorius (Fig. 12.3, no. 7) shows it in four of its six lines, and also as the *alpha* above the encircled *chi-rho*. This inscription is connected, because of its Continental contraction S̄C̄Ī (with contraction-bar above it), *sancti*, with the only others to show such contractions; 391 and 392 from Aberdaron, Caerns. These have PR̄S̄B and PB̄R (*presbyter*) and they also use angle-bar A exclusively.

We have to guess that some other direct introduction from Gaul matching that of the Kirkmadrine stones (which may belong to a community of immigrant clerics)[7] took place in Demetia, but that no relevant EL exemplar happens to have survived. This liking for angle-bar A is a *fashion* – nothing more – linked to memorials as socially desirable exhibitions. The distribution (Fig. 15.6) shows dissemination of the fashion in Demetia, where the personal names involved include some Irish ones (364 QVENVENDAN↵; 368 VENDVBAR↵). The idea could have been introduced, in the form of something noticed in a manuscript, through an ecclesiastical centre. The Life of Samson relates that during the saint's brief period as abbot on Ynys Bŷr (Caldey) there was a visit from some Irishmen,

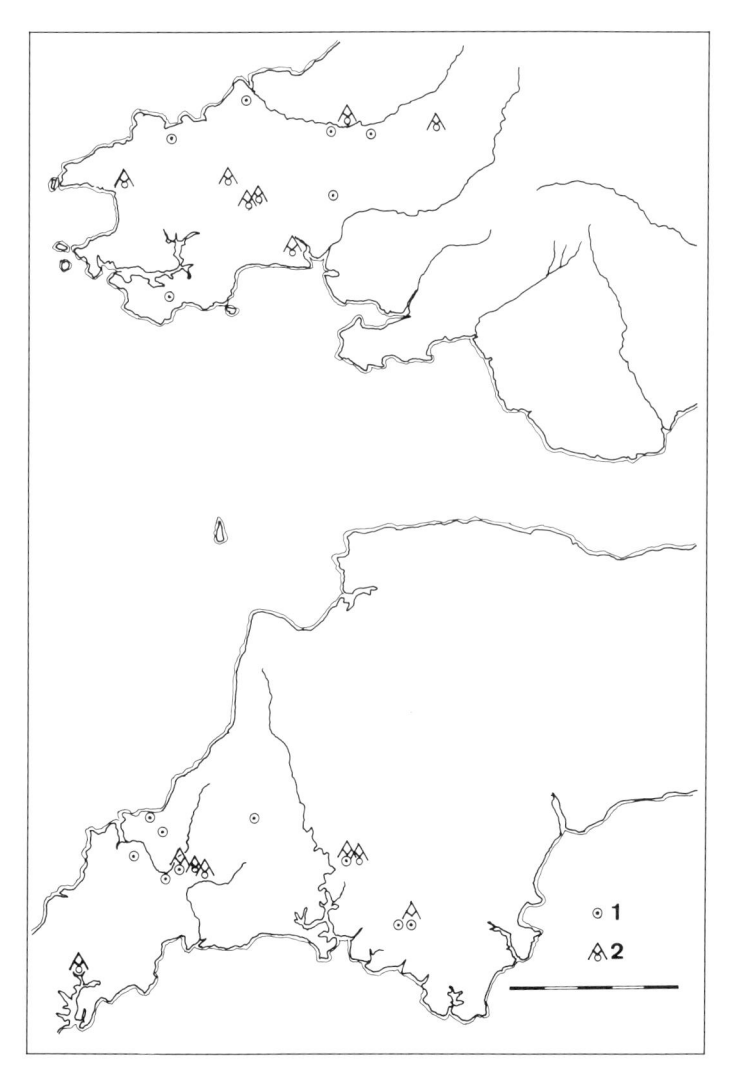

(Left) **Fig. 15.6** The spread of an epigraphic fashion, early sixth century, from Demetia to Dumnonia? **Key**: 1, repetition of personal names (as in Fig. 15.4 above). 2, instances of angle-bar A in inscriptions. Scale 25 miles (40 kms).

(Below) **Fig. 15.7** Two Dumnonian inscriptions (Macalister's *CIIC* drawings); 457, Lancarffe, Bodmin, DVNOCATI, and 473, St Clement churchyard (primary use, VITALI; secondary use, ...IGNI OC). Note angle-bar A in both, and use of Demetian-originating horizontal I.

learned men, *de Roma venientes*.[8] This is about 520. These men were 'coming from Rome' back home again, probably across Gaul and then across Dumnonia, and there must have been other such visiting *phylosophi* 'men of learning'.

The Demetian instances of angle-bar A form the only reasonable source for the repetition of the letter in Dumnonia, where priests as the *ordinatores* or *scriptores* who made up patterns for memorials could easily have established it. In Devon and Cornwall all the stones involved (including 462 QVENATAVCI at Gulval, off the map westward and excluding only the Roman (473) VITALI at St Clement) use the letter in Irish names. All but two of these (460, 489) also have the final horizontal I (as 457 DVNOCAT⊢, Fig 15.7), a related introduction and one almost certainly invented, not adopted from outside, within western Demetia in the later fifth century. Finally the angle-bar A map may narrow the likely points of departure from Demetia. We are now looking at the coastline between Tenby and the Gower.

The whole of this demonstration – epigraphic, onomastic and now palaeographic – allied to the sole narrative source, Samson's *Vita*, points to a migration from Demetia to Dumnonia starting late in the fifth century and affecting mainly the eastern half of Cornwall. It was distinct from, and much more fully evidenced than, any hypothetical smaller migration from Ireland to west Cornwall (chap. 11). Nothing indicates reasons for it. We might speculate that families headed by younger sons had heard of available land in under-exploited parts of Dumnonia, that within Demetia there were anxieties about pressure from adjoining kingdoms like Ceredigion (p. 114) and that there were even circumstances where a given family might have found it prudent to migrate because of dynastic in-fighting (p. 270). All in all, the motives probably *did* lie within what would now be called a socio-economic sphere. Here, they concern us less than another set of inferences and deductions. The newcomers were settlers principally and Christian incidentally, but as Christians they will have been accompanied by priests (*sacerdotes*, presbyters or deacons) and some particularly pious lay folk. The monastery of Docco, followed by Samson's, heads a dimly perceived catalogue of primary Christian sites – Lewannick (p. 313) is one of them – that became enclosed consecrated cemeteries and eventually held churches. Supposedly Christian oriented cist-graves or dug graves, even 'special' graves, went along with inscribed Christian memorials for the more prominent immigrant dead. All of this, growing in scope and variety over two or three generations and independent of the religious character of any peripatetic Dumnonian royal court, marks 'the advent of Christianity' (p. 3) in most of Dumnonia. It also brings into the long and culturally backward peninsula, post-Roman Devon and Cornwall, what the Demetians had already attained in their homeland; the horizons of Christianity, Latinity and relative literacy.

Literacy, but not historicity; and this is the last and very difficult theme to explore. By the Norman period, and for a while before it, there was a minor and particular Welsh interest – arising at the larger monasteries and court circles, among would-be historians, genealogists, bards and collectors of traditions – in a semi-legendary Dumnonian past, the lost glories of other Britons who ceased to be *combrogi*, Cymry, dwellers in one and the same land, when the Anglo-Saxons reached the western shores in the seventh century. Hence the fragmentary reconstructions of a Dumnonian royal succession, the interchange of highly imaginative lives of saints and the partial preservation of epics like that of the Gereint who fell at *Llongborth*. None of these describes any migration in the sixth century. In fact the *Vita Samsonis*, the only 'history' to describe an individual move, does so as a little part of a much longer narrative.

When a noticeable proportion of people in a confined region migrates permanently, the event is likely to be remembered in outline for at least a century. In more recent times the knowledge will rest on both written and oral tradition. I illustrate this, quite fairly, from the case of Cornwall; where there was a very considerable nineteenth-century diaspora, first of working adult males and then of whole families, to the United States and Mexico, Australia, and eventually South Africa and Malaya. The roots were socio-economic, and what was being exported were unique skills in shaft-mining ('hard-rock' mining) and the winning and dressing of all metallic ores. Rather like the Patagonian Welsh, the Cornish took with them a intact package of Wesleyan Methodism, distinctive accents and forms of speech and a closed social system, and parts of this package persisted here and there until the present century. My great-grandfather Edmund Warrington as a youth in the 1860s was sent out to South Australia as a remittance man and told to get a job as a clerk. His father Henry, whose income was probably minimal, was the youngest (eleventh) child of Colonel George Hanmer Warrington (1778–1847), late of the 1st Dragoon Guards, a colourful and improvident man who had married an alleged natural daughter of George IV and who found himself, from 1814, Consul-General in Tripoli. Edmund Warrington obtained work in Kapunda, then an almost exclusively Cornish mining-settlement. He was neither strong nor successful but he had the sense to marry Ann Vivian Moyle, one of many daughters of a Cornish mine-captain (an 'agent' or mine-manager) who had gone out there in the 1840s. Edmund Warrington fathered four children and then died suddenly; his widow, bereft of support, promptly bought a fat cow, got an Irish labourer to slaughter and dismember it and sold the meat to the miners for a profit. In no time, she was proprietor of a butchery establishment and was able to educate and train her children. The eldest, my grandmother, did not return to Cornwall until the 1890s, but did so in considerably better style (on the Union Steam Ship Co.) than that of her parents' nightmare sailing-ship voyages to Down Under. She died aged ninety-eight in 1965 having retained a prodigious memory and having dictated many reminiscences (of Australia, South Africa, the Sudan and other places where her Cornish husband had gone mining). Her early life was passed in an Australia where what is now thought of as 'an Australian accent' (i.e., Sydney-originating) had not emerged, and where most people that she met talked of 'home', meaning

Cornwall. By 1948 she had sailed between Britain and Australia half-a-dozen times.

In Cornwall, this Australian dimension is far from forgotten. It is now about a hundred and fifty years since Captain Thomas Moyle (with family) left Cornwall for ever and landed at what became the city of Adelaide, whence he could expect to get, and did get, the management of a mine in the Yorke Peninsula; in a tight society where Cornishmen would only employ or work with other Cornishmen, for preference those from the same *parish*. Today, in common with a great many other Cornishmen from mining families I have cousins in South Australia, New South Wales and Tasmania to whom I can write or even telephone; to whom a son or nephew can be sent for a long visit, and whose sons would similarly be entertained if they visited Britain. There are thriving 'Cornish Associations' in Australia whose members eat pasties, learn Cornish and wear black kilts if so minded. A permanent feature of libraries and record offices in Cornwall is a crowd of men and women descended from Cornish emigrants, visiting 'home' to research their family history.[9] There is a published literature dealing with all aspects of the Cornish diaspora.[10]

While there can be no direct comparison between the Cornish sailing to Australia and the infinitely shorter passage of the Demetians to Dumnonia, a common factor might be the ways in which traditional knowledge of such happenings are transmitted to future generations. Details with names of the first Cornish miners in South Australia, the picturesque life of Consul-General Warrington and the extent of Thomas Moyle's family can be found only in *written* sources.[11] Against this, my grandmother's reminiscences covered not only family matters – an uncle Edmund Vivian Moyle who became a Senator; how she and her siblings were brought up as Anglicans, not Methodists, because Edmund Warrington's great-grandfather had been a parson;[12] and how when her father married he falsified his age deliberately[13] – but also wider glimpses of Australian life. These included memories of camels(!) as unpopular beasts of burden; attitudes towards the 'low-Irish' (one word) who, poor souls, were assisted migrants employable only as unskilled labour; the embarrassment of 'creamies', the offspring of European fathers and Aboriginal mothers; non-Cornish people on the mines – engineers were often Germans, the doctors Scotsmen (who drank); her work as a trained nurse in tented mining camps during epidemics of typhus; and the staggering contrast, eventually, between the green-ness of Cornwall and the 'bush' or 'outback' with its sun, sand and snakes. Later generations might hear this on tape but it began as *oral* information, much of it recalled three-quarters of a century afterwards.

There is not much point, thirteen or fourteen centuries on, in prolonging discussion about oral tradition of a Demetian migration to Dumnonia. If the essence of the Cornish migration to Australia is scaled right down, the distinction between oral and written records could be applicable. Until at least the end of the sixth century, oral traditions of the first migrants must have circulated in both countries. The *Vita Samsonis* confirms this. It also seems to tell us that, around

600, the author had read Henoc's mid-sixth century written record.[14]

Memories (that can be handed down orally) of happenings that were strung out over a period of time seem more prone to erosion and blurring than do memories centred on famous individuals or, as genealogical recitals, on strings of linked names.[15] In so far as the pre-Norman Dumnonians possessed any grasp of geography, there must have been a limited general knowledge that Wales and Ireland lay vaguely to the north and north-west, just as that Brittany, with its mutually intelligible language, lay to the south or south-east. Underlying the remains of Cornish hagiography is a steady theme to the effect that Christianity was first introduced by sea-travellers from Ireland and Wales, regardless of whether these *sancti* arrived in boats or upon floating millstones and miraculous leaves. (Not unexpectedly, sons and daughters of kings or, at the lowest, of *duces* and *nobiliores*, figure among such missionaries.) For the secular world, *Irlande* was specified by Beroul in his *Tristran* poem, and this may have been drawn from earlier Dumnonian folklore. In the lost opening, Mark's Cornish kingdom was being invaded and attacked. If an attempt is made to supply this from Gottfried von Strassburg's *Tristan*,[16] the details are clouded and geographically imprecise; we might suspect that the enemy was from *Irlant* or, equally so, from *Gales* (Wales). Beroul's story may be meant to suggest that Ireland had once been a victorious opponent – hence the continued Irish exacting of tribute from Cornwall and the potential hostility of an Irish court with its grisly champion *le Morhout*; Ireland is also the land whose princess *Iseut* is intended as Mark's queen. What we do not find anywhere is an echo of non-Cornish groups settling permanently in Cornwall. It is also quite uncertain whether they would have been regarded as in any fashion 'Irish' or simply as other British coming from Wales. The notion that these settlers were *still* speaking Irish when they moved to Dumnonia – most of the time? as occasional bilinguals? – has, in the present writer's view, been grossly over-stated.[17]

As to written sources, we can dismiss the idea of anything with a Dumnonian provenance. If at some date between AD 530 and 570 the deacon Henoc sat down with ink, a writing-implement and vellum and composed (in Latin) an account of the doings of his cousin Samson – and this can be accepted as credible – he did so because he had been educated in sub-Roman Wales, at a centre of literacy like Llanilltud Fawr. Henoc's written memories fall within a horizon of historicity, a mid-sixth-century one focused rather narrowly on Henoc himself. But it can be argued that within one part of Wales, later in the sixth century, localized historicity did just touch upon the Demetian migration.

The 'Brychan Documents' *De Situ Brecheniauc* and *Cognacio Brychan* were examined in earlier chapters. The only points that need to be recapitulated are that components of these medieval versions can be taken back, through identifiable stages, to various older writings – some perhaps as old as the sixth century – and that such reconstructed source-material suggested a knowledge within

Brycheiniog, one that was never up-dated after the end of the sixth century, of a *Damnonia* whose name was textually corrupted to *Mannia* (p. 143). Thus the record of the departed king Brychan's burial on *Enys Brachan*, the isle of Lundy, known to lie *iuxta Manniam* 'next to Damnonia' could be included as a mid-sixth century event, but the removal of his remains in the following century to Hartland and the enshrinement under his latter-day name of 'Nectan' escaped notice.

Though a reasonable reading of the evidence displayed in the maps, Figs. 15.4 and 15.6, and the inscriptions themselves, together show the main thrust of the Dumnonian settlement originating in Demetia with a principal sea-passage between the Camel estuary, and Carmarthen Bay (Tenby east to the Gower, with the mouth of the Tywi in the centre), this does not exclude less well-evidenced contact from other parts of the south Welsh coast. Samson and his father Amon were, strictly, Demetians but much of Samson's life in Wales was passed elsewhere – at Llanilltud, and at other un-named places within today's Glamorgan and Gwent. There are possible indications that it was the group of the earliest (late fifth century) monastic houses all near each other in the South Glamorgan 'bulge' west from Cardiff that first started to look outwards. The foundation of Ynys Bŷr must be linked to Llanilltud; that on Lundy, to one or other house, just possibly the slightly later Llancarfan (Nantcarban); and Docco's monastery at St Kew, perhaps in existence by 500 or so, with Llandough. These are specifically religious feelers, in a way preliminary to a more general settlement from Demetia, but they would widen the nature of the contact.

Brycheiniog was and is land-locked. Access to the coast southwards down several of the long valleys cannot however have posed much of a problem and the reconstructed later life of Brychan would suggest that its inhabitants were just as free in theory to sail south out of Swansea Bay as the Demetians from Carmarthen Bay. In chapter 9, we noted how the Brychan Documents appear to record that a few people were believed to have done so – to have gone to Cornwall, probably in the sixth century. The Norman scribe who copied out *DSB* into Vespasian A xiv may have reproduced a Brecon exemplar almost word for word, line for line, but (as Wade-Evans spotted) his attention slipped among the repetitions and uncouth Welsh names, and a whole line was left out. This was in the 'List of Sons', the roll of twelve male names (p. 142–3), but – on the strength of the text of *CB* – it can be restored [bracketed]:

illi' Clytgeuin. Arthen fil'Brach. Papay.fil'Brach.Kynon.fil'Brac.
[q$^i$.ē.in mannia. Marthaerun.fil' Brach.in keueiliauc.Run.fil'Brach.]
q$^i$.scs.ē. inoccidentali parte p̄dicte mannie. Dynigat. fil'Brach.

The text now tells us of *Kynon qui est in Mannia* 'Kynon, who is in M.' (with *CB*'s *Kynon qui est in Manan*); and of *Run qui sanctus est in occidentali parte predicte Mannie* 'Run, who is a saint in the western part of the aforesaid M.' (alongside

*CB*'s different *Run ipse sanctus ycallet in Manan* 'Run himself a saint *ycallet* in M.'). More specific geography comes with a Berwin whose name could be glossed as *apud Cornubiam* (*CB*), re-written in B.3 for *DSB* as *in Cornwallia*. And from the longer catalogue of women's names, the 'Daughters' (p. 151), we have also Bethan *in Mannia* (*DSB*) or *apud Manau* (*CB*).

Three of these four – Kynon, Run, Bethan – are placed in *Mannia*, or Dumnonia (*Damnonia*). Only Berwin is in Cornwall specifically, though *Cornubia* (VII.3 or VIII) may be simply a later way of noting 'in the western part of Dumnonia' as for Run (p. 143 earlier). The men's names figure in a list interpreted as a diptych for the Mass, and are there in a Christian context. Run is a saint, *sanctus*, a man to be linked to some primary Christian site, and it can be shown that Berwin was also. Kynon, however, is less clearly defined. He cannot be identified as any saint, patronal or otherwise, in present-day Devon or Cornwall. A slightly pompous description as 'a secular adventurer of some standing' might fit him better.

We may be looking again at Breage, *Pembro*, the head-place of its post-Roman *bro* adjoining the hill-fort of (Castle) *Pencair* 'the head fort' (p. 216 and Fig. 11.1). The latter's alternative and locative name Tregonning Hill goes with Trencrom, Chun and others (p. 194). These, replacements for the original designations of ancient fortresses, are the names of the medieval farm-holdings that treated such hills as marginal grazing. John Leland in the 1540s heard other things.[18] 'Cair Kenin, alias Gonyn et Conin, stoode in the hille of Pencair. There yet apperith 2. diches.' The same personal name is contained in Tregonning (1341, *Tregonan*). Leland chose to add an antiquarian note – 'Sum say that Conan had a sun caullid Tristrame' – but this is a separate idea; it suggests inspiration from the well-known Castle Dore inscription, 487 (p. 280 below) with its CVNOMORI and DRVSTANVS and is not a piece of Breage information at all.

There are no Cornish stories about this eponymous Conan (Conin, Gonyn, Kenin). There would be no objection in identifying him with the Brycheiniog *Kynon*. This is not an aspect of any postulated minor Irish settlement in west Cornwall (chap. 11) nor should it be supposed that Castle Pencair or Cair Kenin was Cormac's Dún maic Liatháin. An Irish name *Cunagnas*[19] went alongside a British *Cunignos, Cunegnos*[20] (both mean 'Little-Hound, Little-Wolf') and the range of sixteenth-century recorded forms might in theory represent either, Irish 'Conan' or Welsh 'Cynan, Cynin' (both very common indeed); but the heroic emigrant from Brycheiniog was presumably British. If there is a true link here, it is obviously early and interesting, but a one-off; and well outside the area of settlement outlined in Fig. 15.2.

With the other names, especially in view of the Christian aspect of two of them, some simple questions arise. There would be little difficulty in accepting that a few well-connected Christians in Brycheiniog could have migrated to Dumnonia around the middle of the sixth century. The actual journey was easy enough.

Brycheiniog (in this writer's belief) was already partly Latinate and Christian before 500 and, at least one centre within it, the horizon of historicity was reached somewhat before 600. There was a context in which the names of such emigrants could be written down, qualified by *Damnonia* or even *in occidentali parte Damnonie*. But that is only the transmitting end. At the receiving end the questions are – Is there any record of these few names? and, Do places associated with any such records relate to the areas affected by other settlers from Wales?

Berwin's destination, which may have first been recorded as *in Damnonia*, could be refined at a later date when *Cornubia* was appropriate. As the *Be(...)en*, no. 35 in the tenth-century Vatican List of Cornish saints, restorable as \**Berguen* (where -gu- is for /w/), and as the *Barrianus*, patron of Fowey church (1170 *sancti Barriani*)[21] whose name became inverted as 'Finbar', Fimbarrus, it has already been suggested that he represents an immigrant Welsh head of Samson's monastery, \**Lann-gorthou*, subsequently elevated as patron of successive churches there (p. 232). The daughter Bethan is another who cannot be found as a parochial patron anywhere in Dumnonia. But in the large mid-Cornwall parish of Blisland in Trigg, where the name seems to be only a locative (1177 *Bloiston*, with English *-ton*) and where the patron Protus or 'Pratt' looks like a substituted clerical invention, there is a *Lavethan*. The name is found as early as 1475. There is some slight confusion with other nearby place-names,[22] and there is no knowledge of an appropriately early-looking holy site (which would have stood only a short distance from the church); but, however tentatively, Lavethan might be referred to an older \**Lanvethan* (*lann, Bethan*).

Run, the *ipse sanctus*, was said to be *ycallet in Manan*. This mysterious graph defeated the Anglo-Norman redactor of *CB*, as well it might. At this B.3 stage in reactions of *CB*, *ycallet* stood for the more usual Middle Welsh graph *ygcallet* ( = *yn* + *callet* 'in the greenwood, woodland'; *called, callet*). In so short a gloss the allusion is obviously specific, not generic. Run had gone to the western part of Damnonia, *i.e.* to Cornwall; he was remembered as a *sanctus*; and he became this in the setting of 'The Wood', some feature famous or notorious enough to suggest that in Cornwall and probably also Wales it was known simply as \**Callet*.

This is the most intriguing and the most difficult of the four references.[23] Dark hints, reminiscent of John Buchan's novel *Witch Wood* (1927), seem to lurk here. The solution is that Run is probably the un-named patron of Lanivet, an early church-site just west of Bodmin. There was another separate Dumnonian saint, Rumon – a different name (<*Romanus*) – who figures at Ruan Lanihorne near Truro, Ruan Major and Minor in the Lizard (*Rumon>Ruvan>Ruan*). No life of this man was known and the gap was filled by poaching one of an Irish saint, Ronán, whose cult lay in Brittany. The resulting conflation has an episode in which the hero, born in Ireland, goes to *Cornuguallia* and there builds his oratory *iuxta magnam silvam vocabulo nemeam* 'next to the Great Wood called Nemea'. In Brittany this was, naturally, taken to mean not the primary 'Cornwall' but the secondary, Breton, Cornouailles. How, when and why the Oratory's location was drawn into the Rumon–Ronán identification, and what this had to do with any seventh(?)-century gloss about Run, is unclear; but it is curious that *Run* (*CB* and (missing line?) *DSB*) should have become Run*an* in the later, Jesus College 20, list of the twelve names.

The name of the *magna silva* as *Nemea* may have been taken in that form from a Classical source like Diodorus Siculus (*History*, iv.11 – the valley and temple-grove in the Argolis where Heracles slew the lion) but its likely Celtic name (*Nemet*) takes us back to a term older than *Callet*, and one that still held sinister undertones for early Christians. A *nemet(on)* had been a natural sacred grove or wood, and secondarily such a feature as the site of a pagan or pre-Christian temple or cult-centre.[24] In Roman (and doubtless in pre-Roman) Dumnonia there had been *nemeta* in Devon – a Roman establishment at a place *Nemeto statio* and later place-names like '*Nymet* Rowland' – and apparently in mid-Cornwall, with *Lannived* (< *lann* plus *nimet*) in 1268. Here, the churchyard goes back to a primary Christian site, with its curvilinear enclosure-bank and its sixth-century memorial (465, ANNICV FIL(..) – see p. 265 below). There is a large and imposing granite church and several eleventh-century tall crosses. By Norman times any patronal name had been forgotten; the old locative name was still used; and any *nimet* or *callet*, 'The Wood', had diminished to isolated stands in the surrounding valleys. Yet this may be where Run arrived, founded his Christian site and sought to expunge an earlier heathen aura; and where, so unusually, Run's origin and mission were once remembered both in Brycheiniog and Dumnonia.

Kynon, if connected with Tregonning Hill and *Cair Kenin*, is out of the immediate picture. For Berwin, Bethan and Run, any credence given to the Brycheiniog glosses – allowing them to be as old as *c*. 600, or not much after that – leads us to speculate that as Christian emigrants to Cornwall their association was real as well as literary; they came from the same background, arrived more or less together and remained in the same area. Lavethan is only eight miles from Lanivet, and Lanivet only twelve from Fowey. More to the point, on a map (Fig. 15.8) these three places are not just in the western part of Dumnonia but within the Camel-to-Fowey corridor, and within that swathe of mid-Cornwall indicated by relevant intrusive memorials as the area first affected by settlement from Wales. Save for Berwin's the identifications must remain tentative; but their siting and their proximity looks rather more than fortuitous.

We might therefore conclude that, while in general the arrival of people from Demetia (and marginally, it would seem, from Brycheiniog as well), took place at a period far too early to have yielded a descriptive or allusive account generated in Dumnonia – and has to be defined in other ways – the Brycheiniog element of it was, almost by chance, preserved through incidental references in the Brychan Documents; alongside, that is, the much weightier central note of Brychan's burial on an island *iuxta *Damnoniam*. The possibility that, for Run, some tale of a

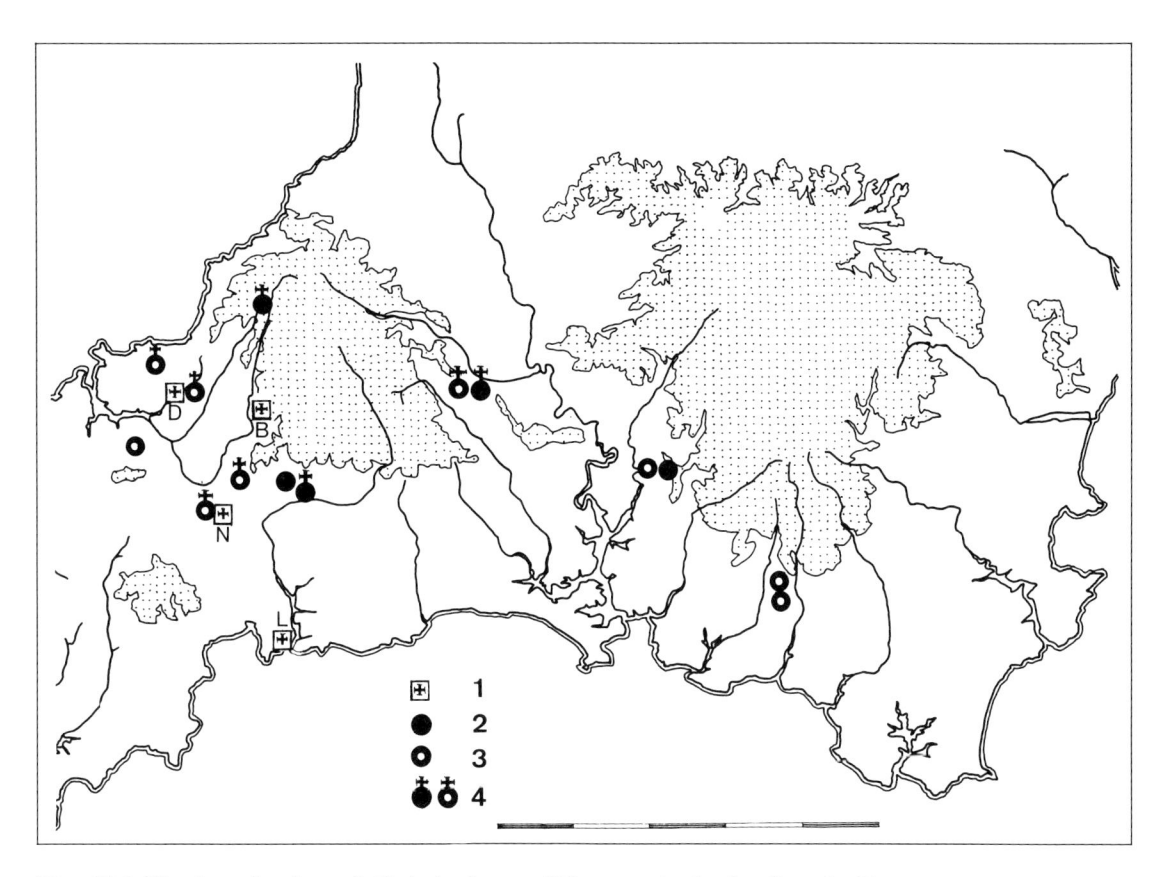

**Fig. 15.8** The introduction of Christianity, *c.* 500 onwards, in the Camel – Fowey corridor and the South Hams (cf. Fig. 15.2). **Key**: 1, D, *Docco*'s monastery; B, Lavethan (*Bethan*?); N, Lanivet (*Run*?) L, Langorthou, Fowey (*Berwin*). 2, memorials with Irish and/or Roman names, and 3, the same where such names also occur in Wales (cf. Fig. 15.4). 4, Christian status – type (d) or single-name. Scale, 25 miles (40 kms).

Christian immigrant born in a distant land who founded a church by the vanishing Great Wood was current in early Dumnonia has not been previously noted; romantic or not, it deserves to be considered. Anything more, if there *was* anything more, was long ago submerged in local folk-tales, hearthside or hagiographic. If we seek additional detail, it can now only be from the mute stones themselves.

253

## References

1. McManus, *Guide*, s.n. ENABARRI.
2. Differing somewhat from Jackson's (*LHEB*) dates for the group, tabulated in McManus, *Guide*, 97–8; the overall context is not considered and some of the datings (e.g. 484 IVSTI; around 600) seem unjustifiably late.
3. One or two of the names are found elsewhere in Wales (Anglesey 326, MACCVDECCETI) but this does not affect the main distribution.
4. *PLRE* i.831–8, ii.1001–16.
5. 'Palaeography' rather than 'epigraphy' here because a single unit of writing is being discussed, not a 'message'.
6. E. A. Lowe, *Codices Latini Antiquiores*, *II* (2nd edn., Oxford 1972), 3–4, no.124; see more widely Knight 1992.
7. This idea is expanded in Thomas 1992.
8. *Vita Samsonis*, cap.37 – the passage makes it clear that they were on their way to Ireland.
9. Source: Cornwall Record Office *Review 1991–2* (Truro 1992) – noting genealogy accounting for 66 per cent of all searches, and non-UK visitors as 8 per cent of total (4 per cent of them from Australasia).
10. For Australia, Oswald Pryor, *Australia's Little Cornwall* (Rigby, Adelaide 1963); Geoffrey Blainey, *The Rush That Never Ended*; *a history of Australian Mining* (1963, 2nd edn., Melbourne Univ. Press 1972); *Pictorial History of Australia's Little Cornwall* (Rigby, Adelaide 1978), *The Cornish Miner in Australia* (Dyllansow Truran, Redruth 1984) and *The Cornish Farmer in Australia* (Dyllansow Truran, Redruth 1987), all by Philip Payton, with numerous articles by same; Phyllis Somerville, *Not Only In Stone* (Angus & Robertson, Sydney 1942), and many smaller items published by the Cornish Association of Victoria, town committees and individuals. No bibliography exists.
11. Hanmer Warrington appears in a good many books, most recently in Ann Schlee's historical novel *Laing* (Macmillan, 1987) – I am most grateful to Miss Schlee for kindly providing additional details of Warrington and his family.
12. This is so; George Warrington (d.1830) was vicar of Hope, Flint, in 1774 and of St Asaph's in 1822.
13. In 1866, claiming to be 'of age'; he may have been barely eighteen but his birth in Tripoli (or Malta?) made such deception easy.
14. Note that, if a seventh-century date for only the Prologue to the Life is accepted, this approximately dated record of Henoc's activity takes on special importance for Insular literacy.
15. Cf. the far-reaching conclusions of David P. Henige, *The Chronology of Oral Tradition. Quest for a Chimera* (Clarendon Press, Oxford 1974).
16. Karl Marold, *Gottfried von Strassburg, Tristan* (1906, 3rd edn. (ed. Werner Schröder), Walter De Gruyter, Berlin 1969); A. T. Hatto, *Gottfried von Strassburg, Tristan, with the 'Tristran' of Thomas* (Penguin, Harmondsworth 1960); summary of lost opening, based on Gottfried, in A. S. Fedrick, *Beroul. The Romance of Tristan* (Penguin, Harmondsworth 1970).
17. The inscriptions – the *only* evidence – show continued use of some Irish personal names in Latin spellings; limited use of ogam; use of a very few formulaic words (466 MEMOR, 489 MAQI and the unusual MAQVI); and no instance anywhere of a genuine Irish declensional termination. A few learned clerical *scriptores* would have accounted for all

18. Toulmin Smith, i.187.
19. Cf. other animal-diminutive names like ogam (100, Cork) ULCCAGNI, (370, Carms.) VLCAGNVS (*ulk-, (probably) 'wolf').
20. Welsh inscriptions show 362 CVNIGNI, 374 CVNEGNI.
21. Olson & Padel 1986, 56–7; the identification has been proposed on a number of occasions.
22. Louden, in next-door St Breward parish, was *Lauedon* (thirteenth cent.); there is also a separate record of *Landvedwen* (1318) that may suggest Lavedden in Bodmin (as *lann*, with *bedewen* 'birch-tree').
23. I summarize what I believe to be the solution here; there is a longer treatment with references in *Brychan Documents.* (chap. 9, note 11).
24. *PNRB* 254–5 (s.n. *Aquae Arnemetiae*, Buxton) offers an instructive discussion with further references.

Note 17 continued: this. McManus, *Guide*, discusses (*passim*) whether any written forms of Irish names in Dumnonia reflect spoken sound-changes; but these (syncope, lenition, etc.) could just as well have arisen through British speech.

# 16

## *The Dumnonian Inscriptions: 'Kittens in the Oven . . .'*

IN NOVEMBER 1874 William Iago, chaplain to the Cornwall Asylum at Bodmin, bought a folio album and wrote in it 'Notes, Extracts, Prints, Photographs, Sketches, Tracings of Sketches, & Memoranda, made, and collected from various sources, & compiled relative to the Most Ancient Inscriptions, discovered in the County of Cornwall by Revd W. Iago BA, LSSA etc., Westheath, Bodmin'. This filled the title-page. Many of us buy large notebooks and compose grand openings; often we get no further than page one. Iago, who had been interested in all this for some time, did rather better. Born in 1836, son of a Cornishman in the Customs Service, he was a keen local historian and after election to the Fellowship of the Society of Antiquaries became its Local Secretary for Cornwall.[1] His first publications on such stones appeared in 1869 and 1871[2] and encouraged by others — Dr C. F. Barham, then President of the Royal Institution of Cornwall, and the mineral agent Nicholas Whitley CE, its Secretary — Iago set to work. He wrote letters to the Cornish newspapers asking for details of any unpublished or un-inspected inscribed stones, and he corresponded with Arthur Evans, Sabine Baring-Gould, Albert Way and (through Barham) with Emil Hübner in Berlin. Arthur G. Langdon gave him much help. As the Asylum chaplain Iago's duties were flexible and he could travel around Cornwall and Devon, producing rubbings and drawings and eliminating reported examples that proved to be medieval or recent. Letters show Iago as kindly and humorous. Fig. 16.1, from a choice little collection, suggests that he took neither himself nor his hobby too seriously. Though the projected volume remained unpublished at his death[3] its compiler's contribution to all later studies, this book among them, is acknowledged with warm gratitude.

Iago and his circle drew on a range of inspiration and hearty encouragement. Arthur Langdon, with Romilly Allen's aid, was compiling his corpus of hundreds of Cornish crosses, a few of them inscribed.[4] The writings in Wales of (Sir) John Rhŷs and others were followed closely, and there were seminal encounters. The Cambrian Archaeological Association came to Cornwall in 1862[5] and again in 1895, when there was a strong emphasis on seeing inscribed stones and sculptured crosses.[6] Great interest was expressed in Celtic philology. The aims lay far beyond the mere compilations of lists and classification — what Glyn Daniel used to call 'the higher philately' of monuments. Iago and his friends were all native

## PICKWICK'S IMMORTAL DISCOVERY.

"There is an inscription here," said Mr. Pickwick. "Is it possible?" said Mr. Tupman. "I can discern a cross and a B. This is important," continued Mr. Pickwick; "this is some very interesting inscription—it must not be lost." All admirers of the great Pickwick should pause and examine the stone, and they will find the words, "BEECHAM'S PILLS." Let them bear this in mind, and they may safely conjecture that on the other side of the stone, not reproduced by the artist, is added, "WORTH A GUINEA A BOX."

**Fig. 16.1** A light-hearted item from William Iago's album (*The Penny Illustrated Paper*, 20 July 1889, page 12); Courtney Library, Royal Institution of Cornwall.

Cornish and a recurrent theme in their writings was the importance of seeing behind the names on inscriptions to 'our distant forbears', 'our Christian ancestors' and in effect to the first records of Dumnonians as *people*.

Three shorter surveys of the Dumnonian memorials preceded Macalister's 1945–49 *Corpus Inscriptionum Insularum Celticarum* volumes. Emil Hübner, a classical epigrapher, brought together some thirty stones from Devon and Cornwall in his *Inscriptiones Britanniae Christianae* (1876).[7] Text and notes were entirely in Latin, as was customary in classical studies (Hübner's letters to Barham, in Iago's album, show a total command of English). Langdon and Allen expanded this in their 'Catalogue of the Early Christian Inscribed Monuments in Cornwall' (1895) with summaries of references and line-drawings at $\frac{1}{24}$th scale, a catalogue willingly accorded room in *Archaeologia Cambrensis*.[8] Macalister himself toured Cornwall, Devon, Somerset and Dorset in 1928–9 and, paying gracious compliments to Langdon's work, gave some corrected readings and fresh drawings in his 'The Ancient Inscriptions of the South of England'.[9] (Following his retirement from the chair at Dublin (1943) he moved to Cambridge (1945?) and did re-visit Devon and Cornwall before 1949; but in poor health and not always showing his former intellectual power.) Finally we can note that very good use of these surveys was made to support his chapter on 'The Dark Ages' in 1931–2 by the young American prehistorian Hugh O'Neill Hencken.[10]

An interest in the inscriptions, especially the personal names, as a philological quarry for the earliest Celtic had been fostered by Rhŷs and in Cornwall was dominated by Rhŷs's vast published output. This rather became lost during the 1920s when another generation turned to the Cornish language. Henry Jenner and, after him, Robert Morton Nance were far more concerned with reviving a 'modern' Cornish from the surviving Middle Cornish texts, and the progression from Late British through Primitive, Old and Middle Cornish[11] was not regarded as particularly relevant; this was, after all, the pre-Jacksonian era. Similarly the memorials as visible objects (some with minimal art) were treated as the oldest stratum of a long sequence of worked and sculptured stones. Arthur Langdon and J. Romilly Allen were the south-western counterparts of P. M. C. Kermode (*Manx Crosses*, 1907), W. G. Collingwood (*Northumbrian Crosses*, 1927) and of course the earlier Allen and Anderson, *Early Christian Monuments of Scotland* (1903). All these great corpora contained some inscriptions, but submerged by greater listings. Nash-Williams's *Early Christian Monuments of Wales* restored epigraphy and language to equal footings with sculptured art but its post-war appearance (1950) seems to have passed unremarked in south-west Britain. When Kenneth Jackson's mighty *Language and History in Early Britain* came out in 1953, the author's central interest embraced the evidence of the inscriptions, a topic with which he had been concerned since youth.[12] But *LHEB* was virtually incomprehensible to the Cornish-language enthusiasts who, like some of their Welsh friends, were otherwise busy inventing neologisms for *aerodrome, bicycle* and *contraceptive*.

The purpose of this cursory survey is certainly not to present the present writer as any kind of pioneer, but to explain why it has taken so long to exploit the Mute Stones of Dumnonia for what they are; historical records, with a linguistic content. The third and perhaps the weightiest reason for delay has been neither artistic nor philological, but a shortcoming of *archaeology*.

Admittedly many of the Dumnonian stones have been moved around (some, several times) since discovery, as have many in Wales; but others have not been, and even for some displaced stones it is often possible to suggest likely original stances. They were features of a contemporary landscape, and a proper understanding requires that they are discussed in landscape-history terms. Moreover, they go with all the other primary or pre-Norman Christian sites and monuments (places of burial, places for worship, monasteries, shrines and church property) in making up a unitary topic that will yield new knowledge only when treated as a specialist landscape-archaeology in its own right; involving other classes of evidence like place-names, working backwards from medieval times as well as forward from Roman times and − because the west of Britain, like Ireland, is an *Atlantic* province − having in mind always the potential of what Emrys George Bowen and his predecessors called 'the Western Seaways'. In Dumnonia these ideas were first and influentially propagated by Dr C. A. Ralegh Radford (who unfortunately never embodied them in book-length form).[13] The present author as Radford's disciple attempted a summary in 1967, in a book that was ostensibly a study of a single parish,[14] and followed this with further essays embedded in parochial guidebooks.[15] Subsequently under the aegis of either the Institute of Cornish Studies (founded in 1961) or the Cornwall Archaeological Unit (1974) younger workers established new guide-lines, taken from work on a massive place-name corpus, cartography, field-work and critical analysis of literary and historical sources, that make it possible to contemplate holistically planned enquiries like this book.[16] As an unexpected bonus the renewal of work at the region's principal post-Roman focus, the site complex at Tintagel, included exploration of the churchyard; the 'sacred space' linked to the sixth-century Dumnonian citadel.[17]

Formulation of an outline model − the hypothetical scheme of origins, events, dates and spatial impact − for the (principally) Demetian settlement in a part of Dumnonia during the sixth century is not, as it might have been fifty years ago, a fluffy little pink-tinged cloud of imagination floating along in the clear blue sky of utter ignorance. It has to be accommodated within the scenario of what we think has been established already, and this will be attempted in the closing chapter. Meanwhile the memorials from Dumnonia, not all of which have been correctly illustrated, can be selectively discussed. The rest of this chapter covers those previously defined (p. 238) as *intrusive*; exhibiting the use of ogam, displaying Irish or continuing-Roman names (or both) and indicating the commemoration of immigrants. There is an inevitable margin of error, perhaps ten per cent or more of the whole, in making the distinction, but chapter 17 can then consider the overlapping and slightly later stones that we might define as *native* or else as 'the Dumnonian response' – memorials portraying the native adoption, entirely within a Christian framework, of an intrusive fashion.

In Cornwall there is a saying, one that goes back to the last century and may (with changes) occur elsewhere, to the effect that 'if a cat has kittens in the oven, that doesn't make them pasties'. It is not necessarily unkind; it means that if your family comes from elsewhere and is called Murgatroyd or Macleod or Malinowski, you will not be seen as truly Cornish just because you happened to be born west of the river Tamar. The concept of differentiation tends to be attached to *names*, not to a child's readily acquired accent or where the home is. When the lack of much else by way of clues forces us back to the small number of inscribed stones as evidence for ethnic differentiation, the presence of the descendants of settlers in the sixth and possibly seventh centuries, it is the *names* on the stones (more numerous than the few instances of the ogam script) that alone assist us to distinguish between Demetians and Dumnonians, kittens and pasties. In shape, absolute sizes, nature and disposition of Roman words and Latin letters the memorials of both regions differ only geologically.

The very simple typology suggested for some Demetian memorials (Fig. 6.2) can at this point be repeated with extra qualifications. Type (a) comprises those with ogam only, generally longer than a single name; pre-Latinate, probably also pre-Christian and in Wales to be regarded as early fifth century. Type (b), the full 'bilinguals', involves mostly vertical inscriptions where the A FILI B (or variants) matches *A MAQI B* in ogam, any differences being those between Latin and Irish expressions of the same. These are Latinate, and date from the second half of the fifth century. Type (c) covers the partly bilingual stones; A FILI B in Roman letters is accompanied by only the deceased's name, *A*, in ogam. As this may mark decline in the knowledge of, and use of, ogam forms, a start in the later fifth century is suggested. (Types (b) and (c) are not necessarily before, or outside, adoption of Christianity, but they are not overtly Christian either.) Type (d) runs parallel to type (c); the A FILI B may still be accompanied by *A* in ogam, but extra wording – (H)IC  IACIT, or simply (H)IC, or some other appropriate word – makes the memorial a Christian one. Beyond (a) to (d) typologically, though possibly overlapping chronologically, are memorials with short vertically set Roman lettering mainly of the concise form 'Of-A FILI Of-B'; the un-typed class.

This slightly expanded classification will be found to cover the Dumnonian memorials. The special case of 479 (*Cunaide*, Carnsew) aside, there is a proviso of a starting-point later than in Demetia; derived from separate considerations, this was outlined earlier (Fig. 8.2). No Dumnonian (a) to (d) stone can securely be portrayed as much earlier than *c*.500. The matter of dating individual inscriptions is not a satisfactory one – it cannot be – and the present author's methods are as subjective as anyone else's. One can give (as has been done already) 'dates' to

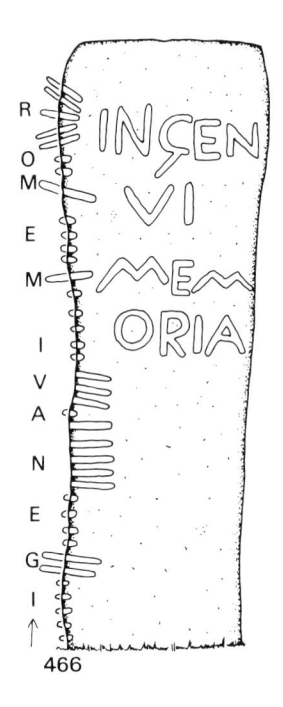

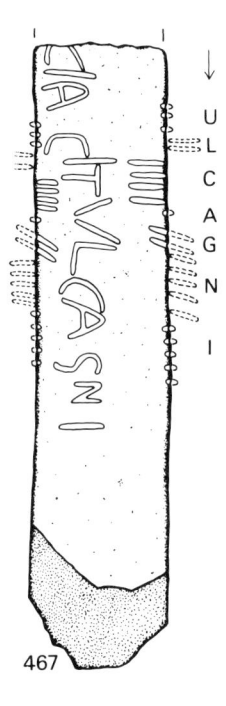

**Fig. 16.2** The Lewannick stones. 466, reddish granite, worn, now in churchyard; 467, now in church (top missing), showing downward-reading ogams – **left**, incorrect, **right**, corrected second attempt.

the nearest third of a century and in the text and figures it saves space to write these as V.3, VI.1, VI.2, VI.3, etc., implying 'a belief that this memorial was made in 470–500, 500–30, etc.'. They are not guesses, but carefully considered estimates based on context, form, epigraphic and linguistic nature, and on such considerations as the appearance on type (d) and the short un-typed memorials of primary *art* – Christian symbols, curved lines and 'cartouches' (p. 293). As to the all-important *names*, the detailed reasons for identifying them in ethnic terms are relegated to the notes so that the narrative is not impeded.

Two memorials relating to the Demetian settlement have already been mentioned. Just west of the Camel estuary at Nanscowe, St Breoke, 472 VLCAGNI FI(LI / SEVER⊢ commemorates an Irish-named settler, son of a Roman-named father[18] (Fig. 15.5). It is un-typed, and early (VI.1), and suggests one of the first incomers. East of the Camel at St Kew the smaller memorial (Fig. 15.3) of Iustus, 484, ogam I)USTI above IVSTI in a cartouche, was suggested as that of a member of Docco's monastery. It is too short to be a proper type (b) and can be dated as VI.2.

Among the more interesting ogams are those at the present churchyard of Lewannick near Launceston, which is twenty-three miles east of the Camel at Wadebridge and which incomers might have reached either by crossing (or skirting) Bodmin Moor, or from a minor north-coast landing like the Haven at

Tintagel[19] or the sheltered inlet at Boscastle. The type (b) granite pillar outside the church, 466 (Fig. 16.2), is unusual in being horizontally set. It reads INGEN/VI / MEM/ORIA 'the *memoria* of Ingenuus' (cf. p. 82 earlier) and in ogam *IGENAWI MEMOR*. The name is Roman, the use of *memoria* is Christian, no parentage is given and this should be a priest's epitaph, dated as VI.1 – perhaps around 500, and an aspect of original settlement. The choice of ogam letters is important. If the -ng- in Ingenuus was spoken /ŋ/ (the sound heard in 'singer', not the double-sound as in 'on-going'), the three oblique lines used in later manuscript tradition for (medial) NG could not be employed because, as McManus shows (Fig. 3.1), at this period they meant the sound /g$^w$/. The *ordinator* therefore chose ogam *G* for /ŋ/. In the ogam for INGENVI the -VI (-ui) included a /w/ sound before the final -i- and this was represented by ogam *A, V* and *I*, spoken as /awi/. MEMOR is a Primitive Irish loan from *memoria*[20] and cannot have been long current.

The second Lewannick stone (467, Fig. 16.2), now in the church, was found in two parts and its present top is missing. Type (d), single-name, it looks to be a little later than 466; late VI.1 or early VI.2. The Latin HI?)C IACIT VLCAGNI was written down the stone. Unusually so, apparently was also the ogam ULCAGNI, but the first try, down the *left* edge, involved a muddle and actually reads UDSAGCI, B-surface and H-surface having become confused, possibly because of writing downwards instead of upwards. The correct second version is given on the right. This is Irish *Ulcagn(us)* already seen in Cornwall on 472. It does not look likely that the inscription was originally any longer than IC or HIC IACIT VLCAGNI, or had another name in the nominative at the start. There is just a chance that a *third* stone outside the churchyard, much damaged, not illustrated but for the moment numbered as 1207, contained a short ogam inscription (single name on its own?).

There are two further type (d) memorials east of the Camel and near the northern coast with similar formulae, 'Of-A here lies, the son of-B'. The large prone awkwardly placed Worthyvale or Slaughterbridge stone, 470 (Fig. 16.3), has two lines LATINI IC IACIT / FILIUS MACARI[21] and on the angle the ogam *LATINI*. Latinus and Macarius are Roman names and the memorial dates to VI.2. Somewhat later (VI.3? around 600?) is the St Endellion pillar or 'Long Cross', reading BROCAGNI IHC IACIT / (.)ADOTTI FILIVS (478). This has been laterally trimmed, the second name's first letter being probably N. Above the vertical two lines is a curved line (p. 294), and above that, a late form of an upright and hooked *chi-rho*. The inscription shows quite a few devolved letter forms. Brocagnus (Primitive Irish *Brocagnas*), 'Little-Badger', is the same name as that of king Brychan (chap. 9); the damaged NADOTTI or RADOTTI suggests nothing elsewhere recorded, but the reading is uncertain (Fig. 16.4).

In the farming district with its sheltered wooded valleys south of Wadebridge, four more inscriptions indicate settlers. The type (d) 457 DVNOCAT↪ HIC IACIT / FILI MESCAGN↪ at Lancarffe near Bodmin (Fig. 15.7) is another that treats an opening genitive as a nominative; 'of-Dunocatus here lies, of-the-son of-

(Above) **Fig. 16.3** The Worthyvale or 'Slaughterbridge' stone, now prone beside the stream. **Above**, the inscription (470) LATINI IC IACIT / FILIVS MACARI; below, ogam *LATINI*. (Photographs: Susanna Thomas.)

(Right) **Fig. 16.4** The 'Long Cross', St Endellion (478) with BROCAGNI IHC IACIT / N(?)ADOTTI FILIVS (type (d)), and hooked *chi-rho* cross over curved line. Drawn *in situ* and from photographs.

Mescagnus'. It shows angle-bar A and horizontal I, with two reversed capitals but no devolved letters; a date of VI.2 is a safe one. Dunocatus (cf. 327 DVNOCATI in Brycheiniog, with ogam, p. 124) is probably Irish; his father's name, a Pr.Ir. diminutive form *Mescagnas.[22] The other three inscriptions (458, 460, 465) are the un-typed sort, all of the shape 'Of-A, (of)-the-son of-B'. Earliest may be the incomplete 465 ANNICV FIL(, inside an oval-topped cartouche, from Lanivet and now in the church; this the Roman *Annicius*, with the *V* as an error for *II* or *I* (*Annicii, Annici*), dated as VI.2. (Fig. 17.15). Just eastward in Cardinham parish are two stones, one preserved in a cross-roads hedge and the other outside the parish church. The former, 460 VAILATHI / FILI VROCHANI, has angle-bar A's and some devolved letters, is topped by a curved line (Fig. 17.14) and is not earlier than VI.3. Both the names are Irish, the Roman letter V being used to represent what, by 600, was possibly an /f/; subsequent versions of these were *Fáelath* 'Howler', perhaps another word implying 'Wolf', and *Fróechán* 'Little-Heather'.[23] The very tall granite pillar by Cardinham church, 458, reads RANOCOR⊢ / FILI MESG⊢ (or MESC⊢), with a large angle-bar A, and above the inscription an, apparently contemporary, deep-cut vertical line that may be the upright of some form of *chi-rho* cross. The second name goes with 457 MESCAGN⊢ at Lancarffe, above; it is difficult to say anything about RANOCORI, if that is the right reading.[24] This is also VI.3, a fairly late sixth-century memorial (Fig. 17.17).

The ten memorials are offered as visible and legible evidence for settlers (and their sons and grandsons) in the north-east part of Cornwall during the sixth century. An origin in Wales can be suggested through the names, Irish or continuing-Roman and including those also recorded in Demetia; and through the epigraphy (the ogam, angle-bar A, horizontal I). None of this can be regarded as indigenous to Dumnonia. The type (d) inscriptions and some primary 'art' indicate Christianity, and both Iustus and Ingenuus may have been priests. The implication that certain find-spots – St Kew, Lanivet, Lewannick, perhaps Cardinham – denote primary Christian sites can be discussed later.

In the overall maps (Figs. 13.3 and 15.1) there are other memorials in south-west Devon. One little group is of very special interest because these inscriptions suggest a second, if minor, Venture to the Interior – a venture that took incomers right across to the desirable land, the western edge of the South Hams, below Dartmoor. Nor was this a slow diffusion to be assigned to the seventh century. It was at least as early as the initial land-takes around the Camel basin.

The Buckland Monachorum stone, 488 (Fig. 16.5), in Tavistock vicarage garden, was found on Roborough Down near Buckland churchtown. It was first inscribed in ogam as *ENABARR*; this has already been examined (p. 237), as an Irish name, and linguistically it is probably VI.1, after 500. The *secondary* use was for the man's son, down the face in three lines; DOBVNN⊢ /FABRI FILII/ ENABARRI 'Of Dobunnus the *faber*, of-the-son of-Enabarrus' (with Latin *faber* as 'craftsman, smith'). The angle-bar A's, horizontal I and 'Of-A of-the-son of-B'

**Fig. 16.5** Tavistock vicarage garden, among shrubs. **Left**, 488, ogam ENABARR (read upwards) and DOBVNNI / FABRI FILII / ENABARRI, with angle-bar A's. **Right**, 492, SABINI FILI / MACCODECHETI, with angle-bar A's and horizontal I's. (Photographs: Susanna Thomas.)

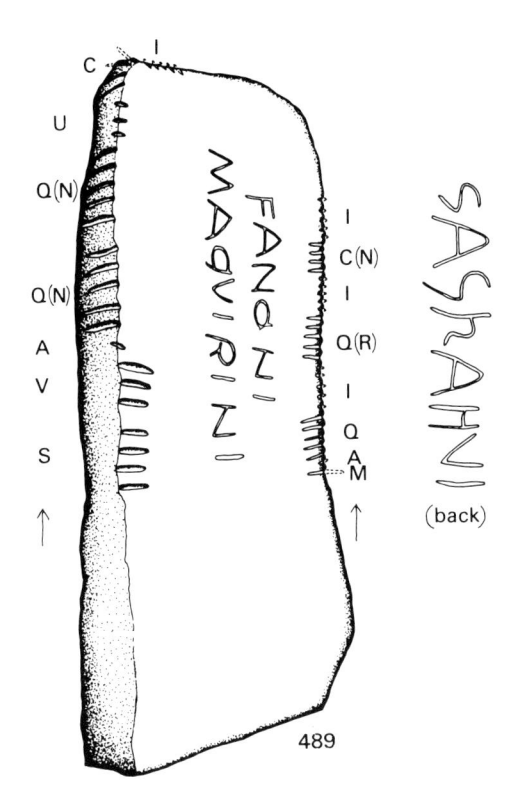

## THE DUMNONIAN INSCRIPTIONS: 'KITTENS IN THE OVEN ...'

**Fig. 16.6** The Fardel, Ivybridge, stone (489) in the British Museum, and drawn from photographs. Primary inscription, FANONI / MAQVI RINI (with unique case of Irish *maqui*, Latinized), has ogam as shown, SWAQQUCI MAQI QICI; bracketed letters show suggested correction as ogam equivalent of the Latin, SWANNUCI (hypocristic form) MAQI RINI. On the back, secondarily, is the single name SAGRANVI.

formulation link this, a generation after *Enabarras* anyhow, to the VI.2 inscriptions in north Cornwall. DOBVNNI, 'of Dobunnus, or Dobunnius', is less obviously Irish.[25] The other stone from Buckland village, also at Tavistock (Fig. 16.5), is 492 SABIN⊢ FIL⊢/MACCODECHET⊢ (angle-bar A, horizontal I, 'Of-A of-the-son of-B') but without ogam, and much the same date (VI.2). Sabinus is Roman, MACCODECHET⊢ an interesting form of an Irish name.[26]

But in this same small-scale movement the would-be settlers pushed south-east a further eleven miles, to Fardel near Ivybridge. The large Fardel stone, 489, is so remarkable a document in the early history of Devon that it seems a great pity that, since being presented in the 1860s, it remains in the basement of the British Museum; at Exeter or Plymouth it would be prominently and properly on display.

It is a proper type (b) bilingual (Fig. 16.6). The face has FANONI / MAQVI RINI – 'Of-F, of-the-son of-R', with letters that may be uncertain but are capitals; ordinary A and no horizontal I. The ogam reads SVAQQUCI MAQI QICI. Since it would be *prima facie* likely that the inscriptions run parallel, the ogam has to be seen as prey to errors; MAQI (*maqʷi* 'of the son') stands, but in the first name the two five-stroke Q's when reversed are five-bar N's – SVANNUCI – and in the second, five-stroke Q should be five-oblique R and the C (4 strokes) is a

267

straight mistake for N – RINI. Primitive Irish *Swannuci*, where the older /sw/ was passing towards the sound of /f/, might have been rendered as FANNVCI; in face, \**Swannucas* must have been a pet-form or hypocoristic of the name Latinized as *Fanonus*, and a reflex is actually seen in Pembrokeshire, 455 FANNVC⊢ (probably VI.2). (The relationship is something like that between 'Johnno' and 'Jacko'.) *Rini* may occur on an ogam inscription (34) in Co. Kilkenny. The inscription has been the subject of previous comments.[27] Another striking feature is that it is the only inscription where the Irish MAQI is rendered not by FILI but by MAQVI (/makwi/) as a Roman-letter equivalent.

On the reverse of the stone, there is a single name, SAGRANVI 'Of-Sagranuus'; it represents Irish *Sagragnas*[28] and is written in relatively devolved lettering (Fig. 16.6). Taking this as a secondary use, it may be VI.2 or even VI.3; the bilingual, longer, inscription then perhaps early VI.2 or even VI.1, certainly early in the sixth century. Between them the Buckland and Fardel inscriptions show us seven personal names, one of which is Roman (*Sabinus*) and six either certainly or probably Irish. As a little group these are Latinate. Some *scriptor* knew the Latin noun *faber*, and (488) the correct FILII for the usual FILI; however, these memorials are not ostensibly Christian, nor is there any primary art. From the early and mid-sixth century they form a rather surprising witness to a minor incursion that, otherwise, left no trace whatsoever.

There are other inscriptions in Devon, east and north of the group, including a few with Roman names. Some date from VI.3 or VII; it is better to reserve discussion for the next chapter since, here, Latinity and Christianity by the late sixth century may be the result of separate inspiration from other regions of sub-Roman Britain. West of an imaginary line from Padstow and Wadebridge down to Fowey, we find mid-Cornwall, and then west Cornwall with the Isles of Scilly. These are imprecise terms for an elongated district, but distributed within it (Fig. 16.7) are a further twenty-five memorials; extant and legible, extant but now illegible, and lost but recorded. There are no ogams, and none that can together match the tight cluster around the Camel basin, but at least five show Irish and/or Roman names within the same inscription-types as those just examined and they have to be seen as intrusive.

A mile or so inland up a small valley ('the Porth stream') that meets the north coast at Trevelgue Porth east of Newquay is the ancient tenement of Rialton, site of an important medieval manor. A large slab of a distinctive close-grained granite must have been brought from the Hensbarrow massif six to ten miles away.[29] It was propping up an outhouse roof at Rialton in the last century and was then built, its top broken off, into a barn of the adjoining farmyard. This is Duchy of Cornwall property and the stone, presented to the Royal Cornwall Museum by HRH The Duke of Cornwall, was removed to Truro in 1991. The vertical inscription is ... F)ILL⊢ TRIBVN⊢, and centred above the *Tribuni* is the word BONEMIMOR⊢; there is no A, but three horizontal I's and (presumably) the

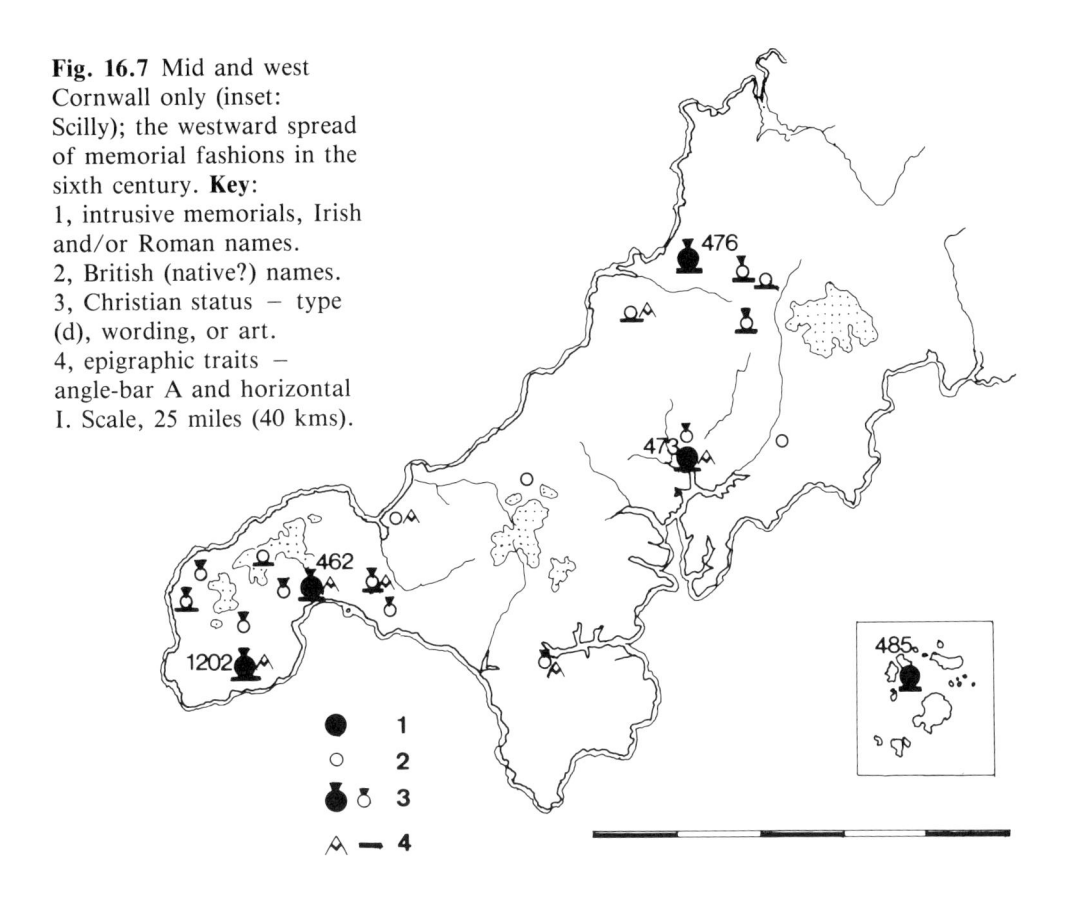

**Fig. 16.7** Mid and west Cornwall only (inset: Scilly); the westward spread of memorial fashions in the sixth century. **Key**: 1, intrusive memorials, Irish and/or Roman names. 2, British (native?) names. 3, Christian status – type (d), wording, or art. 4, epigraphic traits – angle-bar A and horizontal I. Scale, 25 miles (40 kms).

formula 'Of-A, of-the-son of-B'. The letters are confident capitals and the indicated date would be VI.1.

The Rialton stone, 476, has three unusual facets; the epigraphy, the personal name and the situation. BONEMIMOR⊣ is separate, certainly not a name,[30] and is the Gaulish *bonae memoriae*, equivalent to our own 'In Loving Memory (of)', part of the vocabulary associated with the EL (extended Latinate) inscriptions. Since it normally occurs in longer formulae like *Hic quiescit in pace bone memorie X qui vixit annos ...* and since the spelling is erratic it may have been included as an expression that had been heard, rather than read. *Memorie*, long final -*e* (/ay/), for *memoriae* is acceptable for fifth-century provincial Latin; *mimori* would not be (see Fig. 16.8).

Was *Tribunus* a name, or a rank? It did occur as the former; there had been a Tribunus, an envoy from North Africa, and there is a memorial from Lyon with HIC IACET NN (= nomine) TRIBV/NVS, etc.[31] Following the legionary tribunes of the early Empire there were the Late Roman *tribuni* holding administrative ranks into the fifth century and the 'tribune' who met St Germanus of Auxerre in southeast Britain in AD 429 may have been a civilian official, *tribunus ac notarius*, and not 'a man of high military rank'.[32] We might prefer it here as a personal name. A very few Insular inscriptions do exhibit titles – 488 DOBVNNI the *faber*; from

**Fig. 16.8** The Rialton granite slab, now in Royal Cornwall Museum, Truro; top (left) is missing. It reads (476) BONEMIMORI / (missing name) F)ILLI TRIBVNI — memorial of a son of king Triphun, *Tribunus*?

north-west Wales 386 MELI, *medicus*, and 394 MAGLI, *magistratus* (to say nothing of *sacerdotes* and *presbyteres*) — but all of them accompany proper names.

It is at least possible that the subject of 476, his name so annoyingly missing,[33] was a son of *Tribunus* (Triphun), king of Demetia. The dates accord. In the Demetian succession, Triphun preceded Aircol (see p. 55) whose likely son Voteporix, the *Vortipor* of Gildas and the next king, was alive *circa* 540 and was commemorated by the VI.2 stone 358 VOTEPORIGIS. A son of Triphun could have lived until around 520–30 (in VI.1; the epigraphically suitable date of stone 476). The estate of Rialton is sheltered, rich and desirable and as *Rieltone* with 300 acres pasture, 60 of woodland and land for 30 ploughs it is listed in Domesday for St Petroc's large monastery at Bodmin. With English -*ton* excised, the name is *Riel, and this does occur in a record of 1302 (Treneglos, *iuxta Ryel*). There are insufficient dated forms to allow certainty,[34] but a suspicion that the word goes back to a British adjectival *rigal-* 'kingly, royal' (cf. the west Cornish sixth-century name 468 RIALOBRANI, with -*g*- lenited or lost). Was this particular aristocratic settler's estate called 'the Kingly one's land', if only satirically by those who knew that their neighbour's father had been a Demetian king?

Across Cornwall, outside Truro and now by the church of St Clement is a huge (nearly 11 feet) granite monolith (Fig. 17.17), found in a nearby glebe field, with a primary inscription (473) VITAL⊢ FILI TORRICI (one vertical line, angle-bar A, horizontal I, 'of-A, of-the-son of-B'). This can be dated as VI.1 (or perhaps early in VI.2); the pillar was re-used, probably before 600, for a shorter and smaller secondary inscription read as IGNIOC. A *third* use, when both faces of the top end were cut back in the twelfth century to make relief ringed crosses, removed the opening of what must have been ... IGNI OC (for '(Stone) of-*Cunignus*' (or similar name), '*oc*' (for *ic* = *hic* 'here')). *Vitalis* is a Roman name, one of some distinction;[35] *Torricus* (or *Torricius*) is not, and it is hard to see what could be Latinized thus.

In the west of Cornwall the three intrusive inscriptions are all late in the sixth century — a general dating might be VI.2/VI.3 — and though the personal names are apparently Irish, not Dumnonian, they are too few and too far removed in time from any putative early fifth-century (Uí Liatháin?) settlement to be connected with such. They might be regarded as commemorating immigrants, or descendants of immigrants, who had gone forty or fifty miles westward. Two of them are from the main agrarian belt of the Land's End peninsula, the southern coastal shelf. Just outside Penzance at Bleu Bridge (*plu* = parish), Gulval, stands the recently re-sited QVENATAVC⊢ IC / DINVI FILĪVS (462). This must count as type (d). The cutter began with over-large letters and at the end of the vertical first line had to put the ⊢ above the C and squeeze in a tiny raised IC (*ic iacit*). The A's are angle-bar, the second N is H-shaped and final S reversed. *Quenatauci* is Irish, with Pr.Ir. *quen-* 'head'. The Latinized genitive DINVI, for a spoken /dinawi/ — cf. INGENVI and IGENAWI earlier — is certainly not a Roman name and suggests a slightly earlier Primitive Irish *Denawas*[36] (Fig. 16.9).

The inscribed stone found at Vellansajer, St Buryan (Fig. 17.8) now lies below shrubs in a private garden; use as a gatepost, an outhouse lintel and the mount for a small cannon has not improved it and the reading is incomplete.[37] The two vertical lines are partly in a cartouche, with an upper inner compartment that appears to contain unsure versions of A and W, *alpha* and *omega*. The inscription (1202) is, upper line, EVOCAT.., with an unusual ligature of T and final ⊢; lower line, CA(T?).., the space allowing perhaps a FILI. The A's are angle-bar. The first name must suggest 19 *IVACATTOS* (ogam, Co. Kildare).[38]

The stone from the Isles of Scilly forms part of an archway paving at the ruined St Nicholas Priory church in Tresco Abbey gardens. It is incomplete, and the lettering much eroded. Older readings centred upon ... THI FILI/... COC⊢ (485). A new and very careful attempt (Fig. 16.10), a last-chance effort, was made in 1990[39] and though any reading is now inconclusive it might be ... THI FILI and (lower line) ... COL⊢NI (Fig. ). The third letter is certainly no known form of G and an I, horizontally, may have been squeezed in between a curved L and a relatively certain NI. If so this will suggest the Irish compound name, Pr.Ir. *Maqqi-Colini*, represented by (Roman letters) MAQVICOLINE in the late fifth-century Wroxeter inscription.[40]

These few inscriptions from mid-Cornwall and the far west, while individually interesting, have to be seen as not really forming part of the primary, inscriptional or epigraphic, evidence for a *circa* 500 settlement from Demetia in eastern Cornwall with an early offshoot in south-west Devon. What the map, Fig. 16.7, may show is mainly the spread of a fashion for memorials — and they may nearly all be Christian memorials — during VI.2 and VI.3, the mid and later sixth century. The diffusion of horizontal I and angle-bar A can be clearly indicated. The 'native response' — that is, the appearance of inscribed stones on which the names can be called Dumnonian (as opposed to Demetian Irish, or Demetian-

# THE DUMNONIAN INSCRIPTIONS: 'KITTENS IN THE OVEN ...'

**Fig. 16.9** The Bleu Bridge stone, 462; an 1890s view by Gibson of Penzance, by the Gulval stream (stone is now re-sited in overgrown hedge nearby). Note, in the QVENATAVCI IC / DINVI FILIVS of this defective type (d) memorial, angle-bar A, horizontal I and the reversed S (cf. Fig. 15.7).

favoured Roman) – involves memorials from other parts of Dumnonia, memorials whose dates take us into the earlier seventh century.

Before looking at them in detail we might usefully notice how the original sitings of these memorials (insofar as we can establish them now) were only occasionally at what were, or were to become, primary Christian locations. About half of the stones were first found standing somewhere in the landscape. We may well suspect that they were erected where the deceased person's family or clan had settled and, for associated thoughts, we can hark back to chapter 2. A memorial may have been put up on a hillock by someone's home, or on a customary border of a land-holding; the 'entrance' to his estate, the sixth-century equivalent of lodge gates with the family heraldry displayed in stone. At deeper levels of popular belief, did the sight of a tall pillar bearing the name of a prominent and powerful ancestor

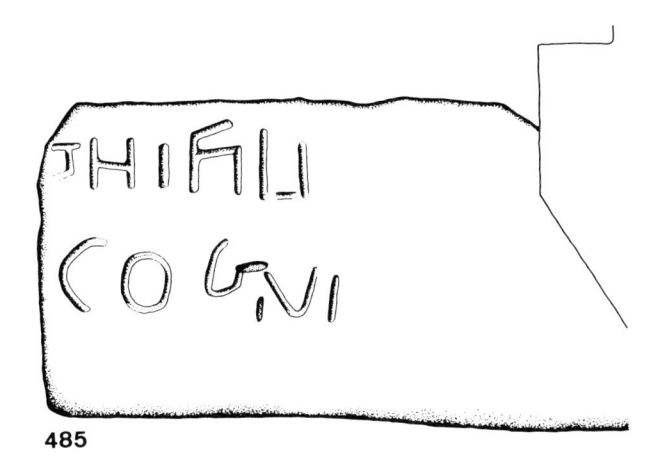

**Fig. 16.10** Tresco, Isles of Scilly; broken granite slab (485) now partly below arched doorway of St Nicholas's priory church (the 'Abbey'). This almost entirely eroded stone is drawn from casts and rubbings; it appears to read ...(T?)HI FILI/...CO(L? horizontal I?) NI (...*thi fili ... colini?*).

ever suggest that the man's spirit continued to reside *within* the stone, there to guard his descendants' acres and to maintain their claim in a legible form? In exploring spatial relationship between overtly Christian memorials and the first Christian sites, we must not lose sight of such older and non-Christian possibilities.

# References

1. Hence the mysterious 'LSSA' instead of 'FSA'.
2. *JRIC* 3 (1868–70); 103–7, a medieval slab at Bodmin, and 318, the Worthyvale LATINI stone (470).
3. William Iago, coincidentally, had like R. A. S. Macalister graduated at St John's College, Cambridge.
4. *Old Cornish Crosses* (Pollard, Truro 1896); 'great assistance ... from the Rev. W. Iago' is noted in the preface.
5. J. T. Blight, *Churches of West Cornwall* (Oxford 1865), 120 ff; 'Two Days in Cornwall with the Cambrian Archaeological Association'.
6. Separate programme of *Forty-Ninth Annual Meeting, to be held at Launceston ... Illustrated programme* (ed. J. Romilly Allen; CAA, London 1895).
7. *Edidit* Aemilius Hübner (Reimer, Berlin: Williams & Norgate, London 1876).
8. *AC* (5th ser., vol.12) 1895, 50–60, 7 pp.illus.; much of this was reproduced in *Victoria County History of Cornwall*, I (ed. W. Page, London 1906), also with tiny illustrations.
9. *AC* 1929, 179–96, with drawings and some photographs.
10. *The Archaeology of Cornwall and Scilly* (Methuen, London 1932). Hencken, a prehistorian who took his BA and (1929) Ph.D. at Cambridge, was generally ahead of his times. With a few noble exceptions (Crawford, Fox, Wheeler), the methodology of prehistory was not applied to post-Roman monuments.
11. As later defined in *LHEB*, chap.I.
12. See his essay in *ECNE*.

13. His published 1974 Holbeche Corfield Lecture (see Radford 1975) summarizes many of his findings.
14. Charles Thomas, *Christian Antiquities of Camborne* (Warne, St Austell 1967).
15. Same author, *Phillack Church. An Illustrated History* (British Publishing Co., Gloucester 1961, and reprints); *Gwithian. Notes on the Church, Parish, etc.* (Earle, Redruth 1964, and reprints).
16. Padel 1976–7; Padel 1985; Preston-Jones & Rose 1986: Olson 1989; Preston-Jones 1992 – these are only the main items.
17. *Cornish Studies* 16, for 1988 (1989) (= Tintagel Papers); Nowakowski & Thomas 1990; id., 1992; general summary at popular level, Thomas 1993.
18. With an Imperial name; *PLRE* i.831–8, ii.1001–6 (49 exx.).
19. Thomas 1993, chap.2, and (*passim*) the evidence that the Haven was used as a landing-place in the sixth century.
20. *LHEB*, 141; McManus, *Guide*, 203 s.v. MEMOR; RIA Dict. M, 98, s.v. *mem(m)ra*, and Vendryes, *Lexique ... MNOP* (1960), M-34 s.v. *membre*. It does not figure on the contemporary Irish inscriptions.
21. In the past, -ARI was read as ATRI, then 'Atry', and 'King Arthur' was dragged into a Last Battle here; hence Slaughterbridge. For the (Greek) *Macarius*, mainly eastern and fourth–fifth cents., see *PLRE* i.524–5, ii.696–7; *Latinus*, ibid. i.495–6, ii.657.
22. In 457 *Mescagni* and 458 *Mesci* (?), there may be an element of the sense of 'excitement, confusion, drunken exaltation'; cf. Vendryes, *Lexique ... MNOP* (1960), M-41, M-42. The proximity of PrIr. \**Mescas* and (dimin.) \**Mescagnas* would suggest one family.
23. McManus, *Guide*, 6.11, 6.28, 6.29, discusses *Fróech, Fróechán*.
24. The initial R- is peculiar; cf., tentatively, the TARICORO of the Aberhydfer stone (p. 119), which must be an Irish name.
25. This neatly illustrates the predicament of some isolated *scriptor*; since his V had to reproduce /w/ and shades of vowel /u/, initial P meant only /p/ and F was confined to fricatives – /f/ and, in 489, perhaps a development of Irish /sw/ – B was the only letter to represent sounds heard as voiced labials. For this \**Dobunn(ius)*, obviously we think of PrIr. (156) DOVVINIAS – McManus, *Guide*, s.n.
26. McManus, *Guide*, 202–3 s.nn., full discussion of various forms.
27. Thurneysen, in *ZCP* 12 (1918), 411–12; Eoin MacNeill, in *Ériu* 11 (1932), 133–5 (with '... cannot offer any explanation of the name *Rini*'). MacNeill also saw this as pointing to Irish settlers 'who preserved the Irish language *or some tradition of it*' (my initials; again, this is not the same as full bilingualism).
28. McManus, *Guide*, 204, s.n.
29. I owe the petrological identification to Mr Courtney Smale, who recognized the variety of granite at once. It needed eight men, a lorry, planks and rollers, etc., to get the stone from Rialton to Truro; it weighs about ·8 of a ton. When, why and how was it dragged from Hensbarrow across country to Rialton?
30. As, unhappily, Macalister thought (*CIIC*.i); *memoria* in this sense differs from that of 466 (and 358) MEMORIA referring to an actual burial and perhaps visible superstructure. The older (Classical) usage is apparent in (CIL.877.58) an epitaph, AD CONSERVANDAM MEMORIAM TANTAE BENEVOLENTIAE 'to the keeping alive of the memory of such great good-will'.
31. *PLRE* ii.1126; I am very grateful to Jeremy Knight (*in litt.*, 1991) for his helpful discussion of what *Tribunus* here might mean.
32. Constantius, *Vita S. Germani*, cap.15, translated by F. R. Hoare, *The Western Fathers* (Sheed & Ward, 1954), at 298.

33. When the stone was still *in situ*, )LLI TRIBVNI could be read; on removal, with mortar cleaned off, )ILLI is clearly visible. A reconstruction as ... *ILLI TRIBVNI* 'Of ... *illius* the tribune' might be argued. I prefer 'Of-A; *filli Tribuni*' on balance for several reasons. Names in *-ill(i)us* are rare — cf.327 TVRPILLI, the sole instance? *Tribunus* ( = Triphun) is acceptable as an inscriptional form. F)ILLI, for *fili* or *filii*, is unusual but by no means unlikely alongside MIMORI, and the tip of the F is, I think, detectable before ILLI on the stone. The pillar may well have originated as a tall menhir elsewhere and the nature of the rock makes it unlikely that only its tip is missing; more probably a metre or so is lacking above the transverse fracture, enough for a disyllabic name at least before F)ILLI.
34. Early forms of 'Rialton' contain *\*riel* rather than *\*rial* (the latter word might be reconstructed from Middle Cornish *ryal*, *real* 'kingly'). The objection is not insuperable because the early forms are relatively late (1086, *c*.1270 Rielton: 1333 Rialton). The suggestion that it might have signified 'a ruler's residence, or capital estate' was in fact made by W. M. M. Picken, *DCNQ* 30.ii (1965), 39 (but without reference to TRIBVNI in any form). The point is not so much what this estate *was*, but what others may have called it.
35. *PLRE* i.970, ii.1177 (*\*Torricus* is presumably Celtic). Repeated inspections — the stone is a half-mile from his house — suggest to this writer that the secondary use represents addition, using slightly smaller letters, of a grandson's name; the whole could be restored as '(Stone of) ...ign(us), OC ( = *ic*, (*h*)*ic*, or for (*h*)*oc in tumulo*), (son) of-Vitalis FILI TORRICI'. Before the cutting-back of the top for a medieval cross-head, there cannot have been much room above VITALI.
36. Assuming that from the context DINVI is more likely to represent an Irish than a British name, see McManus, *Guide*, 203 on 1 MENUEH (Galway: VII or early VIII, a rare instance of book-hand) and its development from *\*Minawicas*. A (divine ?) name DENA- seems to figure in 279 DENAVECA (Waterford, ogam). *\*Denawas* or *\*Dinawas* may be reflected here as DINVI and possibly OIr. *Dinnu* (*CGH*, 589).
37. Author's note, *CA* 19 (1980), 107–9.
38. If not also the Silchester, Berks., ogam with *EBICATO(S)*, *CIIC* i. 496; but for its authenticity see Fulford and Selwood, 'The Silchester ogham stone; a reconsideration', *Antiquity* 54 (1980), 95.
39. By Jeanette Ratcliffe and Rosemary Robertson, Cornwall Archaeological Unit, who kindly provided rubbings and drawings and have allowed reproduction of this figure.
40. McManus, *Guide*, 76–7, with further references (Appendix 2; xxi).

## 17

## *The Dumnonian Inscriptions: The Native Response*

ANY IMPRESSION THAT the sixth-century settlers from Wales were commemorated, and *only* commemorated, through inscriptions having Irish and continuing-Roman names would be too rigid. This cannot have been entirely so, any more than the converse; that all other recorded Celtic names were those of native Dumnonians. In moving onward from epigraphic evidence to historical inference we meet this problem. So far, memorials with ogam, Irish names, Roman names and likely Demetian features have been presented as intrusive, because they lack obvious antecedents in fifth-century Dumnonia and also because distribution in time and space indicates a degree of cultural unity. The so-called intrusive characteristics are linked. 466 *Ingenui*, 484 *Iusti* and 470 *Latini* show Roman names repeated in ogam; vertical disposition and final horizontal I is not foreshadowed by the *Cunaide* memorial or the extended Latinate group; and the Fardel stone (489) shows three Irish names, ogam, and the Irish words MAQI and MAQVI. None of this proves, of course, that there were not also incomers from Wales who bore British names. At the period the vernaculars of Wales, Dumnonia and North Britain were regional forms of what had been one language, British.

Had anything resembling modern-day 'Neo-British' differentiations arisen? When a Rugby team from Wales visits Cornwall it is assumed that some players will be called Ieuan, Dafydd or Haydn, just as the home team may contain Perran, Treve and Garfield.[1] The assumption is not upset by the fact that either side might also have Roy, Wayne and Nigel. For the sixth century all we can say is that, while between them the inscribed stones of Demetia and Dumnonia give us a long list of purely British personal names, there is no overlap. We cannot produce a *British* equivalent to the Irish-Roman map, Fig. 15.4, showing the repetition of names as between Demetia (with Brycheiniog) and Dumnonia. Not a single match can be found. Common elements in names, like *clut-* or *-ual*, are there because of a common origin in (Roman-period) British. We might suspect that by post-Roman times some genuine regional preferences had become established. The chances of onomastic overlap, that British names on Dumnonian stones are Demetian, seem too small to vitiate conclusions; as a margin of error, ten per cent is a generous estimate.

In distinguishing native from intrusive memorials there will be a preliminary observation that, as a class, native memorials with British names appear to be later and may therefore also be culturally secondary – copies of originals. Between thirty and thirty-five monuments are involved. Provided that agreement were possible as to which characteristics are significant and which are not[2] it is theoretically possible to construct a data-base, and subject it to programmes of multivariate analysis. The writer believes that too many characteristics are either now wildly variable or frankly indeterminable, and that intuitive conclusions serve just as well if not better; the largest single characteristic is that of the forms of individual letters and, at the moment, there may be radical disagreement in classifying and time-ordering these.[3]

We know of twenty-one Dumnonian memorials, eight in east Cornwall and Devon, six in mid-Cornwall and seven in west Cornwall. Four more (two on Lundy, two on the north side of Exmoor) fall outwith the main distribution and will be separately noticed. A further four, all in west Cornwall, probably belong to this category but are now illegible, fragmentary or lost. Finally five stones (two from Devon and three from west Cornwall) can be dated to after 600, represent the latest phase of the whole fashion and (apart from 1048, at Madron) show only single names.

In the main group of twenty-one stones a preliminary glance reveals several characteristics that, set against those examined in the discussion of intrusive memorials, point to typological devolution and relative lateness. Only eight, if as many, could be defined as 'type (d)', some with no more than IC (or OC); the rest have the formula 'Of-A, of-the-son of-B', sometimes breaking down grammatically. Epigraphically, while the fully established preference for verticality continues (with horizontal I on twelve memorials), angle-bar A becomes uncommon (four examples), On the five seventh-century inscriptions, both these letter-variants have disappeared. On the other hand 'art' in the sense of any incised motif or line, Christian or not, other than proper lettering occurs on five stones and also on three of the seventh-century memorials.

Even on a map with so few symbols (Fig. 17.1) the archaeological model would be specific diffusion of a new and desirable artefact (a way of commemorating socially prominent parents) followed by limited and peripheral imitation. This may be exactly what the artefacts allow us to suppose. Six miles south-east from Lewannick stands the granite pillar (486) found in 1891 in the adjoining rectory garden and now re-erected in the parish churchyard at Southill or South Hill. It reads CVMRECIN⊣ / FILI MAVC⊣ ('Of-C, of-the-son of-M'; Fig. 17.14) topped by a curved line, below a higher curved line acting as base of a *chi-rho* cross (with a decidedly open *rho*, p. 199).[4] The forms of M, N and R and the general character together suggest late VI.2 or VI.3. The first name is from British *\*Comreginos*, perhaps 'Very-Proud-one'. As mentioned earlier the South Hill dedication to St Samson is interesting, at a now-isolated place that was the mother-church of Callington (and may have been a pre-Norman minster), but insufficient to allow any connection with the historic Samson and his Dumnonian visit (p. 226).

278

THE DUMNONIAN INSCRIPTIONS: THE NATIVE RESPONSE

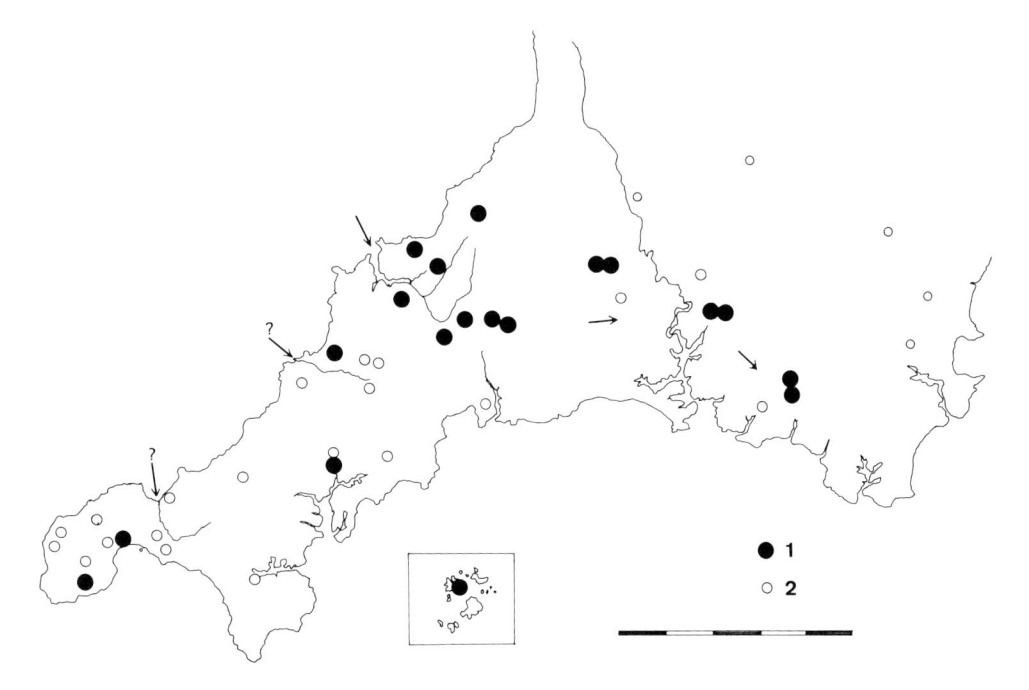

Fig. 17.1 Dumnonian inscriptions; basic archaeological model on 'flat' map of all intrusive (Demetian-originating?) memorials (**key**: 1, with points of access arrowed), and the native-response memorials, partly peripheral to the intrusive clusters (**key**: 2). 479 *Cunaide* and some illegible stones are omitted. Scale, 25 miles (40 kms).

In south Cornwall and now re-sited alongside the main road, a mile and a half north-west of Fowey Church (?*Langorthou*) stands the tall granite menhir – and it probably *was* a prehistoric menhir – called 'the Castle Dore stone' and 'the Tristan stone'. More romantic prose has been written about it than about any other memorial in Dumnonia (Fig. 17.17). The monument, despite its size and great weight, has been moved several times (within a small area). Any connection with the adjoining Iron Age hill-slope fort called 'Castle Dore', where the pre-war excavations claimed to have found large post-Roman timber buildings that might have validated a folkloristic palace of 'King Mark', is irrelevant.[5] On the reverse (south) upper face a large and eroded 'T' in coarse relief (which may or may not be a Christian symbol called a *Tau* cross) could well be both later than, and unconnected with, the inscription.

This, in two vertical lines, is type (d). It reads (487) DRVSTĀNVS HIC IACIT / CVNOMORI FILIVS. In the top line the D is reversed, the open A and N ligatured; in the lower, the M is inverted (like a 'W'). In capitals, it must have been quite legible for centuries (Fig. 17.2). *Drustan-* is the name that became 'Tristan', making this Cornish record of it (the likely date being late VI.2 or VI.3[6]) far and away the earliest, and therefore adding weight to the well-argued idea[7] that the nucleus of

279

*DRVSTANVS HIC IACIT*
*CVNOWORI FILIVS*

**Fig. 17.2** The Castle Dore stone (487); detail of the inscription, drawn *in situ*. With ligatures and reversed letters, it reads DRVSTANVS HIC IACIT / CVNOMORI FILIVS (type (d), VI.2 or VI.3?).

a romance linking Tristan and Yseult or Isolt, *Drustanus* and *\*Adsiltia*,[8] was pre-Norman Cornish.

The inscription may have used a few eccentric letters but it is in correct Latin; A lies here, of-B the son. CVNOMORI is Latinized genitive either of *\*Cuno-mori* 'Hound, Wolf, of-the-sea' or (with vowel-change) *\*Cuno-māros* 'Great Hound'.[9] Legible display of this inscription in post-Roman centuries allowed readers to offer their own deductions, the latest example of which is implied by Leland's note that 'Sum say that *Conan* had a sun caullid *Tristrame*' (p. 250). Visitors from Brittany landing at Fowey are likely to have been shown this stone. The monk Wrmonoc, who wrote the late-ninth-century Life of St Paul Aurelian, eponym of St Pol-de-Léon, had his hero crossing Cornwall in an episode that borrows much from the *Vita Samsonis*.[10] Somewhere in the Fowey area, Paul is made to meet the king of Dumnonia, a man called *Marcus* ('Mark'), *quem alio nomine Quonomorium vocant* 'whom people call by another name, Quonomorius'. In the *Tristan* legend, Tristan is the nephew of Mark king of Cornwall, and the original tale may have depicted him as a son who goes to fetch a young bride for his widowed father and then falls in love with her. The stone says that Drustanus was the son of *Cunomori*. Therefore, it was argued, Mark and *Cunomori* (*Quonomorius*) are alternative names for the same person. A Breton cleric like Wrmonoc, intent on writing a good colourful *Vita* for a saint whose actual history was sketchy in the extreme, would have the added excitement of knowing that there was another local king in sixth-century Brittany with the same name; he figures as *Chonomoris* in Gregory of Tours' History of the Franks and very briefly as *Commorus* (var. *Comorus*) in the Life of St Samson.[11] How if at all the supposed Dumnonian king *Kynwawr* (<*\*Cuno-maros*?) of the Welsh genealogies[12] fits into this is unclear, but also immaterial. Much more interesting would be a deduction that as early as the 880s a Breton writer, who may not himself have visited Cornwall from Landévennec but could well have met others who had done so, believed in a link between a former Cornish king *Marcus* and the legible name *Drustanus*; Mark and Tristan. Such a connection must take Dumnonia's one great legacy to medieval European letters, the romance of *Tristan*, back to the ninth century and firmly within a Cornish milieu.

These are the only two Dumnonian stones around the larger Demetian cluster (Fig. 15.2). Three others, two with inscriptions of the shape 'Of-A, of-the-son of-B', adjoin the narrower area of that early venturous settlement in south-west Devon. Found near Tavistock church, 493 NEPRANI / FILI CONBEVI has as its second name a form, and the date here is probably VI.3, of British *Cunobiuos* 'Quick, or Lively, Hound', the Old Welsh name *Conbiu*.[13] An inscription on a tall pillar somewhere in Buckland parish, 1208, certainly exists even though barely legible.[14] It is just possible to think that it may be type (d) because of starting with IC (the C reversed) and some individual letters (capitals) can be made out. When we continue past Fardel eastward around the southern skirts of Dartmoor, there is a stone now prone in the church porch at Lustleigh, itself a site of some interest.[15] The inscription exhibits both angle-bar A (turned sideways) and horizontal I, is late VI.3 if not slightly after 600, and contains two British personal names; 490 DATVIDOC⊢ / CONHINOC⊢ FILI (the 'FILI' is barely visible). These are from *Cuno-senacos*[16] and *Date-uidacos*, much later the Welsh *dedwyddach* 'lucky, fortunate'.[17] Lastly there is an inscription, once at Bowden House near Totnes, now lost, recorded by Emil Hübner and since then overlooked. Hübner had to take his drawing from an eighteenth century source (Sir John Rhŷs did not see the stone and Macalister omitted it from *CIIC*.i). The inscription (1210) is not wholly irrecoverable (Fig. 17.3); it is pretty clearly of the form 'Of-A, of-the-son, B' and might tentatively be restored as a three-line VALCI / FIL⊢ V.../ ANV̄S, with NV ligatured – note the angle-bar A and horizontal ⊢, indications that a genuine inscription was being sketched. (It is not impossible that the second name was *Vettanus* or less plausibly *Veddanus*;[18] neither name is very informative.)

Two further Devonshire stones contain Roman names, but must both be dated as VI.3; on balance, it may be less likely that they go with the Demetian group than that these are instances of late, but native, Dumnonian inscriptions. The Sourton Cross, which stands incongruously – one hopes, safely – by the large new roundabout at the west end of the Okehampton bypass, is an extremely worn granite pillar whose top was re-shaped and ornamented as a wayside Latin cross in the twelfth or thirteenth century. Macalister read it as PRINCIP⊢ / IVRIVCI / AVDETI (491). Previous suggestions that it commemorates *princeps* 'a prince' would meet the objections voiced in the case of 476 TRIBVNI (p. 270); a title or descriptive word unaccompanied by a name. Alternatively the first word *is* a name, Latin *Principius*.[19] In the last century the inscription was slightly less eroded, and Baring-Gould and Iago were able to read and draw FILIV. (*filius*). The second name is AVDETI; 'of Aude(n)tius'.[20] Above the vertical three lines is a small *chi-rho* cross, the *rho*-hook reversed, standing on a line (cf. Fig.17.16). Much further east, a large two-part block of granite built into East Ogwell parish church[21] has been read as 1209 CAOCI FIL⊢ / POPLIC⊢ (horizontal I, but capitals, and no ligatures; perhaps late VI.2?). The second name is seen as the Roman *Public(i)us*, which gave later Welsh Peblig.

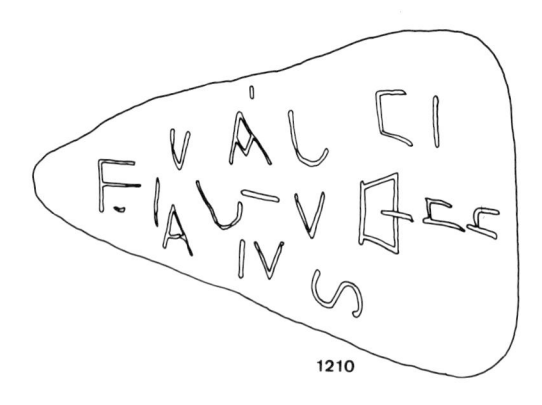

**Fig. 17.3** The lost inscription (1210) from Bowden House, Totnes; Emil Hübner's drawing (*Inscriptiones* ... (1876), no.30). It may have read VALCI / FIL⌐ VETT/A̅N̅V̅S̅.

The Dumnonian inscriptions of mid-Cornwall start with three, all fairly close together, in the St Columb area and thus about twelve miles south-west from the Camel basin. Outside St Columb Major church porch stands a rectangular slab of smooth but extremely coarse-grained local granite. It was found in use as a churchyard gate-post, and on both upper faces are vestigial, angular medieval crosses produced by crude relief-work. When Macalister saw this stone he must have been directed, but was not guided; and, extraordinarily, read and published the *wrong* face (as *CIIC*. i, 475). His IA/CON/IVS does not exist; there are certainly marks, but they are either flaws or the scars of pegmatite crystals. Faint traces of lettering on the reverse face were noted long ago.[22] All that can now be made out (Fig.17.4) is that the inscription was in two vertical lines, and contained ... ADO. ... / ...FIL⌐( ... ? (only the FIL is really certain).

Not far off, and built into the front of a farm outhouse at Bosworgey, an inscription on a very large granite upright was only discovered recently.[23] So far it seems to have defeated interpreters. It is none the less legible (Fig.17.4), despite slight damage resulting from a former existence as a gate-post, and a full reading was made in 1992.[24] It says (1206) DOVITH⌐ ⌐C / FILIVS DOCIDC⌐. Though the C of the 'IC' is reversed, this makes it a type (d) memorial. The first name, *Dovith(us)*, is now represented by Welsh *dofydd* (which, as '*Dofydd*', is one of many synonyms for 'God, *Dominus*, The Lord'). Here a much older secular sense of 'Tamer, Subduer, Lord' is to be seen.[25] The second name suggests a reduplicated *\*Doci-doc(us)*.[26] Standing by the mission-church (St Francis) at Indian Queens is a worn granite stone with CRV̅ARIG⌐ HIC (IACIT? ... (474); this too is type (d) but if there was a second name it is buried and lost, and any lettering becomes illegible after the faint C of HIC (Fig.17.5).

Two of the other three mid-Cornwall inscriptions provide no less than six British names. Built into Cubert church, near the north coast, is a long tapering boulder (in the west wall of the tower, low down) with (477) CONETOC⌐ / FILI TEGERNO /MAL⌐ (Fig.17.17 – angle-bar A, horizontal I's, 'Of-A of-the-son of-B' and

## THE DUMNONIAN INSCRIPTIONS: THE NATIVE RESPONSE

**Fig. 17.4** Two memorials from St Columb Major, mid-Cornwall, drawn *in situ* (1992). **Left**, Bosworgey, pillar in farm-shed (1206) – note peculiar (type (d)) IC, with horizontal I and reversed C. **Right**, by porch of parish church (475; but reverse of Macalister's very doubtful 475 on opposite face). Both have been used as gate-posts; 1206 has an upper battered area, 475 a (twelfth-century?) cross added.

**Fig. 17.5** Memorials from (**left**), St Columb Major, Indian Queens (now by St Francis mission church), CRVARIGI HIC IA(CIT) (474); **right**, Madron, the 'Men Scryfys', RIALOBRANI / CVNOVALI FILI (468) – the small inserted linear cross appears to be an early addition.

several devolved capitals; probably in VI.3). In the first name the internal -T- and -C- represent (by now, lenited) D and G, pointing to *Cune-dagos* 'Good-Hound'[27] while the father's name, *Tigerno-maglos*, surfaces briefly in the *Vita Samsonis* as also that of a bishop to whom the author addressed his Prologue.[28] Similarly built into another church (Cuby, mother-church of Tregony) is a red-granite slab with a long inscription; 461 NONNITA / ERCILIVI / RICATI TRIS FILI / ERCILINCI '(Memorial of) *Nonnita* (fem.), *Erciliuus* (masc.), *Ricatus* (masc.), three children (*tris fili* = *tres filii*) of *Ercilingus*.' (Fig. 17.14). There is a curved

283

line above the four-line vertical inscription, itself a poignant witness to some tragedy late in the sixth century. The inscription is VI.3; N is written as H throughout, the A is inverted and there are a few ligatures. As to the names, *Nonnita* (nominative) is a British feminine; *Erci-liuus* and *Erci-lingus* (<*lengus*) son and father, contain a word meaning 'grey, speckled, etc.' (Welsh *erch*) and British **liuo*, Old Cornish *liu* 'colour'; *Ricatus* goes back to **Rigo-catus* ('kingly' and 'battle').[29] The last inscription is the secondary, smaller one on the tall St Clement stone (473), with ... IGNI OC; its British character is indicated by the diminutive ending *-ign-* (as against Irish *-agnas*, in *Broc(c)agnas*, etc.).

The seven west Cornwall inscriptions are scattered, three being perhaps type (d) and the rest the 'Of-A' variety. A stone from the fabric of Redruth parish church was seen and drawn, albeit as a very tiny sketch, by Dr William Borlase in 1740.[30] Borlase was familiar with such monuments, noted this one as being 3 ft 6 ins long and 10 ins wide, and was able to make out some of the letters (Fig.17.7). A cautious reconstruction would be (1205) MAVORI FI(LI / VITO ... (for *Vitori*?); there is a Roman name *Mavortius*,[31] but a closer match would be that of one of the *sacerdotes, Mavorius*, on the longer Kirkmadrine inscription (516), itself perhaps Gaulish.[32] South from here and on the west side of the Lizard peninsula at Mawgan in Meneage is the pillar called Mawgan Cross. It is now extremely hard to read at all, though Iago was able to make rubbings from it in the last century. Macalister made out (469) CNEGVMI FILI / GENAIVS, the A being an angle-bar one. There are certainly some (contemporary) designs above the vertical two-line inscription; whether they make up (so Macalister) a fantastic *alpha*, a wide *M* (for 'Maria') and a fantastic *omega* is open to question. NE is ligatured, the letters (save for M) are capitals and a date of VI.3 is suggested. The second name is unidentified; *Cnegumi* may be for *Cone-* (<*Cune-*) with an unusual syncope, the second element being uncertain.[33]

Closer to the 'neck' of west Cornwall, the narrowing between Hayle estuary on the north and Mounts Bay on the south, a much-ruined stone (once a gatepost) at Treveneague, St Hilary, was both seen and drawn in the late nineteenth century. It is possible to say that it was vertical, in two lines, contained angle-bar A and probably horizontal and widely-spaced capitals; that it may have been type (d); and that its date might have been VI.2 or VI.3. Beyond that lies the difficulty in re-assembling the actual names from the surviving drawing (Iago's). The first line (482) seems to end in IC, preceded by FILI(?), preceded by the name which began with N. The second line reads NEMIAVS and it is possible that this contained a ligature (NEMIANVS); Fig.17.8.[34]

The Phillack stone (Fig.17.6) was found in the church foundations during the 1856 restorations and stands against the vestry wall. It reads (471) CLOTUALI / MOBRATTI; the letter-forms, despite two enlarged angle-bar A's, are partly from book-hand (L, T, M, B, R) and the whole inscription may be within VII.1 rather than VI.3. Macalister read the lower line as FIL) MOBRATTI, but his FIL) is not

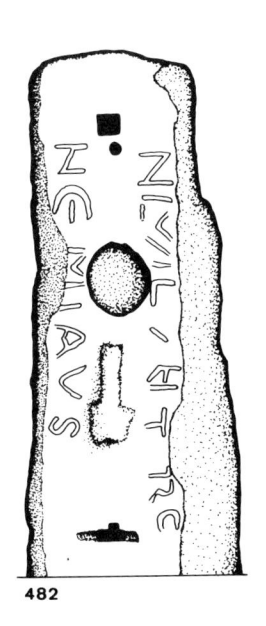

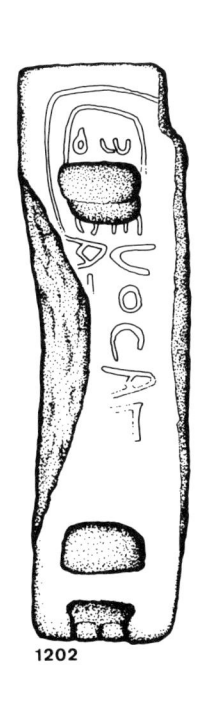

# THE DUMNONIAN INSCRIPTIONS: THE NATIVE RESPONSE

**(Top left) Fig. 17.6** Large coarse granite slab, Phillack churchyard, by vestry, with CLOTVALI / MOBRATTI (471) – note angle-bar A; VI.3 or VII.1.

**(Top right) Fig. 17.7** Dr William Borlase's tiny sketch, enlarged from original in a 1740 MS notebook, of a lost stone (1205) seen by him at Redruth parish church; MAVORI FI(LI? / VITO ... is just possible.

**(Bottom left) Fig. 17.8** Two damaged memorials from west Cornwall. **Left**, 482, lost or destroyed, from Treveneague, St Hilary; Langdon's drawings in W. Iago's album – N ... FILI(?) IC(?) / NEMIA(N?)VS, angle-bar A. **Right**, 1202, Vellansajer (now Boskenna, garden), St Buryan, drawn *in situ* – *alpha* and *omega* in cartouche, EVOCA(TI?) / CA ..., also with angle-bar A.

there; a stepped flaw in the granite (as sketched in 1895 by Langdon) has been misread. The first name, by the seventh century *Clotual* (approximately as /klothwal/), is from **Cluto-ualos*, meaning something like 'Worthy-of-Fame'. The question is whether the second word is like the *faber* in 488 DOBVNNI FABRI, the master-craftsman; an epithet or qualifier. If so, we could suggest that it means 'great-in-judgement' (British **brattos*)[35] and that this person had held some appropriate position in tribal society; it is yet another tiny hint (p. 197) that Phillack was a place of particular importance within post-Roman Cornwall.

In the Land's End peninsula proper, the 'Men Scryfa' or, better, 'Men Scryfys' (written stone) stands in a field near the northern edge of the granite uplands. It has been a landmark for centuries; it reads (468) RIALOBRAN⌐ / CUNOVAL⌐ FIL⌐. These are large bold capitals, the N's as H, and two of the three A's may be open (inverted V), though this is a matter of opinion. A small linear cross, involved with the start of the two vertically set names, has been noticed for a long time; it is certainly there (Fig.17.5) and can be photographed, but it would be surprising if it were contemporary with the lettering on a memorial that could probably be dated as VI.2. These are 'heroic' British names (**Rigalo-branos*, 'Kingly *Bran*' (or 'Raven', **branos*) and **Cuno-ualos* 'worthy, or valiant, as a hound') and in human terms it is easy to see this as commemorating a sixth-century chieftain[36] of an identifiable territory (see below, p. 291).

The inscription at Sancreed (churchyard) is legible but defective and must originally have been set, vertically, near the top of an extremely tall granite pillar that was subsequently inverted and carved into a twelfth-century cross with round head and ornamental shaft (Fig.17.9). (1057) FILIVS IC can certainly be read, showing this to be type (d); remains of an upper line with a name are there, though Macalister's EROCAVI is difficult to sustain. The inscription is in normal capitals, may have been of the shape 'Of-A / Of-B *filius ic*' and need not be later than VI.2 on the strength of what is visible. The last stone in the group is now within the parish church of St Just in Penwith[37] (Fig.17.10) again found built into a wall during last-century restoration. Unusually, two faces of a quadrangular granite pillar are employed. The inscription is (483) SENILVS IC IAC⌐T, with NI being small and superscript as if omitted in error by the cutter, and a curious horizontal I *within* IAC⌐T. On the adjoining wider face is an upright cross with barred terminals and rounded open-*rho* loop, like a crook, all within a rectangular cartouche (Fig.17.15).

There is a puzzling addendum to this. Before 1906, someone signing himself as 'T.W.S.' wrote to a local paper[38] with an account of how, when the stone was set into its present granite block mounting, he and 'a gentleman visitor' who happened to be present both saw, 'in Roman capitals 1½ inches long', the word PRESBYTER right across the bottom of the shaft (we are not told on which face). There is no reason to doubt that something was seen and read; one can certainly doubt that a horizontal *Presbyter* formed part of the original inscription, though this

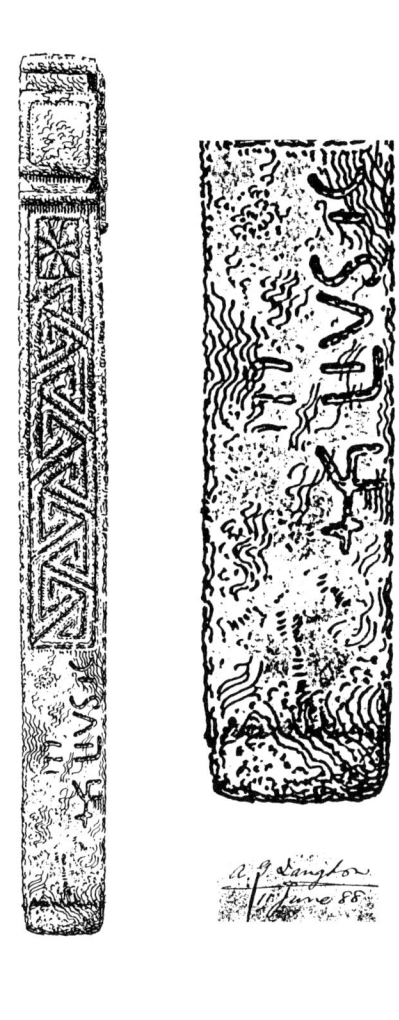

**(Left) Fig. 17.9** Tall granite cross (twelfth century?), Sancreed churchyard; the present east face. The cross represents medieval re-use of an inverted 'menhir', leaving part of an original inscription, 1057, ...... / .. FILIVS IC (?.. Arthur Langdon's own drawing, 1888 (courtesy of the Courtney Library, Royal Institution of Cornwall). Inset right, enlarged detail of the lettering.

**(Below) Fig. 17.10** Two memorials from St Just in Penwith. **Left**, 483, fine granite pillar in church; inscription on one face, *chi-rho* cross in frame on adjoining face. **Right**, 1055, at Boslow, in mound or cairn (cf. Fig. 17.14). Main (compass-W) face has TAET/UERA over very devolved cross-form(?); adjoining (compass-S) face, a contemporary linear cross, VII.1 or VII.2. Drawn *in situ*.

287

memorial may like others with a single name commemorate a priest and the prominent *chi-rho* cross would be opposite.

Four early inscriptions from what might be called the northern fringe of Dumnonia must be mentioned. The two later and vertically-set ones from the Beacon Hill graveyard on Lundy (chap.10) include (1402) POTIT(I?, surmounted by a 'hot-cross-bun' circled linear cross very like that on the Welsh (358) VOTEPORIGIS stone; if this suggests a VI.2 date, the single-name *Potiti* in capitals would would not be out of temporal place. One cannot be sure (Fig.10.3) if the last letter was vertical or horizontal I; the granite broke right across, sharply, here and the writer's belief, examining the stone at length in 1969, is that a vertical I coincided with, and weakened, an existing transverse crack. The interest of the name *Potitus* is that it was also borne by St Patrick's grandfather.[39] The last Lundy stone (1403), also broken, is much larger – it must have been a substantial upright pillar – and now reads ... )IGERN⊢ / (FIL)I TIGERN⊢, the G's and the second E being non-capital forms. Spacing might suggest that the first name was longer than just TIGERN⊢[40] and this late sixth century memorial with its resounding names, perhaps an indication that the cemetery was still in use around 600 for prominent laymen, may have been for a man whose body was brought across from mainland Devon.

Since both 1402 and 1403 would, as to their formulae and letterings, fit perfectly well into the Cornish series further west we meet the puzzle of why so few memorials are known from the much larger Devon. The 'Exmoor' inscriptions, excluding a vague report of a lost stone (1405) from Holwell, are (Fig.17.10)) the Caffin Cross Stone near Lynton (1404) and the only one noticed by Macalister, that from Winford Hill (499). The former (shape, 'Of-A, son of-B') reads CAVVD⊢ FILĪVS C⊢V⊢L⊢; the D is reversed, there is a profusion of the horizontal I, but otherwise this is legible capitals; *Cavudus*, son of *Civilis* (a name borne by a *vicarius Britanniarum* in the fourth century).[41] The Winford Hill inscription is (499) CARĀTACI NEPVS in capitals with reversed N, the AT ligatured by having a bar above the A, and three angle-bar A's. The deceased was *nepus* ('grandson, immediate descendant') of a British *Caratacus* or *Carantacus*, a heroic name in itself.[42] The island of Lundy, given its position and supposed ecclesiastical importance, may in respect of early memorials have been a special case; but these two Exmoor inscribed stones, both perhaps to be dated VI.3, are so far removed from the main Dumnonian concentration as to suggest connections with those of Glamorgan.

The illegible or lost inscriptions from west Cornwall do give us a useful reminder that we deal, perforce, with that unknown fraction of an original total that happens to have survived; beyond that, one can only note them. A granite gatepost at Trevaylor, north of Gulval, has the remnants of a single vertical line of lettering (1201); it came to light about 1890 as the result of William Iago's newspaper appeal and a hundred years later one can just make out odd letters (like .. IVM ..

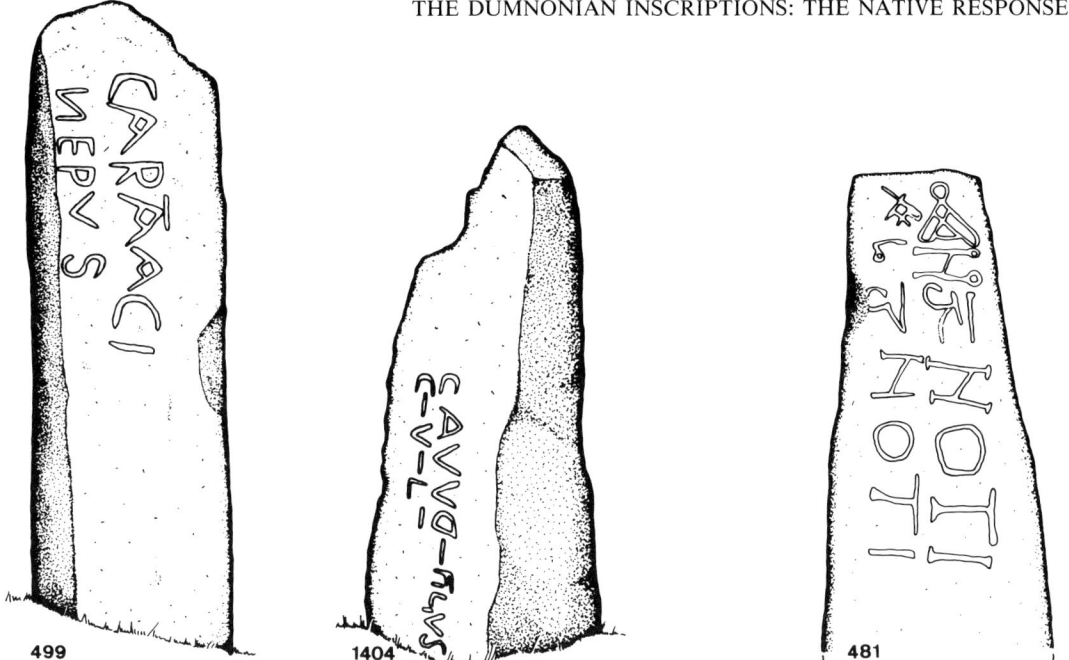

THE DUMNONIAN INSCRIPTIONS: THE NATIVE RESPONSE

**(Left) Fig. 17.11** Inscribed stones from Exmoor, drawn from photographs. Left: 499, from Winford Hill, has CARATACI / NEPVS (note ligatured AT; *Cara(n)taci* – and angle-bar A's). **Right**, 1404, Caffin cross, un-typed with numerous horizontal I's, CAVVDI FILIVS / CIVILI.

**(Right) Fig. 17.12** The 'Noti Noti' stone, west Cornwall, St Hilary churchyard (481); drawn *in situ*. The right-hand line, with devices and NOTI, probably VII, appears to have been copied in the left-hand line.

PI(?).), but that is all. Similarly a larger granite slab, apparently with two vertical lines of lettering, spotted in the 1920s[43] might just begin to be legible (as 1204) if taken out; it is part of a public-footpath stile and annually a great many hundred nailed boots are stamped upon it. The lost stone from Porthgwarra, St Levan, was sketched in the seventeenth century as showing (1200) ... HS SPED, in capitals and also within a rectangular cartouche like the 483 *Senilus* pillar.[44] Very recently a large flake of granite, found[45] in the Kenidjack valley at St Just in Penwith, has what looks like a perfectly genuine scrap, (1203) U(?).S., the tail of the S with a forked serif, and even a hint of another letter from a lower second line.

Several of the inscriptions already mentioned, provisionally dated late in the sixth century (as 'VI.3' or 'late in VI.3'), may belong to the early seventh; this depends upon what typological and/or chronological weight is given, not so much to the limited display of linguistic change, but to the extent to which the use of clear capitals is diluted by (eventually, to be replaced by) letter-forms that can be classified under various names.[46] Such letters were taken from contemporary versions of writing, probably confined to the writing of Latin. This means the use of ink or stylus-lines on parchment, papyrus, wax and prepared wood – *book-hands*, as opposed to monumental script cut large upon stone. Of the five late Dumnonian inscriptions now to be considered, two are entirely in a book-hand; all have characteristics that point to seventh-century dates. Four of the memorials are single-name and all four probably (one, 1055, almost certainly) mark the graves of priests; the fifth (1048) is rather different and is an important memorial for an important person.

The two Devon inscriptions, vertical on large pillars, are at the churches of Yealmpton in south Devon (494: GOREVS, in capitals except for G) and Stowford near Okehampton (1060, GUNGLEI, wholly in very barbarous lettering).[47] They may represent forms of British names but one cannot expand that suggestion. The other three are all in west Cornwall. Found in the fabric of St Hilary church and now inside the churchyard entrance is a tall granite pillar with a 'double' vertical inscription; the (original) upper vertically set line has, in huge letters, (481) NOTI – genitive of *Notus*? – preceded by three elaborate symbols something on the lines of those on the Mawgan Cross (469, above, p. 263). The eye of faith might read them as *alpha*, M and *omega*[48] but cool Reason would be hard put to explain precisely how. They exist, but remain meaningless. The second line is an attempt to reproduce the upper line, and not very competently so; if this is an inexplicable copying, it is also an early copying (Fig. 17.12).

The church of Madron, mother-church of the town of Penzance and contained within the remnants of a large curvilinear enclosure,[49] was partly restored internally in 1935–6. Built into an inner wall-face under nine layers of plastering was a tall slab of fine whitish granite, inscribed face outward and inverted.[50] Attempts to read it at the time were not entirely successful and the stone was placed in a recess in the south-west angle, in very dim light. When Macalister saw it after his retirement to Cambridge, in 1945 or so, he was not in his prime and it is perhaps remarkable that he could see as much as he did (probably by candle-light). He wanted to read two separate inscriptions; a longer, two-line one of FILIA / GVENNCREST, and then another at the other end, with the whole slab inverted, which he saw as HADNOB (is) – there was no comment as to what *language* a name like this could belong. The entire face of the thin slab, over 6 feet long, is ornamented (Fig. 17.13). There are motifs top-and-bottom, a near-complete cartouche, transverse incised lines and various long wavering surface-fissures; the first upright in H(ADNOB) is part of a transverse line, not of a letter. The lettering is almost all there, but much of it was originally cut fairly lightly.

The memorial (1048) starts with a small superscript VIR, and then reads QONFAL FILIV(S / VENNORCIT. In FILIV(S the V is inverted and the S is now barely detectable; in the lower second name, the N's are also reversed, OR is an odd ligature (like capital C and a script R) and the final IT is crammed together. There is a small panel with three vertical lines at the base, and at the top there is a 'paddle-armed' cross standing on a line with looped terminals, a motif that by this time (first half

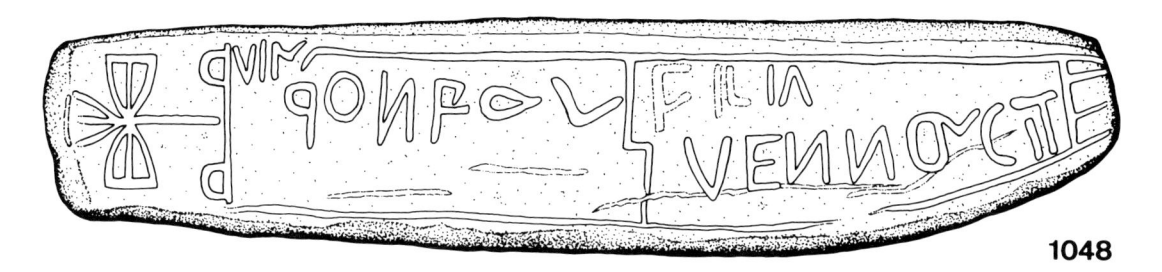

**Fig. 17.13** Madron church, 1048; long thin memorial slab (VII.1?) of fine whiteish granite, with VIR / QONFAL FILIV(S) / VENNORCIT, extended framing, headed by devolved *chi-rho* cross. Drawn *in situ*.

of the seventh century) no longer shows its origin in the *chi-rho* cross with linear base (Fig.17.17).

The opening VIR is unique in Insular inscriptions; it is suggested that it means 'husband' or even '(my) husband' and that a widow denotes the commissioning of the memorial. Better ideas would be welcomed. The second (the father's) name is British, *Uenn-orgit*, a warrior's or nobleman's name and like French *beau sabreur* it would have had the sense of 'Fair Slayer'.[51]

For the first name, the letters – the largest in the inscription – may be uneven in size and form but are quite legibly QONFAL. The question is what the *scriptor* or *ordinator* wanted to convey. If he still knew the convention that medial C (as in *Uennorcit*) had to be used for /g/, albeit by now lenited, he may have selected Q on its own to represent /k/. What seems the likely answer is that his F – instead of V (for /w/) or M (for /m/) – stands for lenited M, /μ/, and that though the A misrepresents a diphthong or a lengthened vowel the name is actually Conmael (< *Cuno-maglos*).[52] The whole monument is still, and must have been designed to be, impressive. Without a tempting excursus into historical landscape-reconstruction, one can raise the idea that the (Norman-period) combined parishes of Madron and the smaller Morvah make up a well-defined north–south territory right across the Land's End peninsula. The Men Scryfys (468) dominates its northern sector. We can envisage Cunowal and Rialobran as successive chieftains, neither necessarily baptized in infancy as Christians; a gap of one or perhaps two generations; and then Uennorgit and Conmael, the latter being accorded a handsome memorial at the most important Christian locale in the southern sector (Madron is also *Landithy*; p. 317).

The last memorial has no special name, is not much visited because it is quite hard to find, and stands on the high granite moorland of west Penwith at the intersection of two trackways of prehistoric origin. The area is part of Boslow common. Yet this stone, an unobtrusive four-sided granite stump, can be as evocative as the mighty Maen Madog (p. 125) or the modern Maen Waldo (p. 12) because, perhaps uniquely in Cornwall, it is in its original stance. The visitor at the right moment can still share, just a little, in the commemoration of a burial thirteen centuries ago. The Boslow stone (1055) is inscribed on one face, a single name split into two vertical lines: TAET/UERA. Below them is a device something

**Fig. 17.14** The mound grave at Boslow, St Just, with the memorial stone of *Taetuera* (1055; see Fig. 17.10). Two views, cleared of vegetation, 1991. (Photographs: author.)

like a cross and something like a schematized human figure (Fig.17.10). On the adjoining (south) face is a large equal-armed expanded-terminals cross and on the face opposite the inscription there is another small medieval or modern linear cross. This monument is firmly embedded in a low mound (Fig.17.14). Probing shows that the mound contains large stones and is a true *congeries lapidum*, almost certainly covering the original burial. When the stone was chosen and erected it was so placed that the inscribed side faces due west and that when the midday sun is at its highest it strikes across the face, throwing the large and deep-cut lettering into relief for about 20 minutes. The large cross, on the south-facing side, is visible as one comes up the track. It is surely contemporary, and the placing of the lettering on one face and a prominent cross on an adjoining face might suggest deliberate copying of the St Just stone, 483 *Senilus*, which stood not far away – two miles SW, over a low hill. TAETUERA is entirely in large straggling half-uncial letters; the final -A may be for an unstressed obscure vowel (like the last -*a* in 'Britannia'), not the mark of a feminine nominative.

All the circumstances point to this as the burial of a priest in the later seventh century at a place that was somehow significant. The name, which by now can be called Primitive Cornish, contains elements meaning 'travel, journey' and 'exalt, or praise'.[53] It may be untranslatable or it may indicate a name-in-religion connected with pilgrimage. This is not all that we can extract from this stone (see p. 298) but it must suffice to end the catalogue.

There have been many references to the minimal art – so minimal that it has been written 'art' on occasions – associated with some of the memorials. Discussion cannot be widened to include Demetia because, except for a very few memorials which can be linked to the EL category, this is a Dumnonian feature. We can pick out three elements – the *curved line* (Fig. 17.15), the frame or '*cartouche*' (Fig.17.16) and developed forms of the upright *chi-rho* cross (Fig.17.17).

The curved line looks like an attempt to define a rounded top to granite pillars whose upper ends are generally irregular and the framing, similarly, to impart a rectilinear outline. Independent invention would be a remote possibility; if in Dumnonia, why not also in south Wales? Imitation of literary models (rectangular frames as the linear borders of folios or pages) would be a notion raising serious problems of date. A third explanation can only be provisional, but does no violence to chronology. The down-curved line probably *is* meant to imply a circular-headed upright or stele, and the rectilinear cartouche to give a more 'Roman' or official appearance to a lettered epitaph. Source of both ideas, neither reflected on Dumnonian memorials before VI.2, may lie in the format of memorials in Christian Gaul if not further afield, and the ideas would have been introduced along with the vocabulary illustrated in Fig.12.4 earlier. Lynette Olson draws attention[54] to Iberian Christian memorials surmounted by a motif like an inverted horse-shoe or Moorish arch, one clearly inspired by older (third – fourth

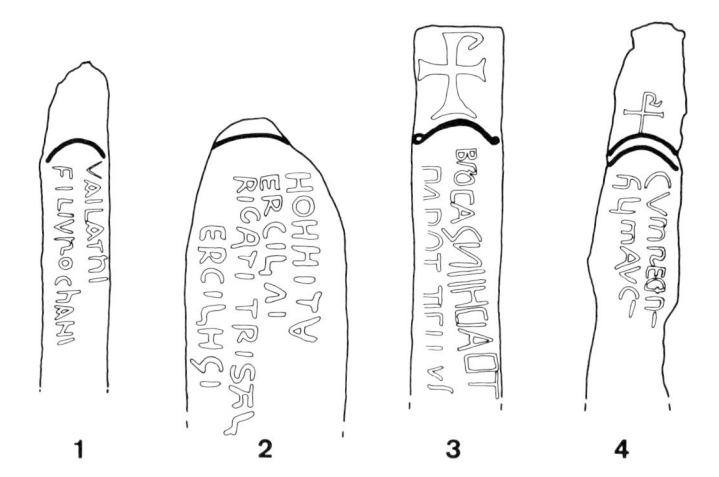

# THE DUMNONIAN INSCRIPTIONS: THE NATIVE RESPONSE

**Fig. 17.15** Art on Dumnonian stones, *(1)*. Curved lines – attempts to define a rounded top, Roman-style? 1, 460 (Cardinham, un-typed, Irish names). 2, 461 (Cuby, un-typed, British names). 3, 478 (St Endellion 'Long Cross', type (d), Irish name). 4, 486 (South Hill, un-typed, British name).

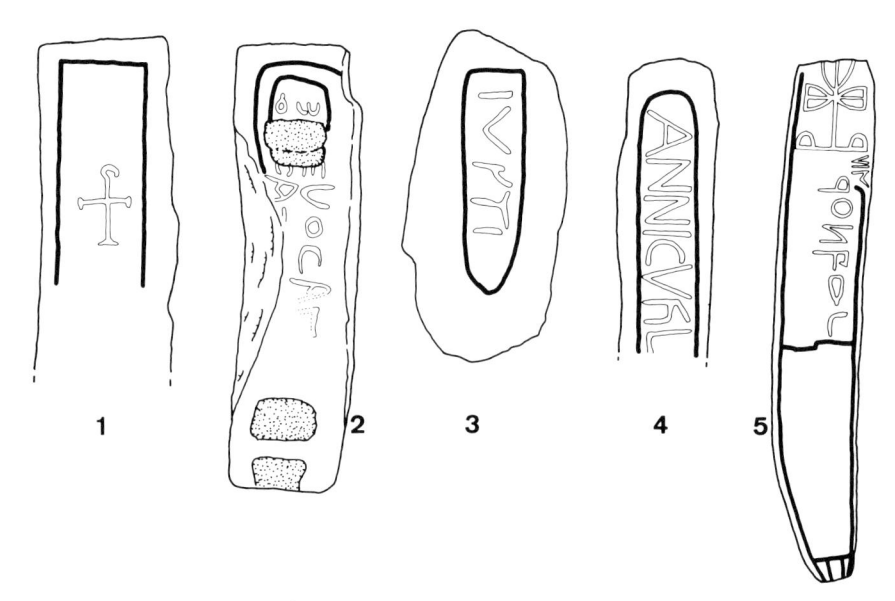

**Fig. 17.16** Art on Dumnonian stones, *(2)*. Use of a 'cartouche' or framing lines, presumably originating in Roman monumental frames or borders. 1, 483 (St Just, side-panel, British(?) name). 2, 1202 (now at Boskenna, St Buryan, Irish name). 3, 484 (St Kew, *Iusti* with Ogam, Roman name). 4, 465 (Lanivet, Roman name). 5, 1048 (Madron, British names).

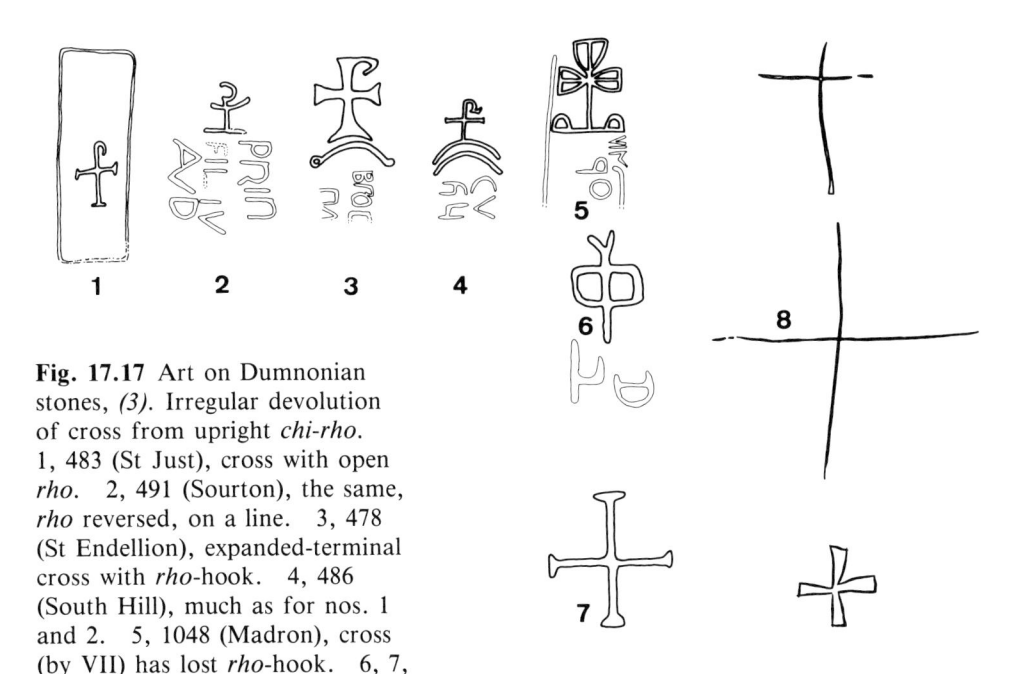

THE DUMNONIAN INSCRIPTIONS: THE NATIVE RESPONSE

**Fig. 17.17** Art on Dumnonian stones, *(3)*. Irregular devolution of cross from upright *chi-rho*. 1, 483 (St Just), cross with open *rho*. 2, 491 (Sourton), the same, *rho* reversed, on a line. 3, 478 (St Endellion), expanded-terminal cross with *rho*-hook. 4, 486 (South Hill), much as for nos. 1 and 2. 5, 1048 (Madron), cross (by VII) has lost *rho*-hook. 6, 7, devices on 1055 (Boslow, *Taetuera*); 6, shown inverted, may be related to no.5, but 7 is a typical linear cross with short bar-terminals of *c.* 600 onward. 8 (for comparison only), late 6th-century(?) 'primary' crosses on slate, associated with cist-grave burials, Tintagel churchyard.

centuries) tombstones in Spain (Fig.2.5). Neat framing of multi-line horizontal inscriptions of all kinds was so common in Roman monumental work that it would be impossible to point to a specific model. It may be significant that the only example of rectilinear framing on a Welsh stone (385, *ECMW* 89; Llanfaglan, Caern.) is from a district where EL inscriptions suggest Gaulish influence.

Among the cases illustrated here, three of the five memorials with framing or cartouches are probably for priests, and four of the five (1202 has an uncertain provenance) come from Christian locations; whereas only one of the four with curved lines (461, Cuby) comes from an actual church. It might be suspected that framing was the more likely outcome of Continental contact in priestly circumstances, and that the curved line was an internal development, one that could have begun with copying part of such an inscription as Lanivet, 465 ANNICV.

Versions of the upright *chi-rho* cross (not arranged in likely chronological order) are shown in Fig.17.17; the fact that the *rho* is hooked throughout, not looped, suggests a fifth-century model from Atlantic Gaul (p. 200). Portable ecclesiastical objects could have formed a mode of transmission. All that can be said is that

295

these few depictions show a Dumnonian familiarity with the motif. They show also its combination with the curved line (which can become a base-line), and eventually (1048) degeneration into an ornate cross where the *rho*-hook is forgotten.

But it is at this point, in the seventh century, that another school of 'primary Christian ornament' becomes involved. The linear cross, at its plainest in such provincial Christianity where on rough stone it is no more than lines incised at right-angles, is difficult to date because of this very simplicity. The natural 'cross' on the (479) *Cunaide* stone, Fig.11.5, may be interesting but is fortuitous; the small incised cross on the Men Scryfys (Fig.17.5) cannot be proved to be contemporary with the lettering. On the memorials, the cross on the Boslow *Taetuera* stone, 1055, may well be the earliest. The idiosyncratic design below the lettering (shown here in Fig.17.17 upside-down) could be, as with 1048 above it, the ultimate derivative of the upright *chi-rho* cross.

Primary, cross-incised grave-markers — smaller stones placed at a grave, larger ones serving as covering slabs for cist-graves — are recorded from many parts of Atlantic Britain and Ireland; and we now know that they were used in sixth–seventh century Dumnonia, from the recent excavations at Tintagel churchyard.[55] Simple crosses, linear and outline, accompanied other designs involving the use of dividers or compasses to make intersecting circles and 'crosses of arcs', as they are called. Some could be as early as VI.2 or VI.3. But when examples, as in Fig.17.17, are placed alongside the inscribed-memorial ornament we can sense that in the seventh century the two traditions had not by then coalesced. Had the erection of inscribed memorials lasted longer, analogies from Ireland suggest that they would have done so.

Throughout the chapters that have discussed the inscribed stones of Wales and the south-west as memorials to the dead, there has been an implication that such pillars and slabs physically accompanied the burials of those so commemorated; that HIC IACIT meant what it said. The example of any modern churchyard or municipal cemetery might raise a general idea that *of course* the inscribed stones stood upright, at the west or head end of a grave. The plain truth is that almost nothing is known about this, and the main reason for ignorance is that almost no inscribed stone still stands where it was first put up.

Verticality of the whole memorial, like the ogam-inspired verticality of the lettered message, was an Insular innovation; this observation is a vital one. In the western provinces of the late Empire the corresponding inscribed slabs (including Gaulish ones) were, as Jeremy Knight reminds us,[56] conventionally prone; horizontally placed, inside churches or in cemeteries. This writer (like many of his archaeological colleagues, long indebted to Mircea Eliade's teachings) makes no excuse for dwelling on modalities of ascension or the connection with uncharted prehistoric beliefs. A good few of the very large Dumnonian granite uprights probably had been pre-Roman menhirs; Fig.17.18, showing stones whose inscribed

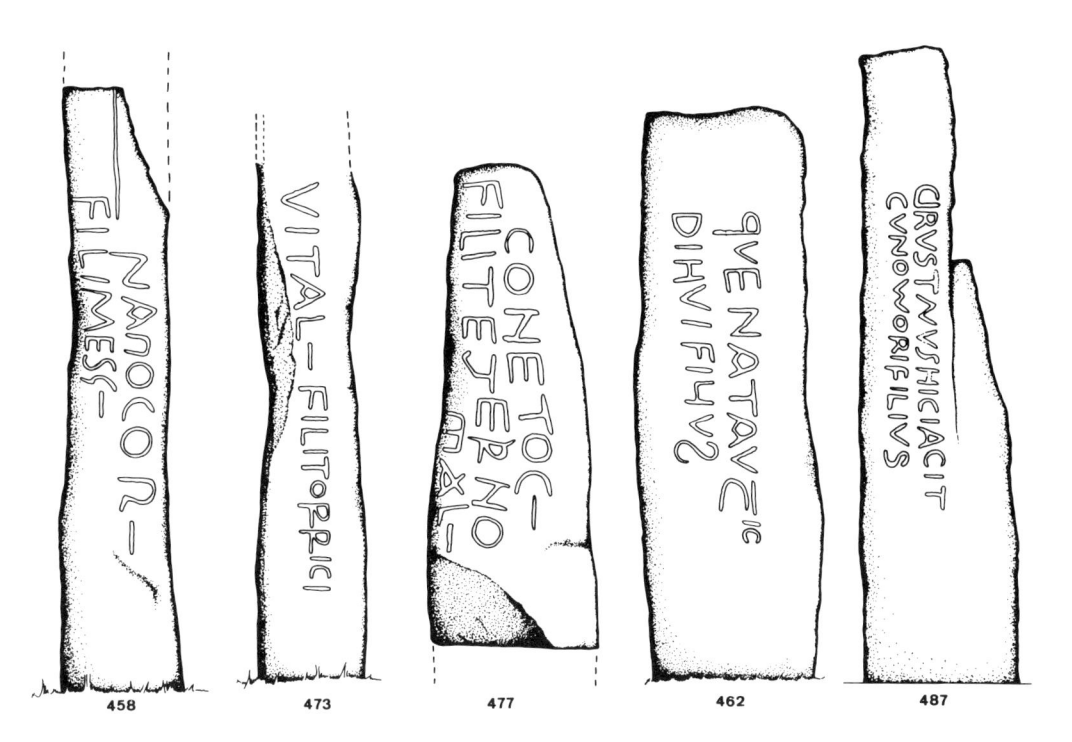

THE DUMNONIAN INSCRIPTIONS: THE NATIVE RESPONSE

Fig. 17.18 Verticality in Dumnonian memorials, a feature over-riding both types of 'message', and ethnic differences of names. **Left to right**: 458, Cardinham, un-typed, Irish names. 473, St Clement (primary inscription), un-typed, Roman name. 477, Cubert, un-typed, British names. 462, Gulval (Bleu Bridge), type (d), Irish names. 487, Castle Dore, type (d), British names.

names cover the range of linguistic differences, also depicts the essential verticality.

This does not altogether exclude horizontal positioning (any more than in today's graveyards, where upright memorials and prone tablets occur together), and a separate Irish series of *recumbent slabs*, beginning perhaps around 700, is well-known.[57] Dumnonia can provide us with a few surprises. The stone for *Iustus* (484) never stood upright; it is a heavy chunk of granite, now 2 ft. 6 in. long, with its IUSTI and ogam I)USTI along the sloping upper surface. One has to suppose that it sat on a grave, or across the end of a grave, and is what Macalister – noting others in Ireland – called a *pulvillar* or pillow-stone. The 1048 QONFAL stone from Madron, as Fig.17.13 indicates, has a face that is inscribed and ornamented from top to bottom; it is also noticeably narrow, and the reverse side is flattish. May this not have been intended to lie prone, full-length along a grave, and (in the seventh century) conceivably inside a small church structure? Had its *scriptor* in mind, even at some remove, the inscribed lid of a late Classical sarcophagus?

297

# THE DUMNONIAN INSCRIPTIONS: THE NATIVE RESPONSE

**Fig. 17.19** The Penzance Market Cross (*CIIC*.ii, 1051), now at Penlee House (Museum), Penzance. **Left**, side-view showing rounded head with roll-bar 'ears', panelling and (bottom) illegible inscription. **Right**, front(?) face, figure, destroyed area, and visible part of main inscription. (Photographs: Susanna Thomas.)

For vertical memorials, it is impossible to generalize. It is apparent from archaeology (though not from historical sources that might have offered a rationale, suggested Mediterranean precedents, and confirmed that venerable tradition[58] of the resurrected corpses sitting up to face the Holy Places and the

Second Coming) that early Christian burials were, overwhelmingly so, laid out east – west with the head at the west end. Modern usages might suggest that an upright memorial stood by a west end. There are only two Dumnonian instances that throw any light on this and they seem to tell their own story. In 1991 the mound in which the *Taetuera* pillar is set was carefully cleared (Fig.17.14). If this was a small mound grave, a pile above a granite cist, then the pillar probably *is* nearer the west end than the east (foot) end; but the inscription faces *westward*, not along the grave. Going back to Fig.11.4, Richard Edmonds' account of the discovery of the *Cunaide* burial (also a mound grave) in 1843 has to be used with care, but implies that the inscribed stone (479) was found, inscription upward, alongside and just south of the grave. Supposing it to have been erected at the west end, then unless in falling this slab twisted, unaided, through 180 degrees it follows that the inscription *also* faced westward. What are we to make of this? Here are two memorials, both admittedly accompanying mounds and both in west Cornwall (13 miles apart), though separated in time by at least two centuries. Was it the norm, or has chance preserved the settings of 479 and 1055 as our only evidence?

The end of the memorial fashion in Dumnonia has been estimated as *circa* 700, with the latest – whichever that is – of the late stones. For Wales, the far bigger corpus presented in *ECMW* was divided into four classes, of which Class IV is medieval. The Nash-Williams scheme rested mainly upon epigraphy, has often been called 'elegant' and has been applied outside Wales, for instance by Radford to the inscriptions of Dumnonia.[59] The inscribed stones, visually distinct from uninscribed stones with 'primary' cross ornamentation (Class II), constituted a Class I of the fifth to seventh centuries, inclusive. Forty years on, it could be said – and earlier chapters of this book may have shown this – that, as a general guide, the scheme is applicable to large groups of memorials but fallible in individual cases. Recently K. R. Dark[60] has given reasons why a different approach, a contextual rather than purely epigraphic (and linguistic) analysis, could yield a more flexible and probably more realistic system of dating. Rightly, he pinpoints the weakness of *ECMW*'s end-datings for the separate classes and the fact that, using *ECMW* criteria, 'Class I' stones exist that could well 'refute the idea of a seventh-century end for the sequence'. None the less, the Dumnonian stones – all of which we have now examined – do, as a funerary fashion, seem to fade away; unless dozens more like 1055 (*Taetuera*) and 1060 (*Gunglei*) have been selectively destroyed, some such date as the late seventh century *is* the apparent end. Why this should be so in Dumnonia (apart from Wales) must be addressed in the last chapter.

There are, as in Wales and Ireland, subsequent inscriptions. They have other purposes and are found on other kinds of monuments. We can note 1054 *doniert rogavit pro anima* (cross-base, late ninth); 1058, on base, *runho(1)* (sculptured cross, late tenth, probably sculptor's name); 1044, + *leuiut iusit hec altare pro anima sua* (altar frontal, mid-tenth). Possibly the most telling example is the

Penzance Market Cross (1051), a tall, almost baroque, granite object with round head, dot-filled panels, human figures in outline and other motifs. Inscriptions occur low down, on a side-panel and front panel. The former has lettering so grotesque as to be unintelligible.[61] The latter, which is larger, was long ago clipped at the bottom (now set in a modern base) and slightly damaged this century at the top, though missing letters are safely recorded.[62] Three lines of writing occur, in an eleventh century book-hand. Despite such extreme ideas as that the message is in Old Cornish (!) or designedly cryptic, it is in Latin. The author's reading (Fig. 17.19) restores the fewest possible missing letters: the obliques represent an incised transverse panelling-line.

p c u m b u i n / f o (r i s

q u i c u m q :/ p a ? (c e

u e n i t h i / c o (r e t

– or, expanding it, *Procumbunt in foris – Quicumque pace venit hic, oret* 'They lie here, in the open – Whosoever comes hither in peace, let him pray' (for their souls). It is a passage with partial parallels elsewhere,[63] and exhortatory in tone. The cross may have been put up (*c.* 1050 ?) at a cemetery of St Clare's on the west side of Penzance and one could guess that its creation was an act of conspicuous piety by an English *thegn* or squire called Alward (who before Domesday held the manor still bearing his name, Alverton) and that an English priest composed the message. *ECMW* lists some elaborate Welsh crosses with rather similar inscriptions. But, with these, we are in the Middle Ages. We are a very long way indeed from anything like a re-used menhir saying CONETOCI FILI TEGERNOMALI.

**References**

1. The name, still widely in use, commemorates James Abram Garfield, 20th President of the United States, elected (and assassinated) in 1881; a popular anti-slavery stalwart, he is supposed to have been the son of poor but respectable Cornish immigrants.
2. E.g., absolute size, geological composition and probably the simple techniques of letter-cutting would have far less significance than the 'shape' (formula employed) in a memorial statement.
3. Cf. K. R. Dark's recent paper (Dark 1992), with a conclusion that formula and 'direction' (disposition?) may be more helpful than 'epigraphy, art history or historical dating' in building relative and absolute chronologies.
4. Macalister's G is CI ligatured. *Com-* as equative or intensive prefix 'very', Ellis Evans, *BBCS* 24 (1972), 419-20. For *regin-* 'stiff, proud, tall', see Jackson, *Britannia* 1 (1970), 78–9; and cf. also 359 (Cynwyl Gaeo) REGIN↦ /FILIVS NUDINTI.
5. P. A. Rahtz, *CA* 10 (1971), 49–54, with further references.
6. Jackson's proposed 'end of the 5th century' (*LHEB* 291) was on linguistic grounds (-MORI

representing *mār(os)*, explained ibid.), but any enlarged context shows that this is really too early.
7. Padel 1981.
8. Allowing *Eselt*<**Adsiltia* 'she who is to be looked-at; "Miranda"' (so Jackson).
9. See n.6 above.
10. Wendy Davies 1982, 215; ed. G. H. Doble, *St Paul (Paulinus) of Léon, Bishop and Confessor* (Lampeter 1941).
11. *Vita Samsonis*, cap.59 (overthrowing of Commorus, unjust oppressor).
12. *EWGT*, 45 (no.10).
13. *LHEB*, 373
14. Appendix (16-17) to Pearce 1982 ('The hitherto unrecorded inscribed memorial stone from Buckland Monachorum', with photograph).
15. M. J. Swanton & S. M. Pearce, 'Lustleigh, S. Devon; its inscribed stone, its churchyard and its parish', pp.139-143 in: S. M. Pearce, ed., *The Early Church in Western Britain and Ireland* (BAR Brit.ser. 102, Oxford 1982).
16. *Sen*- 'old, ancient' (Latin *senex*) with adjectival *-acos*; cf.391 SENACVS (an earlier stone). Though, regularly, /s/>/sh/>/h/, the name 'Henoc' (early VI) in *Vita Samsonis* is probably, as Patrick Sims-Williams points out, the Biblical *Enoch* – Vulgate, Genesis iv & v, has *Henoch* (undeclined).
17. Perhaps also to be translated 'happy, blessed', here.
18. Enlarged 'E' looks likely; if then -TT or DD-, *cf.* (cautiously) the Scottish (Catstane) 510 VETTA(?) or even the Irish 211 ogam VEDDONOS, Co. Kerry. This inscription, if irregular, must have been fully legible and it is a pity no better drawing was made.
19. *PLRE* i.726, ii.905.
20. *PLRE* i.124, ii.185; RIB no.653 has *Audes* for *Audens*, the loss of *-n* in *-nt*, *-ns* being fairly common.
21. C. A. Ralegh Radford, 'An Early Christian Inscription at East Ogwell', *PDAS* 27 (1969), 79-81 illus., with comments by K. H. Jackson.
22. Note, in *JRIC* 4 (1871-3) pt.iv, xxviii; the inscription was just about as illegible then.
23. By Miss Mary Henderson, during her country-wide survey of crosses.
24. I am grateful to Mrs Bill Glanville (president, St Columb Old Cornwall Society) for expert local guidance and for her practical help in obtaining readings of inscriptions 475 and 1206.
25. *GPC*, 1072 s.v. *dofydd*. In the inscription -TH- represented lenited -d- /ð/, using a convention that may well have been brought from Wales since, in the Brycheiniog narrative, the male name no.12 (p. 143) has (*DSB*) *Windouith* (*uuin, douith*) as a sixth-century graph. *LHEB*, 484, with 'in the early inscriptions there is no case of V or U for μ', was penned before this memorial was discovered. Cf. Sir Ifor Williams, *BBCS* 6 (1932), 210, citing Juvencus 9 *douid*(?), for Pr. W *doμið, as the source of *dofydd* ('reading is doubtful', *LHEB*).
26. Assuming that DOCIDCI actually means 'Docidoci', did an O get lost in the cutting?
27. As in the North British, subsequently NW Wales, 'Cunedda' (*Cunedag*). Jackson (*LHEB*, *passim*) regarded 477 as after 600 ('seventh century' not further qualified), which it may well be; VII.i, perhaps.
28. Cf. discussion of the name in *LHEB*, *passim*.
29. *Nonnita*: Melville Richards ('Nynnid'), *AC* 118 (1969), 144-6; *Erciliui*, *Ercilinci*: *LHEB* 575, 582. *Ricatus*: *LHEB* 456-7 (with the suggestion that 'the correct reading may very likely be VIRICATI', but the deliberate arrangement of names in the four lines would not support that).
30. M. Tangye and C. Thomas, notes in *CA* 24 (1985), 171-4.

31. *PLRE* ii.736.
32. This is argued in Thomas 1992, with the names on the Kirkmadrine memorials representing clerical immigrants from the Continent.
33. It is not clear that (Loth, *CB* 178) OBr. *Uuorcomet*, and (833) *Guor-gomed*, contain this element.
34. This must suggest, if British, the various 'Nennius-like' names; 339 (Scethrog, Brecon) NEMNIVS (if correct). The Roman names *Nemesius*, *Nemesianus* (*PLRE* i.621–2, ii.775) may be irrelevant.
35. *LHEB* 633 (for *\*bratos* 'judgement'; no particular reason to see geminate TT here as marking lenition); prefix *mo-* (*\*mog*), implying something like 'accroissement', see Fleuriot, *GVB*, 118 s.v. *cormo*, and also 249 (*mach-*), 250, Gaulish (RO-)MOGILLUS, etc.
36. The hill behind the Men Scryfys is 'Hannibal's Carn'; R. M. Nance suggested that 'Hannibal' was metathesized from an older 'Holiburn' known from local folklore ('Giant Holiburn') and that the second name arose from imprecise reading of the inscription.
37. Brief explanation, by now overdue – the presence in Cornwall of various parishes sharing patronal names requires such distinctions as St Just in Penwith/in Roseland, Mawgan in Meneage/in Pydar, Newlyn (West)/Newlyn East, etc.
38. E. Whitfield Crofts (as 'Peter Penn'), ed., *Cornish Notes and Queries, 1st series* (Penzance 1906), 183–4. 'T. W. S.' was Thomas Walter Sandrey (b.1842), once a schoolmaster at St Just. The stone was found in 1834 and the anecdote may refer to *c*. 1880 or so.
39. *Confessio*, cap.1; there was also a Potitus, *vicarius urbis Romae* in 379–80 (*PLRE* i.721), but it is hardly a widespread name.
40. 'Kentigern' (*\*Contigern-*) and 'Vortigern' are examples; and about three or four missing letters are indicated. The general sense of *\*tigernos* in Dumnonia might be 'landed noble'; not higher.
41. *PLRE* i.205; for Cavudus, cf. (Demetia) 433, 434, both CAVETI, or 417 (Merioneth) CAVOSENI.
42. This is also 363 CARANTACUS, a single-name stone (Egremont, Carms.).
43. By Charles Henderson; MS notes, Royal Institution of Cornwall.
44. A. H. A. Hogg, note in *Proc. West Cornwall Field Club*, 2.5 (1960–61), 246–7 illus., from the seventeenth cent. Stowe MS 1024.
45. Found in summer 1990 by the roadside, by Peter Herring (Cornwall Archaeological Unit, Truro), to whom I am grateful for showing it to me and allowing mention of it.
46. Uncial, then half-uncial (Insular Majuscule), and other terms including the former 'Hiberno-Saxon'. These palaeographical aspects have been side-stepped because, important as the progression from capitals to book-hand may be, over-emphasis upon it as the main (if not only) criterion in dating inscriptions should now give way to wider, *contextual*, considerations (cf. Dark 1992).
47. Macalister (*CIIC* ii) read this as GURGLES; corrected by Radford, in n.21 above.
48. So Macalister; memorials 481 and 469 (Mawgan) are only thirteen miles apart and linked by an old Mounts Bay to Helford road. One of these little extravaganzas surely copies the other.
49. See p. 317; this is the former (?pre-Norman) *Landithy*.
50. H. R. Jennings, *Historical Notes on Madron, Morvah and Penzance* (Penzance 1936), 45–6, and pl.opp.64 (with incorrect reading).
51. *Uenn*<*\*uindo-* 'white, fair, etc.'; for the second element, cf. *GPN* 239–40, *Orgetorix*, *VGB* 277 citing OBr. names like *Eusorgit*.
52. See p. 145 earlier; Professor K. H. Jackson (*in litt.*, 15 Jan. 1961) pointed out the linguistic objection ('f .. could not occur like this in the middle of a name') but, without seeing the

53. TAET-, cf. W *taith* (MW *teith*; OBr. **teith* (*GVB*, s.v. *anteith* (68)), and presumably OCorn.); -UERA, cf.Loth, *CB* 173 (names like *Buduere*, *Ri-uuere*), *GVB* 161 s.v. *en tan guerehetic* (*uere* '..l'idée ancienne de "s'élever, se présenter"..'), and further references. 'He who exalts the journey' may be getting somewhere near a meaning.
54. Olson 1989, 38–9. There is a Demetian stone (440, *ECMW* 335, Llanychaer, Pembr.) known only from a 1698 drawing; it may be safer to omit consideration of its possible curved-line motif.
55. Illustrations, Nowakowski & Thomas 1990 id., 1992.
56. Knight 1992, at 45.
57. P. Lionard, 'Early Irish Grave-Slabs', *PRIA* 61 C (1961), 95–169.
58. St Paul's words, I Corinthians, xv.
59. Consistently in Radford 1965.
60. Dark 1992.
61. Macalister's reading (with drawing), *CIIC* ii, p.181, as *regis ricati crux* 'cross of king Ricatus' is impossible to follow; an eleventh-century Cornish king would need a lot of explaining.
62. Blight, mid-19th cent.; W. Iago (MS album, Courtney Library); G. B. Millett (after C. V. Le Grice's observation in 1850), note in *Trans. Penzance Nat. Hist. Antiq. Soc.*, 2nd ser. iii (Penzance, 1888–92), at 350–1. To some extent early photographs support the former existence of these reported, now missing, letters.
63. Isabel Henderson & Elizabeth Okasha, 'The Early Christian Inscribed and Carved Stones of Tullylease, Co. Cork', *CMCS* 24 (1992), 1–36 illus.; stone no.1 (ninth cent.?) contains *qui cu(m) quae* and *orat*. For the abbreviation of *quicumq*(ue) here, cf. *ECMW* 62 (*Ioruert Ruallaunq*(ue), enclitic *-que*) and 240, the eleventh-cent. Merthyr Mawr cross, with *usq*: for *usque*. A further contraction to *qcunq* appears on 125 (Llanwnnws, ninth cent.). The 'silent' contraction of *-ro-* in **procumbunt* – silent, because the expected r-hook mark is not visible – is rather more credible than omission of the final *-nt*, and I am guessing that this represents some obscure MS usage. The present subjunctive *oret* with exhortatory sense ('let him pray') might be indicated by the spacing, instead of, say, *ora* ('Pray!') or a curtailed *orat*(io) 'prayer for' (as in the common Irish *oroit do*). A similar subj. use, twelfth to fourteenth cents., of *propiecetur* 'may (God) have mercy, be favourable' is widespread on grave-slabs from north Wales.

# 18

# The Church in the Landscape

FIFTY-FIVE DUMNONIAN INSCRIPTIONS have been discussed. If we set aside the Carnsew (*Cunaide*) stone, the four illegible or lost West Cornish ones, and the outlying six from Lundy and Exmoor, out of the remaining forty-four it was possible to classify eighteen as intrusive and of a likely Demetian inspiration; twenty-one as forming the Dumnonian native response; and five late stones that marked the closing stages.

In making distinctions through personal names a small margin of error was accepted. When it comes to the earliest known locations there may be another such error-factor, but it is also containable; a large heavy stone built into a medieval church is more likely than not to have been found at (or very near) the site. The locations can be divided between 'landscape sites' and 'Christian sites'. The first division covers unenclosed ground, proximity to old trackways, proximity to natural boundaries like streams, and present-day farmland. The second includes churches of medieval or pre-Norman foundation with their churchyards and immediate surroundings, and also pre-Norman cemeteries and chapels (extant, or reliably recorded) that failed to develop into full parochial centres.

Of the eighteen Demetian intrusive memorials, nine come from landscape sites, nine from Christian ones. The twenty-one Dumnonian memorials belong to seven landscape and fourteen Christian sites and, of the five late stones, four are from churches and only one (1055 *Taetuera*) in the landscape. Taking the three groups as successive if overlapping, the percentage of the AD 500 to 700 memorials from Christian sites grows through time from fifty, to sixty-six, to eighty. These proportions could tell us other things. Sixth-century Demetian settlers may have preferred to commemorate heads of families, or *nobiliores*, on family estates rather than to have resorted to isolated burial-grounds. There was a handful of Christian sites in north and east Cornwall in VI.1 and VI.2 – Docco's monastery, Samson's second monastery, Lewannick, perhaps Lanivet – but before about 600 there may have been very few; and therefore memorials were placed in a landscape because alternative consecrated sites were not readily found. Our interpretation of the rising line 50–66–80 could be distorted by failure to understand that inscribed pillars may have possessed changing functions. None the less, this record of growth exists.

There is a suspicion among students of pre-Norman Insular Christianity, its history and archaeology, that we know a great deal less than we thought we did. This final chapter, concerned mainly with Cornwall, takes such views into account when discussing a region where those now active in study would agree that models put forward in the 1920s or the 1940s or even the 1970s must be regarded as far too simple.[1] The potential evidence from inscribed memorials, in particular, has seldom been exploited; and yet as a class these make up, not just the largest single group of Early Christian monuments, but in certain respect the *only* group. In Wales, long before the heyday of Principal Sir John Rhŷs, there was an interest in inscriptions as the oldest records of Welsh; a living language and the banner of Welsh nationhood. In Cornwall, with rare exceptions (Edward Lhuyd's visit, Dr William Borlase's eighteenth-century fieldwork, Iago's revival) the stones remained Mute Stones. They were seen, when noticed at all, as picturesque yet enigmatic forerunners to the enormous range of Cornish crosses, most of which fall between the tenth and thirteenth centuries.

In AD 500, Cornwall was barely Christian; in 1200, wholly and organizationally so. The relevance of seven centuries' worth of Christian archaeology to the history of a changing landscape is too obvious to need elaboration; parish churches make up at least half of all surviving medieval buildings. For the pre-1200 period there have been important recent studies aligned to those carried out elsewhere; Lynette Olson's rigorous investigation of the few genuine monasteries, Ann Preston-Jones's continuing survey of the form and siting of all the churchyards and Oliver Padel's elucidations of the main elements found in ecclesiastical place-names.[2] Much of the work now runs parallel to ongoing research in Wales – Heather and Terrence James in Dyfed, Diane Brook over a very large area (both sides of Offa's Dyke, and including Brycheiniog) on early cemeteries and churchyards and of course the survey of Welsh place-names begun by Melville Richards and now maintained by Tomos Roberts.[3] In Cornwall the two outstanding challenges concern any pre-Norman system of minsters – the 'proto-parochial' landscape, interest in which is renewed by recent discoveries at Tintagel and Minster[4] – and the ordering and analysis of the hundreds of worked stone crosses, counterparts of the *ECMW* Classes III and IV to which they are stylistically linked.

It is the Early Christian landscape in Cornwall and Devon – better described, perhaps, as the whole landscape with its occasional Christian features – before AD 700 that remains the least-explored theme. It may seem impenetrable. This writer's initial conclusion (rather more than a suspicion) is that there may not be over-much to penetrate; we deal with a time and place before territorial bishoprics, before the rise of large land-owning monasteries and before the emergence of a system of pastoral care applicable beyond individual clans and estates. The purpose of our closing chapter is to find out what light the inscribed memorials shed upon the seeming darkness, and for this the most effective tool – as O. G. S. Crawford was fond of reminding historians – remains the distribution-map, as the best way to marshal any set of facts spatially.

THE CHURCH IN THE LANDSCAPE

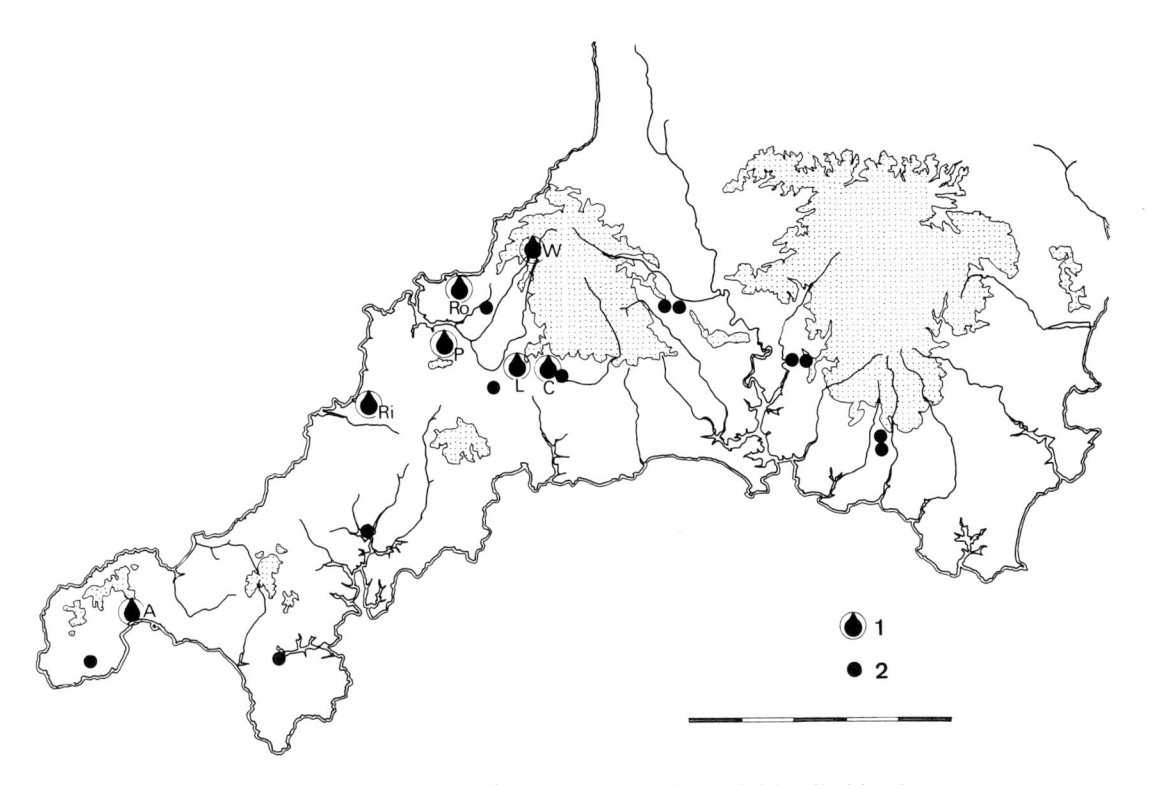

**Fig. 18.1** Sixth-century Dumnonia: Demetian settlers as substantial landholders?
**Key**: 1, intrusive memorials linked to what later became major Domesday manors. Ro, *Roscarrock*. W, *Worthyvale*. P, *Pawton*. L, *Lancarffe*. C, *Cardinham*. Ri, *Rialton*. A, *Alverton* (and/or *Lanisley*). 2, all other intrusive memorials. Scale, 25 miles (40 kms).

Fig.18.1 maps seven intrusive memorials with landscape contexts. A closer look shows that they all mark prime agricultural tenements, and that nearly all of those were named in the Domesday survey,[5] had manorial status, and reveal meaningful placings of the inscribed stones. From north-east to south-west, then, 470 was found where a side-road crosses the stream at the entrance to Worthyvale (manor), DB (Domesday Book) *Guerdevalan*. 478 *Brocagni* stood at cross-roads marking the farm lane opening to Roscarrock (manor), DB *Roscaret*, in the parish of St Endellion described a century ago[6] as 'a first-class agricultural parish ... Roscarrock, the largest farm'. The stone of *Ulcagnus* son of Severus at Nanscowe (472) stood by the track up from the Camel valley to Pawton, DB *Pautone*, the paramount hundredal manor with extensive grazing on St Breoke downs (DB, six by two leagues of pasture). At Lancarffe (manor), DB *Lancharet*,[7] the memorial of *Dunocatus* (457) marks what is still a large private farming estate; and 460 *Vailathi* from Welltown, Cardinham, belonged to farmland just east of Cardinham castle, the Norman seat of the descendants of William I's general Turold, conqueror of the south-west, where the lords of *Dinan* (p. 190) were the most

307

powerful family in twelfth-century Cornwall. The stone of the un-named son of *Tribunus* (476) is from Rialton (manor), DB *Rieltone*, the richest manor (after Pawton) in the hundred of Pydar. Down west, 462 *Quenatauci* served as a footbridge-slab where the valley road crosses the Trevaylor stream, the natural bound between Alverton, DB *Alwaretone* (p. 299) on the west, and Lanisley (manor), DB *Landicle*, south-west portion of Gulval parish.[8]

This is not coincidental. Between them, these sixth-century memorials give us four Roman names and eight or nine Irish ones; if one were to add the venture into the South Hams, the contexts of 488 *Enabarr* somewhere near Buckland and 489 *Fanoni* at Fardel are likely to be similar and these stones supply another five Irish names. What we must be seeing is the advent of Welsh settlers who were not just migrating farmers but the important leaders of important Demetian families. In Cornwall they acquired the *best* estates. How this took place – marriage-alliances as in Brycheiniog (p. 151), share-farming, anything approaching sale or exchange, or armed dispossession – we cannot tell. We lack the detailed paleo-environmental surveys that might suggest new emphases upon stock-rearing (of sheep).[9] What we can deduce is that the incomers were not fobbed off with marginal hill-farms that no Dumnonian would quarrel over. This is the advent of a land-exploiting aristocracy, whose members were probably practising Christians, accompanied by literate priests. And information of this order does not come from the few memorials in Cornwall that have landscape siting and *Dumnonian* names. One such, the Men Scryfys, 468 *Rialobrani*, possesses another sort of positioning altogether. It denotes burial of a tribal chieftain, a man like the *comes* Guedianus in the Life of St Samson (p. 229), up on the wild moors at a high and visible point.

Fig.18.2 directs us towards those stones with Christian sitings. The time-frame embraces about two centuries, 500 to 700, and (omitting those from Devon) memorials with Roman, Irish or Dumnonian British names are plotted together. A necessary further qualification is to denote those inscriptions – all the single-name ones – likely to signify the burials of priests,[10] and this brings in two stones that belong to 'the landscape' rather than to Christian sites, 474 *Cruarigi* (*c*.600) and 1055 *Taetuera* (*c*.700).

Even within Cornwall, only a part of post-Roman Dumnonia, there are discernible clusterings; this is not an all-peninsula distribution and nor would we expect such. Separate clusters – west Cornwall, mid-Cornwall, the Camel–Fowey corridor and around the south of Bodmin Moor to the Tamar valley – could be indicated loosely by lines around the specific distributions, not of *all* memorials, but of the intrusive ones alone. These, not the Dumnonian stones, show the first spread of Demetian-introduced Christianity. The areas are separated by the (largely, granitic) blocs of land over 400 feet OD – the Wendron massif, the china-clay district (Hensbarrow or White-moor) and Bodmin Moor. Lastly, in Fig.18.2, symbols with numbers mark another relevant pattern; the monasteries that Dr Lynette Olson concluded could be shown as 'reasonably certain' to have

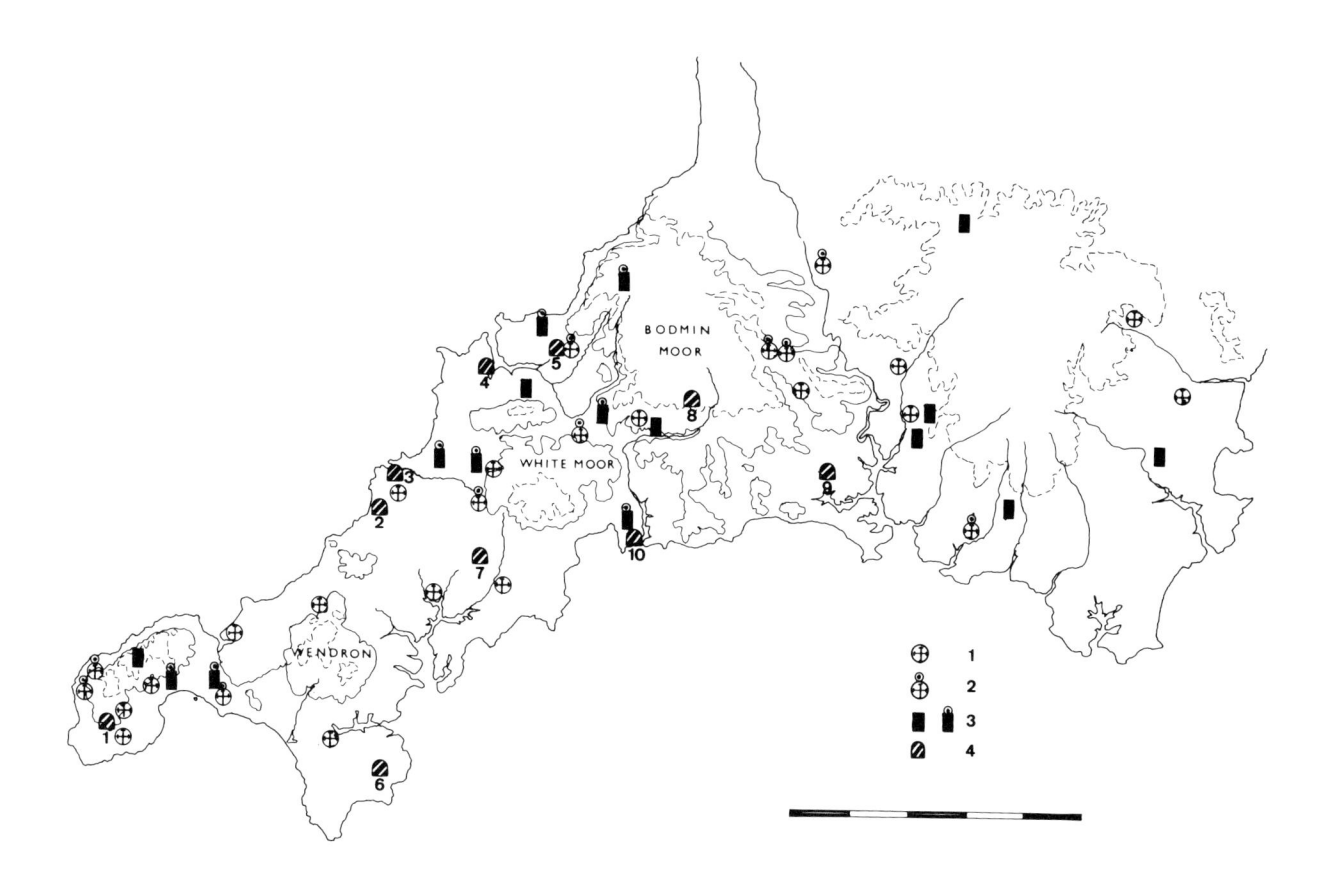

**Fig. 18.2** Dumnonia; sixth–seventh century diffusion of Christianity, as suggested by memorials. **Key**: 1, memorials at ecclesiastical locations (mostly churchyards). 2, the same, single-name memorials (for clerics?). 3, memorials in the landscape with (dotted circle above) type (d) memorials distinguished. 4. B. L. Olson's (1989) 'reasonably certain' pre-Norman monasteries – *1*, St Buryan, *2*, Lanpiran, *3*, Crantock, *4*, Padstow, *5*, Landocco (St Kew), *6*, St Keverne, *7*, Probus, *8*, St Neot, *9*, St Germans; added here, *10*, Langorthou (Fowey). Contours at 600 feet and (Cornwall only) 400 feet. Scale, 25 miles (40 kms).

existed on historical and archaeological grounds (her other category ('significant doubt, but monastic explanation is best') is omitted). The sole adjustment has been to substitute a *Langorthou* at Fowey, p. 232, for her question-marked symbol at Golant.

The outcome is as near as one can hope to get, using present evidence, to a depiction of the initial stage of Christian activity in Dumnonia west of the Tamar. Nothing would be gained by superimposing the bounds of the six ancient hundreds, or denoting places with *lys-* place-names (Fig.13.2), or inserting the few spots like Tintagel which might be called 'high-status defensive sites' of

AD 500–700. We are looking at a map that may be over-simplified – necessarily but not grotesquely so – of, not an Early Christian landscape, but a landscape with evidence for Christian burials and for dispersed ecclesiastical sites. It is certain that comparable maps could be produced for Demetia, AD 450 to 700, but it would have doubled the length of this volume to have included such maps and explanations. For Fig.18.2, perhaps the clearest impression should be of the absence of a hierarchical dimension, or of any spatial reflection of a Church having designated leaders tied to central places (i.e., bishops with diocesan seats); and yet 'pre-organized' would be a more accurate term than 'disorganized'.

The seventh century author of the Life of the sixth-century man Samson may have known that Dumnonia, or at least Cornwall, had no bishops. The mid-Cornish spiritual setting in which he placed Samson was rudimentary and we are given a glimpse (p. 230) of the saint being urged to stay and to accept a bishopric accorded by popular election. Wrmonoc's late-ninth-century Life of Paul Aurelian is not entirely an independent source because a good many aspects of the narrative are lifted from the older *Vita Samsonis*; but again, in what the author may have believed was a period about a century after Samson's visit, 'King Mark' is made to implore Paul similarly to accept a territorial bishopric (*pontificatum suae regionis*). This is again a *regio* of Dumnonia with Christianity *prae novitate huc illucque nutans* 'because of its newness, (still) wavering here and there'.[11] Near-contemporary witness comes from the long letter[12] addressed, c.705, by Aldhelm of Malmesbury to *Geruntius*, king of *Domnonia* (this is the historical Gereint II, p. 213 earlier). Aldhelm was a noted Latin stylist and his choice of synonyms, as of obscure words, reflects this. The letter opens with a reference to a recently held council of *episcopi* 'bishops' ('where from nearly all of Britannia an innumerable crowd of the *sacerdotes* of God came together'). When the churchmen of Dumnonia are mentioned, they are 'your *sacerdotes* and *clerici*' just as in the proem Geruntius is addressed with his *cunctis Dei sacerdotibus per Domnoniam conversantibus* 'encircling *sacerdotes* of God serving with devotion throughout Dumnonia'. This is partly rhetoric; *sacerdos* 'one holding Divine office' could mean both bishop and priest; but the letter, sent from Malmesbury in the expectation of being read out and of enforcing spiritual compliance, was addressed first of all to the king, not to any *episcopi Dumnoniorum* (who are not mentioned). Did Aldhelm's *sacerdotes et clerici* mean 'priests and minor orders' only? While this must be inconclusive, it is not until nearly two centuries later that we encounter bishops of Cornwall, with a see that had shifted from St Petroc's monastery at Bodmin to *Lanalet*, St Germans, before being transferred c.1050 to Exeter and revived at Truro in 1877. Lastly, for the earlier centuries, we have to take note that not once, in over fifty south-western inscriptions, do we find words like *sacerdos* (or even *presbyter*) that occur in Scotland and Wales.[13]

The provisional Early Christian map in Fig.18.2, then, may reflect an ecclesiastical world – small, but real – which had not yet been subjected to any kind of hierarchy, or network, or system; and in the absence of a detectable system we revert to the components from which eventually a territorial and hierarchical system would be built. Apart from the very few sixth-century monasteries (which would have looked like any other sixth-century hamlet with huts, plots and the general mess of a life-support smallholding), the most likely component would have been created when a repetitive and specifically Christian activity became anchored to a particular spot. That activity might take the form of burial in a consecrated plot (a cemetery), communal worship in or around a dedicated building (a church), or a combination of the two. In Dumnonia, as probably over most of Wales, the noun and also the place-name element for this was (Pr.Co., Pr.W) *lann*, the earlier British *landa*. The development of meanings is far from clear but some such sequence as 'rough meadow' > 'small enclosed meadow' > 'enclosure' > 'churchyard, church, monastery' must be approximately right.[14] Early ecclesiastical place-names formed with *lann* are as important in Cornwall (> *lan*) as they are in Wales (>*llan*) but in trying to exploit the evidence we meet with a certain frustration. There *are* by now quite a number of excavated sites, mostly cemeteries, that are demonstrably pre-700; but we do not know by what place-names they were called at that time. There *are* places with names in Lan-, Llan-, acceptable as very early but we cannot now find the, probably very small, physical monuments that bore these names. And when we encounter an embanked curvilinear graveyard enclosure like, say, Lanivet, where there is every chance that Christian activity *and* the original name go back well before 700, a desirable excavation is not possible because – almost by definition – these are Christian sites still in use and thus inaccessible.

In Britain, the religious as opposed to secular names of primary Christian locations have arisen by several routes. One is a patronal name; a first church, leading to a sequence of churches that can end with a cathedral, takes its name from the burial of a holy person, a *sanctus* (St Albans, from the Roman-period martyr *Albanus*), or else does so because an altar incorporates a relic of a saint from somewhere else – some early churches in south-west Scotland (Whithorn? Kirkmadrine?) had a relic of St Martin of Tours,[15] and the Northumbrian monasteries at Jarrow and at Wearmouth had relics of St Paul and the Apostle Peter respectively. But these are figures venerated in more than one European country; universal saints. The patron of Lewannick church happens to be St Martin (of Tours) and that ascription will have been Norman, because Anglo-Norman church founders venerated St Martin.

The Cornish names with *Lan-* may be known to us from records of the twelfth and later centuries but it is a safe assumption that many of them came into use very much earlier. Nearly all have the shape of *Lan* plus a personal name. Locatives or ascriptives, like Lanivet (**lann neved*) and the medieval *Langorthou*, are rare. There are at least three possibilities, all matched in the closely comparable place-names of Demetia (and indeed of Wales generally). We may have the name of the cleric, a priest or subsequent *sanctus*, regarded as the founding figure, whose body, contemporary grave or subsequent shrine, was a central feature of the site. Names of this kind will have been those of extremely local, as opposed to universal, saints; and as patron saints some are with us today. The old church at Perranzabuloe (Perran *in sabulo* 'in the sand-dunes') was *Lanberan* in 1303. Its name began as a compound of *\*lann* and Peran or Piran, with numerous relics of the saint (whoever he was), and retains his patronal name for the parish and the modern church – he is in fact generally considered as Cornwall's patron saint. By no means 'universal', this saint's name also figures in Perranporth, Perran Sands, Perranwell, Perranarworthal, etc., and plenty of little Cornish boys are still christened 'Perran' (spelled various ways).

Oliver Padel's examination of parish-status *Lan-* place-names[16] considered a division, subject of much past speculation, into those where the personal name remains as today's patron saint and often also parish name – Lamorran (969, *Lannmoren*) or Lanhydrock (1299, *Lanhidrok*) – and those where it differs, or is lost, or has been transferred, or is inexplicable; St Erth, patron still 'St Erth', one of the alleged Irish incomers who faced King Teudar (p. 187), was in 1269 *Lanuthno*. Two further possibilities here are, *one*, that '-uthno', in 1204 *Lanuthinoch*, is not a personal name but a locative or district-name;[17] *two*, that it *is* a personal name, deflected from an older form like Breton *Guethenoc* (833, 866), *Uethenoc*[18] and that he was either (a) a pious landowner who first gave and dedicated that plot of land now occupied by St Erth parish church and churchyard, or (b) another early *sanctus* – earlier or later than 'Erth' – whose name was preferentially preserved until a full-size medieval church was built.

The truth is that we have no way of choosing between such alternatives, each of which is supportable as an explanation. Nor is there much enlightenment to be sought from inscriptions. The case of Lewannick comes to mind. Physically, today's parish churchyard contains an inner element which is a partly-oval enclosure, clearly primary, the eastern side of which is still a massive bank. It is the archaeological equivalent of what is meant by *\*lann*. Since the site yields two clerical memorials of *circa* 500–50, 466 *Ingenui* and 467 *Ulcagni*, there is every reason to see it as a Christian location beginning as a burial-place for some Demetian settlers and then native converts; subsequently all or part of it was enclosed in a dug bank surrounding a curvilinear space; this *lann* was 'developed' with one or more small stone churches; a fine new church (whose ornate Norman font is still there) was built after 1100; and it continues to be what it has been for fifteen centuries, the spiritual focus of an arbitrary tract defining the parish.

Supposing that *Ingenuus* and *Ulcagnus* were successive priests, the first such priests, venerated as holy persons; we know both were buried here (*memoria* of the former, the latter *ic iacit*). Yet the name of the sacred site, and of the parish, is neither 'Laneggan' nor 'Lanolfan', which is what these personal names might have yielded in late Middle Cornish. In c.1125 it was *Lanwenuc*.

Who was 'Wenuc'? Here is a wholly imaginary scenario. If we accept a date of around 500 for the existence of the monastery at or near St Kew, under Docco, then a few decades later Samson met a man from there whose name may have been (Latinized) Uiniauus, *Uiniau. The Life suggests that he was the head of this little house. The inland Demetian settlers at Lewannick may have had occasional contact with others around the Camel basin and, as Christians, they may have turned to the monastery of Docco as a principal Christian centre. 'Wenuc' looks like a hypocoristic name; 'Uinoc' is the likely hypocoristic form of Uiniau (as of almost any name starting with Uin(d), Uinn 'fair, blessed, white' >uindo-; St Winnow, east Cornwall, in 1086 San Winnuc, has been explained as a hypocoristic of Winwaloe (Gunwalloe)[19]). Had a real Uiniau gone, later in his career — say in 540 × 550 — from St Kew to Lewannick, and had he ended his life with the spiritual cure of families around Lewannick, then the local fame of his tomb (as 'Uinoc's') might have eclipsed that of his predecessors. A seventh-century *lann* of Uinoc could follow. (The solitary twelfth-century record as Lanwenuc would not preclude this derivation.)

There is no reason to regard the above as anything except as a piece of imagination; it is not easy, either, to detect such place-names where a lay benefactor may be remembered (Llandingad at Llandovery, p. 143, is among a very few possible cases), but there is again nothing to say that 'Wenuc' was not some sixth-century Dumnonian who, after conversion, provided a burial-ground for his locality. Too many alternatives can be adduced for the formation of Christian place-names at a far-distant era when virtually the only names we know are those preserved on inscribed memorials. Nowhere in Cornwall is any such epigraphic name repeated in that of an early cemetery or church-site. The rationale, now beyond detection, of why about twenty Cornish parish-church names consist of *lan*- plus the existing patron saint, and conversely why about twenty show *lan*- plus another name altogether, cannot be explained by distribution-maps. Fig. 18.3 plots the two kinds. It should be realized that there were almost certainly many more names of either sort, names that have been lost because pre-Norman enclosed cemeteries or chapelries failed to attain eleventh-century parochial status, or went out of use. From the contrasting samples, it might be guessed that the pattern of (*lan* plus other-than-patron) names is rather closer to that of all the inscribed memorials together, and to the 'early Christian landscape' map of Fig. 18.2. Does this suggest that name-forms of this non-patron kind, for which (as we saw) there could be any one of several explanations, were by and large formed *earlier*? The upper map (*lan* plus patron) contains more of the names of pre-Norman monasteries; may this not simply mean that a name of a monastic founder, like *Docco*, is inherently likely to have been remembered, revered and preserved?

What we know of the monasteries included in Fig. 18.2, those identified with 'reasonable certainty',[20] comes from a few charters, the Domesday survey, and pre- or post-Conquest status as *collegia* of canons or as priories, and

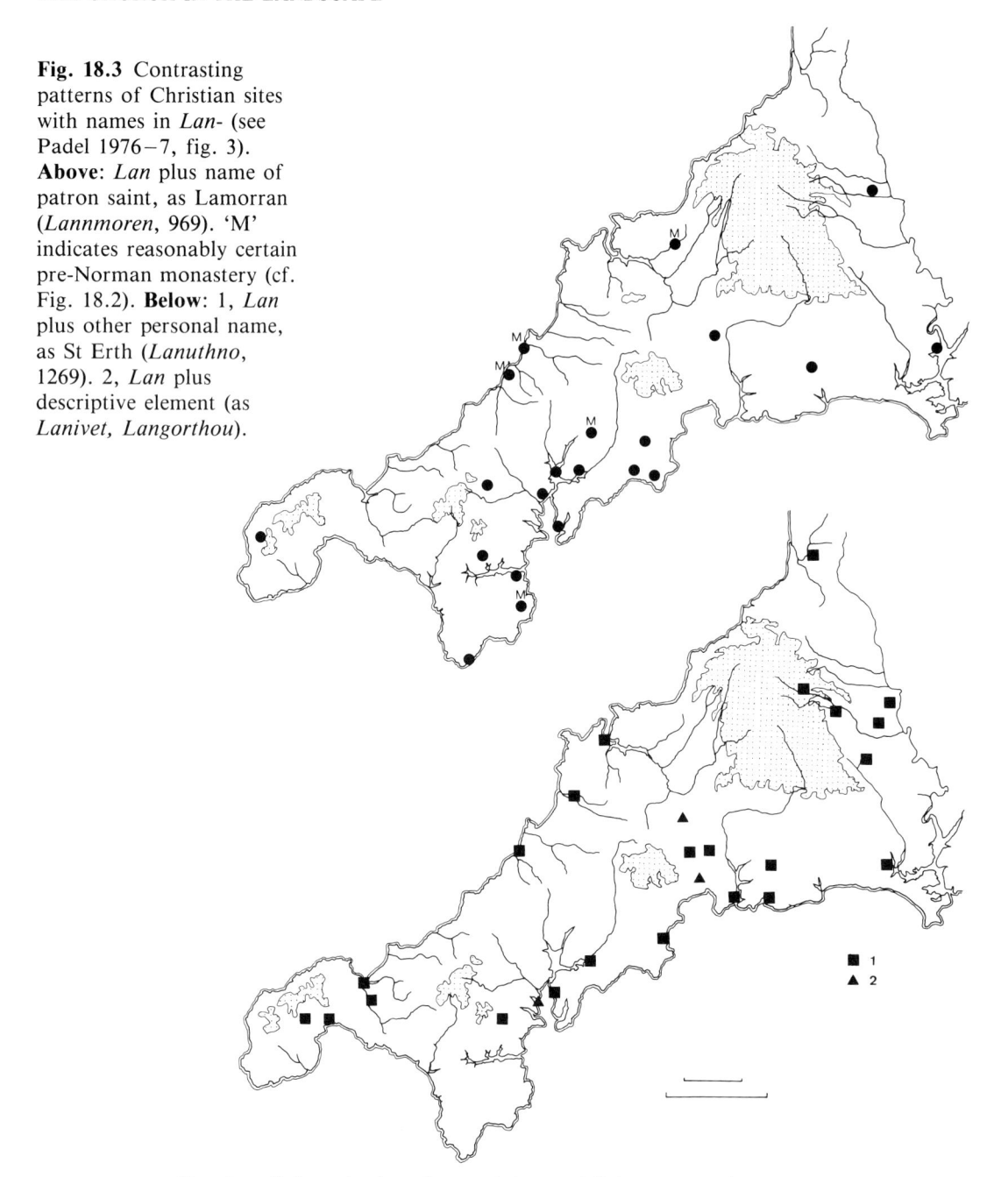

**Fig. 18.3** Contrasting patterns of Christian sites with names in *Lan-* (see Padel 1976–7, fig. 3). **Above**: *Lan* plus name of patron saint, as Lamorran (*Lannmoren*, 969). 'M' indicates reasonably certain pre-Norman monastery (cf. Fig. 18.2). **Below**: 1, *Lan* plus other personal name, as St Erth (*Lanuthno*, 1269). 2, *Lan* plus descriptive element (as *Lanivet, Langorthou*).

medieval tradition. Archaeology might establish when each was founded, but there will be a broad impression that the later sixth and seventh centuries are involved. Here, only those along the northern shores are discussed. From west to east they are: *Ecglosberria* (DB), St Buryan parish church; *Lanpiran* (DB), St Piran, Perranzabuloe Old Church; *Langoroch* (DB), St Carantoc, Crantock parish church; *Lanwenehoc* (DB), *Landwethinoch* (*c.* 1100), St Petroc replacing Wethinoc, Padstow parish church; and *Landochou* (tenth-cent.), Docco, replaced by St Cywa, St Kew parish church.

Given what has been said already, we should expect that medieval traditions concerning the last four might point to south Wales (with an Irish colouring) for founders; and for St Buryan in the Land's End, to Ireland without the intermediacy of Wales. This is precisely the case. Despite the later standing of St Piran or Perran, any Life of him was lost. All that we have is a late-medieval pirating of a life of St Ciaran of Saighir that tells us nothing about Piran. The name *Coroc* (or *Corroc*, or *Carroc*) at Crantock is hypocoristic, from *Carantoc*, the Welsh Carannog. The medieval Welsh *Vita* (*Prima*)[21] makes him a high-born native of Cardiganshire – Llan*grannog* there preserves his name – who lived at the time of Irish invaders, visited Ireland and then sailed to Cornwall to found a church at *Carrum* (Crantock). Before his death he visited *ostium Guellit* and founded another at *Carrou* – this is to explain the Somerset river Willit, and Carhampton. At Padstow we find St Petroc, of royal stock and also a native of Wales (cf. Llanbedrog, or St Petrox, Pembs.) who pays a visit to Ireland.[22] He sails to *amnem Hailem* (the Camel estuary) where he finds the cell of a hermit 'Samson' and a monastery where a bishop Wethinoc lives with his monks (*cella ... cum suis*). *Petroc displaces Wethinoc but allows his name to remain attached to the place (hence, e.g., 1361 Lanwethenek*), founds a small retreat and then journeys inland up the Camel, like Samson. He meets a hermit Guron or Uuron, once more overshadows him, but allows his name to remain attached to this final monastery (*Dinuurin*, at or near Bodmin). The *Vita Petroci* offers explanatory tales for the non-Petroc names of Petroc's monastery, first at Padstow and rather later (*c.* 900?) when it moved to Bodmin. Of *Landochou*, St Kew, all we really know comes from *Vita Samsonis* – 'Docco' may or may not have been a late fifth-century Christian hero[23] – but a connection with Wales, or south-east Wales, seems very likely.

The foundation-stories are set in a local never-never time, a heroic age. Carantoc, landing somewhere near Crantock, meets as joint rulers *Cato* and *Arthur* and there is a mention of their citadel, *Dindraithou*.[24] Petroc encounters a cruel tyrant *Teudur*, who is the 'King Teudar' (p. 197) of Phillack transposed eastwards. For St Buryan all that remains is John Leland's note[25] that 'S. Buriana an holy woman of *Irelond* sumtyme dwellid in this place and there made an oratory', and the twelfth-century *Exeter Martyrology*'s entry for 1 May[26] about *In hibernia sancte Berrione virginis*, 'St Berriona, virgin, (from) Ireland' through whose merits the son of a king was cured of paralysis. We are not disappointed when we read that the king was *Gerentius*, though it matters little if he was the one alive in 705 or his much earlier namesake (p. 212). The tradition here is of a direct link with Ireland; no mention of Wales.

What sort of conclusions can be expected? Lynette Olson sees this south-western evidence as suggesting 'a derivative rather than a primary role for the region in the monastic movement', and that is certainly fair; nothing here matches the world of Dubricius, Illtutus and others in south-east Wales and the plausability of houses like Llanilltud Fawr extant around 500.

Full discussion of the Cornish material would take us far beyond this work's limit of AD 700, but the likely picture may be of certain foundations, possibly of the late sixth century – consolidating an early sixth-century introduction of the Faith – that acquired full monastic status in the seventh century. In this, the monasteries must have differed physically from the very much larger range of *lann* sites, that remained no more than communal burial-places to which the first small churches might be added. And fieldwork begins to permit this interpretation. The model is of a smaller, central (or sometimes off-centre) *lann* of the enclosed-cemetery kind, within a bigger tract that may or may not have been defined by banks and ditches, hedges or other visible bounds. Monastic establishments on such lines were first postulated for much of Ireland[27] and, since exact equivalent *lanns* are a feature of most of early Christian Wales, it is encouraging to know that 'concentric enclosure' sites have now been recognized from the air in Demetia.[28]

*Landochou* may have comprised the present churchyard – near which 484 *Iusti* was, after all, picked up – and attached land stretching as far as the farm tenement of Lanow, a half-mile away. At Padstow, Dr Olson finds traces of what may be an extensive outer enclosure with a bank as *vallum monasterii*, defining land of which Padstow churchyard occupies only a fraction.[29] The evidence from *Langorroc*, Crantock, is considerable though confusing; activity seems to have extended beyond the (quite large) 'Old Churchyard' and as at Phillack there are hints of a pre-Christian burial area.[30]

*Lanpiran* stands in the rolling wastes of Perran Sands. The (seventh-century?) core would have comprised the now re-buried 'St Piran's Oratory', a tenth-century secondary church; and the unenclosed (?) cemetery around it. Not far off is the *lann* itself, a large ovoid enclosure marked by a visible low bank; within it is the abandoned Old Parish Church, whose north-east part is another tenth-century church incorporated into a medieval structure, and also a tall granite cross that appears to be the *cristel mael* in a charter of 960.[31] The churchyard at St Buryan with its late tenth-century cross and medieval church is the nucleus of *Ecglosberria*; a goodly estate of at least seven tenements was attached, surrounding it, one that was later recognized as a boundary sanctuary. The holding was confirmed by Aethelstan in a charter of 925 × 939[32] but, as with *Lanpiran*, this marked a likely re-constitution – not foundation, or re-founding – of an older establishment.

With the others listed by Dr Olson these need not have been all the pre-Norman monasteries in Cornwall. We must allow for foundations that functioned as monasteries for limited periods, or simply closed down and were abandoned, or have left inadequate records.[33] Ann Preston-Jones has shown that Mawgan in Meneage, where the *c.* 600 memorial of 469 *Cnegumi* could stand at a way-in through an outer enclosure stretching far around the parish churchyard,[34] is a likely candidate. And though early nomenclature of all the Christian locations involved other words, probably all post-700 – like *merther* (possessing a corporeal relic of a named saint?), *eglos* (for a full 'proto-parochial' church, perhaps by the tenth century) and even the rare loanword *mynster*[35] – the word *\*lann*, in Dumnonia as in Wales,[36] is at once the most important, the common factor and probably the oldest of the lot. Out of the eleven 'reasonably certain' monasteries, seven – eight if *Langorthou* replaces St Samson, Golant – have names in *Lan-*, today or formerly. Looking again at the map, Fig. 18.2, though in the text the Christian sites, mostly churchyards, have been given their modern names, we can note the following; Madron, *Landithy*; St Just in Penwith, *Lanuste* (1396); Cubert, *Lannowen* (1635) and of course Lanivet and Lewannick. Physically even if no such place-name is recorded 'lanns' constitute the older parts of the churchyards at Sancreed, St Hilary, Redruth, Mawgan in Meneage, (probably) St Columb Major and (emphatically) Cardinham.

Since the *lanns* of both Demetia and Dumnonia share with the inscribed stones the claim to be our oldest archaeological monuments of Christianity it is as well to stress that hardly any have been excavated, and that consequently we rely on surface archaeology alone. As abandoned rural sites, when protected by legislation they are unlikely to be threatened except by internal ploughing or forestry. This generally precludes rescue-excavation; as churchyards still in use, the commonest threat – road-widening – will expose only a small part of a perimeter.[37] A *lann* is thus easier to recognize than to expound in sequential detail. Fig. 18.4, almost a random choice, gives a schematized map of the village of Luxulyan in mid-Cornwall, once a granite-quarry hamlet,[38] and in 1338 *Lansulien*. Dedication of the fifteenth-century church, replacing a Norman one whose font survives, is to Cyricius and Julitta. The shadowy *Sulien* sinks back into obscurity.[39]

One could draw similar maps for fifty or more Cornish churchtowns, as one could in Demetia; Fig.18.5, which avoids poaching from published examples, is a small cross-section including one probable re-used fortified site (Mydrim, as indicated by Heather James). Should this seem to overlook the rest of Dumnonia, Fig. 18.6, taken from Professor Susan Pearce's work,[40] offers a representative sample. Stowford, by the A30, now a picturesque and isolated village, is centred on a well-defined *lann* on a slight slope. By its entrance stands the vertically inscribed pillar 1060 *Gunglei*, a priest's memorial of about 700.

The nature of resemblances – fortuitous or causative? – between sacred and profane sites of similar sizes and shapes could draw us towards religious phenomenology and Eliade's teachings. *Lanns* do resemble the small curvilinear enclosed homesteads of both Dumnonia (the 'round', *ker*, *caer*) and Demetia (the 'rath'). One distinction is that the enclosing bank (often with ditch) of a round can be substantial; a proper stone-faced rampart, shielding a native farm with its children, livestock and possessions from raptors animal or human. The very few

## THE CHURCH IN THE LANDSCAPE

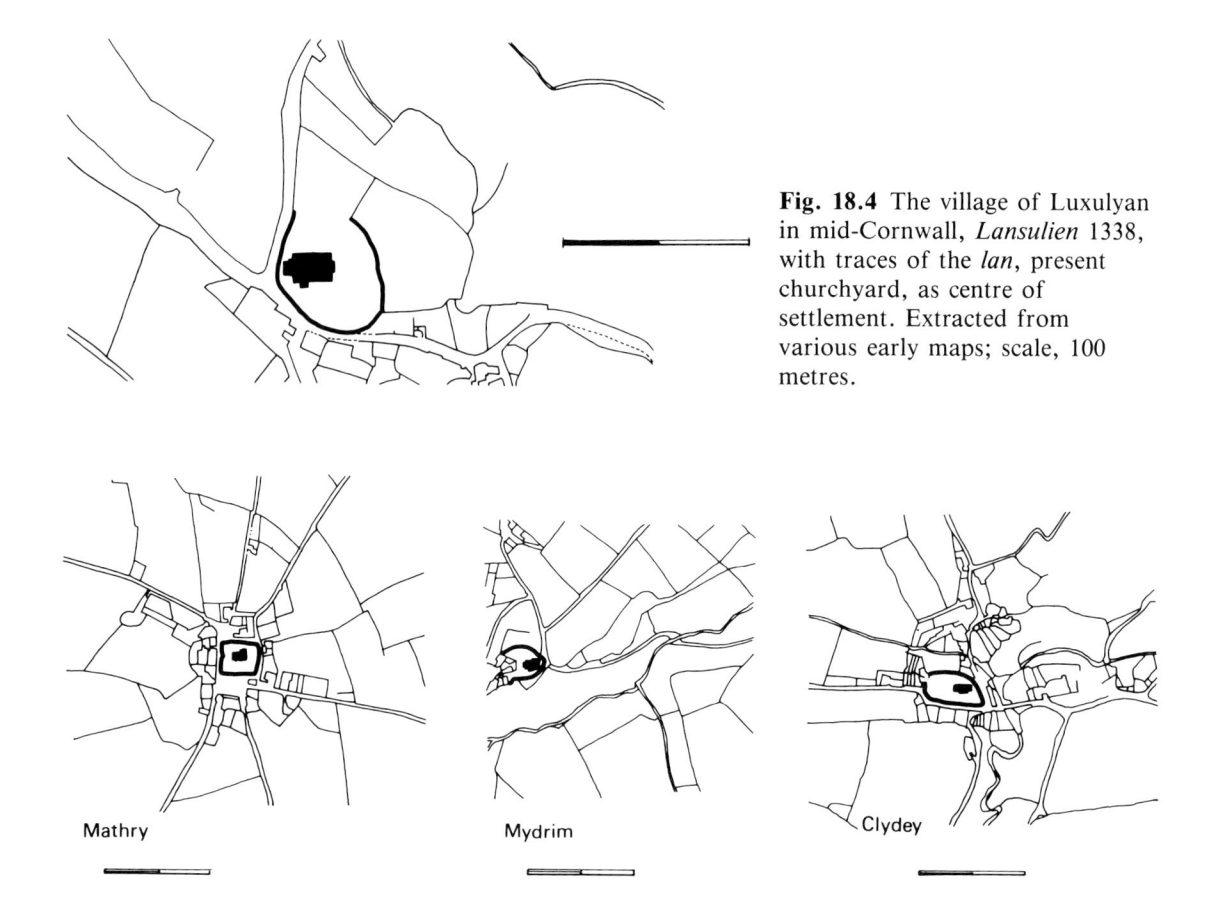

**Fig. 18.4** The village of Luxulyan in mid-Cornwall, *Lansulien* 1338, with traces of the *lan*, present churchyard, as centre of settlement. Extracted from various early maps; scale, 100 metres.

**Fig. 18.5** Demetia; early cemetery enclosures of different kinds as parish churchyards (maplets kindly provided by the Dyfed Archaeological Trust). Mathry, despite shape, should be early; Mydrim (Meidrim) shows re-use of small hill-spur fort; Clydey (Clydai) is probably sixth-century. Scale for all, 200 metres.

sections across the banks of custom-built *lanns* like Beacon Hill on Lundy (p. 165) and now at Tintagel churchyard,[41] indicate rather a symbolic bound – visible, even prominent, but not defensive. As for size and shape Ann Preston-Jones supplies a telling diagram[42] in which near-identical plans of five rounds and twelve *lanns*, from all over Cornwall, are set side by side. If the Cornish round or *ker* be taken in its several hundreds as the standard homestead enclosure of the Roman centuries, the fact that very few can been shown by excavation to have been still inhabited by the fifth and sixth centuries[43] does not negate the further fact that most would have been visible enough to provide a sacred-enclosure model in the sixth, seventh or eighth centuries. The connection may be closer still because, just as there are cases from elsewhere in Britain of abandoned fortifications being

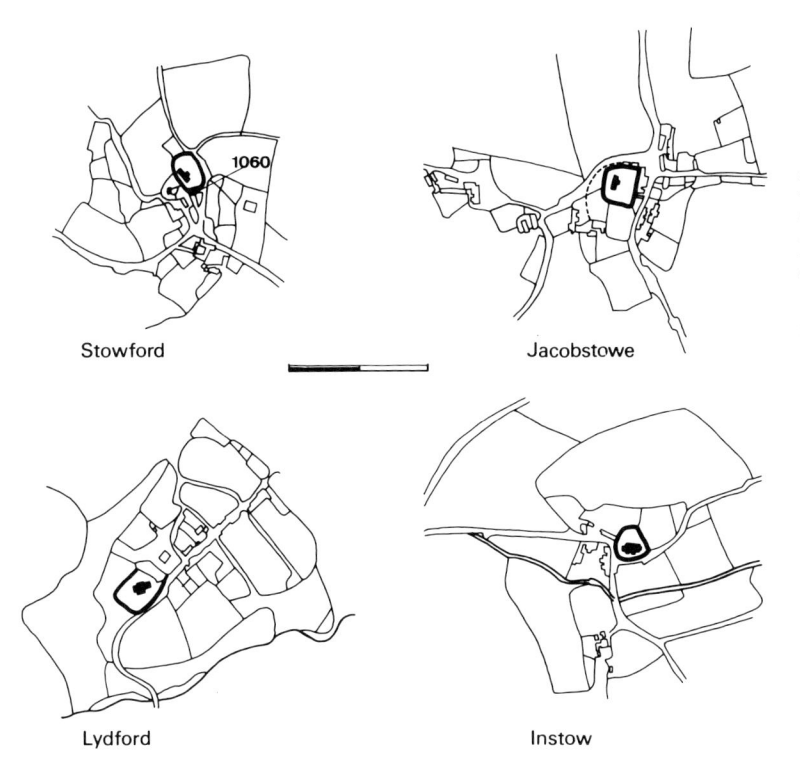

**Fig. 18.6** Dumnonia (Devon only); reasonably certain pre-Norman *lanns* as parish churchyards, from the 1840s Tithe Apportionment maps (Pearce 1985; reproduced with Professor Susan Pearce's kind permission). Note inscribed memorial 1060 at Stowford, and how English *-stow* replaces probable earlier British *\*lann*. Scale for all, 200 metres.

granted to saints for monastic establishments,[44] Dumnonia can provide its own examples. The core of the monastery of the virgin *Berriona* at St Buryan, the parish churchyard, was clipped by road-widening in 1984 (Fig. 18.7); limited excavation allowed the conclusion that inside the present wall the traces of a stone-faced bank, and diagnostic pottery, suggested that this was originally a late Iron Age or Roman-period round. Nothing short of a full exploration would tell us how long before any tenth-century reconstitution of the monastery (p. 316; probably with construction of a new church) Christian use began. Excavation of the pronouncedly oval *lann*, of Merther-Uny near Wendron, some years ago, showed a long ecclesiastical sequence, up to a medieval stone chapel of sub-parochial status. This began around 900 with a tall dedicatory cross at the entrance, dug graves and cist-graves, and some small early church. However, remains of two circular huts with native Roman-period pottery confirmed that the substantial enclosing bank with outer ditch began as a conventional round, abandoned for four or five centuries before being chosen as a Christian cemetery.[45] In mid-Cornwall again the isolated granite hill of St Dennis among the clay-pits is crowned by its parish church. But 'Dennis' is a ghost-patron, some Anglo-Norman muddle from Cornish *dinas* 'fort'; this is a fine stone-ramparted fortlet, as a 1962 trench showed,[46] with remains of a second outer

**Fig. 18.7** Dumnonia; the re-use of deserted secular enclosures as Christian sites. **Left**, St Dennis, mid-Cornwall, bivallate stone-ramparted fort (*\*Dinmelioc*? minor excavations, 1962) with twelfth-century church and churchyard. **Right**, St Buryan, west Cornwall, possibly a small monastery of VII(?), confirmed by charter in X, with medieval parish church, in an older 'round'. Scales for both, 30 yards over 30 metres.

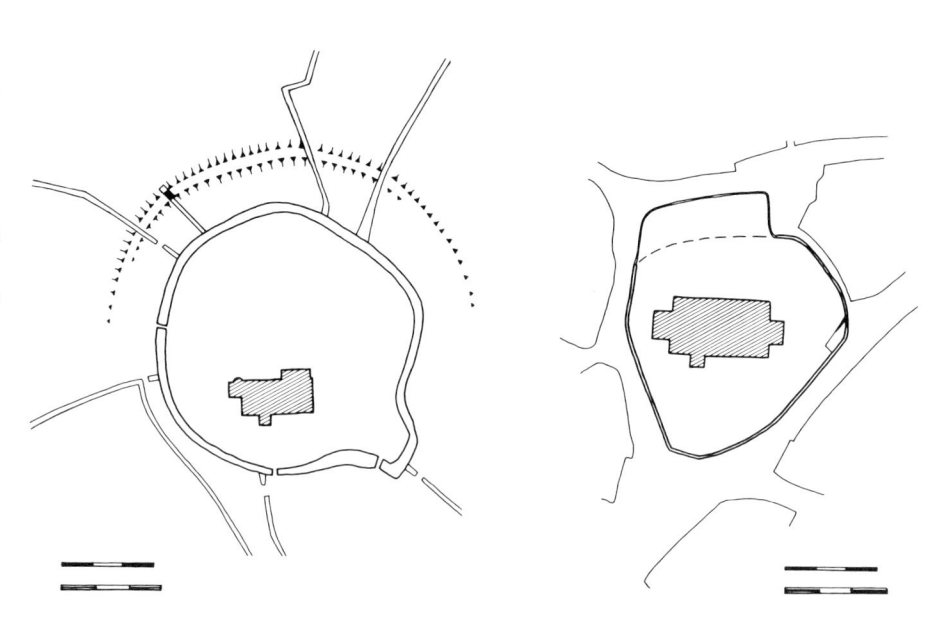

rampart. It is the *\*Dinmelioc* of legend (p. 5). The church is twelfth century (Fig. 18.7). Nothing suggests re-occupation earlier than this horizon. With such Dumnonian sites goes, in Demetia, Heather James's 1979 excavation at Caer, Bayvil, near Caerau (Pembs.);[47] the abandoned Iron Age *caer* or 'rath' was filled by oriented graves that appeared to be set in rows, and graves were even dug into the ramparts. Here a dense but undeveloped cemetery which may eventually have held some 3,400 graves was conveniently located in a ready-made *lann* of Iron Age origin.

What must also not be overlooked in any Early Christian landscape analysis is the shifting-cemetery syndrome; one site may have replaced another without record in the distant past, usually because of threats from natural causes. *Lanpiran* (p. 316) would today still hold the parish church, if encroaching sand had not made it necessary to dismantle that church (1805) and to rebuild it a couple of miles inland.[48] This is, at least, recorded. Lelant church – with fine Norman work in it – stands on the west shore of the Hayle estuary (Fig. 12.1), visible from Carnsew; the patron is St Uny (female), an 'Irish' incomer also commemorated at Redruth and Merther-Uny, and William Worcestre in 1478 – making her *Sanctus* Uny, brother to St Erth – learnt that she *iacet* (lay, was buried; i.e., had a shrine) in the parish church of St Uny *prope villam Lalant* 'next to Lelant town'.[49]

Lelant was, c. 1200, *Lananta*. It is not clear why one local non-universal saint's name should have replaced another; *\*Anta* may appear in the name of some (sunken) rocks near the mouth of the estuary, Chapel-Ainger or Chapel-Annyer, if this is where the 1495 *capella Sancte Ante alias Ansa* once stood.[50] Lelant churchyard is raised internally and substantially embanked, but its sub-rectangular plan (Fig. 18.8) is that of the Norman foundation, not of a *lann* at all. By chance, what may have been the *lann* of *Ansa* or *Anta* was intersected in 1875 when the branch

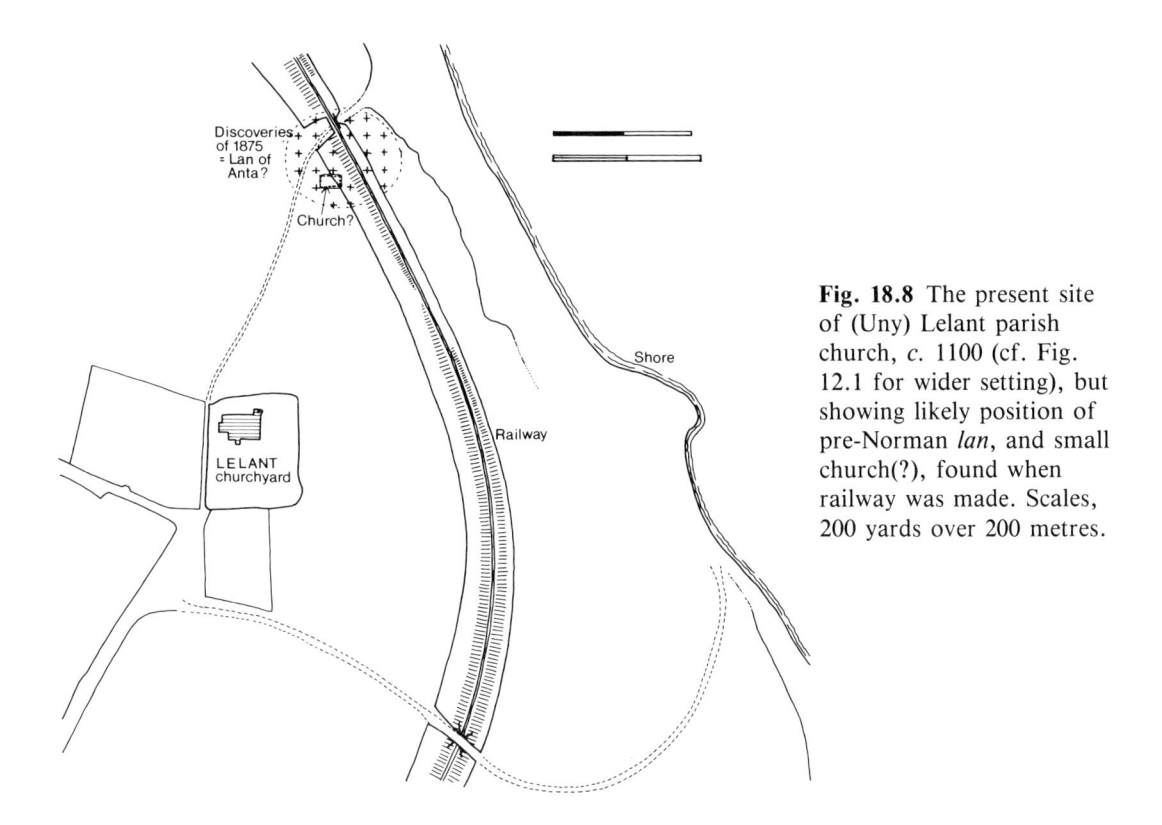

**Fig. 18.8** The present site of (Uny) Lelant parish church, *c.* 1100 (cf. Fig. 12.1 for wider setting), but showing likely position of pre-Norman *lan*, and small church(?), found when railway was made. Scales, 200 yards over 200 metres.

railway was built.[51] The cutting went straight through a cist-grave cemetery and, on the west side, what sounds like part of some small early church. Blowing sand, or an eroding shore-line, induced a removal inland around 1100, probably with Uny's shrine from Anta's *lann* being re-housed in the new Norman church. However, but for 'God's Wonderful Railway', neither this puzzle nor its solution might ever have come to light. We can even forgive the navvies who sought out the Early Christian jawbones with teeth, to preserve them 'as an antidote against the toothache' – a display of sympathetic magic if ever there was one.

In this work the whole range of Dumnonian inscriptions has been presented as ending with the seventh century. A funerary fashion simply died out. The position in Wales may not have been quite the same; but neither were Welsh circumstances, since a far more evolved ecclesiastical system (notably in such old counties as Glamorgan) favoured partial continuity. Nevertheless the typical, vertical, Demetian inscribed memorial gradually went out of use. One could point to intermediate monuments, intermediate in type and probably in date between *ECMW* Group I and the more elaborate inscribed and sculptured Group III ('culminating development of Welsh Early Christian monumental art . . . the cross . . . either in the round . . . or in relief as a shaped cross-slab . . . a number bear inscriptions (as) tombstones or personal memorials') to which a ninth–eleventh century date was allotted. An appropriate inscription to mark this caesura in commemorative styles, certainly for Wales, would be, not the famous Pillar of Eliseg (*ECMW* 182) but the slab naming two Brycheiniog princes – as surely they were – now safely inside the half-forgotten little church at Llanllywenfel or Llanlleonfel; where (a solitary link to the world outside!) Charles Wesley married Sarah Gwynne, 8 April 1749. On the stone, five horizontal lines surround a central cross in the middle of line 3 (Fig. 18.9). The inscription – *ECMW* 62, *CIIC*.ii 986 – is: *In sindone muti Ior/uert Ruallaunq*(ue) / *sepulcris + iudicii / adventum specta*(n)*t / i*(n) *pace tremendum*; 'Silent in the shroud, Iorweth and Ruallaun await in peace the dreadful coming of the Judgement'. [52] Llanllywenfel is not in Brycheiniog, but lies just north of Mynydd Epynt (p. 150), over the high ground and down into the broad vale of *Buellt*, Builth. If as seems likely the two men were brothers and, perhaps further, two brothers who fell in battle together, *Ruallaun* may be the Brycheiniog king fourth after Rein Dremrud son of Brychan;[53] with the marriage of Ruallaun's daughter *Keindrec*, 'Fair of face', to *Cloten*, fifth ruler in line after Guotepir (p. 56), the lines of Demetia and Brycheiniog were merged. This metrical epitaph may, like a reasonable estimate for the death of Ruallaun, belong to near the end of the seventh century. Standing there and reading it, one cannot help being conscious that it captures and preserves a moment of Welsh history and, even more so, that with it we have left behind all the older memorials of AD 400 to 650. The angular book-hand transferred to stone, the neat central cross, the sonorous wording and the inherent *dignity* of the memorial allow us to glimpse a composition by a priest attendant upon the Brycheiniog royal house. It is a fragment of contemporary manuscript cut into rock, and it has no counterpart in Dumnonia at all.

This coincidence, of the disappearance or discontinuation of the older Demetian and Dumnonian memorials, and of the disuse (p. 21) of the Class I Pictish stones – in regions where Christianity had been introduced at a secondary stage in the whole Insular memorial tradition from neighbouring lands already Christian – suggests that we may well look again to Stephen Driscoll's definition of the temporal change as 'the point at which the importance of the Church is outstripping that of the ancestors'. Indeed the memorial of Iorwerth and Ruallaun, omitting as it does parentage and any such words as *rex* or *princeps* (which would almost certainly have been included in VI, or even in VII.1), marks a transition; as perhaps does the resounding Christian closure with *adventum ... tremendum*. In Dumnonia, it was less a case of Death being the Great Leveller, than a likelihood that after 700 all or almost all Christians were being interred, in cist graves or dug graves, amid rows and clusters within enclosed cemeteries like Beacon Hill (p. 163). Social prominence, if marked at all, would not be indicated by inscribed pillars; but in different ways. Ground-level covering slabs with ornamentation, related to shrine coverings, is one idea (p. 177); upright and

**Fig. 18.9** Llanllywenfel or Llanlleonfel church, Brecon (in *Buellt*); large memorial slab, *CIIC* ii.986, *ECMW* no.62, perhaps *c* .700, to the (?) Brycheiniog princes and brothers, *Ioruert* and *Ruallaun*. Precise contemporary function is unclear; vertical memorial? recumbent cover-slab? even frontal panel of 'central cross' type (cf. Thomas, *ECANB*, 183 – 90) for an altar tomb. (Photograph: Susanna Thomas.)

impermanent markers of wood might be another.

If it seems unsatisfying to have to conclude with a depiction of late seventh century Dumnonia as a Christian landscape devoid of traces of internal hierarchy or spatial organization, dissatisfaction is lessened when we accept that the evidence forces one conclusion; this is still too *early* a picture to carry the weight of much detail. The peninsula sketched in Fig. 18.2 may have held at the outside 40,000 people, one-eleventh of its 1993 population. Three centuries on, the story will be very different and much more intricate, but that story belongs to another book. *This* one has left plenty of scope for further research, and plenty of indications about what such work might be. The contentions of our narrative stand firmly. The inscribed memorial stones of south-west Wales, with their vertical modality, owe their inception to Ireland. The style was brought with them by raiders who had turned into settlers, who may have known what Rome stood for but who became Christians (and Latinate) *after* their arrival, through coming into touch with sub-Roman Christian Wales. The conversion of the Dumnonians, similarly, followed a secondary and principally a land-seeking settlement originating in Wales. 'Early Christian Cornwall' and 'The Land of Saints' are resounding phrases but, until the second half of the sixth century, devoid of true meaning. We began with the two great peninsulas as separate political entities within Britannia, Atlantic *civitates* that would give way to post-Roman states; we end with this reminder of the long-ago debt that one peninsula may very well owe to the other.

# References

1. T. Taylor, *The Celtic Christianity of Cornwall* (Longmans, London 1916) with his pupil Charles Henderson's *The Cornish Church Guide* (Blackford, Truro 1928) and many other writings; G. H. Doble's whole series (to the late 1940s) of his *Cornish Saints* numbered booklets; and the present author's *Christian Antiquities of Camborne* (1967), various articles, and in part his *The Early Christian Archaeology of North Britain* (1971).
2. Olson 1989; Preston-Jones 1992; Padel 1976–7, and 1985 *passim*.
3. These are all given as chapters in Edwards & Lane 1992.
4. Nowakowski & Thomas 1992 – Tintagel, foundations of (*c.* 1000?) church north of twelfth-cent. parish church, inferred presence of earlier tenth-cent. church as well; Minster, 'Norman' chancel of church regarded as older late tenth or eleventh cent. church incorporated.
5. Thorne & Thorne 1979 (with Padel's translation and other contributions) is followed here for the forms of names.
6. J. Polsue, *Lake's Parochial History of Cornwall* (Lake, Truro 1867–73), i.336; Roscarrock, then 491 acres, was by Cornish standards large.
7. Possibly *nan(t)* 'valley' and *carrek* 'rock'; there is no trace of any early chapel.
8. I am grateful to Richard Warner (*in litt.*) for pointing out the significance of the Bleu Bridge find-spot of this stone.
9. H. C. Darby & R. Welldon Finn, eds., *The Domesday Geography of South-West England* (Cambridge 1967) includes – in *Cornwall*, by W. L. D. Ravenhill – 338, Fig.77, quantified map of 'sheep on the demesne in 1086' from the Domesday entries; it might well repay more detailed analysis.
10. Memorials (Cornwall, only) are: Demetian, 465 *Annicu*, 466 *Ingenui*, 467

*Ulcagni*, 484 *Iusti* – Dumnonian, 473 ... *igni*, 474 *Cruarigi*, 483 *Senilus* and (late) 481 *Noti*, 1055 *Taetuera*.

11. Wrmonoc, *Vita Sancti Pauli Aureliani*, cap.viii.
12. A. W. Haddan & W. Stubbs, *Councils and Ecclesiastical Documents ... etc.* vol.iii (Oxford 1871), 268 ff. The letter contains an unexpected side-swipe at the *Demetarum sacerdotes*, glorying in the currency of their worldly possessions. It is of course possible that Aldhelm chose to distinguish between *episcopi*, bishops of the converted English, and *sacerdotes* (of the British in Dumnonia and Demetia) of whose regular consecration he had private doubts.
13. Cf. Scotland, 516, two *sacerdotes*; *sacerdos* on the Peebles stone, *PSAS* 101 (1968–9), 127–9; Wales, *presbyteres* on 391 and 392, with 328 *sacerdos* and 384 *sacerdos* (all four from NW Wales).
14. So Rivet and Smith, in *PNRB*, 502.
15. This is contentious ground, but I have argued (Thomas 1992) that a relic of St Martin (d.397) brought from Gaul to Galloway a century or so later best explains subsequent records (e.g., Bede's) of a 'St Martin' church at Whithorn (or Kirkmadrine).
16. Padel 1976–7; Dr Padel also makes the point (p. 25) that Cornwall has certain parishes where it looks very much as if a universal saint has ousted, as patron, an obscure figure whose name may appear in a '*lan* plus non-patron' place-name.
17. Padel 1988, 82.
18. MSS of *Vita Samsonis* give the name as *Juniavum, Uiniavum, Uiniavus*; the equation of it in *britannica lingua* as *lux* 'light' must favour *Uiniau*, which would be Latinized as *Uiniavus*.
19. Padel 1988, 180.
20. Olson 1989, xiv, map A.
21. Piran – G. H. Doble, *St Perran, St Keverne & St Kerrian* (Long Compton 1931). Carannog – Wade-Evans, *VSBG* 143–9.
22. G. H. Doble, *St Petroc, a Cornish Saint* (3rd edn., Long Compton 1938).
23. For an extreme elevation of Docco into the historical realm, see John Morris, *The Age of Arthur* (1973), 350 ff.
24. *Din* 'fort' and (very probably) OCo. plur. *traitou* 'beaches, strands'. *Contra* Morris, op.cit., 645 index, and others before him, this is *not* 'Din(d) Tradui' from Cormac. The place intended was perhaps the Iron Age promontory fort of Trevelgue, between beaches east of Newquay.
25. Toulmin Smith, ed., i.189.
26. Ed. G. H. Doble, 'The Original Exeter Martyrology', in: vol.iv, 1–105, J. N. Dalton & G. H. Doble, eds., *Ordinale Exon*, 4 vols. (Henry Bradshaw Society, 1909–40).
27. Pioneer air-photographic research by Leo Swan; cf. his 'Enclosed ecclesiastical sites ... etc.', pp. 269–94 in: T. Reeves-Smith & F. Hammond, *Landscape Archaeology in Ireland* (BAR Brit.ser.116, Oxford 1983).
28. Terrence James, 'Air photography of ecclesiastical sites in south Wales', pp. 62–76 in: Edwards & Lane 1992.
29. Preston-Jones 1992, 121, fig.11.11.
30. B. L. Olson, 'Crantock, Cornwall, as an early monastic site', pp. 177–85 in: Pearce 1982.
31. C. Henderson's note, in Doble, *St Perran* ... (n.21 above). For the charter, see Sawyer no.684.
32. Sawyer no.450; Olson 1989, *passim*, for problems concerning what was probably a genuine original.
33. Minster, a short way north-east from Tintagel, *Talkarn* (DB), St Materiana – small church

34. Plan, see n.29 above.
35. Padel, 1976–7, discusses these and other words.
36. For *lann* in early Wales, see W. Davies 1978, 1982, *passim*; her analysis says just about all that can usefully be said at present.
37. The last three occasions in Cornwall (Phillack, Pelynt and St Buryan) all arose out of County Council minor road-widening exercises.
38. Luxullianite (so *OED*, 1878) is an attractive variety of granite, in past demand for tombstones, sarcophagi of national heroes, etc.
39. Padel 1976–7, 18; '**lann* and **loc* (Br. *loc*, 'chapel') were evidently interchangeable in this name'.
40. Plans from Pearce 1985, reproduced with her kind permission.
41. Nowakowski & Thomas 1992; 31–5, figs. 23, 24, section across low rubble bank, perhaps 2.5 m wide and a metre high with hint of low vertical external face, but no ditch.
42. Preston-Jones 1992, 115 fig. 11.6.
43. Trethurgy, St Austell, fifth–sixth cents.; Miles & Miles, *CA* 12(1973), 25–9.
44. *ECANB*, 33–4, lists the more obvious (Irish and Northumbrian) cases.
45. Illustrated report; Preston-Jones, *CA* 26 (1987), 153–60.
46. Ditto; Thomas, *CA* 4 (1965), 31–5.
47. H. James 1992 – one grave gave a date of (calibrated) AD 640–883 (CAR-291, 1290± 60 bp).
48. Useful general account, E. W. F. Tomlin, *In Search of St Piran* (Lodenek Press, Padstow 1982).
49. William Worcestre, ed. Harvey 1969, 114–5.
50. C. Henderson MS, RIC; from an episcopal register (Redmayne's).
51. Cyril Noall, 'Nineteenth-century discoveries at Lelant', *CA* 3 (1964), 34–6.
52. Nash-William's translation; *sindōn,-onis* (from Greek), meant textile of fine linen or muslin. Though there are New Testament echoes here – II Peter, iii.12, *exspectantes ... in adventum*, and Hebrews, x.27, *terribilis expectatio iudicii* – the epitaph may be a seventh-century composition, not a full quotation.
53. This note must anticipate a fuller study of Brycheiniog kingship; see now *EWGT* 45 (JC 20, 8) and 11 (Harl.3859, 15; with Dumville's corrections, *CMCS* 10 (1985), 48–50). There are suggestions of Brycheiniog reverses including loss of the Buellt of V and early VI (smaller than the later Buellt, Wendy Davies 1982, *passim*). The 'father'(?) of the Ruallaun here, Idwallawn, two kings later than Rigeneu son of Rein Dremrud, may also have been the *rex Iudguallaun* (*Llan Dâv*, 176–7) whom a *rex Clotri, rupta pace, occidit* 'having broken the peace, slew'. This, at *Garthbenni* (Welsh Bicknor), is undated. A *Clotri* (same man? another?) was granting land at Cemais, *Llan Dâv* 183–4, c.700 (so Wendy Davies 1979, 111), though it seems impossible to identify him in the surviving genealogies.

# Appendix
# The Dumnonian Inscriptions: Hand-list and Concordances

The hand-list is a guide to the Dumnonian inscriptions discussed in this book. Concordances relate mentions of individual stones to references in Jackson, *LHEB*, and McManus, *Guide*, with a two-way key to the numbers in Elizabeth Okasha's *Corpus of Early Christian Inscribed Stones of South-west Britain* (Leicester University Press, September 1993). Her book appeared when the present volume was going to press, and only this concordance could be inserted. Dr Okasha gives long and invaluable bibliographies for the stones, with definitive histories of them all as monuments. Her Preface disclaims any attempt to write a history of the south-west in the early Christian era, still less a work of palaeography or a treatise on Celtic philology (and the division of proper names into linguistic categories, pp. 43–5, will invite criticism from Celticists). Her views on dating (pp. 50–7) set out the view that 'Category 1 stones' ( = *ECMW* Group I) cannot be more closely dated than within two centuries, in a span from the fifth and sixth centuries to the eleventh, the latter *terminus* being based on the linguistic dating of the (early Middle English) Lanteglos by Camelford cross-shaft, a 'fossil' inscription that happens to be predominantly in capitals. In at least fifteen cases Dr Okasha's readings of inscriptions ('texts') are less full, or less confident, than Macalister's or those given here; in a further seven, she describes texts as 'illegible', though that must remain a matter of opinion. Insular post-400 orthographic conventions are not discussed, nor is the handling of the ogams at all convincing. Dr Okasha's aim is to offer a corpus 'accurate in its information and reliable in its reading of the texts'. The present writer, admittedly with the advantage of being able to visit and re-visit the stones of Dumnonia at ease (Dr Okasha writes from, and lives and works in, Cork), is naturally disposed to prefer the system of assigning 'probability dates' closer than a five-century span, and readings derived from long and repeated inspections; the two-way concordance will aid any reader who wants to check inscriptions in the field.

APPENDIX

**A numbered hand-list of inscribed stones of south-west Britain, 1993**

Numbers as far as 1060 are those of Macalister, *CIIC*. i and ii. The rest have been allotted by the author for reference in this book. Entries bracketed are for stones in *CIIC*.i that appear to be much later than the seventh century. In each entry a key name is given for identification, with a locality (correcting in some cases Macalister's locality-names). Stones with numbers from 1500 are cross-ornamented, not inscribed with lettering; are of various dates; and are included because reference has been made to some of them.

*Cornwall*

457 Lancarffe, Bodmin DUNOCATI
458 Churchyard, Cardinham RANOCORI
(459 Tawna, Cardinham – reading uncertain, figure, medieval shaft?)
    (Now mounted in hedge next to 460)
460 Welltown crossroads, Cardinham VAILATHI
461 Church, Cuby (Tregony) NONNITA
462 Bleu Bridge, Gulval QUENATAUCI
    (Now re-set against hedge close to footbridge)
(463 Church, Gulval VRIVI – part of shaft of 10th–11th cent. cross)
(464 Trebyan crossroads, Lanhydrock – medieval or later? cross-base?)
465 Church, Lanivet ANNICU
466 Churchyard, Lewannick INGENUI (with ogam)
467 Church, Lewannick ULCAGNI (with ogam)
468 Men Scryfys, Madron RIALOBRANI
469 Churchtown, Mawgan in Meneage CNEGUMI
470 Worthyvale, Forrabury & Minster LATINI (with ogam)
471 Churchyard, Phillack CLOTUALI
472 Nanscow, St Breoke ULCAGNI
473 Churchyard, St Clement (i) VITALI (ii) ..IGNIOC (*no* ogam)
474 Churchyard, Indian Queens CRUARIGI
475 Churchyard, St Columb Major ...A...FILI
    (Reverse side, Macalister's IA?CON/IUS, probably non-existent)
476 Rialton, St Columb Minor TRIBUNI
    (Now in Royal Cornwall Museum, Truro – 1992)
477 Church, Cubert CONETOCI
478 Doydon, St Endellion BROCAGNI (hooked cross; *no* ogam)
    (Now re-set at road junction inland)
479 Carnsew, Hayle CUNAIDE
(480 Lanhadron, St Ewe LURATECUS(?) – 11th–12th cent. cross-base?)

481   Churchyard, St Hilary NOTI (with symbols above)
482   Treveneague, St Hilary NEMIANUS(?)
          (Recorded, but now destroyed)
483   Church, St Just in Penwith SENILUS (with *chi-rho* cross)
484   Church, St Kew IUSTI (with ogam)

*Isles of Scilly*

485   Abbey ruin, Tresco gardens COLINI(?)

*Cornwall*

486   Churchyard, South Hill CUMRECINI (with *chi-rho* cross)
487   Castle Dore crossroads, Tywardreath DRUSTANUS

*Devon*

488   Buckland Monachorum (i) ENABARR (ogam) (ii) DOBUNNI
          (Now in Tavistock vicarage garden)
489   Fardel, Ivybridge (i) FANONI (with ogam) (ii) SAGRANUI
          (Since 19th century, British Museum (basement, in store))
490   Church, Lustleigh DATUIDOCI
491   Sourton, Okehampton PRINCIPI (with *chi-rho* cross)
          (Now at road-junction, roundabout, W. end Okehampton bypass)
492   Churchtown, Buckland Monachorum SABINI
          (Now in Tavistock vicarage garden)
493   Vicarage garden, Tavistock NEPRANI
494   Churchyard, Yealmpton GOREUS

*Somerset*

499   Winsford Hill CARATACUS

*Cornwall*

1043  Trewint, Altarnun — inscribed(?) medieval cross-base
1044  Fenton-Ia, Troon, Camborne LEUIUT — late 10th cent.(?) frontal
          (Now mounted as side-altar mensa, Camborne parish church)
1045  St James, Treslothan AEGURED — 11th cent.(?) frontal panel
          (Now mounted as side-altar mensa, Treslothan church)
1046  Churchyard, Cardinham ARANI(?) — 10th–11th cent. high cross
1047  Roseworthy, Gwinear RUNHOL — late 10th cent. high cross
          (Now Lanherne convent garden, St Mawgan in Pydar)
1048  Church, Madron QONFAL (with cross above; 7th cent.)

APPENDIX

(1049   Church, Madron URITIN(?) (so Macalister) )
              (Cannot be found; wrong location apparently cited, no other traced)
1050    Waterpit Down, Minster MEUROC – shaft of 11th cent. high cross
1051    Market cross, Penzance P(RO)CUMB(NT) IN (etc.) – 11th cent. high cross
              (Now in garden, Penlee House Museum, Penzance)
1052    St Piran's, Perranzabuloe – ?? – lost, fragmentary, date uncertain
1053    Biscovey, Par ALRORON – shaft of 11th cent. high cross
              (Now outside St Blazey Gate church)
1054    Doniert Stone, St Cleer DONIERT – late 9th-cent.(?) cross-base
              (Now in protective roadside enclosure, Redgate)
1055    Boslow common crossroads, St Just in Penwith TAETUERA
              (With linear cross; 7th cent.)
1056    Church, St Michael Penkivel – unlocated, fragmentary, date uncertain
1057    Churchyard, Sancreed FILIUS IC – 6th cent., re-used as 12th cent. high cross
1058    Churchyard, Sancreed RUNHOL – late 10th cent. high cross
1059    Trevillet, Tintagel AELRIAT – 11th cent. flat decorated cross
              (Now outside Wharncliffe Arms, Tintagel)

*Devon*

1060    Churchyard, Stowford GUNGLEI – 7th cent.

*Cornwall* (pre-700 inscriptions)

1200    Porthgwarra, St Levan ..IUS SPED(?) – lost, possibly genuine
1201    Trevaylor hill, Gulval ..IUMI..(?) – illegible, probably genuine
              (Now a gatepost into field off road)
1202    Vellansagia, St Buryan EVOCATI (with symbols above)
              (Now in garden, Boskenna, St Buryan)
1203    Kenidjack, St Just in Penwith ..S.. – fragment, probably genuine
1204    Trencrom, Lelant – illegible, two lines, apparently genuine
              (Now horizontal in stile between road and Trencrom Hill)
1205    Church, Redruth MAVORI – lost, acceptably genuine
1206    Bosworgey, St Columb Major DOVITHI
1207    Churchtown, Lewannick – ogam only, damaged but probably genuine

*Devon* (pre-700 inscriptions)

1208    Buckland Monachorum – mainly illegible, acceptable as genuine
              (Undisclosed location, to prevent visitors)
1209    Church, East Ogwell CAOCI
1210    Bowden House, Totnes VALCI – lost, recorded, genuine

*Island of Lundy* (pre-700 inscriptions)

1400  Beacon Hill OPTIMI
1401  Beacon Hill RESTEUTA (with circle above)
1402  Beacon Hill POTITI (with encircled cross above)
1403  Beacon Hill ..TIGERNI

*Exmoor (N. Devon & W. Somerset:* pre-700 inscriptions*)*

1404  Caffin Cross, Lynton CAVUDI
1405  Holwell, Parracombe (lost; only possibly genuine)

*Un-inscribed stones with* chi-rho *motifs, Cornwall*

1501  Cape Cornwall, St Just in Penwith (XP *chi-rho*; now lost)
1502  Church, Phillack (XP *chi-rho*; in gable over S. porch)
      (1500, with 1503 onward, are omitted as irrelevant to this book)

*Ogam inscriptions; summary*

*(i) Genuine*

466  Lewannick IGENAVI MEMOR
467  Lewannick ULCAGNI
470  Worthyvale LATINI
484  St Kew I)USTI
488  Buckland ENABARR
489  Fardel ?SVANNUCI MAQI RINI (corrected)

*(ii) Uncertain*

1207  Lewannick

*(iii) Claimed by Macalister, but not detectable*

473  St Clement
478  St Endellion

*Abbreviated references (see also Bibliography) to published post-*CIIC *stones*

1200  A. H. A. Hogg, *Proc. West Cornwall Field Club* II.5 (1960–61), 246–7
1202  C. Thomas, *Cornish Archaeol.* 19 (1980), 107–9
1205  M. Tangye, C. Thomas, *Cornish Archaeol.* 24 (1985), 171–4
1208  S. M. Pearce, *Proc. Devon Archaeol. Soc.* 40 (1982), 16–17
1209  C. A. R. Radford, *Proc. Devon Archaeol. Soc.* 27 (1969), 79–81
1404  J. F. Chanter, *Trans. Devonshire Assoc.* 45 (1913), 270–5; L. V. Grinsell, *The Archaeology of Exmoor* (1970), 104–5 (pl.,108); C. Whybrow, *Antiquary's Exmoor* (1970), 33
1405  L. V. Grinsell, *The Archaeology of Exmoor* (1970), 105 (with refs.)

# APPENDIX

**Concordance of references to Dumnonian stones listed in *CIIC*.i, found in *LHEB* and McManus, *Guide***

| CIIC nos. (* = with ogam) | LHEB (pages) | Guide (sections) (* = footnotes) |
|---|---|---|
| 457 | 171, 188, 319 | 4.12 |
| 460 | 566 | |
| 461 | 188, 192, 456, 570 | |
| 462 | 140, 171, 296 n.2 | 4.12 |
| 466* | 141, 171 n.1, 172, 175, 183, 366, 620 n.2, 622 | 4.11, 4.13, 5.31, 6.25, *4.46 |
| 467* | 171 n.1, 179, 187 | 5.31, *4.46 |
| 468 | 457 | |
| 470* | 171 n.1, 172, 184 | 4.11, *4.46 |
| 471 | 274 n.2, 646 | |
| 472 | 171, 518 n.1 | 4.12 |
| 473 | 171 n.1, 290, 610 | *4.46, Appendix 2 |
| 477 | 274 n.2, 291, 447, 463, 464, 645 | |
| 478 | 171 n.1, 463, 566, 665 n.1 | *4.46, Appendix 2 |
| 479 | 168 n.1, 188, 329 n.1 | |
| 483 | | 7.5 |
| 484* | 171 n.1, 172, 187 | 4.11, 5.31, *4.46 |
| 488* | 171 n.1, 181, 645 | 4.14, 5.31, *4.46 |
| 489 | 171 n.1, 187 | 2.2, 4.11, 5.31, *4.46, 5.44 |
| 490* | 190, 274 n.2, 279, 291, 521, 610, 646 | |
| 492 | 171, 172 n.2, 177 n.1, 181 ff. 518 n.1, 566, 610, 627 | 4.12 |
| 493 | 192, 274 n.2, 373, 646 | |

# APPENDIX

**Double concordance of stones listed in this book, and those (nos.1–79) in Okasha, 'Corpus of Early Christian Inscribed Stones of S-W Britain'**

| Here | Okasha | Here | Okasha | Okasha | Here | Okasha | Here |
|---|---|---|---|---|---|---|---|
| 457 | 18 | 1043 | 72 | 1 | 1053 | 40 | 1502 |
| 458 | 9 | 1044 | 7 | 2 | 1202 | 41 | (d) |
| 459 | 63 | 1045 | 69 | 3 | 1055 | 42 | 1200 |
| 460 | 75 | 1046 | 8 | 4 | 1206 | 43 | 1054 |
| 461 | 66 | 1047 | 20 | 5 | 1210 | 44 | 1205 |
| 462 | 14 | 1048 | 32 | 6 | 1208 | 45 | 476 |
| 463 | 15 | 1049 | 33 | 7 | 1044 | 46 | 473 |
| 464 | 65 | 1050 | 74 | 8 | 1046 | 47 | 475 |
| 465 | 21 | 1051 | 37 | 9 | 458 | 48 | 478 |
| 466 | 23 | 1052 | 38 | 10 | 487 | 49 | 481 |
| 467 | 24 | 1053 | 1 | 11 | 477 | 50 | 1501 |
| 468 | 31 | 1054 | 43 | 12 | 1209 | 51 | 483 |
| 469 | 34 | 1055 | 3 | 13 | 489 | 52 | 484 |
| 470 | 78 | 1056 | (a) | 14 | 462 | 53 | 1058 |
| 471 | 39 | 1057 | 54 | 15 | 463 | 54 | 1057 |
| 472 | 35 | 1058 | 53 | 16 | 479 | 55 | 491 |
| 473 | 46 | 1059 | 64 | 17 | 474 | 56 | 486 |
| 474 | 17 | 1060 | 57 | 18 | 457 | 57 | 1060 |
| 475 | 47 | 1200 | 42 | 19 | 480 | 58 | 493 |
| 476 | 45 | 1201 | (b) | 20 | 1047 | 59 | 492 |
| 477 | 11 | 1202 | 2 | 21 | 465 | 60 | 488 |
| 478 | 48 | 1203 | (b) | 22 | (c) | 61 | (e) |
| 479 | 16 | 1204 | 67 | 23 | 466 | 62 | (e) |
| 480 | 19 | 1205 | 44 | 24 | 467 | 63 | 459 |
| 481 | 49 | 1206 | 4 | 25 | 1403 | 64 | 1059 |
| 482 | 71 | 1207 | (b) | 26 | 1402 | 65 | 464 |
| 483 | 51 | 1208 | 6 | 27 | 1401 | 66 | 461 |
| 484 | 52 | 1209 | 12 | 28 | 1400 | 67 | 1204 |
| 485 | 68 | 1210 | 5 | 29 | 490 | 68 | 485 |
| 486 | 56 | 1400 | 28 | 30 | 1404 | 69 | 1045 |
| 487 | 10 | 1401 | 27 | 31 | 468 | 70 | (f) |
| 488 | 60 | 1402 | 26 | 32 | 1048 | 71 | 483 |
| 489 | 13 | 1403 | 25 | 33 | 1049 | 72 | 1043 |
| 490 | 29 | 1404 | 30 | 34 | 469 | 73 | (g) |
| 491 | 55 | 1405 | 36 | 35 | 472 | 74 | 1050 |
| 492 | 59 | 1501 | 51 | 36 | 1405 | 75 | 460 |
| 493 | 58 | 1502 | 40 | 37 | 1051 | 76 | (h) |
| 494 | 79 | | | 38 | 1052 | 77 | 499 |
| 499 | 77 | | | 39 | 471 | 78 | 470 |
| | | | | | | 79 | 494 |

APPENDIX

*Double concordance: notes on omissions*

(a) Okasha, appendix C – post-1100
(b) Here, 1201-3-7 – not in Okasha
(c) Lanteglos-by-Camelford, cross shaft, eleventh cent.
(d) Plymstock, cross, ninth–eleventh cents.
(e) Both Tavistock, lost, medieval slabs
(f) Trevarrack – age and type uncertain
(g) Tuckingmill – lost, unrecorded
(h) Whitestile – probably post-medieval

# References and Bibliography

**Author's note**  Two highly relevant works, Dr B. G. Charles's *The Place-Names of Pembrokeshire*, 2 vols. (National Library of Wales, Aberystwyth 1992 = here, *PNP*) and Dr Thomas Charles-Edward's *Early Irish and Welsh Kinship* (Clarendon Press, Oxford 1993 = here, *Kinship*) were available only as this book was about to be sent to press; some corrections and a few references could be inserted but any proper consideration of *Kinship*, in particular, was unfortunately not possible.

## Abbreviated references

(See also under Appendix)

| | |
|---|---|
| *Atlas* | William Rees, *An Historical Atlas of Wales* (revised edn., Faber & Faber, London 1959) |
| *BAR* | *British Archaeological Reports*, Oxford – British series |
| *CAn.* | (Sir) Ifor Williams, *Canu Aneirin* (Cardiff, 2nd impr., 1961) |
| *CB* | J. Loth, *Chrestomathie Bretonne* (Paris 1890) |
| *CBA* | Council for British Archaeology, London (as publisher) |
| *CGH* | M. A. O'Brien, *Corpus Genealogiarum Hiberniae, Vol.I* (Dublin 1962) |
| *CIIC* | R. A. S. Macalister, *Corpus Inscriptionum Insularum Celticarum*, 2 vols, i (1945), ii (1949) (Stationery Office, Dublin) |
| *CRB* | C. Thomas, *Christianity in Roman Britain to AD 500* (Batsford, London 1981; rev. impr., 1985) |
| *CT* | (Sir) Ifor Williams, *Canu Taliesin* (Cardiff 1960) |
| *DEB* | Gildas, *De Excidio Britonum* (ed. & trans. Michael Winterbottom, Phillimore, Chichester 1978) |
| *DSB* | *De Situ Brecheniauc* (text and transl., *VSGB*) – with, similarly, *CB* = *Cognacio Brychan* (follows *DSB* in *VSGB*) |
| *ECANB* | C. Thomas, *The Early Christian Archaeology of North Britain* (London 1971) |
| *ECMW* | V. E. Nash-Williams, *The Early Christian Monuments of Wales* (NMW, Cardiff 1950) |
| *ECNE* | K. H. Jackson, 'Notes on the Ogam Inscriptions of Southern Britain', pp. 197–214 in: Cyril Fox & Bruce Dickins, eds., *The Early Cultures of North-West Europe* (Cambridge 1950) |

| | |
|---|---|
| ED | 'The Expulsion of the Déisi' (see chap.5) |
| *EWGT* | P. C. Bartrum, ed. & annot., *Early Welsh Genealogical Tracts* (Cardiff 1966) |
| *GPC* | *Geiriadur Prifysgol Cymru, A Dictionary of the Welsh Language* (Cardiff 1950– , in progress) |
| *GPN* | D. Ellis Evans, *Gaulish Personal Names* (Oxford 1967) |
| *Guide* | D. McManus, *A Guide to Ogam* (Maynooth 1991) |
| *GVB* | L. Fleuriot, *Dictionnaire des gloses en vieux breton* (Paris 1964) |
| *HE* | Bede, *Historia Ecclesiastica gentis Anglorum* (ed. C. Plummer, as *Venerabilis Baedae opera historica*, 2 vols., Oxford 1896) |
| *KGP* | Karl Horst Schmidt, *Die Komposition in Gallischen Personennamen* (repr. from *ZCP* 26) (Tübingen 1957) |
| *Land* | *Liber Landavensis*, The Book of Llandaff (see *Llan Dâv*) |
| *LBS* | S. Baring-Gould & J. Fisher, *The Lives of the British Saints*, 4 vols. (London 1907–13) |
| *Lexique* | J. Vendryes (*et al.*), *Lexique etymologique de l'irlandais ancien* (irregular: *A* 1959, *B* 1981, *C* 1987, *M-N-O-P* 1960, *R-S* 1974, *T-U* 1978 – Dublin & Paris) |
| *LHEB* | K. H. Jackson, *Language and History in Early Britain* (Edinburgh 1953) |
| *Llan Dâv* | J. Gwenogvryn Evans & John Rhys, *The Text of the Book of Llan Dâv* (Oxford 1893, reproduced as facsimile edn., NLW, 1979) |
| *MGH* | *Monumenta Germaniae Historica* |
| *NLW* | The National Library of Wales, Aberystwyth (as publisher) |
| *NMW* | The National Museum of Wales, Cardiff (as publisher) |
| *Onomasticon* | Edmund Hogan, *Onomasticon Goidelicum* (Dublin & London 1910) |
| OD | Ordnance datum (heights above sea-level) |
| OS | Ordnance Survey |
| *PLRE* | *The Prosopography of the Later Roman Empire* – 2 vols., i, AD 260–395, ed. A. H. M. Jones, J. R. Martindale & J. Morris (Cambridge 1971); ii, AD 395–527, ed. J. R. Martindale (Cambridge 1980) |
| *PNRB* | A. L. F. Rivet & Colin (C.) Smith, *The Place-names of Roman Britain* (Batsford, London 1979) |
| RCAHMW *Inv.* | The Royal Commission on Ancient and Historical Monuments in Wales, *Inventory* volumes, by counties |
| RCHME | The Royal Commission on the Historical Monuments of England (as publisher: also *Inventory* volumes, by counties) |
| RIA *Dict.* | Royal Irish Academy, *Dictionary of the Irish Language*, in parts, now complete (Dublin 1913–76) |
| *RIB* | R. G. Collingwood & R. P. Wright, *The Roman Inscriptions of Britain, I, Inscriptions on Stone* (Oxford 1965), numbered entries |
| RIC | Royal Institution of Cornwall, Truro |

Sawyer         P. H. Sawyer, *Anglo-Saxon Charters. An Annotated List and Bibliography* (Royal Historical Society, London 1968)
SEBC           Nora K. Chadwick (*et al.*), *Studies in the Early British Church* (Cambridge 1958)
TYP            Rachel Bromwich, *Trioedd Ynys Prydein, The Welsh Triads* (Cardiff 1961)
VC             *Vita S. Cadoci*, text in *VSGB*
VD             *Vita Beati Davidis*, see James (J. W.) 1967
VSBG           A. W. Wade-Evans, *Vitae Sanctorum Britanniae et Genealogiae* (Cardiff 1944)
WATU           Melville Richards, *Welsh Administrative and Territorial Units* (Cardiff 1969)

*Periodicals (abbreviated refs. only)*

| | |
|---|---|
| *AC* | *Archaeologica Cambrensis* |
| *BBCS* | *Bulletin of the Board of Celtic Studies* |
| *CA* | *Cornish Archaeology* |
| *CMCS* | *Cambridge Medieval Celtic Studies* |
| *DCNQ* | *Devon and Cornwall Notes and Queries* |
| *JCorkHAS* | *Journal of the Cork Historical & Archaeological Society* |
| *JRIC* | *Journal of the Royal Institution of Cornwall* |
| *PBA* | *Proceedings of the British Academy* |
| *PDAS* | *Proceedings of the Devon Archaeological Society* |
| *PRIA* | *Proceedings of the Royal Irish Academy* |
| *PSAS* | *Proceedings of the Society of Antiquaries of Scotland* |
| *SC* | *Studia Celtica* |
| *THSC* / *Trans. Cymmrodor.* | *Transactions of the Honourable Society of Cymmrodorion* (London) |
| *ZCP* | *Zeitschrift für celtische philologie* (Tübingen) |

**Books and articles**

Barley, M. W. & Hanson, R. P. C., eds., 1968 *Christianity in Britain 300–700* (Leicester)
Byrne, F. J. 1973 *Irish Kings and High-Kings* (Batsford, London)
Carney, J. 1971 'Three Old Irish Accentual Poems', *Ériu* 22, 23–80
Charles-Edwards, T. 1971 'The Heir-Apparent in Irish and Welsh Law', *Celtica* 9, 180–90
Charles-Edwards, T. 1989 'Early medieval kingships in the British Isles', pp.28–39 in: S.Bassett, ed., *The Origins of Anglo-Saxon Kingdoms* (Leicester)

# REFERENCES AND BIBLIOGRAPHY

Coplestone-Crow, B. 1981–2 'The Dual Nature of the Irish Colonization of Dyfed in the Dark Ages', *Studia Celtica* 16/17, 1–24

Cuppage, Judith *et al.* 1986 *Archaeological Survey of the Dingle Peninsula* (Oidhreacht Chorca Dhuibhne, Ballyferriter, Kerry)

Dark, K. R. 1992 'Epigraphical, art-historical, and historical approaches to the chronology of Class I inscribed stones', pp.51–61 in: Edwards & Lane 1992

Davies, Wendy 1978 *An Early Welsh Microcosm. Studies in the Llandaff Charters* (Royal Historical Society, London)

Davies, Wendy 1979 *The Llandaff Charters* (Nat. Library Wales, Aberystwyth)

Davies, Wendy 1982 *Wales in the Early Middle Ages* (Leicester)

Davies, W. H. 1968 'The Church in Wales', pp.131–50 in: Barley & Hanson 1968

Driscoll, S. T. & Nieke, M. R., eds., 1988 *Power and Politics in Early Medieval Britain and Ireland* (Edinburgh)

Edwards, Nancy & Lane, Alan, eds. 1988 *Early Medieval Settlements in Wales AD 400–1100* (Bangor & Cardiff)

Edwards, Nancy & Lane, Alan, eds. 1992 *The Early Church in Wales and the West* (= Oxbow Monograph 16: Oxbow Books, Oxford)

Fox, (Lady) Aileen 1973 *South West England 3,500 BC–AD 600* (David & Charles, Newton Abbot)

Haddan, A. W. & Stubbs, W. 1869–78 *Councils and Ecclesiastical Documents relating to Great Britain and Ireland*, 3 vols. (Oxford)

Harvey, John H. 1969 (ed. & annot.) *William Worcestre. Itineraries* (Clarendon Press, Oxford)

Jackson, K. H. 1982 '*Varia*: II. Gildas and the Names of the British Princes', *CMCS* 33, 30–40

James, Heather 1992 'Early medieval cemeteries in Wales', pp.90–103 in: Edwards & Lane 1992

James, J. W. 1967 (ed.,annot.,transl.) *Rhigyfarch's Life of St David* (Cardiff)

Jones, (G. D.) Barri & Mattingly, D. 1990 *An Atlas of Roman Britain* (Blackwell, Oxford)

Kirby, D. P. 1976 'British Dynastic History in the Pre-Viking Period', *BBCS* 27, 81–114

Knight, J. K. 1992 'The Early Christian Latin inscriptions of Britain and Gaul: chronology and context', pp.45–50 in: Edwards & Lane 1992

Krämer, K. 1974 *Die Frühchristlichen Grabinschriften Triers* (von Zabern, Mainz)

Lacy, B. *et al.* 1983 *Archaeological Survey of County Donegal* (Donegal County Council, Lifford)

Nowakowski, J. & Thomas, C. 1990 *Excavations at Tintagel Parish Churchyard, Cornwall, Spring 1992* (Cornwall Archaeol. Unit, Truro)

Nowakowski, J. & Thomas, C. 1992 *Grave News from Tintagel. An illustrated account of archaeological excavations at Tintagel Churchyard, Cornwall 1991* (Cornwall Archaeol. Unit, Truro)

Ó Cathasaigh, T. 1976 'On the LU Version of "The Expulsion of the Desi"', *Celtica*, 11, 150–7

Ó Cathasaigh, T. 1984 'The Déisi and Dyfed', *Éigse* 20, 2–33
Olson, B. Lynette 1989 *Early Monasteries in Cornwall* (Boydell, Woodbridge)
Olson, B. L. & Padel, O. J. 1986 'A Tenth-Century List of Cornish Parochial Saints', *CMCS* 12, 33–71
Orme, Nicholas, ed. 1992 *Nicholas Roscarrock's Lives of the Saints: Cornwall and Devon* (Devon & Cornwall Record Soc., n.s.vol.35, Exeter)
Padel, O. J. 1976–7 'Cornish Language Notes; 5. Cornish Names of Parish Churches', *Cornish Studies* 4–5, 15–27
Padel, O. J. 1981 'The Cornish Background of the Tristan Stories', *CMCS* 1, 53–82
Padel, O. J. 1985 *Cornish Place-Name Elements* (English Place-Name Soc., vol.56/57, Nottingham)
Padel, O. J. 1988 *A Popular Dictionary of Cornish Place-Names* (Alison Hodge, Penzance)
Pearce, S. M. 1978 *The Kingdom of Dumnonia* (Lodenek Press, Padstow)
Pearce, S. M. ed. 1982 *The Early Church in Western Britain and Ireland. Studies presented to C. A. Ralegh Radford* (*BAR* Brit.ser.102, Oxford)
Pearce, S. M. 1985 'The Early Church in the Landscape: Evidence from North Devon', *Archaeological Journal*, 142, 255–75
Pender, Séamus 1947 'Two unpublished versions of the Expulsion of the Déssi', pp. 209–17 in: S.Pender, ed., *Essays and Studies Presented to Professor Tadhg Ua Donnchadha (Torna)* (Cork)
Penhallurick, Roger D. 1986 *Tin In Antiquity* (Institute of Metals, London)
Preston-Jones, Ann 1992 'Decoding Cornish Churchyards', pp.104–24 in: Edwards and Lane 1992
Preston-Jones, Ann & Rose, Peter 1986 'Medieval Cornwall', *CA* 25, 135–85
Radford, C. A. Ralegh 1975 *The Early Christian Inscriptions of Dumnonia. 1974 Holbeche Corfield Lecture* (Cornwall Archaeol. Soc., Truro)
Richards, Melville 1960 'The Irish settlement in south-west Wales – a topographical approach', *Journ. Roy. Soc. Antiquaries of Ireland*. 90, 133–52
Sharpe, Richard 1994 (transl., annot.) *Adomnán of Iona. Life of Saint Columba* (Penguin Books, London)
Thomas, C. 1966 'The Character and Origins of Roman Dumnonia', pp.74–98 in: C. Thomas, ed., *Rural Settlement in Roman Britain* (CBA, London)
Thomas, C. 1989 'The Context of Tintagel: a New Model for the Diffusion of Post-Roman Mediterranean Imports', *CA* 27, 7–25
Thomas, C. 1992 *Whithorn's Christian Beginnings. First Whithorn Lecture 1992* (Friends of the Whithorn Trust, Whithorn)
Thomas, C. 1993 *Tintagel. Arthur and Archaeology* (Batsford & English Heritage, London)
Thompson, E. A. 1984 *St Germanus of Auxerre and the End of Roman Britain* (Boydell, Woodbridge)
Thorne, Caroline & Frank 1979 eds., *Domesday Book. 10, Cornwall* (Phillimore, Chichester)

REFERENCES AND BIBLIOGRAPHY

Toulmin Smith, L. 1907 ed., *Leland's Itinerary in England and Wales*, 5 vols. (Oxford)
Todd, Malcolm 1987 *The South-West to AD 1000* (Longmans, London)
Vives, D. J. 1969 *Inscriptions cristianas de la España romana y visigoda* (2nd edn., Barcelona)

# Indexes

## I

Place-names and subjects. Chapter notes as '15.31'; alternative forms of place-names in brackets; Romano-British and certain other early place-names in italics.

Abbreviations: c., city; co., county; d., district, region, hundred, etc.; DB, Domesday Book (survey) form of place-name; est., estuary; f., fort (any kind); is., island; k., (early) kingdom; mt., mountain; pen., peninsula; pr., province; r., river; tr., 'tribe', people; v., valley.

Abercar 125
Aberdaron 243
Abergavenny 117–18
Aberhydfer 117, 166
Aberystwyth 92
*Alabum* 117–18
Alverton 299, 308
An Daghda Mór 27
'angle-bar' A 74, 96–9, 242–5, 265, 271
Anglesey 43, 201
Antrim, co. 43
Arberth, *see* Narberth
art, Christian, on stones 82–3, 106–7, 278, 290–1, 293–6, 323
Athens 16
Australia 36, 246–7
Axe, r. 209

Bath, c. 156, 6.16
Beacon Hill, Lundy ch. 10, 288, 322
Benni (Benny) 138–40, 148–9
Bergen, Norway 34
Bible, versions of 134, 144, 223
bilingualism 91, 106–7
bishop (rics)
    Demetia 234, 18.12
    Dumnonia 230, 306, 310
Bishop-houses, Demetia 105–6
Black Mountains 145–6
Bleu Bridge 271–2
Blisland 251
Bodmin 103, 229, 257, 270, 315
Bodmin Moor 184, 239, 262, 308–9
Bogomils, art of 18
Bordeaux 5
Boscastle 263
Boskenna 285
Boslow 291–3

Bosworgey 282–3
Bowden House, Totnes 281–2
Braga 184
*Bran coyn* (Bryn gwyn?) 137–9
Brawdy 75
Breage 186, 215–16, 250
*Brecenanmere* 132
Brecon, c. 7, 78, 131–3, 146–7, 152
Brecon, co., *see* Brycheiniog
Brecon Beacons 117
Brecon Gaer (Y Gaer), f. 117–18
Brega, d. 55, 60
'Brehant Dincat' 7.34
*Bremia* 117
Bridell 69–75
*Britannia Prima*, pr. 146, 209, 213
Brittany (*Armorica*) 114, 184, 223–6, 251–2, 280
*Broc(c)anniock* 135, 176–8
Brownslade Burrows 97
Brychan
    'daughters' of 133, 151
    'sons' of 113, 141–51
    'wives' of 139–41
Brycheiniog, chs. 8, 9, 78–9, 91, 113, 2.8, 8.25
Brynich stream 147
Buckland Monachorum 237, 265–7, 281, 308
Builth (Buellt) 113, 150, 322, 18.53
Burgos 19

Caer, Bayvil, f. 320
Caer Drait(h)ou, f. 45
Caerleon on Usk, f. 95, 117
Caer Lydan, f. 190
Caernarfon, co. 43
Caervarchell 9.45
Caffin Cross 288
Cair Kenin (Gonyn, Conin), f. 250–2

Caldey, is. 71–4, 91–2, 97–8, 106, 163–7, 228, 244–5, 249
Callington 278
Camel, est., r. 229–30, 239, 262, 315
Cantref Bychan, d. 106
Cantref Gwarthaf, d. 106
Cantref Mawr, d., 106, 117
Cantref Selyf, d. 113
Cape Cornwall 199
Cardigan, co. 1, 51, 60, 67–8, 80, 114, 315
Cardigan, town 76
Cardinham 187–90, 265, 307, 317
Carew (Castle), f. 76, 97–8, 213
Carhampton 315
Carlisle 202
Carmarthen, co. 1, 57, 68, 91–4, 103, 106
Carmarthen, town 4, 7, 51, 83–4, 93, 114, 117
Carmarthen Bay 249
Carn Ingli 57
Carn Marth 13.26
Carnsew, f. 188–94, 197–206, 238, 320
Cashel 29–30, 44–6
Castell Dwyran 82, 97
Castle Dore, f. 279–80
Castlemartin 97
Castle Pencair, f. 216, 250
Causses, les Grands 9–10, 2.1, 4.25
Cedweli, *see* Cydweli
*cella (memoriae)* 167–74
Cemais, d. 105–6
cemeteries
    enclosed 106, 153–5, 163–7, 226–7, 311–13, 317–19
    gifts of 100–2, 312–13
    older forts used as 316–20

# INDEXES

'shifting' 320–1
*cena* (burnt areas, inferred) 170–1, 192, 205–6
Ceredigion, k. 90, 114, 215
Chapel-Ainger, -Annyer 320
Cheshire, co. 4, 20
Chester, c. 29
*chi-rho* on stones 199–202, 295–6
Chun, f. 194, 250
Cilgerran 122
Cilieni, r. 8.20
Cirencester 146, 156, 209
Cleeve 163
Clegyr Boia, f. 90
climatic disaster, Brycheiniog? 151–3
Clodock 9.33
Clonmacnoise 189
Clydai (Clydey) 75–6, 122, 318
*C(ognacio) B(rychan)* 79–8, ch.9, 248–52
coin-hoards, Roman 188–9
Cologne (Köln) 5, 201
Conerton 215
Corfu, is. 10
Cork, c. 34, 184–5, 232
Cork, co. 62, 205, 7.31
*Cornn* (Cornwall) 184
*Cornovii*, tr. 209
*Cornubia* 143, 155, 176, 250
*Cornuguallia* 251
*Cornwallia* 143, 250
Coygan Camp, f. 97–9
Crai 119
Crantock 309, 314–16
crannog in Llyn Llan-gors 132
Crediton 177
Crickhowell 119, 123
Crowan 186
Cubert 282–3
Cuby 283–4
Cwm Criban, v. 122
Cydweli (Kidwelly) 51, 58, 60, 91, 106, 184
Cyfeiliog, d. 143
Cynwyl Gaeo (Caio) 93, 104, 201, 7.34

Dál Riata, k. 19, 43–6, 58, 107, 183
Dartmoor 239, 265, 281
Daugleddau, d. 105–6
Davesco 14–15
Defynnog 119, 121, 153
Deheubarth, pr. 150
Déisi, tr. 53–64
*Demetae*, tr. 51–2
Demetia, k., defined 1, 42, 51–2

Derry, co. 135
*D(e) S(itu) B(recheniauc)* 79–81, ch.9, 248–52
Devon, co. 1, 4, 7, 135, 155, 175–6, 209, 214
Dindraithou, f. 45, 315, 18.24
Din Drichan (f.?) 138
Dinllaen 43
Din map Lethan, f. 44–6, 186–94
Dinmelihoc, Dimilioc, f., 5, 213, 320
Dinn Tradui, f. 44–6, 57–8
Dinuurin 315
discoidal steles 18
diptychs (names in Mass) 141–51, 250
Dol de Bretagne 218, 223–4
Domellick 5
Domesday manors, Cornwall 215, 307–8, 313
Donegal, co. 11
Down, co. 28
Dumnonia, k.
  defined 1, 209–11
  divisions of 214–18, 229
*Dumnonii*, tr. 209
Dún maic Liatháin, f. 44–6, 183–94, 250
Dún Tredúi, f. 44–6, 57–8, 62, 76, 183
Durham 190
Durocornovium 209
Dyrham (*Deorham*) 104, 153

East (Wivelshire), d. 216
East Ogwell 281
*Eboracum*, see York
Ecglosberria, DB 314, 316
Eglwys Gymyn 75, 7.48
Egypt 18, 176–9, 9.41, 10.23
Elfed, Elmet, d. 122, 8.16
Emlyn, d. 105–6
'Enifernach', see Mynydd Frynach
Enys Brachan, is. 139, 145, ch.10, 249
enshrinement (*translatio*) 172–80
Ep(p)ynt, mt. 150, 322
Erging, k. 143, 9.35
Est Lo ('East Pool'), Hayle 190, 195, 198
*Eubonia*, is. 58
Exe, r. 214
Exeter, c. 77, 103, 209–10, 218
*Exeter Martyrology* 315
Exmoor 218, 278, 288–9, 305
'E(xpulsion of the) D(éisi)', tale 53–6

E(xtended) L(atinate) inscriptions 68–97, 200–5

Fal, est., r. 239
Fan Frynych, mt. 9.46
Fardel 237, 267–8, 308
Fenni, see Abergavenny
Fenni-Fach, see Benni
Fforest Fawr, mt. 91, 117, 124
*Finnaun doudec seint* 151
Fishguard 62, 67, 76, 92
Flat Holm, is. 167
Foel Trigarn, see Moel Trigarn
fosterage 90, 149, 223
Fowey, town, r. 230–3, 239, 251–2, 279–80, 309
France, see Gaul

Galloway 20, 43–5
Gannel, est. 239
Garth Matrun, k. 117, 145–6, 151–3
Gateholm, is. 163, 7.43
Gaul (as N & W France) 84, 96–7, 118, 199–206, 240–3, 269, 284, 295–6
  imports from 97–9, 202–4, 244–5
Germoe 186
Glamorgan, co. 4, 51–2, 78, 93, 249, 288
Glansefin 138–9
Glastonbury 44–6
Gloucester, c. 104, 156
Glywysing, k. 78, 91, 104, 213
*Gobannium*, see Abergavenny
Golant 231–2, 317
Gower, pen. 45, 51, 58, 60, 91, 184, 245, 249
Grisons (Graubünden), canton 14–15
Guerdevalan, DB 307
Gulval 10, 245, 271–2, 308
Gunwalloe 215
Gwaun, v. 56, 67, 8.2
Gwent (= Monmouth), co. 4, 104, 249
Gwinear 186
Gwithian 215
Gwydderig, r. 117
Gwynedd, k. 42, 45

Hartland (Hertilonde) 163, 174–80
Hayle, est., r., town 184–95, 197–206, 284
Helford, est. 188–9
Helsbury, f. 216
Helstone in Trigg 216

342

Hensbarrow, d. 268, 308
hexametric inscription (360), 104
*Hibernia* ( = Irish-settled Demetia) 145, 153
Holcombe 218, 13.43
Holwell 288
'horizons'
  of Christianity 2, 14, 85, 90, 101–3, 127, 132, 147, 218, 240–5
  of historicity 102–3, 128, 132–51, 245–8
  of Latinity 14, 77, 84–5, 101–3, 127, 132, 147, 240–5
horizontal I 70, 93–4, 265, 271
Housesteads 16
*Hryt Eselt* 13.26
Hypocoristic names 231, 268, 313, 315

Iceland 153
*Icht* (?Wight, Isle of) 44
Ilfracombe 163
India (NW Provinces) 107
Indian Queens 282–3
Inscribed stones
  corpora of xix, 257–9, 327
  decay of 7
  disappearance of fashion for 321–3
  modern 23–4, 96
  now illegible 288–9
  Roman, wording of 16–17, 36, 94–5
  sitings of 272–3, 291–3, 296–8
  surviving totals? 240, 288
  typologies of: Brycheiniog 113–17, 237; Demetia 68–71, 113–17, 237; Dumnonia 96, 113–17, 261–2, 278
'internalized' messages 16
*Inventio Sancti Nectani* 176–8
Iona, is. 206
'Irish Sea Culture' 47
Irish settlements
  early, general 41–5
  recent 3–6
  in Cornwall? 43–5, 58, 183–90
  in SW Wales 43–7, ch.5, 71–2, 76, 91–4, 114–15
*Isca, see* Caerleon on Usk
*Isca Dumnoniorum, see* Exeter
Ischir, *see* Ysgir, r.
Ivybridge 267

Jacobstowe 319

Jordanston 74

Kenidjack, v. 289
Kerrier, d. 216–17
Kerry, co. 11, 34, 37, 205
Kidwelly, *see* Cydweli
Kildare, co. 267
Kilkenny, co. 268
kings, post-Roman, categories of 210–14
Kirkmadrine 201–4, 243, 284

La Couvertoirade 18
Lamorran 312–14, 11.22
Lanalet 310
Lananta, *see* Lelant
Lanberan, -piran 309, 312–15, 320
Lancarffe 224, 263–5
Landeuailac, *see* Llandyfaelog (Fach)
Landévennec 280
Landithy 291, 317
Landocco, -dochou 167, 229, 240–1, 309, 314–16
'landscape' sitings, defined 305–8
Lanespetit, *see* Llansbyddyd
Langoroch DB, -gorroc 314–16
Langorthou 232, 251–3, 309–11
Langport (?Llongborth) 213
Languedoc, France 18
Lanhydrock 312
Lanisley 308
Lanivet 102, 251–3, 265, 294, 305, 311, 317
*Lann i doudec seith* 151
Lann Maies, *see* Llanfaes
Lannowen 317
Lanow, Lannowe 231
Lan Semin, *see* Glansefin
Lansulien 317–18
Lantyan (Lancien) 233
Lanuste 317
Lanuthno, -uthinoch 312
La(n)vethan 251–5
Lanwenuc 312–13
Lanwenehoc DB, Lanwethenek 315
Latin, spoken, in Ireland 28–34
*Latium*, d.? 62, 84
Leinster, pr. 28, 34–6, 43, 84, 4.18
Lelant 198, 320–1
Lesnewth, d. 216–17
Lewannick 245, 262–3, 305, 311–13, 317
Lidan, f.? 190, 194
Liscastell, f.? 82, 97

Lives of Saints, *see Vita(e)*
Lizard, pen. 185, 251, 284, 11.20, 13.26
Luxulyan 317–18
Llanbedrog 315
Llanbeulin 101, 132
Llancarfan 78, 178–9, 249
Llandawk(e), 71–4, 98–9
Llanddetti 9.33
Llanddeusant 101, 104–6
Llan Degeman 106
Llandeilo Fawr 104–6, 7.34
Lland(e)ilo Llwydiarth 106
Llanddewibrefi 93, 100, 104–6, 117
Llandingad 124, 150, 313
Llandough 249
Llandovery (Llanymddyfri) 101, 117, 143, 313
Llandrudian 106
Llandudoch, *see* St Dogmaels
Llandyfaelog Fach 139, 141, 152–5, 9.62
Llandysilio West 62–3, 72, 75, 166
Llanfaes 137–9, 148, 153
Llanfaglan 295
Llanfihangel Cwm Du 119
Llangadog 147
Llan-gan 7.48
Llangasty Tal-y-Llyn 132, 144, 151
Llangeler 75, 135
Llangeneu 106
Llan-gors 132–3, 155
Llangrannog 315
Llangwyryfon 7.13
Llangynin 106
Llangynog 7.48
Llanhamlach 9.47
Llanio 117
Llanilltud Fawr (Llantwit Major) 91, 103, 134, 167, 227–8, 248–9
Llanism(a)el, *see* St Ishmael
Llanlleonfel (Llanllywenfel) 322–3
Llanllyr 93, 100
Llansadwrn 201
Llansbyddyd 139, 141, 153–5, 9.62
Llansemyn, *see* Glansefin
Llan Teilaw 106
Llan Teulydawc 106
Llantrisaint 201
Llanwinio 75
Llanychaer 17.54
Lleyn (Llŷn) pen., 43

343

INDEXES

Llynfi, r. 117–18, 145, 151
Llyn Llan-gors 132, 140, 146
Llyn Syfaddan 144, 153, 9.17, 9.40
Llywel 117, 120
Lochdwrffin 72, 82–3
Loire, r. 200
Longbury Bank 97–8, 7.23
Loughor (Llwchwr), r. 51–2, 91
Ludgvan 11.15
Lundy, is. 156, ch.10, 202, 206, 218, 228, 231, 249, 288, 305, 318
Lustleigh 281
Luxulyan 317–18
Lydford 319
Lynton 288
Lyon 199, 201, 243

Mabe 11–12
Madron 283, 290–1, 317
Maenclochog 106
Maes Llanwrthwl 104
*Mainaur Oper Birnich* 126, 138, 147
Man, Isle of 43, 58, 107, 259
'Mannia, Manan' (= *Damnonia*) 139, 142–3, 154–5, 249–50
Mathry 75, 318
Mawgan in Meneage 284, 316–17
Meath, co. 27, 54
Mediterranean imports 97–9, 198, 205–6
Meidrim (Mydrim) 106, 138–9, 147–9, 318
Mellte, r. 117
Menevia (Mynyw) 84, 91, 103, 106, 141, 7.7
menhirs
    Cornwall 10–12, 229–31, 279, 296
    France 9–11
    Wales 12–13
    symbolism of 11–14
Mercia 131–2
Merther Uny 319–20
Merthyr Cibliver (Kyfliuer) 143
Merthyr Cynog 139, 141, 153–5
Merthyr Tydfil 119
Mesocco 15
Milford Haven 230
Minster 306, 10.25, 18.4, 18.33
Moel Trigarn, f. 46, 57–9, 72, 75, 92, 183, 194
monasteries, early
    Demetia 90, 93, 100, 166–7, 227–8, 234, 249
    Dumnonia 213, 226–34, 240, 308–10, 313–17

Monmouth, co., town 51–2, 104, 131
Montgomery, co. 143
*Moridunum, see* Carmarthen (town)
mound-graves 171–5, 191–3, 204–6, 292–3, 298
Munster, pr. 28–30, 34–6, 54–7, 61, 78, 5.18
Mynachlog-ddu 12
Mynydd Frynach, mt. 126, 138, 147
Mynydd Epynt, *see* Epynt
Mynydd Preseli, *see* Preseli
Mynydd Troed, mt. 145–6

names, personal, *see* hypocoristics: repetition of
Nanscowe 262, 307
Nantcarban, *see* Llancarfan
Nant Crew, v. 125
Nant Dincat 124, 126, 150, 7.34
Narberth 72, 82, 92, 98
Neath, r., town 52
Nemea, wood of 251–2
*Nemeto statio* 252
Nevern 57, 63, 74, 92, 136, 166
Newchurch 242–3
New England 36, 3.31
New Grange 27
New Quay 92
Newquay 239, 268
Newport, Gwent 154, 179, 10.37
Newport, Pemb. 75
New Zealand 36
Northumbria 20, 47, 174, 259
Nymet Rowland 252

ogam script
    date 33–4
    invention of 30–3
    models for 34–7
    Primitive Irish sound-values 31–3
    and paganism 32–6, 72–3

Padstow 230, 268, 309, 315–16
*Pagus Tricurius, see* Trigg
parentage, earthly, shunned 22
parish dedications, Cornwall 176–8, 186–8, 311–14
Parrett, r. 210
Pawton 217, 307–8
Pebidiog, d. 80–2, 90, 106, 122–3, 145–8
Pembro (= Breage) 215–16, 250, 13.57
Pembroke, co. 1, 60–2, 77, ch.6, ch.7, 6.8

Penally 97, 99, 106
Penfro, d. 105–6
Penmachno 205
Penmorfa 9.12
Penwith, d. 217
Penzance 298–9
Perran Sands 316
Perranzabuloe 312–14
Peuliniog, d. 7.40
Phillack 190, 197–201, 232, 285–6, 316
Picts 19–25
Place, Fowey 232
Porthcawl 167
Porthgwarra 289
Porth Mawr 90, 92, 138–40, 147, 151
Poundbury 10.14
Powder, d. 215, 217
Powys, k. 138–40, 149
'Pre-Patrician' saints 28
Preseli (Prescelly), mt. 12, 23, 57, 62, ch.6, ch.7
'primary' grave-markers 295–8
Pumpsaint 117–18
Pydar, d. 217–18

Redruth 284–5, 320
regnal lists, Déisi 53–64, 77–83, 90
repetition of personal names
    Demetia–Brycheiniog 122–3, 147–8, 277
    Demetia–Dumnonia 239–43, 249–53, 277
Rhineland 5, 201
Rhos, d. 106
Rhoscrowther 97, 106
Rhuddlan 69
Rialton 217, 268–70, 307–8
Riviere 187, 197–8
Roborough Down 265
Roman Britain (*Britannia*)
    divisions of 51–2, 209–10
Roscarrock 307–8
*Rosina vallis* 89–90
Rome 244–5
Ruan (Lanihorne, Major, Minor) 251

St Albans 311
St Breoke 241–3, 262, 307
St Breward 15.22
St Buryan 271, 285, 309, 314–20
St Clement 245, 270, 297
St Columb Major 281–3, 317
St David's, c. 89, 92, 103, 106, 141

St Dennis 319–20
St Dogmaels 69, 75–6
St Donats 228
St Endellion 263–4, 294–5, 307
St Erth 187, 312
St Germans 309–10
St Hilary 201, 285, 289, 317
St Ishmael 106
St Ives 187–8, 213
St Just 286–7, 289, 293–5, 317
St Keverne 309
St Kew 167, 229–31, 237, 240–1, 249, 262–5, 294, 309, 313–15
St Levan 289
St Neot 309
St Nicholas 106
St Petrox 315
St Pol de Léon 280
St Samson's, Golant 231–2, 317
St Winnow 10.31
Salona(e) 5, 12.30
*Sanas Chormaic* 44–6
Sancreed 286–7, 317
Santa Maria de Bretoña 184
Scilly, Isles of 155, 271–3, 10.8
Seisylling, d. 114
Silchester 16.38
*Silures*, tr. 51–2
Sithney 187
Somerset, co. 155
Sourton 281, 295
South Hams, Devon 214, 253, 265, 308
South Hill 231, 278, 294–5
Spain 10, 18–19, 184, 201, 293, 12.16
Stabio, Ticino 15
Steep Holm, is. 167
Steynton 73, 92
Stoke St Nectan 174–80
Stowford 290, 317–19
Stratton, d. 216–17
Strumble Head 92
*Stuctia*, see Ystwyth, r.
Switzerland 14–15, 201

Taf Fawr, r. 117
Talgarth 146, 152–3, 9.61

tally-sticks 32–4
Tamar, r. 239, 308
*Tau* cross (on 487) 279
Tavistock 265–7, 281
Teifi, r. 51–2, 67–8, 105, 114–15
Tenby 7, 71, 83, 97–8, 150, 245, 7.26
Tintagel 49, 163, 206, 213–14, 218, 233, 263, 295–6, 306–9, 4.23, 13.6, 18.4
Tipperary, co. 39, 3.11
*Ton Ridoch Windouith* 143
Totnes 281
Towy (Tywi), r. 51–2, 91, 98, 105, 114–15, 147, 249
Trallwng 119–21, 153
Trecastle 119–20, 124
Tregonning (Hill) 216, 250–2
Tregony 283
Trencrom, f. 186, 194–5
Trenewith 216
Trevelgue, f. 268, 18.24
Treveneague 285
Trigg, d. 216–17, 229
*Tristan and Iseult (Isolt, Yseult)* 190, 194, 213–14, 248, 279–80
Try, Gulval 10
'*Tuerobis*', see Teifi, r.
Tywardreath 231
Tywi, see Towy, r.

Uí Liatháin, tr. 58–61, 184, 195, 238
Ulster, pr. 19, 43, 45, 4.1
Usk, r. 113, 117–19, 147–52, 179

'Vatican List' 197, 251
Vellansagia, -sajer 271, 285
Vienne 199, 201, 243
*Vitae* (= Lives of Saints)
  *V. sancti Cadoci* 78–81, 231, 9.61, 10.39
  *V. prima sancti Carantoci* 80, 213, 315
  *V. beati Davidis* 80–1, 88–91, 100–2
  *V. Gildae* 80
  *V. sancti Gundleii* 9.16

*V. sancti Iltuti* 175
*V. et passio sancti Nectani martyris* 175–9
*V. Oudocei* 80–1
*V. sancti Pauli Aureliani* 279–80, 310, 7.34
*V. sancti Petroci* 315
*V. Ronani*, *V. Rumonis* 251–2
*V. prima sancti Samsonis* 98, 218, ch.14, 239–48, 280–2, 310, 315
Volterra 16

Wadebridge 229, 263, 268
Warbstow Bury, f. 216
Wareham 218
Waterford, co. 34, 60–2, 71
Wells, c. 10.14
Welltown 307
Wendron 187, 308, 319
Wexford, co. 60–2
Wheal (Alfred, etc.) 6.6
Whitesand Bay 92
Whithorn 202, 311
Wicklow, co. 28
Willit, r. 315
'Wincdilantquendi' 100–3
Winford Hill 288–9
Winnianton 215
Wirksworth 10.25
Wivelshire, E & W, d. 216–17
wolves, menace of 47, 4.25
Worthyvale 170, 263–4, 307–8
Wroxeter 271
Wye, r. 117–18, 152

Yealmpton 290
Ynys Bŷr, see Caldey, is.
Ynys Echni, is. 167
Ynys Wair (Weir), is. 167
York, c. 16–17
Youghal 34
Ysgir, r. 138, 149
Ystradfellte, v. 119, 125
Ystrad Tywi, d. 114
Ystwyth, r. 52, 115

INDEXES

# II

Proper names (those in actual inscriptions as BROCAGNI). Chapter notes as '7.21' (figures are specified). Abbreviations: a., abbot; bp., bishop; e., emperor; k., king; pr., priest; s., saint.

Adomnán, a. 14.8
Aed Brosc, k. 53–5, 79–85, 90, 147, 6.30
Aemilius (Cologne) 5
Aemilius (estate of?) 5
Aethelstan, k. 177, 215
Agricola, k., see Aircol
Aircol, k. 53–6, 80–5, 89–90, 97, 101, 124, 223, 270
Aldhelm, a. 213, 310
Alfred, k. 176
ALKOVINOS 15
Allen, J. Romilly 257–9
Amon 101, ch.11
ANDAGELLI 92
ANICIUS INGENUUS 16
Anlach, k. 78–82, 90, ch.9
Anna, wife of Amon 91, 14.2
ANNICI 125, 132
ANNICU 252, 265, 294
Ann(h)un 'rex Grecorum' 139–40
Antonius Gregorius, praeses 146, 9.41
ANTO(NIUS) STEPAN(US), 16–17
ASAITGEN 100, 7.31
ASKONETI 15
AUDETI 281, 17.20
AVITORIA 75
AVITTORIGES 281

Baillie, M. G. L. 152–3
Banadil, Banadylwed 138–40, 149
Baring-Gould, Sabine 275, 281
BARRIVENDI 74, 98–9, 150, 7.30
Barth, Fredrik 107
Beckerlegge, J. J. 193
Bede 101
Beroul 190, 194, 214, 233, 248
Berwin, s. ch.9, 249–53
Bethan 249–53
BIVADI 75
BIVATIGI 201
BIVVA... 75, 6.20
Blackwell, A. E. 163
BODDIB.. 75
BODIBEVE 73
Boia 90
Borlase, William 284, 306, *Fig. 17.17*
Bowen, Emrys George 68, 260
BRANNUS 93
BRAVECCI 94–5

Breaca, s. 187–8
BRIECI 69, 71–3, 6.11
Brictricus (Brihtric) 177
BROCAGNI (316) 135
BROCAGNI (372) 75, 135
BROCAGNI (478) 135, 263–4, 294, 307
BROCANN 135
Brook, Diane 306
Brychan, k. 78, chs.9 & 10, 248–53, 263

Cadog (Cadocus), s. 78–9, 134, 151, 179, 234
CALUNOVIC(A) 60
CAMAGLI 125
CAMULORIGI 93–5
CANNTIANI 119
CAOCI 281
Carannog (Carantocus), s. 80, 114, 315
CARA(N)TACI 288–9, 17.42
CARAUSIUS 201, 205
Carney, James 30
Carson, R. A. G. 27
'Castanius' ch.9
CATACUS 119
CATICUS 75
CAVUDI 288–9, 17.41
Ceredig, k. 114
Charles-Edwards, Thomas 106, 214–15, *Fig. 7.7*
CIVILI 288–9
Claudius Ptolemaeus 27
CLOTUALI MOBRATTI 197, 284–5, 17.35
Clotri, k. 54–5, 62–4, 74–6, 82–4, 97, 136, 5.17, 5.35, 5.38
CLUTARI 63–4, 69, 136
CLUTORI 62–3, 69, 81–2, 92, 136
CLUTORIGI 62–3, 76, 80–4, 136, 166, 5.35
Clytwyn (Brycheiniog) ch.9
CNEGUMI 106, 137, 250, 17.33
Colenso, J. W., bp. 3
..COLINI 271–3
Collingwood, W. G. 259
Columba, s. 46, 206
Conan, Conin, see Kynon
Conan Meiriadoc 211
CONBEVI 281

CONETOCI 282, 297, 17.27
CONHINOCI 281, 17.16
Constantine I, e. 53, 211
Constantine, k. 5, 212–13, 218
Coplestone-Crow, B. 60
Corath (Corach) 53, 79–80
CORBAGNI 94
Cormac ('Coronac, Gornuc') 79, 138
Cormac mac Cuilennáin, bp. 44, 183–4, 188, *Fig. 4.2*
Crabtree, Joseph 130, 304
Crawford, O. G. S. 306
Crimthann Már, k. 44, 53
CRUARIGI 282–3, 308
CUMRECINI 278, 294, 17.4
CUNACENA 37
CUNACENNI (A)VI ILVVETO 119, 121, 8.16
CUNACI 9.12
CUNAIDE 192–3, 207, 238, 243, 11.27, 11.29, 12.16
CUNATAMI 75, 6.22
Cunedag ('Cunedda') 114, 17.27
CUNEGNI 106, 137, 250
CUNIGNI 75, 250
CUNIOVENDE 94–5
CUNOCENNI 119–21
CUNOGENI 119–21
CUNOMORI 213, 250, 279–80, 297, 17.6
CUNOTAMI 75, 16.22
CUNOVALI 283, 286
CURCAGNI 94
Cynog, s. 79, ch.9, 176–9
Cywa, s. 229

DAARI 93–5
Daniel, Glyn E. 257
Dark, K. R. 298
DATUIDOCI 281
David ('Dewi'), s. 80, 89–91, 100–2, 212
Davies, W. H. 204
DECABAR BALOM 75
DEMETI 69, 76
DENAVECA 16.36
DERVACI 125
De Valera, R. 60
Dillon, Myles 42
DINUI 271–2, 297, 13. 36
Ditmas, E. R. M. 190

DITOC 100
DOBAGNI 74, 6.19
DOBITUCI 76
DOBUNNI 265–7, 269, 286, 297, 16.25
Dochou (Docco), s. 229–31, 315
DOCIDCI 282–3, 17.26
DOMNICI 94–5
Donatus 32
DONIERT 299
DOTHORANTI 9.22
DOVAGNI 74
DOVATUCEAS 76, 6.24
DOVITHI 282–3, 9.22, 17.25
DOVVINIAS 16.25
Driscoll, Stephen 23–4, 322
(D?)RUGNIATO 119–21, 242, 8.13
DRUSTANUS 250, 279–80
Dubricius, s. 234
DUMELEDONAS 74. 98
Dumville, D. N. 183, 211
DUNOCATI (327, Dincat) 119, 123–5, 150, 265
DUNOCATI (457) 224–5, 263–5, 307

Edmonds, Richard 191–3, 298, *Fig. 11.4*
EF(E)SS(A)GNI 71
Eglecta 16–17
Eliade, Mircea 10–11, 317
Elidius ('Ilid', 'Helen'), s. 10.8
ENABARR(I) 237, 265–6, 308
Eochaid Allmuir, k. 53–62, 77–85, 89–95
Eóganacht dynasty 5.34
EQUESTRI 204
ERCAGNI 94–5
ERCILINCI 283–4, 294
ERCILIVI 283–4, 294
ETTERNI 75, 84
EVOCAT... 271, 285, 294, 16.38
EVOLENGI 76

FANNUCI 267–8, 308
FANONI 95, 268
Felec ('Phillack'), s.? 197
Fin(n)bar(r), see Berwin
Flavius Antigonus Papias 202, 12.19
Frantz, Alison 199

GENAIUS 284
GENDILI 73–4, 92, 6.16
Geoffrey of Monmouth 213–14
Gereint (Geruntius), k. 212–13, 310, 315
Germanus of Auxerre, bp. s. 84, 269

Gildas 29, 56, 80–1, 89, 133, 183–4, 204, 212, 218, 223
Giraldus Cambrensis 134, 166
Gladusa 78, ch.9, 176–9
GLUVOCA 119
Glywys, k. 104
Gottfried von Strassburg 248
GOREUS 290
GRAVICA 91
Greene, David 30
Guedianus, comes 229–30
GUNGLEI 290, 317–19
Guo(r)tepir, k. 53–6, 77–85, 167, 270, 6.41
Gwynllyw, k. 234, 10.37
Gytha 175–7

Harvey, Henry 191
Hencken, H. O'N. 259
Henderson, Charles 215
Henoc, deacon 224–5, 230, 248, 17.18
Hockin, Frederick 197
HOGTINIS 69–76
Hübner, Emil 257–9, 281, *Fig. 17.3*
Hughes, Kathleen 226
Hyde, Douglas 224–6
Hywel Dda, k. 54, 113

Iago, William 193, 257–60, 281, 284, 288, 306
IDNERT 100
IGENAWI 262–3, 271
Illtud, bp.s. 175, 227–34, 10.15
INGENUI 204, 237, 262–3, 271, 277, 312
Instantius, bp. 5
IORUERT 322–3
IOVENALI 201
IVACATTOS 271
IUSTI (344) 125, 132
IUSTI (484) 237, 240–1, 262, 277, 294–7

Jackson, Kenneth H. 8, 32–6, 60, 68–71, 73, 94–6, 178, 188, 193, 259, 7.2
James, Heather 306, 317, 320, 7.49
James, J. W. 55, 101
Jenner, Henry 259
Jerome, s. 134, 150
Jones, Francis 108

Ker, W. R. 2
Kermode, P. N. C. 259
Kirby, D. P. 211
Knight, Jeremy 296, 16.31

Kynauc, *see* Cynog, s.
Kynon 137, 249–53

Langdon, Arthur G. 257–9, *Fig. 17.9*
LATINI 237, 263–4, 277
Leland, John 187, 216, 250, 280, 315
LEO 21
LEUIUT 299
Lewis, John 107
Lhuyd, Edward 119, 306
LITENI 60–1
LLONNOCC 147
LOVERNACI 94
(LU)CIUS 118, 166
LUGUDECCAS 7.33
LUNARCHI 9.22
LUPICINUS 201
Lyfring, bp. 177

Macalister, R. A. S. 8, 119, 193, 259, 281–2, 284–90, 297, 6.10
MACARI 237, 263–4, 16.21
MACCODECHETI 266–7
MACCUDICCLI 75
MACCUTRENI SALICIDUNI 119–20
MACUDECETI 94, 122
MACUTRENI (425) 94, 122
MACUTRENI (428) 122
MADOMNUAC 100, 7.31
Maeloc, bp. 184, 11.15
MAGLAGNI 69
MAGL(IA) DUBR(ACUNAS) 74
MAGLICUNAS 63–4, 69
MAGLOCUNI 63–4, 69, 81–2, 92, 5.38
Magnus Maximus, e. 54–6, 211
Mallory, James 107
MAQIDECEDAS(?) 122
MAQUERIGI 94–5
MAQUICOLINE 271
MAQUITRENI SALICIDUNI 119–20
Map, Walter 134
Marchell (Marcella) ch.9
'Mark', k. 213, 248, 279–80, 310
Martin of Tours, s. 311
MAUCI 278, 294
MAVOHENI 94
MAVORI 284–5
MAVORIUS 201, 243, 284
McManus, Damian xix, 32, 36, 119, 263
MELI (368) 270
MELI (453) 106
MENUEH 16.36
MESCAGNI 244, 263–5, 16.22

MESCI 265, 297, 16.22
Mes-Delmonn, k. 84
Miller, Molly, 55, 4.17, 5.20, 7.35
MOINENA MAQI OLACON 37
Morris, John 42–4
Morris, W. Meredith 67

(N)ADOTTI 263–4, 294
Nance, R. Morton 259
Nash-Williams, V. E. xix, 68, 70–1, 201, 259, 298
'Nectan', s. 175–80
NEITANO 178
NEMIA(N)US 284–5
NEMNII 119, 125, 17.34
Nennius 45, 58, 4.23
NEPRANI 281
NETTASAGRI 69, 71–3, 75
NIMNI 125
NONNITA 283–4, 294, 17.29
NOTI 289–90

Ó Cathasaigh, T. 60
OCCON 100, 7.31
OGTENAS 69, 76
O'Kelly, Claire 27
O'Kelly, Michael J. 27
Olson, B. Lynette 197, 211, 229, 293, 306–9, 316, *Fig. 18.2*
OPTIMI 163–6, 10.6
O'Rahilly, Cecile 42
O'Rahilly, Thomas F. 67

PAANI 106, 7.50
Padel, Oliver J. 197, 213, 306, 312
Palladius, bp. 27–8
Patrick, bp.s. 27–8, 44, 91
Paul (Aurelian), s. 280, 310
PAULINI (325) 201
PAULINI (MARINI LATIO) 62–3, 84
PAULINUS (361) 104, 201–2, 7.41
Paulinus (in *VD*) 100–1
Pearce, Susan M. 175, 317, *Fig. 18.6*
Pearson, John Loughborough 132
PECULIA 201
PELEGER 243
Pender, Seamus 53, 55
Per(r)an, Piran, s. 312, 315
Petroc, s. 315
Phaer, Thomas 230
Picken, W. M. M. 231
PIVOTIALUI 14–15
Piro (Pyro), pr. 228
POPLICI 281
POTENTINA 95
POTITI 163–6, 288, 10.6, 17.39

Praust 139–41, 9.30
Preston-Jones, Ann 306, 316–18
Price (Prise), Sir John 131–2, 147, 9.3
PRINCIPI 281
Prosper of Aquitaine 84

QAG...TE 71
QONFAL 290–1, 294, 297, 9.29
QUENATAUCI 245, 271–2, 297, 308
QUENVENDANI 94, 224
'Quonomorius' 280

Radford, C. A. Ralegh 260, 298
RANENI 15
RANOCORI 265, 297, 16.24
REGINI 94, 17.4
Rein (Dremrudd), k. ch.9, 322
RESTEUTA(E) 163–6, 10.7
Rhigyfarch, pr. 80, 89–90, 100–3
Rhŷs, Sir John 67, 257, 281, 306
RIALOBRANI 243, 270, 283–6, 308
RICATI 283–4, 294
Richards, Melville 67, 82, 114, 127, 185, 306, *Fig. 6.1, Fig. 8.1*
Rigeneu, k. 9.38
RINACI 92, 204
RINI 267–8, 16.27
Roberts, Tomos 306
Ronán, s. 251–2
ROSTECE 201
Rowlands, I. W. *Fig. 9.4*
RUALLAUN 322–3
Rumon, s. 251–2
Run, s.(?) ch.9, 249–53
RUNHO(L) 299

SABINI 266–7
SAGRAGNI 75
SAGRANI 75
SAGRANUI 267–9
Samson, bp.s. 89, 102, 134–5, 175, 278, 310, ch.14
Sandrey, T. W. 286–7
SATURNINUS 201
SECUNDI 201
SENACUS 201, 17.16
SENILUS 286–7, 293
SEVERI (373) 84, 242–3, 16.8
SEVERI (472) 241–3
SEVERINI 84, 242–3
Sharpe, Richard 206
SILBANDUS 93, 106
Simon Magus 204
SLANIAI 14–15
SOLINI 95, 122, 242
SWANNUCI 267–8, 16.27

Tacitus 42, 6.46
TAETUERA 287, 291–3, 297, 308, 17.53
TALORI ADVENTI 95
TARICORO 119, 122, 166, 8.12
(T)AUR(I)ANUS 118
Taylor, Thomas 226
Teague, surname 6
TECURI 125
TEGERNACUS 119, 122
TEGERNOMALI 282–3, 297
Tertullian 12.31
'Teudar', k. 186, 197, 213, 312–15
Teuderic, k. ch.9
Teudfall, k. ch.9, 9.29
Thomas, Hugh 134
Thompson, E. A. 183
TIGERNACI 74, 122
TIGERNI 163–6, 288, 17.40
TISIUI 14–15
Todd, Malcolm 5, 211, 214
Tomlin, R. S. O. 118
TORRICI 244, 270, 297, 16.35
TOTAVALI 94
Treffry, J. T. 232
TRENACATUS 69
TRENACCAT(L)O 69, 92
TRENAGUSI 92
TRENALUGOS 71
TRIBUNI 80, 124, 268–70, 16.31, 16.32
TRILUNI 80, 119, 123–5, 8.21
Triphun (Tribunus), k. 53–6, 80–5, 90, 123–4, 223, 270, 16.33
TUNCCETACE 93–5, 7.14
Turold 187, 307
TURPILLI 119, 123–5, 8.21
Uin(n)iavus, pr. 229, 313, 14.17
ULCAGNI (467) 242, 262–3, 312
ULCAGNI (472) 241–3, 263, 307
ULCAGNUS (370) 15.19
Uny, s. 187, 320–1
URSUS 201

VAILATHI 265, 294, 307, 9.22
VALAUNAL 15, 2.13
VALCI 281–2
VEDDONOS 17.18
VELVORIA 95
VENDOGNI 75, 122, 8.17
VENDONI (328) 119, 121, 242
VENDONI (429) 95, 122, 242
VENDUBARI 74, 98–9, 244
VENNISETLI 95

VERKALAI 14–15
VETTA 17.18
VETTANI(?) 281–2
VICTOR 75, 86
VICTORINI 119, 132
VITALI 244–5, 270, 297
VITALIANI (EMERETO) 74, 92, 106, 166, 6.18
VITO... 284–5
VIVENTIUS 201, 243

VOTECORIGAS 82–3
Voteporix, *see* Guo(r)tepir, k.
VOTEPORIGIS 80–3, 106, 204, 212, 270, 288, 6.40, 6.41
VROCHANI 265, 294, 9.22, 16.23

Wade-Evans, A. W. 137, 149, 249, 9.3
Wainwright, Geoffrey 97
Warner, Richard B. 152–3, 214, 3.9

Warrington family 246–7
Westwood, J. O. *Fig. 8.7*
Wesley, Charles 322
White, William 197–8
Williams, Sir Ifor 97, 122
Williams, Waldo 12–13, 23, 57, *Fig. 2.1*
Williams, William, 'Pantycelin' 3
Worcestre, William (of) 187, 320
Wrmonoc, pr. 104, 280, 310

# III

Words and phrases other than in English.

**LATIN**
Words and phrases in the text; the same, used (or also used) in inscriptions *(italics)*, omitting HIC IACIT, FILI and variants thereof.

algor 157
altrix, -ices 223, 7.4
ante ostium 153
antiquo ... stilo conscripta 89–90
apostolicum excipere obsequium 230
architriclinus 139, 9.31
armilla 139–40
barbaris figuris insculptum 177, 10.25
*bone memoriae* 201–3, 269
*bonemimori* 268–70
boni regis 75
capitalis (quadrata) xx, 243
castellum 29, 187, 227
castrum, -a 29, 3.17
cella (memoriae) 168–75
cena 'funeral meal' 205–6
cirografium 10.24
civitas, -ates 51–2, 209–10
clerici 310
comes 229–33
*congeries lapidum* 205, 293
cubicularii 138, 9.27
*cum multitudinem fratrum* 201
curia (regis) 97, 124, 9.61
currus 229, 233, 14.18
decurio 63
diptyca 150, 7.3, 9.55
*dis manibus, D M* 16, 95
domus, -um 'monastery' 224, 231
dux, duces 138, 213, 9.28
*emereto* 74, 106

emeritus 74, 6.18
episcopi 310, 18.12
exercitus 'war-band' 230–2

faber, *fabri* 265–9, 286
*filia* 75, 95
foederati 42

gentilis 'non-Christian' 74, 6.16
grassatores 183
guttur 'windpipe' 7.34

insula 100–1, 7.43
*iudicii adventum spectant* 322–3

magi 90
*magistratus* 63, 270
magna mortalitas 151
magna silva 251–2
marmorarius xxii, 17
martyrium 9.62
*mater* 95
*medicus* 270
medio quadrangularium lapidum 175
*memoria* 82–3, 89, 92, 203–5, 238, 263–3, 16.30
miles Dei 179
monasterium 227–33
*mulier* 95

navis 233
negotiatores 28, 188
*nepus* 288
nequam fili 81
niger, nigri 'swarthy' 9.41
nobilis, -es 147–8
nobiliores 108, 127, 140, 155, 305, 9.32
nomen, -ine, -ina 92, 203–4
*nomena* 99

nomina in sacris diptycis scripta 150, 7.3
numen 295

obses 149–50
occidentali parte, in 143, 249–51
offerentium nomina 150
ordinator, -ores xxii, 102, 135, 245
ordo, ordines 63, 84, 211

*pace, in* 322–3
pagus 215–7, 220
paganus 7.50
patria 156, 213, 10.36
pedis(s)equae 151, 9.39
phylosophi 245
pontifex 'bishop' 234
pontificatum suae regionis 310
*praedium* 100
praeses 146, 9.41
presbiter, presbyter, -eres 204, 228, 243, 286, 8.13
princeps 281
p(ro)cumbu(nt) in fo(ris) 229, 17.63
protector, *protictoris* 82–3, 89, 204, 7.12
provincia, -ae 51
provincia proxima 223
puer 123–4
*puueri* 119

*requiescit, requievit* 193, 201–3, 12.16
respublica (civitatis) 3, 209
rex, regis 89, 210, 212–13, 6.41
Roma venientes, de 244

INDEXES

romanitas 4, 29, 77, 117, 211, 223, 232
*sacerdos, -otes* 201, 245, 284, 310, 18.12, 18.13
sanctus, -a, -i (n. & adj.) 100, 144–5, 150, 171, 243, 249, 311–12
schola 227
scriptor, -ores xxii, 96–8, 102–4, 135, 245
seniores 150, 9.28
*servatur fidaei* 104
*sindone muti, in* 322–3, 18.53
stelae 18

tabella (= diptyca) 150
*tesquitus* 100–1, 7.31
translatio 172–8
transmarini 7.34
tribunus 30, 84, 269–70
triclinia 30
*tris fili* (= tres filii) 283
tumulus, *tumulo* 125, 193, 200–3
tyrannus, -i 89–90, 211

ultra mare 224
*uxsor* 93, 95

vetustissimis ... scriptis 100–3
*vixit annos* 193, 201–3
*vir* 290–1
volumina 135

**CELTIC**
Reconstructed or hypothetical ('starred') names, words and elements; selective index. Ir., Irish ('Goedelic'); Br., British or Brittonic. The meanings can be no more than approximate ones.

-ac-os (-a, -on), adjectival ending
Adsiltia ('Miranda') 17.8
-agn-as, dimin. (Ir.) 75, 135, 250, 15.19, 7.19
anmen 'name' 205
Artu-gen- 9.54

barras 'top, crest, scalp' 237, 7.30
biwa 'lively, alive' 6.20
bou (beu, bu) 'cattle, cow(s)' 185, 9.53
bou-itro 67, 185
bran- 'black bird, raven(?)' 286
broc(c) 'badger' 135
broga 'boundary, defined area' 216
brogo-rix 215
catu- 'battle, conflict'

Catu-maglos 125
clout- 'cleanse' 8.24
clut- 'fame, renown' 277
Cluto-rigi, -rix 55, 5.35
Cluto-ualos 286
Cluto-uindos 55, 9.54
Com-reginos 278, 17.4
corio- 'war-band, muster' 217, 232
cu 'hound, wolf', compositional cun-
Cuno-biuos 281
Cune-dagos ('Cunedda') 282, 17.27
C(u)ne-(gom-, gum-?) 284
Cuno-maglos 291
Cuno-maros 213, 280
Cuno-mori 280
Cuno-senacos 291
Cuno-ualos 286

Date-uidacos 281
Denawas, Dinawas (Ir.) 271, 16.36
dom- 'tame, subdue' 17.25
dumn-os 'deep, secret(?)' 13.5
duno- 'fortress, stronghold' 58
Duno-catos 8.19
duro- 'enclosed settlement(??)' 209

epos 'horse' 9.53
etnas 'bird' 237

gelt 'pasture, grassland' 9.53

-ign-os, -egn-os, dimin.(Br.) 15.19
Ilwetos 'eloquent?' 122

knukko- 'knob, hillock' 7.5

landa 'clearing? enclosure' 101–2, 311, 7.36
litan-os adj. 'wide, broad' 190
liuo- 'colour' 284

magl-os 'great, chief-' 291
Magl-acos (n. & adj.) 'chiefly, princely' 184, 9.62
maqqas (Ir.) 'son'
Matrona 'great, Divine, Mother' 146

neitos 'champion' 72
nemeto- 'sacred grove' 252
nikto- 'clean, washed, pure' 178

orget- 'slay' 17.51

petuariia 'fourth (part)' 218

quen(n)- (Ir.) 'head'
Quenadeccas? 7.33

regin-os (adj.) 'proud, stiff' 17.4
rest- 'roll, run(?)' 10.7
rigal-os (adj.) 'kingly' 270

Rigo-catos 284
Rigalo-branos 286
rix, rig-, ri- 'king'

Samotona (samo 'summer') 153, 9.40
sen- 'old' 17.16
sent- 'path, trackway' 9.53
swan(n)- 267–8, 7.20

Tari-rig? 8.12
tigernos 'landed chief, lord' 17.40
tigern-acos (adj.) 74
Toncetaca ('Fortunata') 93
touto- 'all-the-people, tribe' 215
Touto-maglos 146, 9.29
Touto-rix, -rigi 135–6, 215

uind-os, -a (uinn-) 'white, fair, holy' 75, 291, 313, 10.29, 17.51
uinndi 'holy, blessed house' 100–3, 7.32, 14.17
Uiniau 18.18
Uiro-maros 'Great-man' 212
ulk- 'wolf' 15.19

**IRISH**
ainm 'name' 205
allmuir 'd'outre-mer, étranger' (Vendryes) 53
assait 'accouchement' 7.31
béo, 'alive, living' 7.20
Bóthar 'road' 67
brosc(?) 'fat, stout' (?) 80, 185, 6.30
caiseal, dimin. caisleán 'fort, stone fort' 29
celi, gen. (céile) 'servant, attendant' 124
cell '(priest's) cell, church, monastery' 29
clann 'personal descendants' 53
cnoc 'hillock, hill' 67
corach 'striker, fighter(?)' 79–80, 5.21, 6.30
crich 'territory, confines' 58
cumachta 'dominion, rule (over)' 183

derbfine (lit.) 'true kindred' 147
doe, pl. due, dui 'construction, rampart, mound(?)' 57–8
drong 'crowd, throng' 8.13
dún 'fortress, stronghold' 44, 47

fert, 'mound, grave-mound' 57
fiana, pl. 'bands of warriors' 29, 3.12

filid, pl. 'poet-seers, learned men' 78
foss 'servant, disciple', 8.21
mac, pl. maic 'son' 60
már, mór 'great' 27, 183
membre, mem(m)ra '*memoria*, grave-monument' 16.20

rígdamnae 'royal material, eligible for kingship' 147
tre- 'triple, three-' 57–8
trebun(n) '*tribunus*, tribune' 30, 84
tuath, pl.-a 'kingdom, tribal area' 41

uí, pl. 'descendants'

**WELSH**
Mod. W, Modern Welsh; OW, Old Welsh, equivalents of words; alternative forms with initial f- and g- represent lenitions of b-, m- and c- respectively.

aber 'river-outflow, confluence' 147
ach 'descent, pedigree' 134
afon 'river' 51
bach, fach 'little' 138, 140, 9.48
ban, fan 'mountain-peak' 9.46
banadil (Mod. W. banadl) 'broom-plant' 119
bar(r) 'top, summit (of hill, etc)' 110
bed, pl. beddau (Mod. W bedd) 'grave' 81, 101
breisc (Mod. W braisg) 'fat, stout' 6.30
breuant 'neck, windpipe' 7.34
bro 'territory' 7.34
broch 'badger' 9.21
bychan 'small' 106
caer, gaer, pl. caerau 'fort, (Roman) camp' 47, 97, 117, 9.45
called, callet 'greenwood, trees' 143, 249–51
cantref 'area of 100 trefs, land-division' 215, 9.56
castell 'fort, camp' 97, 3.16
cnwc, cnwch 'hillock, small hill' 67, 115
cors 'swamp, marsh, reed-bed' 131
dedwyddach 'lucky, happy, fortunate' 281

deu (Mod. W dau) 'two' 7.34
din(as) 'fortress, stronghold' 58, 138
dofydd, Dofydd 'Lord (God)' 282, 9.22, 17.25
doudec (Mod. W deuddeg) 'twelve' 151
erch 'speckled, mottled, dun' 284
feid(i)r, meid(i)r 'farm-lane' 67–72, 115, 185
finnaun (Mod. W ffynnon) 'spring, source' 151
ffelaig, ffelyg 'lord, chieftain' 197
garth 'ridge, hill-spur' 145–6
(g)oresgynnaud 'conquered, overcame' 142, 150
Groegwr, pl. -gwyr 'a Greek' 9.41
gwarthaf 'upper' 106
gwas 'servant, follower, disciple' 8.21
(g)wedd 'appearance, visage' 149
gwlad 'homeland, *patria*' 10.36
gwrthrychiad 'nominated successor, formal heir' 146
gwyndy 'holy house, church' 7.32
lann (Mod. W llan, pl. llannau) 'monastery, church site' 75, 101–4, 153, 311, 317–18
loch 'pool, lake, marsh(?)' 82
llyn 'lake' 132, 144
llys (OW lis) 'administrative centre, court' 216

maenor (OW mainaur) 'estate, manorial demesne' 138, 147
map 'son'
mawr, fawr 'great, large' 106, 117, 138
merthyr 'saint's grave, shrine' 139–41, 153, 9.62
mynydd (OW menid) 'mountain, high ground' 138, 145–7

porth 'landing-beach, natural harbour' 138, 147
sant, pl. saint 'saint, holy person' 34, 134
taith 'journey, travel' 17.53
tal 'brow, verge, front of' 132, 146
ti (Mod. W tŷ) 'house, dwelling' 7.32
tir 'land' 67
tri 'three' 58

tud 'kingdom, people' 215
uin(n), fem. uen(n) (Mod. W gwyn) 'fair, holy' 10.29
ynys (OW enys) 'island' 91, 139, 156, 178, 228
ysbyddad, yspyddad 'thornbush, hawthorn' 9.62
ystrad 'broad river-valley' 114

**CORNISH** (Old and Middle)
aradar, pl. ereder 'plough' 215
bar 'top, summit' 7.30
bedewen 'birch-tree' 15.22
bounder 'farm-lane' 67, 185–7
bro 'territory' 215, 250

caer (car-, ker) 'fortified enclosure' 185–9, 216, 250
carn 'rock-outcrop' 190
carrek 'rock' 18.7
castell 'fort' 3.16
chy 'house, home' 194
cor(dd), pl. corddou 'war-band, muster' 216, 232
crom 'curved, crooked (hill)' 194

din(n) 'fortress, strongpoint' 5, 44, 188–94, 18.24
dinas, dinan (dimin.) 'fortress' 189, 319
du 'black' 190

eglos 'substantial church' 314, 317
est 'east' 190

faw 'beeches' 14.27

gol 'feast, festival' 14.29
(g)oon 'downs, upland' 194

hen 'old, obsolete' 216
hryt (rit) 'ford' 13.26

keverang 'administrative hundred' 216

lan(n) 'enclosure, cemetery, monastery' 232, 311–19, 18.39
lidan, lydan 'wide, broad' 190
lis, lys 'administrative centre'(?) 216–17
liu 'colour' 284
lo 'pool, tidal inlet' 190
loc 'chapel, cemetery-area?' 18.39

map 'son' 189
margh 'horse' 13.26

351

INDEXES

merther 'saint's grave, shrine' 317, 9.62
mynster 'mother-church, minster' 317
nant 'valley' 18.7
neved, nived 'grove, pagan centre?' 252, 311
pen 'end, top' *or* 'head, chief' 187, 216, 250
plu 'parish' 271
pou 'territory, *pagus*'
real, ryal 'kingly, royal' 270, 16.34
teg 'fair, beautiful' 6

traitou, pl. 'strands, beaches' 4.23, 18.24
tre(f) 'farm-holding, land tenement' 14, 185, 215
tri, try 'three' 216
tus 'folk, people in general' 215
uin(n), (g)wyn 'white, fair, holy' 10.29, 14.17
wheyl 'working, mine-work' 6.6

**BRETON**

brehant (??) 7.34
Buduere 17.53
cormo 17.35

derch, dre(h) 9.49
Drem-rudd 9.34
Drihic(an) 9.49
drogn- 8.13
Eusorgit 17.51
Guethenoc, Uethenoc 312
Guorgomed (Uuorcomet) 17.33
letan-, litan- 190
loc 18.39
mo- (mog) 17.35
pou 215
Restue 10.7
Ri-uuere 17.53
teith 17.53
uuin(n) 14.17

# IV

Inscriptions, with *CIIC* and (1200 onward) gazetteer (p.327) numbers, cited in the text. Page references as '91, 287'; chapter notes as '15.31'; illustrations, including some map locations, as '**8.3**'.

| | | | | | | |
|---|---|---|---|---|---|---|
| *(Ireland)* | | 341 | 119, 122, 10.25, **8.3, 8.4** | 384 | 18.13 |
| 1 | 16.36 | 342 | 119, 122, **8.3, 8.5** | 385 | 295 |
| 19 | 271 | 344 | 125, 8.22, **8.3** | 386 | 270 |
| 31 | 8.13 | 345 | 119, 124, **8.3** | 391 | 201, 243, 17.16, 18.13, **12.3** |
| 34 | 268 | 348 | 71, 75 | 392 | 18.13 |
| 100 | 15.19 | 349 | 95 | 393 | 201, 243, **12.3** |
| 147 | **3.3** | 350 | 100, 7.15, **7.2** | 394 | 95, 270 |
| 156 | 16.25 | 351 | 7.16 | 397 | 9.12 |
| 167 | 8.13 | 352a | 94–5, 7.13 | 405 | 91 |
| 172 | 7.14 | 353 | 71, 92, 7.12, **6.2** | 407 | 7.40 |
| 194a | 147 | 354 | 7.13 | 410 | 7.40 |
| 199 | **3.3** | 355 | 93, 106, 7.13 | 413 | 10.7 |
| 211 | 17.18 | 356 | 95, 7.16 | 414 | 10.7 |
| 215 | 8.13 | 358 | 55, 71, 82, 97, 106, 204, 212, 270, 288, 6.40, 7.12, 9.23, 16.30, **6.5, 7.5** | 416 | 204 |
| 263 | 7.33 | | | 417 | 17.41 |
| 272–81 | 5.33 | | | 421 | 201, **12.3** |
| 273 | 60 | | | 422 | 75, 122, 8.17 |
| 279 | 16.36 | 359 | 17.4 | 423 | 71 |
| 316 | 135 | 360 | 201, 7.15, **7.2, 12.3** | 425 | 122 |
| | | 361 | 95–6, 104, 7.34 | 426 | 71–2, 75, **6.2, 6.4** |
| *(Wales)* | | 362 | 74–5, 15.20 | 427 | 71, 74 |
| 320 | 201, **12.3** | 363 | 17.42 | 428 | 71, 92, 122, 7.12 |
| 323 | 201 | 364 | 244 | 429 | 122, 242 |
| 325 | 201, 7.40, 8.21 | 365 | 9.22 | 430 | 74–5, 84 |
| 326 | 15.3 | 368 | 71, 74, 98–9, 150, 244, 7.13, **7.6** | 431 | 75 |
| 327 | 80, 119, 123–4, 150, 265, 8.21, **8.3, 8.7** | | | 432 | 74, 122 |
| 328 | 119, 122, 242, 18.13, **8.3, 8.5** | 369 | 7.13, 7.34 | 433 | 71, 92, 7.12, 17.41 |
| | | 370 | 7.13, 15.19 | 434 | 17.41 |
| 329 | 119, 8.16, **8.3** | 372 | 74–5, 135 | 435 | 62, 75, 81–4, 136, 166, 5.35, 7.40, 8.9, 9.23, **5.6** |
| 331 | 125, **8.3** | 373 | 84, 242, **15.5** | | |
| 332 | 126, **8.3** | 374 | 106, 137, 7.16, 15.20 | | |
| 334 | 119, 122, **8.3** | 375 | 9.22 | 436 | 96, 7.13 |
| 339 | 119, 122, 125, 17.34, **8.3** | 376 | 95 | 439 | 71, 95 |
| | | 378 | 74–5 | 440 | 96, 122, 17.54 |

| | | | | | | | |
|---|---|---|---|---|---|---|---|
| 442 | 74–75 | 476 | 80, 268–70, 281, 308, **16.8**, **18.1** | *(Wales)* | | | |
| 443 | 93, 7.13 | | | 986 | 322, **18.9** | | |
| 445 | 74, 92, 166 | 477 | 282–3, 17.27, **17.17**, **17.18** | 993 | 100, 7.15, **7.2** | | |
| 446 | 63–4, 74, 81–2, 92, 136, 5.38, **5.6**, **6.2** | | | *(Dumnonia)* | | | |
| | | 478 | 135, 263, 307, **16.4**, **17.15**, **17.17**, **18.1** | 1044 | 299 | | |
| 448 | 92, 97, 204, 7.13, **7.5** | | | 1048 | 290–1, 297, 8.16, 9.29, **17.13**, **17.16**, **17.17** |
| 449 | 74–5 | 479 | 191–3, 238, 243, 261, 277, 296–8, 8.9, **11.3**, **11.4**, **11.5** | | |
| 450 | 75, **6.2** | | | 1051 | 299, **17.19** | | |
| 451 | 93–5, 7.13 | | | 1054 | 299 | | |
| 452 | 106, 7.16 | 481 | 290, 17.48, 18.10, **17.12** | 1055 | 290–3, 296–8, 305, 308, 18.10, **17.10**, **17.14**, **17.17** |
| 453 | 106, 7.16 | | | | |
| 454 | 95 | 482 | 284, **17.8** | | |
| 455 | 95, 268 | 483 | 286–7, 289, 293, 18.10, **17.10**, **17.16**, **17.17** | 1057 | 286, **17.9** |
| 456 | 73–4, 92 | | | 1058 | 299 | | |
| 001 | (*see* 8.7) 121–4, 166, 8.15, **8.3** | 484 | 237, 240, 262, 277, 297, 316, 15.2, 18.10, **15.3**, **17.16** | 1060 | 290, 298, 317, **18.6** |
| | | | | 1061–4 | 218, 13.42 | | |
| 002 | 125, 8.23, **8.3** | 485 | 271, **16.10** | 1200 | 289 | | |
| 003 | 117–9, 8.7, **8.3** | 486 | 278, **17.15**, **17.17** | 1201 | 288 | | |
| | | 487 | 213, 250, 279–80, **17.2**, **17.18** | 1202 | 271, **17.8**, **17.16** | | |
| *(Dumnonia)* | | | | 1203 | 289 | | |
| 457 | 245, 263–5, 307, 16.22, **15.7**, **18.1** | 488 | 237, 265–9, 286, 308, **16.5** | 1204 | 289 | | |
| | | | | 1205 | 284, **17.7** | | |
| 458 | 265, 8.12, 16.22, **17.18** | 489 | 237, 245, 267–8, 277, 308, 15.17, **16.6** | 1206 | 282, 9.22, **17.4** | | |
| 460 | 245, 265, 307, 9.22, **17.15**, **18.1** | | | 1208 | 281 | | |
| | | 490 | 281 | 1209 | 281 | | |
| 461 | 283–4, 295, 308, **17.14**, **17.15**, **18.1** | 491 | 281, **17.17** | 1210 | 281, **17.3** | | |
| | | 492 | 267, **16.5** | 1400 | 163–6, **10.2**, **10.3** | | |
| 462 | 245, 271, **16.9**, **17.18** | 493 | 281 | 1401 | 163–6, **10.2**, **10.3** | | |
| 465 | 252, 265, 295, 18.10, **17.16** | 494 | 290 | 1402 | 163–6, 288, **10.2**, **10.3** | | |
| | | *(Hampshire)* | | 1403 | 163–6, 288, **10.2** | | |
| 466 | 204, 237–8, 263, 277, 312, 15.17, 16.30, 18.10, **16.2** | 496 | 16.38 | 1404 | 288, **17.11** | | |
| | | *(Northumberland)* | | 1405 | 288 | | |
| 467 | 237, 263, 312, 18.10, **16.2** | 498 | 8.9 | 1501 | 328 | | |
| | | *(Somerset)* | | 1502 | 199–200, **12.2** | | |
| 468 | 243, 270, 278, 286, 291, 308, **17.5** | 499 | 288, **17.11** | *(Roman Britain: numbers from RIB.I (p.336))* | | | |
| 469 | 284, 17.48 | *(Scotland)* | | 359 | 95 | | |
| 470 | 237, 263, 277, 307, 16.2, **16.3**, **18.1** | 510 | 205, 17.18 | 374 | 95 | | |
| | | 515 | 204 | 653 | 17.20 | | |
| 471 | 197, 284–6, **17.6** | 516 | 201, 204, 243, 284, 18.13, **12.3** | 695 | 16, **2.3** | | |
| 472 | 241–2, 262, 271, 307, **15.5**, **16.9**, **18.1** | | | 858 | 5.35 | | |
| | | 517 | 204 | 955 | 202, 12.19 | | |
| 473 | 245, 270, 284, 18.10, **15.7**, **17.18** | 518 | 204 | 1618 | 16 | | |
| | | 520 | 8.9, **12.3** | 1632 | 3.30 | | |
| 474 | 282, 308, 18.10, **17.5** | | | 1823 | 3.30 | | |
| 475 | 281–2, **17.4** | | | 1833–4 | 13.3 | | |
| | | | | 2233 | 201, 12.17 | | |